Variable	English Name	Description
$"	$LIST_SEPARATOR	The output list separator for the print function
$;	$SUBSCRIPT_SEPARATOR	The subscript separator for multidimensional array emulation
$#	$OFMT	The output format for printed numbers
$%	$FORMAT_PAGE_NUMBER	The current page number of the currently selected output file handle
$=	$FORMAT_LINES_PER_PAGE	The current page length (printable lines) of the currently selected output file handle
$-	$FORMAT_LINES_LEFT	The number of lines left on the page of the currently selected output file handle
$~	$FORMAT_NAME	The name of the current format for the currently selected output file handle
$^	$FORMAT_TOP_NAME	The name of the current top-of-page format for the currently selected output file handle
$:	$FORMAT_LINE_BREAK_CHARACTERS	The set of characters after which a string may be separated to fill continuation fields (starting with ^) in a format
$^L	$FORMAT_FORMFEED	The value a format will output for each form feed
$^A	$ACCUMULATOR	The current value of the write() accumulator for format() lines
$?	$CHILD_ERROR	The status returned by the last pipe close, backtick (``) command, or system() operator
$!	$ERRNO	The current numeric or string value of error number (the value returned is determined by the numeric or string context of the operation)
$^E	$EXTENDED_OS_ERROR	Error info rent oper

er

Mastering™ Perl™ 5

Eric C. Herrmann

SYBEX®

San Francisco • Paris • Düsseldorf • Soest • London

Associate Publisher: Richard Mills
Contracts and Licensing Manager: Kristine O'Callaghan
Acquisitions & Developmental Editor: Maureen Adams
Editor: Marilyn Smith
Project Editors: Gemma O'Sullivan, Elizabeth Hurley-Clevenger
Technical Editor: David Medinets
Book Designer: Kris Warrenburg
Graphic Illustrator: Tony Jonick
Electronic Publishing Specialist: PageMasters & Company
Production Coordinator: Susan Berge
Indexer: Ted Laux
Cover Designer: Design Site
Cover Photographer: Michel Tcherevkoff/Image Bank

Mastering is a trademark of SYBEX Inc.

Screen reproductions produced with Collage Complete.

Collage Complete is a trademark of Inner Media Inc.

Netscape Communications, the Netscape Communications logo, Netscape, and Netscape Navigator are trademarks of Netscape Communications Corporation.

Netscape Communications Corporation has not authorized, sponsored, endorsed, or approved this publication and is not responsible for its content. Netscape and the Netscape Communications Corporate Logos are trademarks and trade names of Netscape Communications Corporation. All other product names and/or logos are trademarks of their respective owners.

TRADEMARKS: SYBEX has attempted throughout this book to distinguish proprietary trademarks from descriptive terms by following the capitalization style used by the manufacturer.

The author and publisher have made their best efforts to prepare this book, and the content is based upon final release software whenever possible. Portions of the manuscript may be based upon pre-release versions supplied by software manufacturer(s). The author and the publisher make no representation or warranties of any kind with regard to the completeness or accuracy of the contents herein and accept no liability of any kind including but not limited to performance, merchantability, fitness for any particular purpose, or any losses or damages of any kind caused or alleged to be caused directly or indirectly from this book.

GNU License Information
GNU Texinfo version adapted by Jeff Kellem
composer@Beyond.dreams.org.
Copyright 1989, 1990, 1991, 1992, 1993 Larry Wall Texinfo version
Copyright 1990, 1991, 1992, 1993 Jeff Kellem
Permission is granted to make and distribute verbatim copies of appendices A and B provided the copyright notice and this permission notice are preserved on all copies.

Permission is granted to copy and distribute modified versions of appendices A and B under the conditions for verbatim copying, provided also that the sections "GNU General Public License" and "Conditions for Using Perl" are included exactly as in the original, and provided that the entire resulting derived work is distributed under the terms of a permission notice identical to this one.

Permission is granted to copy and distribute translations of appendices A and B into another language, under the above conditions for modified versions, except that the section "GNU General Public License" and this permission notice may be included in translations approved by the Free Software Foundation instead of the original English.

Library of Congress Card Number: 98-86868
ISBN: 0-7821-2200-0

Manufactured in the United States of America

10 9 8 7 6 5 4 3 2

This book is dedicated in loving memory to my Mom. She raised the three of us by herself on a secretary's salary. I don't know how she managed to be such a happy woman, but she always had a smile and a hug for us. She taught me to never doubt myself. What I accomplish and pass on to my own three children is a result of her wisdom and love.
Thank you, Mom.
Love, Eric

ACKNOWLEDGMENTS

This book could not have been written without the support of my wife and family. For over a year now, my wife has taken care of duties I'm supposed to perform, and she also has typed a major portion of this book. My kids have seen much less of their Dad than they should. Through it all, my family has encouraged me, loved me, and allowed me the exorbitant amount of time required to write this book.

There are not enough words to express my appreciation for Marilyn Smith, my editor. Marilyn did much more than fix my words and grammar, which was no small task by itself. Marilyn helped me craft this book. Marilyn never tried to overwhelm me, but her contributions are a significant reason for my pride in its final contents.

Gemma O'Sullivan was responsible for keeping this book on track. A sweeter boss I have never had. Gemma understood when I tried to do too much in too short a time. Instead of threatening me when I missed a deadline, she helped me define a schedule I could make. Gemma was always ready with a thank you and understanding when I needed it most.

My technical editor, David Medinets, asked the most infuriating questions and caught the most embarrassing mistakes. His questions always led to a better explanation of a particular topic, and the mistakes he caught you will never see. David is the definition of a great technical editor. He is someone who just won't let you get away with an explanation that isn't quite complete.

I've worked with three different publishers so far. Sybex is special. Sybex has a great staff and has allowed me the time I need to write, even when I was behind schedule. Thanks to Richard Mills, associate publisher; Maureen Adams, developmental editor; Elizabeth Hurley-Clevenger, project editor; Susan Berge, production coordinator; PageMasters, electronic publishing specialist; and Tony Jonick, graphic artist.

My co-workers and partners James and Tim always helped, advised, and stepped in when I needed extra time to work on the book. Thanks, guys.

CONTENTS AT A GLANCE

TABLE OF CONTENTS

PART III   Input and Output Handling

PART V   Advanced Perl Programming

INTRODUCTION

Perl 5 is absolutely the best language I've ever encountered. Perl 5 is currently the most popular language for Internet programming.

I think working with code, especially Perl 5 code, is one of the best and most fun jobs in the country. That is the basic philosophy of this book: Programming is fun. It's not mysterious, cryptic, or indecipherable. If you have ever felt that code or the coding process *is* mysterious, cryptic, or indecipherable, then this book is for you.

It is the goal of this book to make sure you understand the fundamentals before moving onto the details. Just understanding the syntax is not enough. Real programming solutions require an understanding of the context in which the language works. This book shows you the context of the code as well as the syntax, providing the foundation you need to master Perl 5.

Programming provides you with multiple approaches for solving the same problem. This book is written to give you the understanding you need to choose the best solution.

Note that this is not just a Unix book or a Unix book with a bit of Windows programming thrown in; it's a complete explanation of Perl 5 from a totally fresh perspective. Perl is a cross-platform language by design, which means that most code runs on both a Windows and Unix platform by default. Most of the programs presented in the book were written on a Windows computer, then run on both Windows and Unix platforms. And although the book's main goal is to teach you how to program using Perl 5, you'll also learn how to build CGI programs that run over the Internet.

Who Should Read This Book

Through the innovative use of a two-track chapter system, this book is designed for both novice and experienced programmers. If you are an experienced programmer who needs something more than a syntax reference but less than an exhaustive explanation, you can go directly to the "jump-start" chapter for each of the main topics covered in this book. By reading the jump-start chapters, experienced programmers can learn Perl 5 in a day. Each jump-start chapter includes a glossary of the terms used in that part of the book plus a jump-start program that demonstrates the major concepts covered.

If you are a novice programmer, you will find careful explanations of concepts and code, without a lot of techno-babble, in the chapters that follow each jump-start chapter. You can look over the jump-start chapter to get a feel for the concepts covered in that part of the book and then read the following chapters for details and examples.

What's in This Book

If you're new to programming, the job may seem confusing because most programming guides skip over bits of essential information. Chapter 1 of this book supplies those missing puzzle pieces. You'll learn how to use the command line and programming editors. However, the first chapter isn't all talk and no action. You'll step through writing and running two programs—one that runs on both Windows and Unix systems and one that runs on the Internet as a CGI program. This first chapter includes information on configuring your web server.

Chapter 2 steps you through the debugging process. If you've ever written code, you know that a good deal of your programming time is spent uncovering and fixing errors, which are called *bugs*. Both novice and experienced programmers make mistakes. If you don't know how to find and fix those mistakes, your early programming experiences can be very frustrating. I don't want that to happen. Chapter 2 explains the fundamentals of debugging your code and includes some useful techniques you can apply to Perl 5 code.

Chapter 3 is the first jump-start chapter, which gets you started with Perl 5 basics. Chapters 3 through 9 focus on the fundamental elements of the Perl 5 language. In these chapters, you will learn about Perl 5 operators, data structures, and control statements.

Chapters 10 through 13 explain the intricacies of I/O (input/output) programming in Perl 5. Chapter 10 is the jump-start chapter for this part of the book, providing an overview of handling I/O, printing and formatting output, and using I/O utilities.

Chapters 14 through 16 cover Perl 5's most powerful features: string processing and regular expressions. Chapter 14 is the jump-start on strings and regular expressions, and the next two chapters provide all the details you need to manipulate strings and interpret regular expressions.

Chapters 17 through 20 explore advanced features and topics of Perl 5. Chapter 17 gives you a jump-start on functional and object-oriented programming, as well as e-mail solutions. You'll learn about symbol tables, data scope, and packages in Chapter 18. Chapter 19 focuses on the object-oriented features of Perl 5. Chapter 20 explains how to create e-mail applications that run on Windows and Unix platforms.

Chapters 21 through 24 are specific to Windows platforms. Chapter 21 provides the jump-start for Windows solutions. Chapter 22 provides details about system administration, including obtaining information about your file system, users, and network. Chapter 23 concentrates on accessing and manipulating the Windows Registry. Chapter 24 explains how to create Perl 5 applications that connect to database engines, such as Microsoft Access, and includes a complete example of exporting your database to the Internet.

Additionally, you'll find a quick reference to Perl 5's variables printed on the inside covers of this book.

About the Examples

Each concept discussed in this book is illustrated and clarified with examples. There are more than 150 code listings in this book, demonstrating how Perl 5 code works to solve real problems. The majority of the programs in this book were built first on my Windows computer and then tested on a Unix platform.

Many of the examples in this book are drawn from actual programming tasks that were implemented by my peers or myself. Several examples are from commercial Internet products my company has launched on the World Wide Web.

All of the programs and examples used in this book are available from the Sybex web site at www.Sybex.com, as well as from the book's companion web site at www.MasteringPerl5.com.

If you have any questions or comments about the examples or other information in this book, you can contact the author at EricHerrmann@MasteringPerl5.com.

Perl 5 Resources

Throughout this book, you'll find references to editors, debuggers, listings, programs, modules, and other Perl 5-related items.

The best information and programs are available from this book's web sites: www.sybex.com and www.MasteringPerl5.com. Along with all the examples presented in this book, the web site also contains lists of Perl 5's built-in functions and modules, the ASCII table, a glossary, and other useful material. Additionally, you can download programming editors and some of the other software mentioned in this book. However, there are many resources for getting the latest information about Perl 5. Here, I have listed some of the resources that have proved valuable to me over my programming career.

Note that newsgroups are *not* a source of online documentation. They can be useful for getting help with a specific Perl coding problem, but unless you enjoy getting nasty e-notes, you should first take advantage of the other resources available. Before you go to the newsgroups to ask your question, check the FAQs, the man pages, the POD pages, and archived newsgroups messages (with the Dejanews search engine).

Frequently Asked Questions (FAQs)

If you are new to Perl and you have a question, check the FAQs first. They are called frequently asked questions because that is exactly what they contain—all the questions that are asked over and over again.

The Perl community has created and maintained some of the best FAQs on the Internet. Tom Christiansen and Nathan Torkington have worked hard to keep their Perl 5 FAQ up-to-date, and it remains one of the better sources of online Perl documentation available. Their FAQ is located at http://www.perl.com/ perl/faq, which is a subdirectory off the main site for Perl documentation, code, and binaries at http://www.perl.com/perl. Be aware that this site is heavily traveled, and the connections are frequently very slow.

One of the drawbacks to the official Perl FAQ is its focus on the Unix implementation of Perl. One of the better FAQs for Windows platforms is Evangelo Prodromou's Perl for Win32 FAQ. This FAQ is a nice overview of the features available for the Win32 platform. You can download the latest version of this FAQ from http://www.ActiveState.com/support/faqswin32.

Recently, I have found ftp://ftp.cdrom.com/pub/perl/CPAN an excellent site for Perl information. This site is maintained by Walnut Creek Software, a commercial company that offers CD-ROMs of freeware and shareware. Walnut Creek Software distributes a CD-ROM of the perl.com/perl site, which is updated semi-annually. Also available from the Walnut Creek Software site is "The Idiot's Guide to Solving Perl CGI Problems" by Tom Christiansen.

Man Pages

The man pages are primarily a Unix documentation tool (if you are not on a Unix machine, the man pages aren't very helpful). The name *man* is short for manual. If you are working at the Unix command line and you want to look at the manual for a particular command, you can request a man page. For example, to see information about the sleep command, simply type:

```
man sleep
```

Unix's man pages are often rather terse. Nevertheless, they are always available for looking up information on any command you can execute from the Unix command line. It's even possible to get online help on Perl, like this:

```
man perl
```

This man request produces pages of information on using Perl.

If your man request for Perl information doesn't return anything, it may be because the MANPATH environment variable isn't set correctly. The man command searches for man pages in the directories listed in the MANPATH environment variable. If the Perl man pages are not installed into one of the standard man directories, then the man command will not be able to find the manual pages. The man pages' default locations are in the directories /usr/man, /usr/contrib/man, and /usr/local/man. If your Perl man pages are in a different directory, set the environment variable MANPATH like this:

```
setenv MANPATH = ($MANPATH /path-to-perl/man)
```

Perl Online Documentation—POD Files

POD stands for Plain Old Documentation. Larry Wall, the father of Perl, wanted a simple documentation tool that made paragraphs look like paragraphs. The simplicity of the POD documentation language allows Perl programmers to build their documentation along with their programs with very little effort. POD documentation can even be embedded directly into Perl scripts.

When you are learning Perl or when you are learning about one of the new Perl modules, Perl POD files frequently are available to help you. To view the POD documentation, use one of the POD translators to convert the embedded POD documentation into a separate documentation file. (POD translators also read script files.)

There are several POD translators available. Some of the ones I have seen on the Internet are pod2text.pl, pod2man.pl, pod2html.pl, and pod2latex.pl. The pod2text.pl translator converts POD documentation to simple text. The pod2man.pl and pod2html.pl translators convert POD documentation to man page format and HTML format, respectively. Both of these programs are available for both the Unix and Windows operating systems, giving you an easy way to create online documentation. If you use pod2html.pl to create HTML documentation files, you can read the Perl documentation using your browser any time you need it. To create HTML documentation from a file that contains POD formatting commands, just type something like this:

```
pod2html.pl filename.pod
```

You can usually create documentation for Perl 5 modules by using the POD documentation embedded in the modules, like this:

```
pod2html.pl modulename.pm
```

HTML Files

One of the most complete HTML documentation sources I've found is included with the ActivePerl build, the Perl 5 build for Windows. Even if you work on a Unix computer, you might want to extract just the HTML pages.

After you install the ActivePerl build, the HTML pages are loaded onto your hard disk, giving you the benefits of HTML hyperlinks without the frustrating delays of Internet connections. On my computer, the HTML index was installed at c:\Perl5\html\index.html. This HTML index page includes links to the official

Perl 5 FAQ, the Win32 FAQ, module documentation, ISAPI (Internet Server Application Programming Interface), and PerlScript documentation. All of these excellent sources of Perl documentation are loaded onto your hard disk when you install the ActivePerl build.

When you have exhausted the HTML documentation on your hard disk, it may seem like it's time to post a question to a Perl newsgroup. However, before you take that step, read the next section to see how you can search newsgroups to discover if the question you want to post has already been answered.

Dejanews

Newsgroups give you the ability to ask your question to anyone who might have already solved your problem. However, it is likely that someone has already asked your question and gotten a useful answer. To find out if this is the case, you can search through all the archived messages of a newsgroup. Unfortunately, searching through the archived messages of a newsgroup can be a slow and tedious task. A great solution is to use Dejanews.

Dejanews is a newsgroup search engine that has archived more than 100 million messages, using more than 175 gigabytes of disk space. Its archive of Usenet messages goes back to March 1995. Dejanews also offers some search tools that let you search for your question and get your answer without needing to read through a bunch of irrelevant messages.

The Dejanews home page is at http://www.dejanews.com. Dejanews calls its home page the Quick Search Page. The Quick Search Page searches the Dejanews current message database, which usually has the last few weeks of messages of all the archived newsgroups. The Quick Search Page tries to match all of the keywords you included in your search. The results will be returned to you in a list, which shows the date of the message, a score, the subject heading of the message, the newsgroup the message is from, and the author of the message. The messages are sorted based on the number of matches to your search words.

Instead of going through the Dejanews home page, you may want to bookmark the Dejanews Power Search Page at http://www.dejanews.com/home_ps.shtml. This page allows you to customize your search criteria to specify the level of information you see (concise or detailed), which database is searched, and other search options. I frequently limit my search to the relevant newsgroups, which are usually comp.lang.perl.misc and comp.infosystems.www.authoring.cgi (the CGI newsgroup).

You also can use the Dejanews Power Search Page to find all of the newsgroups that relate to a particular topic. Just enter your topic name with an asterisk in front of it. Set the From and To fields to the current date, and leave the other fields blank. Select the Create Filter button, and you'll get a list of documents with their newsgroups listed beside them. These are most (if not all) of the newsgroups that have anything interesting to say about the topic you specified.

Perl Newsgroups

Usenet newsgroups are a fantastic resource for staying abreast of what is going on in your field and for getting answers to some difficult questions. Newsgroups also can be a place to get rude, unkind, and unhelpful e-mail. Before you post, please take the time to use the other resources you've just read about.

Now, I must admit, I am a lurker. A lurker is someone who reads the newsgroup but seldom posts. I read newsgroups to find out what problems everyone is trying to solve and because it's fun to watch the group banter over some side topic like Perl versus Java. When you start reading a new newsgroup, I recommend spending about two weeks getting to know the personality of that particular group.

The newsgroup for the best information on Perl 5 is comp.lang.perl.misc. There are some very smart people contributing to this list as well as a few Perl celebrities. Larry Wall, Randal Schwartz, and Tom Christiansen regularly contribute to this newsgroup.

The comp.lang.perl.misc newsgroup is definitely misnamed; this is not a miscellaneous newsgroup. This newsgroup is *only* about Perl programming questions. Everyday someone asks a CGI question in this newsgroup, and that someone gets an e-mail reminder that this is a Perl newsgroup, not a CGI newsgroup. If you have a question about CGI programming, don't post it (or even cross-post it) to comp.lang.perl.misc; post it to comp.infosystems.www.authoring.cgi. However, if you have a Perl 5 problem that you just cannot figure out, you can try posting to comp.lang.perl.misc. Make sure you include your code in the post, because it is impossible to answer a programming question thoroughly without seeing the code.

If you are using Perl 5 for Internet, CGI, database connectivity, or HTML applications, two newsgroups to check out are comp.infosystems.www.authoring.cgi and comp.infosystems.www.authoring.html.

Perl Mailing Lists

Mailing lists are also a good source of Perl programming information. Mailing lists allow you to communicate through your e-mail programs without requiring you to constantly monitor a newsgroup discussion.

Most mailing lists have a feature called digest, which allows you to get a day's, a week's, or a month's worth of messages in one e-mail message. With the digest feature, you can subscribe to an e-mail list without getting tens, hundreds, or thousands of e-mail messages daily.

Useful e-mail lists for Perl and Internet programmers are the Active State admin, database, and user digest lists. You must go to www.ActiveState.com to register for these Win32 mailing lists. Don't be fooled by the Win32 in the Active State mailing list name. These mailing lists, especially the user list, answer all types of Perl questions. Furthermore, unlike some of the newsgroups, the people involved in the mailing lists are very tolerant of newcomers' questions.

PART I

A Quick Start to Perl Programming

CHAPTER
ONE

Writing Your First Program

- An introduction to Perl 5

- A system administration program

- The command-line interface for running Perl programs

- Programmer's editors for Windows and Unix

- Perl program structure and components

- An introduction to CGI and HTTP communications

- A CGI program that runs on a web server

Introductions are important. You can describe someone with words, but a real introduction should be done in person. This chapter provides a personal introduction to Perl 5. You will meet Perl 5 through two programs. The first program, which shows your system configuration variables, demonstrates the simplicity of Perl 5. The second program illustrates Perl 5's most recent application, which is CGI programming. These two programs represent the minor poles of Perl 5: system administration and Internet programming. One program is five lines long; the other program is more than 75 lines. You'll see that Perl 5 is a programming language for a myriad of uses.

This chapter begins with some background on Perl 5 and explains what type of programming language Perl is. It then progresses rapidly through running and editing Perl 5 programs. In the final sections of the chapter, you'll work through a CGI program example. When you're finished with this chapter, you'll have some useful Perl 5 programs and you'll understand how to edit and run Perl 5 programs on your own computer and over the Internet.

Introducing Perl 5

Perl 5 is the most powerful, easy to use, and full-featured programming language available today. That's my opinion, so let me tell you why I think Perl 5 is the best.

Perl was written by a linguist, not a computer scientist, named Larry Wall. Larry built Perl to evolve over time, as a language does. Traditional programming languages evolve slowly and at some point stop changing. Perl, like a spoken language, evolves quickly to meet each new generation's needs.

The Evolution of Perl

Perl stands for Practical Extraction Report Language. Perl's original purpose was to generate reports that tracked errors and corrections to a software development project that involved multiple types of machines and spanned the United States.

The distribution of Perl 5 has always been freely available on the Internet, and that distribution includes the source code. Distributing a language's source code is a bold and uncommon move. It means anyone can modify the language to meet individual needs and goals.

Perl attracted the attention of Unix system administrators, who needed a language that was easier to use than the C programming language and more powerful than scripting languages such as Borne and C-shell. Unix system administrators and others contributed to the language, updating it and submitting free scripts that made their jobs easier. Originally, most Perl users were Unix system administrators and other people with similar needs, who used Perl's text-processing power to generate reports and write scripts that aided in the configuration and monitoring of Unix systems.

In 1994, the World Wide Web, through the Netscape browser, became a new and powerful influence on the jobs of Unix system administrators. They turned to Perl as their tool to help them with their new World Wide Web tasks. As they built new tools, they continued their practice of sharing those tools.

When new users of the web wanted to create dynamic web pages through CGI programming, they were generally working on a Unix web server. Perl was freely available on those Unix web servers, and users started using Perl for their CGI applications. Because Perl was built to process text, and much of CGI programming is processing user input and returning HTML text pages, Perl was a natural fit for this new programming environment.

These new users of Perl continued the tradition of sharing their programs freely throughout the Internet. In the middle 1990s, Perl continued to evolve and went through a major maturation stage with revision five, called Perl 5. Much like the difference between Windows 3.1 and Windows 95, Perl 5 is more than just another upgrade of Perl. Perl 5 is a total rewrite of the original Perl, with many new features. Perl 5 is not just Perl any more than C++ is just C.

Perl was always designed to run on any computer, but because it usually ran on a Unix computer, it had (and still has) a decidedly Unix flavor. In the later half of the 1990s, applications and versions of Perl targeted toward Windows programming environments started appearing. Today, Windows versions of Perl 5 are freely available and are distributed with the main Perl 5 distribution. The programs written for this book are first run on a Windows computer and then tested on a Unix computer, if necessary.

This is the state of Perl 5 today. It is the de facto programming language for dynamic HTML web pages. It is easy to use, and there are thousands of free CGI, system administrative, and text processing programs written in Perl available on the Internet. With the addition of references to Perl 5 (which you'll learn about in Chapter 7), the language is maturing into the mainstream programming world.

A Perl Program

As I said at the beginning of this chapter, the best way to introduce you to Perl 5 is with some Perl code. Listing 1.1 is a little program that lets you see some information about your computer.

Listing 1.1:   **Environment Variables**

```
1. #!/usr/local/bin/perl
2. foreach $key (keys %ENV){
3. print qq|The value of $key is $ENV{"$key"}\n|;
4. }
```

TIP   The program shown in Listing 1.1 is available from this book's companion web pages on the Sybex web site (go to **www.sybex.com**, click on Catalog, then perform a search for the book to go to the companion pages), as are all the examples in this book. However, I recommend typing in most of the listings, except for the long ones. Just the act of typing in a program seems to help you remember what you just read about it. It's easy to just go to sleep reading a technical book. So, here's your opportunity to get some Dilbert-type exercise—make those finger muscles humongous!

The output from Listing 1.1 is shown in Figure 1.1. If you have Perl 5 installed on your computer, you can run this program without compiling it and see the environment variables on your computer.

Environment variables are created each time you run a program. An environment variable contains information about the services, hardware, and data available to your program. The environment variables available to your program vary based on where the program is executing. For example, the environment variables available from an MS-DOS window, a Unix command shell, or a CGI program are different. As you can see in Figure 1.1, environment variables include things like your username, your processor's type, and the name of your operating system.

If you don't have Perl 5 installed yet, see Appendix A. If you don't know how to run this program from your computer, don't worry. You'll learn how to run Perl programs in this chapter. If you don't know what I meant when I said you could run this program "without compiling it," let me explain that Perl 5 is an interpreted language, which means it is not compiled to a binary executable. The difference between an interpreted language and a binary executable is important to Perl programmers, so we will explore those concepts in the next section.

FIGURE 1.1:

Running a Perl program to get environment variables

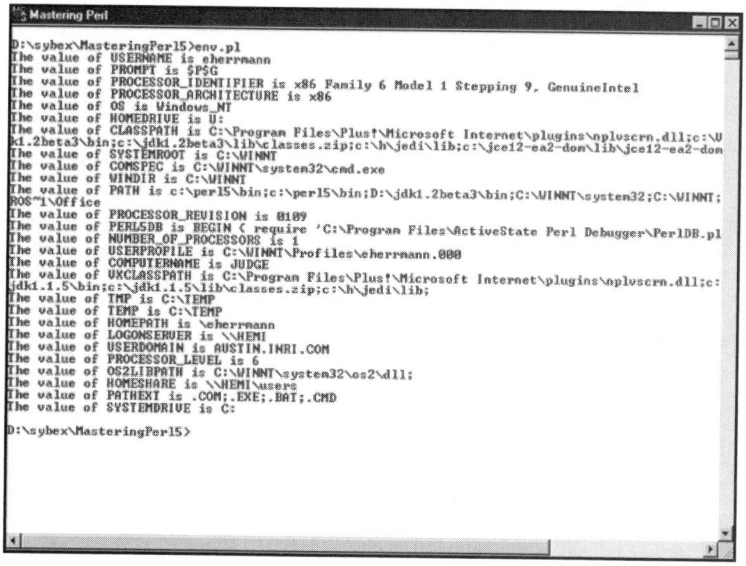

Perl as an Interpreted Language

Perl 5 is an interpreted language. Programs are usually run in one of two forms: as binary executables or as interpreted. *Binary executables* are programs that have been compiled and linked into a format that can run on a computer without the compiler or linker present. Interpreted programs, on the other hand, require the interpreter to be installed on the computer they are running on. But this explanation doesn't make much sense without definitions of the terms compiler, linker, and interpreter.

A *compiler* takes the code you type into a file, like the code in Listing 1.1, and converts it into a series of ones and zeros, or binary numbers, that your computer understands. (You'll learn more about binary numbers in Chapter 4.) However, the compiled program is only a small piece of an overall binary executable.

Modern programs use preexisting library routines to add, subtract, print output, and get input. These library routines are like pieces of a puzzle that need to be linked together with the newly compiled program to create a binary executable. This is the job of the *linker*. A compiled language, such as C, requires you to install a compiler and linker on your computer. You then compile and link your program, which can be a lengthy and painful process. The result of this process, however, produces a binary executable program that runs without the compiler and linker.

A program written in an interpreted language, such as Perl 5, is converted to machine-readable format when the program is run. This means that it does not go through the standard compilation and linking process that binary executables do. Interpreted programs run the code that is in a file just as you see it, as in Listing 1.1. The steps required to run a program—converting the programming language to machine-readable format and then linking in other library routines—still occur. These steps take place when your interpreted program begins execution, and they are handled by the *interpreter*. This means that the interpreter that converts your program must be installed wherever your program runs, which has two main effects.

First, because your program is converted into machine format at the moment it is run, that machine format is more likely to be compatible with the machine it is running on. This is one of the primary features of Perl 5. Your Perl 5 programs are likely to run on any platform without modifications. This is in contrast to binary executable programs. Because binary executables usually contain operating system-specific information, you usually must compile and link a version of your program for every version of each operating system you want your program to run on.

NOTE   Binary executable programs usually need to be run on a computer that has the same operating system and operating system version as the one it was compiled and linked on. Different versions of the same operating system are sometimes compatible, but this is not always the case. MS-DOS, Windows 3.1, Windows 95/98, and Windows NT are versions of the same or similar operating systems that are not compatible. Different operating systems like Unix, Windows, and the Macintosh operating system are seldom compatible.

Second, because your program is converted to machine format when it is executed, most interpreted programs are slower than similar programs that are compiled. It takes time to convert your Perl 5 syntax to machine format. However, since Perl 5 is an extremely optimized and fast interpreted language, it isn't much slower than compiled code. For this small sacrifice in speed, you get a language that is very portable (can be run on different operating systems without modification).

Another benefit of an interpreted language is that the coding and testing process is much easier and faster. With a compiled language, you must write your code, compile it, link it, and then test it. The compiling and linking steps usually take a bit of time and sometimes create additional debugging issues unrelated to the syntax errors in your code. With Perl 5, you just write your code and test it. This process is very quick and leads to a programming paradigm called "code a little; test a little," which is an excellent way to develop programs. (*Paradigm*, by the way, just means a way of doing something; in short, a pattern or a model to follow.)

In summary, every program is eventually converted to a machine-readable format, and supporting libraries are made available for the program's use. Binary executables, such as C programs, are converted to machine format before the program is run. Interpreted programs, such as Perl 5 programs, are converted to machine format when your program starts up or sometimes as the program is run. Binary executables are typically faster than interpreted programs, but Perl 5 code usually performs well in speed performance tests against binary executables. Interpreted code is usually more portable than binary executable code. Finally, the code and test process for Perl 5 programs is easier and quicker than the code, compile, link, and test process necessary for binary executables.

Windows, Unix, and Perl

Perl 5, like the Java programming language, will run on a Unix, Windows, or Macintosh operating system, with little or no change required to the code you've written. This feature is called *portability*. The Java jingle of "Write once, run anywhere" also applies to Perl 5. This portability feature of Perl 5 means the beginning programming skills taught in this chapter must be taught for both the Unix and the Windows operating systems. (I will not be covering the Macintosh operating system.)

The Windows operating system family is currently made up of Windows NT, Windows 98, and Windows 95. I will not be addressing the Windows 3.1 operating system, although I suspect Perl 5 would run just fine on Windows 3.1.

The Unix operating systems brands are too numerous to name. Some of the more widely used Unix operating systems are the HP-UX, Sun Solaris, Linux, and Linux Red Hat. Perl 5 runs on all of these brands of Unix without modification.

Differences between Unix and Windows

The differences between the Unix and Windows operating systems can be traced back to the fundamentally different approaches taken in their development. Here's a comparison:

Windows	Unix
Initially developed by an entrepreneur	Developed by some university grad students
Developed for commercial sale	Though now developed by several vendors for commercial sale, is still available in several free varieties
Developed with one man's vision for its future	Developed by many, many contributors with a variety of visions and goals
Developed for ease of use	Developed for easy access to the operating system

Unix may be powerful, but the user interface is frequently cryptic and unknown. Windows may be weak in many areas, but the user interface is easy to learn and consistent.

As Windows moved away from the DOS interface to support the ease-of-use paradigm, its programming interface became less friendly. Unix has always supported the programming interface, and the tools to support programming have increased over the years. The programming interface is where you will notice the greatest difference between the two operating systems but, of course, that is where you will be working. As you learn to use Perl programs, you will learn the differences between these two operating systems' programmer interface, which is the command line.

Running Perl Programs

You run Perl 5 programs from either an MS-DOS window (from a Windows 95/98/NT computer) or the Unix command shell (if you're running the Unix operating system). Both are referred to as the *command-line interface*. In this section, you will learn the few commands that are necessary on the Windows and Unix operating systems to run Perl 5 programs (such as the one shown in Listing 1.1).

NOTE   You won't be able to run any Perl 5 programs unless you have Perl 5 installed on your computer. If you don't have Perl 5 installed yet, turn to Appendix A for instructions.

You may be thinking that if you're running Windows, you don't need to read the information about using the Unix command shell. However, if you are writing Perl scripts, some of those scripts are likely to be CGI programs that require installation on a Unix server. You'll learn more about CGI programs later in this chapter. For now, you should read through the Unix command shell section so you will be prepared.

Using the MS-DOS Window

The MS-DOS window is an independent window that allows you to enter MS-DOS commands from the keyboard. You open an MS-DOS window by selecting Start ➤ Programs ➤ Command Prompt (or MS-DOS Prompt), as shown in Figure 1.2.

When you open an MS-DOS window, your cursor is placed at the right of the command prompt (>). The *command prompt* is the keyboard interface for issuing MS-DOS commands. The command prompt, by default, displays the current working directory, as you can see in Figure 1.3.

TIP   On a Windows NT computer, you can modify the starting size, background color, and window fonts of the MS-DOS window by right-clicking on the MS-DOS program icon and selecting the Properties menu option.

FIGURE 1.2:

Opening an MS-DOS window

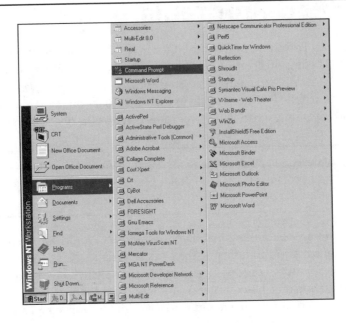

FIGURE 1.3:

The command prompt in an MS-DOS window

There are just a few commands you must know to run Perl programs from the MS-DOS window. You need to know how to view the contents of a directory, change directories, create a directory, and start a program.

Working with Directories

To view the contents of a directory, use the `dir` command. This command lists the directory in long format, which shows each file's eight-character filename and extension, size, last modified date, and full name. To see the directory in abbreviated format, use the command `dir/w`. Abbreviated format shows only the eight-character name and three-character extension of each file in the directory.

To change to a different directory, use the cd command. To tell the command which directory you want to change to, you enter a path name as a command argument. A *path name* is a guide to a location on your computer, including the drive, directory, and subdirectories. A *command argument* is the additional information you supply to the command that specifies how the command should operate or what the command should operate on. The cd command takes either an absolute or relative path name as a command argument. An *absolute* path name starts from the root of the directory tree, represented by a backslash (\), and lists the path all the way to the destination directory. A *relative* path name starts with the current directory and lists the path from there to the one you want.

If you are not starting from the disk drive the absolute path is on, you must change to that particular disk drive. To change disk drives, just type the correct disk drive letter followed by a colon and press Enter (you don't need to type the cd part). For instance, if you want to change to disk drive E, simply type **E:** and press Enter.

To create a new directory, use the mkdir command. Like the cd command, the mkdir command takes an absolute or relative path name as its command argument.

Now that you know what the commands do, you can follow the steps listed below to create a Test directory for your Perl 5 programs, create an MPListings subdirectory under the Test directory, and copy the Listing 1.1 file into the MPListings subdirectory. Here, I assume that you have installed Perl 5 onto your D drive in the directory Perl5 (that's where I have it installed on my computer). If you have installed Perl 5 on another disk drive and/or directory, substitute those names in the following steps. If you haven't installed Perl 5 yet, turn to Appendix A and follow the instructions there first.

1. Select Start ➤ Programs ➤ Command Prompt (or MS-DOS Prompt) to bring up an MS-DOS window. This should put you at the command prompt in some directory on the C disk drive (such as C:\WINDOWS >).

2. Move to the D disk drive by typing **D:** and pressing Enter. (You should press Enter after entering each command, so I won't mention it again.)

When you first change to the D disk drive, you should be at the root directory, which is D:\. If you are not, you can change to the root directory by typing **cd **.

3. To create a Test directory with an MPListings subdirectory, type:

```
mkdir \Perl5\Test\MPListings
```

4. Now copy the file that contains Listing 1.1 into the D:\Perl5\Test\MPListings directory. You can use the copy command from the MS-DOS window, like this:

```
copy environmentVariables.pl
     D:\Perl5\Test\MPListings\environmentVariables.pl
```

Or you can run Windows Explorer and drag-and-drop the environment Variables.pl file into the new directory, which is the method I prefer.

In step 3, we used an absolute path name to create the directory. This command could be executed from anywhere on the D drive. On your Windows computer, you can create a directory node without first creating previous directory nodes. In other words, it is not necessary to create the Test directory before you create the MPListings directory.

NOTE   A *directory node* is another name for any individual directory along a directory path. A *directory tree* is a set of directories that has a beginning node and several nodes that are subdirectories beneath the beginning node. The beginning node of a directory tree is called the *root node*. When you install Perl 5 into the directory D:\Perl5, this creates a directory tree. The root node is Perl5. The subdirectories underneath the root node, such as Test, lib, html, and eg, are branches along the Perl5 directory tree.

You could also create the directories using relative path names, which would look like this:

```
>D:
>cd Perl5
>mkdir test
>cd test
>mkdir MPListings
```

Each of these commands uses a relative path name. The path name is relative to the current working directory. Changing directories to the Perl5 directory is relative to the root directory. Creating the Test directory is relative to the Perl5 directory. Changing directories to the Test directory is relative to the Perl5 directory also. Creating the MPListings directory is relative to the Test directory.

Running a Program

Now you're ready to run a Perl program. To run the program shown in Listing 1.1, follow these steps from the MS-DOS window:

1. Change directories to the MPListings directory using an absolute path name by typing:

   cd \Perl5\test\MPListings

2. If you are on a Windows 95/98 computer, run the program by typing:

   perl environmentVariables.pl

   If you are on a Windows NT computer, type:

   environmentVariables.pl

Now you should see something on your screen similar to Figure 1.1. Getting results without compiling or linking is one of the features I really like about Perl 5.

Using Other MS-DOS Window Commands

There are several other MS-DOS window commands that you might find useful.

If you are on a Windows 95/98 computer, the DOSKEY command will make your life easier. Every time you bring up the MS-DOS window, the first thing you should type is **DOSKEY**. The DOSKEY command tells the MS-DOS window to remember your previously typed-in commands, saving them in a previous command buffer.

With DOSKEY installed, you can use the up arrow key to display your previous commands. You can then press Enter to execute a previous command exactly as you used it last time, or you can modify a previous command to perform a similar but slightly different command. To modify a previous command, press the up or down arrow key until you see the command you want to modify, then use the left and right arrow, Delete, Backspace, and/or regular alphanumeric keys to modify the command to perform the new operation. Once you get used to using the previous command buffer, you'll save a lot of time entering new commands.

The previous command buffer, created by the DOSKEY command on a Windows 95/98 computer, exists by default on a Windows NT computer. In Windows NT, you can access the buffer by pressing the up and down arrow keys or the F7 key. When you press F7 from an MS-DOS window, you get a pop-up window that lets you select the next command to execute.

Another command you might want to use in the MS-DOS window is rmdir, which deletes a directory. The directory must be empty before it can be deleted. Use the rmdir command with relative and absolute path names, in the same way that you use the mkdir and cd commands.

If you want to delete a file, you can use the del command from the MS-DOS window, like this:

```
del fileName.pl
```

Finally, you can get additional help on MS-DOS commands by typing **help** at the MS-DOS command prompt.

Using the Unix Command Shell

Navigating around the Unix command shell isn't a lot different from navigating through the MS-DOS window. However, unlike with the Windows operating system, the Unix command shell is the default interface for the Unix operating system. Some Unix brands, like HP-UX and Sun Solaris, have a more Windows-like environment, but most Unix users start out at the Unix command shell when they log on to a Unix computer.

If you are reading this section, it's probably because you need to install a CGI program on a Unix web server. Your CGI programming interface is likely through a telnet session, which is discussed later in this chapter. The commands you use to run the program in Listing 1.1 on your Unix computer are the same commands that you use to install your CGI program, and they are similar to the MS-DOS commands explained in the previous section.

Working with Unix Directories

The Unix command shell has a command prompt, much like the MS-DOS window. However, the default Unix command prompt is not the current working directory, and it may be something as simple as the right arrow (>). Figure 1.4 shows the Unix command shell. To see the current working directory on a Unix computer, use the pwd (print working directory) command.

To view the contents of the current directory on a Unix computer, use the ls (list) command. The ls command shows the contents of the directory in an abbreviated format, much like the MS-DOS dir/w command. To view more details about the files in the current working directory, add switches to the ls command (a *switch* modifies the basic behavior of a command). To view the contents of the directory in long format, use the `ls -lat` command. These switches tell the `ls` command to list the directory contents in long format (`l`), list all filenames (`a`), and show the times associated with each file (`t`).

FIGURE 1.4:

The Unix command shell

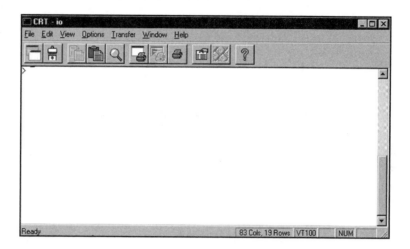

To change directories, use the `cd` command, using the same syntax as described for the MS-DOS `cd` command in the previous section. One difference between the two commands is the separator used in the path name. Unix uses a forward slash (/) directory separator rather than the backslash (\) used by MS-DOS. Another difference is that unlike MS-DOS path names and filenames, Unix path names and filenames are case-sensitive. In other words, the directory *test* is different from the directory *Test*.

The following steps show you how to create a Perl5 test directory and an MPListings subdirectory, then copy the program shown in Listing 1.1 into that subdirectory. Note that the Unix environment is less forgiving than the MS-DOS environment. You need to explicitly create each directory node separately. Also, unlike with Windows systems, I don't recommend creating your test directory in the Perl5 installation directory. It's a better idea to create the MPListings directory underneath the default login directory on your Unix computer. The default login directory is likely to be a directory named after your login user name. For example, on my web server, my default login directory (or *home directory* as it is often called) is ~yawp.

1. Create the MPListings directory node by using relative directory paths. The beginning relative path will be relative to your home directory. Type this:

```
mkdir Perl5
mkdir Perl5\test
mkdir Perl5\test\MPListings
```

2. To copy the file that contains Listing 1.1 to the MPListings directory, type (all on one line):

```
cp environmentVariables.pl Perl5\test\MPListings\
environmentVariables.pl
```

Running a Program under Unix

You could run the program in Listing 1.1 under Unix just as you did from the Windows 95/98 operating system, like this:

```
>perl environmentVariables.pl
```

However, this is not the preferred way of running executable programs on a Unix computer. Unlike MS-DOS, which uses file extensions to associate a file type with a program (the file type of .pl is associated with Perl 5 executables when you install Perl 5 on a Windows computer), Unix associates file types with permissions modes. Permission modes tell the system whether the file is readable, writable, and/or executable.

After the Unix command shell has determined a file is executable, it looks for a line in the file that tells it which program to run with the executable file. Perl 5 programs that run on a Unix computer must include a line that has the path to the Perl 5 installation (as in Listing 1.1), like this:

```
#!/usr/local/bin/perl
```

Unix file permissions are separated into three groups: owner, group, and world. Each group has three privileges that may be turned on or off: read access, write access, and executable access. The Unix chmod command modifies a file-access permission using a three-digit number that assigns a permissions value to the files. The possible permissions values make up a binary number, which is typed in as an octal value. The possible octal numbers and their meanings are shown in Table 1.1. (Binary, octal, and hexadecimal numbers are discussed in Chapter 4.)

TABLE 1.1: Unix Permissions

Binary Number	Octal Number	Meaning
000	0	No permissions
001	1	Execute only
010	2	Write only
011	3	Write and execute
100	4	Read only
101	5	Read and execute
110	6	Read and write
111	7	Read, write, and execute

You set the file permissions for each group using a single octal digit to represent each group's permissions. To set the permissions to read, write, and execute for the owner and to read and execute for the group and world, combine the three permission values like this:

owner = 7, group = 5, world = 5

Therefore, to make your Perl program executable from the command line, you must change its permissions mode to executable (755), using the chmod command, like this:

```
>chmod 755 filename.pl
```

To run the program shown in Listing 1.1, follow these steps from the Unix command shell:

1. Change directories to the MPListing directory by typing:

   cd \Perl5\test\MPListings

2. Make the program executable by typing:

   chmod 755 environmentVariables.pl

NOTE   Remember that Unix filenames are case-sensitive: *environmentVariables.pl* is not the same file as *EnvironmentVariables.pl*.

---

3. To run the program, simply type the name of the executable file (just as from a Windows NT computer):

```
environmentVariables.pl
```

If this doesn't work for you, try including the current working directory, like this:

```
./environmentVariables.pl
```

You should see something similar to Figure 1.1 on your screen. As with the MS-DOS window example, compiling and linking a Perl 5 program is not necessary to run the program file.

Using Other Unix Commands

In the MS-DOS window section, I suggested that you use the DOSKEY command to save your commands in a previous command buffer. Unix has a DOSKEY-like command, called history. To make the history command active, type **set history=100**. To view the history list, type **history**. To use the last command, type **!!**. To use a particular number in the history list, type **!n**. To use the first few unique characters of a previous command, type **!ls**.

The history command is fairly complex. If you want to use this command, I suggest learning more about it by reading the man pages. (Unix online help is always available from the man pages.) The command man is short for manual. To see the online manual for the history command from the command prompt, type **man history**.

The Unix commands for creating and deleting directories are the same as those used in the MS-DOS window: mkdir creates a directory and rmdir removes one. The Unix command for deleting a file is rm, and the command for copying a file is cp.

Using Programmer's Editors

While you are learning Perl, you should be writing and editing the listings in this book. However, I don't recommend using just any text editor or word processing program. If you are working on a Windows computer and using Notepad or Microsoft Word to edit your programs, you are making your job harder, not easier. If you are working on a Unix computer and using vi as your editor, you are making the same mistake. When you are writing Perl programs, you should be working in an environment that enhances your productivity. You should be using an editor that understands the programming language. These types of editors are called language-sensitive or programmer's editors, and they make your programming job a lot easier.

In this section, I will briefly describe four editors that I recommend for writing and editing Perl programs. Each of these programs is available from the companion pages for this book at the Sybex web site (www.sybex.com), as well as from the individual sites mentioned in the following sections, for you to download and test. All of these editors are free, with the exception of Multi-Edit.

Choosing a Windows Editor

For Windows users, I recommend two editors. One of these is free, and the other is a commercial product.

If you want to save money, I highly recommend NTEmacs, which runs on Windows 95/98 systems (despite its name), as well as on Windows NT systems. As shown in Figure 1.5, NTEmacs has all the features of Xemacs, a powerful Unix editor described in the next section. This is a great editor, so don't let the fact that it is free scare you away. NTEmacs is available at www.cs.washington.edu/hones/voelker/ntemacs or ftp://ftp.sunet.selfpublos/Win32/ntEmacs/docs/ntemacs.html.

The other Windows editor I recommend is called Multi-Edit, which costs between $100 and $130. As shown in Figure 1.6, Multi-Edit has a highly configurable user interface. It's easy to use, so you won't waste a lot of time learning the tool, and it has tons of features. A fully functional demo version (it has a nag screen in the demo) of Multi-Edit is available at www.multiedit.com.

If Multi-Edit doesn't know about a filename extension, like .cgi or .notes, you can add extensions and customize existing ones. The keyboard interface is customizable, as is the language-sensitive interface. Multi-Edit has a fantastic file-compare feature, in-line file numbering, a multiple-window interface, and much too much more to list. It makes my programming editing tasks incredibly easier than using Notepad or Microsoft Word.

FIGURE 1.5:

The NTEmacs editor

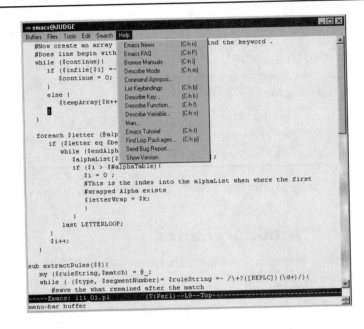

FIGURE 1.6:

The Multi-Edit interface

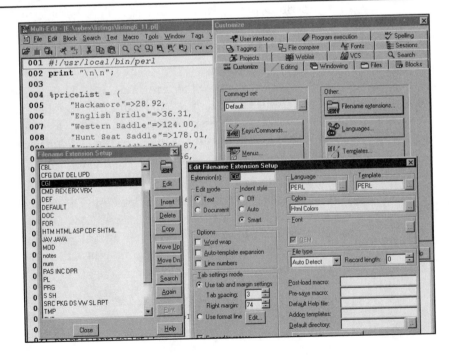

NOTE

In case you are curious, I am not affiliated with Multi-Edit in any way except that I use Multi-Edit daily on both my Windows 98 and NT computers. When I started working regularly on an NT platform, I needed an editor to replace my first love, Emacs. I learned about Multi-Edit after trying to use Notepad and Word as my editor. Multi-Edit found me when I was most vulnerable—lost and cursing my dadgum NT computer. What a relief to find an editor that worked well on the Windows operating system and understood Perl 5, Java, and C++, my three primary programming languages. However, I don't use Multi-Edit when I'm writing a book, and you shouldn't use Word or Notepad when you're working on a program.

Multi-Edit now includes an HTML editor. Personally, I am not a big fan of most HTML editors because I think they try to do too much. But the Multi-Edit HTML editor gives me just the right amount of source code control.

Choosing a Unix Editor

For the Unix platform, I recommend Xemacs or Nedit. I used Emacs for years in a Unix environment. I was always raving to my peers about this wonderful editor, but they waited until it was converted to the Windows-like Xemacs tool.

Xemacs is a free editor with a Windows-like menu-driven command interface. You can find Xemacs precompiled for a variety of Unix systems, as shown in Figure 1.7. Xemacs is available at `www.xemacs.org/ftp-sites.html`.

If you don't like the Xemacs interface, you should try Nedit. The Nedit editor also has a Windows-like user interface, as shown in Figure 1.8.

The Nedit editor has most of the power of Xemacs, and many users think it is easier to use and learn than Xemacs. Like Xemacs, Nedit is freeware and available for a variety of Unix platforms, as shown in Figure 1.9. You can get Nedit at `ftp://ftp.fnal.gov/pub/nedit`.

In this and the previous sections, you learned about four different editors (two for Windows and two for Unix) that will increase your programming productivity. Test these editors or search online for other programmer's editors, but do make sure to take advantage of these powerful editing environments and increase your productivity.

In the next section, you'll make a small modification to the program in Listing 1.1, allowing you to test one of the editors and double-check your Perl 5 installation.

FIGURE 1.7:

Xemacs platforms

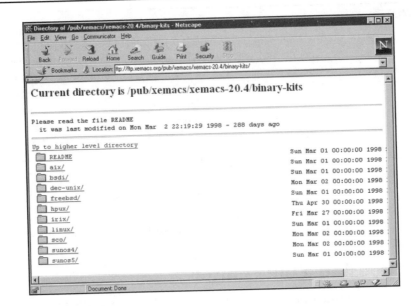

FIGURE 1.8:

The Nedit interface

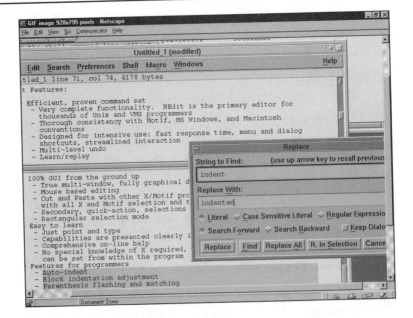

Modifying a Program

The program in Listing 1.1 prints out the environment variables on your Unix or Windows operating system. The environment variables are printed in a seemingly random order. (Actually, the order in which the environment variables are printed is the order in which they are stored in the Perl 5 hash %ENV, which you'll learn about later in the book.) In this section, you are going to modify Listing 1.1 so it prints the environment variables in alphabetical order. This is not a difficult task. The goal of this section is to show you how easy it is to modify and use a Perl 5 program.

FIGURE 1.9:

Nedit platforms

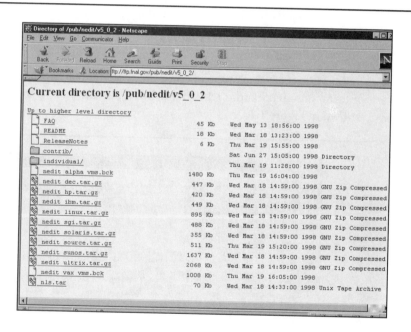

Follow these steps to edit the program:

1. Open Listing 1.1 in your editor of choice.

2. Save Listing 1.1 using a different filename. The filename can be anything, but it should have the extension .pl. I used the filename sortedEnvVars.pl.

3. Modify line 2 by inserting the word **sort** after the opening parenthesis. Make sure you leave a space between the word sort and the word keys, as shown here:

```
foreach $key (sort keys %ENV){
```

4. Save your modified file.

5. Open a command-line interface window (either an MS-DOS window or a Unix command shell). At the command prompt, change directories to the same directory where you saved the modified file.

6. Run the modified file. If you are on a Windows 95/98 computer, type:

    perl sortedEnvVars.pl

    If you are on a Windows NT computer, type:

    sortedEnvVars.pl

    If you are on a Unix computer, type:

    chmod 755 sortedEnvVars.pl
    sortedEnvVars.pl

Regardless of which type of computer you are using, you should see the same information that Listing 1.1 printed, but it should now be in alphabetical order, as shown in Figure 1.10.

FIGURE 1.10:

Sorted environment variables

```
D:\sybex\MasteringPerl5>sortedEnvVars.pl
The value of CLASSPATH is C:\Program Files\Plus!\Microsoft Internet\plugins\nplvscr
k1.2beta3\bin;c:\jdk1.2beta3\lib\classes.zip;c:\h\jedi\lib;c:\jce12-ea2-dom\lib\jce
The value of COMPUTERNAME is JUDGE
The value of COMSPEC is C:\WINNT\system32\cmd.exe
The value of HOMEDRIVE is U:
The value of HOMEPATH is \eherrmann
The value of HOMESHARE is \\HEMI\users
The value of LOGONSERVER is \\HEMI
The value of NUMBER_OF_PROCESSORS is 1
The value of OS is Windows_NT
The value of OS2LIBPATH is C:\WINNT\system32\os2\dll;
The value of PATH is c:\perl5\bin;c:\perl5\bin;D:\jdk1.2beta3\bin;C:\WINNT\system32
ROS~1\Office
The value of PATHEXT is .COM;.EXE;.BAT;.CMD
The value of PERL5DB is BEGIN { require 'C:\Program Files\ActiveState Perl Debugger
The value of PROCESSOR_ARCHITECTURE is x86
The value of PROCESSOR_IDENTIFIER is x86 Family 6 Model 1 Stepping 9, GenuineIntel
The value of PROCESSOR_LEVEL is 6
The value of PROCESSOR_REVISION is 0109
The value of PROMPT is $P$G
The value of SYSTEMDRIVE is C:
The value of SYSTEMROOT is C:\WINNT
The value of TEMP is C:\TEMP
The value of TMP is C:\TEMP
The value of USERDOMAIN is AUSTIN.INRI.COM
The value of USERNAME is eherrmann
The value of USERPROFILE is C:\WINNT\Profiles\eherrmann.000
The value of UXCLASSPATH is C:\Program Files\Plus!\Microsoft Internet\plugins\nplus
jdk1.1.5\bin;c:\jdk1.1.5\lib\classes.zip;c:\h\jedi\lib;
The value of WINDIR is C:\WINNT

D:\sybex\MasteringPerl5>
```

Understanding Perl Syntax Basics

Now that you've run and edited a Perl 5 program, you're ready to learn what Perl expects to see in a program. Here, we'll go over some of the requirements for a program's structure and the components of a Perl 5 program.

All programs do three basic things:

- They manipulate data, which involves storing, retrieving, and modifying data.

- They perform operations (such as adding and subtracting) that modify the data structures created to receive the results of an operation.

- They jump around through branching statements. Branching statements in higher-level languages are called *loop* and *conditional statements*.

A program is made up of many variations on these three basic themes: manipulating data, operating on that data, and jumping around based on testing the contents of a piece of data. The organization of these basic structures makes a program.

Perl Program Structure

Some programming languages require your program to be in a particular format, such as data first, then subroutine declarations, and then the main program. Perl 5 forces very little program structure on you. As you will learn in more detail in later chapters, Perl 5 allows you to declare and define data and subroutines anywhere in your program.

NOTE   A *subroutine* is a reusable piece of code. Subroutines usually are given a name and then referred to as needed throughout a program. When a subroutine is called, your program jumps to the first line of the subroutine. The code in the subroutine runs to completion and then returns control to the calling statement. All subroutines in Perl 5 return a value, which may be saved into a variable. Subroutines that return a value are also called *functions*. You'll learn more about subroutines in Chapter 18.

A subroutine or piece of data that is *declared* is named but not assigned any value. A subroutine or data item that is *defined* is assigned a value and may also be declared at the same time.

A data declaration looks like this:

```
my ($time);
```

The keyword my declares a variable. A *variable* is a name used to store data and refer to that data. The variable in this statement is $time. (The parentheses are not required, but they are convenient if you want to create a definition list.)

A data definition looks like this:

```
my ($length) = 10;
```

This data definition stores the value 10 into the variable $length. You'll learn more about data declarations, data definitions, and variables in Part 2 of this book.

In addition to data and subroutine declarations and definitions, a Perl 5 program includes *statements* (both simple and complex), which you will learn about in the next section.

All Perl 5 programs are part of a package. If the package is undeclared, the package name is main. Packages and program structure are covered in more detail in Part 3 of this book.

Perl Program Components

I'm not really sure why every field—computer programmers, as well as doctors, lawyers, truck drivers, and so on—finds it necessary to change the English language when perfectly ordinary words would work just as well. Nevertheless, there are some terms that you must understand in order to build a program. In this section, you will learn the basic terms used to describe components of Perl 5 programs.

Operators and Lvalues

An *operator* performs a function or operation on a piece of data. For example, the addition operator (+) adds two numbers together, then assigns one value to another data object. The assignment operator (=) takes the value on the right side of the equal sign and stores it into the variable (lvalue) on the left side of the equal sign. Operators are covered in detail in Chapter 4.

The term *lvalue* can be easily translated into left-hand value. It usually refers to the variable on the left side of an assignment operator. An lvalue always refers to some type of modifiable variable. The computer term for modifiable variable is *mutable*. Variables that cannot be modified are called *immutable*. (That's a little bit of geekese you can toss around at parties to awe your friends and attract the fawning attention of the opposite sex, although I must admit that this technique never worked for me.) In Perl 5, the terms *lvalue* and *variable* are interchangeable.

Expressions and Statements

Expression is another one of those computer terms that seems to be used to confuse the uninitiated. Expression in plain English means value. What's unique about an expression is the value is usually the result of some type of operation. An expression may be an operation such as addition, the value returned from a subroutine call, or any other valid Perl 5 operation that returns a value.

A *statement* is made up of an operation and an lvalue. All Perl 5 statements end with a semicolon. (There is an exception to this rule—the semicolon on the last statement of any block, defined in the next section, is optional.) The *syntax* (format) of an assignment statement is:

```
lvalue = expression;
```

For example, you might use this assignment statement:

```
$sum = $subTotal + $tax;
```

This statement adds the values in the variables `$subTotal` and `$tax` together and then assigns the result to the variable `$sum`. Another way to say this is that the lvalue `$sum` is assigned the value of the expression `$subTotal` plus `$tax`.

Blocks

A *block* is a series of related program lines typically used in *control statements*, which are loop and conditional statements used to jump around in programs based on testing the contents of a piece of data. A block begins and ends with opening and closing curly braces. All Perl 5 control statements, such as `if` and `while`, must be formed as a block, like this:

```
if (conditional expression) {

    $lvalue = expression;

}
```

The block of statements may be empty, but it is required. You will learn more about blocks and control statements in Chapters 8 and 9.

Comments

A *comment* is any text in your program that is ignored by the computer, or rather, by the interpreter. Programmers use comments to document their programs, to make it clear to themselves and to other programmers what is being done by the code. A comment in Perl 5 begins with the pound sign (#), like this:

```
# Determine whether the line from the database matches
# the search criteria
```

The pound sign tells the Perl 5 interpreter to ignore everything on the line following the pound sign. A comment may begin anywhere within a line. Everything following the pound sign on that line will be ignored. A newline character terminates the comment. Comments do not affect your code's execution or correctness in any way, but they are extremely important. You'll learn more about comments and other good programming practices in Chapter 8.

Writing a CGI Program

CGI programming is a major application of Perl 5 programming. A CGI program runs on a web server, interfacing with both the web browser and web server. If you've never run a CGI program on your web server, you'll learn how to in this section. Our example uses an HTML registration form and a CGI program that reads registration data to explain the fundamentals of CGI programming.

Before we go into the details of the CGI program, we need to cover some definitions and underlying concepts of CGI programs and the environment in which they work. We'll start with definitions of CGI, client/server model, and HTTP communications. Then we'll get to the web server, HTTP form, and CGI program for the example.

Have you ever started to drink from a water fountain and been squirted in the eye? Prepare yourself to get wet! In fact, the following sections may seem more like trying to take a drink from a fire hose. I have tried to pack in as much information as possible in a limited space.

Defining CGI

CGI programs can create dynamic web pages, which are built in response to a customer profile or query. CGI programs can be obvious, like a complex shopping cart application, or completely hidden, saving or serving data but never creating a line of HTML. CGI stands for Common Gateway Interface, which is the application and interpretation of the HTTP specification. That definition may be complete, but it isn't very informative. Let's see how the terms *Common*, *Gateway*, and *Interface* actually apply.

The Common Gateway Interface is *common* between the client and the server, which is usually your web browser and your web server. All web servers and web clients communicate using HTTP request and response headers. You'll learn more about HTTP headers later in this chapter.

The Common Gateway Interface acts as a *gateway* between the web client and the web server. The gateway program acts as a bridge between the web client and the web server, interpreting and responding to dynamic and data-driven requests from the web client. Without a gateway program, the web server would respond to a URL request by returning a nondynamic, or static, web page. The gateway program assists the web server in returning dynamic web pages, built on the fly, in response to URL and data requests from the web client.

The Common Gateway Interface acts as an *interface* between the web server and other applications on the server machine. The interface program understands the HTTP interface protocols required by the web server and can act as an interface between other computer applications and the web server.

NOTE

Exporting databases is a common CGI task. The CGI program doesn't perform the actual database tasks, but instead acts as an interface program interpreting the incoming data requests into the correct syntax for Microsoft Access, Microsoft SQL Server, Oracle, and other major database applications. When the database responds to the query, the interface program translates the response into the correct format for transmission through the web server to the web client. Exporting databases and e-mail are the two of the larger interface applications of CGI programming, which you will learn about in Part 5 of this book.

To recap, here's how the CGI breaks down:

- *Common* stands for the HTTP protocol used between the web client and the web server.

- *Gateway* stands for the bridge programming used to communicate between the web client and web server.

- *Interface* stands for the programming required to communicate between the web server and large applications such as databases, search engines, and e-mail.

A CGI program is part of the communication between a web client and a web server. This communication is a key element in the client/server interface model, which we will examine next.

Understanding the Client/Server Interface Model

The Internet is the ultimate client/server model. Your web browser, the client, communicates with your server, appropriately called a web server, which is interacting with many other services.

The web browser (client) requests a resource from the web server. The client, your web browser, then waits for the web server to respond. This is the essence of client/server communication.

If you've been around computing at all in the last five years, you've heard the term *client/server model.* This is the paradigm of the Internet (and of the 1990s).

Let's use a restaurant as a client/server analogy. When you go to a busy restaurant and you don't have a reservation, you ask the maitre d' or hostess for a table. At that point, you are the *client* and the maitre d' is the *server.* You have made a request and been placed on a list to be served (seated). When your name pops to the top of the list, you will be served. Your client request has been processed by the server, and the resource you requested has been allocated to you.

Now you are at your table and your waiter (or waitress) is ready to take your order. Your waiter is the server, who takes the order from you, the client. The waiter takes the order to the kitchen and gives the order to the chef. The waiter, your server, has become a client of the chef, and the chef is now the server. The server is always the process that has the resource you, the client, want. In this example, the resource you want is food. However, this resource is not directly available from your server, the waiter. The waiter passes your resource request to another server, which makes the waiter a client to the next server, the chef.

This illustrates the power of the client/server model very well. You need a single-resource dinner. You have a single server—the waiter getting you that resource. That server is specialized, however. The server's only job is to take requests for resources and pass them on to other servers—the chef or bartender in our restaurant analogy. If your server only took care of a single client, you, your server would spend a lot of wasted time waiting for your food to get ready and then for you to eat. Your service from this one server might be very good, but it would be very expensive. Dedicated processes are always more expensive.

Instead of just serving you and wasting time while waiting for something to do, your server serves other clients, and usually stays busier but still takes good care of you. This is the power of the client/server model. The server serves multiple clients, and in a properly balanced system (which isn't necessarily easy to design), the client processes receive the resources they requested in a timely manner.

Obviously, the client and server need to have some way to communicate so that the client can make requests and the server can respond. In the case of the web client and web server, this communication is done using HTTP headers, as explained in the next section.

Understanding HTTP Communications

As you have learned, a client/server communication is usually initiated by the client requesting a service. Figure 1.11 shows a simple client/server HTTP communication. If this communication were initiated from your web browser, you would only see the output shown in Figure 1.12.

To try this yourself, telnet to any World Wide Web site. (For the example shown in Figure 1.11, I used my own virtual domain so I could return a small HTML document, which makes the HTTP headers easier to see.) For example, to telnet to the Yahoo web site, you would use this command:

```
telnet www.yahoo.com 80
```

You must telnet to port 80, which is the default network port where the web server process listens for client requests. This port is similar to the radio frequency HAM radio operators transmit and listen on. The HAM radio operators can transmit and receive on any frequency, but they are more likely to hear and be heard on a commonly known frequency.

To retrieve a document from the web server, you must send it an HTTP request header. In Figure 1.11, you can see the GET header on the fifth line. To retrieve the default document for the document root on a web server, issue this command:

```
GET/HTTP/1.1
```

FIGURE 1.11:

HTTP client/server communication

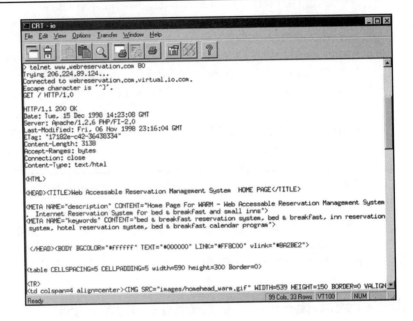

```
> telnet www.webreservation.com 80
Trying 206.224.89.124...
Connected to webreservation.com.virtual.io.com.
Escape character is '^]'.
GET / HTTP/1.0

HTTP/1.1 200 OK
Date: Tue, 15 Dec 1998 14:23:08 GMT
Server: Apache/1.2.6 PHP/FI-2.0
Last-Modified: Fri, 06 Nov 1998 23:16:04 GMT
ETag: "17182e-c42-36438334"
Content-Length: 3138
Accept-Ranges: bytes
Connection: close
Content-Type: text/html

<HTML>

<HEAD><TITLE>Web Accessible Reservation Management System  HOME PAGE</TITLE>

<META NAME="description" CONTENT="Home Page For WARM - Web Accessible Reservation Management System
. Internet Reservation System for bed & breakfast and small inns">
<META NAME="keywords" CONTENT="bed & breakfast reservation system, bed & breakfast, inn reservation
system, hotel reservation system, bed & breakfast calendar program">


</HEAD><BODY BGCOLOR="#ffffff" TEXT="#000000" LINK="#FF8C00" vlink="#8A2BE2">


<table CELLSPACING=5 CELLPADDING=5 width=590 height=300 Border=0>

<TR>
<td colspan=4 align=center><IMG SRC="images/homehead_warm.gif" WIDTH=539 HEIGHT=150 BORDER=0 VALIGN
```

Then press Enter twice to end the HTTP request. A blank line terminates all HTTP client/server header transmissions. This is like the HAM radio operators saying, "Over," when they are finished transmitting to tell the receiver that they have switched their radio set to receive and are now listening for messages. The GET method header is the default method when requesting a URL.

If you have made a valid HTTP request header, you will receive an HTTP status response header of 200 and further information in response to your HTTP request. You can see this response on the line following the blank line after the GET request in Figure 1.11.

The web server's most common HTTP request header is the method request header. This header indicates the type of request the web client is making. The three most common method header types are GET, POST, and HEAD. The HEAD method type is primarily used by the search-bots of the major search engines like Yahoo, Excite, Infoseek, and Lycos. Your browser commonly uses the GET and POST method headers when requesting HTML documents. As you just saw, the GET method header is usually used when you are requesting a URL. The POST method is frequently used when transferring data from the client to the server, as you'll see in our CGI program example, coming up shortly.

FIGURE 1.12:

Web browser client/server communication

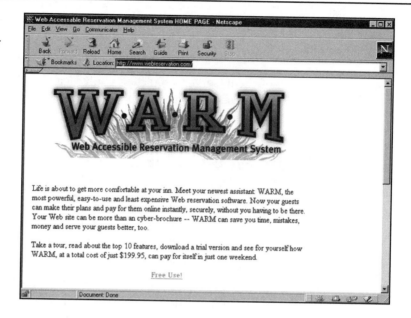

NOTE

Data transferred using the HTTP method GET is available to your CGI program in the environment hash, %ENV, using the hash key QUERY_STRING. Data transferred using the HTTP method POST is available to your CGI program in the STDIN input buffer handle. The amount of data in the STDIN input buffer is available to your CGI program in the environment hash (%ENV), using the hash key CONTENT_LENGTH. You'll see examples of retrieving data in CGI programs in later chapters.

The web server always begins an HTTP response to the client's HTTP request with an HTTP status response header. A valid HTTP status code of 200 means that the web server was able to respond correctly to the client's request.

The primary role of a CGI program is to generate and decode HTTP headers. A CGI program contains two main parts:

- Part one reads any incoming HTTP headers and data from the web client.

- Part two generates any required response from the web server.

Both parts are optional but are usually present. Each of these parts uses the HTTP headers to communicate between the web client and the web server. Your CGI program typically responds with a `Content-Type: text/html` HTTP response header, which tells the browser to expect an HTML document.

The elements of client/server interaction you've learned about are used for the web browser and web server communication in our CGI program example. Now we'll look at the web server configuration for CGI.

Configuring the Web Server

As you've learned, a CGI program is part of the communication between a web client and a web server. The CGI program runs on the web server, usually under a directory called cgi-bin. In this section, you will learn about the web server directories and configuration variables that are necessary for installing and running CGI programs.

The HTML page is served up by the web server to the web client from a directory tree called the document root. The *document root* is the directory path on your web server to the beginning of the HTML directory tree. The HTML directory tree is the directory and subdirectories that contain your web site's HTML documents. The web server begins searching for HTML documents by prepending the document root path to the directory path given after the domain portion of the URL address.

A URL address is made up of three parts: the protocol, the domain name, and the file identifier. These parts contain the following information:

- The protocol indicates the protocol name. The web server handles protocols of type http://, but URL protocols also may be ftp, wais, gopher, telnet, and other types, which are handled by other server-side applications. The protocol name is not case-sensitive.

- The domain name is the machine Internet address your web browser is contacting. The machine Internet address is a unique series of numbers or characters. Like the protocol name, the domain name is not case-sensitive.

- The file identifier is the path (absolute or relative) to the file, beginning from the document root. The file may be any valid filename. The filename extension tells the web server what file type headers to return to the web client. The file identifier is case-sensitive.

How your web server interprets filename extensions, searches for documents, handles CGI requests, and performs other functions is determined by your web server's configuration files. These files are usually located in a configuration directory inside the server root directory tree. The server root, like the document root, is a directory path on the web server. The web server usually stores your configuration, log, and error files within the server root directory tree.

Listing 1.2 is an edited copy of a web server configuration file from one of my virtual domains. Lines 8 and 9 of Listing 1.2 show the definition of the server root and document root. On line 12 of Listing 1.2, you can see a handler defined for CGI scripts.

NOTE   A *script* is another name for a program. Scripts are usually short programs, and typically they are written in an interpreted programming language (like Perl 5) rather than a compiled language.

Listing 1.2:   **Web Server Configuration File**

```
1.   ##### Apache conf file
2.   ServerType standalone
3.   BindAddress www.practical-inet.com
4.   Port 80
5.   ServerAdmin webmaster@practical-inet.com
6.   ServerName www.practical-inet.com
7.
8.   ServerRoot /virtual/customer/practical-inet.com
9.   DocumentRoot /virtual/customer/practical-inet.com/htdocs
10.
11.  DirectoryIndex blocked.html index.html index.htm index.php
     index.cgi home.html home.htm welcome.html welcome.htm
12.  AddHandler cgi-script .cgi
13.
14.  UserDir disabled
15.  FancyIndexing on
16.  XBitHack Full
17.
18.  Alias /icons/ /virtual/customer/practical-inet.com/icons/
19.  ScriptAlias /cgi-bin/ /virtual/customer/practical-inet.com/cgi-bin/
20.
21.  AddIconByEncoding (CMP,/icons/compressed.gif) x-compress x-gzip
```

```
22. AccessFileName .htaccess
23. DefaultType text/plain
24.
25. AddEncoding x-compress Z
26. AddEncoding x-gzip gz
27.
28. AddType text/html .shtml
29. AddHandler server-parsed .shtml
```

Writing the Registration Form

Using a registration form for gathering information over the Internet is another common CGI application. Figure 1.13 shows the Internet registration form we will use in our example. The source code used to generate this HTML registration form is shown in Listing 1.3.

FIGURE 1.13:

An HTML registration form

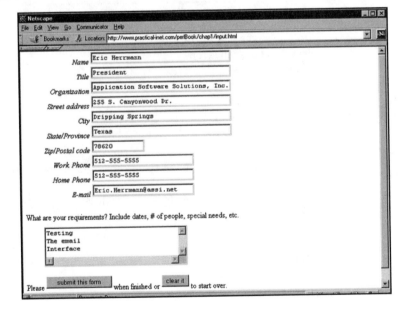

Listing 1.3:　　HTML Registration Form Source

```
<html> <head></head>
<body bgcolor="#FFFFFF" link="#808000">
<p align="center"> </p> <div align="left">
<form
action="http://www.practical-inet.com/cgi-bin/perlBook/
chap1/readInput.cgi"
method="POST">
<blockquote>
    <table border="0">
      <tr>
        <td align="right"><em>Name</em></td>
        <td><input type="text" size="35" name=
            "Contact_FullName"> </td>
      </tr>
      <tr>
        <td align="right"><em>Title</em></td>
        <td><input type="text" size="35" name="Contact_Title"> </td>
      </tr>
      <tr>
        <td align="right"><em>Organization</em></td>
        <td><input type="text" size="35" name=
            "Contact_Organization"> </td>
      </tr>
      <tr>
        <td align="right"><em>Street address</em></td>
        <td><input type="text" size="35" name=
            "Contact_StreetAddress"> </td>
      </tr>
      <tr>
        <td align="right"><em>Address (cont.)</em></td>
        <td><input type="text" size="35" name=
            "Contact_Address2"> </td>
      </tr>
      <tr>
        <td align="right"><em>City</em></td>
        <td><input type="text" size="35" name="Contact_City"> </td>
      </tr>
      <tr>
        <td align="right"><em>State/Province</em></td>
        <td><input type="text" size="35" name="Contact_State"> </td>
      </tr>
```

```
<tr>
  <td align="right"><em>Zip/Postal code</em></td>
  <td><input type="text" size="12" maxlength="12" name=
      "Contact_ZipCode"> </td>
</tr>
<tr>
  <td align="right"><em>Country</em></td>
  <td><input type="text" size="25" name=
      "Contact_Country"> </td>
</tr>
<tr>
  <td align="right"><em>Work Phone</em></td>
  <td><input type="text" size="25" maxlength="25" name=
      "Contact_WorkPhone"> </td>
</tr>
<tr>
  <td align="right"><em>Home Phone</em></td>
  <td><input type="text" size="25" maxlength="25" name=
      "Contact_HomePhone"> </td>
</tr>
<tr>
  <td align="right"><em>FAX</em></td>
  <td><input type="text" size="25" maxlength="25" name=
      "Contact_FAX"> </td>
</tr>
<tr>
  <td align="right"><em>E-mail</em></td>
  <td><input type="text" size="25" name="Contact_Email"> </td>
</tr>
<tr>
  <td align="right"><em>URL</em></td>
  <td><input type="text" size="25" maxlength="25" name=
      "Contact_URL"> </td>
</tr>
  </table>
</blockquote>
<p>What are your requirements? Include dates, # of people,
  special needs, etc.</p>
<blockquote>
  <p><textarea name="comments" rows="5" cols="35"></textarea> <br>
  </p>
</blockquote>
```

```
<p>Please <input type="submit" value="submit this form">
    when finished or <input
    type="reset" value="clear it"> to start over. </p>
</form>
</body>
</html>
```

When submitted, the HTML registration source of Listing 1.3 calls the CGI program `readInput.cgi`, described next.

> **NOTE**
>
> You will need to modify the fifth line of Listing 1.3, `action=http://www.practical-inet.com/cgi-bin/perlBook/chap1/readInput.cgi`, to reflect the URL for your web server.

Creating the CGI Program

The CGI program `readInput.cgi`, shown in Listing 1.4, follows the steps that every CGI program must follow:

- First, a CGI program must decode any incoming data.

- Next, a CGI program uses that data to interface with any server-side programs.

- Finally, a CGI program must return valid HTTP headers.

These three steps are the basics of any web browser-to-web server communication. The web browser and the web server create a classic client/server relationship, as explained earlier. The web browser, through the HTML form in Listing 1.3, calls the web server requesting the resource `readInput.cgi` in Listing 1.4.

> **NOTE**
>
> As I promised you in this book's introduction, the program `readInput.cgi` teaches you Perl and CGI programming in the context of their environment instead of a simple made-for-the-book example. This makes your job a little harder at first but more rewarding in the long run. You will need to confront more new concepts at once, but you can rest assured that the skills you learn are practical and relevant to a real-world programming environment.

Listing 1.4: *readInput.cgi*

```perl
1. #!/usr/bin/perl
2.
3. %postInputs = readPostInput();
4. $dateCommand = "date";
5. $time = `$dateCommand`;
6. open (MAIL, "|/usr/sbin/sendmail -t") || return 0;
7.
8. select (MAIL);
9. print << "EOF";
10. To:    YOUR_ADDRESS\@YOUR_DOMAIN.com
11. From: $postInputs{'Contact_Email'}
12. Subject: $postInputs{'Organization'} Information Requested
13.
14. $time
15. $postInputs{'Organization'} Information Requested
16. Name: $postInputs{'Contact_FullName'}
17. Email: $postInputs{'Contact_Email'}
18. Street Address: $postInputs{'Contact_StreetAddress'}
19. Street Address (cont): $postInputs{'Contact_Address2'}
20. City: $postInputs{'Contact_City'}
21. State : $postInputs{'Contact_State'}
22. Zip: $postInputs{'Contact_ZipCode'}
23. Work Phone: $postInputs{'Contact_WorkPhone'}
24. Home Phone: $postInputs{'Contact_HomePhone'}
25. FAX: $postInputs{'Contact_FAX'}
26. Email: $postInputs{'Contact_Email'}
27. Comments: $postInputs{'comments'}
28.
29.
30. EOF
31.    close(MAIL);
32.    select (STDOUT);
33.    printThankYou();
34.
35. sub readPostInput(){
36.    my (%searchField, $buffer, $pair, @pairs);
37.    if ($ENV{'REQUEST_METHOD'} eq 'POST'){
38.        read(STDIN, $buffer, $ENV{'CONTENT_LENGTH'});
39.        @pairs = split(/&/, $buffer);
```

```
40.        foreach $pair (@pairs){
41.            ($name, $value) = split(/=/, $pair);
42.            $value =~ tr/+/ /;
43.            $value =~ s/%([a-fA-F0-9][a-fA-F0-9])/pack("C",
               hex($1))/eg;
44.            $name =~ tr/+/ /;
45.            $name =~ s/%([a-fA-F0-9][a-fA-F0-9])/pack("C",
               hex($1))/eg;
46.            $searchField{$name} = $value;
47.        }
48.    }
49.    return (%searchField);
50. }
51.
52. sub printThankYou(){
53. print << "EOF";
54. Content-Type: text/html
55.
56. <HEAD>
57. <TITLE>THANK YOU FOR FOR YOUR REQUEST</TITLE>
58. </HEAD>
59. <BODY>
60. <TABLE CELLSPACING=2 CELLPADDING=2 border=0 width=600>
61. <TR><th><BR>
62. <center>
63. <FONT SIZE=+3><B>Thank You $postInputs{'Contact_FullName'}
    </b></font>
64. </center><BR><BR>
65.
66. <CENTER><B><FONT SIZE=+1>
67. <P>For submitting your information.  We will get back with you
    shortly.
68. </P>
69. </FONT></B><CENTER>
70. </th>
71. </table>
72. </BODY>
73. </HTML>
74.
75. EOF
76. }
```

Before you can test this example, you need to know how the installation of a CGI program works. In the next section, you will learn how and where to install your CGI programs.

Installing CGI Programs

To install the HTML registration form shown in Listing 1.3, you must know the document root and the script alias. The script alias identifies the CGI program's directory tree for the web server. The web server will look only within the CGI program directory tree for CGI programs. In Listing 1.2, the script alias is on line 19:

```
ScriptAlias /cgi-bin/ /virtual/customer/practical-inet.com/cgi-bin/
```

The HTML registration form must be installed into a directory underneath your web server's document root. Each web server's document root is unique. Your web server probably has a FAQ (Frequently Asked Questions) list, telling you where to install HTML files. If it doesn't, you'll need to get this information from your web administrator.

Copy the program in Listing 1.3 to your web server using ftp, placing the file into your document root. Now copy the CGI program shown in Listing 1.4 to your web server's cgi-bin directory.

WARNING Whenever you copy files from a Windows to a Unix computer, be sure to set the transfer mode to ASCII. Unix and Windows use different characters to determine the end of a line. If you copy a program from Windows to Unix in the default binary mode, your program may not work.

Next, if you are on a Unix web server, you must set the correct file permissions on the files. As explained earlier, file permissions tell the Unix operating system who can read, write, and/or execute a file.

Your HTML file should have its permissions set to owner = 6, group = 4, world = 4. This gives you permission to read and write to the file; the group and world get read access to the file. Use the chmod command like this:

```
chmod 644 register.html
```

Your CGI program should have its permissions set to owner = 7, group = 5, world = 5. This gives you permission to read, write, and execute the file. The group and world get read and execute access to the file. Use the chmod command like this:

```
chmod 755 readInput.html
```

To test the installation of your CGI program, execute it from the command line, as you learned earlier in this chapter, in the "Using the Unix Command Shell" section. If you have problems, see the next chapter for information about debugging your CGI program.

To test your HTML installation, in your web browser, enter the URL of your web server followed by the filename of the installed HTML file as the location, like this:

```
http://www.yourDomain.com/registration.html
```

Now that you have a working CGI program installed on your web server, let's dissect that program and get a better understanding of how Perl 5 and CGI programs work.

Understanding How a CGI Program Works

You've learned about the client/server interface model, and you put together a CGI application. Now it's time to see how the programming code works. As we work through the code, you'll come across many types of Perl 5 constructs that will probably be new to you. Don't worry if all this is not crystal clear (or even vaguely comprehensible) right now. All of these parts of Perl 5 programs will be covered in detail throughout this book. This is just a quick-start example to show you the power of Perl 5 and make you eager to learn all those details you need to know to write your own programs.

First, your web browser requests a resource from the web server. This happens when you click the submit this form button (in the form shown earlier in Figure 1.13), which has the web browser call the CGI program identified by the action attribute of the HTML registration form tag. The web browser then generates an HTTP method request header. The method type for the HTML registration form in Listing 1.3 is POST, which is also an attribute of the HTML form tag. Here is that HTML form tag from Listing 1.3:

```
<form action=www.practical-inet.com/cgi-bin/perlBook/readInput.cgi"
method ="POST">
```

This means the data submitted by the form will be available for your CGI program at Standard Input, or STDIN (STDIN is a special variable you will learn about in Chapter 12).

Now that the web browser has sent the web server an HTTP request header, the web server will decode and respond to the web client's request. The web server decodes the HTTP request header and determines by looking at the file extension that it must pass the request to a CGI program.

The web server activates the CGI program readInput.cgi. The first thing the CGI program does is read the input data sent by the HTML form. This is done on line 3 of Listing 1.3:

```
%postInputs = readPostInput();
```

This is a subroutine call, which means the program jumps to line 35 of Listing 1.3 and continues execution from there:

```
sub readPostInput(){
```

The subroutine readPostInput is made up of the block of statements that begins with the opening curly brace on line 35 and continues to the closing curly brace of line 50. The subroutine readPostInput verifies that the request header method was POST on line 37 and then reads the data from the HTML form on line 38 into the variable $buffer.

```
if ($ENV{'REQUEST_METHOD'} eq 'POST'){
    read(STDIN, $buffer, $ENV{'CONTENT_LENGTH'});
```

You'll learn about variables in Chapter 5 and about subroutines in Chapter 18. The pattern-matching techniques used in the readPostInput subroutine will be examined in detail in Chapter 15.

The CGI input is passed from the web browser to the web server in URL-encoded name/value pairs. Each name/value pair is directly associated with the HTML form input tag. Each HTML form input tag has a name and value attribute. The name should be set inside the HTML file. Look back at Listing 1.3 and notice that each HTML form input tag contains a name attribute that is set to some unique name, as in these two examples:

```
<td><input type="text" size="35" name="Contact_FullName">
<td><input type="text" size="35" name="Contact_Title"> </td>
```

The value is set by the user's input. When the user clicks on the HTML form's submit button, the browser collects all the data associated with the HTML input tags and URL-encodes the data. This URL encoding converts some characters for safe transfer over the Internet and associates each name and value attribute with an equal sign. Each name/value pair is separated from the next name/value pair by an ampersand (&).

Line 39 of Listing 1.4 separates the name/value pairs into an array named @pairs:

```
@pairs = split(/&/, $buffer);
```

The array is then URL-decoded from lines 42 through 45 and saved into a Perl 5 hash named %searchField. (Remember that this encoding and decoding will be explained in detail in Chapter 15.)

```
$value =~ tr/+/ /;
$value =~ s/%([a-fA-F0-9][a-fA-F0-9])/pack("C", hex($1))/eg;
$name =~ tr/+/ /;
$name =~ s/%([a-fA-F0-9][a-fA-F0-9])/pack("C", hex($1))/eg;
```

The hash is returned to the calling program on line 49:

```
return (%searchField);
```

Perl 5 arrays and hashes are covered in Chapter 6.

Once your CGI program has decoded the incoming data, it can use the data as part of an interface to other programs. On line 6 in Listing 1.4, it creates a connection to the e-mail program sendmail:

```
open (MAIL, "|/usr/sbin/sendmail -t") || return 0;
```

The e-mail message (lines 10 through 29) is sent to the sendmail program via the print statement on line 9:

```
print << "EOF";
```

This print statement, using the heredoc operator (<<), sends everything from lines 10 through 29 to the file handle selected on line 8, which is connected to the sendmail program. The heredoc operator is discussed in Chapter 12, which covers file input and output.

The e-mail message is sent to the e-mail address on line 10:

```
To:   YOUR_ADDRESS\@YOUR_DOMAIN.com
```

The EOF marker on line 30 ends the data transfer initiated by the print statement on line 9. The sendmail program is explained in Chapter 20, which covers e-mail.

The results of the e-mail message generated between lines 10 through 29 are shown in Figure 1.14. The connection to the `sendmail` program is closed on line 31:

```
close(MAIL);
```

FIGURE 1.14:

Registration e-mail

On line 33, the CGI program prepares to respond with a valid HTTP response header by the subroutine call:

```
printThankYou();
```

This subroutine call jumps to line 52:

```
sub printThankYou(){
```

CGI programs are responsible for returning a valid HTTP header. Lines 54 through 56 create the required HTTP response headers:

```
Content-Type: text/html
```

```
<HEAD>
```

The Content-Type: text/html HTTP response header tells the web browser that the remaining data returned by the web server will be HTML text. The results are shown in Figure 1.15.

FIGURE 1.15:

Registration Thank You response

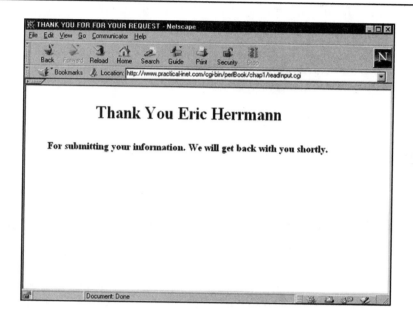

> **NOTE**
>
> The blank line on line 55 of Listing 1.4, following the Content-Type:text/html response header on line 54, is critical. The blank line tells the web browser (client) this is the last HTTP response header. Any data following the blank line is not part of the HTTP header traffic. Your web browser will decode the Content-Type HTTP response header to determine what type of data follows the last HTTP response header.

This completes the HTML communication between the web browser and web server, which I believe deserves a recap. Here are the steps involved in using our sample CGI program:

1. Your web browser, the client, through the HTML form's action field, submits an HTTP request header method of type POST (the type most frequently used when transferring data from a client to a server).

2. The web server decodes the HTTP request header and calls the CGI program identified in the HTTP request header.

3. The CGI program `readInput.cgi` decodes the incoming POST data.

4. The CGI program `readInput.cgi` uses the incoming data to interface with the `sendmail` program and creates an e-mail message.

5. The CGI program `readInput.cgi` completes the client/server transaction by returning an HTTP response header, which is the Thank You HTML page shown in Figure 1.15.

Summary

This chapter began with an introduction to Perl 5. Because Perl was built to evolve, it is changing faster and faster as its user community grows and contributes to Perl 5. Like a snowball rolling downhill, as Perl 5 picks up new users, it grows in contributions to the language and evolves faster to meet new needs.

Next, the chapter explained some fundamental procedures required to accomplish everyday Perl 5 programming tasks. You learned how to run a Perl 5 program from the command-line interface on both Windows and Unix computers and how to edit a program. This part of the chapter used a simple example of a Perl 5 program that shows your computer's environment variables.

The second example in this chapter was a CGI program. CGI programming is a major application of Perl 5 programming, and CGI examples will be used throughout the book to explain appropriate subjects. You learned how your web browser and server communicate using client/server technology and HTTP headers. Then you learned how to install an HTML registration form and the CGI program that reads the form data.

Both of the examples in this chapter are useful, real-world programs. Throughout the book, this will be the rule, not the exception. Practical examples will be used to introduce, explain, and illustrate each new topic.

In the next chapter, you'll learn how to accomplish another fundamental programming task. This task helps you follow a major programming rule: Just writing the code isn't enough—it also needs to do the right thing. Making your code do the right thing is called *debugging*. Before you get frustrated because your code doesn't work, you're going to learn how to fix and avoid the inevitable bugs (errors) that creep into everyone's programs.

Debugging Your Programs

- Syntax errors

- Techniques for avoiding errors

- Runtime errors

- Perl debuggers

- CGI program debugging

When you *debug* your code, you look for coding errors and try to fix them. Inevitably, some bugs will creep into your code. You can use the techniques you'll read about in this chapter to speed up the debugging process.

Coding errors usually come in two forms: syntax errors and logic errors. When looking for errors in programs that you typed in from this book, you can concentrate on syntax errors. Syntax errors are errors created when you fail to follow the required format of a Perl 5 statement. The first section of this chapter explains how to locate and fix syntax errors quickly and painlessly.

Eliminating errors is, of course, what debugging is all about. In the section on avoiding errors, you'll learn about coding practices and techniques that will help you prevent errors in your code. You'll also learn about some mistakes that are commonly made in Perl 5 programs.

Since every program has bugs, every decent language has a debugger. Perl 5 comes with a fully functional Perl debugger. In addition to the free debugger distributed with Perl 5, the builders of one of the Windows versions of Perl 5 offer a Windows Perl 5 debugger, which is also described in this chapter.

What about your CGI programs? The techniques used for standard debugging don't work as well in the CGI environment. Over the years, I've developed a few techniques to help locate my CGI bugs, which you'll learn about in the final section of this chapter.

If you code, you debug, so instead of hiding this chapter at the end of the book, I put it right up front. Learn the rules of debugging, and your Perl 5 coding experience will be a lot less frustrating. As with the first chapter, some of the Perl 5 programming concepts referred to in this chapter have not been discussed in detail yet. In those cases, I've noted where the concept will be covered.

NOTE   Debugging means removing errors from your code. How did the word *bug* get associated with removing errors? Well, back in the early days of programming, computers with less power than your PC took up entire rooms. These computers operated with large servos that opened and closed, defining the bits and bytes of a program. During one of the demonstrations of these ancient dinosaurs, a moth got stuck between one of the servos, causing the computer to malfunction. When the problem was found, someone said "It had a bug in it!" Removing the bugs from your code became and has remained the popular terminology for find and removing coding errors.

Handling Syntax Errors

You will make all kinds of mistakes if you take my advice and type in the programs you're reading about in this book. Don't let those mistakes discourage you from typing in the programs. Not only will that help you learn how to write Perl 5 programs, but it will also help you learn how to debug programs. You know that the examples work, so you only need to concentrate on one kind of coding error—your typing mistakes. Once you become familiar with the typing errors you make, you'll be able to quickly track them down and correct them in your own code.

Let's begin with an example of how Perl 5 reacts when it finds a syntax error. You'll see that Perl 5's diagnostic messages are very helpful, but you need to learn how to interpret them.

Pinpointing Syntax Errors

Figure 2.1 graphically illustrates the effect of just one typo in a program—a missing quotation mark. In Figure 2.1, five different error messages (eight on-screen lines) are printed for a small typing error.

FIGURE 2.1:

Perl 5 syntax error messages

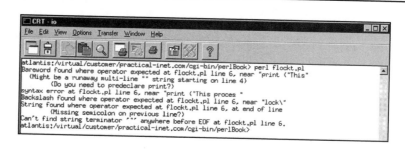

What can you learn from Figure 2.1 that will help you become better at debugging your code?

- One error can create multiple error messages.

- Those error messages usually have the information you need to locate your problem, so don't ignore them.

The last error message in Figure 2.1 is the best clue to the problem. The Perl 5 interpreter is telling you that there is an unbalanced double quotation mark somewhere in the program. It tells you this with the message "Can't find string terminator '"' anywhere before EOF at flockt.pl line 6." When you see this type of message, you know you forgot to include a closing quotation mark at the end of a string (a *string* is character data surrounded by quotation marks, as explained in Chapter 5). Then you just need to locate where the missing quotation mark should be inserted. Perl 5's other messages help you pinpoint the error.

NOTE   The program used for Figure 2.1 is small, so the EOF (end of file) in the "Can't find string terminator" message references line 6. If this program had been 100 lines long, with the error created on line 5, Perl 5 would continue looking for the ending quote until it reached the end of the file at line 100. The EOF condition would still occur, but it would be referencing line 100 instead of line 6.

Listing 2.1 shows the program that generated the error messages in Figure 2.1.

Listing 2.1:   Missing Quote

```
1.  #!/usr/local/bin/perl
2.  use Fcntl ":flock";
3.  open (OUTFILE, ">>flockTest.txt") || warn $!;
4.  # The following line generates the error! Can you find it?
5.  print ("Requesting Exclusive lock\n);
6.  flock(OUTFILE, LOCK_EX) || warn $!;
7.  print ("This process now owns the Exclusive lock\n");
8.  $in = <STDIN>;
9.  flock(OUTFILE, LOCK_UN)|| warn $!;
10. close (OUTFILE);
```

The actual error in this small program is on line 5, where Perl 5 complains about having a bare word where an operator was expected:

```
print ("Requesting Exclusive lock\n);
```

Bare words are character strings without surrounding quotation marks and that do not begin with $, @, or %, which are the variable designators (these designators are discussed in Chapters 5 and 6).

When you begin looking for an error, look for the obvious things first. The messages in Figure 2.1 are generated by a common syntax error made by both experienced and inexperienced programmers. This error is among the most frequently repeated syntax errors, which are listed here:

- Keyword misspelled, such as `if` as `fi` or `elsif` as `elseif`

- Semicolon missing

- Comma missing

- Parenthesis missing

- Curly brace (block delineator) missing

- Quotation mark missing

As you saw in Figure 2.1, a common syntax error (a missing quotation mark) can generate a variety of error messages. Your job as a debugger is to learn to ignore the extraneous information and focus on the important information. For example, the error messages in Figures 2.2 and 2.3 contain important debugging information.

The syntax error messages in both figures give you a good indication of the problem. In Figure 2.2, the error message tells you that you have a syntax error at line 5 near the right parenthesis. In this example, a semicolon was left off the end of the Perl 5 statement on line 4. However, the message identifies line 5. Rarely does the error message identify the correct line when you forgot a semicolon.

In Figure 2.3, the error message tells you that the program is missing a right bracket at line 26. You can believe Perl 5 when it tells you your program is missing a parenthesis or a right bracket, but again, don't believe the line number identification. Perl will match the brackets up out of order until it runs out of brackets.

FIGURE 2.2:

A syntax error message identifying a program line

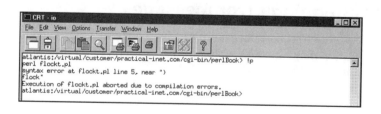

The lesson here is that Perl is kind enough to tell you what the problem is, but it is up to you to find the precise location. Fortunately, Perl usually gets you close enough to the real problem that you should be able to figure it out.

Whenever you see an error message that identifies a line number, you know one thing for certain: The error is not on any line after the line identified in the error message. You also know that the error is likely to be on the line identified or on a previous line. Unfortunately, sometimes the previous line may be 100 or more lines back. Messages about syntax errors that fail to complete a Perl 5 statement—such as missing quotes, right brackets, and missing semicolons—rarely identify the correct line. Messages about syntax errors that are wholly contained within a single statement—such as misspelled keywords or improperly formed conditional expressions—usually correctly identify the line number of the error.

FIGURE 2.3:

Missing braces

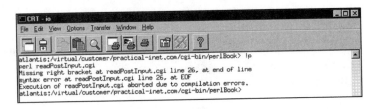

TIP

I hope you like "Where's Waldo?" puzzles, because hunting down bugs in your code is kind of like looking for Waldo in a crowd. Another way to look at debugging is like a treasure hunt to find that missing semicolon or quotation mark. Find the missing operator, and your code magically works. If you take the "it's a game" approach to your debugging, you'll have a lot more success and fun as a programmer.

Understanding Error Messages

As you've seen in the examples, Perl 5 error messages usually contain the information that you need to find the error. A good Perl programmer reads the error messages.

When you see a lot of error messages, realize that usually only the first few messages point to the real error. You should concentrate on the early messages because the later error messages are probably a result of some earlier error. Now, you're probably thinking that I just contradicted myself, since the previous paragraph says that good programmers read the messages, and this one implies that you should ignore the messages at the end of a long list of error messages. The best guideline is a balance of focusing on some of the messages and ignoring others, and achieving this balance comes only with practice.

Perl 5 has almost 500 error messages that you can read at your leisure in the html documentation under the filename perldiag.html. You can find this file under the documentation directory of your Perl 5 installation or at this book's companion page at the Sybex web site. You don't need to read the entire list of error messages, but it is a good idea to know about this file in case you run across a message you don't understand. The following sections describe some of the error and warning messages that you are likely to see early in your Perl 5 programming career.

NOTE   Warning messages appear only when you run your program with the warning switch (-w) enabled. This is a good debugging technique, as explained later in this chapter.

Syntax Errors

Syntax error messages are usually generated by the common syntax errors you just learned about. These messages are frequently interrelated and should be interpreted as Perl's best guess. Use these error messages as clues to help identify and locate the error. Syntax error messages include the following:

- "Missing semicolon in previous line."

- "Can't find terminator before EOF." This message is usually the result of a missing right bracket or quotation mark.

- "Might be runaway multi-line string starting on line *n*." This is usually a missing quotation mark.

- "Missing right bracket."

Did Not Return a True Value

Every required or used file must return a true value as the last line of the file. This means that whenever you write a program that will be included in another program using the `require` or `use` keyword, the last line of the required file must equal some value other than zero or `null`. As you'll learn in Chapter 4, Perl 5 interprets zero and `null` values as false. As you'll learn in Chapter 18, you can write reusable Perl 5 subroutines and include them in your main programs with the `require` or `use` keyword.

To fix this problem, just add the following statement to the end of any file included in other files using the `require` or `use` statement:

```
return 1;
```

Can't Locate Function in @INC

The @INC array is used by Perl 5 to locate library modules and files when loading subroutines. Frequently, this error occurs because you misspelled a function name. Perl 5 dutifully went looking for the misspelled function and couldn't find it.

Look carefully at the error message. If the function name is wrong, correct it. If the function name is correct, you need to modify the locations Perl is searching for library routines. You can modify the @INC array by using the `push` or `unshift` functions (discussed in Chapter 6) to place the correct path into @INC.

Panic: Some System Error

When you see an error that starts with "panic," don't panic. This is an error at the system level instead of at your code level. Several possible problems may have created this type of error. Your program may have used up all of your system resources, which happens when your code doesn't release resources when it finishes using them. Perhaps you initialized a variable to a negative number and it was used as an input to a system function before the variable was properly set.

You cannot fix a system error, but it's likely you are using a reference to an invalid location in memory, building an array in an infinite loop, or using some other resource related to the error. First, determine the type of system error by looking at the panic message. Then look at your code and try to locate the sections that might affect the error identified in the panic message. If there are previous errors before the panic error, solve those problems first.

Missing Comma after First Argument

This error message appears when you forget to type the comma after the first argument of a function. For example, here is an error that I make quite often:

```
@names = split(/:/ @nameList,3);
```

You'll learn how to use various Perl 5 functions and their arguments throughout this book.

String @varName Now Must Be Written as \@varName

You must use the escape character (\) with all literal at signs (@). This error is commonly found in Perl 4 code being upgraded to a Perl 5 installation. In the Perl 4 distribution, you could print e-mail addresses directly in your HTML code. With Perl 5, you will see an error message if you write an e-mail address like this:

```
print "mailto:Recipient@domainName.com";
```

Instead, you must write the e-mail address like this:

```
print "mailto:Recipient\@domainName.com";
```

Use of Function Is Deprecated

Deprecated means that the function has been replaced with a new function or method. A deprecated function works in the currently released version of Perl 5 but may not be supported in future releases of Perl 5.

You'll see this type of warning message when your code uses a function that has been replaced with a newer function, variable, or syntax. The warning message usually includes information on how to fix the error. For example, one of the deprecated messages in the current build is "Use of implicit split to @_ is deprecated." The diagnostic message tells you to "assign the results of a split() explicitly to an array (or list)."

When the warning message isn't helpful enough, you can look up the deprecated function in the online documentation that was delivered with your Perl distribution. Each deprecated function or variable should have an explanation of the newer replacement function or variable.

WARNING Don't write new code with deprecated functions. Your code and the deprecated function will work today, but your program may not run under future releases of Perl.

Use of Uninitialized Value

This warning message tells you that an assignment statement uses a variable that has never been explicitly set in your program. See the "Avoiding Misspelled Variable Names" section later in this chapter for more information about problems that can result.

qw Used Commas in List

The qw operator separates bare words in a list with white space characters (blank, tab, newline, and so on). Putting commas in lists built using the qw operator is unnecessary and creates words that include the comma symbol. (The qw operator is discussed in Chapter 5.)

You will see this type of warning message when your code has initialized an array like this:

```
@trees = qw|Elm, Birch, Cedar, Oak|;
```

Initializing your array this way creates tree names like Elm, when you really wanted names like Elm (without the comma included as part of the name). You probably meant to initialize the array like this:

```
@trees = qw|Elm Birch Cedar Oak|;
```

You'll learn about initializing arrays in Chapter 6.

Name Only Used Once: Possible Typo

Pay attention to this warning message. This error usually occurs when you misspell a variable name. Debugging misspelled variable names can be frustrating and time consuming. See the "Avoiding Misspelled Variable Names" section later in this chapter for more information about this type of error.

Found = in Conditional, Should Be ==

This is another warning message that could save you hours of debugging time. This message says that a conditional expression included an assignment operator (=) instead of the equal to Boolean operator (==). Most conditional expressions test the contents of data instead of making an assignment statement. Making an assignment in a conditional expression is not an error and usually results in a true value, but it's often not what you meant to code. Perl operators are discussed in Chapter 4, and conditional expressions are discussed in Chapter 8.

Avoiding Errors

If it isn't broken, you don't have to fix it! That's pretty obvious, isn't it? You can make sure it isn't broken by taking some preventative maintenance measures in your code. There are some types of errors that can be avoided by setting the correct Perl command-line switch. Other errors can be avoided by following good coding practices. In this section, you will learn a few things you can do that will limit the number of bugs that creep into your code, and thereby reduce the amount of time you spend debugging your code.

Turning On Warning Messages

The first tip for avoiding bugs in your code doesn't even require a coding change. Whenever you change your code, always run it the first time with Perl 5 warnings enabled, like this:

```
perl -w programName.pl
```

This is likely to print out a lot of warning messages. Don't ignore these messages. Warning messages tell you where to look in your code for potential problems. For example, the following types of messages, which were discussed in the previous section, appear only when you run your program with warnings enabled:

- Use of function is deprecated

- Use of uninitialized value

- qw used commas in list

- Name only used once: possible typo

- Found = in conditional, should be ==

Avoiding Misspelled Variable Names

One of the features of Perl 5 is the ability to declare and use variables at any place in your code. Sometimes this feature introduces some hard-to-find bugs. Also, Perl 5 is a case-sensitive language. If you change the case of one character in a variable name, the variables are not the same. For example, the variable names $firstName and $FirstName refer to different storage locations.

If you make a typing mistake in assigning or using a variable name, Perl 5 creates a new variable. Now your code is using the wrong variable name, and either the data you meant to use elsewhere won't be available or the data your code is now using isn't valid. There are two simple steps you can take to avoid this problem (and one of them isn't careful typing). One is to use the warning switch (-w), as described in the previous section.

An alternative to using the warning switch is to use the Perl 5 pragma `strict`. The pragma `strict` tells the compiler to generate three types of errors:

- An error for any variable used before it was declared

- An error if your code uses symbolic references

- An error if your code uses bare words

You can use the pragma `strict` to restrict only the use of variable names, excluding the restrictions on symbolic references and bare words, by adding the following line in your code:

```
use strict 'vars';
```

You can put this line anywhere in your code. Then all the variable names that follow this line must be declared using the keywords `my` or `local`.

You can turn this restriction off by inserting this line:

```
no strict 'vars';
```

If you use the `strict` pragma in your code, you'll never have to debug a variable misspelling because all variables must be declared before they can be used.

WARNING The `strict` pragma can make it difficult for your code to use other modules and programs that don't follow this rule. If you have a problem using other modules, turn off `strict` `'vars'` around the offending module and turn it back on when you need it.

Following Good Coding Practices

Following good coding practices will make it easier for you (and others) to debug your programs. Here are a few tips to get you started.

Comments

Comment your code. My first boss made me comment every single line of code I wrote. That was a bit much, but comments are very important to avoiding and removing bugs. Before you start a new section of code, you should clearly define what you want the new section to do, then write the code the way you described it. You'll see examples throughout this book, and I'll talk more about comments in Chapter 8, which covers conditional statements.

Indentation

Indent your code. This is easy to do if you have a good editor. However, if you aren't using a tool that indents your code for you automatically, you should do it manually. Every time you open a new block of statements with a left curly brace, indent your code some common amount. I like to use three spaces, but the indentation amount doesn't really matter—just be consistent. After you close a block of statements with a right curly brace, outdent a consistent number of spaces. Formatting your code is also discussed in more detail in Chapter 8.

Meaningful Variable Names

Use meaningful variable names. Don't create variable names of one or two characters. Use variable names that reflect the purpose of the variable. You shouldn't go overboard and make every variable half a line long, but every variable should be understandable when you try to read your own code next week (or next year). If you are not very creative with names, just append the data type onto the end of the variable name. For example, `line:`, `$line`, `@line`, and `%line` become `lineLabel:`, `$lineScalar`, `@lineArray`, and `%lineHash`. The little bit of extra typing is worth the time you'll save debugging. You'll learn about variable names in Chapter 5.

Testing Loop and Conditional Expressions

The rule here is to build a little; test a little. Test your code as you write it. Don't wait until you're finished writing the entire program to see if it works. Test each piece as you build it. When you build a new `while` loop, run a couple of tests on it to make sure it stops and starts when you expect it to. As you build each new logical block of code, test it.

Beginning or End of Array Tests

Some places in code are particularly error prone. Loop indexes and any conditional expressions that check for the beginning or end of an array should be carefully tested. In your code, let Perl 5 index through your arrays, like this:

```
foreach (@array){…}
```

instead of explicitly indexing through the array, like this:

```
for ($index=0; $index<$max; $index++){
    $array[$index]; …
    }
```

When your code must explicitly use the beginning or last index, make sure you test those cases. You'll learn about arrays in Chapter 6, conditional expressions in Chapter 8, and for and foreach loops in Chapter 9.

Positive Logic

Another way to avoid errors in conditional expressions is to use positive logic. Don't be negative! That may sound like a philosophy of life, but it should be your programming philosophy also. Every time you write a conditional expression, you have a choice of testing for the existence of some condition or testing for the absence of some condition, like this:

```
while (!red) {…}   #negative
until (red) {…}    #positive
```

Whenever possible, test for the presence of a condition. If you find your conditional logic checks for the negative case, take a moment to look for the positive condition. Every coin has two sides, and every conditional expression has a positive and negative solution. Sometimes the positive condition isn't practical, but that should be the exception in your code. Testing for positive logic makes your code easier to understand, and positive logic usually requires less maintenance. You'll learn more about conditional logic and while and until loops in Chapter 9.

Special Cases

Along with avoiding negative conditions in your conditional expressions, you should also try to avoid handling special cases. This is called *exception handling*. Code that works for every case except one, two, three, or more cases is very prone to errors. There always seems to be one more exception. Look for the solution that doesn't require exception handling.

For example, if you are writing a program that determines when the chicken should cross the road, you might write something like this: Cross the road except when the light is red or yellow, or when there is a vehicle in the way, or when a bicycle is coming.... As you can see, the exception list can get very long. Instead, write something like this: Cross the road when the light facing you is green and the cross traffic is clear. You'll learn more about forming conditional expressions in Chapter 8.

Avoiding Common Perl 5 Mistakes

The tips in this section relate directly to Perl 5. They help you avoid common Perl 5 programming mistakes.

String and Numeric Tests

The testing of scalar data is context-based. If you use a string operator, Perl 5 tests the data in string context. New programmers frequently test for equality using the numeric test operator (==) when they should be using the string equality operator (eq). This isn't an error in Perl 5, but it is likely to produce erroneous results. Most Perl 5 operators have numeric and string counterparts. Make sure you use the correct operator for the correct data context. Operators and string and numeric context are discussed in Chapter 4.

List and Scalar Context

Perl 5 functions and operators perform different operations when operating in list or scalar context. The file input operator (<>) reads an entire file in list context. The same operator reads only one line in scalar context. An array returns its size when used in scalar context, like this:

```
$size = @array;
```

In list context, an array assignment copies the entire array like this:

```
@arrayCopy = @array;
```

Scalar and list context are explained in Chapter 4.

Bare Words

Perl 5, like a natural language, makes a lot of decisions based on context. As explained earlier in the chapter, bare words are character strings that do not begin with $, @, or % characters or have surrounding quotation marks, like this:

```
@languages = (Perl, C, C++, Fortran, Pascal);
```

Perl 5 must decide whether the bare word is a subroutine call (its first choice), a file handle, a label, or a character string. In previous versions of Perl, the default was to treat the bare word as a quoted string unless context clearly determined an alternative. In Perl 5, the bare word defaults to a subroutine call unless context determines another choice. When Perl 5 finds a bare word in your code that it cannot associate with a subroutine, file handle, or label, Perl 5 will treat the bare word as a double quoted string.

TIP   To avoid conflicts with current and future built-in subroutines, when you name file handles or labels, use only uppercase characters. Perl 5's built-in subroutines and functions are named using lowercase characters.

You should avoid using bare words in your code unless the context is obvious. I like to use bare words in initializing arrays (as shown in the example above), because in those cases the context is obvious.

If you run your code at least once with warnings enabled (using the warning switch, -w, discussed earlier in the chapter), Perl 5 will point out all the bare words in our code. You can then decide if these are errors or features.

Default Variables

Perl 5 provides default choices for many functions and operations. Use the default variables, such as $_ and ARGV, only when it is clear by context and convention that the default variables are being used. The use of the default options can make your code hard to understand, error prone, and difficult to maintain. The defaults for various functions and operators are discussed as each function is introduced throughout this book.

The my and local Keywords

Use the keyword my to declare your variables. Using the keyword local creates a variable whose scope includes any called subroutines. If you create a variable with the keyword `local` and then call a subroutine, the subroutine may overwrite the variable or the main routine may overwrite the subroutine's variable, like this:

```
. . .
local $myTemp = 15;
local $yourTemp = 20
doSomething ();
. . .
sub doSomething () {
    $yourTemp = True;
    while ($yourTemp){
        $myTemp++;
        if ($myTemp ==10){
            $yourTemp = 0;
        }
    }
}
```

There is absolutely no way to determine what the real intent of this code might have been, but the calling routine has modified the initial value of $myTemp, and the value of $yourTemp was modified in the subroutine. If the declarations in both the calling routine and the subroutine had used my instead of `local`, the subroutine variables $myTemp and $yourTemp would not have been affected by or would not have interfered with the calling routine's variables. You'll learn more about subroutines and variable scope in Chapter 18.

Global Variables versus Parameters

It seems easier to not pass your variables to your subroutine explicitly. If you don't declare a variable using my, it is global in scope and can be seen by any subroutine you call, as you saw in the example in the previous section.

Using global variables creates code that is hard to modify and has unusual side effects throughout the program. When you call a subroutine, pass the data to the subroutine explicitly, like this:

```
my $myVar=15;
my $yourVar=0;
doSomething($myVar, $yourVar);
. . .
sub doSomething($$){
    my($myVar, $yourVar)=@_;
. . .
}
```

Now an action taken in the subroutine affects only the subroutine. Then your subroutine can explicitly return any data it wants to make available to the calling program. Again, see Chapter 18 for more information about scope and subroutines.

Loop Variable Modification

The foreach statement creates an optional loop variable when processing arrays and lists. The loop variable is a reference to the actual array or list variable. If you modify the loop variable, you are also modifying the actual value. This is a nice feature if you understand it, but it's a big surprise to many programmers who expect the loop variable to be a temporary location. The foreach statement and loop variables are discussed in Chapter 9.

Handling Runtime Errors

If you try to run your program and Perl tells you your program didn't compile, then you have a syntax error, as discussed earlier in this chapter. When your code runs but produces the wrong results, you have a runtime error. This section focuses on runtime errors, which usually take a little more work to fix than syntax errors.

When you don't have a debugger handy, use print statements or some other type of error message to tell you what went wrong with your code. You'll learn about using debuggers a little later in the chapter. Here, we'll look at some other debugging techniques.

Using the System Error Variable

When you perform any system functions, such as opening a file, a special variable ($!) contains information about any failure conditions. This variable always contains the last system error message, which means you should only check it if the last operation you performed failed.

Perl provides two functions, die and warn, that work hand in hand with the system error message variable ($!). Both the die and the warn functions will print the filename and line number in the file where the error occurred or the contents of the specified print list (any data that you want printed when your program stops).

The `die` function causes your program to stop executing, or die. The syntax of the `die` function to output the filename and line number is:

```
die print_list;
```

To output only the contents of *print_list*, include a newline character (\n) at the end of *print_list*, like this:

```
die print_list\n;
```

The following form uses the `die` function with the system error message variable to output the filename and line number:

```
die "$!";
```

In some cases, you want your program to continue executing but still need an error message printed to the screen. In those cases, use the `warn` function, which has the same syntax as the `die` function.

```
warn print_list;
```

I like to use a combination of the system error message variable and the `die` or `warn` function whenever I call a system function. Listing 2.2 (a program named (errorMessage.pl) demonstrates how to use these functions with system calls, and Figure 2.4 shows the output.

Listing 2.2:   **The System Error Message**

```
1.  #!/usr/local/bin/perl
2.  open (FH,"<t.t") || warn "$!\n";
3.  open (FH,"<t.t") || warn "$!";
4.  print "after warn\n";
5.  open (FH,"<t.t") || die "$!";
6.  print "after die";
```

Though Listing 2.2 is a very contrived example, it illustrates the easiest mechanism for calling `die` or `warn`. The OR operator (| |) after the `open` call activates the `die` or `warn` function only if the return value from the `open` function is false (the OR operator is discussed in Chapter 4).

Line 1 of Listing 2.2 illustrates the use of the `warn` function with a newline character in the print list. As you can see in Figure 2.4, the first error message does not include any file information. Line 5 of Listing 2.2 illustrates the result of the `die` function. Line 5 never executes because the die function stops execution of the errorMessage.pl program.

Using the system error message variable

```
 Select Mastering Perl                                             _ □ ×

D:\sybex\MasteringPerl5>perl errorMessage.pl
No such file or directory
No such file or directory at errorMessage.pl line 2.
after warn
No such file or directory at errorMessage.pl line 4.

D:\sybex\MasteringPerl5>
```

Inserting print Statements

One of the most common methods of debugging a program is to insert print statements throughout the program. The print statement can be a simple statement identifying that you reached a particular location in your code. More frequently, however, the print statement includes some variable names that tell you the current state of your program.

I used to insert print statements and then remove them. Then I would need to rewrite the dadgum things all over again the next time a new bug appeared. There is an easier way. Every time you add a debug print statement, use an if $DEBUG clause, like this:

```
print "some Debug Info \n" if $DEBUG;
```

You must initialize the $DEBUG variable at the front of your program, like this:

```
$DEBUG=1 if $ARGV[0]=~/-D(ebug)?/i;
```

This statement will set the variable $DEBUG to 1 only if the first argument from the command line is -d (uppercase or lowercase), followed by an optional ebug. Now when you need to debug your code, you can add print statements and leave them in your code. The only time they will execute is when you add a -Debug argument after you program name, like this:

```
perl errorMessage.pl -d
```

Searching for Bugs

When you have a large program with a runtime error, just finding where the bug is can be a real pain. When trying to locate bugs in a large program, I use a method called *binary search*. The binary search method looks in only one half of the code at one time. For example, here are the steps for using this method with a 100-line program:

1. Copy the last 50 lines to a temporary file and then delete them from your program. (You may need to leave in closing braces or other required statements.)

2. Rerun your program. If the error disappears, the problem is in those last 50 lines of your program; otherwise, it is in the first 50 lines. Let's assume the problem is in the last 50 lines of code.

3. Take the half of the code with the error in it and return it to the main program. Now your main program has lines 1 through 75 and your temporary program has lines 76 through 100.

4. Rerun your program. If the error is still missing, you now know the error is in the last 25 lines.

5. Add one half of the last 25 lines back in and rerun your program. If the error shows up, you know the problem is between lines 76 and 87.

6. Repeat this process until you have identified the exact line that contains the error. You can find the error because you have a much smaller area in which to look.

The ultimate way to find bugs is with a debugger. In the next section, you'll learn about the Perl 5 debugger and a commercial Windows-based debugger.

Using a Debugger

A *debugger* is a tool that allows you to execute your code one or more lines at a time. Every debugger should allow you to view variables and set breakpoints, which stop execution of your code at predetermined locations. Perl 5 comes delivered with a free debugger, which performs these basic functions and more. Here, we'll look at the Perl 5 debugger, including how to use it with the Emacs editor in an interactive window. Then I'll tell you about the ActiveState Windows debugger, which I use to debug my code.

Running the Perl Debugger

The Perl debugger is available with all Perl 5 distributions at no charge. To start the Perl 5 debugger, you must be at the command prompt. From the command prompt, enter:

```
perl-d filename.pl
```

NOTE The examples shown in this section use the DOS command window, but these commands also work from the Unix command shell.

The debugger will be invoked on the file regardless of the filename extension (it doesn't need to be .pl). If your program has syntax errors, Perl will exit with an error message (remember that Perl 5 first compiles your program before running it). You will need to use one of the debugging techniques discussed earlier in this chapter to fix the syntax error before starting the debugger.

If your program is syntactically correct, you will see a beginning debugger screen, which should look like the one shown in Figure 2.5. You can see the debug prompt, DB<1>, on the last line of the opening window.

NOTE Notice in Figure 2.5 that the debugger says "Emacs support available." Many of the commands you will learn here work both from your Emacs editor and the command line. In the next section, I'll explain how to run an interactive Emacs debugging session.

FIGURE 2.5:

The Perl 5 debugger window

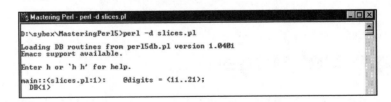

```
Mastering Perl - perl -d slices.pl                                    _ □ ×

D:\sybex\MasteringPerl5>perl -d slices.pl

Loading DB routines from perl5db.pl version 1.0401
Emacs support available.

Enter h or `h h' for help.

main::(slices.pl:1):    @digits = (11..21);
  DB<1>
```

Getting Help

The second line printed by the Perl debugger tells you how to get help. Because your DOS command window on a Windows 95/98 computer may not have a scroll bar, the first thing you need to be aware of is how to get help on help. If you type in h at the debug prompt, all the help information will rapidly scroll off the screen. To get an abbreviated list of the debugging commands, type in h h at the debug prompt. Figure 2.6 shows an example of what you will see.

The help function from the DOS command window provides further help on additional commands. To get help on a particular command, type **h** *command* (where *command* is a help command) at the debug prompt. If you type **h 0**, you get a screen full of information on the various debugger options. Other requests for help just repeat a one-line help statement, which is the same information as shown in Figure 2.6.

FIGURE 2.6:

The Perl 5 debugger's help information

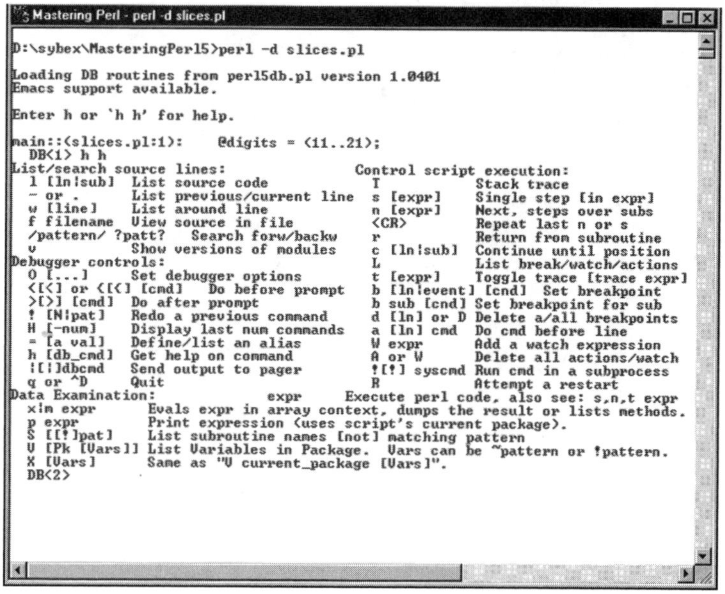

Displaying Source Code

If you're not looking at the help messages, then you probably want to look at your code. The two commands I most frequently use to view my source code in the Perl debugger are list (l) and window (w). These two commands tell the debugger to show you your source code.

As shown in Figure 2.7, you can type l from the debug prompt to list the next ten lines of your program. Each time you enter l, the next ten lines of your source code are printed. The l command starts displaying from the last displayed line. For example, if line 50 were the last displayed line and you entered l, lines 51 through 60 would be displayed.

FIGURE 2.7:

Listing your source code

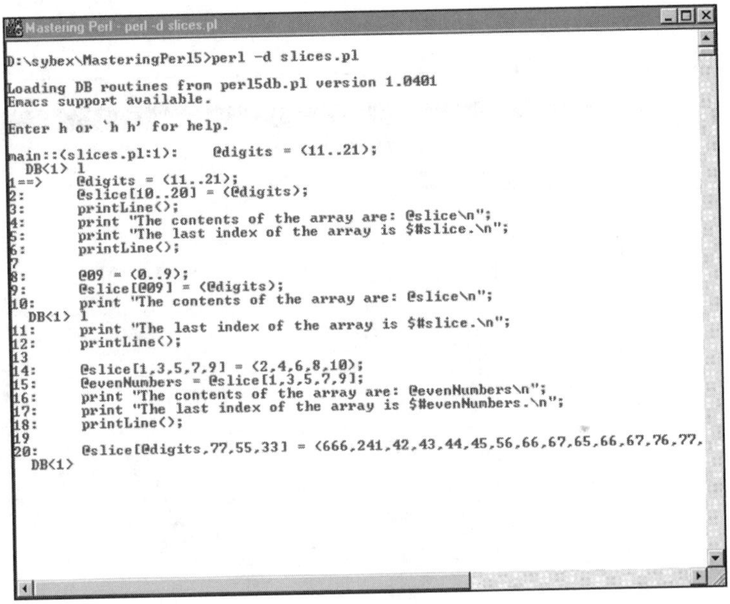

The l command has the following options:

- To display a particular line, enter l *lineNumber*, like this: l 8. This command displays only the requested line.

- To display a range of lines, use the l command with a starting and ending line number. For example, to see lines 21 through 42, enter l 21–42. Alternatively, you could enter the starting line number, a plus sign, and then the number of additional lines you would like. For example, to see line 15 and the following 20 lines, enter l 15+20.

- To list the contents of a subroutine, type l followed by the subroutine name: l *subName*.

When I'm debugging, I usually like to see a few lines surrounding the current line. The w command shows a few lines before the current line and a few lines after the current line. The w command also can be used with a line number to show the lines surrounding a particular location. Figure 2.8 shows an example of each of these forms of the command.

FIGURE 2.8:

Using the window (w) command

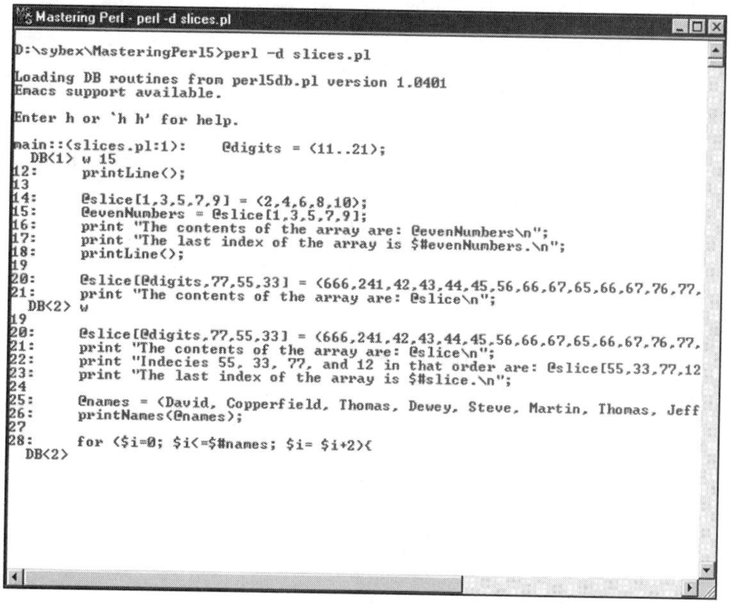

```
Mastering Perl - perl -d slices.pl

D:\sybex\MasteringPerl5>perl -d slices.pl

Loading DB routines from perl5db.pl version 1.0401
Emacs support available.

Enter h or `h h' for help.

main::(slices.pl:1):     @digits = (11..21);
  DB<1> w 15
12:     printLine();
13
14:     @slice[1,3,5,7,9] = (2,4,6,8,10);
15:     @evenNumbers = @slice[1,3,5,7,9];
16:     print "The contents of the array are: @evenNumbers\n";
17:     print "The last index of the array is $#evenNumbers.\n";
18:     printLine();
19
20:     @slice[@digits,77,55,33] = (666,241,42,43,44,45,56,66,67,65,66,67,76,77,
21:     print "The contents of the array are: @slice\n";
  DB<2> w
19
20:     @slice[@digits,77,55,33] = (666,241,42,43,44,45,56,66,67,65,66,67,76,77,
21:     print "The contents of the array are: @slice\n";
22:     print "Indecies 55, 33, 77, and 12 in that order are: @slice[55,33,77,12
23:     print "The last index of the array is $#slice.\n";
24
25:     @names = (David, Copperfield, Thomas, Dewey, Steve, Martin, Thomas, Jeff
26:     printNames(@names);
27
28:     for ($i=0; $i<=$#names; $i= $i+2){
  DB<2>
```

Executing Your Code

The purpose of a debugger is to give you control over the execution of your program. The following are the primary commands for executing your code one or a few lines at a time:

- To execute one line of code at a time, use the step (s) command. To execute the next statement in your program, at the debug prompt, type **s** and then press

Enter. Then you can just press Enter again to continue stepping through your code. The step command shows you the sequential execution of your code. If your code calls a subroutine, you will step into that subroutine, which you can continue to execute one statement at a time.

- To execute the next line of code, stepping over any subroutine calls, use the next (n) command. When you are stepping through your code, you frequently know whether a subroutine works or not. If you want to sequentially execute your code but do not want to enter a subroutine, use the next command.

- To execute until the next program interrupt, use the continue (c) command. The continue command tells the debugger to execute your code until it finds a breakpoint. Your code will execute to completion unless you have set breakpoints to interrupt your program. Setting breakpoints is described in the next section.

- To execute the remaining statements in the current subroutine, use the return (r) command. If you have stepped into a subroutine to view some specific information, but you don't need to step through each line in the subroutine, use the return command. The return command completes the execution of the subroutine and stops execution of your program on the first Perl 5 statement after the subroutine call.

Setting Breakpoints

Executing your code one line at a time gets old very fast. When your code is several hundred lines long, you need to be able to skip the pieces of your program that you've already tested. The breakpoint (b) command allows you to tell the debugger to execute your program until it reaches a particular line number, subroutine, or loading of an external file.

To set a breakpoint at a particular line, enter b *lineNumber*, like this: b 8. To execute until you reach that line, just type **c** at the debugger prompt. Your program will execute up to but not including the breakpoint line.

Conditional breakpoints stop execution of your program only when a specific condition is met. The syntax of conditional breakpoints is like this:

```
B lineNumber condition
```

The condition may be any expression. The breakpoint will stop execution of your program only if the condition evaluates to true. Figure 2.9 shows an example of a breakpoint set on line 8 with this conditional statement:

```
($slice[10] == 11)
```

This means to stop execution of the program when the tenth element of the slice array is equal to 11. (Conditional expressions are discussed in Chapter 8; arrays are covered in Chapter 6.) The breakpoint is set in the middle of Figure 2.9 and looks like this:

```
b 8 $slice[10]==11
```

FIGURE 2.9:

Setting a conditional breakpoint

```
D:\sybex\MasteringPerl5>perl -d slices.pl

Loading DB routines from perl5db.pl version 1.0401
Emacs support available.

Enter h or `h h' for help.

main::(slices.pl:1):    @digits = (11..21);
  DB<1> l
1==>      @digits = (11..21);
2:        @slice[10..20] = (@digits);
3:        printLine();
4:        print "The contents of the array are: @slice\n";
5:        print "The last index of the array is $#slice.\n";
6:        printLine();
7
8:        @09 = (0..9);
9:        @slice[@09] = (@digits);
10:       print "The contents of the array are: @slice\n";
  DB<1> b 8 $slice[10]==11
  DB<2> c
==========================================================================
The contents of the array are:         11 12 13 14 15 16 17 18 19 20 21
The last index of the array is 20.
==========================================================================
main::(slices.pl:8):    @09 = (0..9);
  DB<2> w
5:        print "The last index of the array is $#slice.\n";
6:        printLine();
7
8==>b     @09 = (0..9);
9:        @slice[@09] = (@digits);
10:       print "The contents of the array are: @slice\n";
11:       print "The last index of the array is $#slice.\n";
12:       printLine();
13
14:       @slice[1,3,5,7,9] = (2,4,6,8,10);
  DB<2>
```

To show all the breakpoints you have active in your debugging session, type L. To delete all your breakpoints, type D. To delete an individual breakpoint, type d followed by the line number of the breakpoint, like this: d 8.

I like to include external program files into my code using the require command (the require command includes subroutines into a program from other files on the hard disk). Frequently, I need to set breakpoints in these required files.

You cannot set a breakpoint in a required file unless you are currently executing in the required file. The easiest way to stop your code at a required file is with the breakpoint on load command, like this:

```
b load filename
```

For example, if the required filename is readPostInput.cgi, the breakpoint on load command looks like this:

```
b load readPostInput.cgi
```

The breakpoint command also accepts a subroutine name as a breakpoint value. When you use the breakpoint command with a subroutine name, your program will stop on the first executable line of the subroutine. Breakpoints on subroutine names may also be conditional, like this:

```
b readPostInput $DEBUG == 1
```

This conditional breakpoint will stop here only if the variable $DEBUG is equal to 1.

Viewing Program Data

Once you've stopped your program using the step or breakpoint commands, you need to be able to look at your program's data to determine what is wrong with your code. The print (p) command prints the contents of a variable or expression. The syntax of the p command is like this:

```
p expression
```

For example, if you want to print the contents of an array, enter the command like this:

```
p @arrayName
```

Figure 2.10 shows several examples of printing the contents of an array. Notice the command with quotation marks around the array name:

```
p "@slice"
```

This form inserts a space character between each array cell.

Quitting the Debugger

You will find your debugging sessions are interactive with your programming sessions. Your programming development cycle will begin to look like this: Build a little, test a little, debug a little, fix a little, build a little…. Quite often, the test a little, debug a little, and fix a little cycles take a lot more time than the build a little portion.

Once you have located your coding error in the debugger, there is usually no reason to continue running your program. You exit the debugger by entering the quit (q) command.

FIGURE 2.10:

Printing the contents of arrays

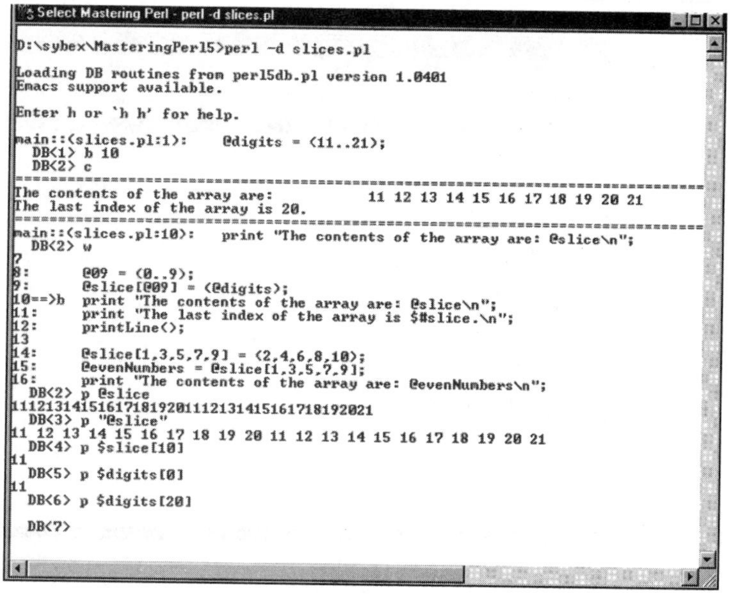

Once you exit the debugger, you will most likely open your favorite editor and modify your program based on the information gathered during your debugging session. After you have made your changes, test your code to see if you have really fixed the error.

As you get more experienced with programming and debugging, you should explore the debug commands in more detail. The commands you have learned here are the basic ones that you will use with almost every debugging session.

Debugging Using Emacs

With the basic Perl debugger, you must continually list the lines of your program. Using either the Unix or Windows Emacs editor (described in Chapter 1), you can invoke the Perl debugger in an interactive window interface.

To begin debugging a program within the Emacs editor, first start an Emacs session and then enter the Emacs command window by typing *meta* **x**. On most computers, *meta* is the Escape key (the only way to be sure you have the correct key is experimenting from your keyboard). Once you are in the command window, type **perldb** and press Enter. You will be prompted for the program you want to debug, as shown in the last line of Figure 2.11.

FIGURE 2.11:

Starting an Emacs debugging session

NOTE   Figures 2.11 and 2.12 show an interactive Emacs debugging session run on a Unix computer. The Emacs commands shown for Unix also will work for Windows computers.

Once you tell Emacs which program you wish to debug, you will be presented with a split-window interface, as shown in Figure 2.12. In the top window, you can enter any valid debugging command. In the bottom window, the next line to execute is identified by a right arrow in the left column. The Emacs editor allows you to switch between these two windows. You can enter debugging commands in the top window and switch to the bottom window when you want to scroll through your program. If you change the contents of the bottom window, you are changing the contents of the actual file.

FIGURE 2.12:

The split-window Emacs debugging interface

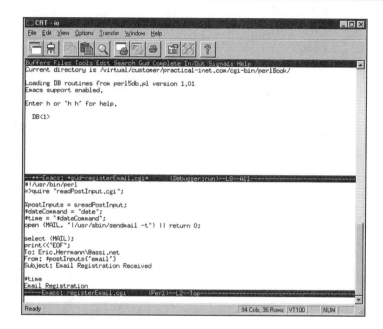

Running the ActiveState Windows Debugger

The Perl debugger has everything you need in a debugger, but it lacks a little in ease of use. Because I spend a good portion of my day writing and debugging code, I use the ActiveState debugger, shown in Figure 2.13. Like the Multi-Edit editor (discussed in Chapter 1), this tool is not free, but it is well worth the cost. This debugger enhances the built-in Perl debugger with an intuitive and easy-to-use interface.

TIP

The ActiveState debugger is available at www.activestate.com and this book's web site. You can run an evaluation copy on your computer at no cost. Instructions for integrating the ActiveState debugger with the Multi-Edit editor are available at the ActiveState web site.

FIGURE 2.13:

The ActiveState Windows debugger

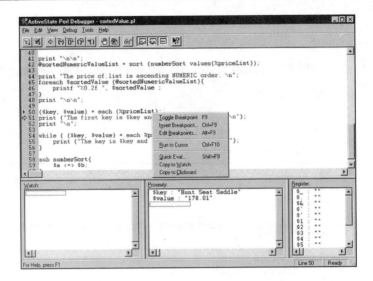

The toolbar buttons and menus across the top of the window allow you to manage your debugging session. From left to right, the buttons perform the following operations: continue, quit, show the next statement, step, step over, step out of, run to cursor, insert breakpoint, and delete all breakpoints. As you can see, these operations are similar to (if not the same as) the free Perl 5 debugger operations.

The right three buttons on the top toolbar (excluding the help button) activate the bottom three windows of the ActiveState debugger:

- The Watch window shows the values of variables you have explicitly requested.

- The Proximity window shows the values of scalar variables surrounding the current execution point of your program. (The current execution point is also called the instruction pointer location.)

- The Registry window shows the contents of the Perl 5 special variables that are relevant to the current instruction pointer.

If you right-click with your mouse, you bring up the pop-up menu also shown in Figure 2.13. (This pop-up menu is the interface I most frequently use.) One of the options on this menu is QuickEval. Selecting that option brings up the Quick-Eval window, shown in Figure 2.14. The QuickEval window allows you to view data and evaluate Perl 5 expressions. Note that to evaluate or view the contents of an array, as shown in Figure 2.14, you must surround the array name with quotation marks. If you evaluate an array without surrounding quotation marks, you are returned the size of the array.

Figure 2.14 also shows the Watch window fully expanded at the bottom of the screen. You can add variables to the Watch window through the QuickEval window. Once a variable is added to the Watch window, its current value is displayed throughout your program's execution.

Here, you've learned about just a few of the main features of the ActiveState debugger. The user interface is intuitive, and as you work with it, you will learn about the other capabilities of this debugger.

Debugging CGI Programs

Debugging CGI programs usually involves creative use of print statements. Here are the three basic steps for the CGI programmer:

- Make sure your code is syntactically correct.

- Test your code with sample data.

- Print the data sent to your CGI program using a debugging interface subroutine.

FIGURE 2.14:

Evaluating data

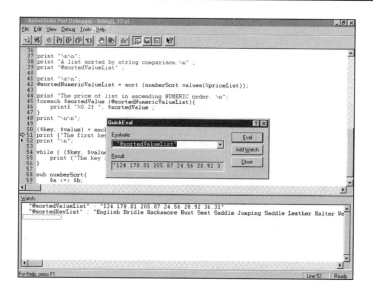

First, make sure that your CGI program compiles without syntax errors before you begin debugging it through your web server. If you are running the program on a Unix computer, make sure that the file permissions are set to 755. Then test the program by running it from the command line.

After you know that your program does not have any syntax errors, you can move onto the next steps. The following sections explain the techniques that I use to debug my CGI programs and include some examples.

Running the Program with Test Data

If the program is free of syntax errors, I run it with special test data. This step is critical because most CGI programs require external data sent via a web page. If this method does not solve the problem, then I modify my CGI program to show the data it is receiving and add print statements as necessary, as described in the next section.

To test my CGI program, I first create a file of debug information. This file should contain data already in the format your CGI program expects. The file shown in Listing 2.3 is a debug data file I used to debug an online reservation program. The debug file is then included in your CGI program using the require command, an example of which follows the listing.

Listing 2.3:	Debug Data

```
%lodgingInfo = (
'ARRIVAL_DATE' => "10/6/98",
'ROOM_PREFERRENCE' => "Red River",
'LENGTH_OF_STAY' => 4,
'PAYMENT_METHOD' => "Credit Card",
'NAME' => "Eric C. Herrmann",
'ADDRESS' => "255 S. Canyonwood Dr.",
'CITY' => "Austin",
'STATE' => "Texas",
'ZIP' => "78620",
'TELEPHONE' => "512-442-2991",
'EMAIL' => "yawp\@io.com",
'OCCASION' => "20th Wedding Anniversary",
'SPECIAL_REQUEST' => "It would be really nice if you would do something
    very nice and let us take the raft down the creek",
'NUMBER_IN_PARTY' => 2,
```

```
'UID' => 62878766310,
'PAYMENT_METHOD' => "onLine",
) ;
$ENV{'QUERY_STRING'}="UID=  14fa7198.49.249.718";
return 1;
```

When I want to test a CGI program I insert a line like this:

```
require "debugConstants.cgi" if $DEBUG:
```

Notice that the last line of Listing 2.3 returns a 1. If the last line of a required file does not return a true value, your program will fail.

This mechanism of testing a CGI program allows you to load and run your program from the command line using your favorite debugger interface.

Adding print Statements

If I need to do further debugging of my CGI program, my next step is to modify the program to show the data it is receiving and add `print` statements as necessary. The first thing I modify the program to do is print the HTTP response header `Content-Type: text/html`. I also modify the program so that it performs this special debug function only when I send it a unique input variable.

As an example, I modified Listing 1.4 of Chapter 1, modifying line 3 to run the `printDebug` subroutine when the input form sends the user's name as Debug, as shown in Listing 2.4.

> **NOTE**   The subroutine `printDebug` may be inserted at any reasonable place into your code. I usually put my subroutines at the end of the file, as shown here.

Listing 2.4:   Debugging CGI Programs

```
1. #!/usr/bin/perl
2.
# REPLACE LINE 3:
# 3. %postInputs = readPostInput();
# WITH THIS LINE:
3. printDebug() if $postInputs{'Contact_FullName'} =~ /Debug/i;
4. $dateCommand = "date";
```

```
5. $time = `$dateCommand`;
6. open (MAIL, "|/usr/sbin/sendmail -t") || return 0;
7.
8. select (MAIL);
9. print<<"EOF";
# ...lines omitted for space purposes

sub printDebug(){
    print "Content-type: text/html\n\n";

    foreach $key (sort keys %postInputs){
      print qq|$key ==> $postInputs{"$key"} <br>|;
    }
    exit(1);
}
```

As shown in Figure 2.15, this allows you to see your incoming CGI data. If you need to see other data in the program, insert print statements as required.

FIGURE 2.15:

Viewing incoming CGI POST data

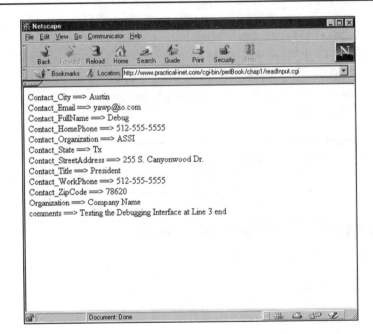

I recommend that you always print your input CGI data as your first online CGI debugging step. The input data is the most likely source of errors. Notice that the subroutine `printDebug` in Listing 2.4 calls the `exit` function after printing the input data. This prevents the remaining portion of the CGI program from running. You should comment out the `exit` statement if you need other parts of your CGI program to execute after you call the `printDebug` subroutine.

Summary

The goal of this chapter is to reduce your frustration as you work through the details of learning Perl 5. Each section is designed to teach you how to deal with the common coding problems you will encounter as you learn Perl 5. If you code, you will debug.

The first types of errors you will encounter are likely to be syntax related. In the section on syntax and error messages, you learned how to separate erroneous error messages from error messages that help you find your bug. The most common error messages were explained in this section.

Of course, it would be nice if you could prevent errors before they occur. In the section on avoiding errors, you learned about programming techniques that help you prevent bugs before they become a problem. These techniques include good programming practices such as commenting and indenting your code and using meaningful variable names. The section on avoiding errors also included how to avoid common logic errors such as boundary conditions and negative logic.

You also learned about the most common Perl 5 mistakes, such as using numeric instead of string conditional logic. Once you become familiar with the language, you may be tempted to use bare words and default variables. When to use these features and when to avoid them were also discussed in the section. Perl 5 allows the programmer wide latitude in variable declaration and use. This section included a discussion of the misuse of global variables and when to use the keyword my.

Even the best programmer writes code that includes errors. In the section on debugging techniques, you learned that the system error message can be used to help locate an error. This section also explained how to apply a binary search to quickly isolate a difficult bug in a large program.

Every good language has a good debugger. You learned about using the built-in Perl debugger, the Emacs interactive window interface, and a Windows-based debugger.

Finally, this chapter included three basic techniques for debugging CGI programs. First, make sure your code is syntactically correct. Next, test your code with sample data. Finally, print the data sent to your CGI program using a debugging interface subroutine.

If you've never coded with Perl before, you're now prepared to enter the Perl 5 programming world. This first section of the book was designed to give you the foundation you need to work though the remainder of the book with confidence. In the next section of the book, you'll learn how to write Perl 5 statements, create variables, and control how your program executes.

PART II

Perl Programming Fundamentals

Jump-Start on Programming Fundamentals

- Perl 5 operators

- Variable rules

- Scalar, array, hash, and reference variables

- Branch-on-condition statements

What do you need to know in order to begin using Perl 5 data and control structures now? That's the heart of this "jump-start" chapter. Just the facts; embellishments not included.

In this chapter, you'll learn about the fundamental elements of Perl 5 programs: operators, variables, and control structures. The jump-start program shows an example of how these elements work together, and the rest of the chapter takes an "in-a-nutshell" approach to explaining the fundamentals.

All those details that help you use the Perl 5 language efficiently, effectively, and effortlessly follow in the remaining chapters of this part. At the end of this chapter, you'll find a guide to help you decide where to go from here.

Jump-Start Definitions

Array	A collection of scalar variables, with its own set of rules for assigning and retrieving the data stored into each cell of the array. An array name starts with an at sign (@).
Assignment operator	A Perl operator that takes the result of an expression (such as `4.2 + 3`) and stores it into the lvalue.
Associativity	The rule used to determine with which expression the operator is bound. For example, the exponential operator (`**`) is right associative, meaning it takes the exponent of the number to its right.
Binary operators	Operators that operate on bits.
Block of statements	A requirement for all Perl 5 control statements. A block of statements can be zero, one, or many lines of Perl 5 code. It is always surrounded by curly braces (`{}`).
Boolean operators	Operators used in conditional expressions to choose the next statement a program should execute. A Boolean value is something that is either true or false.

Branching statement	A type of statement that tells your computer which line in your code to execute next. The computer's choice is based on the results of a conditional expression and the branching command associated with the conditional expression. Branching statements include `if`, `if else`, `if elsif`, `?:`, `last`, `next`, `for`, `foreach`, `while`, `until`, and several others.
Cell	The container within an array that stores each scalar variable separately.
Cell index	The unique identifier (number) for an array cell to reference the scalar data stored within it. A cell index is surrounded by brackets; for example, [0] indicates the first cell of an array.
Conditional expression	An expression that evaluates to either true or false. The true or false value is usually the result of a compare operation, but the expression can be any operation.
Dereferencing	Accessing values referred to by Perl references.
Hash	A mechanism for efficiently storing and retrieving values in a sparse array. A hash table uses an algorithm (a function) to determine the index of where to store or retrieve a data value. The scalar data within a hash is not stored or retrieved in sequential order. A hash name starts with a percent sign (%).
Hash key	The unique identifier assigned to a hash cell to reference the scalar data stored within it. A hash key is any literal, usually a string. Each key is associated with a value when assigning data to a hash.
Label	A marker for the Perl 5 interpreter. A label is usually used to mark the beginning of a new block of statements.

List	One sequential group of scalar variables. A list can contain other lists. Any lists that are originally part of the containing list are always resolved to their scalar list values before the container list completes evaluation. The container that creates a list context can be parentheses or an array.
List context	A Perl 5 context in which the expression being evaluated returns a list of scalar values.
Literal	The actual value expressed in a program, such as the number 10 or the string `"Perl 5"`.
Loop	A special form of branching statement that executes repeatedly until a condition is met.
Lvalue	The value on the left side of the assignment operator, such as a variable.
Multi-dimensional array	A Perl 5 array that contains a reference to another array.
Namespace	A list, or table, of all of the names that the Perl 5 interpreter must keep track of.
Null	An undefined or empty value.
Numeric operators	Operators that perform standard math operations, such as addition (+), subtraction (-), and multiplication (*).
Precedence	The rule used to determine which operation in an expression is performed first. The operator with the higher precedence goes first.
Reference	A Perl 5 scalar variable that keeps track of where another variable (of any type) is stored in memory. Each reference variable takes up only a single address space. A reference variable is created by using the reference operators `\`, `[]`, `{}`, `sub {;}`, and `bless`.

Scalar context	A Perl 5 context in which the expression being evaluated returns only one value.
Scalar variable	A variable that stores only one data item at a time. Perl 5 scalar variables can contain either numeric or string data. A scalar variable name starts with a dollar sign ($).
Sparse array	An array that may have indexes from one to a million but contains only a small number of actual values.
String	A type of data that can be stored into a Perl scalar variable. String data normally refers to single characters strung together to create words. Anything surrounded by quotation marks is considered a character string.
String operator	Perl operators that add and multiply string values or compare strings or character data.
Variable declaration	The process of making a variable part of the namespace table, also called a symbol table. A declared variable has a place in the symbol table but it doesn't have any contents or data associated with it until it is explicitly initialized. Uninitialized but declared variables have the value null in Perl 5.
Variable definition	The process of assigning some value to a variable. Perl 5 allows you to declare and define a variable in one step. Whenever a new variable is assigned a value, it is also declared. The new variable is given a place in the symbol table and assigned a value.
Variable interpolation	Perl 5's process of interpreting characters in a string literal surrounded with double quotation marks. Without variable interpolation (when the string literal is surrounded by single quotation marks), Perl stores the characters exactly as they appear.

Jump-Start Program

The program presented here is a prototype for an online Auto Mall. The program demonstrates many of the concepts in this chapter and prints the HTML page shown in Figure 3.1.

NOTE	In Listing 3.1, as well as in other listings throughout this book, some lines of code are too long to fit on a single line of the printed book page. The runover code for these lines is shown as indented beneath the code with a line number. In these cases, the entire entry should be typed in as a single line of code. In all the listings, the line numbers represent the individual lines of code.

Listing 3.1:   **An Auto Mall Prototype**

```perl
1.    #!/usr/local/bin/perl
2.    #Initialize a global debug variable if we have -debug or some
3.    #version of -debug on the command line.
4.    #When you see if $DEBUG, that line will be executed only
5.    #if -debug was part of the invocation of the program.
6.    $DEBUG = 1 if $ARGV[0] =~ /-d(ebug)?/i;
7.    require "debugData.pl" if $DEBUG;
8.    #Define the constants this program will use
9.    $MAXIMUMSEARCHSIZE = 25;
10.
11.   #Initialize arrays
12.   @carMakes = (Mitsubishi, Geo, Chevrolet, Ford);
13.   @fordModels = (Taurus, Contour, Mustang, Escort);
14.   @MitsubishiModels = ("3000 GT", Diamante, Eclipse, Spyder,
                           Galant, Mirage);
15.   #Initialize hash
16.   %Spyder = (Price =>26000,
17.           Engine =>'2 Liter',
18.           Color =>Red,
19.           Transmission =>Manual,
20.           Brakes =>'Anti-Lock',
21.           DriverAirBag =>Yes,
22.           Turbo =>Yes,
23.           Horsepower =>210,
24.           Name =>"Spyder GS-T",
```

```
25.              img =>'spyder.jpg',
26.              Model =>Mitsubishi);
27.
28.   #Read input from web search
29.   %searchCriteria = readPostInput() if !$DEBUG;
30.
31.   while ($searchCriteria{numberOfSearches} > 0){
32.       #Create lexical variables. They will be initialized to null
33.       #each pass through the while loop.
34.       my ($searchResult, @matches);
35.       if($searchCriteria{maxSearches} > $MAXIMUMSEARCHSIZE){
36.           $searchCriteria{maxSearches} -= $MAXIMUMSEARCHSIZE;
37.       }
38.       if ($searchCritera{carMakes} eq "Any") {
39.
40.           #The $make variable defined by foreach loop is NOT
41.           #visible outside the foreach loop (lexical to loop).
42.           foreach $make (@carMakes){
43.               #Each time processMake runs returns array of hashes.
44.               #push statement puts that array on global match array.
45.               push @matches, processMake($make, $searchCriteria
                                             {maxSearches});
46.           }
47.       }
48.       else {
49.           #In this case. we are only searching one car make, so we
50.           #will get back one array of hashes.
51.           $matches[0] = processMake($searchCriteria{carMakes},
                                         $searchCriteria{maxSearches});
52.       }#end else
53.   }#end while
54.
55.   sub processMake($){
56.       #Read in my parameter list
57.       my ($make, $searchLimit) = @_;
58.       my @matches;
59.       SWITCH:{
60.           #Switch statement calls correct inventory subroutine
61.           #for each car make. Each subroutine returns array of
62.           #hashes for processing at the end of the SWITCH block.
63.           if ($searchCriteria{carMakes} eq "Mitsubishi") {
64.               (@inventory) = getMitsubishiInventory();
```

```
65.            last SWITCH;
66.          }
67.        if ($searchCriteria{carMakes} eq "Geo") {
68.            (@inventory) = getGeoInventory();
69.            last SWITCH;
70.          }
71.        if ($searchCriteria{carMakes} eq "Chevrolet") {
72.            (@inventory) = getChevroletInventory();
73.            last SWITCH;
74.          }
75.        if ($searchCriteria{carMakes} eq "Ford") {
76.            (@inventory) = getFordInventory();
77.            last SWITCH;
78.          }
79.        DEFAULT: {
80.            printInputError($searchCriteria{carMakes});
81.          }
82.      }#end SWITCH
83.       #Print out the detailed match.
84.      printDetailedMatch(\@inventory);
85.
86.      #The $index variable defined in the for loop is defined as
87.      #global variable and is visible outside the for loop.
88.      for ($index = 0; $index <= $#inventory; $index++){
89.          if ($inventory[$index]->{price} <=
                             $searchCriteria{price}  &&
90.              $inventory[$index]->{model} eq
                             $searchCriteria{model}) {
91.              #Put hash reference onto @matches array.
92.              #The @matches array is used in list context.
93.              unshift @matches, $inventory[$index];
94.              #The @matches array is used in scalar context.
95.              last if @matches > $searchLimit;
96.          }
97.      }#end for loop
98.      $searchCriteria{numberOfSearches} = @matches - $index - 1;
99.      return (\@matches);
100. }
101.
102. sub printDetailedMatch (\@){
103.      #This subroutine receives a reference to an array of hashes.
104.      my ($inventory) = @_;
```

```
105.    #The array reference is dereferenced into an array.
106.    my @carInventory = @$inventory;
107.    open (DEBUGFILE, ">carMatch.html") if $DEBUG;
108.
109.    #select statement returns previously selected file handle,
110.    #allowing restore of file handle before subroutine exits.
111.    $originalOut = select (DEBUGFILE) if $DEBUG;
112.
113.    #If we are testing, set the HTTP headers to null and
114.    #open the debug file for output.
115.    #Otherwise, print out the valid http headers before
116.    #we start returning the matches.
117.    $HTTPheader = ($DEBUG)? "" : q|Content-Type: text/html
118.
119. |;
120.
121.        print<<"EOF";
122. $HTTPheader
123. <HTML><head>
124. <Title>Matching Inventory</Title>
125. </HEAD>
126. <body bgcolor="#FFFFFF" link="#0000FF" vlink="#660099">
127. EOF
128.    #Each hash reference from array retrieved by foreach.
129.    #This print statement uses double qoutes after the heredoc
130.    #operator, which means you get variable interpolation.
131.    #The hash reference $carData is retrieved and dereferenced
132.    #throughout the HTML output. Both right arrow notation ->
133.    #and $$ dereference notation is demonstrated.
134.    foreach $carData (@carInventory){
135.
136.        print<<"EOF";
137. <center>
138. <h1>$carData->{Model} $carData->{Name} </h1>
139. </center>
140.
141. <table border="0" cellpadding="0" cellspacing="0" width="100%">
142.
143. <td width="40"> </td>
144. <td valign="top" width="100%">
145. <h2 align="center"><font size="6" face="Arial">
                        $carData{Name}</font></h2>
```

```
146. <div align="center"><center>
147. <table border="0"
148. cellpadding="5" width="95%">
149. <tr>
150. <td valign="top" width="50%"><font size="2" face="Arial">
                                                        <br><br>
151. <B>Make: </B>$carData->{Name}
152. <BR>
153. <B>Model: </B>$carData->{Model}
154. <BR>
155. <B>Engine: </B>$carData->{Engine}
156. <BR>
157. <B>Turbo: </B>$carData->{Turbo}
158. <BR>
159. <B>Horsepower: </B>$carData->{Horsepower}
160. <BR>
161. </table>
162. </font></td><td align="center" valign="top" width="50%">
163. <img src="$$carData{img}" align="top" border="0" alt=
                                        "$$carData{Name}"></A>
164. </table>
165. </body>
166. </html>
167. EOF
168.     close(DEBUGFILE) if $DEBUG;
169.     #Return the original selected output file handle
170.     select($originalOut) if $DEBUG;
171.     }
172. }
173. sub printInputError ($){
174.     my ($error) = @_;
175.     open (DEBUGFILE, ">debug.html") if $DEBUG;
176.     $originalOut = select (DEBUGFILE) if $DEBUG;
177.     $HTTPheader = ($DEBUG)? "" : q|Content-Type: text/html
178.
179. |;
180. print<<"EOF";
181. <HTML><head>
182. <Title>INVALID INPUT</Title>
183. </HEAD>
184. <body bgcolor="#FFFFFF" link="#0000FF" vlink="#660099">
185.     <h2> We are sorry but the input data $error is not valid for
```

```
186.    our database.
187.    </h2>
188. </body>
189. </html>
190. EOF
191.    close(DEBUGFILE) if $DEBUG;
192.    select($originalOut) if $DEBUG;
193. }
194.
```

This program works from both the command line and the Internet by implementing a concept of creating a debug file to test a CGI program (see the "Debugging CGI Programs" section in Chapter 2). If you are testing this program, all data will be read from the debug file and output is sent to a file for later analysis. This is implemented on line 6, where the command line argument array @ARGV is checked for a -debug switch:

```
$DEBUG = 1 if $ARGV[0] =~ /-d(ebug)?/i;
```

FIGURE 3.1:

My matching car

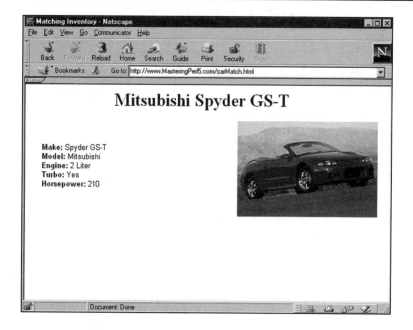

The program initializes global variables in the first few lines and then begins processing user input.

Each request by the user is handled by the `processMake` subroutine called on lines 45 and 51:

```
push @matches, processMake($make, $searchCriteria {maxSearches});
$matches[0] = processMake($searchCriteria{carMakes},
    $searchCriteria{maxSearches});
```

The `processMake` subroutine returns an array of hashes, which are printed in the `printDetailMatch` subroutine that begins on line 102. The `processMake` subroutine calls the correct inventory subroutine for the car make specified by the user input. Invalid user input is handled by the `DEFAULT` block, a `SWITCH` block that begins on line 79. This `SWITCH` block calls an error routine, which returns an error HTML page with the invalid data.

The Perl 5 fundamental elements used in Listing 3.1 are explained briefly in this chapter and in detail in the following chapters in this part of the book.

Operators and Context

Perl 5 is a context-sensitive language and uses a different set of operators for string and numeric operations. That context sensitivity comes in two forms:

Numeric versus string   Whether a scalar variable is treated as a numeric variable or as a string variable is determined by the context of an operation. The data stored in the variable and the operations performed with it determine whether Perl 5 treats the variable as numeric or string. For example, on lines 89 and 90 of Listing 3.1, price is compared in numeric context and model is compared in string context:

```
if ($inventory[$index]->{price} <= $searchCriteria{price}  &&
    $inventory[$index]->{model} eq $searchCriteria{model})
```

Scalar versus list   In scalar context, the expression being evaluated returns only one value. In list context, the expression being evaluated returns a list of scalar values. When Perl sees a list (a group of scalar objects contained by parentheses or an array), any lists that are originally part of the containing list are always resolved to their scalar list values before the container list completes evaluation. In Listing 3.1, the `@matches` array is used in both list context (line 93) and scalar context (line 95):

```
unshift @matches, $inventory[$index];
last if @matches > $searchLimit;
```

Table 3.1 lists each of the Perl 5 operators and separates them into string and numeric categories when context is important. Table 3.1 also shows operator precedence (the order in which operations are performed), from highest to lowest precedence, and associativity (which expression the operator is bound with—the one on the right or the one on the left).

NOTE   Where string and numeric operators have been separated into adjacent rows in Table 3.1 but perform similar operations, the precedence is the same. For example, the precedence of the less-than operators in either numeric (<) or string (1t) context is the same.

TABLE 3.1: Perl 5 Operators, Precedence, and Associativity

Operator	Meaning	Associativity
() `"'` ` functions	Parentheses (grouping), quotes (string), functions	Left
->	Dereference	Left
++ –	Increment/decrement	None
**	Exponential	Right
! ~ \ unary + –	NOT (logical and binary), Escape, sign operators	Right
=~ !~	Bind, not bind	Left
* / %	Multiply, divide, modulus	Left
x	String multiply	Left
+ –	Add, minus	Left
.	String concatenate	Left
<< >>	Binary shift left and right	Left
< > <= >=	Numeric comparison: less than, greater than, less than or equal to, greater than or equal to	None

Continued on next page

TABLE 3.1 CONTINUED: Perl 5 Operators, Precedence, and Associativity

Operator	Meaning	Associativity
lt gt le ge	String comparison: less than, greater than, less than or equal to, greater than or equal to	None
== != <=>	Numeric comparison: equal to, not equal to, compare	None
eq ne cmp	String comparison: equal to, not equal to, compare	None
&	Binary AND	Left
| ^	Binary OR, exclusive OR	Left
&&	Logical AND	Left
||	Logical OR	Left
?:	(Condition)? True: False	Right
= += -= *= /= %= x= <<= >>= &= |= ^= &&= ||=	Compound assignment statements	Right
, =>	Comma, right arrow	Left
not	Logical NOT	Right
and	Logical AND	Left
or, xor	Logical OR, logical exclusive OR	Left

TIP   Use parentheses to make one expression execute before another expression. Parentheses always execute the innermost expression first and work outward.

Variables

Perl 5 variables come in three flavors: scalar, array, and hash. Perl 5 scalar variables also can hold a reference value, which is similar to a C/C++ pointer. The same basic rules for naming, declaring, and defining variables apply to all three types of variables.

NOTE   You cannot declare a variable as an integer, a float, or a character in Perl 5; a variable can be declared only as scalar, array, or hash.

Variable Names

Variable names are preceded by a variable designator character to indicate their type. Perl 5 uses the first character of a variable name to distinguish which namespace to allocate to a particular variable name, as follows:

- Scalar variables begin with the dollar sign ($) character, as in $MAXIMUM-SEARCHSIZE = 25 (in line 9 of Listing 3.1).

- Arrays start with the at sign (@), as in @carMakes = (Mitsubishi, Geo, Chevrolet, Ford) (in line 12 of Listing 3.1).

- Hashes start with a percent sign (%), as in %Spyder = (Price =>26000 (in line 16 of Listing 3.1).

At least one character must follow the variable designator character. Variable names may contain any printable character, except the space character. Perl 5 is a case-sensitive language, which means that the variable $MAXIMUMSEARCHSIZE is different from the variable $MaximumSearchSize.

Variable names that begin with an underscore or an alphabetical character (*A* through *Z*) may be any practical length, although some implementations may limit the variable name length to 255 characters. The characters that follow variable names that begin with an underscore or alphabetical character may be digits, underscores, and alphabetical characters. If a variable name begins with a digit, it may be of any practical length, but it can contain only digits. If a variable name begins with any nonalphanumeric character, it can only be one character long. (Perl 5 has many built-in special variables that are only one character long.)

WARNING   Using single-letter variable names is not recommended because it makes your programs cryptic.

Namespaces and Variable Declarations

Some languages require you to declare a variable before you can define it. In Perl 5, a variable comes into existence the first time it is assigned a value, which means that you can define variables as you need them. Variables are defined by assigning a variable name to a value. Perl 5 also allows you to declare variables (initialize variables before they are used) by using the my and local keywords. Variables declared using my or local are assigned a null value.

NOTE   Each Perl 5 data type reserves a separate namespace in the symbol table. This means a variable with the same name may occupy multiple spaces in the global symbol table. Perl 5 separates variables into the correct namespace based on the first character of the variable name (for scalars, arrays, and hashes) or context (for file and directory handles).

The namespace of variables declared using the keyword my is limited to the enclosing block. The keyword my may be used singularly with a variable name, as on line 58 of Listing 3.1:

```
my @matches;
```

Alternatively, my can be used with a list of variable names, as on line 34 of Listing 3.1:

```
my ($searchResult, @matches);
```

WARNING   If you create a list of my variables, be sure to place parentheses around the list. The comma operator binds tighter than the my operator. The my operator will affect only the first variable in the list when the variable list is not surrounded by parentheses. This means that only the first variable in the declaration list will be a lexical my variable; the remaining variables in the list will be global variables. See Chapter 18 for details about lexical and global scope.

Variables declared using the keyword local are visible to any subroutine called within the declaring scope. The local keyword may be used with a single variable name, like this:

```
local $var;
```

Alternatively, local can be used with a list of variable names, like this:

```
local ($var1, $var2, $var3, $var4);
```

All other variables are part of a package scope, which looks much like a global namespace. A *package* separates the variables and subroutines of one package from another. Every Perl 5 program has a main:: namespace that contains all of the variable names that are part of the main package. You can access any variable in the main package by adding the namespace prefix main:: to the variable name. Unless you declare your program as part of a package namespace, it is part of the package main::. If you declare your program as part of another package, all variables defined during your program, except for variables declared using my or local, are in effect global in scope. They can be accessed at any place in your code regardless of where they are defined.

The my and local keywords are discussed in the chapters in this part; Perl 5 packages and scope are discussed in detail in Part 5.

Scalar Variables

Scalar variables hold only a single item, which can be either numeric or string data.

Perl 5 uses quotes (quotation mark characters) and quote operators to identify string data. Table 3.2 lists the various string delimiters and indicates whether they allow variable interpolation.

TABLE 3.2: Perl 5 String Data Identifiers

Identifier	Meaning
" or qq	Begins or ends a character string. Allows variable interpolation.
' or q	Begins or ends a character string. Does not allow variable interpolation.
` or qx	Begins or ends a system command string. Allows variable interpolation.
qw	Quoted string. Does not allow variable interpolation.

When you use double quotes or the qq operator, Perl interprets the characters in the string literal. In other words, Perl applies *variable interpolation*. Using the qq operator, as in the following example, allows you to use the quote characters (") without special escape (\") syntax:

```
print qq|<INPUT TYPE="SUBMIT" NAME="$submitButton" VALUE="$submitType">
        <INPUT>|;
```

When you use single quotes or the q operator, Perl stores the characters exactly as they appear—it does not apply variable interpolation. For example, Listing 3.1 includes the following code on lines 117 through 119 and 177 through 179:

```
$HTTPheader = ($DEBUG)? "" : q|Content-Type: text/html

|;
```

In this example, the variable $HTTPheader is set to the empty string, or the HTML HTTP Content-Type header. When returning an HTML HTTP header, it is important to return a blank line after the last header. The quote operator q returns exactly the characters between the delimiters, including the blank line in this example.

For numeric data, Perl 5 recognizes integer, floating-point, hexadecimal, octal, and other mathematical notations, as listed in Table 3.3.

TABLE 3.3: Perl 5 Numeric Formats

Type	Format	Example
Integer	NN	12
Floating point	NN.NN	342.176
Scientific	NN.NNENN	42.04E-6
Big number	NN_NNN_NNN	6_000_000
Hexadecimal	0xNNNN	0xFFD3
Octal	0NNN	0374

The result of an operation that involves a scalar variable depends on its context. Perl 5 takes into account whether the variable contains string or numeric data and whether the operator is a string or numeric operator (see Table 3.1) in determining the correct outcome of an operation.

For example, suppose that you assign the letter "A" to a variable and then increment the variable, like this:

```
$var = "A";
$var++;
print "$var";
```

When you run these three little lines, B is printed on the command line. Conversely, you could append the letter C to $var, and $var would then equal BC. Increment $var again, and $var contains BD. Now suppose that you try to add something to the string BD using the numeric addition operator (+). Perl 5 recognizes this as an out-of-context operation. If you try to add a character, $var suddenly contains zero. If you try to add a number, $var contains the value of the number added.

Arrays

A Perl 5 array is a collection of scalar variables. Unlike in most other languages, a Perl 5 array can contain a mixed bag of string data, numeric data, and references.

Arrays are defined using list assignment or by assigning a scalar value to an array cell. When assigning a list to an array, the syntax is:

```
@arrayName = (list of scalars);
```

An example of array list assignment is in line 14 of Listing 3.1:

```
@MitsubishiModels = ("3000 GT", Diamante, Eclipse, Spyder, Galant,
    Mirage);
```

An array may also be assigned the contents of another array, like this:

```
@arrayName = @array2;
```

Here is an example of an array-to-array assignment:

```
@matchedInventory = @carInventory;
```

Perl 5 arrays are created dynamically. If a new array cell is assigned data but skips several intermediate cells, the intermediate cells are created and assigned the value null. Your array grows in size as new data is added to the array.

An array is made up of cells. Each cell contains a scalar value. The cell is identified by a unique, sequential number surrounded by brackets, called its *index*. Array cell indexes begin with [0].

Since each cell of an array is also a scalar value, assigning or referencing a cell in an array uses scalar syntax. For example, line 51 of Listing 3.1 assigns a value to cell number 0 of the @matches array:

```
$matches[0] = processMake($searchCriteria{carMakes},
    $searchCriteria{maxSearches});
```

The dollar sign ($) tells Perl 5 this is scalar context, and the array cell index [0] tells Perl 5 which cell in the matches array should store the results returned from the subroutine processMake.

To retrieve a value from an array, use similar syntax:

```
$make = $carMakes[0];
```

In this case, the scalar variable called $make is assigned the value held in the zeroth cell of the carMakes array.

The current size of the array minus the initial array index number is available in a special variable, called the last cell index variable, that is the array name prepended with $#. If your array is named @carMakes, the index of the last cell of the array is $#carMakes. The length of the array is:

```
$#carMakes - $[ +1;
```

NOTE   The initial array index variable defaults to zero, but you can set it to any value you choose. However, you should not change the starting array cell number unless you have a strong programming reason to do so.

You can add values to the end of an array by referencing a number whose value is one greater than that of the last cell index. For example, on line 13 of Listing 3.1, the @fordModels array was initialized to the four car models:

```
@fordModels = (Taurus, Contour, Mustang, Escort);
```

Now suppose that you want to add the F250 model to the end of the @fordModels array. You can use this syntax:

```
$fordModels[$#fordModels + 1] = "F250";
```

or this syntax:

```
$fordModels[++$#fordModels] = "F250";
```

If you added the new model to the end of the array, like this:

```
$fordModels[$#fordModels] = "F250";
```

you would be overwriting the last value in the array, which was Escort after the original initialization.

You can also reference Perl 5 arrays using negative indexes. The value −1 (negative one) references the last cell of an array. You can iterate backwards over an

array, from the last cell to the first cell, by starting at -1 and decrementing until
-$#*arrayname*.

Arrays also may be accessed in *slices*, which means you don't need to use the
whole array when just a few cells are needed. Because slices are subsets of arrays,
they are not scalar variables. A slice is referenced using the at sign (@) not the dollar sign ($). If you assign values to a slice, they must be assigned in list context. If
the list of scalars includes the range operator (..), each value of the range is given
its own cell in the new array:

```
@newArrayPiece = @array[4..7];
```

The list of scalars may include any of the array assignment examples. If a scalar
list includes an array or an array slice, each scalar of the array or array slice is
assigned to the new array, in list order. Any missing values are inserted into the
slice as null. If an array called digits was initialized like this:

```
@digits = (0..9);
```

and then a slice was assigned some new values like this:

```
@digits[4..7] = (14,17);
```

then the missing values required to fill the array slice are treated as null. The
@digits array now contains these values:

```
0,1,2,3,14,15,null,null,8,9
```

Hashes

A hash is really a hash table. A hash table uses an algorithm (a function) to determine the index of where to store or retrieve a data value. The idea is to produce a
unique index to identify the value's storage location in a potentially large but
sparsely populated array.

A brief analogy might help clarify how a hash works. If you are told to go get a
64-ounce box of BrandX laundry detergent with bleach, you might locate the data
storage place for BrandX like this:

1. Go to the grocery store.

2. Go to the non-food portion of the store.

3. Go to the cleaning supplies aisle.

4. Find the laundry detergent shelf.

5. Find the BrandX area.

6. Locate the 64-ounce box of BrandX with bleach.

A hash uses an algorithm, much like the way you located the BrandX detergent, to produce a key to where the data is stored. If you used a simple array to store the location of the laundry detergent, and the array was required to hold a place for every product sold in the modern world, that would require a very large array. Also, you would hardly ever access most of the items in the array. Furthermore, either you would need to know the exact array location of the 64-ounce BrandX with bleach or you would need to search the entire array. Keeping track of the exact location of the BrandX with bleach detergent in a giant array doesn't sound easy, and searching the entire array each time you need to find a new product isn't very efficient.

The Perl 5 hash is indexed by a key, which is treated as a string literal. You can also use variables as an index to a hash. Just like an array, a hash is a collection of scalar objects. Access to each scalar object uses scalar notation and curly braces ({ }). The curly braces surround the key, which identifies where the data is stored.

Hashes are initialized by a list of key/value pairs. A key must be associated with each value. You can use any scalar value as the value half of a key/value pair. The syntax looks like this:

```
$hash{$key} = literal;
```

For example, you might assign a key/value to a Spyder hash like this:

```
$Spyder{Price} = 25_689;
```

Perl 5 treats characters that are not surrounded by quotes, also called "bare words," as string literals if they are in list context. This makes initialization more convenient, because keys resolve to a string literal value. The initialization list is a comma-separated list of key/value pairs, like this:

```
%Spyder = (Price,26000,
           Engine,'2 Liter',
           Color,Red,
           Transmission,Manual,
           Brakes,'Anti-Lock',
           DriverAirBag,Yes,
           Turbo,Yes,
           Horsepower,210);
```

Perl 5 uses the right arrow (=>) as an alias for the comma. As an alternative, your hash key/value pairs can be written as on lines 16 through 26 of Listing 3.1:

```
%Spyder = (Price =>26000,
           Engine =>'2 Liter',
           Color =>Red,
           Transmission =>Manual,
           Brakes =>'Anti-Lock',
           DriverAirBag =>Yes,
           Turbo =>Yes,
           Horsepower =>210,
           Name =>"Spyder GS-T",
           img =>'spyder.jpg',
           Model =>Mitsubishi);
```

Notice that a space character in the key is acceptable because the key is specified using quotes.

To retrieve the data just do the reverse:

```
lvalue = $hash{$key};
```

For example, you might retrieve the cost of an item in the Spyder hash like this:

```
$itemCost = $Spyder{Price};
```

To retrieve more than one item from the hash, use one of Perl 5's built-in functions: keys, values, or each. Note that the keys and values returned by these functions are not in the same order that you stored them into the hash (because the hash does not store items sequentially).

The keys function, which returns an array containing the keys in a specified hash, can be used like this:

```
@keyList = keys %hash;
```

If you wanted to list all of the items in your carLot hash, you could do something like this:

```
foreach $car(keys %carLot){print "$car"}
```

The values function returns a list of all of the values in a hash. Here is an example of using the values function:

```
foreach $price(values %carPrice){
       $totalCarLotValue +=$price;
    }
```

The each function retrieves key/value pairs. Each new call to the each function retrieves the next key/value pair. When the entire hash has been read, each returns null. If you wanted to print your car inventory with its cost, you could write something like this:

```
while (($carName, $price)=each % carPrice){
        $totalCarLotValue +=$price;
         print "$carName\tt $price\h";
    }
```

References

New in the Perl 5 release, references extend the Perl language, allowing programmers to create complex data types by simulating multi-dimensional arrays.

A *reference* is actually just a scalar variable with a special type of data stored in it. If you are coming to Perl 5 from a language like C or C++, you are familiar with the term *pointer*. A pointer is a variable that contains the address of another variable. In C/C++, you must declare a variable as a pointer type. In Perl 5, a pointer—or *reference* in Perl 5 lingo—is a scalar variable that has been assigned the address of another variable or function.

NOTE   Perl 5 does not contain an aggregate data type, like a C/C++ structure or union.

You can have references to variables (scalar, array, and hash), functions, and even other references. Any reference can be stored into a scalar variable. Perl uses the \ reference assignment operator. For example, \$car is interpreted as a reference to the $car variable. Table 3.4 illustrates the syntax for saving the address of each data type and a few special cases.

TABLE 3.4: Perl 5 Reference Assignments

Data Type	Operator	Example
Scalar	\$var	$car = \$Porsche;
Array	\@array	$allStores[$number] = \@storeInventory;
Hash	\%hash	$storeType = \%stores;
File handle	*FILEHANDLE	$inputReference = *STDIN;

Continued on next page

TABLE 3.4 CONTINUED: Perl 5 Reference Assignments

Data Type	Operator	Example
Constant	\literal	$pi = \3.414;
Subroutine	\&subRoutine	$callBack = \&numericSort;
Symbolic	\$variableName	$var ="var2"; $var2Ref = \$var;

If you store the address of an array into an array, you simulate a two-dimensional array. In Table 3.4, the array example stores the address of an array into another array, creating at least a two-dimensional array.

Listing 3.2 demonstrates a basic use for references: storing the contents of multiple arrays into a single array, or in effect, creating a multi-dimensional array.

Listing 3.2:   References to Simulate Multi-Dimensional Arrays

```
1.   $totalStores = 3;
2.   $store = "StoreX";
3.
4.   for ($num = 1; $num <= $totalStores; $num++){
5.      open (STOREINV, "$store${num}.txt");
6.      my @store = <STOREINV>;
7.      $allStores[$num] = \@store;
8.   }
9.
10.  for ($x=1; $x<= $totalStores; $x++){
11.     $invRef = $allStores[$x];
12.     for ($i=0; $i <= $#$invRef; $i++){
13.        print "$$invRef[$i] ";
14.     }
15.     print"\n";
16.  }
```

A reference stores the address of a variable, not the contents. Each time through the loop, the my keyword creates a new array @store. Even though the arrays have the same name, they each get a new address. That new array address is saved on line 7 at the end of the first for loop.

That address is later retrieved on line 11 of Listing 3.2. If the my keyword was not used on line 6, each new inventory read into the @store array would be stored into the same array. Then when you retrieved the array address on line 11, each retrieval would be the same array address and would contain only the last values that were stored into the array.

To dereference (access) the address of a variable, you use the dollar sign ($), like this:

```
$ten=10;
$variableRef=\$ten;
print $$variable;
```

The $$variableRef syntax works by first finding the address of the item associated with $variableRef. That item is the variable "ten", which is the address of the numeric literal 10. The $$variableRef is first interpreted to the variable $ten. If you substitute ten for the first $variableRef, you get $ten. Then $ten references the literal 10.

Here is an example that applies the concepts of array references to the @MitsubishiModels array in Listing 3.1:

```
@MitsubishiModels = ("3000 GT", Diamante, Eclipse, Spyder, Galant);
$MitsubishiRef = \@MitsubishiModels;
print "@$ MitsubishiRef";
```

References work with hashes, too. Treat the reference variable as a regular variable that contains the address of a hash. A hash is always referred to using the percent sign (%), which leads to this syntax:

```
%farmAnimals=(cow => 3.123,
              sheep => 985,
              chickens => 45);
$farmAnimalsReference = \%farmAnimals;
while (($animal, $number) = each %$farmAnimalsRef){
      print "$animal, $number\n";
}
```

In short, you treat the reference variable just like any other scalar variable and then add the normal syntax for the variable type you are referencing. Table 3.5 shows the Perl 5 dereferencing operators.

TABLE 3.5: Perl 5 Dereferencing Operators

Type	Operator	Example
Scalar	$$reference	$ref = $name; print "$$ref";
Array	@$reference	$arrayRef = \@array; print "@$arrayRef";
Array scalar	$$reference[index]	$ref = \@digits; $nine = $$ref[9];
Array index	$#$reference	$ref = \@digits; $lastIndex = $#$ref;
Hash	%$reference	$ref = %inventory; ($item, $cost) = each %$ref;
Hash scalar	$$reference	$ref = %inventory; $itemCost = $$ref{'BrandX 16oz'};

The right arrow (->), which is left associative, is an alternative dereferencing operator. The right arrow syntax ($hash->{}) and the multiple dollar sign syntax ($$hash{}) are demonstrated in Listing 3.3.

Listing 3.3:   Hash Reference Dereferencing

```
1.   sub printDetailedMatch (\@){
2.       #This subroutine receives a reference to an array of hashes.
3.       my ($inventory) = @_;
4.       #The array reference is dereferenced into an array.
5.       my @carInventory = @$inventory;
6.       #If we are testing, set the HTTP headers to null and open the
7.       # debug file for output.
8.       # Otherwise. we print the valid http headers before we start
9.       # returning the matches.
10.      open (DEBUGFILE, ">carMatch.html") if $DEBUG;
11.      $originalOut = select (DEBUGFILE) if $DEBUG;
12.      $HTTPheader = ($DEBUG)? "" : q|Content-Type: text/html
13.
14.  |;
15.
16.          print<<"EOF";
17.  $HTTPheader
18.  <HTML><head>
19.  <Title>Matching Inventory</Title>
20.  </HEAD>
```

```
21. <body bgcolor="#FFFFFF" link="#0000FF" vlink="#660099">
22. EOF
23.    #Each hash reference from the array is retrieved by the
24.    #foreach statement. This print statement uses double quotes
25.    #after the heredoc operator for variable interpolation.
26.    #The hash reference $carData is retrieved and dereferenced
27.    #throughout the HTML output. Both right arrow notation
28.    #and $$ dereference notation are demonstrated
29.    foreach $carData (@carInventory){
30.
31.        print<<"EOF";
32. <center>
33. <h1>$carData->{Model} $carData->{Name} </h1>
34. </center>
35.
36. <table border="0" cellpadding="0" cellspacing="0" width="100%">
37.
38. <td width="40"> </td>
39. <td valign="top" width="100%">
40. <h2 align="center"><font size="6" face="Arial">
    $carData{Name}</font></h2>
41. <div align="center"><center>
42. <table border="0"
43. cellpadding="5" width="95%">
44. <tr>
45. <td valign="top" width="50%"><font size="2" face="Arial">
                                                 <br><br>
46. <B>Make: </B>$carData->{Name}
47. <BR>
48. <B>Model: </B>$carData->{Model}
49. <BR>
50. <B>Engine: </B>$carData->{Engine}
51. <BR>
52. <B>Turbo: </B>$carData->{Turbo}
53. <BR>
54. <B>Horsepower: </B>$carData->{Horsepower}
55. <BR>
56. </table>
57. </font></td><td align="center" valign="top" width="50%">
58. <img src="$$carData{img}" align="top" border="0"
                          alt="$$carData{Name}"></A>
59. </table>
```

```
60. </body>
61. </html>
62. EOF
63.       close(DEBUGFILE) if $DEBUG;
64.       #Return the original selected output file handle
65.       select($originalOut) if $DEBUG;
66.    }
67. }
68.
```

Control Structures

Perl 5's branch-on-condition statements are the if family (if else, if elsif, and if elsif else), while, until, for, and foreach. The if statements allow your code to follow alternate paths based on the result of a conditional expression (true or false). The while, until, for, and foreach loops allow you to repeat an operation multiple times.

Each type of branching statement follows the same basic syntax:

```
keyword (conditional expression){
    block of statements
}
```

> **NOTE** Perl 5 also contains the straight branching statements that take you to a specified location: next, last, redo, and goto.

The if Family

The if family of branching statements is made up of the if, if else, if elsif, and if elsif else statements. These statements are constructed of the keyword and the conditional expression, followed by a block of statements. The syntax of the if statements is:

```
if (conditional expression){
        block of statements
}
```

```
elsif (conditional expression) {
   block of statements
}
else {
   block of statements
}
```

The else and elsif statements are optional. The if statement may stand alone.

There may be only one else statement associated with an if statement, and the else statement may not stand alone. The else statement has no conditional expression associated with it. The else statement block of statements executes only if all previous conditional expressions of the if and elsif statements (if present) are false.

There may be zero, one, or many elsif statements associated with an if statement, and the elsif statement may not stand alone. Because the conditional expressions are evaluated in sequential order, multiple conditional expressions may be true, but only the block of statements associated with the first conditional expression that evaluated as true executes.

The conditional expression is surrounded by parentheses and may be a single variable or a complex conditional expression. A *conditional expression* is a value that can be either true or false. The true or false value is usually the result of a compare operation, but the expression can be any operation.

If the conditional expression is true, the branch statement takes the true path, executing the true block of statements. When the conditional expression is false, the branch statement takes the false path, executing the false block of statements. The conditional expression is required for the if and elsif statement.

The block of statements that follows the if, elsif, and else statement must be surrounded by opening and closing curly braces ({ }). The block of statements is required, but it may be zero (empty), one, or many Perl 5 statements.

Lines 38 through 53 of Listing 3.1 demonstrate the use of the if else statement to choose a car make:

```
38.      if ($searchCritera{carMakes} eq "Any") {
39.
40.         #The $make variable defined by foreach loop is NOT
41.         #visible outside the foreach loop (lexical to loop).
42.         foreach $make (@carMakes){
43.            #Each time processMake runs returns array of hashes.
```

```
44.            #push statement puts that array on global match array.
45.            push @matches, processMake($make, $searchCriteria
                              {maxSearches});
46.        }
47.    }
48.    else {
49.        #In this case. we are only searching one car make, so we
50.        #will get back one array of hashes.
51.        $matches[0] = processMake($searchCriteria{carMakes},
                              $searchCriteria{maxSearches});
52.    }#end else
53. }#end while
```

The SWITCH Construct

Many languages have a statement that started out as a computed goto and was renamed into something that sounds more civilized, like case or switch. Perl 5 doesn't have any of these constructs. I missed the switch statement, so I developed a reasonable Perl 5 simulation.

This simulation, which I call the SWITCH construct, is made up of labels, the last statement, and if statements, like this:

```
SWITCH:
{
if (conditional expression-1) {
   block of statements
   last SWITCH;
}#end

if (conditional expression-2) {
   block of statements
   last SWITCH;
}#end

if (conditional expression-n) {
   block of statements
   last SWITCH;
}#end

DEFAULT:
{
```

```
        block of statements
        last SWITCH;
    }
}#end SWITCH block
```

The SWITCH construct begins with a label. A Perl 5 label follows the same naming rules as a variable name but ends with a colon (:) instead of beginning with a special character. By convention, Perl 5 labels are uppercase letters, but this is not required. The label may be referred to by commands like next, last, and redo but has no other impact on your code.

To create a block of statements associated with the label, follow the label with an opening curly brace ({). When you have completed your label's block of statements, close with a closing curly brace (}).

The last statement exits the block of statements associated with the accompanying label. If a label is not part of the last statement, the last statement exits the current enclosing loop's block of statements.

The SWITCH construct includes a block of statements labeled DEFAULT. The label and enclosing curly braces are only for readability. If all previous conditional expressions evaluate to false, the DEFAULT block of statements will execute before exiting the SWITCH construct.

Lines 59 through 82 of Listing 3.1 demonstrate a SWITCH construct:

```
SWITCH:{
    #Switch statement calls correct inventory subroutine
    #for each car make. Each subroutine returns array of
    #hashes for processing at the end of the SWITCH block.
    if ($searchCriteria{carMakes} eq "Mitsubishi") {
        (@inventory) = getMitsubishiInventory();
        last SWITCH;
    }
    if ($searchCriteria{carMakes} eq "Geo") {
        (@inventory) = getGeoInventory();
         last SWITCH;
    }
    if ($searchCriteria{carMakes} eq "Chevrolet") {
        (@inventory) = getChevroletInventory();
        last SWITCH;
    }
     if ($searchCriteria{carMakes} eq "Ford") {
        (@inventory) = getFordInventory();
```

```
        last SWITCH;
    }
    DEFAULT: {
        printInputError($searchCriteria{carMakes});
    }
}#end SWITCH
```

The for Loop

The for loop is traditionally used for processing a block of statements a discrete number of times. An index variable is initialized, tested, and incremented inside the control statement's conditional expression. This syntax is supported in Perl 5:

```
for (initialization list;
     conditional expression;
     increment list){
   block of statements
}
```

where:

- The initialization list can be any statement, even an empty statement, but the trailing semicolon is required.

- The conditional expression may also be an empty statement, but again the trailing semicolon is required.

- The increment list may be any statement, even an empty statement. Unlike the initialization list and the conditional expression, the increment list is executed as the last statement of the for loop. This is the same action as occurs in the C language.

The initialization list traditionally assigns zero to the variable incremented in the increment list, because zero is the index of the first cell of an array. In Perl, because you can modify the first cell index value, you may want to set the initialization list, like this:

```
$index = $[;
```

The conditional expression when processing arrays traditionally compares the size of an array to the index value, like this:

```
$index < @array;
```

Recall that the array syntax, @array, used in scalar context returns the number of cells of the array. Because the initial index value ($[) can be modified, you might decide the last cell index special variable ($#arrayName) is a safer variable to test in the conditional expression.

In Listing 3.5, the first for loop never runs because the size of the array is less than the initial index of the array. The second loop works correctly because the comparison is against the last cell index instead of the array size.

Listing 3.5:   The Array Size Indicator

```
$[ = 1501;
#This loop doesn't run because @checksThisMonth returns
#the array size, which is less than 1501.
for ($checkNumber = $[;             #initialization list
    $checkNumber < @checksThisMonth; #conditional expression
    $checkNumber++){                 #increment list
  print "$checksThisMonth[$checkNumber]";
}
#This loop runs because $#checksThisMonth returns
#the last cell index.
for ($checkNumber = $[;
    $checkNumber <= $#checksThisMonth;
    $checkNumber++){
  print "$checksThisMonth[$checkNumber]";
}
```

Because each of the statements of the conditional expression of the for loop may be empty, the for loop is sometimes used to write infinite loops. The syntax makes it clear what you are doing, including that you meant for the loop to be an infinite loop. The syntax of an infinite for loop is:

```
for (;;){
    block of statements
}
```

The foreach Loop

The foreach loop is usually used to process arrays and hashes. The syntax of the foreach loop statement is:

```
foreach $listItem (list){
```

```
        block of statements
    }
```

NOTE   The **for** loop and the **foreach** loop are actually the same command. Whatever you can do with the **for** loop, you can also do with the **foreach** loop. Try substituting **for** and **foreach** in your code, and you will see that it has no effect. However, programmers tend to use the **for** loop to iterate a discrete number of times and the **foreach** loop to process arrays and hashes.

As with the other conditional branching statements, the block of statements may be empty but is required. The list may be only one element but is required. If the $listItem variable is not supplied, each element of list is loaded into the default special variable $_.

The array syntax of the **foreach** loop is:

```
foreach $item (@itemList){
    process $item;
}
```

The **foreach** loop steps through a list or array one element at a time. When the entire array has been processed, a null is returned as the next element in the list and the **foreach** loop exits its block of statements.

Because the **foreach** loop processes a list of items, it can be used to process an array, as in lines 42 through 46 of Listing 3.1:

```
foreach $make (@carMakes){
   #Each time processMake runs returns array of hashes.
   #push statement puts that array on global match array.
   push @matches, processMake($make, $searchCriteria {maxSearches});
}
```

The while and until Loops

The whi1e loop executes while its conditional expression is true. The unti1 loop executes while its conditional expression is false. In both cases, the loop test is performed before the loop is entered. The syntax of these loops is:

```
while/until (conditional expression) {
    block of statements
}
```

Lines 31 through 53 of Listing 3.1 show an example of a while loop:

```
while ($searchCriteria{numberOfSearches} > 0){
    #Create lexical variables. They will be initialized to null
    #each pass through the while loop.
    my ($searchResult, @matches);
    if($searchCriteria{maxSearches} > $MAXIMUMSEARCHSIZE){
        $searchCriteria{maxSearches} -= $MAXIMUMSEARCHSIZE;
    }
    if ($searchCritera{carMakes} eq "Any") {

        #The $make variable defined by foreach loop is NOT
        #visible outside the foreach loop (lexical to loop).
        foreach $make (@carMakes){
            #Each time processMake runs returns array of hashes.
            #push statement puts that array on global match array.
            push @matches, processMake($make, $searchCriteria
                                    {maxSearches});

        }
    }
    else {
        #In this case. we are only searching one car make, so we
        #will get back one array of hashes.
        $matches[0] = processMake($searchCriteria{carMakes},
                                $searchCriteria{maxSearches});

    }#end else
}#end while
```

What Next?

A jump-start chapter is just the essentials. In this jump-start chapter, you learned the essentials of the Perl 5 fundamentals: operators, variables, and branching statements. If that's all you need for now, feel free to skip to the next jump-start chapter (Chapter 10) and learn about input and output (I/O) handling. However, if you're ready for details and a lot more examples relating to any or all of the topics touched on in this chapter, you'll find them in the rest of the chapters in this part.

Chapter 4 is devoted to the myriad Perl 5 operators. It includes detailed discussions of Boolean operations, complete with truth tables to clarify Boolean conditions. It also provides information about binary, octal, and hexadecimal systems, which come into play when you work with the binary operators.

Chapter 5 covers the variable type that is the basis for all Perl 5 variables—scalars. It provides details about string data, including how the quote characters and operators work, as well as the effects of variable interpolation. It also discusses numeric data and presents some solutions for fixed-point calculations with Perl 5. Its final section explains scalar context versus list context, with an example to demonstrate the differences.

Chapter 6 is all about arrays and hashes. If you're not sure you understand how these data structures work, you'll find the analogies and examples in this chapter very helpful. You'll also learn about Perl 5's built-in functions for working with arrays: `push`, `pop`, `shift`, `unshift`, `splice`, `sort`, and `reverse`.

Chapter 7 deals with references. Even if you are an experienced Perl programmer, you may need more information about this new Perl 5 feature. References allow you to simulate multi-dimensional arrays, which are useful for solving complex problems with your programs. In that chapter, you'll learn how to create references and how dereferencing works.

Chapter 8 discusses the conditional branching statements in the `if` family, as well as the `switch` statement simulation outlined in that chapter. You'll learn the details of `if`, `if else`, and `if elsif else` constructions, as well as the difference between `elsif` and nested `if` statements.

Chapter 9 finishes up the part with a discussion of loops. You'll learn how letting the computer repeat operations for you is an efficient way to perform tests and process arrays. This chapter clarifies the difference between `while` and `until` loops and when you might prefer to use one over the other. It also provides details and examples of `for` and `foreach` loops, which are the most commonly used types of loops in Perl 5 programs.

Operators and Programming Fundamentals

- Numeric operators

- Boolean operators

- String operators

- Boolean combination operators

- Binary operators

- Operator precedence and associativity

There is a glue that holds all programming languages together. Glue is that stuff you stick between things to make something new or to bond one object to another. In any programming language, that glue is the *operators*. Operators work between the building blocks of a language.

If you are new to programming, you'll find the explanations of the various Perl 5 operators in this chapter enlightening. The operator fundamentals will help clear up some of the mysteries about the examples you've seen so far. If you are an experienced programmer but new to Perl 5, you will learn about the similarities and differences between Perl 5 operators and those in other languages, as well as how to use Perl 5's operators in context.

Because context is so important in Perl 5 programming, let's examine that concept before getting into the specifics of operators.

Perl 5 and Context

Perl 5 is very context-sensitive. In this way, it is unlike most programming languages. Operators and functions often return different results based on context. Context can be *numeric*, *string*, *list*, or *scalar*.

If you are new to programming, a context-sensitive language should seem natural. If you already program in another language, however, you may find the context-sensitive nature of Perl 5 a little disconcerting. A programmer is used to talking (working) with a computer that does exactly as it is instructed, interpreting each instruction literally (which may be why interpersonal training classes are a requirement in many large corporations). A novice programmer is still used to talking with humans.

In natural language conversations, the meaning of a single word can change with the context of the sentence, body language, or voice inflection. Perl is like a natural language. The action of an operation or function and the result of these operations are often based on the context of the Perl 5 statement. You'll learn about this context-sensitivity in relation to the operators in this chapter. In the next chapter, you'll learn about scalar and list context.

Numeric Operations

We'll begin our tour of Perl 5's operators with the numeric operators. Many of these operations will be familiar to you, but some of the programming concepts involved in using the operators may not be.

Basic Numeric Operations

Table 4.1 lists the basic numeric operators of Perl 5. These are the familiar math operations, which I'll demonstrate in a simple program.

TABLE 4.1: Basic Numeric Operators

Operator	Example	Description
+	`$a = 3 + 4;`	Add the expression on the left of the operator to the expression on the right of the operator.
–	`$a = 3–4;`	Subtract the expression on the right of the operator from the expression on the left of the operator.
*	`$a = 3 * 4;`	Multiply the expression on the left of the operator by the expression on the right of the operator.
/	`$a = 3 / 4;`	Divide the expression on the left of the operator by the expression on the right of the operator.
**	`$a = 2 ** 4;`	Raise the expression on the left of the operator to the power of the expression on the right of the operator.
%	`$a = 36 % 8;`	Modulo the expression on the left of the operator by the expression on the right of the operator.

I know you already understand how to add and subtract, so Listing 4.1 may seem too simple. However, the code does serve its purpose in showing you how the basic numeric operators work.

NOTE   All the listings in this book begin with the line `#! /usr/local/bin/perl`. This line is not required on a Windows computer, but it does no harm. However, the line is necessary for the programs to run on a Unix computer.

Listing 4.1:   **Basic Numeric Operations**

```
1. #! /usr/local/bin/perl
2. printHeader()();
3. $a = 4.2 + 3;
4. print "The result of 4.2 + 3 is $a \n";
5.
6. $a = 4.2 - 3;
7. print "The result of 4.2 - 3 is $a \n";
8.
9. $a = 4.2 * 3;
10. print "The result of 4.2 * 3 is $a \n";
11.
12. $a = 26 / 8;
13. print "The result of 26 / 8 is $a \n";
14. printHeader()();
15.
16. $a = 26 % 8;
17. print "The result of 26 % 8 is $a \n";
18. printHeader()();
19.
20. sub printHeader() {
21.    $header = ("=" x 80);
22.    print "$header\n\n";
23. }
```

The addition, subtraction, and multiplication lines (3, 6, and 9) of Listing 4.1 show a mixture of integer and real numbers. The result of each operation is saved in the correct numeric context, which is a real number. Line 12 illustrates integer operators returning a real number result. Figure 4.1 shows the output from Listing 4.1.

NOTE   Other languages allow the programmer to mix data types, but the variable where the result is eventually stored usually determines the final saved format. In other words, if your storage variable is an integer, the result is saved as an integer. As you will learn in Chapter 5, Perl 5 assigns the data type of the storage variable based on context. There are no facilities in Perl 5 to declare a storage variable as an integer, a string, or a floating point.

FIGURE 4.1:

Using basic numeric operators

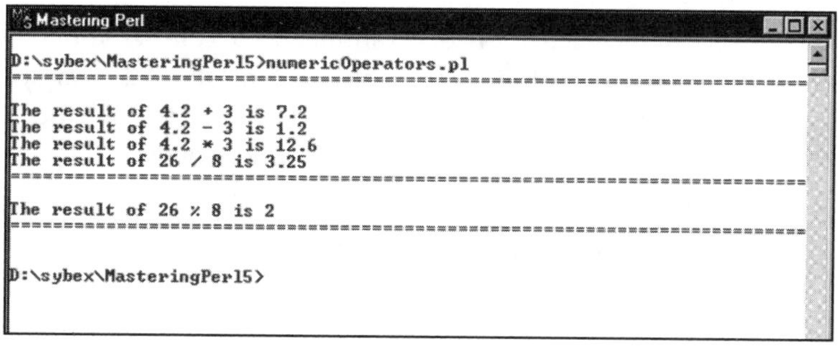

```
Mastering Perl                                              _ □ X

D:\sybex\MasteringPerl5>numericOperators.pl
==================================================================

The result of 4.2 + 3 is 7.2
The result of 4.2 - 3 is 1.2
The result of 4.2 * 3 is 12.6
The result of 26 / 8 is 3.25
==================================================================

The result of 26 % 8 is 2
==================================================================


D:\sybex\MasteringPerl5>
```

The Assignment Operator

The glue that holds together the Perl 5 statements on lines 3, 6, 9, 12, and 16 of Listing 4.1 is the assignment operator, which is an equal sign (=). For example, line 3 reads:

```
$a = 4.2 + 3;
```

The assignment operator takes the result of the expression (4.2 + 3) and stores it into the lvalue ($a). The syntax of the simple assignment statement is *lvalue = expression*. This means that the variable on the left side of the assignment operator (*lvalue*) equals the value on the right side of the assignment operator (*expression*), which is much more readable like this:

```
$variableName = "White Shirt";
$variableName = 22.87;
```

Only an lvalue is valid on the left side of an assignment operator. As you learned in Chapter 1, the term *lvalue* can be easily translated to left-hand value. It usually refers to the variable on the left side of some type of assignment operator. An lvalue always refers to some type of modifiable variable.

The assignment statements of Listing 4.1 should look familiar to you, except that you're probably used to seeing addition and multiplication like this: 8 + 4 = 12. But after you've worked with Perl 5 for a while, you will get used to seeing $x = 8 + 12. Compound assignment statements, which are explained in the next section, look just a bit stranger than the simple assignment statements.

Compound Assignment Operators

As a convenience to the programmer, Perl 5 allows you to use several compound assignment operators, which are listed in Table 4.2. Compound assignment statements are a kind of shorthand for expressions that perform an operation using the lvalue on the left side of the assignment operator. The syntax of this operation is quick and straightforward, like this:

```
$variableName operator = expression
```

TABLE 4.2: Compound Assignment Operators

Operator	Example	Meaning
+=	$a += 3;	Add the expression on the left of the operator to the expression on the right of the operator.
-=	$a -= 3;	Subtract the expression on the right of the operator from the expression on the left of the operator.
*=	$a *= 3;	Multiply the expression on the left of the operator by the expression on the right of the operator.
/=	$a /= 3;	Divide the expression on the left of the operator by the expression on the right of the operator.
**=	$a **= 3;	Raise the expression on the left of the operator to the power of the expression on the right of the operator.
%=	$a %= 3;	Modulo the expression on the left of the operator by the expression on the right of the operator.
.=	$a .= "String Value";	Append the expression on the right of the operator to the expression on the left of the operator.
x=	$a x= 3;	Multiply (replicate) the expression (string) on the left of the operator by the expression (numeric) on the right of the operator.
&=	$a &= 3;	Binary AND the expression on the left of the operator with the expression on the right of the operator.
|=	$a |= 3;	Binary OR the expression on the left of the operator with the expression on the left of the operator.
^=	$a ^= 3;	Exclusive OR the expression on the left of the operator with the expression on the right of the operator.

Continued on next page

TABLE 4.2 CONTINUED: Compound Assignment Operators

Operator	Example	Meaning
<<=	$a <<= 3;	Left shift the expression on the left of the operator by the expression on the right of the operator.
>>=	$a >>= 3;	Right shift the expression on the left of the operator by the expression on the right of the operator.
&&=	$a &&= 1;	Logical AND the expression on the right of the operator with the expression on the left of the operator.
||=	$a ||= 0;	Logical OR the expression on the left of the operator with the expression on the right of the operator.

For example, here's a simple assignment statement:

```
$totalDue = $totalDue + 10;
```

Rather than writing the assignment as shown above, you could use the following compound addition operator:

```
$totalDue += 10;
```

In both versions, the value of $totalDue is determined by your computer before the assignment is made. That value is added to the 10. The result is then stored in the lvalue $totalDue.

As you can see in Table 4.2, Perl 5 allows all operators to become compound assignment operators. Listing 4.2 shows the use of compound assignment operators for some of the basic numeric operations discussed in the previous section, and Figure 4.2 shows the output. The other operations will be explained in the following sections.

TIP

Perl 5 allowing all operators to become compound assignment operators is an example of how Perl follows the all, one, or none rule, also referred to as the 0, 1, or infinity rule. This means that a rule should be true for every case, for only one case, or for zero cases. You can use this concept to figure out how you can accomplish a task using Perl 5 syntax. The more you program, the more you'll learn to appreciate the fact that Perl 5 follows the all, one, or none rule whenever reasonably possible.

Listing 4.2:   **Basic Math Compound Assignment Statements**

```perl
1. #! /usr/local/bin/perl
2. printHeader()();
3. $a = 5;
4. print "\$a equals $a before the operation.\n ";
5. $a += 4.2;
6. print "The result of \$a += 4.2 is $a \n";
7.
8. print "\$a equals $a before the operation.\n ";
9. $a -= 4.2;
10. print "The result of \$a -= 4.2 is $a \n";
11.
12. print "\$a equals $a before the operation.\n ";
13. $a *= 4.2;
14. print "The result of \$a *= 4.2  is $a \n";
15.
16. print "\$a equals $a before the operation.\n ";
17. $a /= 6;
18. print "The result of \$a /= 6 is $a \n";
19. printHeader()();
20.
21. print "\$a equals $a before the operation.\n ";
22. $a %= 6;
23. print "The result of \$a %= 6 is $a \n";
24. printHeader()();
25.
26. sub printLine() { print "\n";}
27. sub print2Lines() { print "\n\n";}
28. sub printHeader() {
29.    $header = ("=" x 80);
30.    print "$header\n\n";
31. }
```

Each of the compound assignment statements has a corresponding simple assignment statement. For example, line 17 of Listing 4.2:

```perl
$a /= 6;
```

could be written as a simple assignment statement:

```perl
$a = $a / 6;
```

FIGURE 4.2:

Using compound math assignment statements

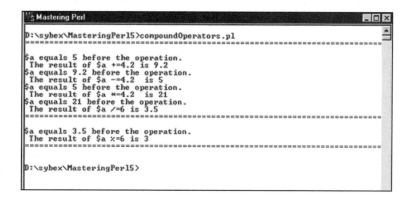

```
Mastering Perl                                              _ □ ×

D:\sybex\MasteringPerl5>compoundOperators.pl
=================================================================

$a equals 5 before the operation.
 The result of $a +=4.2 is 9.2
$a equals 9.2 before the operation.
 The result of $a -=4.2  is 5
$a equals 5 before the operation.
 The result of $a *=4.2  is 21
$a equals 21 before the operation.
 The result of $a /=6 is 3.5
=================================================================

$a equals 3.5 before the operation.
 The result of $a %=6 is 3
=================================================================

D:\sybex\MasteringPerl5>
```

NOTE   You'll see a lot of compound assignment statements in Perl 5 programs. Compound assignment operators are frequently used in a loop when you're adding several values together (loops are covered in Chapter 9).

Increment and Decrement Operators

The increment and decrement operators are unique to programming languages. They came to be because programmers, living up to their reputation as being lazy, prefer to type as little as possible. Instead of writing $a = $a + 1, it's easier to type $a++. The increment and decrement operators are shown in Table 4.3.

TABLE 4.3: Increment and Decrement Operators

Operator	Example	Description
++	$a++;	Increment the scalar variable by one.
–	–$a;	Decrement the scalar variable by one.

It makes a difference whether you put the decrement or increment operators on the left or right side of the variables on which they are operating. When placed on the left side of a variable, the increment or decrement operation is performed first, before any other operation. The increment and decrement operators have precedence over most other operators (the order of operator precedence is described later in this chapter). For example, the line:

```
$a = ++$b;
```

means increment the value of $b and then assign the result to $a.

When the increment or decrement operator is placed on the right side of a variable, the increment or decrement operation is performed after the assignment operation on the left side. For example, the line:

```
$a = $b++;
```

means assign the value of $b to $a and then increment the value of $b.

Listing 4.3 demonstrates the use of the increment and decrement operators, and Figure 4.3 shows its output.

Listing 4.3:   **Increment and Decrement Operations**

```
 1. #! /usr/local/bin/perl
 2. printHeader();
 3. $a=15;
 4. $b = ++$a -15;
 5. $c = $a++ - 15;
 6. print "The increment operation occurs first
           on the left side\n";
 7. print '$b = ++$a - 15 results in $b equal ';
 8. print "$b\n"
 9. print "The increment operation occurs after
           other operations when on the right side\n";
10. print '$c = $a- - 15 results in $c equal ';
11. print "$c\n"
12.
13.
14. sub printHeader() {
15.     $header = ("=" x 80) ;
16.     print "$header\n\n" ;
17. }
```

NOTE Figure 4.3, like most of the figures in this book, is the result of running the program in the listing from the command prompt on my Windows NT computer. The results are the same whether you run the listings on a Unix or Windows computer.

Boolean Operations

A Boolean value is something that is either true or false. Boolean operators are used in a conditional expression to choose the next statement a program should execute (conditional expressions are explained in Chapter 8). Perl uses the number one (1) to indicate true and null to indicate false. The Boolean operators are shown in Table 4.4.

NOTE The values true or false can be implemented in many ways in different programming languages. For example, the C programming language interprets a value of 0 as false and any other number as true. The term null when used by programmers means undefined or the empty string. (The literal meaning of the word null is nothing or having no value.)

FIGURE 4.3:

Using the increment and decrement operators

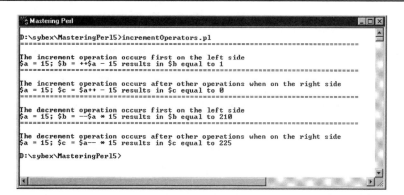

TABLE 4.4: Boolean Operators

Operator	Example	Description
==	$a == 4;	Equal to—if the expression on the left of the operator is numerically equal to the expression on the right of the operator, the result is 1; otherwise, the result is **null**.
!=	$a != 4;	Not equal to—if the expression on the left of the operator is numerically *not* equal to the expression on the right of the operator, the result is 1; otherwise, the result is **null**.
<	$a < 4;	Less than—if the expression on the left of the operator is numerically less than the expression on the right of the operator, the result is 1; otherwise, the result is **null**.
>	$a > 4 ;	Greater than—if the expression on the left of the operator is numerically greater than the expression on the right of the operator, the result is 1; otherwise, the result is **null**.
>=	$a >= 4;	Greater than or equal to—if the expression on the left of the operator is numerically greater than or equal to the expression on the right of the operator, the result is 1; otherwise, the result is **null**.
<=	$a <= 4 ;	Less than or equal to—if the expression on the left of the operator is numerically less than or equal to the expression on the right of the operator, the result is 1; otherwise, the result is **null**.
<=>	$a <=> 4 ;	Compare—if the expression on the left of the operator is numerically less than the expression on the right of the operator, the result is −1. If the expression on the left of the operator is numerically greater than the expression on the right of the operator, the result is 1. If the expression on the left of the operator is equal to the expression on the right of the operator, the result is 0.

Listing 4.4 shows the use of each Boolean operator, and Figure 4.4 shows the results.

Listing 4.4:   **Boolean Operators**

```
1. #! /usr/local/bin/perl
2. printHeader();
3.
```

```
 4. $booleanResult = (4 == 4);
 5. print '  4 == 4;    Results in ';
 6. print "booleanResult = $booleanResult\n";
 7.
 8. $booleanResult = (3 == 4);
 9. print '  3 == 4;    Results in ';
10. print "booleanResult = $booleanResult\n";
11. printHeader();
12.
13. $booleanResult = (4 != 4);
14. print '  4 != 4; Results in ';
15. print "booleanResult = $booleanResult\n";
16.
17. $booleanResult = (3 != 4);
18. print '  3 != 4; Results in ';
19. print "booleanResult = $booleanResult\n";
20. printHeader();
21.
22. $booleanResult = (4 < 4);
23. print '  4 < 4;       Results in ';
24. print "booleanResult = $booleanResult\n";
25.
26. $booleanResult = (3 < 4);
27. print '  3 < 4;       Results in ';
28. print "booleanResult = $booleanResult\n";
29.
30. $booleanResult = (5 < 4);
31. print '  5 < 4;       Results in ';
32. print "booleanResult = $booleanResult\n";
33. printHeader();
34.
35. $booleanResult = (5 > 4);
36. print '  5 > 4;       Results in ';
37. print "booleanResult = $booleanResult\n";
38.
39. $booleanResult = (3 > 4);
40. print '  3 > 4;       Results in ';
41. print "booleanResult = $booleanResult\n";
42.
43. $booleanResult = (4 > 4);
44. print '  4 > 4;       Results in ';
45. print "booleanResult = $booleanResult\n";
```

```perl
46. printHeader();
47.
48. $booleanResult = (4 >= 4);
49. print '  4 >= 4;      Results in ';
50. print "booleanResult = $booleanResult\n";
51.
52. $booleanResult = (3 >= 4);
53. print '  3 >= 4;      Results in ';
54. print "booleanResult = $booleanResult\n";
55.
56. $booleanResult = (5 >= 4);
57. print '  5 >= 4;      Results in ';
58. print "booleanResult = $booleanResult\n";
59. printHeader();
60.
61. $booleanResult = (4 <= 4);
62. print '  4 <= 4;      Results in ';
63. print "booleanResult = $booleanResult\n";
64.
65. $booleanResult = (5 <= 4);
66. print '  5 <= 4;      Results in ';
67. print "booleanResult = $booleanResult\n";
68.
69. $booleanResult = (3 <= 4);
70. print '  3 <= 4;      Results in ';
71. print "booleanResult = $booleanResult\n";
72. printHeader();
73.
74. $booleanResult = (4 <=> 4);
75. print '  4 <=> 4;      Results in ';
76. print "booleanResult = $booleanResult\n";
77.
78. $booleanResult = (3 <=> 4);
79. print '  3 <=> 4;      Results in ';
80. print "booleanResult = $booleanResult\n";
81.
82. $booleanResult = (5 <=> 4);
83. print '  5 <=> 4;      Results in ';
84. print "booleanResult = $booleanResult\n";
85. sub printLine { print "\n" ;}
86. sub print2Lines { print "\n\n" ;}
87. sub printHeader {
```

```
88.     $header = ( "=" x 80);
89.     print "$header\n\n";
90. }
```

Notice in Figure 4.4 that some results, such as that returned by line 8 (3 == 4), are shown as a blank. This means that the result is false, so a `null` is returned.

The compare operator <=> returns -1, 0, or 1 for less than, equal to, and greater than, respectively. The compare operators (`comp` and <=>) are used with Perl sorting routines, as explained in Chapter 15.

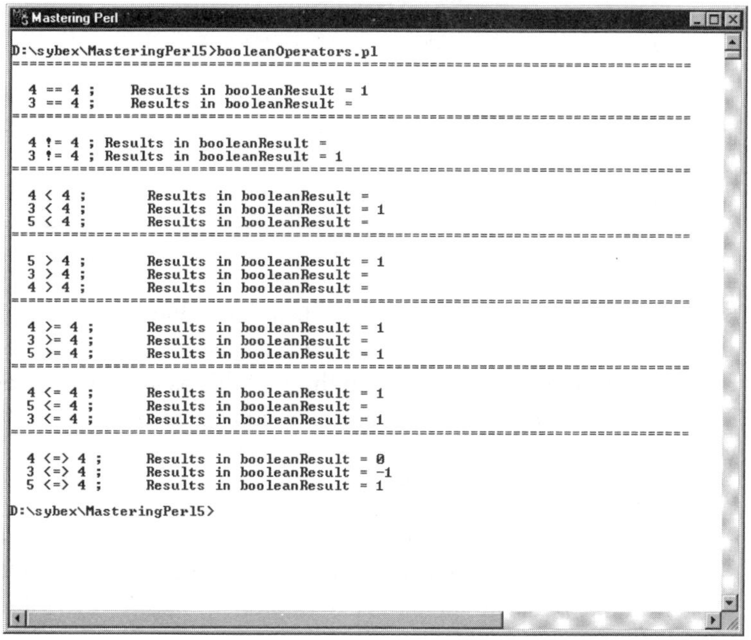

FIGURE 4.4:

Using Boolean operators

```
D:\sybex\MasteringPerl5>booleanOperators.pl
================================================================================
   4 == 4 ;      Results in booleanResult = 1
   3 == 4 ;      Results in booleanResult =
================================================================================
   4 != 4 ; Results in booleanResult =
   3 != 4 ; Results in booleanResult = 1
================================================================================
   4 < 4 ;       Results in booleanResult =
   3 < 4 ;       Results in booleanResult = 1
   5 < 4 ;       Results in booleanResult =
================================================================================
   5 > 4 ;       Results in booleanResult = 1
   3 > 4 ;       Results in booleanResult =
   4 > 4 ;       Results in booleanResult =
================================================================================
   4 >= 4 ;      Results in booleanResult = 1
   3 >= 4 ;      Results in booleanResult =
   5 >= 4 ;      Results in booleanResult = 1
================================================================================
   4 <= 4 ;      Results in booleanResult = 1
   5 <= 4 ;      Results in booleanResult =
   3 <= 4 ;      Results in booleanResult = 1
================================================================================
   4 <=> 4 ;     Results in booleanResult = 0
   3 <=> 4 ;     Results in booleanResult = -1
   5 <=> 4 ;     Results in booleanResult = 1

D:\sybex\MasteringPerl5>
```

String Operations

A *string* is a type of data that can be stored into a Perl 5 scalar variable. String data normally refers to single characters strung together to create words (you'll learn more details about character strings, as well as numeric data, in Chapter 5). Table 4.5 summarizes the Perl 5 string operators.

TABLE 4.5: String Operators

Operator	Means	Numeric Equivalent
.	Concatenate	+
x	Multiply (replicate)	*
eq	Equal to	=
ne	Not equal to	!=
lt	Less than	<
gt	Greater than	>
le	Less than or equal to	<=
cmp	Compare	<=>

The first two string operators listed in Table 4.5 add and multiply string values. The concatenation operator (.) works just like the math + operator—it adds two strings together. You can also think of this as a paste or append operation. The string on the right of the concatenation operator is pasted (or appended) to the end of the string on the left of the concatenation operator, creating a new string. The multiply operator (x) repeats the string the number of times specified.

The remaining operators of Table 4.5 are Boolean operators that compare strings or character data. The Boolean string operators work in the same way as the numeric Boolean operators (see Table 4.4). They return a 1 if true and null if false.

Listing 4.5 demonstrates the use of the string operators, and Figure 4.5 shows the output.

Listing 4.5: **String Operators**

```
1. #! /usr/local/bin/perl
2. printHeader();
3.
4. $booleanResult = ("The" eq "the");
5. print '"The" eq "the"; Results in ';
```

```
 6. print " booleanResult = $booleanResult\n";
 7. $booleanResult = ("the" eq "the") ;
 8. print '"the" eq "the"; Results in ';
 9. print " booleanResult = $booleanResult\n";
10. printHeader();
11.
12. $booleanResult = ("The" ne "the");
13. print '"The" ne "the"; Results in ';
14. print "booleanResult = $booleanResult\n";
15. $booleanResult = ("the" ne "the");
16. print '"the" ne "the"; Results in ';
17. print "booleanResult = $booleanResult\n";
18. printHeader();
19.
20. $booleanResult = ("a" lt "A");
21. print '"a" lt "A"; Results in ';
22. print "booleanResult = $booleanResult\n";
23. $booleanResult = ("A" lt "a");
24. print '"A" lt "a"; Results in ';
25. print "booleanResult = $booleanResult\n";
26. printHeader();
27.
28. $booleanResult = ("a" le "a");
29. print '"a" le "a"; Results in ';
30. print "booleanResult = $booleanResult\n";
31. $booleanResult = ("aa" le "a");
32. print '"aa" le "a"; Results in ';
33. print "booleanResult = $booleanResult\n";
34. printHeader();
35.
36. $booleanResult = ("a" gt "A");
37. print '"a" gt "A"; Results in ';
38. print "booleanResult = $booleanResult\n";
39. $booleanResult = ("a" gt "AA");
40. print '"a" gt "AA"; Results in ';
41. print "booleanResult = $booleanResult\n";
42. printHeader();
43.
44. $booleanResult = ("The" cmp "the");
45. print '"The" cmp "the" Results in ';
46. print "booleanResult = $booleanResult\n";
47. $booleanResult = ("the" cmp "The");
48. print '"the" cmp "The" Results in ';
```

```
49. print "booleanResult = $booleanResult\n";
50. $booleanResult = ("the" cmp "the");
51. print '"the" cmp "the" Results in ';
52. print "booleanResult = $booleanResult\n";
53.
54. printHeader();
55. $a = "The" x 3;
56. print '$a = "The" x 3 ;Results in ';
57. print "a = $a \n";
58.
59. printHeader();
60. $word1 = "The ";
61. $word2 = "beginning";
62. $a = $word1 . $word2;
63. print '$a = $word1 . $word2 ; Results in ';
64. print "a = $a \n";
65. printHeader();
66.
67. sub printLine() { print "\n" ;}
68. sub print2Lines() { print "\n\n" ;}
69. sub printHeader() {
70.    $header = ("=" x 80);
71.    print "$header\n\n";
72. }
```

Line 56 in Listing 4.5 shows the result of multiplying a word or string in Perl 5. The string is repeated as many times as it is multiplied. Skip down in Listing 4.5 to the `printHeader` subroutine between lines 69 and 73. Line 72 is an excellent example of a practical use for the string multiplier; it creates the line of dashes you see in the figures in this chapter.

Line 62 in Listing 4.5 shows the use of the dot (.) operator. Two different strings are stored into two different variables (in lines 60 and 61), and then they are added together (in line 62) to get a new variable that contains both strings in one scalar variable (scalar variables are discussed in Chapter 5).

String Comparisons

You must always remember to use string operators when you want to make a string comparison. Because Perl 5 is a context-sensitive language, if you use numeric operators when you need string operators, you are likely to get rather strange results. As an exercise, try replacing the string operators of Listing 4.5 with numeric operators. I think you will find the results worth your time.

Looking at Figure 4.5, you might be puzzled by what you see. Just what the heck makes "A" less than "a"? And why is "AA" still less than "a"? The answers lie in the ASCII table, as explained in the next section.

FIGURE 4.5:

Using string operators

```
Mastering Perl                                                    _ □ ✕
D:\sybex\MasteringPerl5>stringOperators.pl
=========================================================================
"The" eq "the"; Results in  booleanResult =
"the" eq "the"; Results in  booleanResult = 1
=========================================================================
"The" ne "the"; Results in booleanResult = 1
"the" ne "the"; Results in booleanResult =
=========================================================================
"a" lt "A"; Results in booleanResult =
"A" lt "a"; Results in booleanResult = 1
=========================================================================
"a" le "a"; Results in booleanResult = 1
"aa" le "a"; Results in booleanResult =
=========================================================================
"a" gt "A"; Results in booleanResult = 1
"a" gt "AA"; Results in booleanResult = 1
=========================================================================
"The" cmp "the" Results in booleanResult = -1
"the" cmp "The" Results in booleanResult = 1
"the" cmp "the" Results in booleanResult = 0
=========================================================================
$a = "The" x 3 ;Results in a = TheTheThe
=========================================================================
$a = $word1 . $word2 ; Results in a = The beginning
=========================================================================

D:\sybex\MasteringPerl5>
```

ASCII Characters

As far as your computer is concerned, when it's figuring out whether "A" is less than "a", it's comparing the number 65 against the number 97. Since we all know that 65 is less than 97, it's clear that "A" is less than "a".

Did I lose anybody there? The first time my professors went on about this, I was lost. How the heck was I supposed to understand that the computer thinks *A* is the number 65 and *a* is the number 97? They look like letters to me!

The truth is that your computer can't read. It only understands numbers, so everything you type into your computer must be converted into a number. As far as your computer is concerned, everything you see on your screen is just another number. Makes you feel just a little superior to that hunk of electronics, doesn't it? Well you are. Without people like you, that hunk of metal couldn't do a thing.

Since your computer understands only numbers, there must be some type of conversion of all the letters and symbols you can understand to the numbers your computer understands. The conversion system your computer understands is called the American Standard for Information Interchange, or ASCII (pronounced "Ask'ee") for short.

Table 4.6 shows the ASCII conversion codes for the letters in the alphabet. As you can see, "A", which converts to 65, is really less then "a", which converts to 97.

TABLE 4.6: ASCII Chart for Letters

Decimal	Octal	Hex	Character
065	101	041	A
066	102	042	B
067	103	043	C
068	104	044	D
069	105	045	E
070	106	046	F
071	107	047	G
072	110	048	H
073	111	049	I
074	112	04A	J
075	113	04B	K
076	114	04C	L

Continued on next page

TABLE 4.6 CONTINUED: ASCII Chart for Letters

Decimal	Octal	Hex	Character
077	115	04D	M
078	116	04E	N
079	117	04F	O
080	120	050	P
081	121	051	Q
082	122	052	R
083	123	053	S
084	124	054	T
085	125	055	U
086	126	056	V
087	127	057	W
088	130	058	X
089	131	059	Y
090	132	05A	Z
097	141	061	a
098	142	062	b
099	143	063	c
100	144	064	d
101	145	065	e
102	146	066	f
103	147	067	g
104	150	068	h
105	151	069	i
106	152	06A	j

Continued on next page

TABLE 4.6 CONTINUED: ASCII Chart for Letters

Decimal	Octal	Hex	Character
107	153	06B	k
108	154	06C	l
109	155	06D	m
110	156	06E	n
111	157	06F	o
112	160	070	p
113	161	071	q
114	162	072	r
115	163	073	s
116	164	074	t
117	165	075	u
118	166	076	v
119	167	077	w
120	170	078	x
121	171	179	y
122	172	07A	z

Now for the answer to why "AA" is still less than "a". It seems to me that 6565 is a lot more than 97. It's not, and of course, your computer has a completely logical explanation.

Your computer (actually, the Perl 5 interpreter) knows it is dealing with characters and not numbers, so it doesn't try to create one large character out of the two *A* characters when it makes a comparison. It methodically checks one character at a time to see if it is less than the matching character on the other side of the less-than operator. So when it checks if ("AA" < "a"), it first checks to see if the first "A" is less than "a". It decides the answer is yes, and then it doesn't do any further processing. In other words, your computer compares just the first character of each string, A and a, to determine the answer. The second A of the "AA" string is never used in the operation.

Boolean Combination Operations

In the previous sections, you learned that when you use the Boolean operators for comparing numbers and characters, your computer compares only one character at a time. Let me clarify one point. Your computer may be doing the actual work, but it is following the instructions of the Perl 5 interpreter, which is following the instructions of your code. In other words, the way that your computer compares strings, characters, and numbers depends on the computer language being used and the code you write in that language.

All of the tests you have seen in this chapter have been simple comparisons. You can make more complex comparisons by using the Boolean combination operators, which are listed in Table 4.7.

TABLE 4.7: Boolean Combination Operators

Operator	Means
&&	Logical AND
||	Logical OR
!	Logical NOT

The operators listed in Table 4.7 combine conditional expressions together to create a complex conditional expression. Here are some examples of conditional expressions combined by these operators (remember, you'll get a more in-depth study of conditional expressions in Chapter 8).

The fishing enthusiast's Boolean combination (if today is Saturday or the weather is sunny, let's go fishing):

```
If (today eq Saturday) || (The weather eq sunny)
Go fishing
```

The occasional fisherman's version (if today is Saturday and the weather is sunny, let's go fishing):

```
If (today eq Saturday) && (The weather eq sunny)
Go fishing
```

The workaholic's version (if it's not Saturday or the weather is not sunny, let's go to work):

```
If ! ((today eq Saturday) && (The weather eq sunny))
Go to work
```

NOTE   The parentheses are not required in the first two expressions, but parentheses usually make complex logical expressions easier to understand. Because the NOT operator (!) applies to the entire conditional expression, the parentheses are required for the workaholic's complex conditional expression. You'll learn more about parentheses and precedence later in this chapter.

The Logical AND Operator

As with the comparison of strings, Perl 5 uses a "short-circuit" logical evaluation to determine when to return an answer. The logical AND operator (&&) works like this: Evaluating from left to right (unless parentheses order overrides left-to-right evaluation), the first condition to return a false answer stops any further conditional expressions, and the operation returns a false result. This means that *all* the conditions must be true for the logical AND operator to return a true result. A truth table can help make this clearer.

A *truth table* is a table that lists all of the possible conditions for a particular conditional expression. The two conditions of the previous example are:

1. today eq Saturday
2. The weather eq sunny

The workaholic's truth table with these two conditions is shown in Table 4.8.

TABLE 4.8: A Two-Condition AND Truth Table

Today eq Saturday (A)	Weather eq Sunny (B)	A && B
False	False	False

Continued on next page

TABLE 4.8 CONTINUED: A Two-Condition AND Truth Table

Today eq Saturday (A)	Weather eq Sunny (B)	A && B
False	True	False
True	False	False
True	True	True

Looking at the third column in Table 4.8, you can see that the workaholic only goes fishing when both conditions are true. Now suppose that we add a third condition:

```
The boss must be out of town
```

This three-condition truth table is shown in Table 4.9.

TABLE 4.9: A Three-Condition AND Truth Table

Today eq Saturday (A)	Weather eq Sunny (B)	Boss out of Town (C)	A && B && C
False	False	False	False
False	False	True	False
False	True	False	False
False	True	True	False
True	False	False	False
True	False	True	False
True	True	False	False
True	True	True	True

As you can see from Table 4.9, the logical AND operator returns a true answer only when all conditions are true. Since Perl 5 knows this, it stops evaluating any logical AND expression as soon as it finds the first false condition.

The Logical OR Operator

The logical OR operator (| |) works exactly the opposite of the AND operator. Perl 5 tells your computer to stop evaluating the complex conditional expression as soon as it finds the first true condition. Table 4.10 shows an example of a truth table with the same three conditions as Table 4.9, but with the OR operator replacing the AND operator.

TABLE 4.10: A Three-Condition OR Truth Table

Today eq Saturday (A)	Weather eq Sunny (B)	Boss out of Town (C)	A && B && C
False	False	False	False
False	False	True	True
False	True	False	True
False	True	True	True
True	False	False	True
True	False	True	True
True	True	False	True
True	True	True	True

Just as with the logical AND operator, Perl 5 knows it needs only one true answer to determine the result of any complex OR operation. The first true condition means that the entire complex conditional expression is true. The logical OR operator returns a false answer only if all of the conditions of the expression are false.

The Logical NOT Operator

The NOT operator (!) negates the result of the logical OR and AND operators. If the result of the conditional expression was true and the NOT operator is applied, the result becomes false. Let's revisit the workaholic's Boolean combination, which looks very similar to the occasional fisherman's conditional expression:

```
If ! ((today eq Saturday) && (The weather eq sunny))
```

The truth table for this conditional expression is shown in Table 4.11. Notice that the last column of Tables 4.11 is the inverse of Table 4.8.

TABLE 4.11: A Two-Condition NOT Truth Table

Today eq Saturday (A)	Weather eq Sunny (B)	A && B	! (A && B)
False	False	False	True
False	True	False	True
True	False	False	True
True	True	True	False

If you study Boolean logic (which we are not going to do any more of here), you'll learn about DeMorgan's Law. DeMorgan's Law allows you to apply the mathematical associative theorem to Boolean expressions. This means that:

!(A||B) becomes !A && !B

!(A&&B) becomes !A || !B

!(!A || !B) becomes A && B

!(!A && !B) becomes A || B

The practical application of this theory is that you can determine the real meaning of complex expressions like this:

```
If ! ((today eq Saturday) && (The weather eq sunny))
Go to work
```

which translates into the following expression:

```
If (today ne Saturday) || (weather ne Sunny)
Go to work
```

The result, as you can see in Table 4.11, is that the workaholic goes to work unless it is both sunny and Saturday.

Binary Operations

As you've learned in this chapter, a Boolean value returned from a conditional expression, like if ($a == $b), means true or false. True or false are opposites, just like on and off. *Binary* operations involve ones and zeros, or Boolean true or false conditions.

Before going into the subject of binary operators, you need some understanding of the binary number system and all those ones and zeros. Each binary digit represents a bit in computer memory (you'll learn more about bits in the following sections). If you ever find yourself creating or working with code that operates at the bit level, you must have a rudimentary understanding of binary numbers.

> **NOTE**   Since manipulating bits isn't one of the main jobs of most programmers, I'm providing only an introduction to binary numbers and binary operators, which is all that most Perl programmers really need. Just be aware that there are many more details about this topic.

Another point you should note before you read about binary numbers is that you can represent octal numbers (base 8), decimal numbers (base 10), and hexadecimal (usually referred to as *hex*) numbers (base 16) in Perl 5, but there is no representation for binary numbers (base 2). This means that whenever you use the binary operators, you will need to make a mental conversion from one number system to the binary number system to determine what the result should be. I recommend using hex numbers for binary operations whenever possible. Hex numbers also are covered in this section.

Binary Numbers

Earlier, you learned that your computer only understands numbers. Well, the truth is that your computer is so simple it actually only understands the numbers 1 and 0. Everything your computer does is some combination of the Boolean 1 and 0, which make up the entire number set for the binary number system. Just as your computer changes letters and symbols to numbers, it also changes all numbers to the binary 1 or 0.

You've already learned that your computer translates letters into numbers. Your computer also translates numbers into numbers. The decimal numbers 0 through 9 are translated into the binary numbers 0 and 1. Obviously, there are more decimal numbers than there are binary numbers. Okay, I can hear you snorting and making derisive sounds, because you already know that the numbers zero to nine can be used to make more than ten values.

I suspect you're just waiting breathlessly to get into number theory. You can start breathing again, because we can do without the theory. What you're going to learn is that 10 base 2 means 2 and that 110 base 2 means one 4 and one 2 and zero 1s. Just like the decimal system, binary numbers are position dependent. In the decimal system, you have positions for the ones, tens, hundreds, thousands, tens of thousands, and so on. Each new position is ten raised to the next power. When you see 100, you think of the number one hundred, not ten raised to the power two (10**2), but they are the same number. Table 4.12 shows how the decimal system works with powers of ten.

TABLE 4.12: Decimal System Powers of 10 (Base 10)

Decimal Number	Power of 10
1	10**0
10	10**1
100	10**2
1000	10**3
10000	10**4
100000	10**5
1000000	10**6

If you're like most literate humans, when your brain sees 1000, it thinks one thousand. If you are told that this 1000 is actually a binary number, then you might be able to convert it to the decimal value of eight (I say "might," because only the truly dedicated can convert from binary to anything). Even a calculator is pretty useless for this one. By the time you're done typing in all those ones and zeros, you'll discover that it's probably easier to figure it out on paper. Your poor numerically challenged computer does just the opposite. If it sees, in your code, the number 8, it has to stop and convert that number to the binary 1000. However, although your computer understands only zero and one, it understands zero and one very quickly.

Binary numbers follow the same pattern that you saw in Table 4.12. The binary system powers of 2 are shown in Table 4.13.

Recall that the letter *A* is represented in your computer as the decimal value 65. In binary, decimal 65 is 1000001, which is also two to the sixth power plus two to zeroth power, or 64 plus 1.

TABLE 4.13: Binary System Powers of 2 (Base 2)

Binary Number	Power of 2
1	2**0
2	2**1
4	2**2
8	2**3
16	2**4
32	2**5
64	2**6
128	2**7

Binary numbers are usually grouped into sets of fours. Two groups of four are usually called a *byte*. Decimal 65 or binary 10000001 is usually written as 0100 0001. Each group of four binary digits can represent the decimal numbers 0 through 15. The decimal numbers 0 through 15 are shown in binary, octal, and hex in Table 4.14. Octal is used infrequently these days and is only included in the table for completeness (octal was important when memory was very expensive because it required one less bit of memory).

TABLE 4.14: Decimal Numbers 0–15 in Binary, Octal, and Hex

Decimal	Binary	Octal	Hex
0 0000	000	0	0
1 0001	001	1	1

Continued on next page

TABLE 4.14: Decimal Numbers 0–15 in Binary, Octal, and Hex

Decimal	Binary	Octal	Hex
2 0010	002	2	2
3 0011	003	3	3
4 0100	004	4	4
5 0101	005	5	5
6 0110	006	6	6
7 0111	007	7	7
8 1000	010	8	8
9 1001	011	9	9
10	1010	012	A
11	1011	013	B
12	1100	014	C
13	1101	015	D
14	1110	016	E
15	1111	017	F

Hexadecimal Numbers

As you learned in the previous section, binary numbers are often grouped together in groups of four. In the portion of the ASCII conversion chart shown in Table 4.6 (earlier in the chapter), each character takes two groups of four bits, which makes a byte. The byte is a basic building block in many computer operations. These relationships are all powers of two, which are compactly represented in the hex number system.

The hex number system uses the base 16. This means that hex numbers must have a digit for each of 16 values. The first ten digits of the hex number system are the familiar base ten digits, 0 through 9. The remaining five digits required to make a set of 16 values are drawn from the first five letters of the English alphabet, A through F. These digits, 0 through F (as shown in Table 4.14), can be used together to represent the decimal numbers 0 through 15.

Hex numbers make a convenient translation point between binary and decimal numbers because, as you can see in Table 4.14, four binary bits completely represent a hex digit. Two hex digits require a byte and allow you to represent up to 256 numbers (the original limit placed on ASCII characters).

Perl 5 doesn't have a direct means of representing binary numbers, so when I need to perform one of the binary operations explained in the next section, I usually use a hex number. To represent any hex number in Perl 5, all you need to do is begin the hex number with a zero (0) and the character *x*. For example, 0xFF represents the decimal number 255.

Binary Operators

The binary operators operate on bits. Whether the number is represented in decimal, hex, octal, or binary, the computer is really working with bits in memory.

The Perl 5 binary operators are shown in Table 4.15. The bits on the left of the operator are matched one by one with the bits on the right of the operator to produce a result.

TABLE 4.15: Binary Operators

Binary Operator	Means
&	Binary AND
|	Binary OR
~	Binary NOT
<<	Left shift
>>	Right shift
^	Exclusive OR

The Binary AND, OR, and NOT Operators

The rules are pretty simple for each operator. With the binary AND operator (&), if both bits are ones, the result is one; otherwise, the result is zero. Similar to the logical Boolean operators, the rules for the binary operators are often shown in a truth table. Table 4.16 shows a truth table with all the possible combinations of the two bits in the X and Y columns and the result of the AND operation in the last column.

TABLE 4.16: A Binary AND Truth Table

X	Y	X & Y
0	0	0
0	1	0
1	0	0
1	1	1

The binary OR operator (|) works exactly the opposite of the binary AND operator. If both bits are zero, the result is zero; otherwise, the result is one. Table 4.17 shows a truth table for the binary OR operator.

TABLE 4.17: A Binary OR Truth Table

X	Y	X	Y
0	0	0
0	1	1
1	0	1
1	1	1

In the truth table, notice that the four possible combinations for two bits are the binary numbers 00, 01, 10, and 11, which are the decimal numbers 0 through 3. You can always tell the maximum of decimal value a set of bits can handle by using this formula:

2 ** x - 1

where x is the number of bits you are using. In our truth table, we are using two bits, so the calculation is:

2 ** 2–1, or 4–1 = 3

The exclusive OR operator (^) is not quite as simple to understand as the AND and OR operators. The exclusive OR rule is if only one bit is one, then the result is one; otherwise, the result is zero. Table 4.18 shows the truth table for the exclusive OR operator.

TABLE 4.18: The Exclusive OR Truth Table

X	Y	X ^ Y
0	0	0
0	1	1
1	0	1
1	1	0

The binary NOT operator (~) turns ones to zeros and zeros to ones. It's that simple. This is called "flipping the bits." If you NOT the decimal 15 in four bits, you are actually NOTing the binary value 1111, which produces the results 0000.

Shift Operations

The last two binary operators listed in Table 4.15 are the left shift and right shift operators. Figure 4.6 shows the results of some left and right shift operations.

NOTE Figure 4.6 includes the Perl 5 shift statement on the same line as the result. You can retrieve the sample code from this book's companion pages on Sybex's web site. The filename is shiftOperators.pl.

The left shift operator (<<) can be used to simulate multiplying by powers of 2. The left shift operator moves the bits of the expression on the left of the operator to the left by the value of the expression on the right of the operator. For example, the first six operations in Figure 4.6 show a single bit being shifted left by powers of 2. Remember that the number one is actually bit zero of a 32-bit operating system. Bit one is set to 1, and the rest of the bits are set to 0, like this:

```
0000 0000 0000 0000 0000 0000 0000 0001
```

FIGURE 4.6:

Using left and right shift
operators

The right shift operator (>>) does just the opposite of the left shift operator. The right shift operator moves bits to the right by the value of the expression on the right of the operator. For example, the first six right shift operations in Figure 4.6 show a single bit being shifted right by powers of 2, which simulates division by two. The value being shifted right is the same for each operation. In this case, the starting value is 1073741824, which in binary looks like this:

```
0100 0000 0000 0000 0000 0000 0000 0000
```

If you right shift this number one place, you get one half of its previous value. This results in the number 536870912, which in binary looks like this:

```
0010 0000 0000 0000 0000 0000 0000 0000
```

Precedence and Associativity

Now you know that Perl 5 has a lot of operators. Each operator has a precedence and associativity, which define the order that operators are executed. The operator with the higher precedence goes first.

Associativity affects which expression the operator is bound with and what order the operator is executed. For example, the exponential operator is right associative, so 2**4 means 2 raised to the power of 4. If the exponential operator were left associative, 2**4 would mean 4 raised to the power of 2.

Some operators are nonassociative. This usually means they bind to whichever expression they are adjacent to. For example, the increment (++) and decrement (–) operators are nonassociative, so that $a++ and ++$a both bind to the scalar variable $a.

Table 4.19 lists the associative and precedence properties of Perl 5's operators. The operators with the highest precedence are at the beginning of the table.

NOTE
Some of the operations listed in Table 4.19 have not been covered yet. You will learn about them in later chapters.

TABLE 4.19: Operator Precedence and Associativity

Precedence (Highest to Lowest)	Operators	Associativity
Parentheses, functions, quotation marks	( ) " ' `	Left
Dereference operator	->	Left
Increment/decrement	++ –	None
Exponential	**	Right
NOT (logical and binary), Escape, sign operator	! ~ \ Unary + -	Right
Bind, not bind	=~ !~	Left
Multiply, divide, modulus, string multiply	* / % x	Left
Add, minus, string concatenate	+ - .	Left
Binary shift left, binary shift right	<< >>	Left
Less than, greater than, less than or equal to, greater than or equal to	< > <= >= lt gt le ge	None
Equal to, not equal to, compare	== != <=> eq ne cmp	None

Continued on next page

TABLE 4.19 CONTINUED: Operator Precedence and Associativity

Precedence (Highest to Lowest)	Operators	Associativity
Binary AND	& Left	
Binary OR, Exclusive OR	| ^	Left
Logical AND	&&	Left
Logical OR	||	Left
(COND)? true condition : false	?:	Right
Compound assignment statements	= += -= *= /= %= x= <<= >> = &= |=^= &&= ||=	Right
Comma, arrow	, =>	Left
Logical NOT	not	Right
Logical AND	and	Left
Logical OR, exclusive OR	or xor	Left

Parentheses have the highest precedence in Perl 5, as they do in every programming language. If you're unsure how a statement will be executed, add parentheses to make one expression execute before another expression. Parentheses always execute the innermost expression first and work outward. The following statement illustrates how the computer applies precedence.

```
$a = 3 + 2 * 6 ;
```

$a is assigned the value 15 because the multiply operator (*) has a higher precedence. Perl 5 really performs the operation like this:

- The result of 2 * 6 is calculated and saved into a temporary location.

- Then 3 + the value in the temporary location is calculated and saved into a temporary location.

- Finally, $a is assigned the value of the temporary location.

The statement looks like this inside the Perl 5 interpreter:

```
$temp1 = 2*6;
```

```
$temp2 = 3 + $temp1;
$a = $temp2;
```

If you added parentheses to this statement, you can change the precedence and the result, like this:

```
$a = (3 + 2) * 6 ;
```

Now the variable $a is assigned the value 30 because the parentheses have a higher precedence. Perl 5 performs the operation like this:

- The result of 3 + 2 is calculated and saved into a temporary location.

- Then 6 * the value in the temporary location is calculated and saved into a temporary location.

- Finally, $a is assigned the value of the temporary location.

The statement looks like this inside the Perl 5 interpreter:

```
$temp1 = 3+2;
$temp2 = 6 * $temp1;
$a = $temp2;
```

Summary

A program manipulates data through its operators. In the chapters that follow, you will see the operators introduced in this chapter again and again as you progress from simple to more complex programming problems.

This chapter began with an explanation of the basic numeric operators, which add, subtract, and multiply. The results of those operations were saved into variables using the assignment operator, which was explained next. Perl 5 allows you to combine the assignment operator with most of its other operators. These combined operators are called compound assignment operators.

In the section on string operators, you not only learned which operators are correct for string data, but you also learned why the string character *A* will never equal the string character *a*.

Much of every programming task is centered on testing data in conditional expressions. In this chapter, you learned about the Boolean operators that are used to create conditional expressions (which are the topic of Chapter 8). The section on Boolean combination operators explained truth tables, which can be used to understand complex conditional expressions.

The binary operators operate on bits and bytes. This section about binary operators explained bits and bytes, as well as binary and hex numbers.

Finally, you learned about two concepts called precedence and associativity. Precedence defines the order that an operator will be executed in relation to the other operators. Associativity determines which expression an operator will be bound to.

This chapter included many operators that may be unfamiliar to you. As you learn Perl 5 from this book, each operator introduced here will be explained in further detail elsewhere. The next chapter explains the details of scalar variables, which are the fundamental building blocks used to store and retrieve the results of many of the operators of this chapter.

CHAPTER
FIVE

Scalar Data

- Scalar variables

- String literals

- Numeric literals

- Boolean tests

- Variable definition and declaration

- Scalar context and list context

The simplicity of Perl 5's data structures is part of the beauty of Perl 5. Many languages put a lot of conditions on creating their data structures, making the programming task more tedious. Perl 5 provides built-in functions for manipulating data and puts very few conditions on creating data structures.

You can create data anywhere in your program, and you only need to worry about three types of data structures: scalars, arrays, and hashes. In this chapter, you'll learn about scalar data. The next chapter covers arrays and hashes.

An Introduction to Scalar Variables

There is so much to learn when you begin working with a new language that it can be difficult to figure out where to start. Sometimes, the best approach is to start with a simple example and then move forward from there. Our simple example is in Listing 5.1, which shows how to use a scalar variable to personalize a program. Figure 5.1 shows the output.

NOTE   Remember that line 1 of the listings in this book is not required on Windows machines. Windows NT uses filename extensions to determine which program to run, and Windows 95/98 uses the command line.

Listing 5.1:   **Personalizing a Program**

```
1.  #! /usr/local/bin/perl
2.  $name = "Eric C. Herrmann";
3.  print "The owner of this program is $name\n";
4.
5.  $firstName = "Eric ";
6.  $middleInitial = "C. ";
7.  $lastName = "Herrmann";
8.  print "The owner of this program is $firstName
            $middleInitial $lastName\n";
9.
10. $fName = "Eric";
11. $mInitial = "C.";
12. $lName = "Herrmann";
13. print "The owner of this program is $fName $mInitial
            $lName\n";
```

FIGURE 5.1:

Personalizing with scalar variables

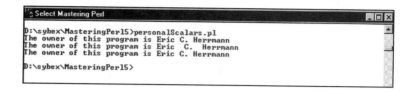

The first scalar variable used in Listing 5.1 is on line 2, $name. It is assigned the data on the right side of the equal sign, which is Eric C. Herrmann. In Figure 5.1, notice that the double quotation marks surrounding Eric C. Herrmann on line 2 of the listing do not show up on the screen. That's because they are not saved in the scalar variable $name. The double quotation marks are used to tell Perl 5 where the data starts and where it ends. Even though it looks like three different names are being assigned—the first name, the middle initial, and the last name—they all are stored in $name as one scalar value. As far as Perl 5 is concerned, only one thing, the string "Eric C. Herrmann", is stored in the scalar variable $name.

We'll revisit Listing 5.1 and see how the other scalar variables in the code work a little later in the chapter, when you learn about character data and quotation marks. I popped it in at the beginning of the chapter to give you a working example before going into those boring but necessary definitions and rules.

What's a Scalar Variable?

A *variable* is a modifiable memory location used to keep information for later use. Since that seems rather abstract, let's try a concrete analogy.

In your closet, you probably have some shoes, and you might even have a shoe-box. If you're really neat, you keep all of your shoes in a shoebox, with one pair of shoes per shoebox. Now, trust me on this, most computer languages are really strict about storage. They demand that you keep only one pair of shoes in each shoebox, and that pair of shoes had better fit the description on the front of the shoebox. Red pumps do not go in the sneakers box! Perl 5 is a lot more relaxed than that. You can mix up the contents of your shoeboxes. You are limited to only one thing per box, however.

Variables are like shoeboxes; they are containers for your data. Perl 5 lets you store two types of shoes in your shoebox: string data (characters) and numeric data (numbers). Scalar means one, and a scalar variable can store only one data item at a time.

The variable, or shoebox, saves your data for later use. Just like with a shoebox, you can replace what is currently in the box with something different. It's called a variable because what's in it can vary over time.

When it comes to scalar variables, remember these three rules:

- A scalar variable can contain only one item at a time.
- Perl 5 scalar variables can contain either numeric or string data.
- Perl 5 determines, based on context, whether a scalar variable contains string or numeric data.

Perl considers the operators, the type of the data, and the variable itself in determining context. The operators, such as `eq` and `==`, usually determine whether the data will be treated as a string or numeric value. The data, such as `99.95` or `"String"`, also plays a part in establishing the context of a variable.

Scalar Variable Names

In Listing 5.1, you saw variable names like `$name`, `$firstName`, and `$fName`. These conform to Perl 5's rules for naming scalar variables. Perl 5 allows you to use alphanumeric and nonalphanumeric characters in your scalar variables, as long as you follow the rules.

All scalar variable names are preceded by a dollar sign (`$`). (The file handle, covered in Chapter 11, is an exception to this rule.) The characters that follow the dollar sign are collectively referred to as the variable name. The following are Perl 5's rules for variable names.

- Variable names cannot contain spaces.
- Variable names may contain any printable character (except the space character), but special rules apply to nonalphanumeric characters.

NOTE The dollar sign (`$`) is a Perl variable designator that determines the variable type as scalar. Perl 5 also uses the at sign (`@`) to distinguish array variable names and the percent sign (`%`) to distinguish hash variable names. Most Perl programmers consider the variable type designator as part of the variable name.

- Variable names that begin with an underscore or an alphabet character (*A* through *Z*) may be any practical length. (Some implementations may limit the variable name length to 255 characters.)

- The characters that follow variable names that begin with an underscore or alphabet character may be digits, underscores, and alphabet characters.

- If a variable name begins with a digit (0 through 9), it may be of any practical length but can contain only digits, as in $982.

- If a variable name begins with a nonalphanumeric character, it can be only one character long.

> **NOTE**
>
> Perl 5 has many built-in special variables that are only one character long. For example, the variable name for the process ID is $$. Perl 5's special variables are covered throughout the book as appropriate and also in Appendix B.

Also, remember that Perl 5 is a case-sensitive language. The variable $A is different from the variable $a.

What's a Literal?

A literal is almost the opposite of a variable. A *literal* is a constant value in your source code and cannot be modified. A *variable* contains a value and can be modified to contain a different value.

In Listing 5.1, `Eric` is a literal—specifically a string literal. The number 10 is a numeric literal. The scalar variable $name could contain anything; the string literal `Eric` and the numeric literal 10 are just two examples of the variable's contents.

Strings and Character Data

Anything surrounded by quotation marks is considered a character string. It's called a *string* because you usually string several characters together to make a word. A single character in quotation marks is called a *character*; multiple characters surrounded by quotation marks are called a *string*. In Perl 5, both single characters and character strings are called strings.

Line 2 of Listing 5.1 is an assignment of a single scalar variable.

```
$name = "Eric C. Herrmann";
```

Only one string of characters is enclosed in the quotation marks.

Lines 5, 6, and 7 of Listing 5.1 illustrate the same concept. One string of characters is assigned to one scalar variable.

```
$firstName = "Eric ";
$middleInitial = "C. ";
$lastName = "Herrmann";
```

The variables $firstName, $middleInitial, and $lastName collectively define the same data as the single scalar variable $name, but the data is divided into three separate character strings—one character string for each scalar variable. Note the space and period in the scalar variable $middleInitial. Both of these characters are as important to the character string as the C. Character data is actually encoded into a computer format called ASCII, as you learned in Chapter 4.

The ASCII code for a letter C is hex 43. The code for a period (.) is hex 2E. The code for the space character is hex 20. You won't normally need to know the ASCII codes, but they illustrate here that the space character is just another number to the computer and of equal importance as the C character to the Perl 5 interpreter. This concept is also important in character string comparisons and other string operations. (Comparing and working with strings are covered in Chapters 15 and 16.)

As I've mentioned, character data in scalar variables is distinguished by surrounding the data with quotation marks. Single, double, or backward quotation marks and the operators q, qq, qx, and qw are ways of distinguishing character data in Perl 5. Each of these types of quotation marks has a special meaning in Perl 5, as explained in the following sections.

Quotation Marks

On your standard computer keyboard, there are three different styles of quotation marks: double, single, and back. You can use two of the three types of quotation marks—double and single—to define string literals (actual values). Each type of quotation mark has a different meaning, as listed in Table 5.1 and explained in the following sections.

TABLE 5.1: Perl 5 Quotation Marks

Quote	Meaning	Variable Interpolation
"	Begins or ends a character string	Yes
'	Begins or ends a character string	No
`	Begins or ends a system command string	Yes

One of the first rules of working with quotation marks is that they always come in pairs. The only exception to this rule is when you use a special syntax, called *escape sequence syntax*. When a quotation mark is preceded by the escape character (\), the quotation mark loses its special meaning and is treated by the interpreter as just another ASCII character. The quotation mark does not need to be paired with another quotation mark, nor do any of the other special quotation mark rules apply.

Escape Sequences

Escape sequences have special meanings to Perl 5. An escape sequence includes the escape character (\) followed by a meta-character, an alphanumeric character with a special meaning, or a quotation mark.

- When paired with a meta-character (a special character for pattern matching, as explained in Chapter 16), the meta-character loses its special meaning.

- When paired with a special meaning alphanumeric character, an escape sequence can transform the character so it can be used in a regular expression as part of a pattern match (also explained in Chapter 16), or it can be used to send printing commands, such as tabs and newline characters, to an output device (explained in Chapter 12).

- When paired with a quotation mark, the quotation mark, like the meta-character, loses its special meaning.

Single Quotes

A single quotation mark, called a *single quote*, at the beginning of a character string tells the Perl interpreter to stop interpreting any character that follows the single quote. This means that Perl does not look at the characters that make up the string literal to see if the characters have any special meaning. This effect continues until the Perl 5 interpreter finds the next single quote. All characters between the pair of single quotes are treated as a single string literal. The single quote must be a forward one, not the backward single quotation mark (*back quote*), because only the forward single quotation mark can be used to define string literals.

The double quotation marks (*double quotes*) around Eric in Listing 5.1 could be replaced with single quotes without any effect. To make this a little more understandable, let's replace all the double quotes in Listing 5.1 with single quotes, as shown in the Listing 5.2.

Listing 5.2:   **Single Quotes Throughout**

```
1.  #! /usr/local/bin/perl
2.  $name = 'Eric C. Herrmann';
3.  print 'The owner of this program is $name\n';
4.
5.  $firstName = 'Eric ';
6.  $middleInitial = 'C. ';
7.  $lastName = 'Herrmann';
8.  print 'The owner of this program is $firstName
            $middleInitial $lastName\n';
9.
10. $fName = 'Eric';
11. $mInitial = 'C.';
12. $lName = 'Herrmann';
13. print 'The owner of this program is $fName $mInitial
            $lName\n';
```

The results of running Listing 5.2 on my Windows 98 computer are shown in Figure 5.2. As you can see, this is quite a drastic change, and all because we replaced the double quotes with single quotes. I know, I just finished saying that replacing $name = "Eric" with $name = 'Eric' would have no effect, and I meant it. However, there is something called variable interpolation occurring on lines 3, 8, and 13, which is profoundly affected by using single quotes rather than double quotes.

FIGURE 5.2:

Using single quotes throughout

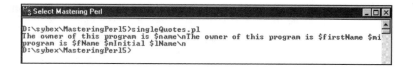

Remember that a single quote tells Perl 5 to treat everything until the next single quote as one string literal. In addition, the single quotes tell Perl 5 not to interpret anything between the pair of quotation marks. So what gets printed is exactly what was typed in after the opening single quote and before the closing single quote. Because each of the `print` statements in Listing 5.2 has single quotes around its character string, you get results like:

```
The owner of this program is $firstName $middleInitial $lastName
```

Obviously, this is not what you want to happen when printing variable names. What you need in these cases is variable interpolation, which is explained in the next section.

Now I was not kidding when I said you could replace the double quotes around `Eric` with single quotes. Take a look at Listing 5.3 and its corresponding output shown in Figure 5.3, which looks just like Figure 5.1.

Listing 5.3:   Single and Double Quotes

```
1.  #! /usr/local/bin/perl
2.  $name = 'Eric C. Herrmann';
3.  print "The owner of this program is $name\n";
4.
5.  $firstName = 'Eric ';
6.  $middleInitial = 'C. ';
7.  $lastName = 'Herrmann';
8.  print "The owner of this program is $firstName
            $middleInitial $lastName\n";
9.
10. $fName = 'Eric';
11. $mInitial = 'C.';
12. $lName = 'Herrmann';
13. print "The owner of this program is $fName $mInitial
            $lName\n";
```

Using single and double quotes

```
Select Mastering Perl                                    _ □ ×
D:\sybex\MasteringPerl5>doubleQuotes.pl
The owner of this program is Eric C. Herrmann
The owner of this program is Eric  C.  Herrmann
The owner of this program is Eric C. Herrmann

D:\sybex\MasteringPerl5>
```

The differences between Listing 5.2 and Listing 5.3 are on lines 3, 8, and 13. On these lines, you need variable interpolation.

Double Quotes and Variable Interpolation

Variable interpolation is not some sort of cryptic programming magic, though I admit that if you are not paying attention it could be a little confusing. With double quotes, Perl actually looks at each character of the string literal to see if it happens to have a special meaning. This is called *variable interpolation*.

> **NOTE**   Most of Perl 5's special characters are also called *meta-characters*. Meta-characters are covered in Chapter 16.

On lines 3, 8, and 13 of Listings 5.1 through 5.3, there are two characters that Perl 5 understands to have special meaning. The escape character paired with the newline character (\n) sends the newline printing command to the output device (more on this in Chapter 12). The dollar sign ($) tells Perl that a scalar variable follows. Hence, on these lines, each of the variables is replaced with the string literals previously stored in them.

The difference between single quotes and double quotes is simple but important. Double quotes allow variable interpolation. Single quotes store exactly the characters that come between them.

> **WARNING**   Using single quotes when you want double quotes or vice versa is a common source of programming bugs. Pay attention to this detail, and you will save yourself some debugging headaches.

Back Quotes

There is a third type of quotation mark that causes the Perl 5 interpreter to do something completely different. The backward quotation mark (`` ` ``), called a *back quote*, tells Perl 5 to interpret the string between the quotation marks as an operating system command. If you want to execute a program from within a program, you can use back quotes.

An operating system command executed within the back quotes always returns some type of data. For some commands, the data may be only a success or failure indication, which is often 1 or 0. For other commands, a long list of data items may be returned. The returned data is stored in the variable on the left side of the equal sign. Listing 5.4 illustrates this concept. Its output is shown in Figure 5.4.

Listing 5.4:   **Back Quotes**

```
1.   #! /usr/local/bin/perl
2.   $name = 'Eric C. Herrmann';
3.   $directory = `dir/w`;
4.   @directory = `dir/w`;
5.   print "Scalar context Directory Listing\n $directory\n";
6.   print "List context Directory Listing\n @directory\n";
```

FIGURE 5.4:

Using back quotes

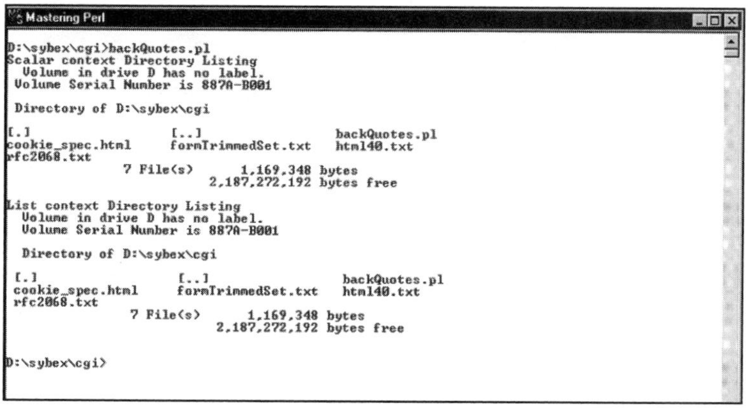

NOTE   Listing 5.4 won't run without modification on a Unix computer, because the directory command on a Unix computer is `ls` instead of `dir`. (System-level commands usually are not portable between operating systems.) To run it under Unix, replace `dir/w` with `ls`.

Line 3 in Listing 5.4 uses back quotes to run the `dir` command to get the contents of the directory, which are printed by lines 5 and 6. This listing also illustrates list context versus scalar context. The `dir` command returns the same information in each context, but the information is stored differently. You will learn more about list and scalar context later in this chapter.

The Quote Operators

If using quotation marks tends to confuse you or you want to print quotation marks to the screen, Perl 5 provides a simple solution. Perl 5 has four operators for replacing quotes: q, qq, qx, and qw. Each of these operators can be used in place of their respective quotation mark characters, as shown in Table 5.2.

TABLE 5.2: Quote Operators

Operator	Meaning	Result	Example
q	Single quote	Noninterpolated string	`print q|The variable $name equals|;`
qq	Double quote	Interpolated string	`print qq#<input type="TEXT" name="NAME">#;`
qx	Back quote	Interpolated command string	`$dList = qx%dir $list-Type%;`
qw	Quoted string	Noninterpolated string	`@familyNames = qw(Eric, Sherry, Steven, Jessica, Scott);`

The quote operators are actually fairly easy to use. Each of these operators works on any characters between the delimiters. The delimiter for a quote operator is the first nonalphanumeric character that follows the quote operator. The space character does not count as a delimiter. Quote delimiters must come in matching pairs, so the closing delimiter must be the same character as the opening delimiter. The delimiters can be any matching pair of nonalphabetic characters. A delimiter is any value used to mark the beginning or end of a statement.

This is a lot clearer with an example, so take a moment to look at Listing 5.5 and its corresponding output in Figure 5.5.

Listing 5.5:   **Quote Operators**

```
1.  #!/usr/local/bin/perl
2.
3.  $singleQuote = q("This is a test." 'He exclaimed!' `Quotes
                     don't count.`);
4.  print "$singleQuote\n\n" ;
5.
6.  $singleQuoteDelimited = q+"This is a test." 'He
                           exclaimed!' `Quotes don't count.`+;
7.  print "$singleQuoteDelimited\n\n" ;
8.
9.  $iValue = 10;
10. $fValue = 11.43;
11. $divValue = 23/7 ;
12. $doubleQuote = qq[Double quotes allow variable interpolation
                   so $iValue,
13. $fValue and $divValue will be printed];
14. print "$doubleQuote\n";
15.
16. $directory = qx!dir/w!;
17. print "qx is just like the back quote. The directory
          is $directory.\n\n";
18.
19. $totalWords = 10;
20. @wordList = qw(Each of these $totalWords words is placed
                  into the array wordlist);
21. print "The number of words are $#wordList.\n\n" ;
22. $index = $#wordList ;
23.
```

```
24. for ( 0 .. $#wordList ){
25.     print "$wordList[$index-] ";
26. }
27. print "\n\n";
```

FIGURE 5.5:

Using quote operators

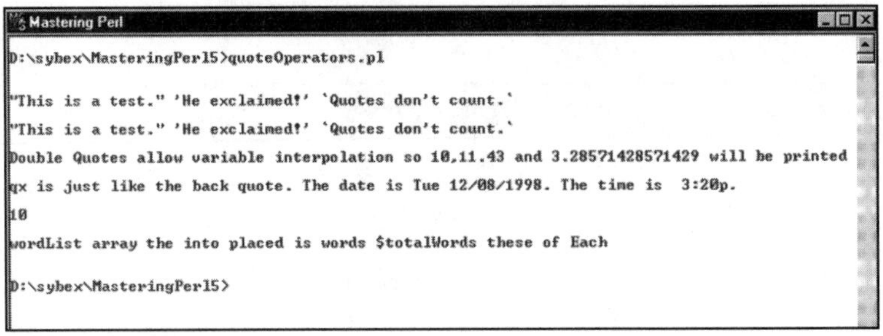

```
Mastering Perl                                                    _ □ X
D:\sybex\MasteringPerl5>quoteOperators.pl

"This is a test." 'He exclaimed!' `Quotes don't count.`
"This is a test." 'He exclaimed!' `Quotes don't count.`
Double Quotes allow variable interpolation so 10,11.43 and 3.28571428571429 will be printed
qx is just like the back quote. The date is Tue 12/08/1998. The time is  3:20p.
10
wordList array the into placed is words $totalWords these of Each

D:\sybex\MasteringPerl5>
```

Lines 3 and 6 show how the **q** operator can be used to create strings with different quotation mark characters embedded in the string. The **q** operator creates a noninterpolated string. The Perl 5 interpreter does not try to interpret anything between the delimiters. On line 3, the delimiter is something you are used to seeing—the left (() and right ()) parentheses pair. The delimiter on line 6 is the plus sign (+).

> **NOTE**   As the example demonstrates, you can use anything as a delimiter with quote operators. However, in your own code, you won't want to use characters that may be misleading, such as plus signs (which can make it look like a math operation is taking place).

The output stored into the $singleQuote and $singleQuoteDelimited variables on lines 3 and 6 is exactly what is typed between the delimiters. You can see this in the first two lines of Figure 5.5.

The **qq** operator is shown in action on lines 12 and 13. I used brackets ([]) as delimiters on line 12 to demonstrate that any nonalphanumeric value can delimit the strings following the quote operators, and those delimiters can span multiple lines. The **qq** operator allows variable interpolation. Notice the long result printed for 23/7.

The qx operator is demonstrated on line 16. It operates just like the back quote character. Again I used the unusual delimiter of an exclamation point (!) on line 16 just so you won't be surprised by this when you see someone else's code.

Finally, the qw operator, demonstrated on lines 20 through 26, returns a list, or array of words (you'll learn more about arrays in Chapter 6). A word is determined by the embedded white space. So the qw operator looks for the space character. Anything separated by a space, or blank, is considered a separate word. The qw operator does not allow variable interpolation. Each word of the word list is treated as if it were surrounded by single quotation marks. That is why the variable $totalWords is printed instead of the numeric literal, 10, which was stored into $totalWords on line 19.

Rules for String Literals

When it comes to string literals, remember these simple rules:

- Single-quoted strings are delimited by paired forward quotation marks (') or the q operator. Single-quoted strings are not interpolated.

- Double-quoted strings are delimited by paired double quotation marks (") or the qq operator. Double-quoted strings are interpolated.

- Back-quoted strings are delimited by paired backward quotation marks (') or the qx operator. Back-quoted strings are interpolated. Back-quoted strings are treated as system commands. The results from system commands are returned in a single string.

- The qw operator returns a list of noninterpolated words.

Numeric Literals

Working with numbers in Perl 5 is straightforward. Basically, what you see is what you get. When you enter a value as 10.10, 10.10 is saved. As shown in Listing 5.6 and its corresponding output in Figure 5.6, Perl 5 allows you to work with numeric literals quite easily.

FIGURE 5.6:

Numeric literal formats

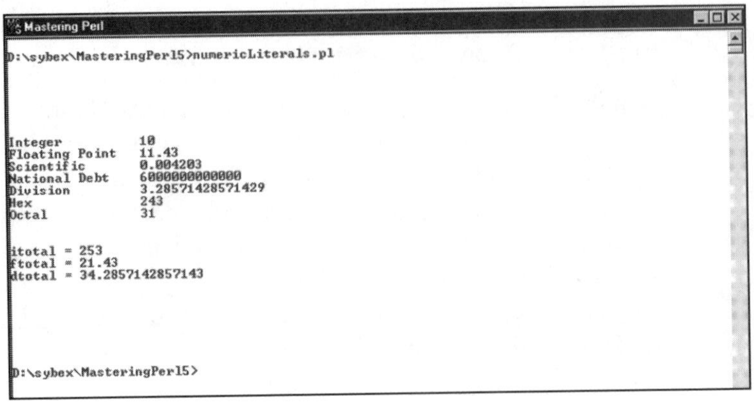

Listing 5.6:   **Numeric Literals**

```perl
1.  #!/usr/local/bin/perl
2.
3.  $integerValue = 10;
4.  $floatingPointValue = 11.43;
5.  $scientificValue = 42.03E-04;
6.  $nationalDebt = 6_000_000_000_000;
7.  $divisionValue = 23/7;
8.  $hexValue = 0x0F3;
9.  $octalValue = 037;
10.
11. $itotal = $integerValue + $hexValue;
12. $ftotal = $floatingPointValue + $integerValue;
13. $dtotal = $divisionValue + $octalValue;
14.
15. print "Integer \t $integerValue\n";
16. print "Floating Point \t $floatingPointValue\n";
17. print "Scientific \t $scientificValue\n";
18. print "National Debt \t $nationalDebt\n";
19. print "Division \t $divisionValue\n";
20. print "Hex \t\t $hexValue\n";
21. print "Octal \t\t $octalValue\n";
22. print "\n\n";
23. print "itotal = $itotal\n";
```

```
24. print "ftotal = $ftotal\n";
25. print "dtotal = $dtotal\n";
```

This listing shows the different formats for numeric literals. Notice in Figure 5.6 that Perl prints everything in the correct format and does the right thing when adding numbers together. Perl is your friend, but like all friends, it does have a few idiosyncrasies. First let's go over the numeric formats that are available.

Numeric Formats

Perl uses the standard mathematical notation for defining numeric literals, as shown in Table 5.3.

TABLE 5.3: Numeric Literal Formats and Notation

Type	Notation	Example
Integer	NN	12
Floating point	NN.NN	342.176
Scientific	NN.NNENN	42.04E-6
Big number	NN_NNN_NNN	6_000_000
Hex	0xNNNN	0xFFD3
Octal	0NNN	0374

Most of this is self-explanatory. The big number format (line 6 of Listing 5.6) is a convenience feature of Perl 5. It's hard to keep track of all those zeros when you are typing them into your program, but each of those zeros is important. Perl 5 allows you to use the underscore character to separate number groups. Normally, you would use a comma to separate your billions from trillions, but commas in numeric literals confuse Perl 5, so underscores seem like a reasonable compromise.

Fixed-Point Number Solutions

Listing 5.6 (lines 11 through 13) also demonstrates that you can mix numeric types and still get the correct answer. Perl just loves making your life easier. It does, however, have one small quirk when it comes to numbers. Perl 5 does not have any built-in way to define rounding, or truncation, for fixed-point number calculations.

This becomes a problem when you're trying to work with currency (perhaps you need to print a total bill for your online catalog customer), and of course, for any other application that requires fixed-point numbers. There are basically three ways you can deal with the need for fixed-point numbers in Perl 5:

- Use the sprintf function to round your result to a fixed-point value.

- Use a regular expression to truncate your result to a fixed-point value

- Create your own rounding function to generate a rounded value that you can control.

The first solution seems like the most reasonable, but the Perl 5 FAQ (Frequently Asked Question list) specifically warns against trusting Perl's rounding capabilities for financial applications. Listing 5.7 and its corresponding output in Figure 5.7 show how the three methods work. As you can see, the sprintf function seems to work just fine. However, you should read the details about each method in the following sections and choose the solution that best suits your needs.

NOTE One of the basic tenets of Perl 5 is that there are a lot of ways to solve a problem. You get to pick the best one for your situation. Perl 5 very seldom forces you to choose a particular solution because of language constraints.

Listing 5.7:   **Rounding Numbers**

```
1.  #!/usr/local/bin/perl
2.  $taxRate = 0.0825;
3.  $totalDue = 9.97 + 4.39 + 8.79;
4.  $tax = $totalDue * $taxRate;
5.  $totalDue += $tax;
6.
7.  #Using the built-in sprintf function for rounding
8.  $roundedValue = sprintf " %0.2f", $totalDue;
9.
10. print "Before rounding the total is $totalDue and the tax
            is $tax.\n";
```

```
11. print "After rounding the total is $roundedValue.\n\n";
12.
13. #Using a regular expression for rounding
14. $totalDue =~ /(\d*\.\d\d)/;
15. $truncatedValue = $1;
16. print "The truncated value is $truncatedValue\n\n";
17. $calculatedValue = $totalDue;
18.
19. if ($calculatedValue < 0 ) {
20.     $negativeResult = "True";
21. }
22.
23. #Using an algorithm for rounding The calculated solution:
24. $calculatedValue = int ( (abs($calculatedValue)
                              /0.01) + 0.5) * 0.01;
25.
26. if ($negativeResult){
27.     $calculatedValue *= -1;
28. }
29. print "The calculated value is $calculatedValue\n";
```

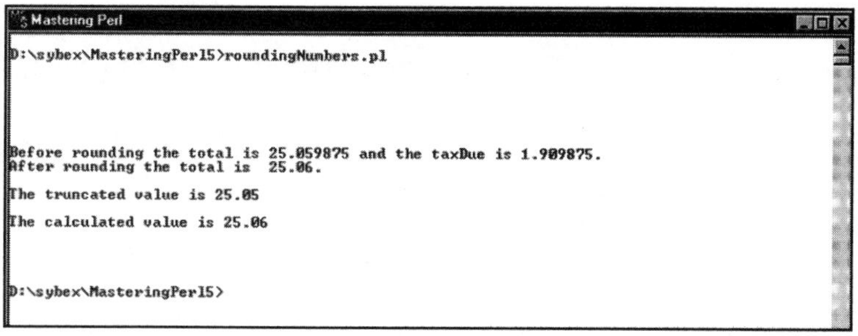

FIGURE 5.7:

Solutions for rounding numeric values

The sprintf Function

Did I lose you as I was describing how the sprintf function seems to work just fine? Don't you know what the sprintf function is? (Sorry, sometimes the geek filter accidentally gets clicked off.)

The `sprintf` function is part of a family of functions used to format data for printing and other display purposes. `sprintf` stands for string print format, which may help you remember it next time you need to format some data.

The `sprintf` function rounds up to the format you request. This function takes two input parameters. The first parameter is a data format parameter. On line 8 of Listing 5.7, that data format is `"%0.2f"`:

```
$roundedValue = sprintf " %0.2f", $totalDue;
```

This parameter tells Perl 5 to format the data as follows:

- The f tells Perl the format should be floating point.

- The .2 tells Perl that two digits follow the decimal point.

- The 0 before the decimal point tells Perl to fill in any missing digits with zeros. Filling in with zeros is called *zero fill*. It results in numbers like 25 becoming 25.00.

The second parameter to `sprintf` is the data that you want formatted. The function returns the formatted output for you to store into an lvalue such as `$roundedValue`, as shown on line 8 of Listing 5.7.

There is a lot more to say for you to understand completely how to use the `sprintf` function. If you need to know everything about `sprintf` right now, turn to Chapter 12, where the `sprintf` and `printf` functions are discussed in detail.

A Regular Expression

Another solution to the rounding problem is to use a regular expression and pattern matching to truncate the digits after the first two digits following a decimal point. Regular expressions are one of the coolest, greatest, most powerful features of Perl 5. You'll spend an entire chapter learning about regular expressions (Chapter 16).

I'll give you the briefest of explanations of regular expressions here because it is important for you to have some understanding of the listing presented in this chapter. (Otherwise, you may look at the listing and feel frustrated because parts of it don't make any sense.)

The regular expression is on line 14 of Listing 5.7:

```
$totalDue =~ /(\d*\.\d\d)/;
```

The regular expression consists of the \d, *, and . between the parentheses. These tell Perl 5 to search the variable on the left side of the pattern-binding operator (=~) for any number of digits (\d*), followed by a period (\.), followed by two digits (\d\d). When Perl 5 finds the pattern, the parentheses surrounding the entire regular expression tell Perl to save the matched pattern into a back reference variable. In this case, the back reference variable is named $1.

A back reference variable contains the characters of the input string ($total-Due) that matched the corresponding portion of the regular expression surrounded by parentheses. The back reference variable is saved into the scalar variable $truncatedValue.

NOTE   Back reference variables are numbered sequentially from 1 to *n*, where *n* is equal to the number of pairs of parentheses in the regular expression. Back reference variables are named in sequential order, corresponding to their regular expression parentheses pair. You can reference the back reference variable both inside and outside the regular expression, which means you can reference back to the pattern you just matched.

For accounting purposes, this is not an acceptable solution. Only the first two digits following the decimal point are saved. This means that all those half cents that should be rounded up and sent off to our ever-needy taxing authorities are being lost. Using the regular expression truncation method, numbers like 25.4567, 25.4588, and 25.4599 all yield the same answer— 25.45—but the tax man thinks the answer should be 25.46 for each of these.

A Calculated Solution

The other solution to the rounding problem, shown on lines 19 through 29 of Listing 5.7, is a calculated solution that the programmer can control. A calculated, or programmer's, solution to a problem is also called an *algorithm*. An algorithm is any solution that is made up of several steps to produce a result. Algorithms are what make programming so much fun. Algorithms are your own ideas solving problems on a computer.

The algorithm on line 24 of Listing 5.7 rounds floating-point numbers to two decimal places:

```
$calculatedValue = int ( (abs($calculatedValue)
                   /0.01) + 0.5) * 0.01;
```

When you first look at this line, you may not understand it, but you already have all the knowledge you need to figure out how this rounding algorithm works. To understand any algorithm, you just need to keep breaking the solution down into smaller steps until you understand each step. This is the same process you use to create an algorithm.

To create an algorithm, you break the problem down into smaller and smaller steps until you can see a coding solution for each step. As an example, let's break the rounding algorithm down into understandable steps. Let's assume that we are rounding the number –30.4557. The input to the first step is the entire algorithm:

```
int ( (abs(-30.4557) /0.01) + 0.5) * 0.01;
```

The input to the remaining steps will be the output from the previous step.

1. Remember from the discussion of operators in Chapter 4 (Table 4.19) that parentheses and functions have the highest precedence and execute from the innermost parenthesis out. That means the first step of the rounding algorithm is to take the absolute value of the scalar variable $calculatedValue, or in our example –30.4557. The absolute value function is abs, which returns the positive or absolute value of a number. The output of this step is:

    ```
    int ( (30.4557 /0.01) + 0.5) * 0.01;
    ```

2. Divide the result of step one by 0.01. Remember that dividing a number by a fraction is the same as multiplying by the inverse. So this has the effect of multiplying the result of step 1 by 100. You want to use division by 0.01 because this forces Perl to use floating-point numbers. Multiplying by 100 has the effect of shifting the decimal place two digits to the right. So 30.4557 becomes 30445.57. The output of this step is:

    ```
    int (3045.57 + 0.5) * 0.01;
    ```

3. The third step continues to use the parenthesis precedence rule. Perform the simple addition to get the output of this step:

    ```
    int (3046.07) * 0.01;
    ```

4. Functions have precedence over the multiplication operator. The int function forces numbers to become integers. The digits to the right of the decimal point are lost, so 3046.07 becomes 3046. The output of this step is:

    ```
    3046 * 0.01;
    ```

5. Multiplying by a fraction is the same as dividing by the inverse. Multiplying by 0.01 moves the decimal place two digits to the left. The output and solution to the rounding algorithm is:

```
30.46
```

Once you understand an algorithm, you have control over the algorithm. You can make it work however you want.

Each of the solutions in Listing 5.7 handles the rounding of numbers differently. You can choose which solution best fits your needs. Personally, I like to use the rounding algorithm solution. The built-in `sprintf` function seems to work, but because I don't know the algorithm that the `sprintf` function uses, I can never be sure why it works. The rounding algorithm is something I understood fully. If I need to explain to an auditor how I calculated my taxes, I'm a lot more comfortable with something I understand versus an unknown algorithm that seems to work.

Boolean Values

As I stated at the beginning of this chapter, Perl 5 has only two data types: string and numeric. Perl 5 does not have a Boolean data type. However, as you learned in Chapter 5, it does have Boolean operators that determine whether a result is true or false, so the basic capabilities of Boolean values can be simulated in the language.

On line 26, I check the variable `$negativeResult`:

```
if ($negativeResult){
```

Line 26 isn't actually testing for the truth of `$negativeResult`, but rather for its existence. If the result of this check is true, the next line of code sets the calculated value as negative. The check on line 26 works because of the way Perl 5 allows you to define variables.

In Perl 5, variables come into existence the first time they are declared or something is stored into them. In this example, the calculated value is positive, so the `if` condition on line 19 fails, and line 20 never executes. Here are those two lines:

```
if ($calculatedValue < 0 ) {
    $negativeResult = "True";
```

When line 26 executes, the variable $negativeResult has never been defined. Therefore, $negativeResult meets the third Boolean false condition of undefined. Remember, there are three ways a variable can be false:

- The value is zero (0).

- The value is null.

- The variable is undefined.

Everything else evaluates to true.

If the calculated value had been negative, the scalar variable $negativeResult would have been set to the string "True". I could have set $negativeResult to any value other than zero, or to null, and still gotten the result I wanted. Setting $negativeResult to true just makes the code a little easier to understand.

Boolean data types are usually used to keep track of a particular condition for a later check in a conditional statement. This is exactly how I used $negativeValue in Listing 5.7. The condition is checked and saved on lines 19 through 21. The results are checked on line 26. (Conditional expressions are covered in Chapter 8.)

In each of the programs in this chapter, you've seen variables pop into existence seemingly out of thin air. Experienced programmers may find this a bit disconcerting. I know I did when I first started learning Perl. New Perl programmers might not have even noticed that the variable $roundedValue on line 8 of Listing 5.7 didn't exist before line 8. In fact, if you look back at Listing 5.7, you'll see that none of the variables are declared in a traditional programming sense. This is the natural Perl 5 way of programming, which you are going to learn about in the next section.

Variable Declarations

In Perl 5, a variable comes into existence the first time it is assigned a value. In languages like C, variables are usually defined at the top of the file before any executable code. (This used to be a requirement in C; now it is a C programming style, even though most C compilers no longer require variables to be declared in a particular location in a file.) In Perl, you can define variables as you need

Programming Style

Everybody has an opinion and a style. Programming languages seem to develop characteristics just like people. Perl 5 is no exception. Throughout this book, you'll learn about Perl 5's style.

Usually, it's a good idea to work within the style of the language. If you work within the style of a language, your code will be more readily understandable by other programmers that also work regularly in the language. Here are three good reasons to conform to Perl's style:

- Your code will be easier to integrate into other Perl 5 code.

- It will be easier to integrate other Perl 5 code into your new code.

- It will be easier for you to understand other Perl 5 code.

them. This lends to a programming style where new variables appear throughout the code.

Perl 5 does allow you to declare variables, which is an important attribute of a language that allows you to initialize variables before they are used.

I'm sorry, I've done it again. I've been blathering along as if you should understand what defining variables and declaring variables mean. Variables exist in two states: declared and defined. Now I hate to do this, but in order to give precise definitions of declaring and defining variables, I've just got to use some techno-babble. I can't help myself!

Variables and Namespaces

When Perl 5 begins running, it creates things called *namespaces*. A namespace is a long list, or table, of all of the names that the Perl 5 interpreter must keep track of. One of those namespaces is `main::`. Every Perl 5 program has a `main::` namespace that contains all of the variable names that are part of the main package. You can access any variable in the main package by adding the namespace prefix `main::` to the variable name. Right now, all of your variables are part of the main package. (In Chapters 18 and 19, you'll learn more about namespaces and packages.)

When you *declare* a variable, it becomes part of the namespace table. This namespace table is also called a *symbol table*. A declared variable has a place in the symbol table but it doesn't have any contents or data associated with it. A declared variable has the value null in Perl 5—not zero, but null.

A *defined* variable has been assigned some value, even if that value is zero. In some languages, you must declare a variable before you can define it. Perl 5 allows you to declare and define a variable in one step. Whenever a new variable is assigned a value, it is also declared. The new variable is given a place in the symbol table and assigned a value.

The my and local Keywords

If you wish, you can declare a variable in Perl 5 without defining it by using the keyword my or local. A variable declared but not initialized will be preset to null.

You declare variables using my and local like this:

```
my $variableName;
local $variableName;
my ($var1, $var2, $var3, $va4);
local ($var1, $var2, $var3, $va4);
```

When you use the my keyword, a new instance of the variable is created each time the line of code is executed, even if the declaration is within a loop. You'll learn more about using the my keyword in loops in Chapter 9.

TIP

A variable declared with my is limited in scope to the enclosing block. A variable declared with local is limited in scope to the enclosing block but is also visible to any subroutines called from that enclosing scope. When a variable is defined without using my or local, it is given global scope. When you get to the more advanced topics and learn more about the scoping capabilities of my and local (in Chapter 18), you may be tempted to start declaring your variables at the top of the program or subroutine. Resist the dark side. Declaring and defining your variables as you need them is very object-oriented. Newer languages like Java and C++ also use this style.

The Case against Recycled Variables

There is one more variable declaration issue I would like to address that is not directly related to Perl 5. This issue is about a lesson from that lovely school of hard knocks. It's a lesson I learned over years of programming experience, pulled hair, and numerous cursing matches with my computer.

Let's return to several key lines on Listing 5.7:

```
8.  $roundedValue = sprintf " %0.2f", $totalDue;
15. $truncatedValue = $1;
17. $calculatedValue = $totalDue;
```

Each of these lines declares a new variable to perform a different type of calculation. This isn't strictly necessary. You could reuse the $totalDue variable for the rounding, truncation, and calculated value code. I strongly recommend against this, however. I have learned, through the experience of painful debugging, that using the same variable for different tasks inevitably ends up creating errors in the code.

Code that uses the same variable for different purposes is harder to understand. Also, frequently the reused variable is needed for its original purpose later in the code.

Variables are cheap. They don't cost any setup time in Perl 5. They make your code more readable. They cost very little in space. So when you need a variable for a slightly different task from what the old variable was used for, create a new one, just as I did on lines 8, 15, and 17 of Listing 5.7. You'll feel better about it (or I will anyway), and you'll spend less time fixing runtime errors.

Scalar Context versus List Context

As you learned in Chapter 4, Perl is a context-sensitive language. Context comes in two flavors: scalar and list. As you've seen in this chapter, scalar context affects whether your data is manipulated as a string or a number. List context is sometimes more subtle. List context can affect the data returned from an assignment operation, and it often has an impact on subroutine parameters and the result the subroutine returns.

A list, as you know, is a series of things—names, sentences, or words—collected in a container. A grocery list is a series of items to be purchased, collected together on a piece of paper. But if you store that series of items to be purchased in a computer file, it would still be a grocery list. The list is in the computer instead of on a piece of paper, but it's still a list.

A list in Perl 5 works the same way. A list is a series of scalar variables held in a container. The container that creates list context can be parentheses like this:

```
my ($day, $month, $year);
  ($day, $month, $year) = `date %d%M%Y`;
```

Or the list context can be an array container. (In earlier versions of Perl, list context was built around a list of scalar variables inside a pair of parentheses, but now list context is much more commonly used with arrays.)

A list is a group of scalar objects, but a list can contain other lists. Perl 5 resolves this conflict by turning the list inside the containing list into its group of scalar objects. The final list is always a one-dimensional list of scalar objects. This is very important because it affects the way that subroutines work, so let me restate this rule. A list is always one sequential group of scalar objects. Any lists that are originally part of the containing list are always resolved to their scalar list values before the container list completes evaluation.

Let's use an example with arrays to clarify list context. Suppose that you have three arrays:

- An array of first names:

  ```
  @firstNames = (Eric, James, Scott);
  ```

- An array of last names:

  ```
  @lastNames = (Martin, Swallow, Peacock);
  ```

- An array of ages:

  ```
  @ages = (45, 16, 21);
  ```

You can place all of these arrays into a list like this:

```
@list = (@firstNames, @lastNames, @ages);
```

Before the list of lists is assigned to the lvalue @lists, each list in the list of lists is resolved to its group of scalars. The list (@firstNames, @lastNames, @ages) becomes:

```
(Eric, James, Scott, Martin, Swallow, Peacock, 45, 16, 21)
```

Each list is resolved into its scalar values, one list at a time and in order from left to right. If there are nested lists, they will be resolved from left to right in turn. For example, for a simple subroutine call to the sort function (which, as its name suggests, sorts a list into order), this means sort is not receiving three lists and sorting each list. The sort function receives and sorts only one list. This is always true, regardless of the complexity of the list. You'll learn more about arrays and the sort function in Chapter 6.

Many of the functions in Perl 5 are actually two functions with one name. If you call the function in scalar context, the function returns a scalar result. If you call the function in list context, the function returns a list result. When a function can be called in two contexts, it is clearly stated in the syntax definition of the function.

List context can also be defined by the called subroutine, and that context can propagate to other subroutines called from the main subroutine. Sometimes the context of a subroutine can be hard to determine. Listing 5.8 contains a subroutine that will show you whether a subroutine is operating in list or scalar context. Figure 5.8 shows the output. (Subroutines are discussed in detail in Chapter 18.)

Listing 5.8:   **Scalar Context versus List Context**

```
1.  #!/usr/local/bin/perl
2.
3.  #list context when lvalue is an array
4.  @array  = isListOrScalar("lvalue is an array: ");
5.  #scalar context when lvalue is a scalar
6.  $scalar  = isListOrScalar("lvalue is a scalar: ");
7.  @array = split(/:/,isListOrScalar("lvalue is
                    an array inside the split function: "));
8.  reset (isListOrScalar("The reset function: "));
9.  print (isListOrScalar("printing: "));
10. print "\n";
11. kill (isListOrScalar("The kill function: "));
12. print "==\n";
13. grep (isListOrScalar("The grep function parameter 1: "),
            isListOrScalar("The grep function parameter 2: "));
14. print "==\n";
15. grep (1,isListOrScalar("The grep function parameter 2 and
            parameter 1 is a constant: "));
```

```
16. print "==\n";
17. grep (isListOrScalar("The grep function parameter 1 and
           parameter 2 is a constant: "),1);
18.
19. sub isListOrScalar($){
20.     my ($callingString) = @_;
21.     if (wantarray){
22.         print "$callingString LIST\n";
23.     }
24.     else {
25.         print "$callingString SCALAR\n";
26.     }
27. }
```

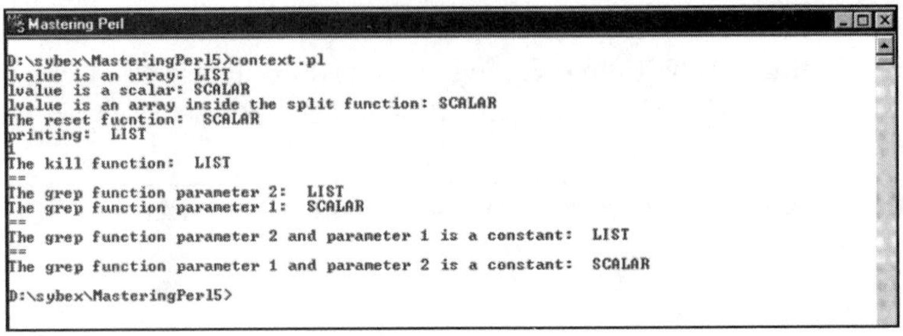

FIGURE 5.8:

Distinguishing between scalar context and list context

```
D:\sybex\MasteringPerl5>context.pl
lvalue is an array: LIST
lvalue is a scalar: SCALAR
lvalue is an array inside the split function: SCALAR
The reset fucntion:  SCALAR
printing:   LIST
==
The kill function:  LIST
==
The grep function parameter 2:   LIST
The grep function parameter 1:   SCALAR
==
The grep function parameter 2 and parameter 1 is a constant:  LIST
==
The grep function parameter 1 and parameter 2 is a constant:  SCALAR

D:\sybex\MasteringPerl5>
```

Notice that when the subroutine is first called, on line 4 of Listing 5.8, it returns list context. The same call when the result is returned to a scalar variable, on line 6 of Listing 5.8, returns scalar context. Most of these functions operate as you would expect. Functions that take expressions operate in scalar context; functions that operate on lists run in list context.

You can force scalar context with the `scalar` operator. For example, the following statement forces `@array` into scalar context, which is the size of the array:

```
scalar (@array);
```

Lists are not quite arrays, but arrays are lists. A list is a series of values, separated by commas, which are enclosed within parentheses. An array is a Perl 5 data type, which refers to a series of values. A list is not a Perl 5 data type. Although the concept of scalar context versus list context is very important, you will spend most of your programming time working with arrays rather than with lists. Just remember that an array can always be thought of as a list of scalars. Arrays are the topic of the next chapter.

Summary

In this chapter, you learned about scalar variables, the workhorse of Perl 5's data types. We began with some definitions. A *variable* is a modifiable memory location. A *scalar variable* is a variable that can only contain one item. In Perl 5, that item can be either a string or a numeric value.

Then you learned about string and numeric literals. A *literal* is a constant value in your source code. String literals are created using paired double quotes and forward single quotes. Perl 5 applies variable interpolation to string literals surrounded by double quotes. A string surrounded by back quotes will be treated as a system function call. In addition to the three types of quotes, Perl 5 has four quote operators—q, qq, qx, and qw—which can be used in place of the paired quotation marks.

Numeric literals are numbers in your Perl 5 source code. Numeric literals can be represented in the mathematical notations of integer, real, scientific, hexadecimal, and octal. In addition, large numbers may use the underscore character instead of a comma as a place separator. Perl 5 does not have a Boolean data type, but Boolean numbers can be simulated by treating null and zero values as false and all other values as true.

Next, you learned about variable definition and declaration. A Perl 5 variable is defined by assigning a new variable name a value. Perl 5 variables may be defined or declared at any location in your program. Perl 5 variables are declared using the keywords my and local. A variable declared using the keyword local is visible to subroutines called within the enclosing block. Variables declared using the keyword my are limited in scope to the enclosing block. Using the my keyword, a new instance of the variable is created each time the line of code is executed.

The final topic covered in this chapter was scalar versus list context. Scalar variables can contain only one item. A list or array contains multiple scalar objects. Surrounding scalars with parentheses creates a list. In the next chapter, you will learn the details of building lists and arrays in Perl 5.

CHAPTER

SIX

Arrays and Hashes

- Array cell and list assignment

- The last cell index variable

- Array slice operations

- Perl 5 array functions

- Hash keys and values

- Perl 5 hash functions

If you can't tell by now, let me say it clearly: I'm a big fan of Perl 5. Its easy-to-use data structures are one of the reasons. You can create data anywhere in your program, and you only need to worry about three types of data structures: scalars, arrays, and hashes. In the previous chapter, you learned about scalar data. This chapter covers arrays and hashes. As you'll learn here, even though Perl 5 uses simple data structures, it still provides some of the most powerful array-processing features in programming land.

We'll begin with an introduction to arrays, and then move through the details you need to program with arrays. The second part of the chapter provides similar information about hashes. Also in this chapter, you will start to learn about how Perl 5's built-in functions simplify your life. It includes details about the built-in functions that support arrays and hashes.

An Introduction to Arrays

An *array* is kind of like a shoe organizer in your closet. Remember that I compared a scalar variable to a shoebox that holds one pair of shoes. A shoe organizer holds a lot of shoes. An array holds a lot of scalar variables.

Just as the scalar variable starts with the special character of a dollar sign ($), the array starts with the special character of an "at" sign (@). Arrays follow the same naming conventions as scalar variables (see Chapter 5)—@A, @b1, and @FamilyNames are all valid array names.

Listing 6.1 shows a simple example of scalar data saved into an array and then retrieved from the array. Figure 6.1 shows its output.

Listing 6.1:   **Scalar Data in an Array**

```
1.  #!/usr/local/bin/perl
2.
3.  @FamilyName = ("Steven", "Michael", "Herrmann");
4.
5.  print $FamilyName[0];
6.  print $FamilyName[1];
7.  print $FamilyName[2];
8.  print "\n\n";
9.
10. print "$FamilyName[0] $FamilyName[1] $FamilyName[2]";
```

FIGURE 6.1:

Storing scalar data in an array

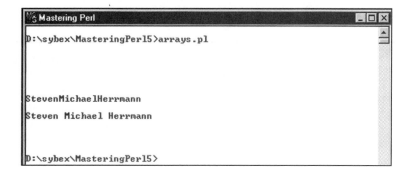

By now, you may have noticed that I like to start with simple examples. Listing 6.1 is a straightforward demonstration of creating an array to hold a full name. On line 3, the array @FamilyName is assigned three string literals: "Steven", "Michael", and "Herrmann". These three string literals make up a list. The list is started by the left parenthesis (() and ended by the right parenthesis ()). A comma separates each item of the list.

Any data type may be part of a list, including scalar variables, other arrays, references, numeric literals, and string literals. The example in Listing 6.1 shows a list of string literals assigned to an array. However, as you will learn in this chapter, assigning a list to an array is only one of the ways to assign data to arrays.

Each array can hold as many scalar variables as your machine's memory and disk space can handle. However, each scalar variable is kept in a separate *cell*. Just like monks in a monastery, one per cell. (I would use jail cells as an analogy, but there are more criminals in one cell at a time.) Each array cell has a unique identifier, or *index*, to reference the scalar data stored within it. An array's scalar values are stored sequentially. The array index identifies the array cell number being accessed.

Like many programming languages, Perl 5 starts counting from zero (0), so the first array cell starts at location 0. To tell Perl 5 that you want to refer to the first element of an array cell, you put square brackets around the cell index; [0] indicates the first cell of an array. As shown on line 5 of Listing 6.1, to access the first array cell of array @FamilyName, you combine the scalar variable name with the array index to get $FamilyName[0]. This accesses the first string literal stored in the array @FamilyName on line 3, which is "Steven".

Lines 5 through 7 and line 14 of Listing 6.1 are accessing the data in the array @FamilyName. The only difference between lines 5 through 7 and line 14 is the printed format of the data. Lines 5 through 7 print exactly what is stored in each array cell. Line 14 adds a space between each cell.

NOTE   An array can contain only scalar values. Perl 5 treats each array cell as a scalar variable. All scalar variables begin with a dollar sign. Hence, using the variable name `FamilyName` with the scalar type indicator (`$`) and the specific cell index zero syntax (`[0]`), you get `$FamilyName[0]`. Scalar variables always begin with a dollar sign, even when you are referring to the scalar value of an array cell.

Just remember that an array is simply a collection of scalar variables, with its own set of special rules for assigning and retrieving the data stored into each cell of the array. That should help you as you learn about the various means of storing data into and retrieving data from Perl 5 arrays.

Array Data Storage and Retrieval

On line 7 of Listing 6.1, you saw the most common means of initializing an array:

```
@FamilyName = ("Steven", "Michael", "Herrmann");
```

This is a list assignment to a Perl 5 array. Although list assignment may be one of the most common methods of building an array, it may not be the easiest to understand. So, rather than starting with an explanation of list assignment, let's begin with array cell assignment. After you see how simple it is to assign data to each cell in an array individually, we can move onto assigning lists to arrays.

Array Cell Assignment

Probably the most straightforward mechanism to store data in an array is array cell assignment. To assign any type of data to an array, all you need to do is identify the cell into which you want to store the data.

You can mix data types in a single array, as shown in Listing 6.2. Figure 6.2 shows the output.

Listing 6.2:   **Mixed Data Assigned to Array Cells**

```
1.  #!/usr/local/bin/perl
2.
```

```
3.  $cellIndex = 0;
4.
5.  $mixedData[$cellIndex] = \@mixedData;
6.  $mixedData[2] = 876;
7.  $mixedData[6] = "The last cell";
8.  $mixedData[4] = 3.41467;
9.
10.
11. foreach $value (@mixedData){
12.     print "Cell number $cellIndex = $value \n";
13.     $cellIndex++;
14. }
15.
16. print "\n\n";
17. print "The last cell of the array mixedData is
            $#mixedData";
18. print "\n\n";
```

FIGURE 6.2:

Assigning data to array
cells

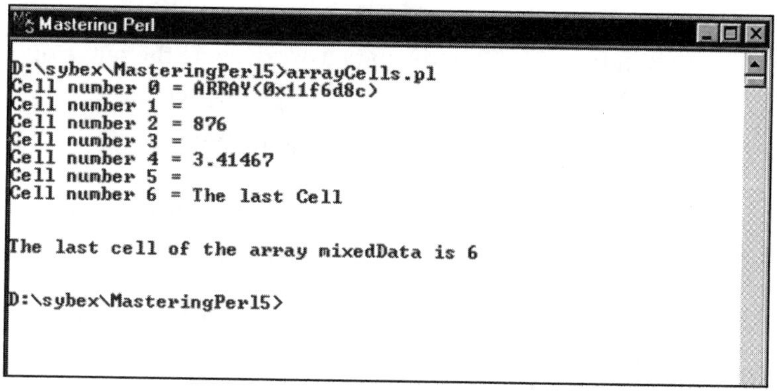

```
Mastering Perl                                          _ □ ×

D:\sybex\MasteringPerl5>arrayCells.pl
Cell number 0 = ARRAY(0x11f6d8c)
Cell number 1 =
Cell number 2 = 876
Cell number 3 =
Cell number 4 = 3.41467
Cell number 5 =
Cell number 6 = The last Cell

The last cell of the array mixedData is 6

D:\sybex\MasteringPerl5>
```

In this listing, the array @mixedData is assigned a reference data type on line 5 (references are covered in the next chapter), a numeric literal on line 6, and a string literal on line 7. Since an array is just a collection of scalar variables, this should not be a surprise to you. If you are coming to Perl 5 from another language, however, this mixing of data types into a single array may take some getting used to.

Try to remember that each array cell is actually a scalar variable. An array is just a convenient means of collecting and referring to a lot of scalar variables using a common naming structure. Since each cell of an array is a scalar variable, each cell is addressed using scalar variable rules. All scalar variables begin with a dollar sign, so the reference to an array cell must begin with a dollar sign. The square brackets ([]) tell Perl 5 it is working with an array, and the cell index identifies exactly which cell in the array is assigned the new value.

In Listing 6.2, notice that the assignment to array cells is neither consecutive nor sequential. As each cell of the array is assigned data, Perl 5 makes space for it. If some cells are skipped between assignments, as illustrated on lines 6 and 7, Perl 5 doesn't complain; it allocates the required numbered of intermediate cells between the last cell defined and the new cell definition. As each intermediate cell is created, it is assigned the value null. Then if you want to store something in one of those intermediate cells, you simply assign data to it, as shown on line 8.

Also notice that adding new cells to an array does not create a problem. Perl 5 extends the array whenever an array cell is added to the end of the array. The dynamic nature of Perl 5 arrays is a very convenient feature that you will learn more about later in this chapter.

Indexes into an array must be numeric. However, you can use scalar variables that contain numeric values. You can also index an array in ranges using the range operator (..). Indexing an array using the range operator is called *slicing*, which also will be covered later in this chapter.

Here are the rules of array cell assignment:

- The syntax of assigning to an array cell is this:

    ```
    $array[cellIndex] = scalar;
    ```

- The value assigned to an array cell must be a scalar or a variable that resolves to a scalar.

- The cell index must be a scalar or a variable that resolves to a scalar. (If the cell index is a range, you are performing array slice assignment and the syntax is different, as explained later in this chapter.)

- The square brackets are required and identify all array assignments.

- The dollar sign ($) takes the place of the at sign (@), because you are performing scalar assignment.

- Assignment to array cells that skip over array cells that have not been assigned initializes all skipped array cells to null.

- Arrays grow in size as new cells are added.

Array List Assignment

Lists and Perl 5 seem to go together. Certainly, using lists to assign data to Perl 5 arrays is a frequent programming task. Lists, like arrays, can be of mixed types. String literals, numeric literals, scalar variables, arrays, array slices, and references are all valid pieces of a single list that can be assigned to an array. All of the data assigned between lines 5 and 8 of Listing 6.2 could be assigned with a single list assignment.

Listing 6.3 shows various ways to assign lists to arrays, and Figure 6.3 illustrates the results.

Listing 6.3: Lists Assigned to Arrays

```perl
1.  #!/usr/local/bin/perl
2.
3.  @mixedData = (\@mixedData,,876,,3.1467,,"The Last Cell");
4.  printArray(@mixedData);
5.
6.  @mixedData = (\@mixedData,'',876,'',3.1467,'',"The Last Cell");
7.  printArray(@mixedData);
8.
9.  @pieces = @mixedData[4..8];
10. printArray(@pieces);
11.
12. @all = @mixedData;
13. printArray(@all);
14.
15. sub printArray {
16.     my @localArray = @_;
17.     $cellIndex = 0;
18.     foreach $value (@localArray){
19.         print "Cell number $cellIndex = $value \n";
20.         $cellIndex++;
21.     }
22.     print "The last cell of the array is $#localArray";
23.     print "\n\n";
24. }
```

Line 3 of Listing 6.3 seems like the most natural approach, but it does not build a six-element array, as did Listing 6.2. Perl 5 recognizes that there is no data between the empty commas and does not create an array cell for the missing data. If you want to create an empty, or null, array cell, you must put quotation marks between each comma, as in line 6 of Listing 6.3, which creates a six-element array. You cannot use a list to create out-of-sequence elements, as you saw on line 8 of Listing 6.2.

FIGURE 6.3:

Assigning lists to arrays

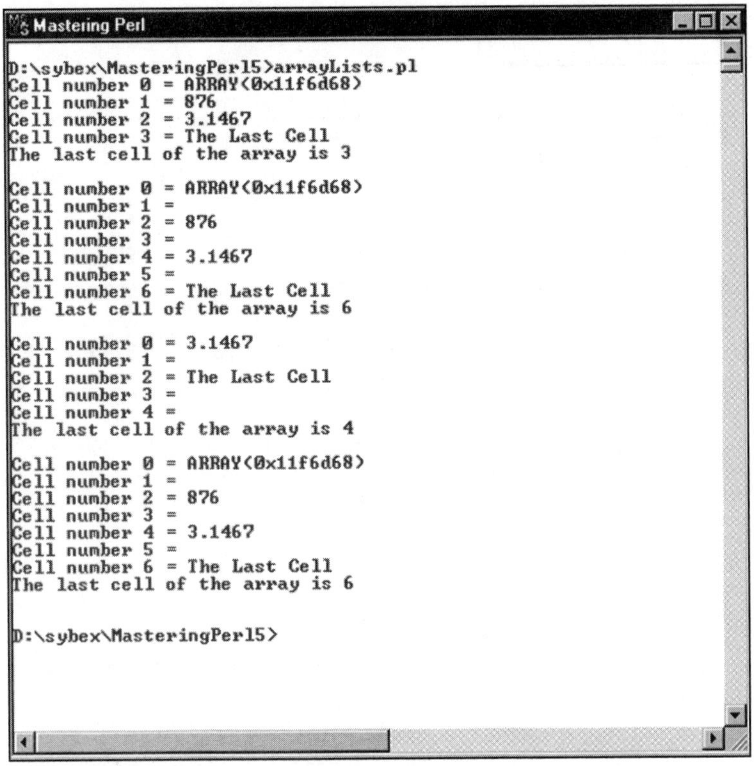

```
D:\sybex\MasteringPerl5>arrayLists.pl
Cell number 0 = ARRAY(0x11f6d68)
Cell number 1 = 876
Cell number 2 = 3.1467
Cell number 3 = The Last Cell
The last cell of the array is 3

Cell number 0 = ARRAY(0x11f6d68)
Cell number 1 =
Cell number 2 = 876
Cell number 3 =
Cell number 4 = 3.1467
Cell number 5 =
Cell number 6 = The Last Cell
The last cell of the array is 6

Cell number 0 = 3.1467
Cell number 1 =
Cell number 2 = The Last Cell
Cell number 3 =
Cell number 4 =
The last cell of the array is 4

Cell number 0 = ARRAY(0x11f6d68)
Cell number 1 =
Cell number 2 = 876
Cell number 3 =
Cell number 4 = 3.1467
Cell number 5 =
Cell number 6 = The Last Cell
The last cell of the array is 6


D:\sybex\MasteringPerl5>
```

Line 9 of Listing 6.3 shows a technique called array slicing. The value on the right side of the equal sign @mixedData[4..8] is a slice of the array @mixedData. The array cells number 4 through 8—five array cells in all—are sliced out of array @mixedData and assigned to array @pieces. Perl 5 counts the number of cells of the slice and creates an array large enough to hold the slice. Even though cells 7 and 8 of the array @mixedData do not exist, Perl creates space for them in the array @pieces, as you can see in Figure 6.3.

The last array assignment on line 12 of Listing 6.3 shows how to copy one array to another array. Perl 5 makes an exact copy of the data in the array on the right side of the assignment statement and puts it into the array on the left side of the assignment operator.

The printing of the arrays is done through a simple subroutine call on lines 4, 7, 10, and 13. Each time the `printArray` subroutine is named, lines 15 through 24 are executed and the array is printed. Subroutines will be covered in detail in Chapter 18.

The rules of array list assignment are as follows:

- You assign a list to an array like this:

    ```
    @array = (1, "string", 4.5, \@arrayZ);
    ```

- You assign an array to an array like this:

    ```
    @array1 = @array2;
    ```

- You assign an array slice like this:

    ```
    @array1 = @array2[1…6];
    ```

- The array grows in size to accommodate the new data.

- Assignments made to existing arrays, as in the example shown below, over-write the original array; `@array1` now contains the same values as `@array2`:

    ```
    @array1 = (1 .. 0);
    @array2 = (11 .. 20);
    @array1 = @array2;
    ```

Array Sizing

The end of an array is defined by the special variable $#*arrayName,* where *array-Name* is the actual array name, such as $#FamilyName, $#pieces, or $#mixedData. This is illustrated on line 17 of Listing 6.2, where the array name is mixedData:

```
print "The last cell of the array mixedData is $#mixedData";
```

This returns the index of the last cell of the named array. The $#*arrayName* variable is referred to as the "last cell index variable" because it is always an index to the last cell of the array.

Variable Name Variety

In introducing the special variable for the last cell index, I used the variable name $#*array-Name*. Later in this chapter, you will see other variable names, such as $#*array*, $*scalar*, and $*scalarSize*, in explanations and examples about retrieving array information.

In most of these cases, I could replace the variable name with the term *lvalue* or consistently use the same variable name throughout the book. However, I think this would be a mistake. A typical beginning programmer misconception is associating a variable name such as $scalar with some special meaning. Also, you might get the idea that a term like *lvalue* actually belongs in your code.

A variable name can be any sequence of characters. You cannot infer anything about the purpose or contents of a variable from its name any more than you can infer anything about a person from his or her name (though you may choose your variable names to help make your code more understandable).

I will use various variable names throughout the book to refer to similar variables. This is not to confuse you, but to make it clear that the variable name, other than the symbols that precede it (such as the $# for the last cell index variable), has no special meaning. Also, in a few cases, I will use the term *lvalue*. However, you should keep in mind that you will never see *lvalue* in any Perl 5 code.

Setting Array Size

If you're dealing with small arrays, Perl 5's ability to add new cells onto the array is a fantastic convenience. However, it can slow down your program if you are building a very large array.

For example, suppose that you are creating a catalog program and need to load a large price list into memory from a file. You could simply load one element of the file into the array at a time. Perl 5 would extend the array as each new element is added. Because it takes a bit of processing each time the array is extended, this turns out to be very slow when working with large arrays. When you know the eventual size of the array you are going to create, you can initialize the size of your array by setting the $#*arrayName* variable.

Let's say you have 3000 items in your catalog. Your price list array will contain 3000 cells. Your program will be more efficient if you initialize your price list array before reading data from a file into the price list array. Initialize the price list array like this:

```
$#priceList=3_000;
```

If the array turns out to be larger, Perl 5 will add new array cells as it needs to. If the array is smaller, you've wasted a little memory, but it only requires one integer's worth of data space for each empty array cell.

Adding Cells to an Array

As you just read, you can set $#*arrayName* to any value, initializing all unassigned array cells up to the last cell index to null. You can also use the last cell index variable as a means of adding cells to the end of an array. Just increment the last cell index before assigning a new value, and your array will grow in size to accept the new value. The syntax for this type of array growth is:

```
$arrayName[++$#arrayName] = $var;
```

or

```
$arrayName[$#arrayName+1] = $var
```

Both operations are equivalent. This is very similar to pushing elements onto your array, which you can do with Perl 5's built-in push function, described later in this chapter.

Deleting Cells from an Array

You can also use the last cell index variable to shrink the size of your array. You can delete cells from the end of an array by decrementing the last cell index, like this:

```
$#arrayName-;
```

If you have a ten-digit array named @digits, like this:

```
@digits = (0 .. 9);
```

and then decrement it, like this:

```
-$#digits;
```

when you access $digits[9], you get the value null. As you decrement the last cell index, each deleted cell is assigned the value null.

If you want to reinitialize an array to all `null` values, set the last cell index to negative one, like this:

```
$#digits = -1;
```

Then the array will be an empty array.

You can also delete elements from the end of an array with the `pop` function or from the middle of an array using the `splice` function, as you'll learn later in this chapter.

Changing the First Cell Index

If you are uncomfortable with Perl's numbering scheme for array cell indexes (the first cell is [0], the second is [1], the third is [2], and so on) or have some special programming need, Perl 5 lets you change the starting number of an array.

The special variable `$[` defines the first index of an array cell. This variable defaults to 0, but it can be set to any number. Each subsequent array cell can be accessed by adding one to the previous array cell's number. Note that regardless of what the first index variable `$[` equals, the last index variable (`$#arrayName`) is always an index to the last cell of the array.

I do not recommend changing the starting array cell index unless you have a strong programming reason to do so. Your code will be difficult for other people to use and understand. Also, if you get used to using a different starting array cell index, you may have a hard time using other programmers' code.

Calculating the Array Size

You can calculate the size of an array using the last cell index variable, with this formula:

```
$#arrayName - $[ + 1;
```

However, there is an easier way. You can create an array in scalar context, like this:

```
$arraySize = @array;
```

The scalar variable `$arraySize` will be assigned the number of elements in the array `@array`, counting from 1.

Array Data Retrieval

When you learned how to assign data to an array cell, you also learned how to retrieve data from an array. The following are the rules of array cell reference:

- Retrieve a single cell of an array in scalar context, like this:

  ```
  $scalar = $array[cellIndex];
  ```

- If you want to retrieve all or part of an array, use list context, like this:

  ```
  @array = @array2[2 .. 4];
  ```

- You can copy a complete array, a contiguous slice of cells, or a random list of cells by referencing an array in list context, like this

  ```
  #Copy an entire array
  @newArray = @oldCopy;
  #Copy an array slice
  @newArray = @oldCopy[5 . . 20];
  #Copy pieces of one array
  @newArray = @oldCopy[0,4,2,10..14,20..24,5];
  ```

As these rules indicate, you can retrieve data from an array in scalar or list context. Be careful to use the correct context. The receiving value, or lvalue, determines context. Use scalar context to retrieve a single element from an array, as noted in the first rule above.

WARNING   Don't forget and use scalar context when you mean list context like this: `$scalar = @array;`. This form retrieves the size of an array, not the contents of an array.

In Chapter 9, you'll learn that retrieving array data in a loop is built into the language. Perl gives you at least three ways to index through an array.

- Process the array in list context:

  ```
  foreach $item (@arrayName) {
      DO STUFF;
  }
  ```

- Index from the front to the rear of the array (as with traditional programming languages):

  ```
  for ($index = 0;
  ```

```
        $index <= $#arrayName;
        $index++) {
    $item = $array[$index];
  }
```

- Index from the end of the array to the front:

```
for ($index = -1;
     $abs ($index)  <= $#array +1;
     $index-;){
  $item = $array [array[index];
}
```

WARNING
If you modify the first cell index variable ($[), your **for** loops must take this into account. Change your loops like this:

```
for ($index = -1;
     $abs($index) <= $array - $[ + 1;
     $index-){
  DO STUFF;
}
```

Array Slices

Not every programming language allows you the convenience of assigning one array to another using one simple statement like @array1 = @array2;. Perl 5 does, of course. The convenience of removing sections, or slices, from an array is even rarer. (Honestly, I'm not familiar with another language that provides this rich programming feature.)

The array slice follows the same rules as an array follows. All slice operations are limited to list context, however. You can reference an individual cell using an array slice, but I don't recommend it.

WARNING
When you code, don't try to be cute or tricky. Write your code to be as self-explanatory as possible. Don't write $var = @array[0]; using slice syntax just because you can. When you're trying to debug your own code months later, you'll appreciate knowing each line of code is written to perform as written, not because of an obscure side effect.

All the rules you learned about assigning and referencing arrays apply to slices, plus the following:

- An array slice is always accessed in list context:

    ```
    @arrayName[listOfScalars];
    ```

- An array slice can be used as an lvalue:

    ```
    @arrayName[@digits]=(11 . . 20);
    ```

- An array slice does not need to reference consecutive elements of an array:

    ```
    @oddNumber = @digits[1,3,5,7,9];
    ```

- An array slice can reference elements out of order:

    ```
    @randomNumbers = @digits[3,0,15,7];
    ```

- You can combine the previous rules creating an array slice using out-of-order lists and elements:

    ```
    $crazySlice[1,20..40,2,0,15,10 ..14] = @digits[0..20, 88, 44, 30 .. 50];
    ```

You can try this last example from your own computer. It works; Perl 5 just drops the cells that don't fit.

Each of the rules of array slices contains a little twist that deserves a bit of explanation. A slice is defined by the use of the at sign (@) and the square brackets ([]). Regardless of the size or content of the list of scalars inside the array index brackets, when you use an array with the at sign and the brackets, you are using an array slice. If the list of scalars contains only one element, Perl treats your array slice as a one-element array.

The list of scalars inside the array index brackets follows the same rules as any list in Perl 5. The list may contain scalars, scalar variables, and arrays—anything that resolves to a scalar value. When an array is used in list context, the array elements become the list and are assigned to the slice using the rules of array assignment. Listing 6.4 shows some examples of assigning array elements to a slice, and Figure 6.4 shows the results.

Listing 6.4:   **Array Elements Assigned to a Slice**

```
1.  @digits = (11..21);
2.  @slice[10..20] = (@digits);
3.  printLine();
4.  print "The contents of the array are: @slice\n";
```

```perl
5.  print "The last index of the array is $#slice.\n";
6.  printLine();
7.
8.  @09 = (0..9);
9.  @slice[@09] = (@digits);
10. print "The contents of the array are: @slice\n";
11. print "The last index of the array is $#slice.\n";
12. printLine();
13.
14. @slice[1,3,5,7,9] = (2,4,6,8,10);
15. @evenNumbers = @slice[1,3,5,7,9];
16. print "The contents of the array are: @evenNumbers\n";
17. print "The last index of the array is $#evenNumbers.\n";
18. printLine();
19.
20. @slice[@digits,77,55,33] = (666,241,42,43,44,45,56,
                                66,67,65,66,67,76,77,888);
21. print "The contents of the array are: @slice\n";
22. print "Indexes 55, 33, 77, and 12 in that order
            are: @slice[55,33,77,12]\n";
23. print "The last index of the array is $#slice.\n";
24.
25. @names = (David, Copperfield, Thomas, Dewey, Steve, Martin,
              Thomas, Jefferson);
26. printNames(@names);
27.
28. for ($i=0; $i<=$#names; $i= $i+2){
29.    @names[$i+1, $i] = @names[$i, $i+1];
30. }
31. printNames(@names);
32.
33. sub printNames (@){
34.    my (@names) = @_;
35.    printLine();
36.    for ($i=0; $i<= $#names;){
37.        print "$names[$i++], $names[$i++]\n";
38. }
39. sub printLine (){
40.    $line = "=" x 80;
41.    print "$line\n";
42. }
43.
44. }
```

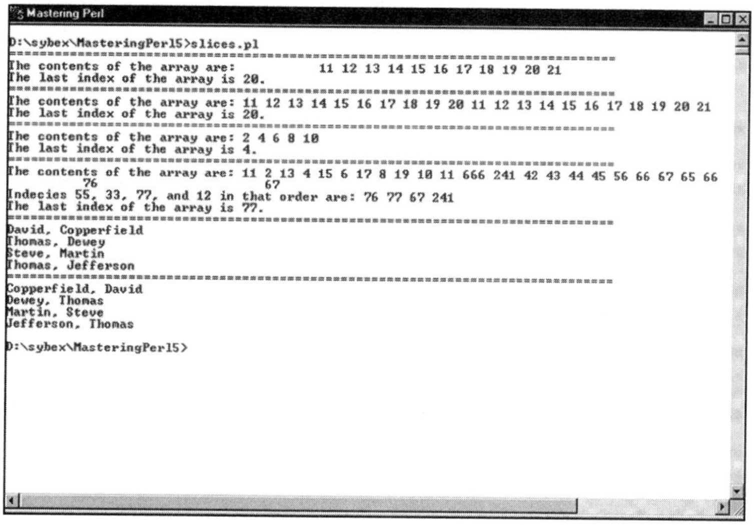

FIGURE 6.4:

Assigning array elements to
a slice

When you use the array inside the array index brackets, the array resolves to a list of scalars. That list of scalars becomes the indices into your array slice. You can see an example of this on line 9 of Listing 6.4, which uses the `@digits` array:

```
@slice[@09] = (@digits);
```

Perl 5 also allows you to reference your slice in nonconsecutive cells in a list, as shown on line 14 of Listing 6.4:

```
@slice[1,3,5,7,9] = (2,4,6,8,10);
```

Each element of the slice is assigned the values in the expression on the right of the assignment operator. If you then use that slice as an assignment to an lvalue, you create a new array that has the contents of that slice. You can see this on line 15 of Listing 6.4, which creates a new array that has the five even numbers of the array slice.

```
@evenNumbers = @slice[1,3,5,7,9];
```

Line 20 of Listing 6.4 illustrates how far Perl 5 allows you to go with slices:

```
@slice[@digits,77,55,33] =
(666,241,42,43,44,45,56,66,67,65,66,67,76,77,888);
```

The array grows in size to the largest index, and the array elements are assigned in the order listed.

If you want to swap array elements, array slice syntax is perfect for the job. For example, the array @names is initialized with a list of first and last names on line 25 of Listing 6.4:

```
@names = (David, Copperfield, Thomas, Dewey, Steve, Martin, Thomas,
Jefferson);
```

If you decide you don't like the way those names are stored in your @names array, you can swap them using array slices. Line 29 of Listing 6.4 swaps the names so the last name is printed before the first name:

```
@names[$i+1, $i] = @names[$i, $i+1];
```

Built-In Functions for Working with Arrays

You already know how to do most of what you'll learn in this section. But just as a power saw has value to the craftsman who knows how to use a handsaw, Perl 5's built-in functions are valuable to a programmer who knows how to perform the tasks manually. The functions you will learn about in this section make your programming life easier. How you use these functions depends on what you need to accomplish with your programs and your personality. Perl gives you freedom of choice, providing a variety of ways to accomplish the same task (and that's why I love this language!). Each of the functions you will learn about in this section comes with the standard distribution of Perl 5.

Stack and Queue Functions

Somewhere near the dawn of programming time, less than 50 years ago, someone thought that an array was like a stack of plates. You added plates to the stack at one end and took them off at the other end. This truly confused me in my introductory database class in college. At our cafeteria, plates were added and removed from the same end of the stack. Now I now that this type of arrangement is actually called an LIFO queue.

A *queue* usually is a list of items to be processed. The key word here is *list*. An array is a list of scalars. So an array can also be thought of as a queue or a stack.

The word *queue* is a British term for line, as in waiting in line. The British are always standing in a queue, not a line. In computer science terms, a queue is very much like a line.

LIFO stands for Last In, First Out. In this type of queue, if you push a plate onto the stack, the first plate that gets taken out of (or popped from) the stack is the plate on top, which was the last one pushed onto the stack.

The other type of queue is called an FIFO queue, for First In, First Out, and is what my database professor was talking about. This is a lot like standing in a line. The person at the front of the line is served first from (or popped from) the line. The person at the end of the line must wait his or her turn, until everyone in front has been served, or popped from the stack.

Processing queues is something you will do a lot of with a language like Perl. Perl provides four functions to help you with processing queues, stacks, or arrays (since they are all the same things). These functions are shift, unshift, pop, and push. For example, you can implement an FIFO queue using the unshift and pop functions. You can implement an LIFO queue using the Perl 5 push and pop functions or the unshift and shift functions. Let's see how each of these functions works.

The push Function

Simply put, push adds an element to the end of an array, like this:

```
push @array, element;
```

The element may be a scalar variable or an array, as shown in the examples that follow. Earlier in the chapter, you learned that you can add an element to the end of an array with the last cell index variable ($#*arrayName*) like this:

```
$array[++$#array] = $var;
```

However, using the built-in function push is more efficient than using the last cell index variable. Also, with push you can add an array onto the end of your array. So something like this becomes possible:

```
@digits09 = (0 .. 9);
@digits1019 = (10 .. 19);
@digits2029 = (20 .. 29);
```

```
push @array, @digits09;
push @array @digits1019;
push @array, @digits2029;
```

The unshift Function

The unshift function performs a similar operation to the push function, using the same syntax. The difference is the unshift function puts its elements into the first cell index of an array ($[]) instead of the last cell index ($#*arrayName*) of the array. Each element that was previously in the array is now moved to the next cell, and its index is one cell index number greater. For example, suppose that you have an array like this:

```
@digits02 = (0..2);
```

which means that:

> 0 is at $digits02[0]
>
> 1 is at $digits02[1]
>
> 2 is at $digits02[2]

and then do this:

```
unshift @digits02, 3;
```

the array elements are in these positions:

> 3 is at $digits02[0]
>
> 0 is at $digits02[1]
>
> 1 is at $digits02[2]
>
> 2 is at $digits02[3]

The unshift function works with arrays just like the push function, except unshift inserts at the front.

```
unshift @digits, (3, 4, 5, 6);
```

The pop Function

The pop function takes elements off the end of an array. It performs the same function as this:

```
$var = $array[$#array-];
```

The last element of the array is removed, and the array is shrunk by one element.

Use pop like this:

```
$var = pop @array
```

You can use pop along with the unshift function to move elements from the end of an array to the front of an array.

NOTE   The pop function has two default conditions. The first default condition works with the @ARGV special variable. The @ARGV special variable contains a list of all of the command-line arguments your program was started with. You'll learn about the @ARGV array and command-line processing in Chapter 11. The other default condition has to do with the special parameter array (@_) and subroutines, which are covered in Chapter 18.

If the array that pop is working on is empty, pop returns undefined. (The value undefined is different from the value null or zero.)

The shift Function

The shift function performs the same operations that pop performs with the same default operators as pop. However, the shift function works on the first index of the array instead of the last index. As with the unshift function, elements are moved toward the first index by one each time the shift function is used. Consider the same array you saw for the unshift function example:

```
@digits02 = (0..2);
```

then:

> 0 is at $digits02[0]
>
> 1 is at $digits02[1]
>
> 2 is at $digits02[2]

If you use shift like this:

```
$digit = shift @digits02;
```

then the element list looks like this:

> 1 is at $digits02[0]

2 is at $digits02[1]

$digits02[2] is undefined and $digit contains the value 0.

NOTE   If no array is specified when shift is called, the shift function operates on the first index of the @ARGV array in package main scope. It operates on the first index of the @_array in subroutine scope. You'll learn more about these operations in Chapters 11 and 18.

Tailoring Directory Searches with the Stack Functions

If you're wondering about some practical uses for the stack functions, and you don't want to wait until later in the book when we get into subroutines and such, I'll give you a quick preview. These functions are useful for working with the @INC array, which is a special variable

built into Perl. The @INC array contains a list of directories for Perl to search in for Perl 5 libraries and for Perl scripts included in your program using the require and use keywords.

If you want to add to the end of the @INC array a local directory you want Perl search in, you can use the push function, like this:

```
use Cwd;
push @INC, cwd();
```

Cwd is a Perl 5 built-in module that contains the function cwd (), which returns the current working directory. It works on both Unix and Windows NT platforms. (The Cwd module is discussed in Chapter 13.)

When I'm testing a modified piece of software that is part of a larger project, I modify the @INC special variable to include my test directory. Perl 5 then looks first in my test directory before it looks in the project directory. For example, if I modify a version of cgi.pm to test for my own needs, I unshift the directory where I keep my modified version cgi.pm into the @INC array. Perl 5 will use the first subroutine it finds when searching the @INC path list, as shown in the following example.

If you have your own version of cgi.pm in a test directory and your web server has cgi.pm in the Perl bin directory, you must modify the @INC array to get Perl to use your version instead of the library version. You can use unshift like this:

```
unshift @INC, "/user/local/test";
```

Continued on next page

Now Perl will look in `user/local/test` before it looks in any other directory during its subroutine search.

The current directory is identified by the special variable dot (`.`). The dot directory is included at the end of the `@INC` array. Because the dot directory is at the end of the `@INC` array, Perl 5 will search the directory you start your Perl 5 programs from last. If you want Perl to look first in the current directory, which is probably the directory you started your program in, you can use the `pop` function, like this:

```
$dotDirectory = pop @INC;
unshift @INC, $dotDirectory;
```

By the way, do you wonder how I know what the `@INC` array contains? You, too, can "see" what is in the `@INC` array, and in every other special variable, simply by writing what I call a test script, like this:

```
print "@INC"
```

Pretty simple, eh?

List Modification with the splice Function

You can use the `splice` function to modify or delete elements from an array. Because you have so many ways to modify elements in an array, you may not use `splice` very often in that mode. You may, however, find `splice` one of the simplest means for deleting elements from a list.

The `splice` function takes a starting cell index, the number of cells to modify, and a list of items to modify in those cell locations. If you omit the list of elements to modify, `splice` removes the number of elements you specify. If you do not give `splice` a number of elements to remove, it removes all of the elements to the end of the array, beginning with the cell index you gave it.

For example, suppose that you want to remove the fifth element of the `@digits` array. You would do this:

```
@digits = (0..9);
splice @digits, 5,1;
```

The array `@digits` now contains 0, 1, 2, 3, 4, 6, 7, 8, 9.

If you want to remove all of the elements after and including the fifth element, do this:

```
@digits = (0..9);
splice @digits, 5;
```

The array @digits now contains 0, 1, 2, 3, 4.

If you want to modify the fifth element in the array, do this:

```
@digits = (0..4, 6..9);
splice @digits, 5, 1, 5;
```

This creates the following list of elements: (0, 1, 2, 3, 4, 5, 7, 8, 9). The fifth element, which was the number 6, is now the number 5.

The splice function does not insert new elements into an array; it only modifies the existing array. The splice function replaces the contents of each cell with the list of elements. However, splice does actually decrease the size of the array if you use it to delete elements.

Array Sorting Functions

Are you familiar with the A-Z sort option in the pull-down menus of various Microsoft Office products? With a mouse click, you can sort your table, row, column, or whatever. Perl 5 provides you with a similar function for your arrays. Like the Microsoft sort utility, the sort function provides a lot more functionality than just sorting arrays. Here, we'll go over some of the basics of the sort function and the reverse function. You'll learn more about sorting in Chapter 15.

The sort Function

You can use the sort function on arrays, like this:

```
@names = (Eric, Tom, James, Pete, Cindy, Carol, Sherry);
@names = sort @names;
```

The @names array is now sorted into the following order: Carol, Cindy, Eric, James, Pete, Sherry, Tom. The sort routine uses the very efficient quick-sort algorithm, which sorts on character strings. This means that you have a problem if you're sorting numbers, but there is a workaround. The solution is to write your own subroutine that sorts numerically, and then tell Perl to sort using your subroutine. Listing 6.5 shows how to sort characters and numbers, and Figure 6.5 shows its output.

Listing 6.5:   **Character and Number Sorts**

```
1.  @names = (Eric, Tom, James, Pete, Cindy, Carol, Sherry, Steven,
               Jessica, Scott);
2.  @names = sort @names;
3.  print "@names\n";
4.  @numbers = (12,45,36,14,258,361,124,2785,1,2,4,);
5.  @numbers = sort @numbers;
6.  print "@numbers\n";
7.  @numbers = sort sortNumbers @numbers;
8.  print "@numbers\n";
9.
10. sub sortNumbers(){
11.    $a <=> $b;
12. }
```

FIGURE 6.5:

Sorting characters and numbers

```
Mastering Perl                                                    _ □ ×
D:\sybex\MasteringPerl5>sorting.pl
Carol Cindy Eric James Jessica Pete Scott Sherry Steven Tom
1 12 124 14 2 258 2785 36 361 4 45
1 2 4 12 14 36 45 124 258 361 2785

D:\sybex\MasteringPerl5>
```

Since sorting is based on character codes, 1 is always less than 2, even when 1 is part of 124 and 2 is all by itself, as you can see in the second line of output in Figure 6.5. Now notice that the last line of output in Figure 6.5 has the numbers sorted numerically. I did this by telling the sort routine to sort based on numbers. To have Perl 5 sort using a different algorithm, I inserted a subroutine between the array and sort, as you can see on line 7 of Listing 6.5:

```
@numbers = sort sortNumbers @numbers;
```

You will need to write the sortNumbers subroutine. You'll learn more about how the sortNumbers subroutine efficiently sorts numbers in Chapter 15, where sorting is discussed in more detail.

The reverse Function

That sort option in Microsoft Office applications also includes a one-click reversing capability. Perl's reverse function works similarly. Just give it the array, and it swaps the indexes. Listing 6.6 demonstrates how to use reverse, and Figure 6.6 shows the output.

Listing 6.6:   **Sorts**

```
1.  @names = (Eric, Tom, James, Pete, Cindy, Carol, Sherry, Steven,
              Jessica, Scott);
2.  @names = reverse @names;
3.  print "@names\n";
4.  @numbers = reverse @numbers;
5.  print "@numbers\n";
6.  $names = reverse @names;
7.  print "$names\n";
8.  sub sortNumbers(){
9.      $a <=> $b;
10. }
```

FIGURE 6.6:

Reversing the order

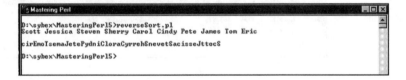

Notice in Figure 6.6 that reverse also works in scalar context. In this context, the order of each cell in the array is not reversed, just the contents of each cell are reordered. Each name has been reversed—*Carol* become *loraC*, *Scott* becomes *ttocS*, and so on. The function reverse in scalar context reverses each element of the array or string and returns one string, which is stored into the scalar lvalue.

An Introduction to Hashes

Even more amazing than the manipulations you can make with Perl 5 arrays is what you can do with Perl 5 hashes. Hashes are cool. In other languages, I have had to build pseudo hashes when I wanted the simplicity of data access that hashes allow. (Java contains a hash data object, but Perl 5 had it first.) The more you work with Perl 5, the more you'll come to love, admire, and depend on the hash data structure.

You'll start your relationship with hashes in this chapter, learning how to work with key/value pairs using the `keys`, `values`, and `each` functions. Your relationship with hashes will continue throughout this book. Hashes are the primary data structure for CGI data objects, and they are a natural data structure for many business applications.

NOTE   In older Perl literature, you may see hashes referred to as *associative arrays*. I like the term associative array, because it's more descriptive of how a hash works. A hash associates a string literal with a value. It's like a two-dimensional array, but the indexes are in English. The Perl community has accepted the term hash, so throughout the book, I will also use the term hash.

Hash is a computer term used to describe a mechanism for efficiently storing and retrieving values in a sparse array. A *sparse array* is an array that may have indexes from one to a million but contains only a small number of actual values. A hash table uses an algorithm (a function) to determine the index of where to store or retrieve a data value. The idea is to produce a unique index to identify the value's storage location in a potentially large but sparsely populated array. Since Perl 5 hides all the algorithm stuff so you don't need to deal with it, I won't say any more. Suffice it to say that a hash is really a hash table, and a hash table has a key for looking up the address of where the data associated with that key is stored.

As you've learned in this chapter, in regular arrays, this key is called an index, and indexes are sequential values used to access the contents of the array's cells. With hashes, the index is called a *key* and it is linked to the value associated with it. These keys and values are referred to as *key/value* pairs. Like arrays, hashes are dynamically created, but hashes do not have a last cell index variable as do regular arrays. The mechanisms for declaring hashes, using `my` and `local`, are the same as previously described for declaring variables in general (in Chapter 5). The mechanisms for storing and retrieving data using key/value pairs are different from those used with regular arrays, as explained in the next section.

Hash Data Storage and Retrieval

One of the key differences between hashes and regular arrays is the way that they store and retrieve values. Values are retrieved from a regular array using a numeric index. Each value of a regular array can be retrieved sequentially. You cannot retrieve your data from a hash sequentially. Remember that a hash uses some type of algorithm to determine where in the array is the best place to store the data. This algorithm is supposed to guarantee quick access and efficient data storage, which Perl 5 hashes provide, but it does not use sequential storage.

Hash Keys

Since keys are the way that data is stored into hashes, that is the first thing you should learn about. A hash key is any literal that is convenient for you to use to look up your value. Usually, hash keys are string literals. If you are building an inventory, you might want to use descriptive names or serial numbers as your hash keys. Listing 6.7 demonstrates initializing hashes using lists. The output is shown in Figure 6.7.

Listing 6.7: **Hash List Assignment**

```
1.  #!/usr/local/bin/perl
2.  print "\n\n";
3.
4.  %priceList = (
5.      "Hackamore"=>28.92,
6.      "English Bridle"=>36.31,
7.      "Western Saddle"=>124.00,
8.      "Hunt Seat Saddle"=>178.01,
9.      "Jumping Saddle"=>205.87,
10.     "Leather Halter"=>24.56,
11. );
12. printAA(%priceList);
13.
14. print "You could print a hash cell like this $priceList{'Western
    Saddle'}\n";
15.
16. %priceList = (
17.     1358=>28.92,
18.     1359=>36.31,
19.     1965=>124.00,
20.     1966=>178.01,
21.     1977=>205.87,
22.     1357=>24.56,
23. );
```

```
24.
25. print "Or like this $priceList{1965} \n\n";
26.
27. printAA(%priceList);
28. sub printAA {
29.     my %myPriceList = @_;
30.
31.     foreach $key (keys(%myPriceList)){
32.         print "The price of item $key is $priceList{$key}\n";
33.     }
34.     print "\n\n";
35. }
```

FIGURE 6.7:

Assigning hash keys

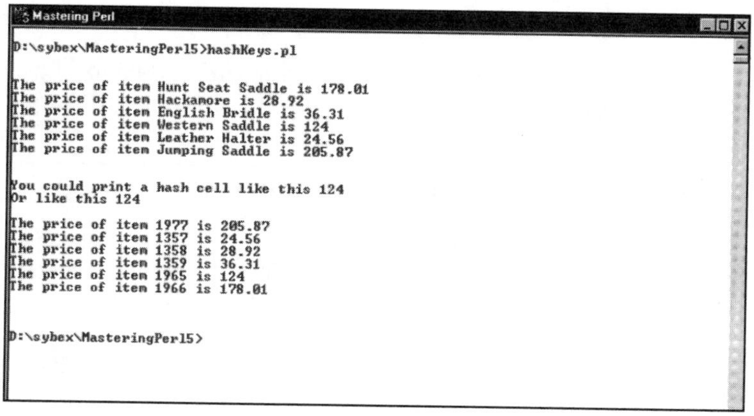

Each key is associated with a value when assigning data to a hash. The key is the item on the left of the associative operator (=>), and the value is on the right side. Lines 5 through 10 in Listing 6.7 illustrate using string literals as keys. For example, line 5 has the statement:

```
"Hackamore"=>28.92,
```

The key in this list assignment is "Hackamore" and the value is 28.92.

Lines 17 through 22 of Listing 6.7 illustrate using numeric literals as keys. For example, line 17 has the statement:

```
1358=>28.92,
```

The key in this list assignment is 1358 and the value is 28.92.

Very quickly, you should notice some of the similarities and differences between hashes and regular arrays. (I always hate it when an author implies I should be able to figure out something in the text and I am clueless; I hope you don't take offense here.) First, all hashes begin with a percent sign (%), as illustrated on lines 4, 12, 14, 16, 25, and 31 of Listing 6.7, just like all regular arrays begin with the at sign (@).

Next, notice on line 28 that the value of a hash cell is retrieved by a scalar variable that begins with a dollar sign ($), just like with regular arrays. Perl 5 distinguishes between references to regular array cells and hash cells by the different characters surrounding the cell index. Hashes use curly braces ({ }) around the array key, as in $*arrayName*{"*key*"}. Remember that regular arrays use square brackets ([]) around the cell array index, as in $*arrayName*[$*index*]. Line 31 uses the built-in keys function, which you'll learn about a little later in the chapter.

A more common means of assigning string data to a hash is by using a variable as the key. Listing 6.8 demonstrates this approach.

Listing 6.8:   **Hash Variable Assignment**

```
1.   sub readPostInput(){
2.       my (%searchField, $buffer, $pair, @pairs);
3.       if ($ENV{'REQUEST_METHOD'} eq 'POST'){
4.           # How many bytes are we supposed to receive?
5.           read(STDIN, $buffer, $ENV{'CONTENT_LENGTH'});
6.           # make a list of keyword/value pairs
7.           @pairs = split(/&/, $buffer);
8.           # cycle through each pair and decipher the values
9.           foreach $pair (@pairs)
10.              # get the name/value pair strings
11.              ($name, $value) = split(/=/, $pair);
12.              # translate "+" to a space
13.              $value =~ tr/+/ /;
14.              # decipher ASCII hexadecimal escaped
15.              $value =~ s/%([a-fA-F0-9][a-fA-F0-9])/
                          pack("C", hex($1))/eg;
16.              $searchField{"$name"} = $value;
17.              #   print "val = $value name = $name <br>";
18.          }
19.      }
20.      return (%searchField);
```

```
21. }
22. return 1;
23.
```

Lines 3, 5, and 16 use hashes to retrieve and store information. For example, line 16 looks like this:

```
$searchField{"$name"} = $value;
```

The rules for assigning values to hash cells, listed below, are similar to those for array cell assignments, which you learned earlier in this chapter.

- The syntax of hash cell assignment is:

    ```
    $hash{key} = scalar;
    ```

- The dollar sign identifies the assignment as scalar.

- The curly braces identify the assignment to a hash.

- The key may be a numeric or string literal or a scalar variable.

- If the key resolves to a string literal that includes spaces, the string literal must be surrounded by quotation marks.

- Only scalars may be assigned to a hash cell.

- The syntax of hash list assignment is:

    ```
    %hash = (key/value pair list)
    ```

- The percent sign is required in hash list assignment.

- The parentheses are required around the key/value pair list.

- The key/value pair list is a comma-separated list. Each key is an index into the hash and must be associated with a value.

- Perl 5 uses the associative operator (=>) as a convenience operator in place of the comma. This allows key/value pairs to be written like *key=>value* instead of the equivalent *key, value*.

Hash Value Retrieval

As explained earlier, you cannot retrieve the values stored in your hash in the same sequential order in which they were stored in the array. Look back to

Listing 6.7. Notice that the same data is stored into the same array in the same order in lines 5 through 10 and lines 17 through 22. Now notice that when that data is printed in Figure 6.7, the values are not printed in the same order in which they were stored. Finally, notice that the values of the array stored with string literal keys are retrieved in one order and the values stored with numeric keys are retrieved in a different order.

The primary reason hashes are so popular in Perl 5 is the easy and intuitive access to the data. For example, retrieving catalog prices by product name or serial number is much easier than creating some artificial association between a numeric index of a regular array and a product name or serial number.

The same basic rules for storing and retrieving data you learned about in the regular arrays section generally apply to hashes. In short, to retrieve a value from a hash, you use this syntax:

```
$hashName{"key"}
```

Built-In Functions for Working with Hashes

Keeping track of your hash keys can be a pain in the neck. So, in its usual helpful way, Perl 5 provides several convenient functions that allow you to easily get at the keys and values of hashes.

Key Retrieval Functions

You have already seen one of Perl's key retrieval functions in Listing 6.7. The keys function takes a hash and returns a list of the keys or indexes in the hash. The values function operates exactly like the keys function, except that it returns all of the values of a hash. In order to keep the example simple and focused on the functions, Listing 6.9 uses the same array as Listing 6.7 to demonstrate the keys and values hash-processing functions. Figure 6.8 shows the output.

Listing 6.9:   **Hash Key and Value Retrieval**

```
1.  #!/usr/local/bin/perl
2.  print "\n";
```

```
3.
4.   %priceList = (
5.        "Hackamore"=>28.92,
6.        "English Bridle"=>36.31,
7.        "Western Saddle"=>124.00,
8.        "Hunt Seat Saddle"=>178.01,
9.        "Jumping Saddle"=>205.87,
10.       "Leather Halter"=>24.56,
11.  );
12.
13.  @keyList = keys %priceList;
14.
15.  print "@keyList";
16.
17.  foreach $index (keys(%myPriceList)){
18.      print "The price of item $key is $priceList{$index}\n";
19.  }
20.
21.  print "\n\n";
22.  foreach $key (@keyList){
23.      print "The price of item $key is $priceList{$key}\n";
24.  }
25.
26.  @valueList = values %priceList;
27.
28.  print "\n";
29.  print "@valueList";
30.
```

FIGURE 6.8:

Retrieving hash keys and values

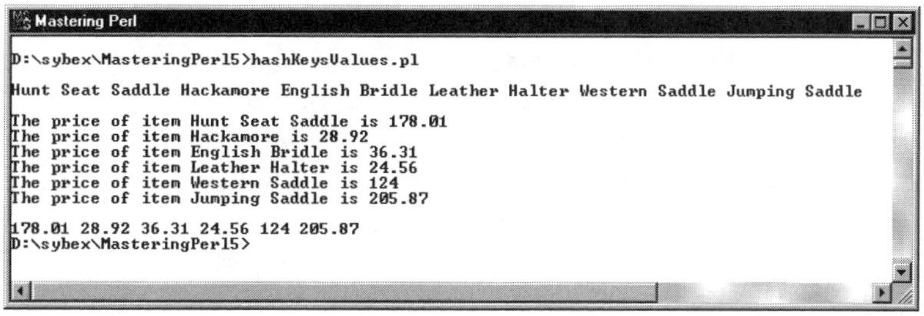

The keys Function

The keys function is used on line 13 of Listing 6.9:

```
@keyList = keys %priceList;
```

I have left out the parentheses I usually use after the keys function to illustrate that the parentheses are not required. You can use the keys function with parentheses, like this:

```
@list = keys(%hash);
```

Or without parentheses, like this:

```
@list = keys %hash;
```

Since the keys function returns a list, that list can be stored into an array for later use, such as printing it (line 15 of Listing 6.9). Usually, the list returned by the keys function is processed in some type of loop and is never stored into an array. The foreach loop on lines 17 through 19 of Listing 6.9 is a common usage of the keys function:

```
foreach $index (keys(%myPriceList)){
    print "The price of item $key is $priceList{$index}\n";
}
```

In the foreach statement, the keys function is executed first, and only once, returning a list. The list is then processed one element at a time by the foreach statement. Although this is the way you will normally use a foreach statement in your code, the foreach loop on lines 22 through 24 is a better illustration of what is actually happening:

```
foreach $key (@keyList){
    print "The price of item $key is $priceList{$key}\n";
}
```

On line 22, you can see the list of keys or indexes retrieved back on line 13 of the hash, %priceList, explicitly being processed. Each cell of the array @keyList is accessed and stored iteratively into the variable $key. Then the key into the hash %priceList is used on line 23 as both an identifier, in English, as to what the value in the hash %priceList is ($key) and as an identifier, in Perl, as an index or key into the hash %priceList ($priceList{$key}).

You'll learn more about the foreach statement in Chapter 9. The thing you need to remember about the keys function is that it returns a list of all of the keys or indexes into the hash.

The values Function

The syntax of the values function is:

```
values %hash;
```

The list returned from the values function is in exactly the same order as the list returned from the keys function.

Line 26 of Listing 6.9 illustrates the use of the values function:

```
@valueList = values %priceList;
```

The values function returns the contents, or values, of the hash cell. In our example, if you weren't interested in the item but just wanted a total of the inventory value, you could use the values function to iterate over your inventory to get a total inventory value, like this:

```
@priceList = values %priceList;
foreach (@priceList){
   $total += $_;
}
```

NOTE The $_ variable is one of the many Perl 5 special variables you will learn about in this book. The $_ variable is the default source and destination variable for several system functions and operations. In this case, $_ takes the place of the lvalue argument of the **foreach** statement.

The each Function

The each function returns a single key/value pair, unlike the keys and values functions, which return a list of all of the keys or all of the values of the hash, respectively.

Both the keys and the values functions return a complete list of all the hash keys or values. If your hash is an inventory of a million or more items, that list can use a significant chunk of your computer's memory.

The each function, on the other hand, allows you to iterate through a hash one key/value pair at a time. You may also find it easier to use because it returns both the key and the value in one step. Listing 6.10 demonstrates the use of the each function.

Listing 6.10:   **Hash Key-Value Pair Retrieval**

```
1.  $separator = "=" x 80;
2.  while (($key, $value) = each %ENV){
3.      print "$key \t\t==> $value\n";
4.  }
5.  print "$separator\n";
6.  foreach $key (sort keys %ENV){
7.      print qq|$key \t\t==> $ENV{"$key"}\n|;
8.  }
```

The each statement can be used in a loop, as shown on line 2 of Listing 6.10:

```
while (($key, $value) = each %ENV){
```

The loop will terminate at the end of processing the hash because each returns a null list when the list is completely read. If you contrive to use the each function after the null list is returned, each will start processing the hash all over again, beginning with the first key/value pair in the hash. You'll learn more about while loops in Chapter 9.

The each function iterates through the entire list, starting from the first element and moving to the next element after each subsequent call. The keys, values, and each functions all share the same index to traverse the hash and return the hash in exactly the same order. This means a call to keys or values has an impact on the each function. The each function processes through the entire hash unless the hash index is reset by calling either the keys or values function on the hash that the each function is currently processing.

I included lines 6 through 8 of Listing 6.10 to illustrate processing a hash in a sorted order:

```
foreach $key (sort keys %ENV){
    print qq|$key \t\t==> $ENV{"$key"}\n|;
}
```

You learned how the sort and reverse functions work with arrays earlier in this chapter. You can also use them with hashes to create an alphabetical or a numerically sorted list.

Item Removal with the delete Function

Now that you've got your hash built, how do you remove items from the hash? Suppose that you did something like this:

```
$Inventory{'OLD PRODUCT'} = NULL;
```

Although this sets the key to null, it does not delete the item OLD PRODUCT from the %Inventory hash.

The only way to remove items from a hash is to use the delete function, like this:

```
delete $Inventory{'OLD PRODUCT'};
```

Now the item referenced by the key 'OLD PRODUCT' does not exist in the %Inventory hash. The delete function removes the key 'OLD PRODUCT', as well as any values referenced by 'OLD PRODUCT' from the hash.

Item Verification with the exists Function

You can tell if an item exists in a hash by using the exists function. Even if the key references a null value, the exists function will return true if the key is part of the hash. You use exists like this:

```
$result = exists $hash{$key}
```

For example, to check on an inventory item, do this:

```
$inTheInventory = exists $Inventory{'OLD PRODUCT'};
```

You can also use exists in an if conditional expression, like this:

```
if (exists $Inventory{'OLD PRODUCT'}){
   block of statements;
}
```

You'll learn about using if conditional statements in Chapter 8.

Summary

In this chapter, you learned that arrays are lists. The principle thing you want to remember about arrays is their sequential data-storage structure.

Perl 5 provides a multitude of ways for you to manipulate arrays. The built-in functions push, pop, shift, and unshift add and remove elements from either end of an array. Perl 5 also provides the splice, sort, and reverse functions, giving you a variety of built-in functions for manipulating the internals of arrays.

Arrays should be used for sequential data storage, but when you want to store something using a familiar name, the hash should be your choice. As you become familiar with the hash structure, you'll wonder how you ever did without it. (Luckily, I'm coding in either Perl or Java now, so I've always got the hash handy, but I don't know what I'll do on my next C++ project.)

Perl 5 distinguishes between hash and array cells based on the characters you place around the cell index. Hash cells are indexed using curly braces ({}), and array cells are indexed using square braces ([]).

The hash stores its scalar data using a lookup key. Perl 5 supplies the keys, each, and values functions to help you retrieve your data from a hash. The utility functions delete and exist let you remove keys and determine if a key already is part of a hash, respectively.

Both the hash and the array structures can store only scalar objects and are always one-dimensional arrays. The world is not one-dimensional and neither are most programming problems. In the next chapter, you'll learn about Perl 5 references, which really unleash the power of Perl 5. References depend on arrays and hashes to provide the foundation to solve complex problems, and they are frequently used to create multi-dimensional hashes and arrays.

CHAPTER
SEVEN

7

References

- Symbolic references

- Direct references

- Dereferencing techniques

- Multi-dimensional arrays

- Anonymous references

The reference data type is one of the new features in Perl 5. In the old days before references, creating multi-dimensional arrays and data structures that contained other data structures in Perl was difficult. This new ability to support complex data objects via references may be more important than the efficiency of references. The addition of complex data objects to Perl promotes it from a first-class text-processing language to a world-class language capable of solving both large and small problems. In my opinion, references are the single most important change to Perl in many years.

Creating references may be relatively straightforward, but using references can be confusing. This chapter will help you to understand how to use references properly.

An Introduction to References

A *reference* keeps track of where a variable is stored in memory. A reference can keep track of any type of variable—simple scalars, arrays, hashes, file handles, subroutines, and even literals that act like constants. Each reference variable takes up only a single address space in your computer and can keep track of where large lists of objects are stored in memory.

NOTE   If you are coming to Perl 5 from another language, such as C, you might be familiar with the term *pointer*. If you have looked at some other books about Perl, you may have seen mention of a *thingy*. Both pointer and thingy are other names for a reference.

When you create a regular variable, you are actually creating a storage location for a piece of data. This is a lot like getting a storage container from the kitchen cabinet to save some leftovers. The storage container for your leftovers may be a baggie, a bowl, or something larger. You can think of choosing the appropriate storage container type as declaring a scalar variable, hash, or regular array. You can think of removing that storage container from the kitchen cabinet as taking a container variable from the computer's memory.

Next, you put your leftovers in the container. This is the same as assigning some data to a variable, like this:

```
$baggie = "peas";
```

Finally, you put the storage container into the refrigerator. Later, you will get the storage container back from the fridge to study mold spores for a science project.

The difference between a regular variable and a reference variable is what is stored in a reference variable. A reference variable does not store peas like the storage container in our analogy. Instead, a reference variable stores the location of where the storage container with peas in it is stored.

This may not make a lot of sense in your fridge. You know exactly where the peas storage container is hiding in your refrigerator. But consider a large warehouse where you are storing a lot of different storage containers. A separate storage container that tells you where each storage container is located would be helpful.

Now consider the case where you need to inventory everything in the warehouse. If you had something that you could pass to different employees that told them where each different storage container was located, you could delegate and organize your inventory procedure. Employees who know about peas are given the list of where all the different peas are located. The peas employees go do the peas inventory. Employees who know about meat get a list of where all the meat is stored, and they go do the meat inventory.

Are you beginning to wonder what peas and meat have to do with references? Well, here is the answer: It is a lot more efficient to pass around a list of where things are to the people or subroutines that specialize in that area than to pass the entire contents of the stored inventory. References act like lists of where things are stored in memory. Passing references to subroutines that specialize in peas inventory is more efficient than passing the entire inventory to the subroutine.

References can be simply addresses of where a single scalar variable like $baggie is stored in memory, or they can refer to subroutines, arrays, and hashes, which may contain references also referring to other arrays, hashes, or subroutines.

Continuing with our food storage analogy, you could create an array where each cell contains a vegetable you want to have in your warehouse. This array could be a hash indexed by the vegetable type or a regular array indexed by the number of the items stored. Your array could even contain the locations of all of the lists of where everything is stored in the warehouse—a kind of list of lists.

To sum up, a reference keeps track of where a variable is stored in memory. A reference can keep track of any type of variable. A reference variable is always a scalar variable that contains the address of another object. A reference variable takes up a single address space in your computer, whether it's storing the location of a single scalar variable or the location of a large list of objects.

Reference Operators

You create a reference variable whenever you use the "address-of" operators: \,
[], {}, sub {;}, and bless. (The operator bless is a special case and isn't strictly
a reference operator.) Table 7.1 shows the different ways to create references.

TABLE 7.1: Perl 5 Reference Assignments

Data Type	Operator	Example
Scalar	\$var	$car = \$Porsche;
Array	\@array	$allStores[$number] = \@store-Inventory;
Hash	\%hash	$storeType = \%stores;
File handle	*FILEHANDLE	$inputReference = *STDIN;
Constant	\literal	$pi = \3.414;
Subroutine	\&subRoutine	$callBack = \&numericSort;
Symbolic	\$variableName	$var ="var2"; $var2Ref = \$var;
Anonymous array	[LIST]	$colors = ["RED", "BLUE", "GREEN"];
Anonymous hash	{List of name/value pairs}	$hexCodes = {RED=>0XFF0000, GREEN=>0X00FF00, BLUE=>0X0000FF};
Anonymous subroutine	sub {};	$hitCounter = sub {print "This page has been called $hits times";};
Object reference	bless $self;	sub new {self ={}; bless $self; return $self; }

Types of Reference Variables

There are six variations of reference variables, determined by the type of address
stored into the reference variable:

- Direct reference
- Constant reference

- Subroutine reference

- Symbolic reference

- Anonymous reference

- Object reference

References allow Perl 5 to extend arrays to contain references to other references. This mechanism is often used to create complex data structures—in particular, array cells that refer to other arrays.

Technically, Perl 5 doesn't have multi-dimensional arrays. However, by allowing you to construct arrays that contain references to other arrays, you can achieve an effect that is the same (or very similar to) multi-dimensional arrays. You'll explore the use of multi-dimensional arrays later in the chapter, after you learn about using simpler reference structures.

Direct Reference Variables

Direct reference variables refer directly to other variables, including scalar, array, hash, file handle, and other reference variables. Direct reference variables can modify the contents of the variable they refer to, and the contents of the reference variable may also be modified. A direct reference uses the backslash operator (\).

Direct reference variables are the most commonly used reference method. You'll learn the details of creating these types of variables in this chapter.

Constant Reference Variables

Constant reference variables also use the Perl 5 backslash operator, but they refer to literals rather than variables. You can modify the constant reference variable (an oxymoron, if I've ever seen one), but you cannot modify the literal referred to by the constant reference variable. Literals are normally kept in a special, protected portion of computer memory. For example, only one copy of the literal 10 is kept in computer memory, and you are not allowed to modify the value of 10.

NOTE   The computer term for a variable that is modifiable is *mutable*. All Perl 5 variables are mutable. The constant reference variable is the closest Perl 5 comes to an immutable variable, which is a variable that is not modifiable.

Subroutine Reference Variables

Subroutine reference variables are a hybrid of the direct reference variable and the constant reference variable. You cannot use the subroutine reference variable to modify the subroutine referred to by the subroutine reference variable. However, you can modify the subroutine itself. When creating a subroutine reference variable, you must use the ampersand (&) operator to tell Perl 5 you are referencing a subroutine instead of a literal. You'll explore the methods for creating subroutine references in Chapter 18.

Symbolic Reference Variables

Symbolic reference variables are unique to Perl 5 (at least, in my experience). The symbolic reference variable is a variable that contains the literal name of another variable. You use the backslash operator with the variable name to assign a symbolic reference to it. This mechanism is a little bit tricky, which means that it's prone to creating errors in your code. As demonstrated in Listing 7.1, by using symbolic reference variables, you can create a variable without first defining or declaring it!

Listing 7.1:   References

```
1.  $color = "red";
2.  $$color = 0xFF0000;
3.  print "$red\n";
4.  $color = "blue";
5.  $$color = 0x0000FF;
6.  print "$blue\n";
7.  $color = "green";
8.  $$color = 0x00FF00;
9.  print "$green\n";
```

Listing 7.1 assigns the literal "red" to the scalar variable $color. On the next line, the scalar variable $color is treated as a reference variable, storing the hex value 0xFF0000 into the variable referred to by color. You might have observed that the scalar $color does not contain a reference to a variable; it contains the string "red". This observation, though true on line 1 of Listing 7.1, is false once the scalar variable is treated as a reference on line 2. The string referred to by $color becomes defined as a variable as soon as it is used as a variable.

In Perl 5, when a variable is used, it springs into existence. In this case, $$color treats the value contained in $color as a variable, so it is a variable, as demonstrated on line 3. Line 3 prints the value contained in the variable $red, 0xFF0000, which is the hex value that represents red for your computer. The remaining lines of Listing 7.1 repeat the act of creating scalar variables from scalars that contain strings.

In Perl 5, a symbolic reference occurs when you dereference a scalar variable that contains a string. The string may be the name of an existing variable or may become a new variable when referenced. Dereferencing is explained shortly.

Anonymous Reference Variables

Anonymous reference variables allow you to create references to objects that are never given names. These objects are also called orphaned objects. Anonymous reference operators ([], {}, and sub{;}) are context sensitive; they only create references when assigning a value to a scalar variable. The anonymous subroutine operator (sub{;}) requires an ending semicolon inside the subroutine definition. The anonymous subroutine reference works because Perl 5 treats the reference as single statement with a particular location in memory. You'll learn more about anonymous arrays and hash references later in this chapter.

Object Reference Variables

Object reference variables are really nothing more than anonymous hash references. Perl 5 provides the bless operator, which creates a link between the reference object and the class the object is created within. (*Classes* are packages that contain related subroutines, called *methods*.) An object reference variable is usually created in a subroutine called new, like this:

```
sub new {
    $self = {}; # create an anonymous hash
    bless $self; # link the hash to the class
    return $self; # return a reference to the hash
}
```

You'll explore the methods for creating object references in Chapter 19.

Direct References and Dereferencing

You learned about the scalar, array, and hash data structures in the previous chapters. As mentioned earlier, direct references to these structures are the most commonly used types of references. The following sections explain how to use direct scalar, array, and hash references.

Direct Scalar References

As usual, you'll begin your exploration of this topic with a straightforward example. Listing 7.2 demonstrates references to scalar variables, which are the simplest form of references. The code in Listing 7.2 creates references to standard HTML tags and attributes and then uses those tags to create an HTML file.

Listing 7.2:   **Direct Scalar References**

```
1.  $title = "Reference Color";
2.  $bodyColor = "FF0000";
3.  $HTMLHead = "<html> <head> <title> $title </title> </head>";
4.  $HTMLBodyColor="<body bgcolor=$bodyColor>";
5.  $headReference = \$HTMLHead;
6.  $bodyReference = \$HTMLBodyColor;
7.  open (OUTFILE, ">refColor.html");
8.  print OUTFILE <<eof;
9.  $$headReference
10. $$bodyReference
11.
12. <test>
13. </body>
14. </html>
15. eof
16. close(OUTFILE);
```

The direct scalar references are created on lines 5 and 6 of Listing 7.2:

```
$headReference = \$HTMLHead;
$bodyReference = \$HTMLBodyColor;
```

Each reference is created by assigning the location in memory of another object to a scalar variable. That's easy enough. Now let's see how to retrieve the values referred to by the direct scalar references.

Accessing values of the variables referred to by references, called *dereferencing*, is demonstrated on lines 9 and 10 of Listing 7.2:

```
$$headReference
$$bodyReference
```

To get at the value in memory that a reference variable is ultimately referring to, you must tell the Perl 5 interpreter to look where the container of the memory is located. You must tell Perl 5 to look at the address contained in the reference variable as the container of the value.

The simple rule is that each dollar sign is a container of a value. Perl 5 interprets the dollar sign from right to left or from inside to outside in a simple machinelike manner. Each time it sees a dollar sign, it treats the object to the right of the dollar sign as a container of a value. For example, the reference `$$headReference` on line 9 of Listing 7.2 is read by the interpreter in two steps:

1. Perl 5 starts at the rightmost, or innermost, dollar sign. It tells Perl 5 the following object is a container of a value. Perl 5 fetches the value in the object `$headReference`, which is an address.

2. Perl 5 sees that the second object also has a dollar sign. This means that the object is also a container of a value. Perl 5 has already retrieved the first object's value, which was the address. Since the first object contained a second object (the address) that was a container of a value, Perl 5 fetches the value contained (or pointed to) in the first object (the address) it fetched.

This may sound like circular logic, and in a sense it is. This process can actually go on indefinitely. In step 1, Perl 5 retrieves the value of the first container object. In step 2, Perl looks to see if it has anything else to do. If the retrieved value is identified as a container object (by a dollar sign), then Perl 5 repeats step 1.

The following are some more examples of reference assignments and some dereferencing values:

```
$variable = "ANYTHING";
$reference =\$variable;
Dereference
print "$$reference";
yields "ANYTHING";

REPEAT 1 AND ADD
$doublereference =\$reference;
Dereference
print "$$$doubleReference";
yields "ANYTHING"

REPEAT 2 AND ADD
$tripleReference = \$doublereference;
Dereference
```

```
print "$$$$tripleReference";
yields "ANYTHING"
```

I hope you're yawning by now. The third example may look complex, but just take one container at a time, and you have the answer.

There are not many variations on this theme. If you have created a reference to a scalar variable, treat it like a variable and use the dollar sign ($) to dereference it.

Direct Array References

Direct array references are created in the same manner as direct scalar references, except that they assign the address of an array, like this:

```
$reference=\@array;
```

Dereferencing is just as simple:

```
print "@$reference";
```

Perl 5 starts on the rightmost, or innermost variable, and retrieves it. It then looks to see if it should repeat this operation. In the case of a direct array reference, you have told it that the value it just retrieved is the address of an array by placing the at sign (@) before the variable value, so it goes and retrieves the array. Try it yourself by creating an array, saving it into a reference variable, and then printing it, like this:

```
@array = ("1","2","3","4");
$arrayRef = \@array;
print qq|Array Ref = @$arrayRef\n|;
```

Listing 7.3 shows an example of creating direct scalar and array references and accessing those references via the print function. It includes examples of accessing individual array cells and referencing the last array cell, which you'll learn about in the following sections. Figure 7.1 shows the output.

Listing 7.3:   **Direct Reference Techniques**

```
1.  #!/usr/local/bin/perl
2.
3.  $var = "AnyThing";
4.  #Save address of scalar variable $var
5.  $ref = \$var;
```

```
6.  #Dereference $ref printing value of $var
7.  print "Value = $$ref\n";
8.  #Save address of scalar $ref, itself a reference
9.  $doubleRef = \$ref;
10. #Dereference $doubleRef, then dereference contained reference
11. print "Double Reference Value = $$$doubleRef\n";
12. #Save address of scalar $doubleRef, itself a reference
13. $tripleRef = \$doubleRef;
14. #Dereference $tripleRef, then dereference contained references
15. print "Triple Reference Value = $$$$tripleRef\n";
16. @array = ("1","2","3","4");
17. print "Array @array\n";
18. #Save address of array
19. $arrayRef = \@array;
20. #Dereference array reference $arrayRef, using appropriate syntax
21. #for dereferenced variable
22. print "Array Reference @$arrayRef\n";
23. print "0 $$arrayRef[0], 1 $$arrayRef[1], 2 $$arrayRef[2],
            3 $$arrayRef[3]\n";
24. print "The last index of the array is $#$arrayRef\n";
25. # $#$arrayRef is last index of derefenced array @array
26. for ($i=0; $i <= $#$arrayRef; $i++){
27.    #This prints the dereferenced scalar value
28.    print "The value at array cell $i is $$arrayRef[$i]\n";
29.    }
```

Dereferencing Individual Cells

Dereferencing an individual cell of an array is just as straightforward as dereferencing an entire array. Recall that an array cell is a scalar variable. If you remember this rule, then you will always remember how to dereference an array cell.

You normally access an array cell like this:

```
$array[0];
```

To access an array cell when the variable is a direct array reference, dereference the direct array reference variable first and then treat it like a regular array, like this:

```
$$arrayRef[0];
```

FIGURE 7.1:

Direct references and
dereferencing

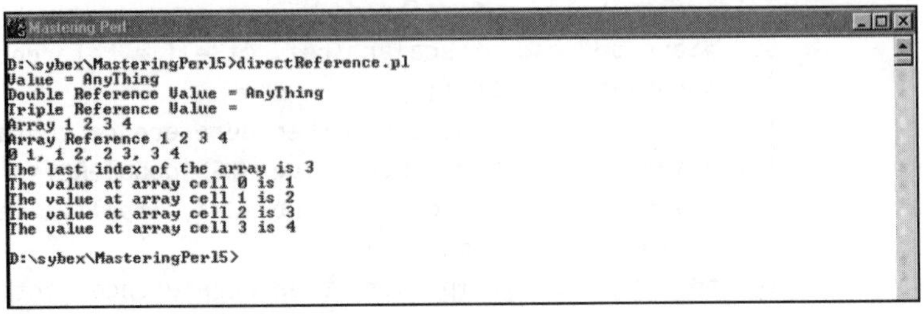

```
Mastering Perl                                                    _□×
D:\sybex\MasteringPerl5>directReference.pl
Value = AnyThing
Double Reference Value = AnyThing
Triple Reference Value =
Array 1 2 3 4
Array Reference 1 2 3 4
0 1, 1 2, 2 3, 3 4
The last index of the array is 3
The value at array cell 0 is 1
The value at array cell 1 is 2
The value at array cell 2 is 3
The value at array cell 3 is 4

D:\sybex\MasteringPerl5>
```

Remember that Perl 5 works from right to left, or from inside to outside. The previous example works like this:

1. Find the rightmost (or innermost) dollar sign. Get the value contained in that object or variable. In this case, that is $arrayRef, which contains the address of @array.

2. Repeat step 1.

Since step 1 retrieved the address or location in memory of @array, you can now think of the outside dollar sign as working on @array. The next dollar sign is a direct scalar reference to a scalar value in array cell 0.

Lines 23 and 28 of Listing 7.3 demonstrate dereferencing individual cells:

```
print "0 $$arrayRef[0], 1 $$arrayRef[1], 2 $$arrayRef[2],
      3 $$arrayRef[3]\n";
   print "The value at array cell $i is $$arrayRef[$i]\n";
```

Perl 5 provides a couple of alternative ways to refer to array references that help clear up the clutter of multiple dollar signs and at signs. You'll learn about those a bit later in the chapter.

Referencing the Index of the Last Array Cell

As you'll learn in Chapter 9, the for loop is traditionally used for processing a block of statements a discrete number of times. The following example shows how to loop through an array from the first cell to the last cell:

```
for($i = 0; $i <= $#array; $i++){block of statements}
```

If you read Chapter 6, you should understand the second conditional expression ($i <= $#array;) in this for loop. The conditional expression returns true as long as the variable $i is less than or equal to the last cell index variable (`$#array`). The `for` loop continues as long as this conditional expression remains true.

You can access the same last index variable through a direct array reference. Just remember the inner to outer, right to left rule. Dereference the direct array reference first, then treat the dereferenced array as if it were a normal array.

The last index of an array through an array reference looks like this:

```
$#$arrayRef
```

An example of this type of reference is shown on line 26 of Listing 7.3:

```
for ($i=0; $i <= $#$arrayRef; $i++){
```

Direct Hash References

The rules you have learned for direct array references apply to direct hash references as well:

- Hash references are created like this:

  ```
  $reference = \%hash;
  ```

- Hash references are dereferenced like this:

  ```
  %$reference
  ```

- Hash references cells are accessed like this:

  ```
  $$reference{'RED'}
  ```

- Hash reference cells are assigned like this:

  ```
  $$reference{'RED'}= 0xff000;
  ```

A Quick Recap

References can get very complex, but the rules for creating references and dereferencing remain the same regardless of the complexity or the data types being referenced. You use the dollar sign to dereference a reference variable, which is always a scalar, and then you use the type indicator, (**$**, **@**, or **%**) of the variable being referenced to access the value of the variable your reference variable contains.

If your reference variable contains a scalar variable, use a dollar sign to retrieve the value of the scalar variable. If your reference variable contains an array, use the at sign or the appropriate syntax to reference array cells and other array variables. If your reference variable contains a hash, use hash syntax, and so on.

You'll spend the rest of the pages in this chapter studying the variations of references, but you already know the fundamentals.

Perl 5 provides several alternatives to the dollar sign as dereferencing operators for more complex dereference operations. In the next section, you'll learn about these dereferencing alternatives.

Dereferencing Alternatives

The dollar sign works in all cases as a dereference operator. However, sometimes all those dollar signs are not a pretty sight—$#$arrayRef or $$arrayRef[0] is just a little hard on the eyes. Larry Wall, the father of Perl, recognized the ugliness of unrestrained dollar signs and created several convenience dereference operators.

Each of the alternatives is just a cosmetic substitution for the dollar sign. However, in some cases, they are left associative instead of right associative, as you would expect when using the dollar sign. These operators—curly braces ({ }), the adjacent square brackets ([] []), and the right arrow operator (->) are lovingly referred to by Larry as syntactic sugar. They make your code just a little sweeter to the eye.

NOTE   If you have experience programming in C++ or Java, you will be comfortable using the right arrow and square bracket operators. Although these are new in Perl 5, they look like C or Java syntax, so they will be familiar to you.

Curly Braces

The curly brace ({ }) helps clarify your code. The curly brace has no actual impact on your code when it's used with variable names. Its only affect is to make it easier for you or your fellow programmers to read your code.

If you place the curly braces around the reference variable, the reference variable returns the object it contains, and the variable operators outside the curly brace pair are executed. The array index variable $#$arrayRef becomes $#{$arrayRef}, and the array variable @$arrayRef becomes @{$arrayRef}. The curly braces help point out that the variable between them is an item that executes before the operator outside the curly braces.

If you have problems remembering whether the array reference refers to the array cell or to the array name, try using curly braces: the array cell reference $$arrayRef[2] becomes ${$arrayRef}[2]. The array reference inside the curly brace occurs first. Then the retrieval of the value of array cell 2 occurs.

You can also use the curly braces to clarify dereferencing multi-dimensional arrays. However, the more common mechanism for accessing multi-dimensional arrays is the right arrow operator, which you'll learn about in the following section.

The Right Arrow Operator

As I mentioned earlier in the chapter, references can contain references to other arrays, which work much like multi-dimensional arrays. Before we get to the topic of using multi-dimensional arrays, you need to recognize the dereferencing operator commonly used with multi-dimensional arrays—the right arrow operator.

The right arrow operator works like the dereferencing dollar sign, but unlike the dollar sign, the right arrow operator is left associative. (Remember that left associative means the operator affects the symbol to the left of the operator.) This boils down to the following rule: Whatever is immediately to the left of the right arrow is assumed to be a reference variable and is dereferenced. The right arrow dereferences the object on its left. This means that $$arrayRef[2] becomes $arrayRef->[2].

The right arrow operator allows syntax like $array[0]->[2]. The value stored in an array cell 0 ($array[0]) is dereferenced and treated as an array. The value in array cell 2 of the dereferenced array is then accessed. You'll see some examples of the right arrow operator in action soon, right after we talk about the remaining dereferencing operator.

Square Brackets

Another way to dereference an array is with square brackets, like this: $array[0][2]. Because Perl 5 knows that you can store only an array reference and not an array into an array cell, it assumes that the first array cell must be a reference to an array. This means that the right arrow operator is not required between square brackets or multi-dimensional array references.

The following three formats are equivalent:

```
${$array[0]}[2]
$array[0]->[2]
$array[0][2]
```

Multi-Dimensional Arrays

As you read earlier, a multi-dimensional array in Perl 5 is actually an array with a reference to another array in it. Listing 7.4 gives you some simple examples of multi-dimensional arrays. Figure 7.2 shows its output.

Listing 7.4:   **Multi-Dimensional Arrays**

```
1.  #!/usr/local/bin/perl
2.  $spacer = "=" x 60;
3.  $spacer .= "\n\n";
4.
5.  #Create arrays of decimal digits and uppercase letters
6.  @numbers = (0 .. 9);
7.  @letters = (A .. Z);
8.
9.  #Save address of letters array into cell 0
10. @lettersAndNumbers[0] = \@letters;
11. #Save address of letters array into cell 1
12. @lettersAndNumbers[1] = \@numbers;
13.
14. #Dereference lettersAndNumbers array cell 0, which references
15. #numbers array; then dereference cell 2 of numbers array, which
16. #is letter C,using various dereferencing formats
17. print "${$lettersAndNumbers[0]}[2], $lettersAndNumbers[0]->[2],
            $lettersAndNumbers[0][2]\n";
18. print $spacer;
19.
20. #Loop through lettersAndNumbers
21. #Initialize starting loop index to value in numbers array
22. # cell 9, which is 9
23. #Loop while loop index is greater than or equal to
24. #value in numbers array cell 0, which is zero
25. #Decrement loop index by one each time through loop
26. for ($index = $lettersAndNumbers[1]->[9];
```

```
27.                    $index >= $lettersAndNumbers[1][0];
28.                    $index-){
29.
30.        #Derefence $lettersAndNumbers array cell 0, which contains
31.        #reference to numbers array
32.        print "The number ${index}'s letter is
                      ${$lettersAndNumbers[0]}[$index]\n";
33. }
34. print $spacer ;
35.
36. #Build 4-element array, each with references to another array
37. @words = (wobble, go, pint, test, drink, trail, shove, quick,
                      twelve, somber, );
38. @codeNumbers = (5,3,1,7,2,0,9,8,4,6);
39. @codeLetters = (W,O,P,S,N,R,H,K,L,B);
40. @codes[0] = \@words;
41. @codes[1] = \@codeNumbers;
42. @codes[2] = \@codeLetters;
43. @codes[3] = \@lettersAndNumbers;
44.
45. #Dereference cell 3 of codes array, which contains reference to
46. #lettersAndNumbers array
47. #Dereference lettersAndNumbers cell 1, which contains reference
48. #to numbers array
49. #Retrieve value cell 0 of numbers array, which is zero, and set
50. #$index to that value
51. #Loop while loop index is less than or equal to last index
52. #number of letters array
53. #Increment loop index by one each time through loop
54. for ($index = $codes[3]->[1]->[0] ; $index <= $#{$codes[3]
                      ->[1]}; $index++){
55.
56.        #Dereference cell 1 of codes array, which contains
57.        #reference to codeNumbers array
58.        #set codeIndex to value retrieved from codeNumbers array
59.        $codeIndex = $codes[1][$index];
60.
61.        #Dereference cell 0 of codes array, which contains
62.        #reference to words array
63.        #set codeWord to value retrieved from words array
64.        $codeWord = $codes[0][$codeIndex];
65.
66.        #Dereference cell 2 of codes array, which contains
```

```
67.     #reference to codeLetters array
68.     #Dereference cell 1 of codes array, which contains reference
69.     #to codeNumbers array
70.     #use number retrieved from the codeNumbers array as index
71.     #into value retrieved from cell 2 of codes array, which is
72.     #index into codeLetters array
73.     $codeLetter = $codes[2]->[$codes[1][$index]];
74.
75.     print "The code word is $codeWord\t its letter is
                $codeLetter\n";
76.     }
```

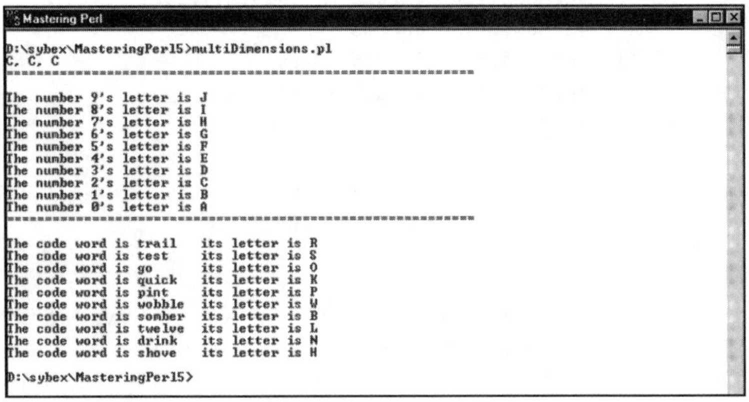

FIGURE 7.2:

The results of arrays with
references to other arrays

The first multi-dimensional array examples are on lines 10 and 12 of Listing 7.4:

```
@lettersAndNumbers[0] = \@letters;
@lettersAndNumbers[1] = \@numbers;
```

References to the arrays created on line 6 and 7 are stored in the $lettersAnd-Numbers array.

Line 17 illustrates the three equivalent methods of dereferencing multi-dimensional arrays in Perl 5:

```
print "${$lettersAndNumbers[0]}[2], $lettersAndNumbers[0]->[2], $letters
AndNumbers[0][2]\n";
```

Each reference on line 17 refers to the third array cell, index number 2, of the @letters array on line 7. The output of line 17 is the first line (after the command prompt) in Figure 7.2, which is the letter C repeated three times.

Let's see how each of the dereferencing methods work on line 17. The first example uses curly braces:

```
${lettersAndNumbers[0]}[2].
```

Perl 5's first step is to decode the value between the curly braces $lettersAndNumbers[0]. This returns an array reference to the @letters array. Perl 5 next dereferences the @letters reference and fetches the scalar value from the third cell, or index number 2. The result is the letter C.

The second example illustrates the right arrow operator:

```
$lettersAndNumbers[0]->[2]
```

The right arrow operator is left associative, so Perl 5 dereferences the value in array cell 0 of the @lettersAndNumbers array. This is the reference to the @letters array. Perl 5 then retrieves cell 2's value from the @letters array.

The third example uses square brackets:

```
$lettersAndNumbers[0][2]
```

Perl 5 takes the same steps as with the right arrow operator. The right arrow operator is always assumed when two array cell reference operators—the square brackets ([])—are placed beside each other.

The for loop in lines 26 through 28 of Listing 7.4 illustrates the same three ways to construct multi-dimensional array references:

```
for ($index = $lettersAndNumbers[1]->[9];
        $index >= $lettersAndNumbers[1][0];
        $index-){
```

NOTE   In Listing 7.4, I mixed the different methods of dereferencing multi-dimensional arrays so that you can see how they each work in practice. You should now be able to choose the method you prefer. I recommend choosing a single style and sticking with that whenever possible. Mixing methods of referencing arrays, as I have done in Listing 7.4, is confusing. I have only done it for illustrative purposes.

Beginning on line 54 of Listing 7.4 are examples of dereferencing one level deeper, into three-dimensional arrays. The following sections explore these techniques.

Three-Dimensional Array Dereferencing

An example of dereferencing a three-dimensional array appears in line 54 of Listing 7.4:

```
for ($index = $codes[3]->[1]->[0] ; $index <= $#{$codes[3]->[1]};
$index++){
```

The following part of the line indexes through a three-dimensional array:

```
$codes[3]->[1]->[0]
```

Remember that this syntax is equivalent to $codes[3][1][0], which is more compact, but does not show as clearly that each array cell is a reference. The three-dimensional reference is decoded with these steps:

1. The value at $code[3] is retrieved.

2. The right arrow operator ->[1] is associated with the value in step 1 (remember that this operator is left associative), creating a reference to the $lettersAndNumbers array.

3. The value in cell [1] is retrieved

4. The right arrow operator is associated with the value in step 3, ->[0], creating a reference to cell [0] of the @numbers array.

5. The value in cell [0], which is the number zero, is retrieved.

This is the Rube Goldberg way of assigning zero to the start of a for loop if I've ever seen one. However, it's also a decent example of three-dimensional referencing. (You'll learn easier ways to assign values to the start of for loops in Chapter 9.)

The Last Cell Index for Loop Control

The next example on line 54 of Listing 7.4, using the last index of the array variable ($#) for loop control, is very common. This example retrieves the size of a referenced array:

```
$#{$codes[3]->[1]}
```

The curly braces don't really accomplish anything, except to help clarify the association of variables. The following form is equivalent, just not as clear:

```
$#$codes[3]->[1]
```

This portion of line 54 is decoded like this:

1. The value in $codes[3] is retrieved

2. The right arrow operator is associated with the value in step 1, ->[1], creating a reference to the @lettersAndNumbers array.

3. The value in cell [1] is retrieved

4 The array size or last cell variable $# is associated with the value returned in step 3. This returns the index of the last cell of the @lettersAndNumbers array.

Multi-Dimensional Arrays as Indexes

Line 73 of Listing 7.4 indexes through the @codeLetters array by dereferencing the @codeNumbers array:

```
$codeLetter = $codes[2]->[$codes[1][$index]];
```

First, the interpreter recognizes $codes[2]-> as an array reference to the @codeLetters array:

```
$codes[2]->[$codes[1][$index]
```

Next, it recognizes [$codes[1][$index] as an index into the @codesLetters array.

The index is inside the $codes[1][$index] reference. The interpreter decodes this reference as a reference to the @codeNumbers array. The value retrieved from the @codeNumbers array is based on the [$index] variable.

Each time $index is incremented, the next cell in the @codeNumbers array is retrieved. This number is then used as an index into the @codeLetters array.

Taken as a whole, it work like this:

1. $codes[1][$index] is treated as a single value. If $index = 0, the value is retrieved and creates the expression $codes[2]->[5].

2. $codes[2]->[5] is a reference to the value located in cell 5 of the array references located in cell [2] of the @codes array.

3. The value in cell 2 is the @codeLetters array. The value in cell 5 of the @codeLetters array is R, which you can see is the first letter presented in the code word list in Figure 7.2.

With the examples and explanations in this section on multi-dimensional arrays, you should be able to build and understand multi-dimensional arrays of any size in Perl 5.

Anonymous Arrays and Hashes

You can create arrays and hashes without an array name. Normally, an array is created by assigning values to cells of a named array, like this:

```
@arrayName = (1, 2, 3);
```

You can create an anonymous array like this:

```
$arrayReference = [1, 2, 3];
```

The array reference can then be saved into another array, creating a multi-dimensional array, like this:

```
$arrays[0] = $arrayReference;
```

When you create a multi-dimensional array, you assign the reference of one array to the cell of another array, like this:

```
@codes[1] = \@codeNumbers;
```

The array @codeNumbers must be created first before being assigned to the @codes array. Anonymous arrays allow you to skip the step of creating the intermediate array, by using the anonymous array operator ([]), like this:

```
@codes[1] = [5,3,1,7,2,0,9,8,4,6];
@codes[2] = [W,O,P,S,N,R,H,K,L,B];
```

Listing 7.5 demonstrates the use of anonymous arrays. Functionally, the listing is the same as Listing 7.4. You can compare the two listings and decide which syntax you prefer.

Listing 7.5:   **Anonymous Arrays**

```
1.  #!/usr/local/bin/perl
2.  $spacer = "=" x 60;
3.  $spacer .= "\n\n";
4.  #Save address of anonymous arrays into cells 0 and 1 of
5.  #lettersAndNumbers array
```

```
6.  @lettersAndNumbers[0] = [A .. Z];
7.  @lettersAndNumbers[1] = [0 .. 9];
8.  print "${$lettersAndNumbers[0]}[2], $lettersAndNumbers[0]->[2],
            $lettersAndNumbers[0][2]\n";
9.  print $spacer;
10. for ($index = $lettersAndNumbers[1]->[9];
11.             $index >= $lettersAndNumbers[1][0];
12.             $index-){
13.     print "The number ${index}'s letter is
            ${$lettersAndNumbers[0]}[$index]\n";
14. }
15. print $spacer;
16. #Use anonymous arrays to build codes array
17. @codes[0] = [wobble, go, pint, test, drink, trail, shove,
                quick, twelve, somber, ];
18. @codes[1] = [5,3,1,7,2,0,9,8,4,6];
19. @codes[2] = [W,O,P,S,N,R,H,K,L,B];
20. #This is equivalent to lettersAndNumbers array
21. @codes[3] = [
22.             [A .. Z],
23.             [0 .. 9]
24.             ];
25.
26. for ($index = $codes[3]->[1]->[0] ; $index <= $#{$codes[3]
                ->[1]}; $index++){
27.     $codeIndex = $codes[1][$index];
28.     $codeWord = $codes[0][$codeIndex];
29.     $codeLetter = $codes[2]->[$codes[1][$index]];
30.     print "The code word is $codeWord\t its letter is
            $codeLetter\n";
31.     }
```

Lines 6 and 7 of Listing 7.5 show that the first step of creating an intermediate array is unnecessary.

```
@lettersAndNumbers[0] = [A .. Z] ;
@lettersAndNumbers[1] = [0 .. 9];
```

Lines 21 through 24 of Listing 7.5 show how you can use the anonymous array reference operator to create multi-dimensional arrays:

```
@codes[3] = [
```

```
        [A .. Z],
        [0 .. 9]
    ];
```

Whenever you use the anonymous array reference operator with the assignment operator, you create an anonymous array reference in the scalar variable being assigned to it. You can use the anonymous array reference operator anyplace you would normally use the array reference operator (\@arrayName). Note that the anonymous array reference operator does not act as a reference operator inside a quoted string.

Treat the anonymous array reference operator as a convenience operator during initialization. In my own code, I do not normally use the anonymous array reference operator outside of array initialization. You must decide for yourself whether it makes your code less or more understandable.

The anonymous hash operator ({}) follows exactly the same rules as the anonymous array operator ([]). You can use the anonymous hash operator anywhere you would normally place the hash reference operator (\%hash), as shown in Listing 7.6 and Figure 7.3.

Listing 7.6:   **Anonymous Hashes**

```perl
1.  #!/usr/local/bin/perl
2.
3.  $hashCodes = {5=>W, 3=>O, 1=>P, 7=>S, 2=>N,
                  0=>R, 9=>H, 8=>K, 4=>L, 6=>B};
4.  foreach $code (sort keys %$hashCodes){
5.     print "The code letter for $code is $$hashCodes{$code}\n";
6.  }
```

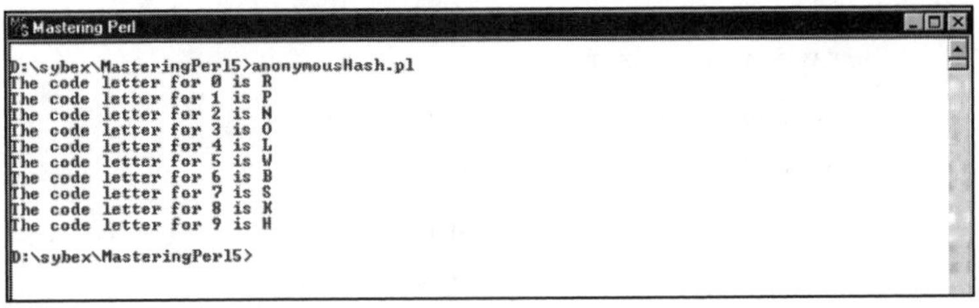

FIGURE 7.3:

A sorted hash

```
D:\sybex\MasteringPerl5>anonymousHash.pl
The code letter for 0 is R
The code letter for 1 is P
The code letter for 2 is N
The code letter for 3 is O
The code letter for 4 is L
The code letter for 5 is W
The code letter for 6 is B
The code letter for 7 is S
The code letter for 8 is K
The code letter for 9 is H

D:\sybex\MasteringPerl5>
```

Summary

In this chapter, you learned about references, which are an important new feature of Perl 5. References are typically used for programming efficiency. It's a lot quicker to pass the address of an array between subroutines than to pass the array itself. With the speed of today's processors, only the most complex problems demand the efficiency of references. Array references, like all complex structures, are used when they are required—in complex problems such as encoding an electronic data format for translation to a legacy data format.

The chapter began by explaining the concept of references. A reference is a scalar variable that contains the address of another variable. Perl 5 references may refer to any Perl 5 data structure. A reference is created by using the address-of operator (\) preceding the variable whose address is being saved. Perl 5 also has anonymous reference operators for arrays ([]), hashes ({}), and subroutines (sub {};).

Next, each of the six types of reference variables—direct, constant, subroutine, symbolic, anonymous, and object—were explained with brief examples. Then you learned the details of creating and dereferencing direct reference variables. The dereferencing operator is the dollar sign ($), which should be preceded by the type indicator of the variable being dereferenced. Using the dollar sign as the dereference operator occurs because a reference variable is a scalar variable. The dollar sign dereferences the scalar variable, and the type indicator ($, @, %, or &) dereferences the variable referred to by the reference variable.

Next, you learned that Perl 5 provides several alternative operators for dereferencing references contained in arrays and hashes, which may point to other arrays and hashes. Programmers familiar with the C language may prefer to simulate multi-dimensional arrays using square brackets, like this: $array[0][0]. Object-oriented programmers can use the right arrow operator, like this: $array[0]->[0]. The right arrow is left associative, so it dereferences the left array cell first.

Finally, this chapter covered anonymous array and hash operations. When used with an assignment statement, the anonymous hash and array operators allow you to initialize multi-dimensional arrays in a single statement.

In the next chapters, you'll learn about conditional branch clauses, the if clause and loops. You'll learn more about using array references in loops in Chapter 9.

CHAPTER

EIGHT

8

Conditional Statements

- Simple and complex conditional expressions

- `if else` statements

- `if elsif else` statements

- Nested `if` clauses

- A `switch` statement simulation

- The ternary operator (?:) to replace `if else`

Telling your computer what to do next is one of the basic things you will do as a programmer. Branching statements tell your computer which fork in the road to take. Branching statements include `if`, `if else`, `if elsif`, `?:`, `last`, `next`, `for`, `foreach`, `while`, `until`, and several others.

In the previous chapters, you've seen code examples that include `if` statements. In Chapter 4, the Boolean operators section used a conditional expression about fishing to explain the logical operators AND (`&&`), OR (`||`), and NOT (`~`).

In this chapter, you'll study the `if` family of branching statements (`if`, `if else`, and `if elsif`) and some related topics, including coding practices, labels, simulating `switch` statements, and eating an elephant. To become a good programmer, you need to learn the correct way to eat an elephant, so you'll spend a little bit of time learning new culinary techniques (just seeing if you're paying attention).

An Introduction to Branching Statements

Look at a tree and you'll understand a branching statement. Each tree branch is a different path to a different location. A cat climbing the tree must pick a branch to choose the next direction to travel. Without branch statements, your code would look like a telephone pole—it would always go to the same location.

Your code is read by the computer from left to right, line by line, like a book. Your code is executed one line after the other until the computer has to choose which line to execute next. The computer's choice is based on the results of a conditional expression and the branching command associated with the conditional expression.

As usual, I'll introduce branching statements with an example. You'll see the `if` statement beautifully illustrated by the single `if` clause in Listing 8.1.

NOTE   Listing 8.1 is part of a larger property management program. I wanted to include the whole program in the book, but eight pages of code were just too much. I have included the larger program on this book's web site, so you can study the surrounding environment of Listing 8.1 and the other program segments that are discussed in this chapter.

Listing 8.1:   **A Single if Statement**

```
1.   # Determine whether the line from the database matches
2.   # the search criteria
3.   #
4.   $unitMatched = "NO";
5.   if ( ( $line1[$pos{'RENTALRATE'}] <= $maxRentalRate + 5000)
6.   && ( $line1[$pos{'RENTALRATE'}] >= $minRentalRate) ) {
7.       $unitType = $line1[$pos{'TYPEOFUNIT'}];
8.       if($desiredUnits{$unitType} eq "TRUE"){
9.           if ( $line1[$pos{'BEDROOMS'}] >= $minBedRooms ){
10.              $totalBaths = $line1[$pos{'FULLBATHS'}] +
                         ($line1[$pos{'HALFBATHS'}]/2);
11.              if ( $totalBaths >= $minBathRooms ) {
12.                  $unitMatched = "YES";
13.                  if ($petsDesired eq "YES") {
14.                      if ($line1[$pos{'PETSALLOWED'}] eq "NO") {
15.                          $unitMatched = "NO";
16.                      }#end pets allowed
17.                  }#end pets desired
18.              }#end total baths
19.          }#end bedrooms
20.      }#end type of unit
21.  }#end rental rate
```

Now I hope you did a double take when you read that last sentence of the previous paragraph. How can 21 lines of code, which includes five different if statements, be just one if clause?

Listing 8.1 should help you understand that a single if statement begins with the keyword if, which is followed by a conditional expression, which is followed by a block of statements. The syntax is:

```
if (conditional expression) {
    block of statements
}
```

Simple Conditional Expressions

As you've learned in previous chapters, an *expression* returns a value. The value can be the result of several operations, it can be a scalar variable, or it can even be a literal, such as the number 10. A *conditional expression* is a value that can be either true or false. The true or false value is usually the result of a compare operation, but the expression can be any operation.

A simple conditional expression looks like this:

```
if (true) {block of statements}
```

If the conditional expression is true, the branch statement takes the true path, executing the true block of statements. When the conditional expression is false, the branch statement takes the false path, executing the first statement following the true block of statements.

Line 14 of Listing 8.1 contains an example of a simple conditional expression that is a compare operation:

```
if ($line1[$pos{'PETSALLOWED'}] eq "NO")
```

The variable `$line1[$pos{'PETSALLOWED'}]` is compared to the string literal `"NO"`. If the `$line1[$pos{'PETSALLOWED'}]` variable contains exactly the characters NO, the compare function will return a 1; otherwise, it will return `null`. The `if` statement will execute the block of statements that follows the conditional expression only if the compare operators of the conditional expression return true. (Remember that your computer considers any expression that is not false— false is 0, `null`, or the empty string ""—as true.)

Blocks of Statements

After the `if` statement's conditional expression, which is always surrounded by parentheses, comes a block of Perl 5 statements. A block of statements is always surrounded by left and right curly braces ({ }). That is why the `if` clause that begins on line 5 of Listing 8.1 doesn't end until the closing curly brace on line 21. The opening curly brace for the `if` statement on line 5 is at the end of line 6. So the block of statements actually begins with the opening left curly brace ({) on line 6 and ends with the matching closing curly brace (}) on line 21. The `if` statement in Listing 8.1 contains six distinct blocks of statements.

A block of statements can be zero, one, or many lines of Perl 5 code. A block of statements must follow the `if` family of conditional clauses. The conditional expression following the `if` keyword must be surrounded by parentheses, and the block of statements must be surrounded by curly braces. The block of statements that follows the conditional expression may be empty or have thousands of lines of code, but it is required. A block of statements may occur anywhere in your code and is always distinguishable by a matching pair of curly braces.

NOTE

The block of statements creates its own namespace in the symbol table, which means variables declared using my or local have scope to the enclosing block of statements. You'll learn more about variable scope in Chapter 18.

Complex Conditional Expressions

A complex conditional expression is a conditional expression that is made up of two or more simple conditional expressions. Complex conditional expressions are built using the logical Boolean operators you learned about in Chapter 4.

The if statement on lines 5 and 6 of Listing 8.1 contains a complex conditional expression:

```
if ( ( $line1[$pos{'RENTALRATE'}] <= $maxRentalRate + 5000)
&& ( $line1[$pos{'RENTALRATE'}] >= $minRentalRate) ) {
```

Notice that this conditional expression has two opening left parentheses. The first left parenthesis begins the overall complex conditional expression. The first inner simple conditional expression begins with the second left parenthesis and ends with the first right parenthesis. The first conditional expression is:

```
( $line1[$pos{'RENTALRATE'}] <= $maxRentalRate + 5000)
```

And the second conditional expression is:

```
( $line1[$pos{'RENTALRATE'}] >= $minRentalRate)
```

The two conditional expressions are joined by the Boolean AND operator (&&). As you learned in Chapter 4, && operates like a short-circuit operator—if the first conditional expression is false, Perl 5 never tries to evaluate the following conditional expression.

The truth table logic you learned in Chapter 4 can be applied to any complex conditional expression. To apply truth table logic to this complex conditional expression, substitute the letter A for condition 1 and the letter B for condition 2, and the complex conditional expression becomes A && B— a two-condition truth table.

The Case against goto

Just 20 years ago, the most commonly used branch statement was the evil goto statement. The goto statement got a bad reputation because it was used in a very unstructured manner.

The goto command, which Perl 5 does contain, tells the computer to resume executing at, or branch to, a particular label (a marker) in your code. The syntax of the goto statement is goto *LABEL*;.

The goto statement usually hops to another section of code. This hopping around can turn your program into what is commonly referred to as *spaghetti code*—you can't figure out how you got to a particular location in your code or where you will go next. The goto command frequently makes your code harder to follow, because the branch location isn't clearly related to the current location in your code. Since code that uses goto statements is extremely hard to debug and maintain, we will focus on Perl 5's more structured if family of branching statements in this book.

Good Coding Practices

Before you go on to learn about the various branching statements, let's revisit a topic introduced in Chapter 2. In the earlier chapter, I explained that following good coding practices helps you in debugging your programs. Now you will see how these rules apply in practice, using Listing 8.1 as a guide. When you start programming branching statements, comments, indenting, and using scalar constants to reference array indexes become important to clarifying your code.

Commenting Your Code

A comment line begins with the pound sign (#). A comment can begin anywhere on a line. Everything following the pound sign will be ignored by the computer. Since comments are not interpreted, they don't slow down your code.

NOTE   Remember that you don't write comment lines for your computer's benefit; you write them for yourself as well as to help other programmers who will look at your code.

Every book these days has something noble and chiding to say about commenting your code. It begins to sound like your parents telling you what is good for you. As a parent of three wonderful kids (though, Scott, now 20 and a sophomore at Texas A&M University, can hardly be called a kid), I know that kids never listen to their parents. Still, heavy sigh, you have to try.

Don't touch that hot stove!!

Or in this case:

Comment your code!!

The value of commenting your code is not immediately apparent when you're writing the code. Of course, you know what that variable is for and why that if statement is needed right now. But trust me, 3 months, 6 months, or 2 years and many thousands of lines of code later, you will forget why you chose to write that line of code in that particular manner. By adding comments, you will save yourself countless hours trying to remember what you meant to do with a particular block of code.

Use comments to summarize what a block of code is supposed to do. For example, lines 1 through 3 of Listing 8.1 outline the if clause from lines 5 through 23.

```
# Determine whether the line from the database matches
# the search criteria
#
```

Just two simple lines explain to a programmer (including the one who wrote those lines) what an if block is supposed to accomplish.

As another example of using comments, lines 16 through 21 of Listing 8.1 have ending comments to denote where each if clause ends:

```
            }#end pets allowed
          }#end pets desired
        }#end total baths
      }#end bedrooms
    }#end type of unit
  }#end rental rate
```

Comments should be used to explain the purpose of sections of code and, as necessary, to keep track of where you are in a loop or a conditional expression. Occasionally, you need comments to explain some complex statement.

On the other extreme of not commenting code at all is over-commenting code. It's not true that because a little is good a lot must be better. Don't put a comment on every single line of code. The appropriate use of comments, along with informative variable names, will make the purpose of your code understandable. If you get into these good coding habits, most of your time will be spent writing code, not trying to turn each line of code into English.

Indenting

Indenting your code provides a visual guide to where each conditional statement begins and ends. This can be important when you are trying to figure out why a piece of code isn't working. One of the more common coding errors is forgetting to add the closing curly brace to an if block of statements. When you have nested if statements, as in Listing 8.1, it is easy to lose track of where each if statement is finished. Proper indenting helps you keep track of nested code. (Nested if statements are explained later in this chapter.)

Indenting does not have to be a big chore. I set up my favorite Windows editor, Multi-Edit (covered in Chapter 1), to indent three spaces, and it takes care of getting things lined up for me.

In the listings in this book, you can see the indenting style I prefer. However, there are many different styles of indenting your code. Here are several common styles of formatting the if clause.

```
if (conditional expression){
    block of statements}

if (conditional expression){
    block of statements
}

if (conditional expression){
    block of statements
    }

if (conditional expression)
    {
    block of statements
    }
```

It isn't really important which style you use; it's just important to pick a style and stay with it. The first style I listed is probably the most popular with C programmers. I personally prefer the second style.

After the next four-hour, hair-pulling debugging session that comes down to a nesting problem that could have been prevented if you had just indented your code, you'll remember my advice and start indenting your code with care.

Using Variable Names as Array Indexes

In addition to Listing 8.1 appearing a little unusual because one `if` statement covers 21 lines of code, you may be scratching your head over the array indexes. Array indexes are supposed to be numeric literals. The arrays in Listing 8.1 look like they are being indexed by a hash, such as on line 5:

```
if ( ( $line1[$pos{'RENTALRATE'}] <= $maxRentalRate + 5000)
```

So far, you've seen arrays indexed with numeric literals, which is called *hard coding* the array index. Rather than hard coding array indexes, you should assign a value to a variable and use the variable as the array index throughout your code. This technique has two main advantages:

- Variable names can convey meaning; numeric literals cannot.

- Variable names are easier to maintain than numeric literals.

NOTE
Most languages provide a convenient method of making variables constant values, which means you can assign a value to the variable at declaration but never again. Perl 5 doesn't have such a means of making variables constants, so you just need to use programmer discipline. You, not the compiler, must enforce the practice of not modifying variables you have designed as constants.

In Listing 8.1, I took this technique one step further and assigned each value to a hash cell. This forced me to keep all of the common array indexes in one location. The first few lines of this hash are shown below, so you can see how I initialized the hash. The actual hash goes on for many, many more hash indexes.

```
# The pos array ties field names to their position
# in record.
%pos =(
     UNITID          =>0,
     ADDRESS         =>1,
     RENTALRATE      =>2,
     ZIP             =>3,
     MLSAREA         =>4,
```

MLSSUBAREA	=>5,
GRIDNUMBER	=>6,
DIRECTIONS	=>7,
TYPEOFUNIT	=>8,
STYLEOFUNIT	=>9,
HEATEDSQFEET	=>10,...

The array @line1 contains the contents of a property manager's database. That database is an old system that was converted to a colon-separated file. Each row of the database contains fields for the location, price, and characteristics of each property. I could have just hard coded a number for each field in the row, and then Listing 8.1 would look something like this:

```
1.    # Determine whether the line from the database matches
2.    # the search criteria
3.    #
4.    $unitMatched = "NO";
5.    if ( ( $line1[0] <= $maxRentalRate + 5000)
6.    && ( $line1[0] >= $minRentalRate) ) {
7.        $unitType = $line1[1];
8.        if($desiredUnits{$unitType} eq "TRUE"){
9.            if ( $line1[2] >= $minBedRooms ){
10.               $totalBaths = $line1[3] + ($line1[4]/2);
11.               if ( $totalBaths >= $minBathRooms ) {
12.                   $unitMatched = "YES";
13.                   if ($petsDesired eq "YES") {
14.                       if ($line1[5] eq "NO") {
15.                           $unitMatched = "NO";
16.                       }#end pets allowed
17.                   }#end pets desired
18.               }#end total baths
19.           }#end bedrooms
20.       }#end type of unit
21.   }#end rental rate
```

Some of you may be thinking this makes the code more compact, and you're right. However, with this version, it's much harder to figure out what each conditional expression is checking for. The English-like variable names in Listing 8.1 help you see what is going on in the if clause.

As I mentioned, the second advantage of using variable names instead of numeric literals as array indexes is maintainability. For example, suppose that you need a prototype to sell a concept to your customer. If you hard coded your array indexes, after you win the contract, you will need to go back through the code to find every array index and change it to the correct value. When you use variables as array indexes, you can change the variable name's value, and poof, all the array index references in your code are updated to the new value. Furthermore, after your system is deployed, you can easily update your arrays to accommodate later changes (and your customers will be very impressed that you are able to make such a rapid fix).

TIP

The technique of using variable names as array indexes can be used for other numeric literals as appropriate. One of the popular numeric literals that gets assigned to a variable is the value of pi, 3.1416. This keeps the precision of the value the same throughout your code.

Now that you've learned how good coding practices can help your code (and probably had enough of my preaching), let's get back to the if family of branching statements.

The if Family

As you've learned, when you use an if statement, your computer evaluates the conditional expression associated with that statement. If the conditional expression is true, your computer executes the block of statements immediately following the conditional expression. If the conditional expression is false, your computer finds the end of the true block of statements and begins execution at the first statement following the true block of statements, as shown in Figure 8.1.

Lines 14 through 16 of Listing 8.1 are a nice example of a simple if statement. This statement has one simple conditional expression and only one line of code in its block of statements:

```
if ($line1[$pos{'PETSALLOWED'}] eq "NO") {
    $unitMatched = "NO";
}
```

Line 17 is the next line to execute if the conditional expression on line 14 is false. Each line following line 15 is the end of a true block of statements for the previous conditional expression. Each true block of statements is given the opportunity to perform further operations, but in Listing 8.1, no further operations occur, so the operation continues at whatever line follows line 21. You can check this out by looking at the code for the entire example, which performs further operations if the variable $unitMatched is "YES".

FIGURE 8.1:

The if statement

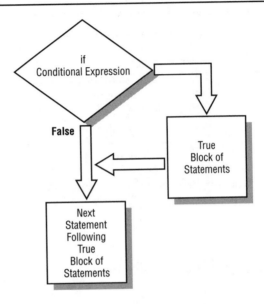

The other `if` family branching statements are `if else` and `if elsif else`. These branching statements follow the zero, one, or many rule:

- Only one `if` statement is allowed with a conditional expression.

- An `if` clause may have zero or one `else` blocks.

- An `if` clause may have zero, one, or many `elsif` clauses.

The `else` and `elsif` clauses and nested statements are discussed in the following sections.

if else Statements

An example is worth a thousand words. Listing 8.2 is another snippet of code from the property management program. This `if else` block is a nice contrast to your first example in Listing 8.1. That single if statement took 24 lines. This if else statement, including two lines of comments, takes only nine lines.

Listing 8.2:   **An if else Statement**

```
1.   # Handle case where there were no entries
2.   # found
3.   if ($totalUnitsFound == 0) {
4.       printNoUnitsFound();
5.   }
6.   else{
7.       printAllMatches();
8.       printTail();
9.   }
```

The else clause is executed only when the if statement is false. It may seem like the else statement is redundant, but it isn't, as illustrated in Figure 8.2.

FIGURE 8.2:

The if else statement

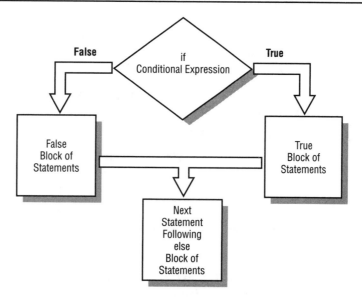

When an if conditional expression is true, it executes the block of statements following the closing curly brace *unless* the next statement is an else statement.

In that case, it skips to the end of the else block of statements and executes the first statement following the else block of statements.

An if statement can exist without an else block, but the else clause cannot stand alone. The else block must be preceded by an if statement. An if clause may have only one else block. The syntax of the if else clause is:

```
if (conditional expression){
        block of statements
}
    else {
        block of statements
    }
```

As with the if statement, the else clause must have a block of statements, and that block of statements may have zero, one, or many lines of code.

if elsif else Statements

The last member of the if family branching statements is the if elsif else clause. The if elsif statement in Perl 5 allows you to have a conditional expression after a false result from the if clause. The elsif clause can come in a variety of forms, but like the else clause, the elsif clause must be preceded by an if statement, as shown in Figure 8.3.

The elsif clause must come before the else clause if an else clause is associated with the if statement. You can have as many elsif clauses associated with an if clause as desired.

The syntax of the elsif statement is:

```
if (conditional expression){
        block of statements
}
elsif (conditional expression) {
    block of statements
}
Optional additional elsif clauses
Optional else clause
```

You'll see an example that uses elsif clauses in the next section, which explains the differences between elsif clauses and nested if clauses.

FIGURE 8.3:

The if elsif else statement

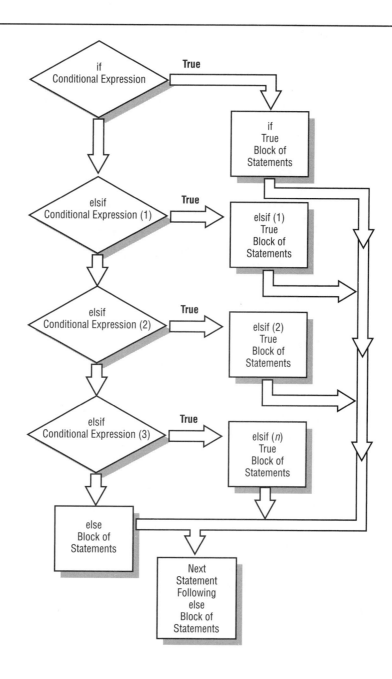

Nested if Clauses versus elsif Clauses

A nested if statement is one with an if else if clause. A nested if clause executes within the block scope of the enclosing else clause.

The difference between the nested if clause and an elsif clause may not be obvious. Both the nested else if clause and the elsif clause execute only if the previous if condition is false. The primary difference occurs when the else if clause completes and the code starts to exit each enclosing nested if clause. As the nested else if clause is completed, the code branches to the end of its enclosing scope, allowing additional statements to execute as each if else if clause completes its block of statements. Figure 8.4 shows how nested if statements work.

The enclosing scope of the if elsif clause is easier to understand because the elsif clause is directly related to its parent if clause and is not related to its sibling elsif clause(s) or the optional else clause. When the elsif clause completes execution, it branches past all sibling elsif clauses and the trailing optional else clause.

The nested if else if clause, on the other hand, is directly related to its parent else clause. This relationship causes the completion of the execution of the nested if else if clause to return to its parent clause and creates a more complex exit path.

WARNING Nested if statements occurring in an if else if else if format can become extremely complex. Complexity is not necessarily bad, but you should simplify whenever possible. The more complex a statement, the harder it is to understand. The harder it is to understand, the greater the potential for errors.

Let's look at a couple of examples that illustrate the nested if else if clause and the if elsif clause. When the nested if conditional expression returns false, other statements inside the else's block of statements can be executed, like this:

```
if (Today is Wednesday){
    Do the laundry
else {
    if (Today is Sunday){
        Sleep
    }
    watch TV for 2 hours
    eat
    sleep
}
```

FIGURE 8.4:

The nested if else if statement

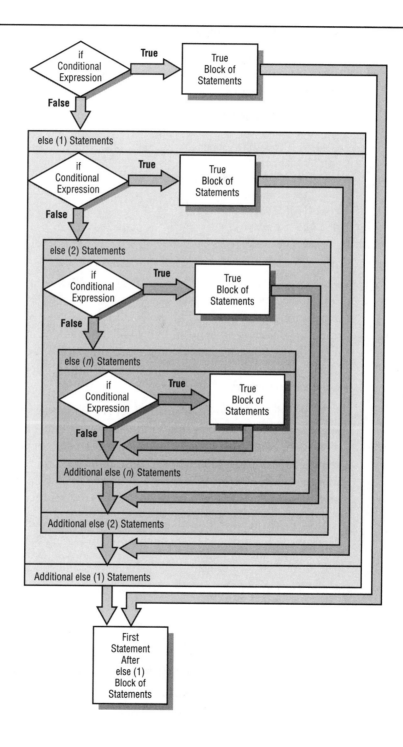

All of the statements inside the `else` block of statements are executed whether today is Sunday or not.

With an `elsif` clause, only the statements inside the `elsif` block of statements are executed. It works like this:

```
if (Today is Wednesday){
    Laundry}
elsif (Today is Sunday){
    sleep}
elsif (Today is Saturday){
    go to races}
elsif (Today is Friday){
    go to movies}
else {
    eat
    sleep}
```

Only the code inside the block of statements that follows the conditional expression that are true will be executed. In the case where none of the conditional expressions are true and an `else` statement exists, the `else` block of statements is executed. The eating and sleeping in the `else` clause happen only on Monday, Tuesday, and Thursday. That's not an eating and sleeping pattern I would recommend.

Notice that you can have multiple `elsif` statements following a single `if` statement. The single opening `if` statement is required, just as it is with the `else` statement. Also notice that a single `else` statement is acceptable but not required. The `else` statement acts as a default for the `if elsif` block of statements—when nothing else is true, do the `else` block of statements. The `else` statement follows the `if` statement, just as it does in a simple `if else` clause.

Now that you have looked at a contrived example, let's look at something real. The subroutine `printAllMatches`, shown in Listing 8.3, generates the text of the web page shown in Figure 8.5.

Listing 8.3:   elsif Blocks

```
1.   sub printAllMatches(){
2.       if ($sortBy =~ /Rent/){
3.           for $index (0 .. $#userDataArray){
4.               $rentArray[$index] = $userDataArray[$index]
                         {'Rent'} . $index;
```

```perl
5.          }
6.          @sortedRent = sort sortRent @rentArray;
7.      }
8.      elsif ($sortBy =~ /Type/){
9.          for $index (0 .. $#userDataArray){
10.             $typeArray[$index] = $userDataArray[$index]
                                    {'Type'} . $index;
11.         }
12.         @sortedType = sort sortType @typeArray;
13.     }
14.     elsif ($sortBy =~ /Beds/){
15.         for $index (0 .. $#userDataArray){
16.             $bedsArray[$index] = $userDataArray[$index]
                                    {'Beds'} . $index;
17.         }
18.         @sortedBeds = sort sortBeds @bedsArray;
19.     }
20.
21.     for $index (0 .. $#userDataArray){
22.         if ($sortBy =~ /Rent/){
23.             $sortedRent[$index] =~ /(\$\d+\.\d\d)(\d+)/;
24.             $sortedIndex = $2;
25.         }
26.         elsif ($sortBy =~ /Type/){
27.             $sortedType[$index] =~ /(\w+)(\d+)/;
28.             $sortedIndex = $2;
29.         }
30.         elsif ($sortBy =~ /Beds/){
31.             $sortedBeds[$index] =~ /(\d)(\d+)/;
32.             $sortedIndex = $2;
33.         }
34.         #$sortedIndex = chop $sortedRent[$index];
35.         $currentLine = $userDataArray[$sortedIndex]
                            {'currentLine'};
36.         $rent = $userDataArray[$sortedIndex]{'Rent'};
37.         $typeOfUnit = $userDataArray[$sortedIndex]{'Type'};
38.         $beds = $userDataArray[$sortedIndex]{'Beds'};
39.         $totalBaths = $userDataArray[$sortedIndex]{'Baths'};
40.         $petsAllowed = $userDataArray[$sortedIndex]{'Pets'};
41.         $address = $userDataArray[$sortedIndex]{'Address'};
42.         $zip = $userDataArray[$sortedIndex]{'Zip'};
43.
44.         print<<"eof";
45. <td><a href="http://www.practical-inet.com/cgi-bin/
```

```
                     trlawing/Details.pl? $currentLine"> Details </a>
46. <td> $rent
47. <td> $typeOfUnit
48. <td> $beds
49. <td> $totalBaths
50. <td> $petsAllowed
51. <td> $address
52. <td> $zip
53. <tr>
54. eof
55.     }#end for loop
56. }
57.
```

FIGURE 8.5:

Using elsif clauses

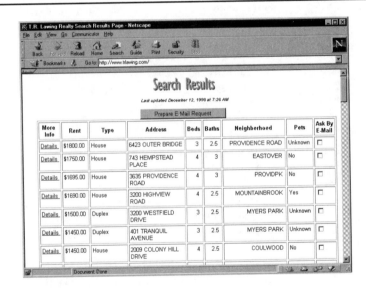

The if conditional expression on line 2 is a pattern-matching expression:

```
if ($sortBy =~ /Rent/){
```

The conditional expression returns true if the variable $sortBy contains the pattern or characters Rent. You'll learn about pattern matching in Chapters 15 and 16.

The subroutine contains two elsif clauses on lines 8 and 14:

```
elsif ($sortBy =~ /Type/){
elsif ($sortBy =~ /Beds/){
```

Each of the conditional expressions on lines 2, 8, and 14 is checked in order. The block of statements following the first conditional expression to return true is executed. Any elsif conditional expression following the first conditional expression to return true is not executed.

If the conditional expression on line 2 is true, the block of statements from lines 3 through 7 is executed and then lines 8 through 19 will be skipped. Line 21 will be the first line executed after the block of statements following whichever conditional expression returns true. The for statement on line 3 is a loop statement, which you'll learn about in Chapter 9. The for statement is processing an array. Each cell of the multi-dimensional array is accessed and stored into a simple array, @rentArray. The array is then sorted on line 6 by calling the sort routine sortRent. You'll learn about these subroutines and creating custom sort routines in Chapter 15.

Once the if elsif block is executed between lines 2 and 19, the for loop starting on line 21 and ending on line 56 begins execution. The same if elsif condition executed between lines 2 and 19 is repeated between lines 22 and 33 with different operations happening inside each elsif block of statements. Each elsif enclosing block of statements uses a different regular expression to extract an index from the simple array @sortedRent.

Line 23 is performing a pattern match on a cell of the array @sortedRent. Each matching pattern is returned in the special pattern-matching variables $1 and $2.

NOTE   Pattern-matching variables are based on the number of opening and closing parentheses. On line 23 of Listing 8.3, there are two patterns enclosed in parentheses, so these are two pattern-matching variables, $1 and $2. Remember, you'll learn the details of pattern matching in Chapter 16.

The index $sortedIndex is used between lines 35 and 42 to retrieve a single row of information from the complex array @userDataArray. The information is retrieved into the understandable variable names $rent, $typeOfUnit, $beds, $totalBaths, $petsAllowed, $address, and $zip. The variables are used on lines 46 through 52. Note that it isn't necessary to use the shorter names for the variables. Each variable could be replaced with its longer name, like this:

```
<td> $userDataArray[$sortedIndex]{'Rent'}
<td> $userDataArray[$sortedIndex]{'Type'}
<td> $userDataArray[$sortedIndex]{'Beds'}
```

```
<td> $userDataArray[$sortedIndex]{'Baths'}
<td> $userDataArray[$sortedIndex]{'Pets'}
<td> $userDataArray[$sortedIndex]{'Address'}
<td> $userDataArray[$sortedIndex]{'Zip'}
```

I went through the extra step because I find the shorter variable names easier to understand at a glance.

As you may have already surmised, lines 45 through 55 are the lines that actually print a single row of the web page table shown in Figure 8.5.

The subroutine printAllMatches can be broken down into the following three basic parts:

- First, the index is retrieved into the variable $sortedIndex.

- Then the index is used to retrieve data from the complex array between lines 35 and 42.

- The data retrieved from lines 35 to 42 is then printed from lines 44 through 54. You'll learn about the print command in Chapter 12.

This completes the discussion of the if family of branch statements. In the next section, you'll learn how to use labels and the if statement to simulate a switch statement.

Writing Defensive Code

Listing 8.3 is a good example of an if elsif block in real-world code, but it has a bug in it, which was removed from the delivered code. I left the bug in this example to show the potential problems your code must take into account. This code breaks a guideline of good programming practice. Can you determine why this code fails?

The problem is that two if elsif clauses in Listing 8.3 do not have any else statements associated with them. Not having a default condition or else clause associated with an if elsif block is generally considered poor programming practice. In this case, the programmer felt that the $sortBy variable should always be set. When it is not set, a program error will occur and the correct HTTP heading will not be returned to the web server.

Continued on next page

This will cause the CGI program to fail and the user to see the infamous internal server error, "Contact Your Web Administrator."

A better solution is to add an `else` clause that prints an error message and sends an e-mail to the programmer or owner of the script with debugging information. That way, when the script changes or fails for some reason, you get enough information to help you debug the process.

This example points out that you should never count on your data being correct. If it can go wrong, it will go wrong. You should take the time to write defensive code.

Switch Simulation

If you have ever programmed in C, C++, Pascal, Ada, Java, or some other language, you might notice that Perl 5 is missing a feature that many other languages have. This feature goes by names like computed `goto`, `case`, or `switch`. A `switch` statement (like the computed `goto` and `case` statements) branches to a single block of statements among many statements. Once the block of statements, called a switch block, has completed execution, the code branches to the end of the `switch` statement, as illustrated in Figure 8.6.

The `switch` statement is favored over the `if else if` or `if elsif` clauses by some programmers for at least two reasons:

- The `switch` statement can change a long list of `if else if` or `if elsif` clauses into clearly separated logical groups. Sometimes it can be hard to determine where one `if else if` clause actually ends and the next conditional expression should begin. The switch block's beginning and end is easy to distinguish. Each switch block begins with a label and ends with the block's closing curly brace.

- It's easy to change the conditional expressions that control each switch block. Adding or deleting an individual conditional expression has no effect on the other switch blocks. Each switch block, by design and implementation, is not affected by the actions of the other switch blocks. This is not the case with `if else if` statements. The nested `if` statement is directly affected by the enclosing conditional expressions.

FIGURE 8.6:

The switch statement

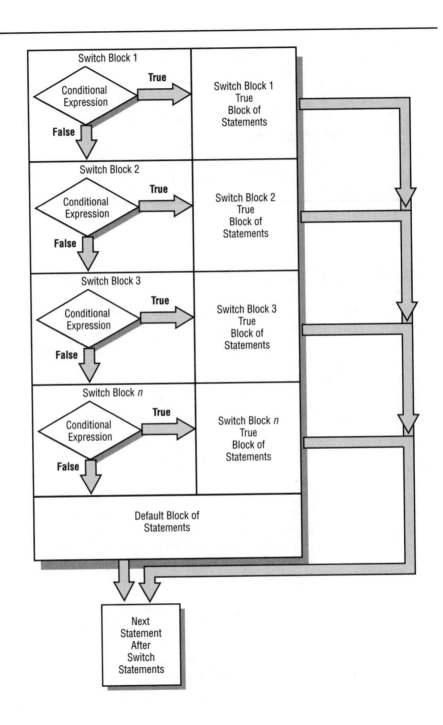

Perl 5 may not include a built-in switch statement, but what you can do with Perl 5 is simulate a switch statement. Listing 8.4 illustrates one way to simulate a switch statement. As always, there are an infinite number of ways to solve just about any coding problem. This is just one implementation of a switch statement that is simple, efficient, and easy to implement.

Listing 8.4:   A switch Simulation

```
1.    SWITCH:
2.    {
3.
4.
5.    if ($line =~ /Segment:/) {
6.       #note that the parentheses are REQUIRED
7.       ($s, $st, $segmentComment) = split(' ',$line,3);
8.       last SWITCH;
9.    }#end if segment
10.
11.   #Position Line
12.   if ($line =~ /Position:/){
13.      ($trash, $position) =  split (' ',$line,2);
14.      last SWITCH;
15.   }#end if position line
16.
17.   #Loop Line
18.   if ($line =~ /Loop:/) {
19.      ($trash, $loop) =  split (' ',$line,2);
20.      chop $loop;
21.      last SWITCH;
22.   }#end if loop line
23.
24.   #Level Line
25.   if ($line =~ /Level:/) {
26.      ($trash, $Level) = split (' ',$line,2);
27.      chop $position;
28.      $tmsg = "1".$position if $Level =~ /Heading/;
29.      $tmsg = "2".$position if $Level =~ /Detail/;
30.      $tmsg = "3".$position if $Level =~ /Summary/;
31.      last SWITCH;
32.   }#end if level line
33.
```

```
34.  #Usage Line
35.  if ($line =~ /Usage:/) {
36.     ($trash, $Usage) = split (' ',$line,2);
37.     if ($Usage =~ /Optional/) {
38.        $MinUse = 0;
39.     }
40.     else {
41.        $MinUse = 1;
42.     }
43.     last SWITCH;
44.  }#end if usage line
45.
46.  #Max Use Line
47.  if ($line =~ /Max Use:/) {
48.     ($w1, $w2, $MaxUse, $trash) = split (' ',$line,4);
49.     $maxUseLine = 1;
50.     last SWITCH;
51.  }#end if max use line
52.
53.  #Purpose Line
54.  if ($line =~ /Purpose:/) {
55.     ($Purpose, $PurposeComment) = split (' ',$line,1);
56.     last SWITCH;
57.  }#end if purpose line
58.
59.  #Notes Line
60.  if ($line =~ /  Notes:/) {
61.     ($Notes, $NotesComment) = split (' ',$line,2);
62.     last SWITCH;
63.  }#end if notes Line
64.
65.  #Syntax Notes Line
66.  if ($line =~ /Syntax Notes:/) {
67.     ($s, $SyntaxNotes, $SyntaxNotesComment) = split
         (/(\w+)/,$line,2);
68.     last SWITCH;
69.  }#end if syntax notes line
70.
71.  #Semantic Notes Line
72.  if ($line =~ /Semantic Notes:/) {
73.     ($s, $SemanticNotes, $SemanticNotesComment) =
         split (' ',$line,2);
```

```
74.     last SWITCH;
75.  }#end if semantic notes line
76.
77.  #Comments Line
78.  if ($line =~ /Comments:/){
79.     ($s, $Comments, $CommentsComment) = split (' ',$line,2);
80.     last SWITCH;
81.  }#end if comments line
82.
83.  #End of header statements.
84.  if ($line =~ /Data Element Summary/) {
85.     $headers = 0;
86.     $fields = 1;
87.     &printHeaders;
88.     last SWITCH;
89.  }#end if data element summary line
90.
91.  DEFAULT:
92.  {
93.     print<<"eof";
94.
95.     There was an error parsing the headers.
96.     All of the switch blocks failed their conditional
        expression.
97.     The line being processed was:
98.     $line
99.     ===================================
100. eof
101.   last SWITCH;
102. }
103. }#end SWITCH block
```

<table>
<tr><td>NOTE</td><td>The example in Listing 8.4 is relatively long, but it shows off the SWITCH block in its best format. A SWITCH block is most suitable for long if else if or if elsif blocks, usually three or more. Additionally, a SWITCH block is recommended when you expect the conditions of the if else if block might change. The SWITCH block, by its design, makes it easy to add and delete the blocks. Each logical SWITCH block should be disconnected from the other SWITCH blocks, which means removing or deleting a SWITCH block should never cause a change in another SWITCH block.</td></tr>
</table>

A traditional language `switch` statement allows you to segment code into easy-to-identify logical groups. The SWITCH construct in Listing 8.4 gives you that advantage.

A traditional `switch` statement is extremely fast. It computes the correct branch in one check at the beginning of the `switch` clause and immediately begins executing the correct block of code. This Perl 5 SWITCH simulation does not do that.

A traditional `switch` statement requires you to use a constant expression, usually an integer, when computing the correct block of statements to begin execution. The Perl 5 SWITCH simulation allows you to use any conditional expression to determine which block of statements will be executed.

So, for the sake of a little speed, you gain a tremendous amount of flexibility. Most computers are so fast today that you'll never notice the speed loss.

The SWITCH simulation includes a SWITCH label, conditional expressions as required, and a DEFAULT label that executes in the event that all conditional expressions evaluate to false. Here is the structure of the SWITCH simulation:

```
SWITCH:
{
if (conditional expression-1) {
   last SWITCH;
}#end

if (conditional expression-2) {
   last SWITCH;
}#end

if (conditional expression-n) {
   last SWITCH;
}#end

DEFAULT:
{
   last SWITCH;
}
}#end SWITCH block
```

When true, the conditional expressions begin executing their associated block of statements. The SWITCH command is denoted by a block of statements identified with an opening label. (A *label* is a marker for the Perl 5 interpreter, as explained in the next section.)

Each conditional expression in the SWITCH block of statements is evaluated in order. The ending statement of every SWITCH block of statements is the last command. The last command is discussed in more detail shortly.

When the conditional expression is evaluated as true, the block of statements following the conditional expression is executed. At the end of the conditional expression block of statements, but before the closing curly brace, the last SWITCH command causes the entire SWITCH block of statements to be exited. Any Perl 5 statements in the SWITCH block following the last statement will not be executed.

If each conditional expression in the SWITCH block evaluates to false, the DEFAULT block of statements on lines 89 through 100 will be executed. The DEFAULT label identifies the purpose of the block of statements between lines 90 and 100. The label is not required, but it makes the code more readable, so it's easier to follow and debug or modify.

Labels

A label is a marker for the Perl 5 interpreter. It identifies a particular line in your code. Perl 5 statements may then refer to that particular line by the label's name.

A label is usually used to mark the beginning of a new block of statements. In Listing 8.4, the SWITCH block is marked by the label SWITCH: and the opening and closing curly braces on lines 2 and 103, respectively. All of the code between lines 2 and 103 is part of the SWITCH block.

Here are the rules for Perl 5 labels:

- A label can go on any line.

- A label must begin with a character followed by any combination of letters or numbers that end with a colon. The ending colon is required.

- You cannot use reserved words like if or else as labels.

- Labels are case-sensitive, just like variable names. The labels SWITCH: and Switch: are not the same. By convention, labels are usually uppercase letters to make them easily recognizable.

WARNING   Although you can use the same characters for a label, a scalar, an array, and a hash (for example, line:, $line, @line, %line) and Perl 5 will understand that they are different things, you shouldn't do this. You might easily type a colon or a dollar sign when you shouldn't or forget to type them when you should. Your program will run, but because you are using a variable as a label or vice versa, your code will not perform correctly. The same rule about creating a different variable name for each new task, presented in Chapter 2, applies to labels.

The SWITCH block in Listing 8.4 works because the Perl 5 last command exits whatever block of statements is referenced by its label. The syntax of the last command in the listing is like this:

```
last LABEL;
```

However, the label is not required with the last command. You can use the last command like this:

```
last;
```

When used without a label, last exits its block of statements. You'll learn more about the last command in Chapter 9.

WARNING   Use the last command with caution. The command can be used to create structured and easy-to-follow code, like the SWITCH block in Listing 8.4. However, when used without caution, the last command will create unstructured code that is hard to understand and debug. This happens when you exit a block of statements unexpectedly from multiple locations.

The split Function

The split function is used for string manipulation and will be explained in detail in Chapter 15. However, it shows up in many examples in this book (because it's such a handy function), including in Listing 8.4, so let's take a moment to see how it works.

The split function searches an input string for a pattern. The pattern may be a regular expression or a simple string. Each time it finds the pattern, it splits the search string into two parts. The first part is returned, and the second part is searched for the next occurrence of the search pattern. This operation is repeated until all of the search string has been searched and split apart or until the maximum number of splits is reached.

The `split` function takes three parameters: the pattern to split on, the search string, and the maximum number of times to split the search string. The syntax of the split function is:

```
lvalue = split(/pattern/, expression, maximumSplit);
```

If the lvalue is a list, each returned string will be saved into the corresponding list variable. If the lvalue is an array, each returned string is stored into its own cell in the receiving array.

For example, on line 48 of Listing 8.4, the `split` function's lvalue is a list:

```
($w1, $w2, $MaxUse, $trash) = split (' ',$line,4);
```

The `split` function searches and splits up to the maximum number of splits identified in the third parameter, which is 4 in this example. Once the `split` function has found the maximum split value, the remainder of the string is returned without modification. In this example, the fourth variable, $trash, receives the remainder of the search string $line.

The `split` function also works with a pattern, which can be a regular expression, as on line 67 of Listing 8.4:

```
($s, $SyntaxNotes, $SyntaxNotesComment) = split (/(\w+)/,$line,2);
```

The `split` function, other functions for working with strings, and regular expressions are covered in Part 4 of this book.

if Blocks versus Simulated switch Statements

Let's look at a program that uses `if else` and `if elsif` blocks, and then see how it can be translated to use SWITCH blocks. The program shown in Listing 8.5 determines the hour of the day and then prints a simple greeting.

Listing 8.5: **Time of Day**

```
1.  #! /usr/local/bin/perl
2.  #month range 0-11, weekday range 0-6
3.  #dayLightStandardTime 0=false, 1=True
4.  ($sec, $min, $hr, $dayOfMonth, $month, $yr,
5.  $weekday, $dayOfYear, $dayLightStandardTime) = localtime(time);
```

```
6.
7.   #is the month December and the day the 23rd or 24th?
8.   if ( ($month == 11) && ($dayOfMonth == 23 || $dayOfMonth == 24) ){
9.      print "Merry Christmas World \n";
10. }
11. else {
12.     # is it after 6pm
13.     if ($hr > 18){
14.       # is it after 6pm and before 9pm
15.       if ($hr < 21){
16.          print "Good Evening World\n";
17.       }
18.       # then it must be after 9pm but before midnight
19.       else {
20.          print "Good Night World\n";
21.       }
22.     } #end if hour > 18
23.     elsif ($hr > 12){
24.        print "Good Afternoon World\n";
25.     }
26.     elsif ($hr > 6) {
27.        print "Good Morning World\n";
28.     }
29.     # if is between 6am and midnight
30.     else {
31.        print "Go to BED already! \n";
32.     }
33. }
```

NOTE   If you are wondering about the `time` on line 5, it is a Perl 5 function that uses the system time and returns the list of time parts shown on lines 4 and 5. The list is returned in this specific order.

Listing 8.5 can be broken down into these simple blocks of statements:

Lines 8–17

```
if (conditional expression){
    block of statements 1
}
```

Lines 18–20

```
elsif (conditional expression){
    block of statements 2
}
```

Lines 21–23

```
elsif (conditional expression) {
    block of statements 3
}
```

Lines 24–27

```
else {

    block of statements 4

}
```

This program could be rewritten with SWITCH blocks. The elsif clauses would be replaced as simple if clauses, and the trailing else block would be replaced as the default condition. The program would then look like the one in Listing 8.6.

Listing 8.6: Switch Time

```
1.   #! /usr/local/bin/perl
2.
3.   #The weekday and the month are range from 0-6 & 0-11,
4.   #respectively
5.   ($second, $minute, $hour, $day_of_month,
6.   $month, $year, $weekday, $day_of_year, $daylight_standard_time)
         = localtime(time);
7.
8.    SWITCH:{
9.       # is it after 6pm
10.      if ($hour > 18){
11.          # is it after 6pm and before 9pm
12.         if ($hour < 21){
13.            print "Good Evening World\n";
14.         }
15.         # then it must be after 9pm but before midnight
16.         else {
17.            print "Good Night World\n";
18.         }
19.         last SWITCH ;
20.      } #end if hour > 18
21.
22.      if ($hour > 12){
```

```
23.          print "Good Afternoon World\n";
24.          last SWITCH ;
25.      }
26.
27.      if ($hour > 6) {
28.          print "Good Morning World\n";
29.          last SWITCH ;
30.      }
31.
32.      DEFAULT:{
33.      # if is between 6am and midnight
34.          print "Go to BED already! \n";
35.          last SWITCH ;
36.      }
37.  }#END SWITCH
```

Take a few minutes to compare Listings 8.5 and 8.6. Look at the different blocks of statements to see how they relate. Notice that the else clause in Listing 8.5 is changed to a DEFAULT block in Listing 8.6. This points out that the else clause is always executed whenever everything has tested false for its conditional expression.

NOTE   When the code is converted to use SWITCH blocks, it becomes a longer program. Sometimes that's okay. In this case, I don't believe converting the code to a SWITCH construction adds much value. This code barely meets the three or more if else if blocks criteria, and the logical blocks are not disconnected. I hope you learn through examples such as these and others in this book that coding is not about hard-and-fast rules. You'll need to use your judgment to pick from many choices, which may each have merit.

Now that you've seen both complex and simple examples of branching statements, you are ready to learn about an operator created for the two-finger typists among the programming crowd. Back in the days of goto statements and single-character variables, programmers created code that could be understood by only the truly obtuse. Most code written today uses variable names that are somewhat understandable; goto statements and the like are not used often. However, I must admit, some conditions just demand the sparse elegance of the ?: operator (pronounced the operator that was formerly known as if then else).

The Ternary Operator

Do you hate to type? Do you prefer code that you and you alone understand? Do you think the following `if else` clause takes up to much space?

```
if (conditional expression){
        block of statements
}
else  {
    block of statements
}
```

Perl 5 contains a built-in alternative to the traditional `if else` clause especially designed for programmers who think just like you.

The ternary operator (`?:`) replaces the entire `if else` construct. It works like this:

```
(conditional expression)? true expression: false expression ;
```

Either the true expression or the false expression becomes the value of the entire expression based on the true or false value of the initial conditional expression.

The ternary operator is very convenient when determining a maximum value. The conventional maximum number logic looks like this:

```
if ($currentMax < $newNumber){
    $max = $newNumber;
}
else{
    $max = $currentMax;
}
```

The ternary operator syntax looks like this:

```
$max = ($currentMax < $newNumber) ? $newNumber : $currentMax;
```

The ternary operator has one distinct advantage over the `if else` construct: It can be embedded into other single-semicolon statements. This syntax looks just a little different:

```
((conditional expression) ? $trueVariable : $falseVariable ) =
$assignmentVariable;
```

This is an example of both embedding the `?:` operator and assigning a variable based on the result of a conditional expression. The conditional expression is evaluated and the `$assignmentVariable` is assigned to the true or false expression, determined by the true or false result of the conditional expression.

The `ctime` subroutine included with Perl 5 uses the ternary operator like this:

```
# Determine what time zone is in effect.
# Use GMT if TZ is defined as null, local time if TZ undefined.
# There's no portable way to find the system default time zone.

$TZ = defined($ENV{'TZ'}) ? ( $ENV{'TZ'} ? $ENV{'TZ'} : 'GMT' ) : '';
($sec, $min, $hour, $mday, $mon, $year, $wday, $yday, $isdst) =
        ($TZ eq 'GMT') ? gmtime($time) : localtime($time);
```

The first example sets the time zone variable $TZ GMT or the empty string based on the environment settings of your computer. The next statement uses the time zone variable, $TZ (set in the previous statement), to choose which system function should be used to get the current time.

Summary

In this chapter, you learned about branch statements. Branch statements are usually built around a conditional expression. The result of the conditional expression chooses the next block of statements to be executed. If the conditional expression is true, the block of statements immediately following the conditional expression, called the true block of statements, will be executed. If the conditional expression is false, the next statement following the true block of statements will be executed.

The next statement may be an `else` block, an `elsif` block, or neither. Both the `else` and `elsif` blocks affect the flow of control of your program, changing which statement will be executed next. The `if` statement can be followed by zero or many `elsif` statements and zero or one `else` statements.

The `if else if` and `elsif` statements can become cumbersome to modify and understand as they grow in size. One solution to the complexity of multiple `if else` and `elsif` blocks is the `switch` statement. However, Perl 5 does not include the `switch` statement. In this chapter, you learned how to build your own, using SWITCH blocks. The simulated `switch` statement should be used when you have three or more `if else if` blocks and the blocks can be logically separated. The

SWITCH construction doesn't decrease the length of your code, but it does make your code easier to understand and modify.

This chapter included some long, short, good, and bad code examples. This book presents a variety of programming solutions so you will become comfortable with the idea of choosing the best fit for each programming job's circumstances. The good programming practices explained in this chapter—indenting, commenting, and choosing meaningful variable names—are part of the many choices you must make as you solve real programming problems.

CHAPTER
NINE

9

Loops

■ while loops

■ until loops

■ do statements

■ for and foreach loops

■ Loop control modifiers

Welcome to learning how to do the same thing over and over and over again. Sorry if that sounds like a job. The nice thing about this is you get to have someone else do all those repetitions.

In this chapter, you'll learn about while and until loops, for and foreach loops, and something that kind of acts like a loop—the do statement. Along the way, you'll learn a little bit more about processing arrays and see a couple of practical CGI programming examples.

Perl 5 includes several loop modifiers—the last, continue, next, and redo statements—which you'll learn about at the end of this chapter. All in all, by the time you are finished with this chapter, you should have a good understanding of the fundamentals for programming with Perl 5.

An Introduction to Loops

In previous chapters, you've learned how to tell your computer what to do. If you were trying to teach your computer to walk, no simple feat (pun intended), you could write some code like this:

```
take one step forward
if (a brick wall is in the way){
    take one step to the right}
else take one step forward
if (a brick wall is in the way){
    take one step to the right
else take one step forward
if (a brick wall is in the way){
    take one step to the right}
else take one step forward
if (a brick wall is in the way){
    take one step to the right
else take one step forward
```

This gets rather tedious and would take a lot of code just to take a few steps forward. In fact, you could easily end up going in circles. You need a tool that lets you repeat the same statement over and over again. You need something that would allow you to do the following:

```
while (still going){
   take one pink hop forward
     if (something in the way){
         turn right}
}
```

This is not a very elegant piece of code. For one thing, there is nothing in the code to tell it when to stop, so it will keep going and going (like that pink, battery-powered bunny). Nevertheless, this is the basis of a loop statement.

A loop is like a circle that has a beginning, a middle, and an end. The beginning is the conditional expression, the middle is the block of statements, and the end is the closing curly brace. The beginning, middle, and end can be executed repeatedly, round and round again.

Loop clauses allow you to make the computer repeat an operation multiple times. The loop statements are a special type of branching statement. They usually branch or return to the top of the enclosing block of statements when their conditional expression evaluates to true.

A loop begins by first testing the conditional expression. If the conditional expression passes the test, the block of statements executes. When the block of statements reaches the closing curly brace, execution begins again at the conditional expression. As long as the conditional expression continues to pass its test, the block of statements associated with the loop continues to execute. A loop is nothing more than a conditional expression with a `goto` statement, which is always executed, as the last statement of the block of statements.

Here's a simplified example of how a loop works:

```
LOOPBEGIN:
if (conditional expression){
   block of statements;
   goto LOOPBEGIN;
}
```

All loops operate under these principles. One loop is distinguished from another primarily by the way that the conditional expression is tested.

The two main types of loops are `while`/`until` loops and `for`/`foreach` loops. Here's how they compare:

while/until	**for/foreach**
Continues to execute as long as its conditional expression remains true (`while`) or false (`until`)	Continues to execute as long as the conditional expression within the control expression remains true
Control variable modified inside the loop's block of statements	Control variable modified in the control expression
Usually used to process files	Usually used to process arrays

while/until Loops and do Statements

I used to wonder why there were so many different types of hammers. There are roofing hammers, carpenter's hammers, fencing hammers, and hammers of different weights. There must be at least a hundred different types of hammers. "Good grief," I said to myself, "They all hit the nail on the head, don't they?" Twenty-five years, several barns, a couple of roofs, too many fences, and a lot of bruised thumbs later, I understand that even with as simple a tool as a hammer, specialized tools make specialized tasks easier.

The same specialization rule holds true for Perl 5's loop statements. You could solve all of your iteration problems with one type of loop statement, but that would be like using only one type of hammer. You'll still be able to hit the nail on the head, but you'll spend more effort than necessary to get the job done.

The `while` and `until` loops are good tools for handling file and user input and output (I/O). They keep executing while or until a particular condition occurs. The do statement allows you to initialize your data during the first pass through the do block. Each of these tools lets you hit that nail a little more precisely.

while Loops

The `while` loop looks a lot like an `if` statement. The syntax of the `while` loop is:

```
while (conditional expression){
    block of statements
}
```

The difference, other than the while instead of the if, is that instead of executing the block of statements once if the conditional expression is true, the while loop will execute as long as the conditional expression remains true.

If the conditional expression is not true the first time it is checked, the block of statements following the while conditional expression will never be executed. If the conditional expression is true when it is first tested, the block of statements following the while conditional expression will be executed. When your computer gets to the closing right curly brace of the while block of statements, it will return to the while conditional expression and test it again. If it is still true, your computer will repeat the execution process it started with. Your computer will continue to test and execute the while conditional expression and block of statements until the conditional expression tests false.

If the conditional expression is never false, the while block of statements will execute forever, or until you do something drastic (like bringing up the Task Manager and ending the process, typing control C, or rebooting your computer). Programmers call code that never stops executing a loop block of statements an *infinite loop*. Infinite loops are usually a programming error, but not always. Infinite loops are quite common for system processes, such as those that read input from a user's keyboard, process data from another computer process, and other tasks that happen over a long period.

Listing 9.1 illustrates three different while loops with increasingly complex conditional expressions. (The loops in Listing 9.1 are drawn from different portions of the same program.)

Listing 9.1:   **Some while Loops**

```
1.    #Now create an array of the data until you find the keyword .
2.    #Does line begin with .
3.    while ($continue){
4.        if ($infile[$i] =~ /^\./){
5.            $continue = 0;
6.        }
7.        else {
8.            $tempArray[$k++] = $infile[$i++];
9.        }
10.   }
11.   LETTERLOOP:
12.   foreach $letter (@alphaTable){
13.       if ($letter eq $beginAlpha) {
14.           while ($endAlpha ne $alphaTable[$i]) {
```

```
15.                $alphaList[$k++] = $alphaTable[$i++];
16.                if ($i > $#alphaTable){
17.                    $i = 0;
18.                    #This is the index into the alphaList
19.                    #where the first wrapped Alpha exists
20.                    $letterWrap = $k;
21.                    }
22.                }
23.            last LETTERLOOP;
24.        }
25.        $i++;
26.    }
27.
28. sub extractRules($$){
29.     my ($ruleString,$match) = @_;
30.     while ( ($type, $segmentNumber)= $ruleString =~
                /\+?([REPLC])(\d+)/){
31.         #save what remained after the match
32.         $ruleString = $';
33.         my @segmentList;
34.         #separate the numbers into 2 digits each
35.         (@segmentList) = ($segmentNumber =~/(\d{2})/g);
36.         $x = 0;
37.         $rule = "";
38.         foreach $segment (@segmentList){
39.             #Does this rule apply to this segment?
40.             if ($match == $segment){
41.                 #R At least one of the pairs is required
42.                 if ($type =~ /R/){
43.                     for ($y=0; $y<=$#segmentList; $y++){
44.                         if ($y != $x){
45.                             $rule .= "| PRESENT
                                        ($segmentList[$y]) ";
46.                         }
47.                     }#really process the segments
48.                     $rule = 'PRESENT($) ' . $rule;
49.                 }#end rule R
50.
51. #ELC rules deleted for space considerations
52.
53.                 #P If any present then all required
54.                 if ($type =~ /P/){
55.                     for ($y=0; $y<=$#segmentList; $y++){
56.                         if ($y != $x){
```

```
57.                        $rule .= "& PRESENT
                                 ($segmentList[$y]) ";
58.                    }
59.                }#really process the segments
60.                $rule = 'PRESENT($) ' . $rule;
61.            }#end rule P
62.
63.            #This last must occur when we have a segment match
64.            last;
65.
66.        }#end we have a segment we are interested in
67.        #keep track of segment processing in segment array
68.        $x++;
69.      }#end processing segment numbers
70.
71.
72.    $rules[$q++] = $rule;
73.    }#end while we have a string to extract
74.    return @rules;
75. }#end extract subroutine
76.
```

The first while loop, on lines 3 through 6 of Listing 9.1, uses a single loop control variable, $continue:

```
while ($continue){
    if ($infile[$i] =~ /^\./){
        $continue = 0;
    }
}
```

This loop is processing file data one line at a time. The loop stops processing when it finds a line that begins with a dot (.).

The second while loop conditional expression, on line 14, compares a preset value $endAlpha with a value modified inside the loop:

```
while ($endAlpha ne $alphaTable[$i]) {
```

The third while loop conditional expression, on line 30, is more complex than the other two:

```
while ( ($type, $segmentNumber)= $ruleString =~ /\+?([REPLC])(\d+)/){
```

This loop continues to execute as long as the variable $ruleString contains a letter R, E, P, L, or C followed by one or more digits. If this pattern is matched, the matched position is saved into the variables $type and $segmentNumber using pattern-matching variables. The variable $ruleString is replaced with the unmatched portion of $ruleString on line 32. You'll learn more about pattern matching in Chapter 16.

TIP

As you'll learn in Chapter 16, using the post-match variable ($`) on line 32 of Listing 9.1 creates processing overhead that slows down your code. A better idea is to use the global pattern modifier (**g**) in scalar context, like this:

```
while ( ($type, $segmentNumber)= $ruleString =~
/\+?([REPLC])(\d+)/g){
```

This matches each occurrence of the regular expression in the pattern-match variable ($ruleString). Each new pattern check starts at the position just after the last match.

---

until Loops

There really isn't much difference between the while loop and the until loop except the way that the conditional expression is checked. The syntax of the until loop is the same as the while loop syntax:

```
until (conditional expression){
    block of statements
}
```

With the while loop, the block of statements is executed while the conditional expression is true. The until loop continues until the conditional expression is true. That is no different from saying the while loop continues until the conditional expression is false and the until loop continues while the conditional expression is false. Now I know that it sounds as if I am trying to confuse you. The fact is that the while loop and the until loop are mirror images.

- The while loop tests for true conditional expressions.

- The until loop tests for false conditional expressions.

To understand how the until loop works, consider how two of the while loops in Listing 9.1 could be replaced with until loops. The first while loop on line 3 looks like this:

```
while ($continue){
    if ($infile[$i] =~ /^\./){
        $continue = 0;
    }
```

This `while` loop could be rewritten as an `until` loop like this:

```
until (($infile[$i] =~ /^\./){
    $tempArray[$k++] = $infile[$i++];
}
```

The `until` loop version allows you to see when the loop will stop executing by looking at the first line. I prefer this version of the loop. The loop control variable `$continue` used with the `while` version forces you to read further into the loop block of statements to determine how the loop terminates. That makes the code just a bit more difficult to understand. Everything you can do to make the code easier to understand makes it easier to debug.

The second `while` loop in Listing 9.1 is on line 14:

```
while ($endAlpha ne $alphaTable[$i]) {
```

This loop's conditional expression could be written using an `until` loop like this:

```
until ($endAlpha eq $alphaTable[$i]) {
```

Again, I prefer the `until` loop's conditional expression because it uses positive logic, which is usually easier to understand. As explained in Chapter 2, if you can test for the negative condition, you usually can also test for the positive case.

The choice of when to use the `while` or `until` loop is based on programmer preference and the particular conditional expression. Unfortunately, programmers tend to use either the `while` or `until` loop exclusively. This can produce code that is just a bit more obtuse than a considered choice of which loop is the more suitable for a specific conditional expression.

From the examples of `while` and `until` loops, you should begin to see the main feature of these types of loops: their versatility. You can use `while` or `until` loops in a wide variety of circumstances, ranging from simple tests that use a single variable, such as `$continue`, to complex tests that check and set a variable in the same statement. You'll see more examples of `while` and `until` loops in the next section, which discusses the do statement.

The do Statement

The do statement is not actually a loop statement, but it is usually used with `while` or `until` constructs. The do statement allows you to always execute the block of statements in a loop at least once. The do loop's syntax looks like this:

```
do {
    block of statements
```

```
} until (conditional expression);
```

or

```
do {
      block of statements
} while (conditional expression);
```

Using the keyword while or until, called do loop modifiers, is not required. If you use the do statement without a do loop modifier, it acts like a simple block of statements. The do statement when used with a loop modifier or as a simple statement has these limitations:

- You cannot add a label modifier to a do block of statements.

- You cannot use the next, redo, or last commands inside a do block of statement's until construct.

This leaves you with a working, but somewhat limited, alternative loop construct.

Listing 9.2 shows the while loop, the until loop, and the do statement used in a program. Figure 9.1 shows the output.

Listing 9.2:   **The while, until, and do Statements**

```
1.  #!/usr/local/bin/perl
2.  print "\n\n";
3.  while ($count < 4){
4.      print "Inside the while loop the count is $count\n";
5.      $count++;
6.  }
7.  print "\n\nCount is incremented one more time in the while loop,
                so it is now $count\n\n";

8.
9.  until ($count > 7){
10.     $count++;
11.     print "Inside the until loop the count is $count\n";
12. }
13.
14. print "\n\nCount is NOT incremented one more time in the until
                loop, so it is now $count\n\n";

15.
16. do {
```

```
17.    print "The do statement is always executed at least once.
              The count is $count\n";
18.    $count++;
19. } until ($count >7);
20.
21. do {
22.    print "The do statement is always executed at least once.
              The count is $count\n\n";
23.    $count++;
24. } while ($count < 4);
25.
26. do {
27.    print "The do statement can act as a loop.
              Here the count is $count\n";
28.    $count++;
29. } while ($count < 14);
```

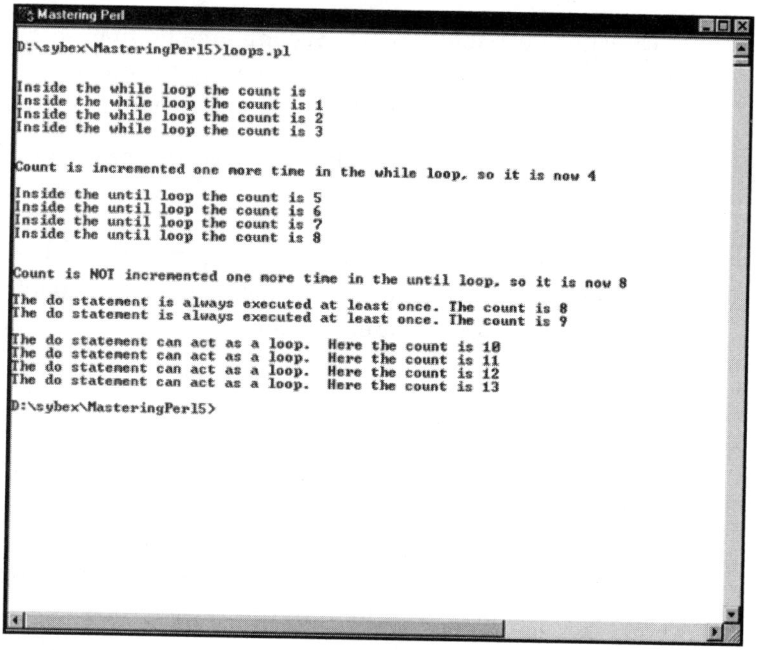

FIGURE 9.1:

Using while and until loops
and do statements

Before looking at the loop constructions in Listing 9.2, let's take a moment for a refresher on how Perl 5 handles undefined variables. Notice that the variable $count is undefined the first time through the conditional expression on line 3 of Listing 9.2:

```
while ($count < 4){
```

Perl 5 takes this in stride. Any time an undefined variable is used in a conditional expression, the test returns 0.

NOTE   Perl 5 initializes all variables to 0 (zero) the first time they are used. If an undefined variable is used in a conditional expression, the test will return 0 for numeric tests and an empty or a **null** string for string tests. You can check this yourself by running this simple program:

```
if ($count == 0) {
   print "yawp!";
)
```

Undefined variables, such as $count, aren't actually assigned a value. Perl 5 doesn't yet know whether the undefined variable should be treated as a string or a number, so it doesn't actually put any value into the $count location.

Then the program uses $count as part of a string expression on line 4:

```
print "Inside the while loop the count is $count\n";
```

Perl substitutes the empty string instead of the number 0. As you've learned in earlier chapters, Perl 5 chooses whether to treat the variable as a number or string based on the context of the expression.

On line 5, it becomes clear that $count will be used as an integer value:

```
$count++;
```

Notice that once $count is used as a number, Perl 5 continues to treat it as a number. Remember that ++ is the increment operator, so line 5 is shorthand for $count = $count +1. Perl 5 substitutes 0 for $count on the right side of the assignment expression, and the expression becomes $count = 0 + 1; $count is assigned 1. The next time through the loop, the expression looks like this:

```
$count = $count +1
```

or

```
$count = 1 + 1;
```

Now take a look at the results of the `while` loop in Figure 9.1. Since the value being tested for true is incremented inside the `while` loop's block of statements, the loop actually executes four times. You might expect it to execute just three times since the conditional expression checks for less than four. If you wanted the loop to execute only three times, you would check for < 3 or initialize your counter to 1.

Line 9 of Listing 9.2 clarifies the semantic difference between the `while` and `until` loops:

```
until ($count > 7){
```

If you reverse the conditional expression, the `while` and `until` loops easily substitute for one another. In the previous section, you learned a more practical difference between the two loops: In some cases, one type of loop allows you to use positive or clearer logic in the conditional expression, which makes your code easier to understand.

By the time the do statement on line 16 of Listing 9.2 is reached, the variable `$count` is greater than 8. Nevertheless, lines 17 and 18 are still executed and `$count` is incremented one more time.

The same thing happens with the do `while` loop from lines 21 through 24:

```
do {
    print "The do statement is always executed at least once.
        The count is $count\n\n";
    $count++;
} while ($count < 4);
```

Even though `$count` is not less than 4, the do statement executes at least once.

So what's the point of adding a do statement? The do statement has one very practical purpose: It allows you to initialize data at the beginning of a loop. When the conditional expression is based on data read from a file, you usually end up writing the setup code for your conditional expression twice—once outside the loop to handle the first time the loop is entered and then a second time inside the loop to handle each line as it is read. The do statement allows you to avoid this because you can use it to execute the loop's block of statements before testing the conditional expression of the `while` or `until` statements.

The do statement gives you one more convenient way to write clean, readable code. In the next section, you'll learn about Perl 5's `for` and `foreach` commands, which are the most commonly used loop statements in Perl 5.

The for and foreach Loops

for and foreach are actually the same command; they are synonyms. Whatever you can do with the for loop, you can also do with the foreach loop. Programmers tend to separate their use into two categories:

- The for loop is used to iterate a discrete number of times.

- The foreach loop is used to process arrays and hashes.

I think Perl included the C-like syntax of the for loop because it is familiar to so many programmers. I also believe the array and hash processing format of the foreach loop is just so convenient you can't help but make that your default format.

Because it's less confusing, you'll learn about the for and foreach statements as if they were different commands. But keep in mind that the for and foreach statements are identical as far as your computer is concerned.

for Loops

The for loop is traditionally used for processing a block of statements a discrete number of times. In this traditional format, an index variable is normally initialized, tested, and incremented all inside the control clause's conditional expression. This syntax is supported in Perl 5 with the following structure:

```
for (initialization list;
    conditional expression;
    increment list){
  block of statements
}
```

A standard for loop contains a simple initialization list, a conditional expression, and an single increment statement, like this:

```
for($i=0; $i<10; $i++){
    print $i;
  }
```

The initialization list can be any statement, even an empty statement, but the trailing semicolon is required. The initialization list is executed only once, before any other for loop statement, as the loop begins execution. The initialization list is always executed, even if the conditional expression evaluates to false and the for loop's block of statements never executes. The initialization list can be any valid expression, but it is usually used to assign an initial value to the loop increment variable. The loop increment variable is visible outside the for loop's block of statements.

You may string zero, one, or many statements together in an initialization list, separating each statement by a comma. This has practical purposes when you are manipulating matrices and need to initialize and increment multiple indexes, like this:

```
for ($i = 0, $j = 0 ; $j < 1000; $i++, $j++){
    block of statements
}
```

The conditional expression may also be an empty statement, but again the trailing semicolon is required. The conditional expression, as always, determines if the block of statements associated with the for loop will execute.

As with all control statements, the block of statements is executed only if the conditional expression is true. The conditional expression can be extended by adding parentheses, where necessary, like this:

```
for (i=0,j=0; (i<10)&&(j<10); i++,j++){
    print "$i, $j\n";
    }
```

The increment list follows the same syntactical rules as the initialization list. There may be zero, one, or many increment expressions. The increment expression may be any valid expression. A comma must separate multiple increment expressions. Unlike the initialization list, the increment list is executed each time the block of statements is executed as the last statement of the for loop.

As a general programming rule, a for loop's conditional expression variable should not be modified inside the for loop's block of statements. The for loop's conditional expression variable is normally modified in the increment list. This is the reverse of the while and until loops, where the conditional expression variable is normally modified within the loop's block of statements, preventing an infinite loop.

Each of the three statements inside the for list is optional. The semicolons in this format are not optional, however. If you don't include a conditional expression, the for statement is evaluated as true. You can write an infinite loop like this:

```
for (;;) {block of statements}
```

A common use the `for` loop syntax is to retrieve the index variable in an array instead of the cell value itself. As shown here, the variable $i is used to iterate through the array @roomList:

```
for ($i=0; $i <= $#roomList; $i++){
    ($thisRoom = $roomList[$i]) =~ s/[^a-zA-Z0-9]//g;
```

Listing 9.3 contains three different `for` loops drawn from an online reservation program, named WARM (which my company, ASSI, sells over the Internet).

Listing 9.3:   **for Loops**

```
1.   # Construct the array that shows which year a certain
2.   # month is in (Dec 1997, Jan 1998)
3.   #
4.   $saveYear  = $thisYear;
5.   $saveMonth = $thisMonth;
6.   $saveDay   = $thisDay;
7.   for ($i = 0; $i < 12; $i++,$thisMonth++) {
8.       if ($thisMonth > 12) {
9.           $thisMonth = 1;
10.          $thisYear++;
11.      }
12.      $yearList[$thisMonth] = $thisYear;
13. }
14.
15. for ($roomNumber = 0;
16.        $lodgingInfo{'ROOM_PREFERENCE'} ne $roomList
                                              [$roomNumber];
17.        $roomNumber++){}
18.
19. my (@roomList) = split(/:/,$configData{'ITEM_NAMES'});
20. $roomNumber = -1;
21. ($cleanRoom = $registrationInfo[$ROOM])=~ s/[^a-zA-Z0-9]//g;
22. for ($i=0; $i <= $#roomList; $i++){
23.      ($thisRoom = $roomList[$i]) =~ s/[^a-zA-Z0-9]//g;
24.      if ($cleanRoom =~ /$thisRoom/i){
25.          $roomNumber = $i;
26.          last;
27.      }
28.  }
```

The first for loop begins on line 7 and illustrates a practical use for multiple expressions in the increment list:

```
for ($i = 0; $i < 12; $i++,$thisMonth++) {
```

The loop creates an array of years associated with the months from 1 to 12; hence, the loop increments 12 times from 0 to 11.

A difficulty arises because the initial month may be any value from 1 to 12, and each month must be associated with the correct year. Each cell is loaded by the beginning month variable $thisMonth. If $thisMonth begins with 12, cell 12 of the @yearList array is loaded with $thisYear, say 1998, and then the increment statements, $i++,$thisMonth++, are executed. The variable $thisMonth now equals 13. The conditional expression on line 8 evaluates to true:

```
if ($thisMonth > 12) {
```

The variable $thisMonth is set to 1, to indicate January, and the year is incremented to 1999. The conditional expression variable $i is not modified, which makes sure the loop processes the correct number of times.

The second for loop, on line 15 of Listing 9.3, illustrates an empty block of statements:

```
for ($roomNumber = 0;
```

The loop determines the correct room number stored into the variable, $roomNumber. This loop illustrates that the increment list is only executed if the loop's conditional expression evaluates to true. The variable $roomNumber is incremented until a match is found. The conditional expression evaluates to false, and the loop's increment variable is available outside the loop for further use.

The for loop on line 15 also illustrates a programming concept called side effects. The normal purpose of a loop is to execute a block of statements. A side effect of the process is the incrementing and testing of the increment variable, $roomNumber. However, in this example, the side effect of incrementing the variable until the conditional expression evaluates to false is the actual purpose of this code.

WARNING Coding for side effects is normally considered poor programming practice, because it is frequently obscure, providing a potential hiding place for bugs. You may also forget the actual purpose of the code, which is hidden in the side effect, so your code is harder to maintain and debug. Use this programming technique judiciously. In this case, the side effect nature of the code is relatively clear.

The third loop, which begins on line 22 of Listing 9.3, illustrates exiting from the loop from multiple locations:

```
for ($i=0; $i <= $#roomList; $i++){
    ($thisRoom = $roomList[$i]) =~ s/[^a-zA-Z0-9]//g;
    if ($cleanRoom =~ /$thisRoom/i){
        $roomNumber = $i;
        last;
    }
}
```

The primary exit is the conditional expression; the secondary exit is the last statement on line 26. You'll learn more about exiting a loop from multiple locations later in the chapter, in the section about loop modifiers.

This third loop implements the same functionality as the loop on line 15. Because the data comparison includes potential modification by a human, the variable comparison is more complex. The regular expressions on lines 21 and 23 remove all characters that are not the letters A through Z or the numbers 0 through 9. You'll learn more about regular expressions in Chapter 16.

Listing 9.3 should give you an idea of how to use for loops. In the next section, you'll learn the syntax of handling lists, arrays, and hashes using foreach loops.

foreach loops

The syntax of the for statement when processing lists, arrays, or hashes is normally expressed using the synonym foreach, like this:

```
foreach $listVariable (list){
    block of statements
}
```

The list syntax of the foreach loop is the same for processing an array or a hash. Perl 5 converts the array or hash into a sequential list and processes the list of elements sequentially.

List Processing with foreach Loops

The foreach loop steps through a list one element at a time. When the entire list has been processed, a null is returned as the next element in the list, and the foreach loop exits its block of statements.

The list variable ($listVariable) is optional. The following syntax is also valid:

```
foreach (list){
    block of statements
}
```

When the list variable is omitted, the special default variable ($_) is assigned the value of each element in the list, iteratively. A foreach loop that prints each of its elements could be written explicitly, like this:

```
foreach $number (1 .. 10){
    print "$number";
}
```

or implicitly, like this:

```
foreach (1 .. 10){
    print;
}
```

Unlike the increment variable in the for loop syntax, the list variable's scope is local to the foreach block of statements. The list variable does not modify variables of the same name whose scope is exterior to the foreach block of statements, as illustrated here:

```
$number = 55;
foreach $number (1 .. 10){
    print "$number ";
}
print "$number\n";
```

This code will print the numbers 1 through 10 and then the number 55.

The foreach loop executes once for each element in the list, unless some other statement like last causes an early exit from the loop. So if you have ten elements in your list, the loop will execute ten times, like this:

```
foreach $number(1,2,3,4,5,6,7,8,9,10){
    print "$number W";
}
```

If you have a sequential list, you can use the range operator, like this:

```
foreach $number (1 .. 10) {
    print "$number"'
    }
```

You can mix the range operator and the comma operator in a list, like this:

```
foreach $element (a,b,c,1 .. 10,e,f,g,Q .. Z){
    print $element
}
```

Anything that is valid in a list is valid in a `foreach` loop list. As with all list processing, any embedded list, like 1 .. 4, within a list is first expanded into its element list. By the time the list is actually processed by the `foreach` statement; the list (1 .. 4) has been processed into its element list (1, 2, 3, 4). In other words, the lists with embedded lists and the lists where each element is explicitly stated are identical to the `foreach` statement.

Array Processing with foreach Loops

When you process an array in a `foreach` loop, each element, or cell of the array, will be processed by the loop as if it were part of a list. If the array contains references to another array, those references will not be followed to the referenced array because they are considered a scalar element of a list. Using references in loops is discussed later in the chapter.

The syntax for processing an array with a `foreach` loop is:

```
foreach $arrayElement (@array){
    block of statements
}
```

As with the list syntax of the `foreach` loop, if `$arrayElement` is omitted, the default special variable ($_) will be set to the value of each element of the array.

Listing 9.4 points out a powerful and somewhat dangerous feature of processing an array using the `foreach` syntax: If you change `$arrayElement` inside the `foreach` loop, you are also changing its corresponding value in the array.

Listing 9.4:   **foreach Loop Array Processing**

```
1.  #!/usr/local/bin/perl
2.  @digits = (1..10);
3.  foreach $number (@digits){
4.      print $number;
5.      $number += 10;
6.  }
7.  print "\n\n@digits";
```

When the @digits array is printed on line 7, it prints the numbers 11 through 20. You may find this surprising. It happens because the array element variable is a reference to the array cell, not a copy of the array cell value. If you change the array element variable's value, as line 5 of Listing 9.4 does, you change the contents of the array.

Hash Processing with foreach Loops

When I first learned Perl, I thought hashes were just fancy two-dimensional arrays. With that in mind, I tried a foreach loop using the regular array format to get at the data. It didn't work. As you learned in Chapter 6, a hash is more than a two-dimensional array, and you cannot access the data by just using a single foreach loop.

Because a hash is a hash table, the indexes into the hash are not stored sequentially, nor are they retrieved sequentially. When you process a hash with a foreach loop, you should use the helper function keys or values, which also were discussed in Chapter 6.

The basic syntax for accessing any hash using a foreach loop and the keys function is:

```
foreach $index (keys %hash){
     print $hash{$index};
}
```

The keys function creates a list of the indexes into a hash.

The values function returns a list of the data in a hash. If you only care about the contents of your hash, use this format:

```
foreach $value (values %hash){
     print $value ;
}
```

Because the keys and values functions return information about the hash in the same order, they can be used together to print the values of a hash, with their keys in sorted order.

Listing 9.5 demonstrates using the keys and values functions with foreach loops. This program prints the environment variables of your computer. The %ENV hash always contains the environment variables of the process where the program is running. Figure 9.2 shows some of the results of running the program in Listing 9.5 on my computer.

Listing 9.5:   **foreach Loop Hash Processing**

```
1.  #!/usr/local/bin/perl
2.  print " SORTED INDEXES OF THE HASH %ENV \n";
3.
4.  foreach $key (sort (keys %ENV)){
5.     print "key = $key and retrieves: $ENV{$key}\n";
6.  }
7.  print "\n  SORTED VALUES OF THE HASH %ENV \n";
8.
9.  foreach $value (sort (values %ENV)){
10.    print "value = $value}\n";
11. }
```

FIGURE 9.2:

Processing hashes in
foreach loops

The foreach loop on lines 4 through 6 sorts the indexes retrieved using the keys functions. If you want to retrieve your data in sorted order, use the format in lines 8 through 11. (The sort function used on lines 4 and 9 is covered in Chapter 6.)

Listing 9.6 demonstrates the use of the hash %ENV in a CGI program, and Figure 9.3 shows the output from running the program on my virtual domain at www.practical-inet.com.

Listing 9.6:   foreach Loop Hash Processing in a CGI Program

```perl
1.  #!/usr/bin/perl
2.  print<<'eof';
3.  Content-Type: text/html
4.
5.  <html>
6.  <head><title>CGI Environment Variables</title></head>
7.  <body>
8.
9.  eof
10.
11. foreach $index (keys %ENV){
12.     print "$index => $ENV{$index} <br>";
13. }
14.
15. print<<'eof';
16. </body>
17. </html>
18. eof
```

FIGURE 9.3:

Processing hashes with a foreach loop in a CGI program

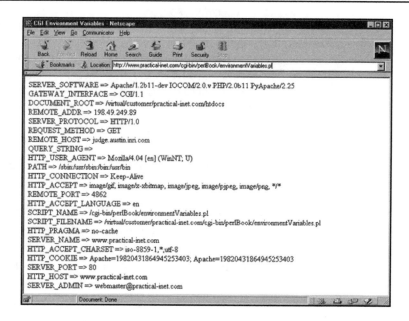

You'll notice that the results are dramatically different from those shown in Figure 9.2. The %ENV hash is always available to your process, whether it's running on a Unix or Windows operating system. Figure 9.2 showed the results of retrieving the %ENV hash on my Windows NT server. Figure 9.3 shows the results for my virtual domain, which is a Unix system. You can see that Listing 9.6 was actually accessed via a web browser by examining the environment variables in Figure 9.3. For example, the environment variable HTTP_USER_AGENT tells you what type of browser called the program. The environment variable SCRIPT_FILENAME tells you the location and script name that the browser accessed to produce the output.

Since Listing 9.6 is meant to be accessed via a web browser, line 3 prints out the required HTTP headers, and lines 5 through 7 print the HTML information.

Line 11 accesses the %ENV hash using the keys function in a foreach loop, which means that it is actually accessing a list of the indexes into the hash $ENV one element at a time:

```
foreach $index (keys %ENV){
```

The keys function returns a list. The foreach loop statement then processes that list. You could also look at line 11 as processing the list shown here (the list produced when the keys function processed the $ENV hash on my web server):

```
foreach $index (SERVER_SOFTWARE, GATEWAY_INTERFACE,
                DOCUMENT_ROOT,
        REMOTE_ADDR, SERVER_PROTOCOL, REQUEST_METHOD,
          REMOTE_HOST,
        QUERY_STRING, HTTP_USER_AGENT, PATH, HTTP_CONNECTION,
        HTTP_ACCEPT, REMOTE_PORT, HTTP_ACCEPT_LANGUAGE,
        SCRIPT_NAME, SCRIPT_FILENAME, HTTP_PRAGMA, SERVER_NAME,
        HTTP_ACCEPT_CHARSET, SERVER_PORT, HTTP_HOST, SERVER_ADMIN) {
    print "$index => $ENV{$index} <br>";
}
```

Line 12 of Listing 9.6 produced all of the data shown in Figure 9.3:

```
print "$index => $ENV{$index} <br>";
```

As the foreach statement processes each element of the list returned from the keys function, the element is stored into the $index variable. That variable is printed on line 12 and is used to access the data in the $ENV hash. The <br> at the end of the print statement acts like a newline character in HTML.

Listing 9.7 shows a practical example of `foreach` loop processing. This program determines if a browser can understand Java 1.2 classes, using a programming concept called *table-driven code*. With table-driven code, instead of trying to handle every possible condition with an `if` check, some of the possibilities are placed into a data structure (a table), often an array. Then the data structure is used to help determine which path the code should execute.

NOTE

The program shown in Listing 9.7 was written by my partner, Tim Coats, to determine whether to show the Java 1.1 or 1.2 version of our web page. At the time the code was written, only the HotJava 1.0 browser could understand Java 1.2 classes. Because Tim used table-driven code, the logic of the program needs to be written only once, and the table can be modified as new browsers become capable of handling Java 1.2 classes.

Listing 9.7: **What Is the Browser Type?**

```
1.   #!/usr/local/bin/perl
2.   # This array specifies all of the browsers that are capable of
3.   # properly displaying our web page.
4.   # It is arranged as browser:version where this is the name
5.   # of the browser reported in the HTTP_USER_AGENT
6.   # environment variable and version is the least capable version
7.   # of the browser that can support our needs.
8.
9.   @allSupportedBrowsers = (
10.      "Mozilla:5.0",
11.      "HotJava:1.0",
12.      "Internet Explorer:4.0"
13.   );
14.   ################################################
15.   # Main routine that determines the capabilities of the
16.   # user's browser then displays the appropriate web
17.   # page
18.   ($usersBrowser, $usersVersion) = split(/\//,$ENV
                                  {'HTTP_USER_AGENT'});
19.
20.   # Remove everything from the version other than the first
21.   # occurrence of a version number in the form
22.   # digits.digits
23.   $usersVersion =~ /([0-9]+\.[0-9]+)/;
```

```
24.  $usersVersion = $1;
25.
26.  # Determine whether the user's browser (including version)
27.  # can support our web page.
28.
29.  $canBrowserBeUsed = "NO";
30.  foreach $supportedEntry (@allSupportedBrowsers) {
31.     ($supportedBrowser, $supportedVersion) = split(/:/,
                                                    $supportedEntry);
32.     if (($usersBrowser eq $supportedBrowser) &&
                            ($usersVersion >= $supportedVersion)) {
33.        $canBrowserBeUsed = "YES";
34.        last; # break out of foreach loop
35.     }
36.  }
37.  # Determine which version of the web page to display
38.  if ($canBrowserBeUsed eq "YES") {
39.     &printForSupportedBrowser;
40.  }
41.  else {
42.     &printForNonSupportedBrowser;
43.  }
44.  ##################################################
45.  # Construct the version of the web page for
46.  # Java 1.2 enabled browsers
47.  sub printForSupportedBrowser(){
48.     &printTop;
49.     &printMiddleForJava11EnabledBrowser;
50.     $printBottom;
51.  }
52.
53.  ##################################################
54.  # Construct the version of the web page for
55.  # Java 1.2 deficient browsers
56.  #
57.
58.  sub printForNonSupportedBrowser(){
59.     &printTop;
60.     &printMiddleForNonJava11EnabledBrowser;
61.     $printBottom;
62.  }
63.
64.  ##################################################
```

```
65.   # Output the top, common portion of the web
66.   # pages.
67.
68.   sub printTop(){
69.   print<<"eof";
70.   Content-Type: text/html
71.
72.   <html>
73.   <head><title>Application Software Solutions, Inc.</title></head>
74.   <body>
75.   <center>
76.   <img src="images/assiLogo.gif" border=2></a>
77.   <h1>Application Software Solutions, Inc.</h1>
78.   <hr>
79.   <p>
80.   Application Software Solutions, Inc. does custom programming,
81.   which means any type of JAVA, PERL, or  C++ application.
82.
83.   </center>
84.   <p>
85.   eof
86.   }
87.
88.   ##################################################
89.   # Output the middle portion of the web page for
90.   # Java 1.2 enabled browsers.
91.
92.   sub printMiddleForJava11EnabledBrowser(){
93.   print<<"eof";
94.   <p>
95.   <center>
96.   <hr>
97.   <APPLET ARCHIVE="Downloading.jar" CODE=
                       "assi/awt/DownloadingApplet"
98.   WIDTH=0 HEIGHT=0 NAME="ASSIDownloading">
99.   <PARAM NAME=AppletBeingDownloaded VALUE="ASSI Applet">
100.  </APPLET>
101.  <table border=5>
102.  <tr>
103.  <th>
104.  <APPLET ARCHIVE="assi.jar,symantec.jar" CODE=
                       "ASSI/login/ASSIApplet"
105.  WIDTH=100 HEIGHT=40>
```

```
106. <PARAM NAME="DownloadWindowAppletName" VALUE="ASSIDownloading">
107. </APPLET>
108. </th>
109. </tr>
110. </table>
111. </center>
112. eof
113. }
114. ###############################################
115. # Output the middle portion of the web page for
116. # non Java 1.2 enabled browsers.
117. #
118. sub printMiddleForNonJava11EnabledBrowser(){
119. print<<"eof";
120. <p>
121. <center>
122. <hr>
123. <table border=5>
124. <tr>
125. <th>
126. The ASSI applet requires a Java 1.2 capable browser.
127. </th>
128. </tr>
129. </table>
130. </center>
131. eof
132. }
133.
134. #########################################
135. # Output the bottom, common portion of the web
136. # pages.
137. sub printBottom(){
138. print<<"eof";
139. <hr>
140. <a href="mailto:yawp\@io.com, jamartin\@io.com">
141. <img src="images/mailbutt.gif" align=center> <i> Send mail to
             ASSI</i>
142. </a>
143. <hr>
144. </body>
145. </html>
146. eof
147. }
```

The key to this table-driven program is in the table-initialization code between lines 9 and 13:

```
@allSupportedBrowsers = (
    "Mozilla:5.0",
    "HotJava:1.0",
    "Internet Explorer:4.0"
);
```

This program can be used for many practical purposes, such as determining if a browser is frames-compliant or if it allows cookies, handles, Java, or any other browser-specific function. You can put different browsers and versions in this table, and the code will work just fine.

TIP

You can use this program as a framework for verifying a browser's compliance with your site's requirements. For example, If you are interested in making sure the browser supports frames, just change the browser values to Mozilla 3.0 and Internet Explorer 2.0. Add any other browser you're interested in, and you have the tools to check if the browser supports frames.

Line 18 uses the CGI environment variable HTTP_USER_AGENT to determine the browser type and browser version. As in Listing 9.6, it accesses the hash %ENV to get a CGI environment variable:

```
($usersBrowser, $usersVersion) = split(/\//,$ENV{'HTTP_USER_AGENT'});
```

Lines 23 through 24 use pattern matching to set a formatted version number:

```
$usersVersion =~ /([0-9]+\.[0-9]+)/;
$usersVersion = $1;
```

The pattern match can be read as, "Find at least one number followed by a period followed by at least one number. (Pattern matching is covered in detail in Chapter 16.)

Line 29 initializes the conditional variable, $canBrowserBeUsed, to "NO" before the loop is started. The loop only checks to see if it can find one match in the list of compliant browsers. If it finds one valid match, it sets the conditional variable to "YES" and exits the loop.

The foreach loop on lines 30 through 36 steps through the array @allSupported-Browsers one element at a time:

```
foreach $supportedEntry (@allSupportedBrowsers) {
```

```
    ($supportedBrowser, $supportedVersion) = split(/:/,$supportedEntry);
    if (($usersBrowser eq $supportedBrowser)
        && ($usersVersion >= $supportedVersion)) {
      $canBrowserBeUsed = "YES";
      last; # break out of foreach loop
    }
  }
```

The `foreach` loop reads the array one array cell at a time. Each array cell contains the browser type and browser version that supports Java 1.2 classes. The Java 1.2 compliant browser is compared with the calling browser. If the calling browser can handle Java 1.2, a variable is set indicating compliance.

If the browser supports Java 1.2 classes, the loop is exited on line 34 using the `last` command, and the Java 1.2 web page is sent. If a Java 1.2 compliant browser isn't found, the flag variable `$canBrowserBeUsed` remains equal to `"NO"` and an error page is sent.

Perl 5 does all the work of incrementing through the array for you. When every element in an array is processed, the `foreach` loop exits automatically. So if this code is called to handle a browser that does not support Java 1.2 classes, the variable `$supportedEntry` will be set once to each value of the array. It is separated into browser and version number on line 31. The `if` test on line 32 will fail and `$canBrowerBeUsed` will never be set to `"YES"`. The `else` portion of the `if else` clause between lines 38 and 43 will be executed:

```
if ($canBrowserBeUsed eq "YES") {
  &printForSupportedBrowser;
}
else {
  &printForNonSupportedBrowser;
}
```

The HTML for the non-supported browser will be printed.

If the browser is a HotJava browser, the `foreach` loop will be exited on the second pass. On the first pass, the variable `$supportedEntry` will be set to `Mozilla 5.0` (it isn't `Mozilla:5.0` because the data is separated on line 31 by the `split` function, which was introduced in Chapter 8). On the second pass, `$supportedEntry` will be set to `$HotJava 1.0`. The `if` check on line 32 will pass. The variable `$can-BrowserBeUsed` will be set to `"YES"` on line 33. Finally, the `last` statement will cause the loop to be exited. Line 39 will then be executed, and the HTML for a Java 1.2 browser will be printed.

In this listing, as in Listings 9.1 and 9.3, the `last` command exited the `for` and `foreach` loops instead of the conditional expression causing the loop exit. You'll learn more about using the `last` command, as well as the `next`, `continue`, and `redo` commands, later in the chapter.

Array References in Loops

In Chapter 7, you learned about Perl 5 references and how they can be used to create multi-dimensional arrays. Referencing arrays in loops can be tricky. Consider these facts:

- A reference is a location of a value in memory.

- An array name is the starting location of multiple values that are retrieved based on the starting location in memory.

These two facts mean that if you make multiple references to the same starting location in a loop or any other context, you have not created multiple array references. Each array reference refers to the same place. As an example, look at this code:

```
for $line (@book) {
        @words = split(/\wi1, $line);
        @wordList [lineNumber++] =\@words;
    }
```

In the third line, multiple copies to the same starting location are saved into an array, so it does not create multiple array references. The `@words` array is loaded each time through the `for` loop with a new list of words, and the previous word list is destroyed by the new word list.

If you want to keep copies of each array as it is created, you must create a new copy of the array to be referenced each time through the loop. You can accomplish this by using the `my` keyword, which creates a new variable each time it is called. Here is a revised version of the code above:

```
for $line (@book) {
        my @words = split(/\wi1, $line);
        @wordList [lineNumber++] =\@words;
    }
```

Notice the difference on the second line. Variables that are prefixed with the my prefix are created each time that the line they are on is executed. The curly braces on the first and fourth lines do not restrict the regular variable created on the second line. (Curly braces create a block of statements for the variable declared using the my keyword.) A new copy of the @words array is created and loaded with a new list of words.

An alternative is to also use the anonymous array operator ([], discussed in Chapter 7):

```
for $line (@book) {
     my @words = split(/\wil, $line);
     @wordList [lineNumber++] = [@words];
  }
```

When used in this manner ([@words]), the @words array is copied into a new anonymous array and a reference to the new anonymous array is stored in @wordList.

Either method will work. I personally prefer using the my keyword. It is a little more efficient because an array copy is not required.

As a more complex example, the foreach loop in Listing 9.8 accesses an array reference inside a hash. I have included the subroutine that creates the %expanded-Codes hash so you can see everything in context.

NOTE   Listing 9.8 is small piece of a much larger program that uses arrays and hashes to decode a standard message format used for transmitting electronic messages.

Listing 9.8:   **Referencing an Array inside a Hash**

```
1.  foreach $idKey (sort numericSort (keys (%expandedCodes))){
2.      print "$idKey: ";
3.      $arrayReference = $expandedCodes{$idKey};
4.      for ($idKeyIndex = 0; $idKeyIndex <=
             $#{$arrayReference}; $idKeyIndex++){
5.        print "$expandedCodes{$idKey}[$idKeyIndex] ";
6.        #print "$arrayReference[$idKeyIndex], ";
7.      }
8.      print "\n";
9.  }
```

```
10.
11. sub processCodes(){
12.     my ($code) = @_;
13.     my ($id, $values, @idValues, $idValue, $i, $idOnly,
            $endOfCodes);
14.     my (@beginCode, @endCode, $k, $wrap);
15.
16.     local (@allCodes, $allCodesIndex, %codeValues);
17.     ($id,$values) = split(/=/,$code);
18.     @idValues = split(/,/,$values);
19.     #have we processed this code previously?
20.     if ($expandedCodes{$id}){
21.         return ;
22.     }
23.
24. IDLOOP:
25.     foreach $idValue (@idValues){
26.         if ( $idValue =~ /[:%]/){
27.             if ($idValue =~ /%/){
28.                 $endOfCodes = 1;
29.                 ($idValue) = split(/%/,$idValue);
30.                 if ($idValue =~ /:/){
31.                     &expandCodes($idValue);
32.                 }
33.                 else{
34.                     $allCodes[$allCodesIndex++] = $idValue;
35.                 }
36.             }
37.             else {
38.                 &expandCodes($idValue);
39.             }
40.         }
41.         else {
42.             $allCodes[$allCodesIndex++] = $idValue;
43.         }
44.         if ($endOfCodes){
45.             last IDLOOP;
46.         }
47.     }#end foreach
48.     $expandedCodes{$id} = \@allCodes;
49. }
```

As you can see from line 5 of Listing 9.8, the right arrow operator is not required to dereference the array reference stored in a hash:

```
print "$expandedCodes{$idKey}[$idKeyIndex] ";
```

The following syntax is equivalent:

```
$expandedCodes{$idKey}[$idKeyIndex]
$expandedCodes{$idKey}->[$idKeyIndex]
```

The right arrow operator is always assumed when accessing two- or three-dimensional arrays, whether they are regular arrays or hashes.

Notice in line 16 of Listing 9.8 that an array is created with the `local` keyword:

```
local (@allCodes, $allCodesIndex, %codeValues);
```

The `local` keyword follows rules similar to the `my` keyword rules. The major difference is the variables created with the `local` keyword are visible to subroutines called with enclosing braces or blocks of code. Variables created with the `my` keyword are not visible to subroutines called from within enclosing braces. You'll learn more about subroutines and scope in Chapter 18.

The nice thing about hashes is their ability to come into existence when they are needed. This really makes sense when you don't know what type or how many objects you need to process. Lines 20 through 22 of Listing 9.8 take care of determining if `$id` has already been processed:

```
if ($expandedCodes{$id}){
    return ;
}
```

If the hash has already created a slot for an ID, the `if` check will return true and the code will return.

The last thing to focus on in Listing 9.8 is line 48:

```
$expandedCodes{$id} = \@allCodes;
```

The array created on line 16 with the `local` keyword is saved by reference on this line.

Now that you've learned about the different types of loops and how to use references in loops, you're ready to learn about the commands that modify loops. The next section describes four commands that can change a loop's control flow.

Loop Modifiers

The title of this section is a bit of a misnomer. Only two commands, `continue` and `next`, of the four discussed here are limited to modifying loops. The `last` and `redo` commands operate on any block of statements. However, all of these commands are traditionally used to modify a loop's flow of control.

The Structured Programming Case against Multiple Exits

In the early 1980s, structured programming was the technique of choice. In the 1990s (and beyond, I'm sure), object-oriented design is the technique of choice. Object-oriented programming doesn't change structured programming techniques; it just repackages them, so the rules of structured programming usually still apply to the newer methodologies of object-oriented programming.

One of the rules of structured programming required every block of statements to have one exit point and only one exit point. The concept of forward-flow, single-point exits developed as a response to the spaghetti-code-creating `goto`, which was everywhere in programming of the 1970s.

Over the years, I rigidly followed the one exit point rule. Now don't get me wrong, this rule has its practical uses, but programmers need to be flexible. Sometimes, it's just plain natural to jump around a little (just look at my 9-year-old-son, Steven).

On one hand, jumping around in your code, modifying the forward flow of execution, can create code that is hard to follow. On the other hand, using only forward-flow, single-point exits can create extra variables (called *flags*) that are incorrectly initialized and maintained.

Balance is the best approach. A little judicious common sense should be applied with the loop/block of statement modifiers `last`, `redo`, `continue`, and `next`.

The continue Block

Earlier in the chapter, you learned that the `for` loop's increment list executes after the loop's block of statements. The `continue` block of statements is equivalent semantically to the increment list.

The `continue` block of statements can be added to the `while`, `until`, and `for-each` syntax, like this:

```
while (conditional expression){
    block of statements
}
continue {
    block of statements
}
```

The `continue` block of statements is just a different way of showing the increment list, so you cannot have an increment list and a `continue` block of statements in the same loop. The following syntax is illegal and will not compile:

```
for (;;){
    block of statements
}
continue {
    block of statements
}
```

The `continue` block of statements is affected by the loop modifiers `next`, `redo`, and `last`, as follows:

- The `next` loop modifier executes the `continue` block of statements before returning execution to the top of the loop.

- The `last` loop modifier exits the enclosing block of statements without executing the `continue` block of statements.

- The `redo` loop modifier executes the first line of the loop's block of statements without executing the `continue` block of statements.

The last Command

The `last` command works with or without a label modifier:

```
last;
```

or

```
last LABEL;
```

You've seen examples of using the `last` command with a label modifier in a `SWITCH` block in Chapter 8 (Listing 8.4) and in Listing 9.1 at the beginning of this chapter. Listings 9.3 and 9.7 show the `last` command used without a label modifier.

When the `last` command is used without a label modifier, it exits the current block of statements. When the `last` command is used with a label modifier, it exits the block of statements associated with the label modifier. The block of statements being exited may be several levels above the current block of statements. Be aware that if the `last` command is executed within a `for` loop with an increment list or `continue` block of statements, neither the increment list nor `continue` block of statements will be executed.

next

Unlike the `last` and `redo` loop modifiers, which can operate with a bare block of statements, the `next` command works with only a loop block of statements. The `next` command executes any associated `continue` block of statements or increment list before returning control to the loop's control block of statements.

The `next` command operates with or without a label:

```
next;
```

or

```
next LABEL;
```

Without a label, the `next` command returns execution to the enclosing block of statements `for`, `foreach`, `while`, or `until` loop's control block of statements. With a label, the `next` command exits to the loop associated with the accompanying label.

Listing 9.9 (another excerpt from the online reservation program, WARM) demonstrates the use of the `next` command without a label.

Listing 9.9:	The next Command

```
1.    foreach $line (@$ref){
2.        if ($lineNumber == $index++){
3.            #If status request is a REMOVE don't print reservation
4.            my @reservation = split(/:/,$line);
5.            #ONLY REMOVE RESERVATION if it has already been deleted
6.            if ( ($reservation[$STATUS] =~ /DELETED/) &&
                    ($status =~ /REMOVED/)){
```

```
7.                    next;
8.                }
9.                $reservation[$STATUS] = $status if $status !~
                                        /REMOVED/;
10.               foreach $item (@reservation){
11.                   print GUESTINFO "$item: ";
12.               }
13.               print GUESTINFO "\n";
14.           }
15.       else{
16.           print GUESTINFO "$line";
17.       }
18.   }
```

On line 7, the next command causes the remaining code to be skipped and the loop resumes execution at the foreach statement's control clause. In this loop, the next command performs the primary task of removing a reservation from the database.

The redo Command

The redo command is more like a goto command than a loop modifier, and it is not used often in practice. This command does not return execution to the loop control block of statements, nor does it execute the continue block of statements or the increment list. It jumps to the first statement of a block of statements.

Like the other commands discussed so far, the redo command operates with or without a label:

```
redo;
```

or

```
redo LABEL;
```

Without a label modifier, the redo command jumps to the first statement of the enclosing block of statements. With a label modifier, it jumps to the first statement of the block of statements associated with the label.

The redo command works within any enclosing block of statements. The redo command creates its own loop syntax and can be substituted for a while or until loop, like this:

```
{
block of statements
redo if conditional expression;
}
```

This block of statements executes exactly like a while or until loop except the block of statements executes at least once prior to encountering the redo statement.

Summary

In this chapter, you learned the syntax and details of Perl 5's loop control statements. We began with the while and until loops, which are mirror images of each other. The while loop stops executing when its conditional expression evaluates to false. The until loop stops executing when its conditional expression evaluates to true. As you saw in the sections on while and until loops, the logic is sometimes easier to understand and more succinct depending on which loop command you chose. Judicious use of both the while and until commands can lead to more maintainable code.

Next, you learned about the for and foreach loops, which are identical as far as your computer is concerned. For the average programmer, however, the for loop traditionally handles a block of statements a discrete number of times. The foreach loop traditionally handles arrays and hashes.

The details and variety of ways to handle lists, arrays, and hashes are part of what makes the Perl language so much fun. You learned in this chapter that modifying the array element variable inside a for loop's block of statements actually modifies the array, and you learned processing hashes using the keys and sort function is a simple and straightforward task.

Amazingly enough, as you finish this chapter, you have covered the core of Perl 5. Unlike other programming languages, however, Perl 5 has a lot more to offer than just data structures and branching statements. In the next part of this book, you'll learn the details of reading from the command line, printing, and file I/O. Until I learned Perl 5, I found these programming tasks rather arduous. Perl 5 makes programming I/O a breeze, as you'll learn in the following chapters.

PART III

Input and Output Handling

Jump-Start on Input/Output

- File input

- File output

- Directory handling

No matter how much time you spend solving a problem, if you cannot communicate the results, your program is useless. Getting data into and out of your program is called I/O programming. Depending on the computer language you are working with, I/O programming can be a simple or very complex portion of your program. With Perl 5, I/O programming is so easy it often seems like magic.

Perl 5's I/O features are the easiest to use of a dozen or so languages I'm familiar with. I strongly recommend you take the time to learn the Perl 5 I/O details covered in Chapters 11 through 13. But if you need to get started tonight, this chapter will show you how to get data into and out of your program.

Jump-Start Definitions

@ARGV

A standard Perl 5 array, created by the Perl 5 interpreter at startup, that contains all data from the command line after the program name and up to when the Enter key was pressed.

Buffered I/O

A type of I/O that reads or writes data into a larger block of memory (called a *buffer*) during I/O operations. During read operations, an optimized size of the file is read into memory. Subsequent reads from the file access the memory buffer until the buffered data is exhausted, thereby limiting the actual times the disk is accessed. During write operations, the data being written to disk is written to memory until an optimized amount of data is in the buffer for writing to the disk. The data in the memory buffer is then written to disk, thus limiting the actual number of times the disk is accessed.

Directory handle

A link between your computer program and the directory on your disk.

Effective ID

The ID your program is currently executing under.

Epoch time

The number of seconds from some fixed date, usually midnight (00:00:00), January 1, 1970 GMT.

File descriptor number

A system number associated with an open file handle. The default file handles STDIN, STDOUT, and STDERR are the first file handles opened for a program. They are assigned the file descriptor values 0, 1, and 2, respectively.

File handle	A direct link from your computer program to the file on your disk, created with the open function. The file handle also keeps track of the last position read in a file.
File locking	A mechanism for handling multiple users accessing a file simultaneously. The file-lock modes include shared lock (more than one process may own the shared lock simultaneously), exclusive lock (only one process may own the file lock), unlock (release the file lock), and nonblocking lock (do not block the process from execution if it does not own the lock).
File test operators	Perl 5 operators that test for file characteristics, such as file permissions, type, size, and existence.
Filename	The path and name of a file. To work with a file, most programs require the directory path name to the filename, the filename itself, and the filename extension.
Group ID (gid)	An ID assigned to multiple users that share something in common, such as their job title, educational status or party affiliation.
Inode	Each file and directory on your computer is assigned a unique number that the operating system uses to keep track of that file. That number is called the inode.
Module	An addition to the core Perl 5 distribution, which can contain many methods (also called functions). For your program to use a module, it must include the use or require keyword and the name of the file, as in use Cwd.
Permissions mask	Parameters that set the read, write, and execute privileges for Unix files. A permissions mask must be in octal format, made up of read, write, and execute bits. A zero means the permission is off, and one means the permission is on. The read permission is bit 0, the write permission is bit 1, and the execute permission is bit 2. For example, read, write, execute (or RWX) in binary is 111, which is octal 7.
Real ID	The ID assigned to your login name.
STDIN	A default file handle opened by Perl 5 at startup. STDIN (Standard Input) is normally set to your computer keyboard. You use this file handle whenever you read input with your program from the input argument array @ARGV.

STDERR	A default file handle opened by Perl 5 at startup. STDERR (Standard Error) is usually initialized to your computer monitor.
STDOUT	A default file handle opened by Perl 5 at startup. STDOUT (Standard Output) is initially set to your computer monitor.
Switch	A default parameter set for a program before the program begins general processing. Switches allow you to turn off or on various features in your program.
Symbolic link	A filename that contains the location of the actual file. A symbolic link is not a copy of a file; it's a pointer to a file, much like a shortcut on your Windows desktop.
Umask	A Unix setting associated with the owner of each file that sets the maximum allowable read, write, and execute privileges for a file. A umask is an octal number. Each bit of the umask clears the associated bit of the permissions mask. For example, if your permissions mask is 777 and your umask is 022 (which clears the write permission for group and world), the resulting permissions mask assigned the file is 755.
Unbuffered I/O	A type of I/O that reads or writes to the disk each time a read or write operation is used in your program.
User ID (uid)	The ID of the person logged in to your computer.

Jump-Start Program

The program in Listing 10.1 reads from the command line a list of files to modify. Each line of the file is searched for a number. If a number is found, the number is formatted into a six-digit number with two decimal places. This program can be used to format ledgers and other files that contain rows of numbers that should be in a specific format. The program demonstrates many of the features discussed in this chapter.

Listing 10.1:   **File Formatting**

```
1. #!/usr/local/bin/perl
2. use Cwd;
```

```
3.   use File::Copy;
4.   #Get the current directory
5.   $dir = cwd();
6.   #Read from the command line the list of files to modify
7.   while (<>){
8.      #If this file is a symbolic link, skip the file
9.      next if -l $ARGV;
10.     #If this is the first time we read from this file,
11.     #make a copy of the file
12.     if ($ARGV ne $oldargv){
13.        #Let the user know we are modifying the file
14.        print "processing $ARGV ...\n";
15.        #Make a copy of the file
16.        copy($ARGV, $ARGV . '.old') || warn $!;
17.        $oldargv = $ARGV;
18.        #Open the file for writing
19.        #This creates a blank file
20.        open (OUTFILE, ">$ARGV");
21.        #Set the default output file
22.        select OUTFILE;
23.     }
24.     #Find a digit in the line
25.     if (/(\d+\.?\d*)/){
26.        $prev = $`;
27.        $post = $';
28.        $digit = $1;
29.        #format the digit
30.        printf "$prev % 6.2f $post", $digit;
31.     }
32.     else{
33.        print;
34.     }
35.  }#end while
36.  #Open the temporary directory
37.  opendir(DIR, "d:\\sybex\\temp");
38.  #Save the contents of the directory file
39.  @dirList = readdir(DIR);
40.  closedir(DIR);
41.  #Set the default output to STDOUT, the screen in this case
42.  select STDOUT;
43.  print "The following files have been modified\n";
44.  foreach $file (@dirList){
```

```
45.    #If the file has a .old extension, then it was modified
46.    if ($file =~ /\.old$/){
47.        #Print the filename, preceded by two tabs
48.        print "\t\t$file\n";
49.    }
50. }
```

Command-Line Input

Perl 5 makes data from the command-line interface available to your program. Like other languages (C/C++ in particular), Perl 5 loads a special variable with the contents of the command line.

Every time you start a Perl 5 program, the Perl 5 interpreter reads the contents of the command line and loads the command-line argument array @ARGV. The variable ARGV, which stands for argument vector, is actually a set of Perl 5 special variables. As you learned in Part 2 of this book, Perl 5 uses a separate variable namespace for arrays, scalars, and file handles. As shown in Table 10.1, the command-line interface variables span the scalar, array, and file handle namespaces.

NOTE If you are familiar with the global variable argc and argv, of the C/C++ programming language, then you have a head start in understanding Perl 5 command-line input. Perl 5's @ARGV isn't an exact equivalent of the C/C++ argv and argc global variables, but the information and structure of the global variable @ARGV contains similar information.

TABLE 10.1: Command-Line Interface Variables

Variable	Description
$0	The name of your program
ARGV	The file handle used when processing the @ARGV array
$ARGV	The file associated with the ARGV file handle

Continued on next page

TABLE 10.1 CONTINUED: Command-Line Interface Variables

Variable	Description
@ARGV	The array loaded with the command-line arguments
$#ARGV	The number of elements in the @ARGV array, counting from 0

When your program begins execution, it has the variables listed in Table 10.1 available for processing. The primary source of command-line input is the @ARGV array. The @ARGV array contains everything typed in at the command line when your program is started, excluding the program name. The program name is available in the special variable $0.

Each cell of the @ARGV array is loaded with a single item from the command line. An item is anything that is delineated (separated) by a space character from any other ASCII character entered at the command line. Place quotes around any list of items that contain spaces, and that list will be loaded as a single item into the @ARGV array. To see how this works, type in the following code and save it to a file named `testArgv.pl`:

```
$NUM = @argv
print $num;
```

Now run this code by typing the filename and some command-line arguments, as shown below (press Enter after the closing quote):

```
testArgv.pl  1 ABC - 3 4 5 "6 6 6"
```

The number 5 will be printed on the command line after this line is executed. You can replace the two lines of code in `testArgv.pl` with the following and get identical results:

```
print $#ARGV + 1
```

This test code demonstrates that the @ARGV array is immediately available to your program. Also, the @ARGV array contains one input for each input on the command line after the program name, and an input with spaces (such as "6 6 6") will be loaded as a single item if it is surrounded by quotes.

The file handle and filename variables, ARGV and $ARGV, are created as result of processing command-line inputs using the file input operator (<>), as demonstrated by line 7 of Listing 10.1:

```
while (<>){
```

Whenever the file input operator is used with a null file handle, the variable $ARGV is loaded with the name of the file currently being read, which you can see on line 14:

```
print "processing $ARGV ...\n";
```

Using the file input operator with a null file handle also associates the file handle ARGV with the file currently being read. The file input operator and its relationship with ARGV are explained in more detail later in this chapter, in the "Reading from a File" section.

By default, Perl 5 assumes input command-line arguments are filenames. If your program also needs to process command-line switches, you should process the @ARGV array within your program before using @ARGV to process filenames.

NOTE   If you need to read the command line for switch input, Perl 5 provides an interface to several varieties of the C switch interface program called **getopt**. The **getopt** function and modules offer an easier way to process switches than reading the @ARGV array to process program switches. Using the **getopt** function is discussed in detail in Chapter 11.

File Input

If your program's input doesn't come from the command line, a second major source of program input is from a file. Reading data from a file is similar to reading a book. First, you pick up the book and then you open it. Usually, you start reading from the front of the book. Some people (like my wife) flip to a few pages before the end of the book and read to the end before they start at the beginning. Most books are for reading only. "Don't write in my book!" Some books, like a diary, are both for writing and reading. A few books might be for writing only. These are all things you can do with a file.

Opening a File

Opening a file requires you to pick up the file and choose how you are going to read or write to the file. These choices are made in the **open** function.

A file, like a book, is picked out from other files by its name. Unlike a book, however, a file requires both the file's location and the file's name for unique identification. The file location, also called the file path name, is used as part of the filename when opening a file.

A file handle is the program connection to the file. Like a bookmark, the file handle acts as a position keeper of the last position read in a file. To create the file handle connection, you use the **open** function.

The **open** function requires a file handle and a filename. The syntax of the **open** function is:

```
open(FILEHANDLE, "filename");
```

The file handle is associated with the filename when the file is opened. A file handle follows the standard rules for variable names, except it does not begin with a dollar sign. Use all uppercase letters to distinguish your file handles from Perl 5's reserved words, which are all lowercase.

The filename may include file path information. If file path information is not included, the program looks in the current working directory of the process. When you include a file path on a Windows computer, you need to add an escape character (\) before each directory separator (\) to prevent Perl 5 from interpreting the directory separator as its escape character. In other words, file path names should have the double backslashes (\\), like this:

```
open(INFILE, "C:\\PerlBook\\Chapt10\\arrays.pl");
```

The default **open** mode is read-only. To open a file in another mode, include the appropriate **open** operator, as listed in Table 10.2, before the filename. For example, to open a file for writing, use the syntax demonstrated on line 20 of Listing 10.1:

```
open (OUTFILE, ">$ARGV");
```

TABLE 10.2: open Operators

Operation	Operator
Read	<
Write (overwrite any existing data)	>
Append (write to end of existing file)	>>
Read/write	+

Continued on next page

TABLE 10.2 CONTINUED: open Operators

Operation	Operator
Write to a program	`|filename`
Read from a program	`filename|`

Reading from a File

Of the multiple ways to read data from a file in Perl 5, the file input operator (<>) is the most straightforward. In scalar context, the file input operator reads one line from the file into the scalar variable. The syntax is:

```
$scalar = <FILEHANDLE>;
```

When the file input operator reaches an end-of-file condition, it returns `null`, which is interpreted in a conditional expression as false. The file handle (*FILE-HANDLE*) is optional.

In array context, the file input operator reads the entire contents of a file into memory in one statement, like this:

```
@allLines = < FILEHANDLE >;
```

If a file handle is not supplied, Perl 5 looks for a filename to open in the @ARGV array. That filename is loaded into the variable $ARGV and associated with the file handle ARGV. This bit of Perl magic leads to code that can open, close, and read from a list of files using just one line of code. Lines 7 through 22 of Listing 10.1 illustrate the relationship between the file input operator (<>) and $ARGV:

```
while (<>){
    #If this file is a symbolic link, skip the file
    next if -l $ARGV;
    #If this is the first time we read from this file,
    #make a copy of the file.
    if ($ARGV ne $oldargv){
        #Let the user know we are modifying the file
        print "processing $ARGV ...\n";
        #Make a copy of the file
        copy($ARGV, $ARGV . '.old') || warn $!;
        $oldargv = $ARGV;
```

```
        #Open the file for writing
        #This creates a blank file
        open (OUTFILE, ">$ARGV");
        #Set the default output file
        select OUTFILE;
}
```

Listing 10.1 will read from an infinite number of files, opening, reading, and closing each file. As each file is opened, $ARGV is assigned the filename, and the file handle ARGV is opened for reading. All of this action takes place on line 7.

As described previously, when the file input operator reads from the null file handle, the default file list is taken from @ARGV. The while loop, on line 7, reads from the null file handle, creating the association with the file list in @ARGV.

Once the file is opened, Perl 5 continues to read from the file until the file handle reaches the end of the file. Then Perl 5 closes the file and checks the @ARGV array for another filename. If the @ARGV array contains another filename, Perl 5 repeats the process, opening the next file in the @ARGV array, associating the open file handle with the global variable ARGV, and assigning the filename to $ARGV. Once all the global ARGV variables are set up, Perl 5 reads from the file into the special variable $_.

The read, using the file input operator (<>) is in scalar context, which means one line at a time is read into memory. The context of the read is scalar because the default special variable $_ receives the data from the file input operator unless another variable is assigned the result of a read. The statements while ($_ = <>) and while (<>) are equivalent.

Here is a summary of the steps Perl 5 takes when processing the while (<>) statement:

- The filename is shifted out of the @ARGV array into the $ARGV special variable, like this: $ARGV = shift @ARGV;

- The filename is opened for reading, associating the file handle ARGV with the newly opened file, like this: open (ARGV, "<$ARGV");

- The file handle ARGV is read from, one line at a time, and the data is stored into the special default variable $_, like this: $_ = <ARVG>;

- When the end of the file is reached, the file handle ARGV is closed, like this: close (ARGV);

File Output

Sending data to a file, standard output (usually your computer's screen), or even a socket requires only one command: `print`. If you want to format that output, you can use special print escape sequences or the `printf` function.

Outputting Program Data

Perl 5's basic mechanism for sending data from your program to an output device is the `print` function. The syntax of the `print` function is:

```
print FILEHANDLE outputList;
```

Both the file handle and output list are optional. If you don't specify a file handle, the `print` function sends output to the default file handle, which is initially set to `STDOUT` (for Standard Output) by the Perl 5 interpreter. (The default file handle can be explicitly set, as you will learn in the next section.)

If you don't specify an output list, the `print` function prints the contents of the default input special variable `$_`. Therefore, when you see this Perl 5 code:

```
while (<>) {
    print;
}
```

you know that the default special variable `$_` contains a line from the current open file and that line is being printed to the default selected file handle, which is most likely `STDOUT`. This code sends the contents of each file that is part of the command line argument list to the computer monitor. This is because, as you learned earlier in this chapter, `while (<>)` is reading from the default input argument array `@ARGV`, and it is reading into the default input special variable `$_`.

You can include an output list as a string or a list of strings. When the output list is surrounded by double quotes, variable interpolation occurs within the output string. Frequently, when I am printing some type of HTML output, I like to use the double quote operators around my output string, like this:

```
print STDOUT qq|<a href="www.assi.com">$home<\a>|;
```

In this example, I used the `qq` operator with vertical bars instead of double quotes so that the `href` line does not confuse the `print` function and the variable `$home` will be variable interpolated by Perl 5.

Setting and Closing File Handles

The file handle STDOUT is initially set to your computer monitor. Your program can set STDOUT to another output device, but I don't recommend it. If you want to change where the output from your program is going, don't change STDOUT; change the default output file handle using the select function, as shown on line 22 of Listing 10.1:

```
select OUTFILE;
```

The select function sets the default output file handle and at the same time returns the current default file handle. The syntax of the select function is:

```
select FILEHANDLE;
```

If the file handle parameter is omitted, the select function will just return the current default file handle.

When modifying the default output file handle, it's a good idea to keep track of the previous default file handle. Then when you complete your work, you can return the default file handle to its previous value, like this:

```
open (OUTFILE, "Results.html");
$prevFH = select (OUTFILE);
print<<"eof";
 anything goes here...
eof
close (OUTFILE);
select ($prevFH);
```

The heredoc (short for here document) operator (<<) prints output to the currently selected file handle. Its syntax is:

```
print<<heredoc-marker;
```

The trailing heredoc marker (eof in this example) identifies where the print function should stop printing.

The example also demonstrates using the close function, which you should use after you've completed working with a file handle. The syntax of the close function is:

```
close FILEHANDLE;
```

Perl 5 will close your file handles automatically if it can. When your process exits, all file handles are also closed. However, if you do not explicitly close all open file handles, you are likely to leave an input or output buffer unflushed, which means your output data may be lost.

When you use the `close` function with a file handle, it flushes the output or input buffer, guaranteeing that all data that was supposed to be written is written. The `close` function also resets the special variable line counter (`$.`).

Formatting Output Data

As you learned in Part 2 of this book, Perl 5 doesn't have floating-point, fixed, or integer data types. The interpreter, based on context, sets a scalar variable's format. If you want your output in a particular format, you can use Perl 5's `printf` function. You can also use Perl 5's special print escape sequences to add basic formatting, such as tabs and carriage returns.

The syntax of the `printf` function is:

```
printf FILEHANDLE "%formatCode", $unformattedVariableList;
```

The format code must be paired with a variable. The format code may be embedded in an output string, as shown on line 30 of Listing 10.1:

```
printf "$prev % 6.2f $post", $digit;
```

The format code is made up of four fields:

- The first character of a format code must be the percent sign (%).

- To align the output to the left, use the plus or minus sign in the second field. To align numbers to the right, place a blank in the second field. The plus character begins positive numbers with a plus sign; otherwise, positive numbers begin with a blank.

- The third field is the width specifier, which is made up of a total output size, a decimal point, and the number of decimal places (this field is 6.2 in the example, for a width of six characters with two decimal places).

- The fourth field is the conversion format. The data formats of the fourth field are character (c), decimal (d), exponential (e), floating point (f), compact (g), octal (o), string (s), and hex (x).

As you've seen in many of the examples in this and preceding chapters, you can use special print escape sequences for some output formatting. Commonly used codes are \n to start a new line, \t to insert a tab, and \r to return to the start of the line, as shown on line 48 of Listing 10.1:

```
print "\t\t$file\n";
```

If you need to format large amounts of data, you can use the `write` command with `format` statements. Creating `format` statements is discussed in detail in Chapter 12.

Directories

How do you find a file on your hard disk? If you're at the command prompt, you use the MS-DOS directory command `dir` or the Unix command the `ls`. If you're writing a Perl 5 program, you must open and read from a directory handle. Your programs can create, read, and delete directories.

Reading a Directory

The most common directory task is reading the contents of a directory. Three directory functions—`opendir`, `readdir`, and `closedir`—should be used each time you access an individual directory. Much like the file `open` command, the `opendir` function associates a directory handle with a directory name, as shown on line 37 of Listing 10.1:

```
opendir(DIR, "d:\\sybex\\temp");
```

The syntax of the `opendir` command is:

```
opendir (DIRECTORYHANDLE, 'directoryPath');
```

The directory handle has the same variable naming rules as the file handle and is, by convention, all uppercase characters. The `opendir` command returns 1 for success and `null` for failure.

NOTE   If you are working on a Windows computer, your directory path includes the back-slash character (\\), which is also the Perl 5 escape character. You must escape the directory separator character (\\), for the directory path to be interpreted correctly, as discussed earlier in this chapter, in the "Opening a File" section.

Once you open an association between the directory name and the directory handle, you must use the `readdir` function to read the directory contents. The `readdir` function has both a scalar and a list context, similar to the file input operator (`<>`), as shown as line 39 of Listing 10.1:

```
@dirList = readdir(DIR);
```

When the lvalue receiving the results of a readdir is a scalar variable, only one line of the directory's contents is returned. When the lvalue receiving the results of a readdir is an array, the remaining contents of the directory are returned. The syntax of the readdir function is:

```
$dirName = readdir (DIRECTORYHANDLE);
@dirList = readdir (DIRECTORYHANDLE);
```

Unlike when you use the file input operator, the directory handle position does not reset to the start of the directory list after the readdir function has read to the end of directory handle. The readdir function returns 0 when it reaches the end of the directory list or when it reads an empty directory handle. To reset the directory handle to the front of the directory list, use the rewinddir function, whose syntax is:

```
rewinddir (DIRECTORYHANDLE);
```

When you have completed your work with a directory, you should always close the directory handle using the closedir function, as shown on line 40 of Listing 10.1:

```
closedir(DIR);
```

The syntax of the closedir function is:

```
closedir (DIRECTORYHANDLE);
```

Once you have the tools necessary to read from a directory, the next logical task is moving around on your hard disk, creating and deleting directories.

Creating, Deleting, and Changing Directories

To create a new directory, use the mkdir function. The mkdir function requires two parameters: the directory name, which may be relative or absolute, and the permissions mask. The syntax of the mkdir function is:

```
mkdir ('directory', UNIXPermissionsMask);
```

The permissions mask sets the read, write, and execute privileges for the new directory, limited by the user's umask. If you are working on a Windows computer, the permissions mask value is required but ignored; you can use any number.

To delete a directory, use the rmdir function. The rmdir function takes as a parameter the relative or absolute path to the directory being deleted. The syntax of the rmdir function is:

```
rmdir ('directory');
```

The rmdir function returns 1 upon success and 0 on failure.

To move around on your hard drive, use the chdir function. The chdir function accepts as a parameter a relative or absolute directory name. The syntax of the chdir function is:

```
chdir ('directoryPath');
```

The chdir command returns 1 for success and 0 for failure.

NOTE

In each of the syntax examples for the directory functions, I have used parentheses to surround the arguments to the function. I prefer this format, but the parentheses are not required. Each of the functions—chdir, closedir, opendir, mkdir, readdir, and rewinddir—can be called without using parentheses.

File and Directory Modules

The Perl 5 directory and file modules provide an object-oriented interface to the Perl 5 functions, as well as making your programs more portable. Table 10.3 lists these modules.

TABLE 10.3: File and Directory Modules

Module	Description
Cwd	Get the current directory
Fcntl	Export file symbols
File::Copy	Copy and move files
FileHandle	Interface to IO::* classes
File::Spec	Platform-specific interfaces
IO::File	Interface to file-open functions
IO::Handle	Base class for IO classes
IO::Seekable	Get the file descriptor

To include a module in your program, use the `use` or `require` command, as on line 3 of Listing 10.1:

```
use File::Copy;
```

Then you can use the module function in your program, as on line 16 of Listing 10.1:

```
copy($ARGV, $ARGV . '.old') || warn $!;
```

What Next?

In this chapter, you learned how to get data into and out of your program. This chapter, like all of the jump-start chapters, provides just the information you need to get started using Perl 5's I/O capabilities. The rest of the chapters in this part give you all the details on the techniques covered here, plus a lot more information about other ways to handle I/O and many examples to demonstrate all the possibilities.

Chapter 11 covers getting command-line input and working with files. It provides an in-depth description of the ARGV special variables. It also describes a more efficient way to read program switches from the command line—the `getopt` function and the `Getopt::Long` module. Other techniques covered in this chapter include using the `seek` command to move your file handle forward and backward throughout the file and modifying an existing file using either the hard disk or memory as the workspace. The final section describes how to use file test operators to check for particular file characteristics, such as whether it is a text or binary file, whether the file exists, and what privileges are required to open or read from a file.

Chapter 12 covers a variety of printing techniques. Along with details on the `printf` and `sprintf` functions, you'll learn a neat trick for printing arrays and how to format large amounts of output using the `write` command and `format` statements. Although the format codes take a bit of work, the results of properly formatted page headings and neatly aligned columns of data are worth it.

Chapter 13 takes you a step past the basics to cover the directory and file functions and modules that come with a Perl 5 distribution. You'll learn how to use the Cwd module to get the current directory on any platform and details about all the functions for working with directories. It also describes how to use file functions for reading and writing to a file, getting and setting file information, and Unix-only functions. Finally, you'll learn about all the file modules that provide portability and object-oriented interfaces.

CHAPTER
ELEVEN

11

Input and Output Basics

- Command-line arguments and switches

- File open operations

- File handle positioning

- File modification

- File test operations

Most programs need to read input data from the command line and use files. This chapter shows you how to use Perl 5's command line and file input and output (I/O) capabilities in your programs.

You'll start by learning all about reading input from the command line. Perl provides the ARGV special variables to simplify getting command-line arguments and the getopts function for getting command-line switches to set program options.

After you learn about the command line, you'll learn how to work with files through your Perl 5 programs. This chapter covers opening files, moving around in files, modifying files, adding to existing files, closing files, and deleting files. Finally, you'll learn about the file test operators, which perform checks for file permissions, type, size, existence, and more.

Command-Line Input

A good program should be configurable from the command line at runtime so it can get the information it needs to run in different situations. Most of the programs you have seen so far in this book are good enough for their current application, but you would need to edit the source code to make them work for something just a little different. Rather than changing your code each time your program needs to open a different file, for example, you can have it accept command-line input.

NOTE   As you learned in Chapter 1, the command line is another name for the MS-DOS window or Unix command shell. The command line is the window that lets you tell the operating system which program you want to run and how to run it.

As usual, Perl 5 provides convenient facilities for getting input from the command line. One way is through the special ARGV variables, which are especially suited for manipulating files. Another way is through the getoption function, which accepts command-line switches for setting program options. The following sections describe both of these methods.

Command-Line Arguments

Perl 5 likes making things easy for you, and certainly nothing could be easier than using the ARGV (which stands for argument vector) special variables to get information from the command line. There are no special statements required. Perl 5 automatically takes everything on the command line after the name of the Perl program and before the Enter keypress and creates the @ARGV array with it. This allows you to write a simple program like the one shown in Listing 11.1 without a lot of command-line overhead at the start of your program. The program in Listing 11.1 gets the names of files from the command line and returns the access rights for those files. Figure 11.1 shows part of its output.

NOTE   Listing 11.1 is a copy of the example that comes with the `Win32::File-Security` module, which you'll learn about in Chapter 22. Listing 11.1 runs only on a Windows NT operating system.

Listing 11.1:   **The Argument Vector @ARGV**

```
1.  #Gets the rights for all files listed on the command line
2.  use Win32::FileSecurity;
3.  foreach( @ARGV ) {
4.      next unless -e $_ ;
5.      if ( Win32::FileSecurity::Get( $_, \%hash ) ) {
6.          while( ($name, $mask) = each %hash ) {
7.              print "$name:\n\t";
8.              Win32::FileSecurity::EnumerateRights( $mask, \@happy );
9.              print join( "\n\t", @happy ), "\n";
10.         }
11.     } else {
12.         print( "Error #", int( $! ), ": $!" );
13.     }
14. }
```

The `foreach` loop on line 3 of Listing 11.1 processes the command-line arguments in the @ARGV array:

```
foreach( @ARGV ) {
```

FIGURE 11.1:

Results of accepting
command line arguments

On line 4, each file in this array is tested to see if it exists:

```
next unless -e $_;
```

The −e operator returns true if this file exists. It is one of the file test operators that you will learn about later in this chapter. The $_ variable is the special default variable, which contains the results of the last Perl 5 operation. The $_ variable is used as the default input for many of Perl's functions. If the file does not exist, the rest of the loop is skipped using the next statement, and the next file in the @ARGV array is processed.

Now let's take a closer look at the @ARGV array and the special variables that Perl 5 creates for handling command-line arguments.

The ARGV Variables

The @ARGV array is a standard Perl 5 array, and it is created by the Perl 5 interpreter at startup. The Perl 5 @ARGV array (unlike the argv and argc variables of the C language) does not contain the name of the calling program. Perl 5 keeps the name of the calling program in the special variable $0. The @ARGV array contains everything on the command line after the name of the Perl program, up to and including the Enter key.

Each cell of the array contains one space-separated item from the command line. You can load a string of information by surrounding an input string with quotes. If you called Listing 11.1 like this:

```
argv.pl context.pl env.pl "fibonacci Rev2.pl" fileInfo.pl
```

the @ARGV array would contain four array cells. Each cell of the @ARGV array would contain a filename, because each filename is separated by a space character. The filename `fibonacci Rev2.pl` is stored in cell 2. (Remember that array cells count from 0.) Without the quote characters surrounding the filename, the filename would have been separated into two array cells, which means that cell 2 would contain `fibonacci` and cell 3 would contain `Rev2.pl`, and neither would refer to an actual file.

Created along with the @ARGV array are the following special variables:

- $#ARGV holds the number of elements in the @ARGV array (it's the normal last cell index variable associated with every Perl 5 array).

- ARGV contains the name of the file handle when your program uses the @ARGV array to open a file.

- $ARGV contains the filename associated with the ARGV file handle.

NOTE   The file handle is a direct link from your computer program to the file on your disk. You'll learn more about file handles later in this chapter.

The @ARGV Array and while Loops

Perl 5 assumes that most of the work you do from the command line is associated with manipulating files. When you use the @ARGV array in a `while` loop, Perl 5 will process each element of the array as if it were a file.

Listing 11.2 demonstrates using the @ARGV array in a `while` loop. This program requires at least three command-line arguments: an old word, the word which will replace the old word, and a file list. It copies each original file into a backup file and then reads the original file, changing each occurrence of the old word to the new word. For example, if you wanted to change the name of an employee from James E. Eastern, to Jim W. Western, you would type in this:

```
sub.pl "James E. Eastern" "Jim W. Western" employees.txt
```

Listing 11.2:   A File-Substitution Program

```
1.  #!/usr/local/bin/perl
2.  if ($#ARGV < 2){
3.      print<<"end_tag";
4.
5.  $0 opens a file for reading and changes a name in the file.
6.  use: $0 OLD_NAME NEW_NAME FILE_LIST
7.      param 1 is the old value
8.      param 2 is the new value
9.      param +2 is file list. There is no programmatic
        limit to the number of files processed.
10. The original file will be copied into a .bak file.
11. The original file will be overwritten with the substitution.
12. The script assumes the file(s) to be modified are in the
13. directory that the script was started from.
14. SYMBOLIC LINKS are NOT followed.
15. end_tag
16.    exit(1);
17. }
18.
19. $OLD = shift; # dump ARGV[0]
20. $NEW = shift; # dump ARGV[1]
21. #Now ARGV has just the file list in it.
22.
23. while ($ARGV = shift){
24.    next if -l $ARGV; #skip this file if it is a sym link
25.    print "\nprocessing $ARGV ...";
26.    $count = 0 ;
27.    open(INFILE, $ARGV);
28.
29.    while (<INFILE>){
30.       $count++ ;
31.       print "." if (($count % 10) == 0);
32.       if ($ARGV ne $oldargv){ #have we saved this file?
33.          #$ARGV is one of those magic Perl variables; it contains
34.          #the name of the current file when reading from <ARGV>
35.          #which can be written as <>
36.          rename($ARGV, $ARGV . '.bak'); #move file to backup copy
37.          $oldargv = $ARGV;
38.          open (OUTFILE, ">$ARGV"); #open file for writing
```

```
39.         }
40.         s/$OLD/$NEW/go;  #perform substitution
41.                         #o - only interpret the variables once
42.         print OUTFILE;  #dump the file back into itself with changes
43.     }
44. }
```

In Listing 11.2, lines 3 through 17 are a different style of program comments. These comments are designed as help information for people who use your code. They appear at the top of your program and print only if your program is called with an invalid list of arguments.

Line 2 checks the special variable $#ARGV for number of arguments on the command line:

```
if ($#ARGV < 2){
```

This program requires at least three arguments. Since the $#ARGV variable is actually the index of the last argument in the @ARGV array, the conditional expression on line 2 is for the number of required arguments minus one. If the program doesn't have at least three arguments after the program name, lines 5 through 14 are printed to the standard output (STDOUT), which is usually the screen.

Notice that lines 5 and 6 use the $0 variable to name the program:

```
$0 opens a file for reading and changes a name in the file.
use: $0 OLD_NAME NEW_NAME FILE_LIST
```

Figure 11.2 shows the program output when it is called without any arguments. Notice that the $0 variable name of the program includes the entire path and program name. This can sometimes be a great debugging aid.

The shift function on lines 19 and 20 of Listing 11.2 operates on the @ARGV array by default:

```
$OLD = shift; # dump ARGV[0]
$NEW = shift; # dump ARGV[1]
```

As you learned in Chapter 6, the shift function removes the first element of the array ([0]) and then moves each element of the array up to the previous array cell. The zeroth element is assigned to the lvalue on the left of the equal sign, as shown on lines 19 and 20. Since the zeroth element is replaced when the array is shifted down one, the element is lost unless it is stored into a new variable location.

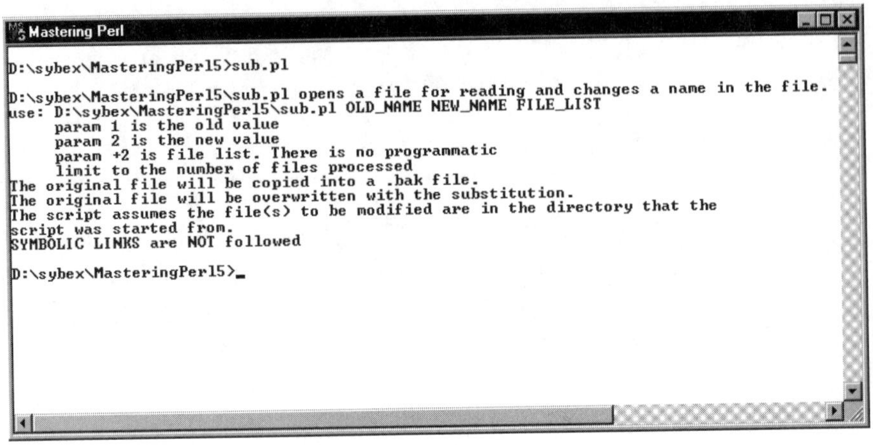

FIGURE 11.2:

Running the name
substitution program
without arguments

```
  Mastering Perl                                                         _ □ ×

D:\sybex\MasteringPerl5>sub.pl

D:\sybex\MasteringPerl5\sub.pl opens a file for reading and changes a name in the file.
use: D:\sybex\MasteringPerl5\sub.pl OLD_NAME NEW_NAME FILE_LIST
      param 1 is the old value
      param 2 is the new value
      param +2 is file list. There is no programmatic
      limit to the number of files processed
The original file will be copied into a .bak file.
The original file will be overwritten with the substitution.
The script assumes the file(s) to be modified are in the directory that the
script was started from.
SYMBOLIC LINKS are NOT followed

D:\sybex\MasteringPerl5>_
```

Line 23 performs the shift of the first filename into the $ARGV variable:

```
while ($ARGV = shift){
```

Line 24 applies only to Unix operating systems. If the file is a symbolic link, it
will not be modified. The file test operator -l on line 24 will be explained later in
this chapter.

Line 27 opens the file for reading:

```
open(INFILE, $ARGV);
```

You'll learn more about the file handle INFILE and the
open(INFILE, "*<filename*") syntax later in the chapter.

Line 29 reads each line of the file:

```
while (<INFILE>){
```

The angle brackets (<>) are the file input operator, which is used to read files, as
explained later in the chapter.

Lines 32 through 39 are used to allow this program to overwrite the original file
without losing the original file contents.

```
if ($ARGV ne $oldargv){ #have we saved this file?
    #$ARGV is one of those magic Perl variables; it
    #contains the name of the current file when reading from <ARGV>
    #which can be encrypted as <>
```

```
    rename($ARGV, $ARGV . '.bak'); #move file to backup copy
    $oldargv = $ARGV;
    open (OUTFILE, ">$ARGV"); #open file for writing
}
```

The first time through the while loop, the variable $oldargv is not equal to the current value of $ARGV. Line 36 uses the Perl 5 rename function to rename the existing file to the same name with the additional extension of .bak.

Because file handle INFILE was opened before the file was renamed, it can still read from the original file. The variable $oldargv is set to the current value of $ARGV on line 37, so the next time through the while loop, the conditional expression on line 32 will fail. Line 38 opens the original filename for output using the file handle OUTFILE. The old file handle INFILE is actually reading from the .bak file.

Line 40 makes the substitution:

```
s/$OLD/$NEW/go; #perform substitution
```

Line 42 prints the modified line to the output file:

```
print OUTFILE; #dump the file back into itself with changes
```

The modified line is stored in the $_ variable, which the print function uses when it isn't assigned anything else to print.

Now let's look at an alternative way for processing your command-line variables as a file list, which seems to work like magic.

The while (<>) File-Processing Code

The simple syntax for processing your command-line variables as a file list is:

```
while (<>)
```

Amazingly enough (and yes, it does seem like magic), this code opens, reads, and closes files. It works like this:

- The @ARGV array is shifted one element at a time into the $ARGV variable.

- The $ARGV variable is used to open the file handle ARGV.

- Each line of the file associated with ARGV is read, one line at a time, into the special variable $_.

- When the entire file has been read, the ARGV file handle is closed and the first step is repeated.

Listing 11.3 performs the same tasks as Listing 11.2, but uses while (<>) instead of the standard while loops.

Listing 11.3: **The while (<>) Syntax**

```
1.  #!/usr/local/bin/perl
2.  if ($#ARGV < 2){
3.      print<<"end_tag";
4.
5.  $0 opens a file for reading and changes a name in the file.
6.  use: $0 OLD_NAME NEW_NAME FILE_LIST
7.      param 1 is the old value
8.      param 2 is the new value
9.      param +2 is file list. There is no programmatic
        limit to the number of files processed.
10. The original file will be copied into a .bak file.
11. The original file will be overwritten with the substitution.
12. The script assumes the file(s) to be modified are in the
13. directory that the script was started from.
14. SYMBOLIC LINKS are NOT followed.
15. end_tag
16.     exit(1);
17. }
18.
19. $OLD = shift; # dump ARGV[0]
20. $NEW = shift; # dump ARGV[1]
21.
22. while (<>){
23.     $count++ ;
24.     next if -l $ARGV; #skip this file if it is a sym link
25.     print "." if (($count % 10) == 0);
26.     if ($ARGV ne $oldargv){ #have we saved this file?
27.         print "\nprocessing $ARGV ...";
28.         $count = 0;
29.         rename($ARGV, $ARGV . '.bak'); #move file to backup copy
30.         $oldargv = $ARGV;
31.         open (OUTFILE, ">$ARGV"); #open file for writing
32.     }
```

```
33.    s/$OLD/$NEW/go; #perform substitution
34.    print OUTFILE; #dump the file back into itself with changes
35. }
```

In this version, the `while (<>)` on line 22 replaces the `while` loops on lines 23 through 29 of Listing 11.2. Line 22 is actually opening and closing the file handle ARGV, setting the $ARGV variable, and reading each line of the file.

In Listing 11.3, line 24 is less efficient than as used in Listing 11.2, because symbolically linked files will still be opened and ready; they just will not be modified.

Although the special ARGV variables are convenient for file handling, using them to deal with command-line switches for setting program options is not simple. Reading each element of the @ARGV array, determining which value goes with each switch, and deciding when you have a file to process can be a painful process. Perl 5's `getoption` function provides an easier way, as described in the next section.

Command-Line Switches

Suppose that you want to set a few parameters in your program from the command line before your program begins general processing. These parameters are called *switches*, and they allow you to turn off or on various features in your program. You can do this by using one of Perl 5's switch-processing functions, as explained in the following sections.

The C programming language provides a function called `getopt,` which reads single-character switches from the command line. Perl 5 has used that C function as a template for reading command-line switches, but Perl provides more options.

The getopt.pl Program

The simplest of the switch-processing functions, GetOpt is part of the `getopt.pl` program. You can include this function in your program by using the `require` statement, like this:

```
require getopt.pl;
```

The GetOpt function accepts one argument. The argument passed to the GetOpt function defines the single-character switches in your program that also take an input parameter. For example, suppose you had a program that entered names into a database, and you called the program by identifying the first, middle, and last names, using the switches f, m, and l. Your program would call the GetOpt function like this:

```
GetOpt(fml);
```

This tells the GetOpt function to look for three switches on the command line that take a parameter. Your database program would be called like this:

```
addNewNames.pl -fMarilyn -l Smith
```

Your addNewNames program would call the GetOpt function, like this:

```
GetOpt(fml);
```

This sets two global variables: opt_f equal to Marilyn and opt_l equal to Smith. If you called your database program like this:

```
addNewNames.pl -d -lLeafcutter -fRed -mQ.
```

and then called the GetOpt function with GetOpt(fml), the GetOpt function would set four global variables: opt_d to 1, opt_f to Red, opt_m to Q, and opt_l to Leafcutter. As you can see from this example, switches that do not take a parameter are set to the value 1 and are not passed as an input parameter to the GetOpt function.

Here are the rules for switches using the GetOpt function:

- Switches begin with a dash character (-).

- Switches that take a parameter may or may not have space between the switch name and the switch value.

- Switches are not required to be in any order.

- Switches are case-sensitive; the switches -f and -F are different.

The GetOpt function compares the data in the command-line argument array @ARGV with the input parameters it receives when your program calls it (GetOpt(fml)). If the first character following the dash character is a character in the input parameter string (fml in our example), any characters following the switch character are assigned to the $opt_SWITCH\_CHARACTER$ variable.

If the switch character is not a character in the input parameter string, the $opt_SWITCH\_CHARACTER$ variable is set to the value 1, and any characters on the command line following the switch character are treated as additional switch characters. This means the following command-line inputs are equivalent (assuming the call is GetOpt(fml)):

```
addNewNames.pl -dlLeafcutter -fRed -mQ.
addNewNames.pl -d -lLeafcutter -fRed -mQ.
```

Because the -d is not an input parameter to GetOpt, the GetOpt function does not expect an input parameter. The data following the -d is treated as additional switch characters and processed accordingly.

The GetOpt::Std Module

The GetOpt::Std module contains two functions: getopt and getopts. The getopt function is identical to the GetOpt function described in the previous section. The getopt function only allows you to define the switches that take an input parameter.

The getopts function allows you to also define the switches that do not require a parameter. Switches that do not require a parameter are passed to the getopts function following a colon, like this:

```
getopts(fml:d);
```

The d switch does not take a parameter, but it is explicitly defined for the getopts function.

Unlike the getopt function, which considers any character preceded by a dash as a switch that does not take a parameter, the getopts function requires that all command-line switches be defined by the input parameter string. Any characters preceding the colon define a switch character that takes a parameter. Any characters following the colon define a switch character that does not take a parameter.

The GetOpt::Long Module

The GetOpt::Long module allows you to use the basic single-character syntax of the GetOpt function or a vastly richer set of features. The function you call when parsing your input parameters using the GetOpt::Long module is GetOptions. The GetOpt::Long module includes several configuration variables, which are shown in Table 11.1.

TABLE 11.1: GetOpt::Long Configuration Variables

Variable	Meaning	Default
autoabbrev	Allow switch names to optionally be abbreviated to a unique value. If GetOptions("Debug=") is used (and no other), then -Debug, -Debu, -Deb, -De, and -D are all valid values for the switch name.	True (1); to set to false, set the environment variable POSIXLY_CORRECT to a nonzero value
bundling	Interpret switch names preceded by a single dash as a series of single-character switch names. Long switch names must be preceded by a double dash. For example, –Type would be interpreted as four switches (T,y,p,e) unless entered as --Type.	False (0)
debug	Turn on verbose debug output.	False (0)
error	An internal error flag.	Null
getopt_compat	Allow + as a valid switch prefix.	True (1); to set to false, set the environment variable POSIXLY_CORRECT to a nonzero value
ignorecase	Ignore command-line case when matching switch names with GetOptions switch names.	True (1)
order	Allow mixing of switches and non-switch parameters.	True ($PERMUTE); to set to false, set the environment variable POSIXLY_CORRECT to a nonzero value
passthrough	Unknown options are left in the @ARGV array instead of being flagged as errors.	False (0)
VERSION	The version number of GetOpt::Long.	

The GetOptions Function

The GetOptions function needs to know the name of the input switches, the data type of the input switches, and optionally, the variable name to store the switch value. The GetOptions function accepts the input parameter as a list, a hash, or a combination of hash and list. The function accepts long names for switches (and also short names if you leave the autoabbrev configuration variable set to its default of true).

NOTE
> You can use double dash (--), dash (-) or plus (+) switch syntax in front of your command-line options. For example --**Debug**, -**Debug**, and +**Debug** are all valid. Note that no space is allowed between the +, --, or - and the option name.

The GetOptions function lets you define the syntax for each switch, as shown in Table 11.2. Special switch syntax is not required. If you leave the switch syntax value blank, the default switch syntax is assumed. The default switch syntax is no switch argument. If the switch exists, its variable will be set to 1.

TABLE 11.2: GetOptions Switch Syntax

Switch Syntax	Description	Example	Command Line
Blank	Set the default syntax.	GetOptions("Debug=");	None
=!	Allow the option to be negated. To negate an option, prefix it with **no**.	GetOptions("Debug=!");	*programName*.pl -noDebug
=s	Set the input option to include a mandatory string argument.	GetOptions("exten-sion=s");	*programName*.pl -extension "*string*"
:s	Set the input option to include an optional string argument.	GetOptions("exten-sion:s");	*programName*.pl -extension
=I	Set the input option to include a mandatory integer argument.	GetOptions("Type=i, \$fileType");	*programName*.pl -Type *number*

Continued on next page

TABLE 11.2 CONTINUED: GetOptions Switch Syntax

Switch Syntax	Description	Example	Command Line
:I	Set the input option to include an optional integer argument.	`GetOptions("Type:i, \$fileType");`	`programName.pl -Type`
=f	Set the input option to include a mandatory real-number argument.	`GetOptions("rate=f, \$interestRate");`	`programName.pl +rate realNumber`
:f	Set the input option to include an optional real-number argument.	`GetOptions("rate:f, \$interestRate");`	`programName.pl +rate realNumber`

The option and the argument will be parsed from the @ARGV array. If a variable name is not supplied, the variable $opt_*SWITCH_NAME* will be set. The variable $opt_*SWITCH*_NAME is created inside the namespace of the calling program. For example, if you use the option `GetOptions("extension=s")`, the string will be parsed from the @ARGV array and a variable $opt_extension will be set to the string.

As an example, suppose that you want to add new employees to a database program. You could use `GetOptions` like this:

```
use GetOpt::Long;
GetOptions("first=s","middle:s","last=s","age:i","salary=f");
```

The command line would look like this:

```
addEmployee.pl -first Gemma -last O'Sullivan -salary 1000000.45
```

This would set the variables $opt_first to Gemma, $opt_last to O'Sullivan, and $opt_salary to 1000000.45. The input parameters middle and age are optional.

Alternatively, you can supply a variable name, and the value of the switch will be stored in that variable, as described next.

Switch Variable Names

You can supply the variable name as a reference to scalar, array, hash, or subroutine. If you wish to use the $opt_*SWITCH_NAME* syntax with hash or array input values, append % or @ to the switch data type, like this:

```
optionName=i@
```

or

```
optionName=s%
```

The variable @opt_*SWITCH_NAME* or %opt_*SWITCH_NAME* will be loaded appropriately.

For example, you can put the switch values in an array like this:

```
program.pl -Type 1 -Type 2 -Type 1 file.txt program.exe program.data
...
use GetOpt::Long;
GetOptions("Type=i@,");
```

This creates the array @opt_Type with the values 1, 2, 1. The @ARGV array after the call to GetOptions contains the program names file.txt, program.exe, and program.data in $ARGV[0], $ARGV[1], and $ARGV[2], respectively.

If you use the hash syntax, separate your hash key and value using *key=value* format, like this:

```
program.pl -TypeName binary=program.exe
...
use GetOpt::Long;
GetOptions("TypeName=s", \%TypeName);
```

This sets the hash %TypeName as:

```
$TypeName{'binary'} = "program.exe";
```

If you use a subroutine reference, the subroutine is passed the option name and option value in the @_ array.

Now that we have finished with the command-line input details, it's time for the real fun of working with files and file handles. In the next section, you'll learn how to use all this data you now have waiting in your program.

Opening Files

When you open a file for reading or writing, you need to know its filename and its file handle. The filename comes first. You can't have a file handle without a filename, but you can have a filename without a file handle. So what's the difference between a filename and a file handle? Let's clear that up before getting into the specifics of the open function.

Parts of a Filename

The filename is the actual path and name of the file. For example, when you open a file using Microsoft Word, you have to give Word the full path and name of the file to open. You usually do this by clicking through the directories until you see the file you want. The filename might look something like this:

```
C:\MyDocuments\report.doc
```

Now you may be thinking that the filename is simply report.doc. C:\MyDocuments\ is the directory name or path name, not the filename. However, when referring to file handles, the filename includes the directory or path to the actual file.

To see the individual pieces that make up the filename, run the program in Listing 11.4. Listing 11.4 uses the module File::Basename (a module distributed with Perl 5), which allows you to separate the filename, directory path, and the extensions of the filename. Figure 11.3 shows an example of the output.

NOTE The *extension* is the last set of characters after the period at the end of the filename. Windows machines use filename extensions to associate programs with particular filenames. For example, my Windows installation has a file association between the filename extension .doc and the application Word. When I double-click on a file with the .doc extension, Windows starts the Word application for that file extension. You can look at the current filename associations in Windows Explorer by selecting View Options and then selecting the File Types tab.

Listing 11.4:   **File::Basename**

```
1.  use File::Basename;
2.  if ($#ARGV < 1){
```

```
3.      print<<"EOF";
4.      Please enter the type of computer you are on, as
        the first parameter.
5.      Choose from one of the four listed operating systems:
6.      VMS, MSDOS, MacOS, UNIX
7.
8.      The second parameter should be a filename.
9.  EOF
10.     exit(1);
11. }
12. $computerType = shift;
13. $filename = shift;
14. fileparse_set_fstype($computerType);
15. ($filenameOnly, $pathName, $fileExtension) =
        fileparse($filename, '\..*');
16.
17. print<<"EOF";
18. The file $filenameOnly is located in the directory
19. $pathName,
20. and has the file extension $fileExtension.
21. EOF
```

FIGURE 11.3:

Using the File::Basename
module to parse a filename

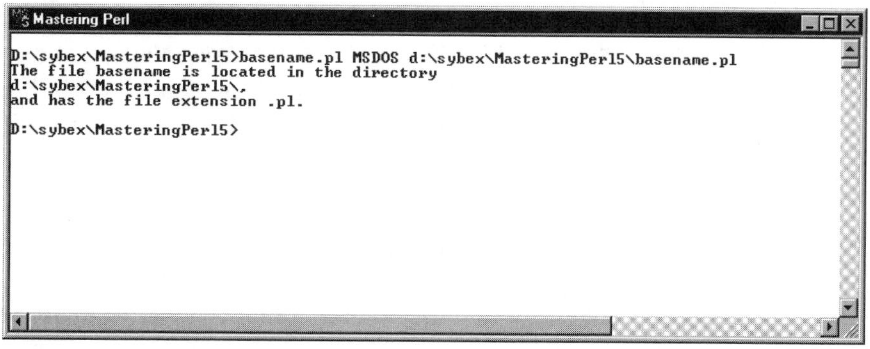

```
D:\sybex\MasteringPerl5>basename.pl MSDOS d:\sybex\MasteringPerl5\basename.pl
The file basename is located in the directory
d:\sybex\MasteringPerl5\,
and has the file extension .pl.

D:\sybex\MasteringPerl5>
```

To use the `File::Basename` module, you must first tell it what type of operating system you are using. Your choices are VMS, MSDOS, MacOS, and Unix (the check is not case-sensitive, so *MsDos* is the same as *MSDOS*). Line 14 tells the Basename module your operating system type. If you don't provide a type, the default is Unix.

Line 15 reads the input filename and returns the filename path name and extension. To use `fileparse`, you must tell it what type of extension to look for. The second parameter to `fileparse` identifies the file extensions. The pattern `\..*` says the file extension begins with a period and is followed by any number of alphanumeric characters. You'll learn how to build patterns like this in Chapter 16.

NOTE   Keep in mind that most of your programs require all three pieces to run: the directory path name to the filename, the filename itself, and the filename extension.

File Handles

The file handle is a direct link from your computer program to the file on your disk. The file handle is used to read and write to a file. The file handle is created when you use the **open** function, discussed in the next section.

To use an analogy, think of the **open** function as dialing a phone number on your telephone. The `$filename` is the phone number to dial. When someone picks up the phone associated with the phone number you dialed, you think of the connection to the other phone, not the phone number. When you speak and listen on your end of the phone, you are sending and receiving information over the phone connection. This is like the connection through the file handle to your file on your computer disk. Once your program has connected to the filename (the phone number) on your hard disk using the **open** function, your program then "speaks" to the "phone number" using the file handle. When your program speaks to the file handle it is writing; when your program listens on the file handle, it is reading.

A file handle follows the standard rules for variable names, except it does not begin with a dollar sign. It can be any combination of alphanumeric characters, both uppercase and lowercase. However, it's a good idea to use all uppercase letters, so your file handles will not conflict with any of Perl 5's reserved words, which are all lowercase. Using uppercase letters for file handles is not too large a restriction, and you can save yourself some painful debugging time.

Perl 5 opens three default file handles at startup:

- The file handle STDIN (for Standard Input) is normally set to your computer keyboard. You use this file handle whenever you read input with your program from the input argument array @ARGV.

- The file handle STDOUT (for Standard Output) is initially set to your computer monitor. You can use this file handle with the print function to send your program's results to an output device.

- The file handle STDERR (for Standard Error) is usually initialized to your output screen also. If you want your program to keep track of errors, set STDERR to an output error file, like this:

```
close (STDERR);
open (STERR, "error.log");
```

The file handle for a file is created by the open function, which completes the connection from your program to the file. You'll learn about the open function in the next section.

The open Function

How many ways can you open a file?

- Read

- Write

- Append

- Read and write

When you open a file and make the connection to the file handle, you tell the computer whether you are going to read, write, or both. (Wouldn't it be nice if you could open a phone connection like that—open Mother-In-Law Talk-to-Only, and you wouldn't have to listen for a change.)

If you open a file for reading, you cannot write to it. If you open a file for writing, you destroy any existing data in the file and can only write to the new file. If you want to add to an existing file, you use append mode.

The syntax of the open function requires a file handle and a filename:

```
open (FILEHANDLE, "filename");
```

By default, your program will try to open a connection to the file by looking in the directory in which the program began execution. If you want the program to look in a different location, you must prepend the directory path information onto the filename. Referring back to the phone analogy, if you dial a phone number and use only the local-area seven digits, the phone network looks in the local calling area. If the network can't find the number, you get an error message. To make the phone network look in a location outside your local calling area, you must prepend that location's area code to the seven-digit number. Similarly, you must prepend the directory path to look outside the local directory.

You tell your computer how you want the file opened by putting a special symbol in front of the filename. The **open** operators and syntax are shown in Table 11.3. If you do not tell your computer how to open the file, it will open it for reading only. (That seems to be the default in real life also—most people want you to listen only while they talk.)

TABLE 11.3: Open Operators

Operation	Syntax	Description
Read	`open(INFILE,"<filename");`	Read from the file.
Write	`open(OUTFILE, ">filename");`	Destroy any existing file and write to a new file.
Append	`open(APP, ">>filename");`	Write to the end of an existing file.
Read/write	`open(RW, "+<filename");`	Read and write from an existing file.
Write to a program	`open(PIPEOUT, "|filename");`	Send data to a program or command. Also called opening a program pipe.
Read from a program	`open(PIPEIN"filename|");`	Receive data from a program or command.

You can use a variable name in place of the string name shown in the syntax portion of Table 11.3. Also, you can place the read, write, and append symbols at the end of the filename. Most programmers put the symbols at the front, however, as shown in Table 11.3.

Your program can fail to open a file because it doesn't have the correct permission, the file doesn't exist, the path to the filename is incorrect, or something else is wrong, so I recommend using syntax like this:

```
open (FILEHANDLE, "$fileName") || die "$!, couldn't open file
$fileName";
```

The `die` function and special variable `$!` give you error information from the Perl 5 interpreter, as you learned in Chapter 2.

After you've opened a file, there are several ways you can move through it, as explained in the next section.

Moving through Files

Listing 11.5 demonstrates two ways of moving through a file. The first mechanism assumes you have fixed-length records and skips forward to a particular record position using the `seek` function. The second mechanism uses computer memory to read the entire file, manipulates the file in memory, and then writes it back out. These mechanisms are explained in the following sections. Listing 11.6 contains the data used for testing Listing 11.5.

Listing 11.5:   **Moving through a File**

```
1.  #ARGV contains the line to read
2.  $lineNumber = shift;
3.  $bytesToSkip = $lineNumber * 30;
4.  $lineSeparator = "=" x 60;
5.  open(INFILE, "Listing9_8.txt") || die "$! can't open file";
6.  #read the last name in the file
7.  #each name takes 30 bytes
8.  seek(INFILE, -($bytesToSkip), 2);
9.  #read one line
10. $name = <INFILE>;
11. print $name;
12. print "Is $lineNumber line(s) from the end of the file\n";
13.
14. seek(INFILE, $bytesToSkip, 0);
15. #read one line
16. $name = <INFILE>;
17. print $name;
18. print "Is $lineNumber line(s) from the front of the file\n";
19. close (INFILE);
20. print "\n$lineSeparator\n\n";
21.
22. open(INFILE, "fixedLength.txt") || die "$! can't open file";
```

```
23. @allFile = <INFILE>;
24. print $allFile[$#allFile-($lineNumber - 1)];
25. print "Is $lineNumber line(s) from the end of the file\n";
26. print $allFile[$lineNumber];
27. print "Is $lineNumber line(s) from the front of the file\n";
28. close (INFILE);
```

Listing 11.6:	Test Data for Moving within a File

```
Steven    M.    Herrmann
Jessica   A.    Herrmann
Scott     E.    Herrmann
Sherry    A.    Herrmann
Eric      C.    Herrmann
```

Positioning with the seek Function

The seek function allows you to position the next place your program will read from or write to a file. Normally, when you open a file for reading, the file handle is positioned at the start of the file. As you read a line of the file, the file handle is moved forward to mark where you stopped reading. You can position your file handle at the end of a file by opening the file in append mode. But what if you want to skip to the end to find something important and then return to the beginning to start reading again? To accomplish this type of reading, you need to use the seek function.

The seek function allows you to move your file handle forward and backward throughout the file. The seek function has three basic positions from which you can specify offsets: the start of the file, the current position, or the end of the file. From these basic positions, you can move forward or backward throughout the file.

To move forward in a file, you provide the seek function with a positive number that identifies the number of bytes you want to skip. To move backward, you use a negative number to identify the number of bytes to skip. You cannot move the file handle above the beginning of the file or past the end of the file.

The syntax of the seek function is:

```
seek (FILEHANDLE, BytesToSkip, StartingLocation);
```

StartingLocation can be one of three values: 0 for the beginning of the file, 1 for the current location, or 2 for the end of the file.

Think of *BytesToSkip* as the characters in a book you want to skip. Each letter or punctuation mark counts as one byte.

NOTE
Counting each byte as an ASCII character will get you started. As you work with different computer systems, you'll learn that different languages and operating systems change the size of a standard byte.

Line 3 of Listing 11.5 sets `$bytesToSkip` to 30 bytes times the number of lines (each line is 30 bytes long):

```
$bytesToSkip = $lineNumber * 30;
```

Line 8 of Listing 11.5 sets the file handle at the end of the file because the starting file handle location in the **seek** function is set to 2. Then the file handle is moved backward the number of lines requested to skip:

```
seek(INFILE, -($bytesToSkip), 2);
```

The file is read one line at a time from the open file handle on lines 10 and 16, using the file input operator (<>):

```
$name = <INFILE>;
```

The file input operator is context-sensitive. The file handle is moved forward one line each time a line is read. The file input operator returns 1 each time a new line is read. It returns 0 when it tries to read past the last line in the file (called the end-of-file condition, or EOF).

NOTE
As you learned earlier in the chapter, the file input operator is frequently used in `while` loops like this: `while (<INFILE>) {…};`. Each time through the `while` loop, one line is read from the file associated with the **INFILE** file handle. The line is stored in the special variable **$_**. The `while` loop continues until the file input operator (<>) returns a zero at the end of the file.

Line 14 of Listing 11.5 resets the file handle to the beginning of the file by setting the starting file handle location to 0 and then moves the file handle forward by 30 bytes:

```
seek(INFILE, $bytesToSkip, 0);
```

Notice that the file is not closed or reopened between seek functions. This increases the speed of moving around the file.

The major drawback of using the seek function is simply having to move around a file in bytes. Because byte size is not always the same between different computers or operating systems, your program may not run on a different computer. The program is not portable. But even more important, in order to know where you should be in a file, the file must be a fixed-record-length file. That means that if you have a file of people's names, each field in the file must be a certain length. In Listing 11.6, each field is 10 bytes long, making a total of 30 bytes available for each name. This mechanism of storing names is very inflexible and error prone.

The tell function returns the current position of the file handle. The syntax of the tell function is:

```
tell FILEHANDLE;
```

You can use this along with the seek function to return to a particular location, like this:

```
$position = tell INOUTFILE;
seek(INOUTFILE, $position, 0);
```

The additional operations required to move the file pointers is not normally an efficient method of managing files; therefore, it will not discussed any further here. In Chapter 24, you will explore the Win32::ODBC module and SQL, which provide efficient mechanisms for modifying large database files.

Reading the File into an Array

The second method of moving around a file is illustrated on lines 22 through 28 of Listing 11.5:

```
open(INFILE, "fixedLength.txt") || die "$! can't open file";
@allFile = <INFILE>;
print $allFile[$#allFile-($lineNumber - 1)];
print "Is $lineNumber line(s) from the end of the file\n";
print $allFile[$lineNumber];
print "Is $lineNumber line(s) from the front of the file\n";
close (INFILE);
```

The entire file is read into an array on line 23:

```
@allFile = <INFILE>;
```

Using the file input operator, the file is read one line at a time. Each line makes a new array cell entry into the array `@allFile`. Different lines in the array file are accessed by line number instead of bytes, as illustrated on lines 24 and 26.

NOTE   The file handle is set to the end of the file after reading `INFILE` into an array. If you want to read the file again into another array, you must set the file handle back to the beginning of the file by using the `seek` function, like this: `seek (INFILE, 0,0);`.

This method of moving around files is much easier than using `seek`, but it has one major drawback: When you are working with a large file, reading in the entire file is not practical. Database files can easily reach gigabytes in size. Your computer probably doesn't have gigabytes of memory available.

Now that you know the basics of moving around in a file, it's time to learn how to make some modifications to a file, as explained in the next section.

Modifying Files

Modifying files requires a little more care and effort than simply reading and writing to files. When you modify a file you must be sure to modify the correct data and not lose any information in the file.

As an example, let's say you need to change all the middle names in Listing 11.6 to middle initials. Listing 11.7 shows how to make this modification using two different techniques. One method uses the hard disk as the workspace for modifying your file, and the other method uses memory as the workspace. Although using memory is faster, it may present problems with large files if your computer doesn't have lots of spare memory.

Listing 11.7:   Modifying a File

```perl
1.  #!/usr/local/bin/perl
2.  use File::Copy;
3.  $filler = " ";
4.  $notOpened = 1;
5.  $index = 0;
```

```
6.   #Open the file for reading
7.   open(INFILE, "<ModifyFile.txt") || die "can't open file";
8.   #using the File::copy method copy the file to a backup file
9.   copy ("ModifyFile.txt", "ModifyFile.bak");
10.  #Read from the INFILE file handle one line at a time
11.  #Because no lvalue is associated with the read operators, the
12.  #incoming data is read into the default input variable $_
13.  while (<INFILE>){
14.      #Only on the first pass is $notOpened equal to true
15.      if ($notOpened){
16.          $notOpened = 0;
17.          #You can open a file of the same name of the file you are
18.          #reading from. Once you have an open file handle, you can
19.          #read from the file until you close it
20.          open(OUTFILE, ">ModifyFile.txt") || die "can't open file";
21.      }
22.      #Separate on non-word characters
23.      ($first, $middle, $last) = split(/\W+/);
24.      #Remove the first character from the variable $middle
25.      $middleInitial = substr($middle, 0 , 1 );
26.      #Append a period
27.      $middleInitial .= '.';
28.      #Fix the length of each name to a fixed length of 10 characters
29.      #The space character is added as a pad character at the end of
30.      #each variable
31.      $first .= $filler x (10 - length($first));
32.      $middleInitial .= $filler x (10 - length($middleInitial));
33.      $last .= $filler x (10 - length($last));
34.      print OUTFILE "$first$middleInitial$last\n";
35.  }
36.  #Close both file handles
37.  close (INFILE);
38.  close (OUTFILE);
39.  #Create a copy of the text file
40.  copy("ModifyFile.txt", "ModifyFile.txt.m1");
41.  #Copy the backup file to the actual filename
42.  copy ("ModifyFile.bak", "ModifyFile.txt");
43.
44.  #Open the file for read and writing
45.  open(INOUTFILE, "+<ModifyFile.txt") || die "can't open file";
46.  #Read the entire file into memory
47.  @allFile = <INOUTFILE>;
```

```
48. #Reset the file pointer to the beginning of the file
49. seek(INOUTFILE, 0, 0);
50. #Now modify the filenames as described previously
51. for $name (@allFile){
52.     ($first, $middle, $last) = split(/\W+/,$name);
53.     $middleInitial = substr($middle, 0 , 1 );
54.     $middleInitial .= '.' . $filler;
55.     $first .= $filler x (10 - length($first));
56.     $middleInitial .= $filler x (10 - length($middleInitial));
57.     $last .= $filler x (10 - length($last));
58.     $tempArray[$index++] = "$first$middleInitial$last\n";
59. }
60. #You can now write back to the same file. The old data will
61. #be overwritten because the file pointer has been set
62. #to the beginning of the file.
63. print INOUTFILE @tempArray;
64. close (INOUTFILE);
```

Line 2 of Listing 11.7 refers to a Perl 5 module, File::Copy, that works well with the both Windows and Unix file systems. Listing 11.7 illustrates modifying the same file twice, so we need to make an extra copy of it.

Using the Hard Disk as Workspace

To demonstrate using the hard disk as the workspace for modifying your file, the input file is opened for read-only on line 7 of Listing 11.7:

```
open(INFILE, "<ModifyFile.txt") || die "can't open file";
```

At that time, the system creates its own internal link to the file so that any changes to the physical file will not affect the file while this program is reading the file. This program counts on that feature, which is fine for small- to medium-sized files but not recommended for larger files. An alternative technique is to write to a different file and then copy the modified file over the original.

Line 13 reads one line at a time from the input file:

```
while (<INFILE>){
```

The line is read into the special variable $_.

If the output file has not been opened previously, lines 14 through 21 will open a file by the same name as the input file for writing:

```
#Only on the first pass is $notOpened equal to true
if ($notOpened){
    $notOpened = 0;
    #You can open a file of the same name of the file you are reading
    #from. Once you have an open file handle, you can read from
    #the file until you close it
open(OUTFILE, ">ModifyFile.txt") || die "can't open file";
}
```

On the disk, the output file ModifyFile.txt is cleared and initialized for output.

The split function on line 23 separates the default special variable $_ using the regular expression W+:

```
($first, $middle, $last) = split(/\W+/);
```

The regular expression W+ tells the split function to separate the string in $_ on any non-word characters, which is any character that is not A–Z, 0–9, or the underscore character. The split function was covered first in Chapter 8 and is covered again in Chapter 15.

On line 25, the substr function pulls one character—the first character out of the variable $middle—and stores the results in $middleInitial:

```
$middleInitial = substr($middle, 0 , 1 );
```

The substr function syntax is:

```
substr ($variable, startingLocation, length);
```

The *startingLocation* parameter tells the substr function where to start taking characters from the parameter $variable. The length parameter tells the substr function how many characters to extract from the $variable parameter. In this case, you only want the first character of the middle name, so your starting location is position 0 and the length is 1. The substr function is covered in more detail in Chapter 15.

Line 27 adds a period to the $middleInitial, and lines 28 through 33 make sure that the output file remains a fixed-length file:

```
#Fix the length of each name to a fixed length of 10 characters
#The space character is added as a pad character at the end of each
```

```
#variable
$first .= $filler x (10 - length($first));
$middleInitial .= $filler x (10 - length($middleInitial));
$last .= $filler x (10 - length($last));
```

Remember that each field in the sample file should be ten characters long. The length of each variable is subtracted from the required size of the field. If the length is less than 10, then a filler string will be appended onto the end of the field variable.

Line 32 works like this:

- The length of $middleInitial is calculated to 2: one character for the initial and one character for the period added on line 27.

- The filler variable $filler is multiplied times (10 - 2) or 8, creating a string of eight blanks.

- The eight blanks are appended to the $middleInitial variable using the .= operator.

- The new $middleInitial variable is "M.bbbbbbbb", where each b represents a blank.

All of the modified variables are then written back out the file on line 34:

```
print OUTFILE "$first$middleInitial$last\n";
```

After the entire file is read and modified, each file is closed on lines 37 and 38:

```
close (INFILE);
close (OUTFILE);
```

Lines 40 and 42 create copies of the modified file and restore the original file to illustrate a second technique for modifying the files.

Using Memory as Workspace

The rest of Listing 11.7 demonstrates the technique of using memory as the workspace for modifying your file.

Line 45 opens a file for reading and writing using the read/write operator (+<):

```
open(INOUTFILE, "+<ModifyFile.txt") || die "can't open file";
```

The entire file is read into memory on line 47:

```
@allFile = <INOUTFILE>;
```

After line 47 is executed, the file handle is pointing to the end of the file. Line 49 resets the file handle to the beginning of the file:

```
seek(INOUTFILE, 0, 0);
```

Now when the modified data is written to the file, it will start at the beginning of the file and overwrite the old data.

Lines 52 through 58 modify the names, just as on lines 23 through 34. Line 58 stores the data into a temporary array in memory:

```
$tempArray[$index++] = "$first$middleInitial$last\n";
```

You don't want to write the data out to the file until the entire file is processed.

Even though your operating system will try to optimize reads and writes to a file by buffering the data, manipulating a file on the disk is a slow process. Always limit the number of times you read or write to the disk. Line 36 is an excellent example of limiting the disk access of a program. Line 36 uses a temporary variable to store intermediate modification. When all the modifications are complete, only one disk access (write) is required.

NOTE   When a file system buffers data, it creates a temporary storage location in memory called a *buffer*. The buffer is usually some large number of bytes, which can be synchronized with the file system for optimal reading and writing to a hard disk or other I/O device. If you are writing to a file, the buffer in memory is written to first until the data you are writing to the file has reached a minimum size. When the memory buffer is full, at some minimum value, or you close the file handle, the data you were writing to the file, which was actually written to the memory buffer, is then written to the file. This limits the number of times your program actually writes to the hard disk.

Line 63 writes the modified data to the file.

```
print INOUTFILE @tempArray;
```

Finally, line 64 closes the file. Novice programmers frequently forget this step. Usually, when your program exits, all open file handles are closed, so why bother explicitly closing files? You'll find the reason in the next section.

Writing and reading data from a file, as illustrated in the first part of Listing 11.7, is time-consuming. Whenever practical (if your machine has enough memory), do all the work you can in memory, as in the second part of the listing.

Closing Files

The `close` function closes file handles and flushes all input and output buffers associated with the file handles. The syntax of the `close` function is:

```
close(FILEHANDLE);
```

Your operating system will usually keep all of the output to a file handle in a system buffer until the file handle is closed or the buffer fills up. This is one of the optimization methods employed by your operating system.

Sometimes, if you don't close a file before your program exits, the system buffers associated with your open file handles are not flushed. The data in your program may be correctly calculated but not saved to your file as you intended. Always close open file handles. You'll save yourself trouble in the long run.

Appending Data

In the section on modifying files, you learned how to modify an existing file using the read/write operator (+<). If you just want to add data to a file, you should use the append operator, using this syntax:

```
open (FILEHANDLE, ">>fileName");
```

A file that is commonly appended to is an error log, like this:

```
open(OUTFILE, ">>c:\temp\error.log");
```

Since creating error logs and other log files is a common practice, these files can create a disk storage problem over time. If you need to clean up old log files that your program creates, use the `unlink` function, as described in the next section.

Deleting a File

I am not sure why Perl 5 tries to hide the function for deleting files; everything else seems so logically named. To delete a file in Perl 5 use the `unlink` function. The syntax of the `unlink` function is:

```
unlink filename;
```

or

```
unlink fileList;
```

The unlink function uses a special syntax for wildcard filenames. If you want to delete all of the files in a directory that have a .doc extension, for example, you need to surround the wildcard file list using the angle brackets, like this:

```
unlink<*.doc>;
```

Why Deleting Is Unlinking

There is an explanation for naming the delete file function unlink, of course. The unlink function doesn't actually delete the file from your hard disk—which, by the way, is true of most standard delete functions

Files are blocks of records on your disk. The filename is actually an entry in a special file called a directory. The directory file contains a list of all the files it is responsible for. When you remove a filename from the directory file, no record of the block of records that contains the data referred to by your filename exists. So, in effect, the file is deleted. However, the data isn't ever removed from the disk. The area the data exists in is made available in the file allocation table (FAT). When the system needs some space for new data, it will eventually overwrite the old "deleted" data. Until that happens, the data is still on your disk.

So, the first reason for naming the unlink function *unlink* instead of *delete* is that it actually unlinks the directory file from the data associated with the filename by removing the filename from the directory file.

The second reason the function is named unlink is because of symbolic links on the Unix system. In the Windows world, these symbolic links are called *shortcuts*. Shortcuts and symbolic links are additional ways of referring to the same physical data on the disk. A symbolic link is a copy of the original disk reference information in a second or additional directory file. If you remove the symbolic link or shortcut reference to the file from the directory file, you do not actually delete the entire file. The original reference to the file exists in some other directory file, and so the file has not been deleted.

I think what really happened is someone built a delete function and then got harassed because it did not remove all references to a filename. Instead of explaining why it did not, the developer just decided to skip the arguing and renamed the function unlink. That made things easy for the developer but harder for the programmers trying to figure out how to delete a file.

Using File Test Operators

When you're writing code that accesses the file system, whether on a Unix or Windows computer, you'll run into all types of files and all types of file problems. Here are some of the questions you may need to answer:

- Do you have the privileges necessary to open or even read a file?

- Is the file a text or binary file?

- Is this a directory?

- How big is this file?

- Does this file even exist?

- When was this file last modified?

All of these questions are answered by Perl 5's various file test operators.

The syntax of Perl 5's file test operators is straightforward:

```
operator $filename
operator FILEHANDLE
```

If the test is true, the operator returns a one. If the test is false, the operator returns an empty string. File test operators are frequently used in conditional expressions, like this:

```
if (-e $filename)
```

or like this:

```
$file = $filename if -e $filename:
```

The −e returns true if this file exists.

Listing 11.8 demonstrates using the file test operators for debugging and error-handling purposes. The operators are explained in more detail in the following sections.

TIP   Opening files when writing CGI programs or stand-alone programs can present all kinds of problems. You can use Listing 11.8 when you want to get some additional information about why your program is failing.

Listing 11.8:   File Test Operations

```perl
1.   #!/usr/local/bin/perl
2.   &fileStatus($ARGV[0], $ARGV[1]);
3.
4.   sub fileStatus(){
5.     #This program will print the file status to STDOUT.
6.     #If $HTML equals 1 then the output will be in HTML format
7.     my ($HTML, $filename) = @_;
8.     my $message = "The file $filename:";
9.     my $newLine;
10.    my $tab;
11.    open (FILE, $filename);
12.    if ($HTML){
13.       $newLine = '<br>';
14.       $tab = '<dt>';
15.    }
16.    else{
17.       $newLine = " \n ";
18.       $tab = "\t ";
19.    }
20.    if (-e $filename){
21.       #Table 11.4 file test operators
22.       $message .= "$newLine $tab NOT readable by the effective
                          uid/gid."  unless -r $filename;
23.       $message .= "$newLine $tab NOT writable by the effective
                          uid/gid."  unless -w $filename;
24.       $message .= "$newLine $tab NOT executable by the effective
                          uid/gid."  unless -x $filename;
25.       $message .= "$newLine $tab NOT owned by the effective
                          uid/gid."  unless -o $filename;
26.
27.       $message .= "$newLine $tab NOT readable by the real
                          uid/gid."  unless -R $filename;
28.       $message .= "$newLine $tab NOT writable by the real
                          uid/gid."  unless -W $filename;
29.       $message .= "$newLine $tab NOT executable by the real
                          uid/gid."  unless -X $filename;
30.       $message .= "$newLine $tab NOT owned by the real
                          uid/gid."  unless -O $filename;
31.
```

```
32.        #Table 11.5 file test operators
33.        $message .= "$newLine $tab has the setuid bit set."
                        if -u $filename;
34.        $message .= "$newLine $tab has the setgid bit set."
                        if -g $filename;
35.        $message .= "$newLine $tab has the sticky bit set."
                        if -k $filename;
36.
37.        #Table 11.6 file test operators
38.        $message .= "$newLine $tab is a plain file."
                        if -f $filename;
39.        $message .= "$newLine $tab is a directory."
                        if -d $filename;
40.        $message .= "$newLine $tab is a symbolic link."
                        if -l $filename;
41.        $message .= "$newLine $tab is a block special file."
                        if -b $filename;
42.        $message .= "$newLine $tab is a character special file."
                        if -c $filename;
43.        $message .= "$newLine $tab is a text file."
                        if -T $filename;
44.        $message .= "$newLine $tab is a binary file."
                        if -B $filename;
45.
46.        #Table 11.7 file test operators
47.        $message .= "$newLine $tab has zero size."
                        if -z $filename;
48.        if ($size = -s $filename) {
49.            $message .= "$newLine $tab has size: $size.";
50.        }
51.
52.        #Table 11.8 file test operators
53.        $dayMod = -M $filename;
54.        $dayAcc = -A $filename;
55.        $dayNode = -C $filename;
56.
57.        if ($dayMod < 0){
58.            $dayMod = abs($dayMod);
59.            $message .= "$newLine $tab was modified $dayMod
                        days after this script started"
60.        }
61.        else{
```

```
62.            $message .= "$newLine $tab was modified $dayMod
                              days ago.";
63.        }
64.        if ($dayAcc < 0){
65.            $dayAcc = abs ($dayAcc);
66.            $message .= "$newLine $tab was accessed $dayAcc
                              days after this script started"
67.        }
68.        else{
69.            $message .= "$newLine $tab was accessed $dayAcc
                              days ago.";
70.        }
71.        if ($dayNode < 0){
72.            $dayNode = abs ($dayNode);
73.            $message .= "$newLine $tab The inode was changed
                              $dayNode days after this script started"
74.        }
75.        else{
76.            $message .= "$newLine $tab The inode was changed
                              $dayNode days ago.";
77.        }
78.        #Table 11.9 file test operators
79.        # The socket test requires a file handle, so it is not
           # demonstrated.
80.        $message .= "$newLine $tab is a name pipe."
                              if -p $filename;
81.        $message .= "$newLine $tab is connected to a tty."
                              if -t $filename;
82.
83.    }
84.    else{
85.        $message = "The file $filename does not exist";
86.    }
87.
88.    if ($HTML){
89.        print<<"eof";
90. Content-Type: text/html
91.
92.        <html>
93.        <head>
94.        <title>File Status </title>
95.        </head>
96.        <body>
```

```
97.        $message
98.        </body>
99.        </html>
100. eof
101.    }
102.    else{
103.        print $message;
104. }
105. close(FILE);
106. }
```

Although it was designed to demonstrate the various file test operators, Listing 11.8 can be used as a diagnostic tool for determining the precise access status your program has for an individual file. If you add the subroutine fileStatus (which begins on line 4) to your code, you can call it whenever you wish to determine the details of your program's access to a file. This subroutine will work both in a CGI environment and a standard output environment, based on the first input parameter, which is decoded on line 12. Lines 12 through 19 check the lexical variable $HTML:

```
if ($HTML){
        $newLine = '<br>';
        $tab = '<dt>';
}
else{
        $newLine = " \n ";
        $tab = "\t ";
}
```

If the variable is nonzero, then the HTML newline <br> and tab <dt> characters will be used in the file messages; otherwise the standard newline (\n) and tab (\t) characters are used.

Line 20 checks to see if the input filename exists:

```
if (-e $filename){
```

Then each file test operator is used to determine the exact characteristics of the file. For example, line 22 uses the -r file test to see if the effective uid/gid can read the file:

```
$message .= "$newLine $tab NOT readable by the effective
                     uid/gid."  unless -r $filename;
```

If the test fails, the message between the quotes is added to $message. This general structure of adding to $message each time a file test fails is repeated throughout the program. At the end of the program, the message is printed in the proper format. If an HTML message is required, a proper HTTP header is returned along with a complete diagnostic message:

```
if ($HTML){
     print<<"eof";
Content-Type: text/html

<html>
<head>
<title>File Status </title>
</head>
<body>
$message
</body>
</html>
eof
}
else{
     print $message;
}
```

Otherwise, the diagnostic message is printed using the standard newline and tab characters.

File Privileges Tests

Unix has user IDs and group IDs, often referred to as the *uid* and *gid*. Windows has usernames and group names that also apply to files. You are assigned a user ID and group ID with Windows NT.

There are two types of user and group IDs: effective ID and real ID. Your login ID is called the *real ID*. The *effective ID* is the ID currently assigned to the executing process, which can be changed during execution of the program. If your Perl 5 program resets the user and group ID, then that becomes the effective ID of the process. The effective ID usually is used to allow additional file access privileges to a process, but each file has specific privileges for both the effective ID and real ID.

Table 11.4 shows the different file test operators for testing to see if your program's effective ID or real ID has privileges to read, write, or execute a particular file. These operators work for both the Windows and Unix platforms.

TABLE 11.4: File Tests for Privileges

Operator	Meaning
-r	Returns true if this file is readable by the effective ID (user ID and group ID).
-w	Returns true if this file is writable by the effective ID (user ID and group ID).
-x	Returns true if this file is executable by the effective ID (user ID and group ID).
-o	Returns true if this file is owned by the effective ID (user ID and group ID).
-R	Returns true if this file is readable by the login ID (real user ID and group ID).
-W	Returns true if this file is writable by the login ID (real user ID and group ID).
-X	Returns true if this file is executable by the login ID (real user ID and group ID).
-O	Returns true if this file is owned by the login ID (real user ID and group ID).

There are three other identifiers that associate with how the file identifies its owner, group, and user IDs. These are called the *sticky bit*, the *setgid bit*, and the *setuid bit*. If the setgid or setuid bits are set, then when the file is executed, the user ID and group ID of the file will be the same as its owners. If these bits are not set, the user ID and group ID of the executing file will be the group and user ID of your Perl program. The sticky bit works the same way, except that it affects the file ownership ID.

All of the bits are important if the file is some type of program, like a CGI. program. Frequently, programs need special privileges to perform a particular task. Generally, the web server starts a CGI program. The web server usually runs as user NOBODY. User NOBODY is just a special account with very limited privileges. If your CGI program needs additional privileges, you can set the setuid, gid, or sticky bit to allow it special user privileges.

WARNING   Allowing a program special privileges is usually considered a security risk. Be very careful giving your programs these extra privileges.

You can test for these privileges using the file test operators shown in Table 11.5.

TABLE 11.5: File Tests for Execution

Operator	Meaning
-u	Returns true if this file will execute with the user ID of the file.
-g	Returns true if this file will execute with the group ID of the file.
-k	Returns true if this file will execute with the privileges of the user ID of the file.

File Type Tests

There are lots of different file types, particularly if you're working on a Unix system where every I/O device is considered some type of file. Even on a Windows machine, there are directories, text files, and binary files. If you are traversing a directory structure or copying files, it is important to know what type of file you are working with. To test for all of the different file types, use the file test operators shown in Table 11.6.

TABLE 11.6: File Tests for Type

Operator	Meaning
-f	Returns true if this file a plain file.
-d	Returns true if this file is a directory.
-l	Returns true if this file is a symbolic link (for Unix systems).
-T	Returns true if this file is a text file.
-B	Returns true if this file is a binary file.
-b	Returns true if this file is a block special file.
-c	Returns true if this file is a character special file.

File Existence and Size Tests

When your trying to read or write to a file, sometimes all you want to know is if the file exists. If it exists, does it have any data in it? Table 11.7 lists the file test operators that show whether a file exists and how large the file is.

TABLE 11.7: File Tests for Existence and Size

Operator	Meaning
-e	Returns true if this file exists.
-s	Returns true if this file has nonzero size.
-z	Returns true if this file has zero size.

File Modification Tests

If you're writing a program that monitors your system, such as a program that keeps track of errors or modifications to the password file, you need to know when that file was last modified in relation to your program. To test to see if a file has been modified since your program has been modified, use the file test operators listed in Table 11.8. Each of these file test operators returns a time in days relative to when your program started. For example, if a file was modified 36 hours before your program started, the file test operator −M will return 1.5. If the file has been modified since your program started, the operators will return a negative value.

TABLE 11.8: File Tests for Age

Operator	Meaning
−A	Returns the number of days since last access relative to the program's beginning execution time.
−C	Returns the number of days since last inode change relative to the program's beginning execution time (for Unix systems).
−M	Returns the number of days since last modification, relative to the program's beginning execution time.

Unix File Handle Type Tests

If you are working on a Unix system, you know that all I/O devices are considered files. The file test operators listed in Table 11.9 tell your program whether the file is a socket, a named pipe, or a tty device.

TABLE 11.9: File Tests for Unix File Handle Types

Operator	Meaning
-p	Returns true if this file is a named pipe.
-S	Returns true if this file is a socket.
-t	Returns true if this file is a tty device.

Summary

Perl 5 is one of the richest I/O languages I've encountered. It's no surprise that it takes so many pages just to cover the basics of command line and file I/O.

In this chapter, you learned that Perl automatically loads an array called @ARGV with all of the command-line data that follows the program name. The program name is in the special variable $0 (unlike in the C language, where it is in the array). You also learned that Perl 5 includes several ways to handle command-line switches. Included in the standard Perl 5 distribution are the four permutations of getopts, a program for handling command-line switches. In this chapter, you learned the details of handling program switches, names, and options using the Perl 5 module GetOpt::Long.

Next, you learned about handling files, beginning with the distinction between filenames and file handles and the various options for opening a file. Then you used both the seek function and arrays to understand how to manipulate files. You also learned the advantages and disadvantages of modifying files in memory and on the disk. You learned why it's important to close file handles and how to delete files. At the end of this chapter, you learned about the large set of file test operators Perl 5 offers to you, the programmer.

Now that you know how to get the data into your program, it's time to learn how to format the data for output. Formatting data and printing to files and the user window are common programming tasks that frequently get overlooked. Chapter 12 gives you the details you need to make sure the final results of all of your work don't get trashed on output.

CHAPTER
TWELVE

Printing and Formatting Techniques

- The print function

- The heredoc operator

- The printf and sprintf functions

- The write function and format statements

In this chapter, you'll learn about the basic methods of printing and formatting your data. First, you'll learn more about the `print` function, including its syntax and how to select file handles. You'll also discover how to use the heredoc operator (<<) and the `printf` and `sprintf` functions, which make your printing job easier.

If the `print` function methods of formatting data for output don't suit your needs, Perl also includes a special syntax for formatting output for reports. If you need to print reams of data in column format, you can use Perl 5's `write` function and `format` statements. You'll learn how to create `format` statements to set up headers and data formats in the second part of this chapter.

Using the print Function

You have seen examples that use the `print` function throughout the previous chapters. You use the `print` function to save data to a file, to print results to your screen, and to help you debug a script. The various forms of the `print` function are shown in Table 12.1.

TABLE 12.1: Syntax for the print Function

syntax	Description
print *FILEHANDLE list*;	Print to *FILEHANDLE* the data in *list*
print *FILEHANDLE*;	Print the contents of the default special variable $_ to *FILEHANDLE*
print *list*;	Print to the default selected file handle the data in list
print;	Print to the default selected file handle (STDOUT at startup) the contents of the default special variable $_

The standard syntax for `print` is:

```
print FILEHANDLE list;
```

However, as you might have noticed in previous examples, you can use the `print` function without specifying a file handle. You also can leave out the list. This means that you can use the `print` function by itself, like this:

```
print;
```

Then `print` uses the default file handle and the default output source.

The default output source is the default special variable $_. The default file handle at startup is STDOUT. If you print like this:

```
print "Location: www.assi.net\n\n";
```

the function really works like this:

```
print STDOUT "Location: www.assi.net\n\n";
```

The default file handle is initialized by the Perl 5 interpreter at startup, but you can also set the default file handle in your program, as explained next.

Setting the Default File Handle

Quite often, you'll use the `print` function with the default file handle STDOUT. As you learned in Chapter 11, STDOUT is one of three file handles opened by Perl 5 at startup.

The file handle STDOUT is initially set to your computer monitor. Your program can set STDOUT to another output device, but I don't recommend it. If you want to change where the output from your program is going, don't change STDOUT—change the default output file handle using the `select` function.

The syntax of the `select` function is:

```
select (FILEHANDLE);
```

The default file handle is a global variable. Whenever you modify a global variable, it is good programming practice to save the previous value of the global variable. When your subroutine is finished using the global variable, the subroutine should return the global variable to its previous value. That way, other programs that depend on the global variable will not be affected by the operations in your subroutine.

WARNING   If you don't return the default file handle to its previous value, the system function `write`, which you'll learn about later in this chapter, will not work correctly. This is called a side effect. Side effects can create subtle errors in your program that can be hard to find. Save yourself some trouble later on by always returning global variables to their previous values.

Using the Heredoc Operator

The heredoc (short for here document) operator (<<) prints output to the currently selected file handle. Many Perl 5 programmers expect the default file handle to always be STDOUT and write their programs to depend on the default file handle remaining STDOUT. As you will learn later in this chapter, you can set the default file handle using the select function. If your program will be included in larger programs or use other programs that might reset the default file handle, you should write code that explicitly sets and restores the default file handle.

The syntax of the heredoc operator is:

```
print<<heredoc-marker;
```

You can have spaces after the print function and before the starting <<, but no spaces are allowed between the << and the starting heredoc marker.

WARNING   Leaving a space between the << and the starting heredoc marker is an easy mistake to make. This mistake is difficult to track down because it isn't an error. The space after the << is treated as the null character and matches the first blank line. In later Perl 5 releases, this will be treated as an error. Right now, leaving a space after the heredoc operator is deprecated. (*Deprecated* means a function or syntax will be invalid in the future but is still supported in the current release to maintain compatibility with previous releases.)

You can use any ASCII text identifier you like as the heredoc marker, but you cannot use a variable name. For my heredoc marker, I usually use the characters eof or eop. The eof is traditionally used for the end-of-file marker, and eop seems like a natural end-of-print marker.

The starting heredoc marker takes one of three forms, corresponding to the forms of quoted strings (discussed in Chapter 5):

- For no variable interpolation, surround the heredoc marker with single quotes:

    ```
    print<<'EOF';
    ```

- For variable interpolation, surround the heredoc marker with double quotes or no quotes:

    ```
    print<<"EOF";
    ```

- For command execution, surround the heredoc marker with back quotes:

    ```
    print<<`EOF`;
    ```

If you don't enclose your heredoc marker with any type of quotation marks, the effect is the same as using the single quote on a single word. However, this syntax, like other bare word syntax, is not recommended.

The trailing heredoc marker identifies where the `print` function should stop printing. The trailing heredoc marker must appear on a line by itself beginning in the far-left column of the line, without any quote characters.

I like to use the heredoc operator in my CGI programming. Instead of using a `print` function for each line of an HTML file, I can use the heredoc operator to print an entire header. This technique is demonstrated in Listing 12.1, which prints the header for an HTML page.

Listing 12.1:   **The Heredoc Operator without Variable Interpolation**

```
1.   sub printHeaders(){
2.       print<<'eof';
3.   Content-Type: text/html
4.
5.   <HTML>
6.   <HEAD>
7.   <TITLE>T. R. Lawing Realty E-Mail Request Page</TITLE>
8.   </HEAD>
9.   <BODY background="images/tr_back.gif">
10.  eof
11.      return (1);
12.  }
```

Listing 12.1 uses the heredoc operator to print the HTTP header content type to tell the browser that data following the header will be HTML syntax. Line 2 uses the heredoc operator and the no variable interpolation form of the heredoc marker (eof):

```
print<<'eof';
```

The blank line on line 4 is required after the last HTTP header sent to the browser. It tells the browser the program has received all of the HTTP headers and to accept any remaining data to conform to the information sent in the HTTP headers. In this case, the program sends only one header to the browser: `Content-Type: text/html`. Notice that `Content-Type` starts in the far-left column. If you allow any space before `Content-Type`, the browser will not recognize the header.

The remaining data is not position dependent. Each line is printed to STDOUT just as it is shown on the line in the file. Each line is printed until the heredoc marker (eof) is reached on line 10.

All CGI output headed for the browser should be directed to the STDOUT file handle. It's better programming practice to select the file handle your subroutine needs to use, as you learned in the previous section. You'll see this done in Listing 12.2, which demonstrates using variable interpolation with the heredoc marker.

NOTE   Listing 12.2 is part of an online property management program. The customer was worried about complying with federal housing disclosure rules and felt that logging all the requests for property listing information was necessary. Listing 12.2 logs all requests for property listing information to a local file.

Listing 12.2:   The Heredoc Operator with Variable Interpolation

```
1.   sub openLogFiles(){
2.      $date = `date +%m%d%y`;
3.      $searchFile = 'search_' . $date . '.log';
4.      $searchFile =~ s/\s//g;
5.      open (CRITERIALOG, ">>$HOME/www/VACANCY/" . $searchFile) ||
           die "Can't open $searchFile file h=$HOME";
6.   }
7.
8.   sub closeLogFiles(){
9.      close (CRITERIALOG);;
10.  }
11.
12. sub printLog(){
13.    $prevFH = select (CRITERIALOG);
14.    print<<"eop";
15. ----------;
16. User IP Address: $ENV{'REMOTE_ADDR'}
17. Date/Time:       $dateTime
18. Search Criteria:
19.    Min Beds:       $minBedRoomsStr
20.    Min Bath:       $minBathRoomsStr
21.    Min Rent:       $minRentalRateStr
22.    Max Rent:       $maxRentalRateStr
23.    Pets Allowed:   $petsDesiredStr
24.    Types Desired:  $desiredUnitsStr
```

```
25.    Search Results:
26.        Unit Id:      $unitid
27.        Address:      $address
28.        Rental Rate: $rent
29. eop
30. select($prevFH);
31. }
32.
```

In Listing 12.2, each of the variable names from lines 16 through 28 is interpreted by Perl 5 and printed out as its value, not as its variable name. This is because the variable interpolation form of the heredoc marker is used on line 14:

```
print<<"eop";
```

NOTE   As explained in Chapter 5, variable interpolation means that Perl will look at each character of the string literal to see if it has a special meaning. In practice, this means variable names will be replaced with their values, and other special characters will be processed by the Perl 5 interpreter. Variable interpolation occurs from the opening heredoc marker to the closing heredoc marker.

Now that you've learned about the `print` function, the default file handle for output, and the heredoc operator, let's look at Perl 5's functions for basic formatting.

Using Print Formatting Functions

Perl 5's two print formatting functions are `sprintf` and `printf`. Although these functions work well for basic formatting of strings and numbers, you do need to know the proper codes to use with them to get the output to look the way you want. Other codes that you can use for some simple formatting, such as adding carriage returns and tabs to your output, are called print escape sequences. You'll learn about using the print formatting functions and escape sequences, as well as the special list separator variable when printing arrays, in the following sections.

Formatting with printf and sprintf

The `printf` and `sprintf` functions perform almost identical functions—they both produce a formatted output based on a format code. The `sprintf` function is normally used for forcing a specific format on one or more variables. The variables may then be used elsewhere in the program. The `printf` function is normally used for printing a string that includes variables that need some specific format. The formatted variables are not available for further use in the program.

The `sprintf` function returns the formatted variable in a string. You usually see `sprintf` used like this:

```
$formattedVariable = sprintf "%formatcode", $unformattedVariable;
```

The format code is optional. If a format code is specified, the `sprintf` function uses it on the `$unformattedVariable`, and the resulting formatted string is saved in `$formattedVariable`. A percent sign precedes the format code.

NOTE   I was first introduced to `sprintf` and `printf` when I learned the C programming language. Both of these functions behave the same way in Perl 5 as they did in C. C is a wonderful and flexible programming language, but like Unix, it can be a little cryptic occasionally. These two functions, `sprintf` and `printf`, can also be a little cryptic.

The `printf` function prints formatted output to the specified file handle. The `printf` function is usually used like this:

```
printf(FILEHANDLE "format", formatVariableList);
```

The `printf` function takes three parameters:

- An output file handle, which is optional
- A format string, which can include the format codes
- The variables to be formatted

Remember to exclude the comma after the file handle parameter. If a file handle is not provided, `printf` uses the default file handle, which is usually STDOUT.

The format code for both the `sprintf` and `printf` functions can be made up of a format flag, a width specifier, and a data format code. You can use the format flags of `sprintf` and `printf` to specify the variable's alignment and the type of sign character to use. The width specifiers are the digits that follow the flags to indicate the number of spaces to be used in formatting. The width-specifier digits can be two parts: a total field size and the number of decimal places. The two parts are separated by a period, like this:

```
total-field-size.number-of-decimal-places
```

The number of decimal places plus one (for the decimal point) is normally subtracted from the total field size to determine the number of spaces available for the integer value or scientific notation. The format flags and examples of width specifiers are shown in Table 12.2.

TABLE 12.2: Format Codes for the sprintf and printf Functions

Flag	Description	Example
Blank (default)	Positive numbers begin with a blank. Negative numbers begin with a minus sign. Align characters to right. Pad from left with blanks.	`printf FH "% 04.2\n", $D;`
-	Positive numbers begin with a blank. Negative numbers begin with a minus sign. Align characters to left. Pad from right with blanks.	`$V = sprintf "%-4.2",$D;`
+ -	Positive numbers begin with a plus sign. Negative numbers begin with a minus sign. Align characters to right. Pad from left with blanks.	`$V = sprintf "%+4.2", $D;`

NOTE

A large portion of the C format codes is involved with the data type of the unformatted variable. Since Perl 5 decides the input data type based on context, those data type codes don't matter in Perl programs.

The data type format code tells Perl 5 what type of data format to display. You can force Perl 5 to display data in integer, hexadecimal, character decimal, scientific notation, and other formats, as listed in Table 12.3.

TABLE 12.3: Data Formats for the sprintf and printf Functions

Format	Description
c	Character format
d	Decimal format

Continued on next page

TABLE 12.3 CONTINUED: Data Formats for the sprintf and printf Functions

Format	Description
e	Exponential format
f	Floating-point format
g	Compact format
ld	Long decimal format
lo	Long octal format
lu	Long unsigned decimal format
lx	Long hexadecimal format
o	Octal format
s	String format
u	Unsigned decimal format
x	Hexadecimal format
X	Uppercase hexadecimal format

You can use multiple format codes associated with multiple variables and insert text between the multiple format codes. The `printf` and `sprintf` functions look for a percent sign (%) to begin a new format code. Each format code must have a corresponding variable, which follows the comma that follows the format code list. Here is an example of using multiple format codes:

```
$unformatted=19.86;
printf "%+16.2fUse the +/- signs \n%-16.2f Left align characters\n%
16.2f Blank/- signs \n",  $unformatted, $unformatted, $unformatted;
```

This example prints the following output:

```
        +19.86Use the +/- signs
19.86             Left align characters
        19.86 Blank/- signs
```

A format of %-16.2f tells the `sprintf` or `printf` function to format a string with up to 16 spaces. The numbers are left aligned. Two spaces are allowed for the decimal point numbers and one space for the decimal point, which leaves three spaces for the integer. If the integer value does not need three spaces, it is padded with blanks on the right. The same function without the minus sign (%16.2f) aligns the number to the right and pads with blanks on the left.

Listing 12.3 demonstrates how to use each of these codes with similar numbers, and Figure 12.1 shows the results.

Listing 12.3:   printf Data Formats

```
 1. #!/usr/local/bin/perl
 2. printf "% 16.2c 16.2c   - character format\n", 0xF7;
 3. printf "% 16.2d 16.2d   - decimal format\n", 82.33;
 4. printf "% 16.2e 16.2e   - exponential format\n", 82.33;
 5. printf "% 16.2f 16.2f   - floating point format\n", -82.33;
 6. printf "% 16.2g 16.2g   - compact format\n", 82.33;
 7. printf "% 16.2ld 16.2ld  - long decimal format\n", -82.33;
 8. printf "% 16.2lo 16.2lo  - long octal format\n", 0xF7;
 9. printf "% 16.2lu 16.2lu  - long unsigned format\n", -82.33;
10. printf "% 16.2lx 16.2lx  - long hex format\n", 0xF7;
11. printf "% 16.2o 16.2o   - octal format\n", 0xF7;
12. printf "% 16.2s 16.2s   - string format\n", 0xF7;
13. printf "% 16.2u 16.2u   - unsigned format\n", -82.33;
14. printf "% 16.2x 16.2x   - hex format\n", 0xF78;
15. printf "% 16.2X 16.2X   - upper case hex format\n", 0xF7;
```

Listing 12.4 demonstrates using data format codes (see Table 12.3) to print ASCII character codes to the screen. Figure 12.2 shows the output.

FIGURE 12.1:

Using printf formats

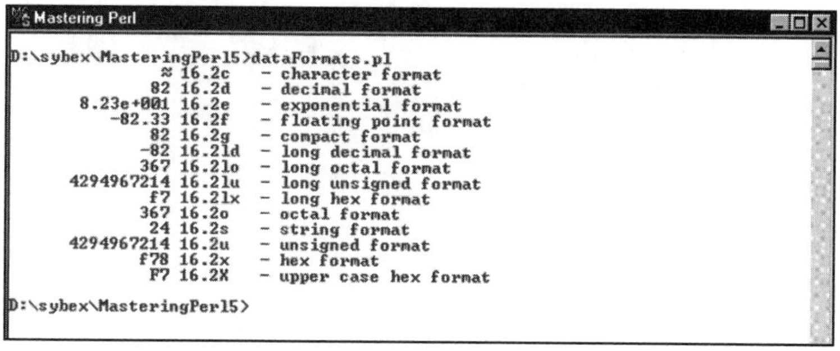

```
D:\sybex\MasteringPerl5>dataFormats.pl
          ≈ 16.2c    - character format
         82 16.2d    - decimal format
   8.23e+001 16.2e    - exponential format
      -82.33 16.2f    - floating point format
         82 16.2g    - compact format
        -82 16.2ld   - long decimal format
        367 16.2lo   - long octal format
 4294967214 16.2lu   - long unsigned format
         f7 16.2lx   - long hex format
        367 16.2o    - octal format
         24 16.2s    - string format
 4294967214 16.2u    - unsigned format
        f78 16.2x    - hex format
         F7 16.2X    - upper case hex format

D:\sybex\MasteringPerl5>
```

TIP

The program in Listing 12.4 is handy for displaying the character codes on your computer. If you want to see the hex or octal values from 0 to 256, just change the %c on line 6 to %o or %x (for hex) or %0 (for octal).

Listing 12.4: **ASCII Character Codes**

```perl
1.  #!/usr/local/bin/perl
2.  for ($i = 0; $i<256; $i++){
3.      if (($i%8)==0){
4.          print "\n";
5.      }
6.      printf "%d %c\t",$i,$i;
7.  }
```

FIGURE 12.2:

Displaying ASCII character codes

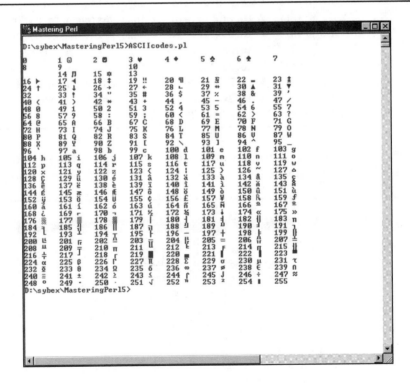

Notice that the second and third lines of Figure 12.2 aren't formatted correctly. That is because some of the character codes between decimal 7 and 15 are control codes that send special signals to your computer. For example, if you have Perl 5 use the character code 7, the program rings the bell; a 13 resets output to the beginning of the line. (The escape sequences \a and \r correspond to the control codes of 7 and 13, respectively.)

Also notice that Listing 12.4 uses two special escape sequences with the `print` function—\t and \n—as you have seen in many examples in this book. These special printing functions are discussed in the next section.

Remember that you can use the data format codes to print or to format your variables before using them in a calculation. When you use `sprintf` for formatting your data, you have essentially added new data types to Perl 5.

NOTE   As explained in Chapter 5, because Perl 5 chooses your data type for you, there is no way to force a number into a particular format or force rounding. Numbers can be strings and strings can be numbers, but it is hard to make a number into $86.12. The simplest way to format or round numbers in Perl 5 is with the `printf` and `sprintf` functions. However, if you are developing a program to sell products and require rounding of dollars and cents, I recommend building your own rounding function. See Chapter 5 for details.

Using Print Escape Sequences

The `print` and `printf` functions send data to a file handle. When that file handle is set to STDOUT, the data is sent to your computer monitor. The print escape sequences described here are used with the `print` function to control the position of the next output character (except for the bell) on the selected file handle. When the file handle refers to your computer monitor, you can see these escape sequences control the placement of the cursor.

As explained in Chapter 5, an escape sequence is the backslash character (the escape code) followed by a single character. Lines 4 and 6 in Listing 12.4 use the \n and \t escape sequences to print a newline and a tab, respectively:

```
print "\n";
printf "%d %c\t",$i,$i;
```

The print escape sequences are listed in Table 12.4

TABLE 12.4: Print Escape Sequences

Code	Description
\a	Ring the bell (alert)
\b	Backspace one position
\e	Add the escape character (Esc key)
\f	Eject the current page (form feed)
\n	Start a new line (newline)
\r	Return to the start of the line (carriage return)
\t	Add a tab space

You can use the printing commands in Table 12.4 to format your output. This is handy for simple or small printing tasks. However, when you have several pages of data to print, it's much easier to use the `write` function and `format` statements, which are discussed a little later in this chapter.

Printing Arrays

Before we leave the `print` statement topic and enter the magical world of the `write` function and `format` statement, there is just one more printing trick I would like to show you. Perl 5 contains a special variable called the list separator (`$'`). Whenever you `print` an array using double quotes around the array, the list separator is placed between each cell of the array. If you print the array without quotes, the list separator will not be placed between each array cell, so the array cells will be jammed together.

The list separator variable can be handy if you want to export some data in various delimited formats. If you want colons, commas, or something else, just set the list separator to the desired value.

WARNING Like the default file handle, the list separator (`$'`) is a global variable that every subroutine uses. If you change the default, remember to set it back to its previous value!

Listing 12.5 demonstrates using the list separator variable with arrays, and Figure 12.3 shows the output.

Listing 12.5:   The List Separator Variable

```perl
1. #!/usr/local/bin/perl
2. (@array) = (1..5, "Apples", "Oranges", "and Peaches");
3. print STDOUT "The default behavior of array printing with
                   double quotes.\n";
4. print STDOUT "@array\n\n";
5. print STDOUT "The behavior of array printing without quotes.\n";
6. print STDOUT @array;
7. print "\n\n";
8. #set list separator to null for printing of rules
9. my $listSeparator = $";
10. $" = ':' ;
11. print STDOUT "The list separator is a colon \n";
12. print STDOUT "@array\n\n";
13. $" = ',' ;
14. print STDOUT "The list separator is a comma.\n";
15. print STDOUT "@array\n\n";
16. $" = '' ;
17. print STDOUT "The list separator is the empty string.\n";
18. print STDOUT "@array\n\n";
19. #return to previous value
20. $" = $listSeparator;
21. print STDOUT "The list separator returned to its previous
                   value.\n";
22. print STDOUT "@array\n\n";
```

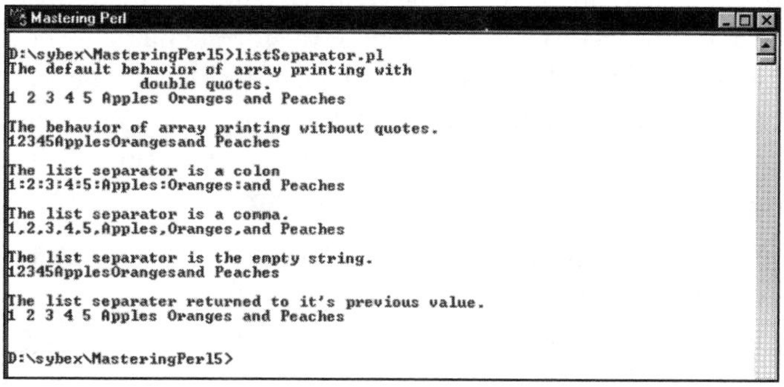

FIGURE 12.3:

Printing arrays using the list separator variable

The techniques you've learned so far work just fine when you want to print a couple of formatted lines, but sometimes you need to format a lot of data for output. In the next section, you'll learn how to use Perl 5's report-formatting techniques.

Writing Formatted Output

How do you write reams of formatted output in a single statement? The function that does the work is called `write`. The syntax of the `write` function is similar to the syntax of the `print` function:

```
write FILEHANDLE;
```

or

```
write;
```

If you don't give the `write` function a file handle, it uses the default or selected file handle. The file handle should have a `format` statement associated with it, which is where all of the formatting is encoded.

The syntax of a `format` statement is:

```
format FORMATNAME =
      output definition
    .
```

This syntax is made up of three parts. The first part is the declaration of the format name:

```
format FORMATNAME =
```

The keyword `format` starts the format declaration. It is followed by the format name, which can be any name (with the same character restrictions as a normal variable, discussed in Chapter 5). If the format name is the same as a file handle, it will be used as the default data format for that file handle. If a format name has the same name as a file handle with the keyword _TOP appended to its name, that format will be used as the default top-of-form format (header) for that file handle. The equal sign (=) follows the format name.

The second part of the format declaration is the definition of what will be printed to the file handle.

The third part of a format definition is its ending statement. All formats end with a period (.) in the left-hand column on a line by itself.

With one simple `write` function and properly built `format` statements, you can send pages of formatted data to a file or your screen. For example, you can print each page with the proper header and all of the data in neatly aligned columns. As an example, Listing 12.6 modifies the output format using `format` statements. Figure 12.4 (though relatively uninteresting) shows how a simple `write` function can send columns of formatted data to the screen.

Listing 12.6: **The write Function and format Statement**

```
1.  #!/usr/local/bin/perl
2.  $unitid = 123456;
3.  $address = "8501 Lancer";
4.  $rent = 875.00;
5.  $dateTime = "3:42 PM";
6.  $ENV{'REMOTE_ADDR'} = "207.456.28.28";
7.  &openLogFiles;
8.  for ($i=0; $i<100; $i++){
9.     &printLog;
10. }
11. &closeLogFiles;
12.
13. sub openLogFiles(){
14.    $searchFile = 'search_' . $date . '.log';
15.    $searchFile =~ s/\s//g;
16.    open (CRITERIALOG, ">>e:\\perlbook\\chapter10\\" .
              $searchFile) || die "Can't open $searchFile
                                file h=$HOME";
17. }
18.
19. sub closeLogFiles(){
20.    close (CRITERIALOG);;
21. }
22.
23. #This format is associated with the FH CRITERIALOG
24. format CRITERIALOG_TOP =
25.
26. Unit ID Address          Rent     Time    IP ADDRESS
27. ====================================================
28. .
29.
30. #This format is associated with the FH CRITERIALOG
31. format CRITERIALOG =
32. @<<<<<<<@<<<<<<<<<<<<<@#####.##@>>>>>>>@>>>>>>>>>>>>>
```

```
33. $unitid, $address,        $rent,     $dateTime, $ENV{'REMOTE_ADDR'}
34. .
35.
36. sub printLog(){
37.     write CRITERIALOG;
38. }
39.
```

FIGURE 12.4:

Formatting output

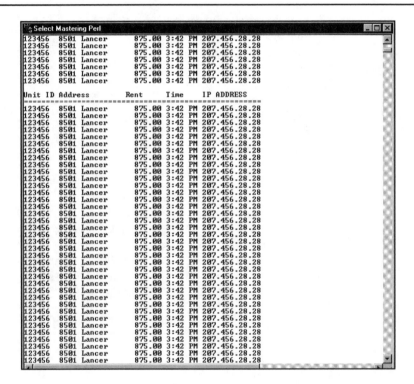

NOTE   The variable that controls the number of lines per page is $FORMAT_LINES_PER_PAGE. This and other special variables that you can use with the `format` statement are discussed a little later in the chapter.

The following sections explain how the `format` statements in Listing 12.6 work.

Naming Formats

By naming the formats the same as the file handles, the format becomes associated with the file handle. There are two types of formats in Listing 12.6:

- The top-of-form format is printed at the top of each new page of data. The top-of-form format is associated with a file handle by appending the keyword _TOP after the file handle name. (The top-of-form format association is case sensitive—it must be _TOP, not _Top or _top.) You can see this name on line 24:

    ```
    format CRITERIALOG_TOP =
    ```

- The format used for the actual data printed on the page is associated with the file handle because it is named the same as the file handle. This appears on line 31:

    ```
    format CRITERIALOG =
    ```

The Perl 5 interpreter is not confused by having two things named the same. Just as Perl 5 understands that $variable, @variable, and %variable are all different things, it understands that format *FILEHANDLE* and open (*FILEHANDLE*) are different variables. The keywords open, select, and format help Perl 5 keep track of what it is supposed to do when it sees the name CRITERIALOG.

Associating a format statement with a file handle by name is not required, but it is handy—it allows you to use a write function like the one on line 37 of Listing 12.6:

```
write CRITERIALOG;
```

This write function prints the formats associated with the file handle CRITERIA-LOG. There are other ways than filename association to use formats, which you'll learn about after the next section on format output definitions.

Defining Format Output

The format statement's format output definition defines what will be printed by the write function. It begins after the format statement's equal sign and ends just before the closing period. Lines 25 through 27 of Listing 12.6 demonstrate a simple format output definition:

```
Unit ID Address       Rent    Time    IP ADDRESS
=========================================================
```

This output definition is made up of a blank line, some column headers, and a separator made up of equal signs (=). In Figure 12.4, you can see the formatted header at about the middle of the screen.

Lines 32 and 33 of Listing 12.6 illustrate the second type of format output definition:

```
@<<<<<<<@<<<<<<<<<<<<<<<@#####.##@>>>>>>>@>>>>>>>>>>>>>
$unitid, $address,      $rent,   $dateTime, $ENV{'REMOTE_ADDR'}
```

Line 32 is called a position line. In this example, it defines five variable alignment fields. Perl 5 uses the position line to determine which column to begin printing the variables of the following variable line (line 33 in Listing 12.6) on and how many output characters to allocate to each variable.

The position line is made up of special characters that tell Perl 5 when to start printing a variable and how to align that variable in its column position. The characters that tell Perl 5 when to start printing a new variable are the at sign (@) and the caret (^). For most formatting tasks, you will begin each alignment field with an at sign. The caret tells Perl 5 to reuse the variable associated with the caret (this is explained in more detail a bit later in the chapter, in the section on long data lines). A variable must appear in the variable line for each at sign in the position line.

The following are the four alignment characters that can be used in the position line:

<   Align left

>   Align right

| Align center

Align right (numeric characters only)

.   Used with the # character in an integer.decimal format

The alignment characters must follow the variable characters (the @ or the ^). Each alignment character reserves one space in your output field. The alignment characters are only associated with the variable character (@ or ^) that they follow.

The pound sign (#) is a special case of the right-alignment character (>). The pound sign tells Perl 5 to treat a variable as a number. An additional special character, the decimal point, can be used with the pound sign. The integer value of the variable is printed before the decimal point, and the decimal value of the variable is printed after the decimal point.

The alignment characters also tell Perl 5 how many columns to allow for each variable. A column in the output form is reserved for each alignment character that follows a variable character. Variables that exceed their allocated column size are right truncated. Since each alignment character takes up one space on the form, what you type into your program is what you see when it is printed. This is an early form of WYSIWYG (what you see is what you get) formatting.

In the example in Listing 12.6, there are exactly five variables on the variable line (line 33), which are associated with the variable alignment fields on the previous line.

Formatting with Special Variables

Perl 5 usually allows you multiple ways to do almost any task. In the previous section, you learned how to associate format variables with file handles. In this section, you'll learn about several alternatives and the special variables that make these alternatives possible.

The special variables include $^ (top-of-form format), $~ (data format), $= (number of lines per pages), and several others. At this point, you might be wondering how you will remember what all of Perl 5's special variables represent. In this case, Perl 5 provides an alternative. One of the very nice modules that comes with Perl 5 is English.pm. Add this line to the top of your Perl 5 code:

```
use English;
```

Then instead of using $^ to set your top-of-form format variable and $~ to set your data format variable, you can use $FORMAT_NAME and $FORMAT_TOP_NAME, respectively.

Table 12.5 lists all of the special variables associated with formats in both their English and special variable name format.

TABLE 12.5: The format Statement Special Variables

English	Code	Description
$FORMAT_AUTOFLUSH	$|	Auto flush on/off flag
$FORMAT_FORMFEED	$^L	Character string to output before a new page (excluding the first page)
$FORMAT_LINE_BREAK_ CHARACTERS	$:	Format line break characters
$FORMAT_LINES_LEFT	$-	Number of lines left before this format page starts a new page
$FORMAT_LINES_PER_PAGE	$=	Number of lines per page

Continued on next page

TABLE 12.5 CONTINUED: The format Statement Special Variables

English	Code	Description
$FORMAT_NAME	$~	Format name
$FORMAT_PAGE_NUMBER	$%	Current format page number
$FORMAT_TOP_NAME	$^	Top-of-form name

Flushing the Buffer

If you not familiar with the terms *flushing* and *buffer* (in the context of I/O, of course), or if you are curious about the auto flush special variable, take a moment to read the following paragraphs.

When your program uses a function, such as print, that sends data to an output device, the data is usually not written immediately. Modern computer memory and CPUs are thousand and sometimes millions of times faster than any input or output device, such as your hard disk, tape drive, or computer monitor. Each time your program stops to send something to an output device (a peripheral), it must wait for the output device to return control of the CPU to your program. If you do this a lot, it can slow your program.

All compiler writers know that I/O devices are much slower than the CPU, so they try to limit the number of times a program writes to peripherals. They do this by sending data to output devices only when an internal variable, called the *output buffer*, contains at least the minimum amount of data (as defined by the system). Each time you use the `print` function or some other means of sending data to an output device, the data goes into the output buffer first. When the output buffer has enough data in it, the data is sent to the correct peripheral, which is called *flushing the buffer*.

The $FORMAT_AUTOFLUSH or $| special variable sets the auto flush flag on or off. The default mode for this variable is off, which is zero or **null**. When the auto flush flag is on (set to a nonzero value), Perl 5 will call the system flush function each time a print or other output request is made, thereby flushing the buffer. I sometimes set the auto flush flag to on for my CGI programs that perform other I/O tasks after they have built and printed the HTML response page. This speeds up the CGI program's response to the calling web browser by forcing the system to flush the printed HTML page.

As with other system and global variables, modify the auto flush variable with caution. If you do change it, be sure to reset it to its previous value as soon as your program is done with it.

Handling Long Data Items

As you've learned, when you use `format` statements, each column of data is set to a particular size. This allows all of your data to line up in rows and columns. However, if you want to print an extra long piece of information, you need to use one of these special characters in the format line (format output definition): caret (^), tilde (~), or an at sign and asterisk (@*).

The caret, when used in the position line where you would normally put the at sign, tells Perl 5 to reuse the variable associated with the caret. Each time the variable is referenced in a data line, all the columns assigned to that variable are filled with the contents of the variable. The contents that were printed are then removed from the variable. Because the variable is actually modified each time it is used, it is always a good idea to use a temporary variable in your data format line.

If you put two tildes (~~) together on a single line, Perl 5 does not modify the output variable.

The easiest method for printing a field of undetermined length is to use the at sign with an asterisk (which I'll call an *at asterisk*) to print everything in the scalar variable `$temp`. A variable printed using an at asterisk in a format position line will start printing wherever the at asterisk is originally positioned, but the output just continues to wrap onto the next line. When you use an at asterisk inside a `format` function, I recommend placing it in the left-hand column on a line by itself.

Listing 12.7 shows how to use each of these special characters for printing long fields, and Figure 12.5 shows the output.

Listing 12.7:   Format Lines

```
1.  #!/usr/local/bin/perl
2.  use English;
3.  $longTestLine = "1 Test line 1";
4.  $longTestLine .= "2 Test line 2";
5.  $longTestLine .= "3 Test line 3";
6.  $longTestLine .= "4 Test line 4";
7.  $longTestLine .= "5 Test line 5";
8.
9.  $printedLine = $longTestLine;
10. format at =
```

```
11.
12.
13. A format line using the at sign and asterisk
14. ------------------------
15.
16.                                      @*
17. $printedLine
18. .
19.
20. $FORMAT_NAME = at;
21. write;
22. $printedLine = $longTestLine;
23. format caretp =
24.
25.
26. A format line using the caret symbol
27. ------------------------
28.
29. ^>>>>>>>>>>>
30. $printedLine
31. ^>>>>>>>>>>>
32. $printedLine
33. ^>>>>>>>>>>>
34. $printedLine
35. ^>>>>>>>>>>>
36. $printedLine
37. ^>>>>>>>>>>>
38. $printedLine
39. ^>>>>>>>>>>>
40. $printedLine
41. ^>>>>>>>>>>>
42. $printedLine
43. .
44.
45. $printedLine = $longTestLine;
46. $FORMAT_NAME = caretp;
47. write;
48. format tt =
49.
50.
51. A format line using the tilde tilde symbol
52. ------------------------
```

```
53.
54. ^>>>>>>>>>>>>>>>>>>>>>>>>>>>>>>>>>>>
55. ~~ $printedLine
56. ^>>>>>>>>>>>>>>>>>>>>>>>>>>>>>>>>>>>
57. ~~ $printedLine
58. .
59.
60. $printedLine = $longTestLine;
61. $FORMAT_NAME = tt;
62. write;
63. format t =
64.
```

FIGURE 12.5:

Using at asterisk, caret, and tilde codes on format lines

> **NOTE**   The documentation says that you can suppress lines that would print as blank lines by placing a tilde (~) anywhere on the line. However, this doesn't work for me. When I put a tilde on a single line, both my Windows NT and Unix computers print a complete line of unreadable characters. You can see an example of this at the bottom of Figure 12.5

Summary

In the previous chapters, you've seen various programs that print and format data for output. In this chapter, you learned the details and syntax of printing data to files and your computer monitor.

The chapter began with an explanation of the `print` function syntax and how to change the default output file (file handle) without disrupting other subroutines. If you need tighter control over data formats, you now know that you can use the `printf` and `sprintf` functions with format codes. You also learned how to use print escape sequences and how to change the list separator for formatting array output.

Next, you learned the details of formatting output with the `write` function and `format` statements. You learned that a format is just a data declaration you can place anywhere in your program. You can name a format anything you want and then refer to it by setting the format name. When a format is not associated with a file handle by name, you associate the format with the current default file handle by setting the special variable $~ or the English name $FORMAT_NAME. Finally, you learned about the format special variables that are associated with each file handle.

In the next chapter, you'll learn about the built-in functions and modules provided with Perl 5 to help you navigate through directories, files, and file handles.

CHAPTER

THIRTEEN

Directories and System I/O Utilities

- Modules for working with directories

- Directory handle operations

- Functions for working with files

- Modules for working with files

Now that you know the basics of I/O programming, it's time to learn about all the I/O bells and whistles that come with a Perl 5 distribution. The Perl 5 directory and file functions and modules give you many options to extend your program's basic I/O capabilities.

In this chapter, you'll learn what these I/O tools do and how to use them. It begins with functions related to directories, and then covers functions and modules related to files. Most of the functions and modules work on both Unix and Windows platforms. The functions and modules that run only on Windows systems are covered in Part 6 of this book rather than in this chapter.

Directory Modules and Functions

It's always a good idea to know where you are. Perl 5 has a nice set of tools to keep the directory path visible to your program. Table 13.1 lists the functions and module covered in this section, and Listing 13.1 demonstrates their use. Figure 13.1 shows the output of Listing 13.1.

TABLE 13.1: Directory Functions and Module

Name	Description
chdir	Change the current directory
closedir	Close the directory handle
mkdir	Create a new directory
opendir	Open a directory handle
readdir	Get the contents of the directory
rewinddir	Reset the directory handle to the start of the directory listing
rmdir	Delete the directory
seekdir	Set the directory handle to a particular byte offset
telldir	Get the directory handle's current byte offset
Cwd	Get the current directory (platform-independent module)

—

Listing 13.1:   Directory Functions

```perl
1.  #! /usr/local/bin/perl
2.  use Cwd;
3.  $dir = cwd;
4.  print "dir=> $dir\n";
5.
6.  chdir ('D:\\sybex');
7.  $dir = cwd;
8.
9.  print "dir=> $dir\n";
10. chdir ('listings\\chap13');
11. $dir = cwd;
12.
13. print "dir=> $dir\n";
14. mkdir ('D:\\sybex\\MasteringPerl5\\newdir',000) ||
15.    warn "mkdir failed $!";
16. mkdir ('newdir2',000) || warn "mkdir failed $!";
17. rmdir ('newdir');
18. print "\n\n";
19.
20. opendir(THISDIR, "$dir");
21. @dirList = <THISDIR>;
22. print "OPEN @dirList\n";
23.
24. @dirList = readdir THISDIR;
25. print "READ @dirList\n";
26. print "\n\nThe directory listing after using readdir\n";
27. foreach $dir (@dirList){
28.    print "$dir\n";
29. }
30. print "\nThe location of the directory handle after reading
31.       through the directory\n";
32. $loc = telldir THISDIR;
33. print "Before Rewind Loc ==> $loc\n";
34.
35. print "\nUsing rewinddir the directory handle is reset.\n";
36. rewinddir THISDIR;
37. $loc = telldir THISDIR;
38. print "After Rewind Loc ==> $loc\n";
39.
40. rewinddir THISDIR;
41.
```

```
42. do {
43.    $tellSpot[$i++] = telldir THISDIR;
44. } while (readdir THISDIR);
45. print "\n\nUsing seek to reset the directory handle\n\n";
46. for ($i = 2; $i <= $#tellSpot; $i++){
47.    seekdir (THISDIR,$tellSpot[$i]);
48.    $fn = readdir THISDIR;
49.    print"$fn\n";
50. }
51.
52. closedir THISDIR;
```

FIGURE 13.1:

Using directory functions

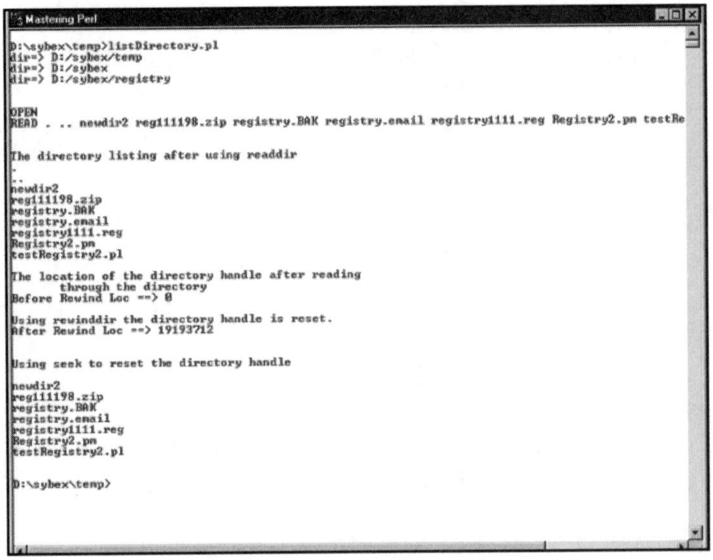

Working with Directories

The directory functions for getting the current directory, changing the directory, creating a new directory, and removing a directory take a directory path as a parameter. The directory path supplied with the directory functions may be a scalar variable, string, or expression. The parentheses are not required. If you are using a variable, remember to use double quotes for variable interpolation.

If you are working on a Windows computer, your directory path includes the backslash character (\), which is also the Perl escape character. You must escape the directory separator character for the directory path to be interpreted correctly, as shown here:

```
chdir ('listings\\chap13');
mkdir ('c:\\temp\\listings\\chap13',000);
rmdir ('e:\\sybex\\testDir');
opendir ('listings\\chap13');
```

Getting the Current Default Directory

A module can contain many methods, which are also called functions. The Cwd module contains the methods listed in Table 13.2. Each method in the Cwd module returns the current working directory. Your program searches in the current working directory for file and directory names that have no path information associated with them. To include the Cwd module in your program, you must use the use command, like this:

```
use Cwd;
```

or the require command, like this:

```
require Cwd;
```

TABLE 13.2: The Cwd Methods

Method	Description	Syntax	Restrictions
abs_path	Get the absolute path of the input parameter	$absolutePath = abs_path(*FILENAME*);	Uses the platform's implementation of the getcwd() function
cwd	Get the current working directory	$directory = cwd(); or $directory = cwd;	None
fast_abs_path	Get the absolute path of the parameter	$fastabsPath = fast_abs_path (*FILENAME*);	May change the current working directory
fastcwd	Get the current working directory		May change the current working directory
getcwd	Get the current working directory	$directory = getcwd(); or $directory = getcwd;	Uses the platform's implementation of the getcwd() function

---

I recommend using the **cwd** method of the **Cwd** module, as shown on lines 2, 6, and 10 of Listing 13.1. The **cwd** method works on both Unix and Windows platforms. I have never had problems porting my code when it included the **cwd** method.

The fast_abs_path method runs faster than the abs_path method, and the fastcwd method runs faster than the other Cwd methods that return the current working directory. However, both of these methods can inadvertently change the current working directory. These methods will always try to return your program to the directory they started in, but because of directory access privileges, they may fail. If the function fails to return your program to its original working directory, your program will die, displaying the message "Unstable directory path."

Changing the Current Directory

When you want to change your program's default working directory, use the chdir (change directory) command. This command is familiar to Unix users. DOS users are used to using the equivalent cd command.

The chdir command accepts one parameter: the directory, relative or absolute, you wish to set as your program's default directory. The syntax is:

```
chdir ('directoryPath');
```

The chdir command returns 1 for success and 0 for failure.

Creating a New Directory

To create a new directory, use the mkdir command. The mkdir command requires two parameters: the directory name and the permissions mask. The syntax is:

```
mkdir ('directory', UNIXPermissionsMask);
```

The mkdir command returns 1 for success and 0 for failure.

The absolute path may include the drive as part of the path name, as shown on line 13 of Listing 13:

```
mkdir ('e:\\sybex\\listings\\chap15\\newdir',000) || warn "mkdir failed
$!";
```

If the drive is not included in an absolute path, the directory will be created on the drive of the current default directory.

The *UNIXPermissionsMask* sets the read, write, and execute privileges for the new directory on a Unix computer. If you are working on a Windows computer, the value is required but ignored. You can use any number for the permissions mask.

On a Unix computer, the permissions mask is affected by your umask (discussed in the "File Functions" section of this chapter). On my virtual domain, I was able to set a permissions mask only for user, not for group and world. I set user to read, write, and execute by using the permissions mask of 0777. The leading zero is required to make Perl interpret the number as octal.

Deleting a Directory

To delete a directory, use the rmdir command. The rmdir command takes one parameter: the relative or absolute path to the directory being deleted. The syntax is:

```
rmdir ('directory');
```

The rmdir function returns 1 for success and 0 for failure.

The rmdir function does not accept wildcards or arrays, which means deleting multiple directories must be done in conjunction with the readdir function (discussed in the "Reading from a Directory" section of this chapter). Follow this procedure:

- Read the directory listing into a scalar variable using the readdir function.

- Use a regular expression to match the directory you wish to delete.

- Call the rmdir function on those directories that match your regular expression (discussed in Chapter 16).

Listing 13.2 shows an example of deleting multiple directories.

Listing 13.2:   **Deleting Multiple Directories**

```perl
1.  #!/usr/local/bin/perl
2.  mkdir ("e:\\sybex\\Testlistings",0)||warn "$!";
3.  for ($i = 0; $i < 10; $i++){
4.    mkdir ("e:\\sybex\\Testlistings\\rmdir$i",0)||warn "$!";
5.  }
6.
7.  chdir ("e:\\sybex\\Testlistings");
8.  use Cwd;
9.  $dir = cwd();
```

```
10.
11. opendir (DH, $dir) || warn $!;
12. while ($dirName = (readdir(DH))){
13.    if ($dirName =~ /^rm/){
14.        print "Removing $dirName\n";
15.        rmdir ("$dirName") || warn $!;
16.    }
17. }
```

Working with Directory Handles

A *directory handle* is equivalent to a file handle. A directory handle is a link from your computer program to the directory on your file system. A directory is itself a file with a special format, which contains information about the locations of the files on your computer.

The directory handle has its own namespace separate from the file handle namespace. The directory handle has the same variable naming rules as the file handle and is, by convention, all uppercase characters to avoid naming conflicts with built-in functions (all Perl 5 built-in functions are lowercase).

In order to use the readdir, telldir, seekdir, and closedir functions, you must first open the directory handle using the opendir function.

Opening a Directory Handle

The opendir command takes as parameters the directory handle name and the directory, relative or absolute, you wish to open:

```
opendir (DIRECTORYHANDLE, 'directoryPath');
```

The opendir command returns 1 for success and null for failure. After you open a directory handle with the opendir function, you can use the functions discussed in the following sections. When you're finished using the directory handle, remember to close it with the closedir function.

Reading from the Directory Handle

The readdir function reads the contents of a directory listing from a directory handle. The readdir function takes one parameter: the directory handle. Its syntax is:

```
$dirName = readdir (DIRECTORYHANDLE);
```

```
@dirList = readdir (DIRECTORYHANDLE);
```

In scalar context, this function returns the next directory listing. In list (array) context, this function loads the array with the remaining contents of the directory handle. The parentheses are not required.

Unlike with the file handle operators, the directory handle position does not reset to the start of the directory list after the readdir function has read to the end of directory handle. The readdir function returns 0 when it reaches the end of the directory list or after reading an empty directory handle. Repeated reads after the readdir function has reached the end of the directory handle and returned a 0 continue to return a 0.

The readdir function only moves forward through a directory handle. You must use the seekdir or rewinddir function to reset the directory handle to the beginning of the directory or a specific position, respectively. The current position of the directory handle before or after a readdir call is returned by the telldir function. These functions are discussed in the following sections. Listing 13.1 includes an example that uses the telldir, seekdir, readdir, and rewinddir functions to manually move through a directory handle:

```
rewinddir THISDIR;

do {
    $tellSpot[$i++] = telldir THISDIR;
} while (readdir THISDIR);
print "\n\nUsing seek to reset the directory handle\n\n";
for ($i = 2; $i <= $#tellSpot; $i++){
    seekdir (THISDIR,$tellSpot[$i]);
    $fn = readdir THISDIR;
    print"$fn\n";
}
```

Getting the Directory Handle's Current Position

The telldir function takes one parameter, a directory handle, and returns the current byte position of the directory handle. Its syntax is:

```
$byteOffset = telldir (DIRECTORYHANDLE);
```

The parentheses are not required.

The telldir function gives an interesting insight into directory implementations. The byte value returned by the telldir function is not an offset from an open file handle, but some value that appears to be a byte offset from a master listing. You can calculate the next byte offset as shown in Listing 13.3. The next byte value returned by telldir is always the length of the filename returned by readdir plus one, as you can see in Figure 13.2. The last value returned by the telldir function in this example is 0.

Listing 13.3:   **Calculating Byte Offsets with telldir**

```
1.  #!/usr/local/bin/perl
2.  chdir ("d:\\sybex\\temp");
3.  use Cwd;
4.  $dir = cwd();
5.
6.  opendir (DH, $dir) || warn $!;
7.  $sByteOffset = telldir DH;
8.  $pbo = $sByteOffset;
9.  while ($dirName = (readdir(DH))){
10.     $dirNameLength = length($dirName);
11.     $byteOffset = telldir DH;
12.     $diff = $byteOffset - $pbo;
13.     $totalSize = $pbo - $sByteOffset;
14.     print "$dirName is $dirNameLength characters long at $pbo
15.            which is $diff bytes\n";
16.     $pbo = $byteOffset;
17. }
18. print "Total directory bytes is: $totalSize\n";
```

Resetting the Directory Handle

The rewinddir function resets the directory handle to the start of the directory listing. The rewinddir function accepts the directory handle as its single parameter. Its syntax is:

    rewinddir (DIRECTORYHANDLE);

The starting byte address of the directory handle is available from the telldir function.

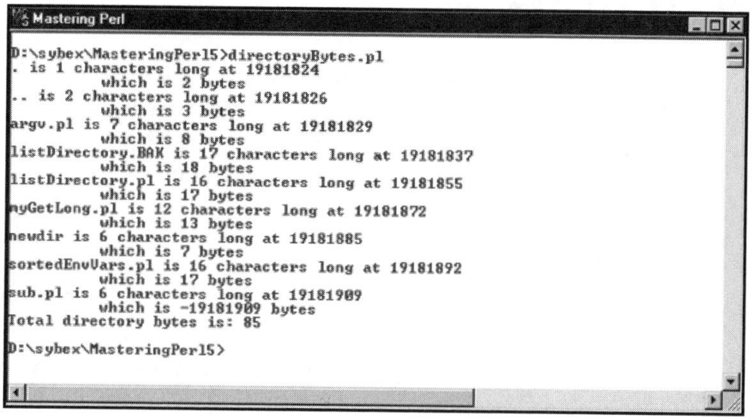

FIGURE 13.2:

Calculating byte values
with telldir

Setting the Directory Handle Position

The seekdir function sets the directory handle position to the specified byte off-set position. It takes two parameters: the directory handle to be set and the value, a byte offset, to assign to the directory handle. Its syntax is:

```
seekdir(DIRECTORYHANDLE, byteOffset);
```

The byte offset must be a value returned by the telldir function (see Listing 13.3). The parentheses are not required.

NOTE   Unlike the seek function used on file handles, the seekdir function does not use a byte offset relative to the beginning or end of the file. The byte offset of the seekdir function is an absolute byte value.

Closing a Directory Handle

Use the closedir function to close a directory handle when you're finished using it. Closing the directory handle makes sure you do not corrupt the direc-tory structure on your computer's file system. The closedir command accepts a directory handle as its single parameter. Its syntax is:

```
closedir (DIRECTORYHANDLE);
```

The directory handle must be a directory handle opened by the opendir com-mand. The parentheses are not required.

File Functions

Perl's basic I/O capabilities, covered in Chapters 11 and 12, are sufficient for most of your general programming tasks. Every now and then, you need to do something special that requires just the perfect tool, however. The file functions in this section are a complete set of special tools that let you do file-system–specific jobs.

Most of these functions work on both the Unix and Windows operating systems. However, even when a function works on both platforms, the results from using a function may differ between platforms. The `stat` function is a good example of a function that works on both platforms but returns different values. Some of the attributes returned by the `stat` function on a Unix system don't exist on a Windows computer.

Perl 5, in its wisdom, doesn't require a special interface to accommodate platform differences. Even when functions return different structures, Perl 5's function interface remains the same. This allows you to write your code once and run it on both the Windows and Unix platforms, which is a very nice feature. Table 13.3 lists the file functions covered in this section.

TABLE 13.3: File Functions

Name	Description	Platform
`binmode`	Read and write the file handle in binary mode	Both
`eof`	Return true if the next character is the end of the file	Both
`fcntl`	Modify the file handle's mode flags	Both
`fileno`	Get the file descriptor of the file handle	Both
`flock`	Set the file lock flags	NT and Unix (not Win95/98)
`getc`	Read the next character from the file handle	Both
`ioctl`	Manipulate low-level device functions	Both
`link`	Create a symbolic copy of the file	Unix
`lstat`	Get the file status of the symbolic link	Unix
`readlink`	Get the actual filename from the symbolic link	Unix
`rename`	Change the name of a file	Both

Continued on next page

TABLE 13.3 CONTINUED: File Functions

Name	Description	Platform
read	Read from the file handle	Both
sysopen	Open the file	Both
sysread	Read from the file handle	Both
sysseek	Set the file handle pointer	Both
syswrite	Write to the file handle	Both
stat	Get the file statistics of the specified file	Both
symlink	Create a symbolic link	Unix
truncate	Restrict the file length to the specified length	Both
umask	Set the default file privileges.	Both
utime	Set the file's last modified time	Both

NOTE   Whenever you see a Perl function starting with `sys`, you know you are getting close to the operating system. Functions that operate at the system level are typically faster but have the potential of being less portable. If you decide to use these `sys` functions, they will not all operate the same across Unix and Windows platforms. Each operating system takes a different approach to the implementing the file system, and these functions are where those differences start to show up. If you include the `Fcntl` module, you can have speed and portability also. The `Fcntl` module is covered later in this chapter, in the "Platform-Independent File Symbols" section.

Opening a File

You can use the `sysopen` function to open a file, setting modes and permissions. The `sysopen` function takes four parameters: the file handle, the filename, the read and write options, and optionally, the access permissions for the file. The syntax is:

```
sysopen(FILEHANDLE, "fileName", ReadWriteMode, Permissions);
```

The file modes are shown in Table 13.4.

TABLE 13.4: File Modes

Read/Write Mode	Description
O_CREATE	Open the file for write only, destroying any previous file contents, same as open(FH, ">fn.txt");
O_RDONLY	Open the file for read only, same as open(FH, "<fn.txt");
O_RDWR	Open the file for read and write, same as open(FH, "+<fn.txt");
O_APPEND	Open the file in append mode, setting the file handle pointer to the end of an existing file, same as open(FH, ">>fn.txt");

The fourth parameter, the file permissions parameter, sets the read, write, and execute privileges for owner, group, and world on a Unix computer. The permissions parameter must be in octal format. A permissions mask is made up of read, write, and execute bits. A zero means the permission is off, and one means the permission is on. The read permission is bit 0, the write permission is bit 1, and the execute permission is bit 2. Read, write, and execute (or RWX) in binary is 111, which is octal 7. The default value if you omit the fourth parameter is 0666, which is read and write access for everyone. The permissions parameter is modified by the file's umask. A umask is associated with the owner of each file (the umask function is discussed later in the "Setting the Default File Permissions Mask" section).

NOTE   If you are still curious about file permissions masks, return to Chapter 1 for more information about Unix file permissions and Chapter 5 for more information about binary operations.

Reading and Writing to a File

Reading and writing byte arrays and other specially buffered data can be a pain. The reading and writing functions described here make that special type of reading much easier.

Reading a Fixed Amount of Data

The read function allows you to read a fixed amount of data from the file handle. The read function takes four parameters: the file handle to read from, a scalar variable to read the data into, the number of bytes to read, and the location to store the data in the scalar variable. The last parameter is optional and can be used to pick up where the last read left off. The syntax is:

```
read(FILEHANDLE, buffer, length, offset);
```

If you are reading from STDIN or a file, you may want to get data in chunks. After each read, you can continue to read into the same scalar variable by incrementing the offset by the amount of data last read, as shown in this code fragment:

```
until (eof()){
        read(INFILE, $buffer, 1024, $offset);
        $offset += 1024;
}
```

The scalar variable will grow as you append new data to the end of it, which only requires you to increment the offset value by the number of bytes last read.

The sysread function is functionally the same as the read function. The sysread function is faster than the read function but less portable. The sysread function takes four parameters: the file handle, the scalar variable to read the data into, the amount of data to read in bytes, and an optional offset to define the starting position in the buffer to put the data. Its syntax is:

```
sysread(FILEHANDLE, buffer, length, offset);
```

The sysread function performs unbuffered input, unlike the standard I/O functions. As explained in Chapter 11, buffered I/O uses a block of memory to optimize the actual read and write operations to the disk. For read operations, this usually means reading an optimized size of a data file into memory, even if the individual read operation only requests one line of data from the file. Subsequent reads of a single line of data from the file actually read from memory until the input buffer is empty.

Unbuffered reads from the disk access the disk each time a read operation is requested. This can slow your program down significantly if the unbuffered read occurs frequently and reads unnecessarily small pieces of data from the file. If you are using the sysread function, do not use the <> operator or print, printf, tell, write, or seek on the same file handle. The sysread function modifies the file handle's file position pointer in a manner that is not compatible with these functions.

Writing a Fixed Amount of Data

The syswrite function allows you to write a fixed amount of data to the file handle. The syswrite function takes four parameters: the file handle to write to, a scalar variable to write, the number of bytes to write from the scalar variable, and the location to start reading the data. The last parameter is optional and can be used to pick up where the last write left off. The syntax of syswrite is:

```
syswrite(FILEHANDLE, buffer, length, offset);
```

If you want to write data in chunks, this is the correct function to use. After each syswrite, you can continue to write from the same scalar variable by incrementing the offset by the amount of data last written.

A negative offset can be used to decrement through the scalar variable from the end to the front. A negative offset skips the offset number of bytes from the end of the scalar data.

Like the sysread function, the syswrite function performs unbuffered output. If you are using the syswrite function, do not use the <> operator or print, printf, tell, write, or seek on the same file handle. The syswrite function modifies the file handle's file position pointer in a manner that is not compatible with these functions.

Getting and Setting File Information

Perl 5 provides various functions for getting and setting file information, as well as changing file attributes. For example, the stat function returns an array that contains a file's attributes, the binmode function sets a file to binary mode, and the rename function changes the name of a file.

Getting File Statistics

The stat function takes the file handle as a parameter and returns a 13-element array of the file's attributes. Its syntax is:

```
@attributes = stat(FILEHANDLE);
```

Table 13.5 lists each returned element, its meaning, and its position in the array. The returned values are system dependent.

TABLE 13.5: The stat Array Elements

Array Cell	Meaning
0	The device number
1	The inode number
2	The file type and permissions
3	The number of hard links to the file
4	The file's user ID number
5	The file's group ID number
6	The device ID
7	The file size in bytes
8	The last access time
9	The last modification time
10	The inode change time
11	The system-preferred block size
12	The allocated blocks

Listing 13.4 demonstrates using the stat function to get the file attributes on a Windows NT system, and Figure 13.3 shows an example of its output.

Listing 13.4:   The stat Function for Windows NT File Attributes

```
1.  open(FH, "io.txt");
2.  @fileAttributes = stat (FH);
3.  close (FH);
4.  foreach $attribute (@fileAttributes){
5.     print "==> $attribute\n";
6.  }
7.  @accessTime = localtime($fileAttributes[8]);
8.  @modifyTime = localtime($fileAttributes[9]);
9.  @inodeTime = localtime($fileAttributes[10]);
10. $month = $accessTime[4] + 1;
11. print "Access time = $accessTime[2]:$accessTime[1]:
                        $accessTime[0], $month/$accessTime[3]/
```

```
                                              $accessTime[5]\n";
12. $month = $modifyTime[4] + 1;
13. print "Modify time = $modifyTime[2]:$modifyTime[1]:
                              $modifyTime[0], $month/$modifyTime[3]/
                              $modifyTime[5]\n";
14. $month = $inodeTime[4] + 1;
15. print "Inode time = $inodeTime[2]:$inodeTime[1]:
                              $inodeTime[0], $month/$inodeTime[3]/
                              $inodeTime[5]\n";
```

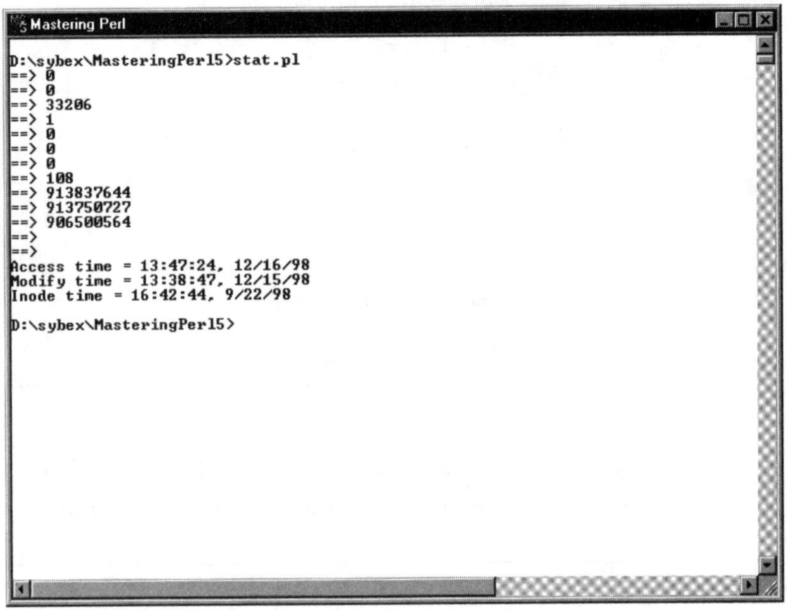

FIGURE 13.3:

Using the stat function to get Windows NT file attributes

Getting the File Descriptor Number

The file descriptor number is a system number associated with an open file handle. There is a finite number of file descriptor numbers available on each system and to each process. Each time you open a file handle, a new file descriptor number is assigned to the open file handle. Each time you close a file handle, that file descriptor number is returned to the list of available file descriptor numbers. The operating system tries to use the lowest available file descriptor number each time you open a new file handle. This means that your process may open and close multiple files, but as long as it closes a file before opening the next one, it may always be using the same file descriptor number.

The default file handles STDIN, STDOUT, and STDERR are the first file handles opened for your program. They are assigned the file descriptor values 0, 1, and 2 respectively. If you close and open the STDIN, STDOUT, and STDERR file handles, they will be assigned the next available file descriptor number. If you opened a file handle between the time you closed and then reopened one of these default file handles, the file descriptor associated with STDIN, STDOUT, or STDERR is likely to be a value different from 0, 1, or 2.

The function fileno takes the file handle as its parameter and returns the system file descriptor number. Its syntax is:

```
$fd = fileno(FILEHANDLE);
```

Getting the EOF Character

The eof (end of file) function optionally takes the file handle as a parameter. If no parameter is supplied, the eof function reads from the last read file handle. Its syntax is:

```
eof(FILEHANDLE);
```

The eof function returns true if the next character is the end of the file or the file handle is not open.

The eof function is a comfort blanket for traditional C programmers who are used to using the eof() function to determine when to stop reading. Reading from a file is much easier in Perl, and the eof function is not particularly efficient. I recommend using the while loop syntax you learned in Chapter 11 instead of the eof function:

```
while( <FILEHANDLE> )
```

or

```
while ($line = <FILEHANDLE>)
```

Getting the Next Character

Sometimes you just need one and only one. The getc function optionally takes the file handle as a parameter and returns a single character from the file handle input stream. Its syntax is:

```
$scalar = getc(FILEHANDLE);
```

If a file handle is not provided, the getc function reads from STDIN. If no data is available, the getc function returns null.

NOTE

The getc function is a C programming tool that was frequently used to read from the command line. Old game programs used this function to read keyboard input. I hate to admit that Perl isn't the best at everything, but if you are down at the device-driver level, using Perl and getc, you are probably using the wrong language. On the other hand, if you occasionally need to get a single character or you want to prototype some device-level code, you'll need getc and some of the other functions discussed in this chapter.

Setting the File Handle Position

The sysseek function works like the seek function (discussed in Chapter 11), setting the file handle pointer at the beginning (0), current position (1), or end of file (1), plus or minus a byte offset value. The sysseek function is faster than seek but less portable. The sysseek function takes three parameters: the file handle, an offset, and a starting position. Its syntax is:

```
sysseek(FILEHANDLE, offset, startingPosition);
```

If you are using the sysseek function, do not use the <> operator or the print, printf, tell, write, or seek function on the same file handle.

TIP

To increase portability, you can import the IO::Seekable constants, SEEK_SET (0), SEEK_CUR (1), SEEK_END (2). The module IO::Seekable is covered later in this chapter.

Setting the File Handle to Binary Mode

A file is usually classified as a binary or ASCII (text) file type. The default mode for reading on a file handle is ASCII. Most programs, images, and compressed files, to name a few, are binary files. The files that Microsoft Word creates are binary files. The files that Notepad can read are ASCII or text files. Text files can be read and printed without a running a special program.

When you are moving a binary file type—such as an image, a compressed file, or a program—use binary mode. The file transfer will corrupt the file if it is not in binary mode.

The binmode function takes the file handle as parameter and changes the format of the data, read from or written to the file handle, to binary. Its syntax is:

```
binmode(FILEHANDLE);
```

WARNING   When you transfer a file between a Unix and a MS-DOS system, use ASCII mode for text files. The end-of-line character, which is different between the two systems, is automatically converted to the correct value when you transfer your files in ASCII mode.

Setting the File System Lock Flags

The flock function is helpful when multiple users may simultaneously access a file. (It does not apply to Windows 95/98 systems.) The flock function, when used along with the Fcntl module (discussed later in the chapter) allows you to write portable file-locking code.

The flock function takes two parameters: the file handle and the lock mode to apply to the file handle. It syntax is:

```
flock(FILEHANDLE, lockMode);
```

The file-locking modes are shown in Table 13.6.

TABLE 13.6: File Lock Modes

Lock Mode	Number	Description
LOCK_SH	1	Shared lock—more than one process may own the shared lock simultaneously
LOCK_EX	2	Exclusive lock—only one process may own the file lock
LOCK_UN	8	Unlock—release the file lock
LOCK_NB	4	Nonblocking lock—do not block the process from execution if it does not own the lock

Preventing two processes or threads from modifying the same file is often a difficult problem. Without the flock mechanism, you must use some other means of file locking. Both flock and an alternative method are shown in Listing 13.5.

Listing 13.5:   **The flock Function**

```
1.  #!/usr/local/bin/perl
2.  use Fcntl ":flock";
3.  open (OUTFILE, ">>flockTest.txt") || warn $!;
4.  print ("Requesting Exclusive lock\n");
5.  flock(OUTFILE, LOCK_EX) || warn $!;
6.  print ("This process now owns the Exclusive lock\n");
7.  $in = <STDIN>;
8.  flock(OUTFILE, LOCK_UN)|| warn $!;
9.  close (OUTFILE);
10. #ALTERNATIVE WITHOUT FLOCK AVAILABLE
11. while (-e "flockTest.lck") { print "waiting for lock\n";
    sleep(1.0); }
12. open (LOCK, ">flockTest.lck") || die "Lock error $!";
13. open (OUTFILE, ">>flockTest.txt") || warn $!;
14. print ("This process now owns the Exclusive lock\n");
15. $in = <STDIN>;
16. close (OUTFILE);
17. close (LOCK);
18. unlink ("flockTest.lck");
```

The flock method of locking a file is implemented on line 5:

```
flock(OUTFILE, LOCK_EX) || warn $!;
```

The program will pause at line 5 until it receives the file lock. The lock is released on line 8:

```
flock(OUTFILE, LOCK_UN)|| warn $!;
```

If the flock method is not available on your operating system, you can use the method illustrated on lines 10 through 18. Line 11 checks to see if a lock file (flockTest.lck) exists (any name can be used for the lock file, as long as all files that are using this locking system use the same filename):

```
while (-e "flockTest.lck") {sleep(1.0); print "waiting for lock\n";}
```

If the lock file exists, this means that another process is accessing the file this program wishes to access. The program prints a message indicating that it is waiting for access to the file and then uses the sleep method to pause for one second. This while loop will continue until the program that created the lock file deletes it from the disk. As you can see, it would be easy for a program to get stuck in this loop forever if the lock file is not deleted.

When the file test fails, indicating the lock file no longer exists, the program continues, opening the lock file (flockTest.lck):

```
open (LOCK, ">flockTest.lck") || die "Lock error $!";
```

By opening the file for writing, the file is created on the file system, thereby locking out other programs that will wait in the same manner for the lock file to no longer exist.

Now that the program has signaled, by creating the lock file, that it will be modifying the file protected by the lock file, it opens the actual file for appending:

```
open (OUTFILE, ">>flockTest.txt") || warn $!;
```

When the program is done writing to the file, it closes the file on line 16:

```
close (OUTFILE);
```

and then closes and deletes the lock file on lines 17 and 18:

```
close (LOCK);
unlink ("flockTest.lck");
```

By deleting the lock file, the program has signaled that it has finished modifying the actual file. Although this procedure works, in practice it is more cumbersome than the flock method. The flock method requires only a line of code (line 5) to wait for the file lock:

```
flock(OUTFILE, LOCK_EX) || warn $!;
```

And then one other line (line 8) to release the lock:

```
flock(OUTFILE, LOCK_UN)|| warn $!;
```

Setting the Default File Permissions Mask

The umask sets the maximum allowable read, write, and execute privileges for a file. A umask is an octal number. Each bit of the umask clears the associated bit of the permissions mask. For example, if your permissions mask is a wide-open 777 and your umask is 077, the resulting permissions assigned the file would be 700. If your umask is 022 (a more common umask that clears the write permission for group and world), then the resulting permissions assigned the file are 755.

The umask function takes one optional parameter. The parameter sets the umask value for the process the program is running within. The umask function also returns the process's current umask value. Without the optional parameter, the umask function can be used to get a process's current umask value. Its syntax is:

```
$oldUmask = umask(MASK);
```

This can be a handy debugging aid, particularly for CGI programs. Frequently, web programs and processes have restricted privileges. Before you spend hours debugging your CGI program, call the umask function and get your process's file privileges. If your process umask restricts any of these capabilities, you'll know why your program isn't running properly.

Renaming a File

The rename function allows you to change the name of an existing file. It takes two parameters: the old filename and the new filename. Its syntax is:

```
rename("oldName", "newName");
```

Truncating a File

The truncate function allows you to restrict the length of a file to a maximum value. It takes two parameters: the file handle and the maximum length for the file specified by the open file handle. Its syntax is:

```
truncate(FILEHANDLE, byteLength);
```

If the file is greater than the specified maximum, the data following the maximum value will be discarded. Files that exceed the maximum file-size value will have their file size reset to the maximum value.

Modifying File Mode Flags

The function fcntl is a low-level system command that allows you to manipulate file handle modes based on a command and command parameters. The capabilities of this function are quite broad and system-specific. The fcntl function's first parameter is the file handle, the second parameter is the file command, and the third argument is optional and dependent on the type of file command. Its syntax is:

```
fcntl (FILEHANDLE, command, commandArgument);
```

The file commands and arguments allow you to copy the file handle, set the file handle mode to append, set and get file locks, and more. See the Unix man pages for further information.

Modifying File Times

You can use the utime function to modify the file list's access and last modified time. This function takes three or more parameters: a file's access time, a file's modification time, and the files to modify. Its syntax is:

```
utime($time, $time, "filenameList");
```

The times must be in epoch format, which is the format returned by the time function. To get an epoch time in the correct format, just do this:

```
$epoch = time;
```

The epoch time is the number of seconds from some fixed date, usually midnight (00:00:00), January 1, 1970 GMT, which is a magic time for most Unix gurus. The inode time of the file will be set to the current process time.

Using Unix-Only Functions

Several Perl 5 functions apply only to Unix systems. These are the ioctl function for controlling the device parameters of special files and the functions that have to do with Unix symbolic links.

Controlling Low-Level Devices

The ioctl function is a system-dependent function that allows you to control device parameters of special files. It takes a file handle, a command, and a scalar variable as parameters. Its syntax is:

```
ioctl (FILEHANDLE, command, commandArgument);
```

The command parameter tells ioctl which function to perform on the file handle and affects the actions on the scalar variable parameter. Some commands return information in the scalar variable parameter, and others use the scalar variable as an input parameter.

The function ioctl requires the use of ioctl.ph, which defines the services ioctl performs on your system. On Unix computers, the ioctl.ph file should be in the directory /usr/local/lib/perl.

Creating a Symbolic Link

The link function creates the new filename with no contents. After the new filename is created, any actions on the new filename that try to access the contents of the new filename are actually accessing the contents of the old filename. The new filename is only a pointer, or a link, to the old filename. The link function takes two parameters: the old filename and the new filename. It syntax is:

```
link("oldFilename", "newFilename");
```

The link function creates a hard link to the old filename. If the old filename does not exist, link returns an error. Actions that access the file-level modes of the new filename, such as removing or changing permissions, do not affect the old filename modes.

The symlink function also creates a new file using a new filename. The new file is a symbolic link to the old file. However, unlike the link function, which creates a hard link to an existing file, symlink creates a symbolic link even if the old filename does not exist. Its syntax is:

```
symlink("oldFilename", "newFilename");
```

Getting Symbolic Link Information

The readlink function returns the filename of the file the symbolic link is associated with. It takes the symbolic link name as a parameter. Its syntax is:

```
$fileName = readlink("linkName");
```

If the link name does not exist, a null value is returned.

The lstat function returns the file-level attributes of a symbolic link. If you used the stat function on a symbolic link, you would receive the attributes of the file the symbolic link points to. The lstat function takes the file handle as a parameter. Its syntax is:

```
@linkAttributes = lstat ("FILEHANDLE");
```

File Modules

The file modules covered in this section, listed in Table 13.7, provide two major features:

- An object-oriented interface to the Perl 5 functions
- Additional portability features

An object-oriented interface to the file system provides a natural approach to working with a file object. Each file system operation is usually on a particular file handle—the object. By using an objected-oriented approach, the file handle's state is encapsulated within each object, where it belongs. An object-oriented approach allows you to write code that deals with multiple file system objects without requiring you to create multiple variables to keep track of each file handle's state.

NOTE
Object-oriented programming in Perl 5 is covered in Chapter 19. If you are unfamiliar with terms such as *class*, *inherit*, and *constructor*, refer to Chapter 19 for definitions.

For example, by using the methods of the IO::* classes, you get a common interface for opening, reading, and writing on a file handle. That common interface still allows you to get at the special features of I/O functions like sysread, however. Most of the features of the multitude of similar but slightly different I/O functions listed in the previous sections can be accessed through a common method in the IO::* classes.

The additional portability added by these modules is at least as important as the object-oriented interface. For example, the Fcntl module exports POSIX-compliant constants to file modes, permissions, and locks. If you use the constants exported by the Fcntl module, your code has a much better chance of working on every platform on which it runs without any modification. Each of the other modules extends the portability prospects of your code.

TABLE 13.7: File Modules

Module	Description
Fcntl	Export platform-independent file symbols
File::Copy	Copy and move files and file handles
FileHandle	Front-end interface to IO::* classes
File::Spec	Platform-specific interfaces
IO::File	Module interface to **open** and **sysopen** functions
IO::Handle	Base class for IO classes
IO::Seekable	Get the file descriptor of the file handle

Platform-Independent File Symbols

The Fcntl module loads the system's symbols for file permissions, modes, and lock flags. Import this module's variables to your namespace when using methods and functions that access file permissions modes and lock flags. The modes and permissions constants (F_*, O_*) are loaded by default. You must import the lock flags like this:

```
use Fcntl ":flock";
```

The module's constants are listed in Table 13.8.

TABLE 13.8: Fcntl Constants

Constant	Description
F_DUPFD	Get a new file descriptor, using the conditions associated with an additional argument
F_GETFD	Get the close on execute flag; if the flag is 1, the file will be closed upon execution of exec(); if the flag is 0, the file will remain open
F_GETFL	Get the file handle's descriptor flags, O_APPEND, O_ASYNC, O_NONBLOCK
F_GETLK	Get the file lock
F_GETOWN	Get the process ID
F_RDLCK	Get the read lock
F_SETFD	Set the close-on-execute flag
F_SETFL	Set the file handle's descriptor flags, O_APPEND, O_ASYNC, O_NONBLOCK
F_SETLK	Set or clear the file lock
F_SETLKW	Set or clear the file lock; if the request cannot be satisfied because another process owns the lock, wait until the request can be satisfied
F_UNLCK	Unlock the file
F_WRLCK	Write lock the file
LOCK_SH	Set a shared lock
LOCK_EX	Set an exclusive lock
LOCK_UN	Release the file lock
LOCK_NB	Set a nonblocking lock
O_APPEND	Force the write operation to the end of the file

Continued on next page

TABLE 13.8 CONTINUED: Fcntl Constants

Constant	Description
O_ASYNC	Enable signal I/O handling (SIGIO) for the process; the process will be signaled when data is ready for reading
O_CREAT	Open and create the file for write only
O_EXCL	Open and create the file only if the file does not exist
O_EXLOCK	Open and set the exclusive lock flag
O_NDELAY	Open but do not block
O_NOCTTY	Do not access the file as a controlling tty device
O_NONBLOCK	Open the file but do not block; set blocking read and write operations to nonblocking; Read or writes that would have blocked will return a negative one (-1)
O_RDONLY	Open the file for reading only
O_RDWR	Open in read/write mode
O_TRUNC	Open the file, truncating the file if it is greater than the maximum size argument
O_WRONLY	Open the file for writing only
SEEK_CUR	Set the file handle to the current position
SEEK_END	Set the file handle to the end of the file
SEEK_SET	Set the file handle to the beginning of the file

Platform-Independent Copying and Moving

The File::Copy module provides a platform-independent way to copy and move files. The syntax for the copy and move methods is:

```
use File::Copy;
copy("oldFile", "newFile");
copy(FILEHANDLE, NEWFILEHANDLE);
move("oldFile", "newFile");
```

The copy method takes two parameters: the file to copy from and the file to copy to. You may use either file handles or filenames as parameters to the copy method. However, the documentation recommends that you use filenames, because file handles may lose data on some systems. The filenames may include path information. The copy method takes an optional third parameter, which defines the number of bytes to hold in memory during copying. The default buffer size is the size of the file being copied, up to a default maximum of 2MB. Files are copied in binary mode.

The move method renames files across directories. The file will either be renamed directly or, if necessary, the file will be copied to the new location and then the old file will be deleted.

Here is an example of using the copy and move methods:

```
use File::Copy;
copy("io.txt", 'c:\\temp') || warn $!;
copy("io.txt", 'ioOLD.txt') || warn $!;
copy("io.txt", 'c:\\temp\\io2.txt') || warn $!;
move("ioOLD.txt", 'c:\\temp') || warn $!;
```

I/O Interfaces

The FileHandle module provides a complete interface to most I/O functions and to the IO::File, IO::Seekable, and IO:Handle modules. The constructor, new, returns a file handle object and passes any parameters to the FileHandle::open method.

Table 13.9 lists some of the methods available through the FileHandle module.

TABLE 13.9: The FileHandle Methods

Method	Description
new	Create a file handle object
open	Open a file handle
print	Print on the file handle
printf	Formatted printing

Continued on next page

TABLE 13.9 CONTINUED: The FileHandle Methods

Method	Description
getline	Read one line of data from the file handle.
getlines	Read all available data from the file handle

Here are some examples of using the `FileHandle` module:

- Create a new file handle object:

    ```
    use FileHandle;
    $fh = new FileHandle;
    ```

- Create a new file handle object. The returned object contains the open file handle to `FileName.txt` in write mode to `FileName.txt`:

    ```
    use FileHandle;
    $fh = new FileHandle ">c:\\temp\\FileName.txt";
    ```

- Create a new file handle object. The returned object contains the open file handle to `FileName.txt` in read-only mode to `FileName.txt`:

    ```
    use FileHandle;
    $fh = new FileHandle "c:\\temp\\FileName.txt", "r";
    ```

- Create a new file handle object. The returned object contains the open file handle to `FileName.txt` in read/write mode to `FileName.txt`. The file handle is set to the end of the file:

    ```
    use FileHandle;
    $fh = new FileHandle "e:\\FileName.txt", O_WRONLY|O_APPEND;
    ```

Open Method Interface

The `IO::File` module provides a common interface to the open and sysopen methods, described earlier in this chapter. The open method accepts the file modes and permissions of the system-specific functions. The open method takes three parameters:

- The filename to open, which uses the same syntax as the open method

- Optionally, a Perl read (<), write (>), append (>>), or read/write (+<) symbol; a POSIX read (r), write (w), append (a), or read/write (r+ or w+) symbol, or a

numeric code corresponding to one of the 0_* constants exported through
Fcntl

- Optionally, the file permissions explained in the discussion of the sysopen
  function in the "File Functions" section (Table 13.4)

Here are some examples of using the IO::File module:

- Create a new file handle object:

  ```
  use IO::File;
  $fh = new IO::File;
  ```

- Create a new IO::File object. The returned object contains the open file
  handle to FileName.txt in write mode to FileName.txt:

  ```
  use IO::File;
  $fh = new IO::File ">c:\\temp\\FileName.txt";
  ```

- Create a new IO::File object. The returned object contains the open file
  handle to FileName.txt in read-only mode to FileName.txt:

  ```
  use IO::File;
  $fh = new IO::File "c:\\temp\\FileName.txt", "r";
  ```

- Create a new IO::File object. The returned object contains the open file
  handle to FileName.txt in read/write mode to FileName.txt. The file
  handle is set to the end of the file:

  ```
  use IO::File;
  $fh = new IO::File "e:\\FileName.txt", O_WRONLY|O_APPEND;
  ```

The syntax used by the constructor may also be used with the open method,
like this:

- Open the file in read-only mode:

  ```
  use IO::File;
  $fh = new IO::File;
  $fh->open(">c:\\temp\\FileName.txt");
  ```

- Open the file in append mode:

  ```
  use IO::File;
  $fh = new IO::File;
  $fh->open("c:\\temp\\FileName.txt", ">>");
  ```

- Create the file in write-only mode with file permissions of at most owner equal to read, write, and execute, and group and world equal to read and execute. The process `umask` may further restrict the file permissions:

```
use IO::File;
$fh = new IO::File;
$fh->open("e:\\FileName.txt", O_CREAT, 755);
```

Object-Oriented I/O

The `IO::Handle` module provides an object-oriented method to use most of the built-in I/O functions covered in this chapter. Table 13.11 lists the methods.

TABLE 13.11: IO::Handle Methods

Method	Parameters	Description
fdopen	*handle, mode*	Open the first parameter, which may be a file handle, a file number, or a `IO::Handle` object, using the *mode*(s) passed in the second parameter
opened	None	Return true if the `IO::Handle` object contains a valid file descriptor
getline	None	Return only one line of data, regardless of context
getlines	None	Return the remaining contents of the `IO::Handle` object (this function must be called in list context)
ungetc	*ordinal*	Push the ordinal value (character) onto `IO::Handle` object input stream
write	*scalar, length, offset*	Use *scalar* as an input buffer and write from *scalar* the amount of bytes specified in the parameter *length* beginning from position *offset*
flush	None	Flush the `IO::Handle` file handle
error	None	Return the last error condition
untaint	None	Set the `IO::Handle` file handle as taint-clean
clearerr	None	Clear the last error condition

The syntax to create a new `IO::Handle` object is:

```
use IO::Handle;
$fh = new IO::Handle ">c:\\temp\\FileName.txt";
```

The returned object contains the open file handle to `FileName.txt` in write mode to `FileName.txt`.

Once the `IO::Handle` object has been created, the methods of `IO::Handle` are accessed using the object returned from the constructor, like this:

```
use IO::Handle;
$fh = new IO::Handle;
#Initialize the IO::Handle object to FileName.txt
$fh->open("c:\\temp\\FileName.txt");
#Set the mode of the file handle to read and write
$fh->fdopen($fh, "r+");
#Verify that the file is open
if ($fh->opened){
    #Get a single line of data even though in array context
    @lines = $fh->getline;
    #Get the remaining lines
    @lines = $fh->getlines;
}
else{
    #Get the error condition
    $error = $fh->error;
    #Clear the last error condition
    $fh->clearerr;
}
```

NOTE The `IO::Handle` module is the base class for most of the `IO::*` modules and many of the `File` modules. This class is not intended to be directly instantiated. You can look to this class to get much of the documentation on the `IO::*` classes because the derived classes do not repeat the documentation of the methods they inherit.

Object-Oriented Seeking

The class `IO::Seekable` gives you an object-oriented interface to the `seek` and `tell` built-in functions, which were discussed in Chapter 11. The `IO::Seekable` class does not include a constructor. You get access to this class only by instantiating one of the other `IO::*` classes that inherit from the `IO::Handle` class. Once you have instantiated one of the `IO::*` classes, you also have access to the `IO::Seekable` methods of `seek` and `tell`.

A File System Operations Interface

The File::Spec module provides a platform-specific interface to file system operations. You must use the platform-specific module as shown in Table 13.10. You may call native methods using this module as the interface.

TABLE 13.10: Platform-Specific File::Spec Modules

Module	Platform
File::Spec::Mac	Macintosh
File::Spec::OS2	IBM OS/2
File::Spec::UNIX	Unix
File::Spec::VMS	Vax VMS
File::Spec::Win32	Windows

Summary

In this chapter, you learned about Perl 5's I/O functions and modules. Perl 5 is constantly growing and includes a seemingly infinite number of functions and modules. This chapter included the functions and modules that work on Unix and Windows platforms (with a few exceptions) and that and most likely to be used by most programmers. The Windows-only functions and modules are covered in Part 6 of this book.

This chapter began with a discussion of the directory modules and functions. The directory module Cwd tells your program the current working directory. Opening and reading a directory is similar to opening and reading a file, but you must use the opendir, readir, and closedir functions.

Next, you learned about some of the system-level file I/O functions, such as sysread and syswrite. These functions use unbuffered I/O operations, which allow your program to read and write a byte-specific amount of data.

Finally, in the section on modules related to file I/O methods, you learned about platform-independent methods of copying and moving files. Perl 5 file I/O modules include methods that provide an object-oriented interface for reading and writing to files.

PART IV

Data Manipulation

CHAPTER

FOURTEEN

Jump-Start on String Functions and Regular Expressions

- ■ String function basics

- ■ Pattern matching

- ■ Regular expression elements

For manipulating strings and patterns, Perl is the easiest and fastest language among Assembly, C/C++, Java, Prolog, Lisp, and Ada—to name several popular languages. In this chapter, you will learn the syntax and basics of searching through, splitting apart, and modifying strings, as well as the basics of regular expressions. The jump-start program demonstrates string-manipulation techniques, and the rest of the chapter provides concise descriptions of the string functions and regular expression elements.

The power of Perl is in its string manipulation. I encourage you to read the two chapters that follow this chapter so that you understand the details. However, if you need to start writing code today, this chapter will give you the necessary introduction to Perl's string functions and regular expressions.

Jump-Start Definitions

Atom	A fundamental building block of regular expressions. An atom is any single item in a pattern.
Back reference variable	A special variable created when an atom in a regular expression is surrounded by parentheses. A back reference contains the string matched by the pattern enclosed by the parentheses. Back reference variable are named $1 to $n. (n is equal to the number of the parentheses pairs used in the regular expression).
Bound string	The expression on the left of the bind operator (=~) or the NOT bind operator (!~), which is bound to the operation on the right of the operator. The bind operator is used to change the default action of Perl utilities that use the $_ variable as a default input parameter. The bind operator forces the pattern-match operator to look for a match in the bound string. The NOT bind operator forces the pattern-match operator to match anything not found in the bound string.

Escape character	The \ character, which is used to change the meaning of the character following it. The escape character is always paired with another character in a regular expression. The escape character allows you to match digits, words, and space characters and to match the ASCII character value of a meta-character.
Greedy match	The default match mode of the regular expression engine. The regular expression engine finds the longest possible string it can match and then begins backtracking, trying to find the first valid pattern match.
Match quantifier	A meta-character that matches a pattern a specific number of times. The zero-or-more quantifiers are *, ?, and +. The specific number, minimum, and maximum quantifiers are enclosed in curly braces, like this: {*Min, Max*}; either one is optional.
Meta-character	A character with special meaning used to build regular expressions. Meta-characters allow you to match just the character or characters you want.
Pattern modifier	A modifier appended to a regular expression after the trailing delimiter, which affects the entire regular expression. For example, you can change the regular expression so that it ignores case, matches across the entire input string instead of just the first occurrence, or compiles the regular expression so it is evaluated only the first time it is encountered.
Regular expression	A series of characters used to match a pattern that may be repeating. A *pattern* is a series of characters.
Substring	A string within another string.

Jump-Start Program

Listing 14.1 is a CGI program that reads input from the QUERY_STRING CGI environment variable. Most CGI programs get their input through the POST method, but the QUERY_STRING variable is handy for special circumstances, such as passing data through an HTML link.

You can pass data to a CGI program through an HTML link by appending data after a question mark, as in this example:

```
<a href=http://www.webreservation.com/cgi-
bin/warm/admin/ratesHTML.cgi?fileName=$name>
```

Everything before the question mark is part of the link to the HTML reference. Everything after the question mark becomes part of the CGI environment variable QUERY_STRING; the question mark is discarded. In this example, the link is to http://www.webreservation.com/cgi-bin/warm/admin/ratesHTML.cgi. The QUERY_STRING data is fileName=$name, which is one name/value pair. The name is fileName, and the value is the value in the scalar variable $name.

The CGI program in Listing 14.1 is called through an HTML link and uses this data to determine a room rate for an online reservation system.

Listing 14.1:   **Reading and Formatting the Query String**

```
1.  #!/usr/local/bin/perl
2.  #
3.  my (%rateData);
4.  #Only process the QUERY STRING if something is
5.  #in the string to process
6.  if (length ($ENV{'QUERY_STRING'}) > 0 ){
7.      my ($buffer) = $ENV{'QUERY_STRING'};
8.      #Separate all the name/value pairs at the &
9.      my (@pairs) = split(/&/, $buffer);
10.     my ($name, $value);
11.     foreach $pair (@pairs){
12.         #Separate each name/value pair at =
13.         ($name, $value) = split(/=/, $pair);
14.         #Convert each plus character to a space character
15.         $value =~ tr/+/ /;
16.         #Substitute the hex value for a character
17.         $value =~ s/%([a-fA-F0-9][a-fA-F0-9])/pack("C", hex($1))/eg;
```

```
18.        #Save the result into the hash %rateData
19.        $rateData{$name} = $value;
20.    }
21. }
22. #If the data was not defined, use the default
23. if (defined $rateData{'fileName'}){
24.    #The filename of the rate is defined in the link
25.    #
26.    $fileName = $rateData{'fileName'};
27. }
28. else {
29.    $fileName = "Base.rates";
30. }
31. #Prepare for output the new HTML page
32. #Get the position in the filename where .rates begin
33. $position = index($fileName, "\.rates");
34. #Beginning at position 0 read until the location of .rates
35. $fileNameOnly = substr($fileName,0,$position);
36. #Read the configuration data
37. local (%configurationData) = readConfiguration();
38. $temp    = $configurationData{"TYPE_OF_ITEM"};
39. #Separate each item on a single space
40. @temp    = split(" ",$temp);
41. #In scalar context get the number of items
42. $number = @temp;
43. foreach $item (@temp) {
44.    #Get just the first letter of each item
45.    $first  = substr($item,0,1);
46.    #Get the total length of each item
47.    $length = length($item);
48.    #Get everything after the first character
49.    $temp   = substr($item,1,$length-1);
50.    #Convert the first character to uppercase
51.    $first  =~tr/a-z/A-Z/;
52.    #Create a new string separated by spaces,
53.    #with the correct format
54.    $newtemp = $newtemp . " " . $first . $temp;
55. }
```

String Functions

Perl 5's string functions allow you to manipulate the contents of strings, translate characters, separate strings, and join strings. Table 14.1 lists the standard string functions.

TABLE 14.1: Perl 5 String Functions

Function	Syntax	Description
chomp	`lvalue = chomp($scalar);`	Removes only a newline character from the end of a string
chop	`lvalue = chop($scalar);`	Removes the last character of each element of the input list
chr	`lvalue = chr(number);`	Translates a number into a character
index	`lvalue = index (searchString, substring, beginningSearchPosition);`	Returns the first position of a substring
join	`lvalue = join(delimiter, list);`	Creates a single delineated string from an input list
lc	`lvalue = lc(expression);`	Changes all the characters in the expression to lowercase
lcfirst	`lvalue = lcfirst(expression);`	Changes only the first character of the expression to lowercase
length	`lvalue = length(expression);`	Returns the number of characters in a string

Continued on next page

TABLE 14.1 CONTINUED: Perl 5 String Functions

Function	Syntax	Description
ord	`lvalue = ord(expression);`	Converts ASCII characters into their numeric value
pack	`pack TEMPLATE, inputList;`	Takes one or more character codes and translates the corresponding character(s) to the format specified
rindex	`lvalue = rindex (searchString, substring, beginningSearch Position);`	Returns the last position of a substring
split	`lvalue = split(/pattern/,expression, maxSplit);`	Separates the expression into parts
s/ (substitute)	`$searchString =~ s/oldPattern/ newPattern/;`	Substitutes one string for another string
substr	`lvalue = substr(expression, startingPosition,length);`	Returns or modifies a substring
tr (translate)	`$input =~ tr/searchString/ replacementString/`	Exchanges each occurrence of a character in the search string with its matching character in the replacement string
uc	`lvalue = uc(expression);`	Changes all the characters in the expression to uppercase
ucfirst	`lvalue = ucfirst(expression);`	Changes only the first character of the expression to uppercase

The length Function

Line 6 of Listing 14.1 uses the length function to determine if any data was passed via QUERY_STRING:

```
if (length ($ENV{'QUERY_STRING'}) > 0 ){
```

This program uses a default value on line 29 if the QUERY_STRING variable contains no data. I usually use the defined function (defined ($variableName);) to determine if a variable has been assigned a value. The defined function returns true if a variable has been declared using the keyword my or local or is assigned a value. However, this doesn't work with the CGI environment variable QUERY_STRING because it is always a key in the %ENV hash, which means the defined function returns true whether or not QUERY_STRING has been assigned data. The length function works here because it reads the contents of a scalar variable and returns the number of characters the variable contains.

If the length function is used on a variable that has not been declared or defined, it returns 0.

The split Function

The split function separates an expression into a list. The expression will be interpreted as a string. The expression may be a scalar variable, string literal, or an expression that returns a string. If the expression is omitted, the default special variable $_ will be used. The lvalue can be a scalar, but it is usually a list or an array. In scalar context, the split function returns the number of times the pattern is matched.

The maximum split parameter defines the maximum number of times the expression may be separated. If this value is omitted, Perl 5 will separate the expression as many times as available for assignment plus one. If the assignment list is greater than or equal to the maximum split value, the remainder of the expression will be saved into the last variable in the list.

Multiple name/value pairs can be appended after the HTML link by separating each name/value pair with an ampersand. Line 9 of Listing 14.1 separates each name/value pair, using the split function:

```
my (@pairs) = split(/&/, $buffer);
```

When the pattern is a regular expression, as shown here, the pattern follows the same regular expression rules and syntax outlined later in this chapter and explained in detail in Chapter 16.

The `split` function also can be used to delineate simple strings, as shown on line 13 of Listing 14.1:

```
($name, $value) = split(/=/, $pair);
```

Line 13 separates the scalar $pair at the equal sign (=), creating a list made up of the scalar variables $name and $value.

The translate Function

The translate (`tr`) function exchanges each occurrence of a character in the search string with its matching character in the replacement string. The translate function modifies the string it is bound to via the bind (=~) or not bind (!~) operator. If the bound string is omitted, the translate function modifies the default special variable $_.

Data passed via the QUERY_STRING variable is URL-encoded, which means that all space characters are converted to the plus sign (+) and several other characters are converted to the ASCII hex equivalent. Line 15 of Listing 14.1 uses the translate function to convert the plus characters to space characters:

```
$value =~ tr/+/ /;
```

The substitute Function

The substitute (`s///`) function searches the search string for the input pattern and replaces it with the replacement pattern. Unlike the translate function, the substitute function operates on regular expressions and follows the general rules of regular expressions. The variable $searchString, which may be any valid expression, is searched for the old pattern. The first occurrence of the old pattern is replaced with the new pattern. If a variable is not bound to the substitute function, the function operates on the default input variable $_.

Line 17 of Listing 14.1 uses the substitute function, back reference variables, and the pack function (which translates characters to a specified format) to convert hex values to their character equivalents:

```
$value =~ s/%([a-fA-F0-9][a-fA-F0-9])/pack("C", hex($1))/eg;
```

The index Function

The index function returns the first position of a substring in a string. The search string and the substring may be a variable or a string literal. The value returned by the index function is actually the first occurrence of the substring after the off-set position. If the substring is not found in the search string, the index function returns –1.

In Listing 14.1, the index function on line 33 is used to locate the occurrence of a string within a string:

```
$position = index($fileName, "\.rates");
```

The substr Function

The substr function is used to extract a substring from another string. The string being extracted may be any valid expression. The substr function, beginning at the starting position and for as many characters as defined by the parameter length, copies that portion of the string into the lvalue. The length parameter is optional. If the length is not supplied, the substring is copied from the starting position to the end of the string.

In Listing 14.1, the substr function on line 35 uses the position returned by the index function on line 33 to extract the filename only from the variable $fileName:

```
$fileNameOnly = substr($fileName, 0 ,$position);
```

Character-Case Functions

The uc, lc, ucfirst, and lcfirst functions change character case. The lvalue will be assigned the value in the expression, with the character case changed to the uppercase or lowercase equivalent. If you use these functions without an expression, the default special variable $_ will be used as the expression.

Lines 43 through 55 of Listing 14.1 format the data from the input file, converting the first character of an input list to an uppercase character:

```
foreach $item (@temp) {
    #Get just the first letter of each item
    $first  = substr($item,0,1);
    #Get the total length of each item
```

```
    $length = length($item);
    #Get everything after the first character
    $temp    = substr($item,1,$length-1);
    #Convert the first character to uppercase
    $first  =~tr/a-z/A-Z/;
    #Create a new string separated by spaces,
    #with the correct format
    $newtemp = $newtemp . " " . $first . $temp;
}
```

Rather than the approach shown here, you could use one of the character-case functions. Lines 43 through 55 could be replaced with the following code:

```
foreach $item (@temp) {
    $newtemp = ucfirst($temp);
}
```

> **NOTE** Lines 43 through 55 are included in Listing 14.1 to illustrate the value of reading the details of string manipulation in Chapter 15. Although these lines are functional, they can be vastly simplified with a little more knowledge of Perl 5.

Regular Expressions

Regular expressions are useful for decoding user input, matching strings, manipulating file I/O, and many other tasks. A regular expression is a string of meta-characters, regular characters, and match quantifiers, which create a pattern. The pattern is designed to match part or all of a character string. By the time you see a regular expression in someone else's code, the regular expression has probably been built one atom at a time, until you get a rather complex pattern, like this:

```
$var =~ /([;<>\*\/'&\$!#\(\)\[\]\{\}:'"])/;
```

This regular expression is designed to match the standard Unix shell meta-characters, which are slightly different from the Perl 5 meta-characters. Though this pattern looks rather complex, it is simply using the atom list meta-characters ([]) and the escape meta-character (\) to search for Unix shell meta-characters.

The Pattern-Match Function

Perl 5 has three primary functions that use regular expressions: `split`, substitute (`s///`), and pattern-match (`m//`). You were introduced to the `split` and substitute functions in the previous section. When used with regular expressions, each of these functions follows the same rules.

The syntax of the pattern-match function is:

```
m/pattern/;
```

The pattern is tested against the default input variable $_ or an input string bound to the pattern, like this:

```
$inputString =~ m/pattern/;
```

The bind operator (=~) associates the expression on the left of the operator with the operation on the right of the operator. If the pattern is matched in the input string, the match function returns true. The pattern-match function can be used without the beginning m, and it is frequently used in conditional expressions, like this:

```
if (/pattern/){
```

The pattern can be a simple character string or a series of meta-characters designed to match a range of possible values.

Elements of Regular Expressions

Regular expressions are made up of atoms. Each atom is its own pattern. An atom is any single item in a pattern and can be any of the following:

- A single character or digit, *A–Z, a–z, 0–9*
- An escaped meta-character
- An escaped special-meaning character
- An octal, hex, or control code (such as \077, \xFF, \cD)
- A regular expression enclosed in parentheses
- A list of atoms enclosed in square brackets
- A back reference to a previous pattern match

You can use any of the Perl 5 meta-characters in your regular expressions. The meta-characters are listed in Table 14.2.

TABLE 14.2: Perl 5 Meta-Characters

Character	Meaning
\	Do not interpret the following meta-character (escape)
|	Match either of the alternatives (OR)
()	Create a single expression or atom
{}	Define the minimum and or maximum repetitions of an atom
*	Match an atom zero or more times
+	Match an atom one or more times
?	Match an atom zero or one times
^	Match an atom at the start of the string
$	Match an atom at the end of the string
[]	Match one of the enclosed atoms
.	Match any character
\A	Alternative to meta-character ^
\Z	Alternative to meta-character $
\b	Word boundary
\B	Not word boundary
\d	Digit
\D	Not digit
\e	Escape
\f	Form feed
\n	Newline
\r	Carriage return
\s	Space character (space, \t, \n, \r, \f)

Continued on next page

TABLE 14.2 CONTINUED: Perl 5 Meta-Characters

Character	Meaning
\S	Not space character
\t	Tab
\w	Word
\W	Not word
\oNN	Octal
\xNN	Hex
\cC	Control character

The Perl 5 match quantifiers are meta-characters that affect the number of times the atom that precedes them will be matched. As shown in Table 14.2, the meta-characters *, +, and ? tell the Perl 5 interpreter to match the previous atom a pre-defined number of times. The match quantifiers using the curly brace meta-characters work as follows:

{*matchNumber*}	The preceding atom must occur exactly *matchNumber* of times.
{*minimum,*}	The preceding atom must occur at least minimum number of times.
{*minimum,maximum*}	The preceding atom must occur at least minimum number of times, up to and including maximum number of times.

The parentheses meta-characters are used for creating a single atom from multiple elements and also have the effect of creating back reference variables. A *back reference variable* is a variable created during a regular expression pattern match. The back reference variable contains the string matched by the pattern enclosed by the parentheses. Each pattern match that is enclosed by a pair of parentheses is remembered in a back reference variable. The back reference variable is always a variable of the name *$1* to *$n* (where *n* is always equal to the number of the parentheses pairs used in the regular expression). The number of the parentheses pairs are determined by counting the pairs of parentheses in a regular expression beginning from left to right and starting with the number 1.

Pattern modifiers, which are listed in Table 14.3, affect the action of the entire pattern. They are appended to a regular expression.

T A B L E 1 4 . 3 : Perl 5 Pattern Modifiers

Modifier	Meaning
g	Instead of matching only the first occurrence of the pattern, the pattern will be matched repeatedly against the input string.
I	Ignore character case when matching the pattern.
m	Treat the input string as if it were multiple lines.
o	Compile the pattern and only interpret it the first time it occurs.
s	Treat the input string as if it were a single line.
x	Allow comment characters in the pattern.

A Regular Expression Example

To demonstrate how to use Perl 5 regular expressions, let's examine the following regular expression:

```
$line =~ s!<NET>\s*(.*?)\s+(.*?)<ENDNET>!<a href="$1">$2</a>!ig;
```

This regular expression reads a line like this one:

```
You can contact <NET> Eric.Herrmann@assi.net Eric Herrmann <ENDNET> via
email or visit his <NET> http://www.assi.net company's <endNet>home
page.
```

and converts the line to an HTML link, like this:

```
You can contact <a href="Eric.Herrmann@assi.net"> Eric Herrmann </a>
via email or visit his <a href="http://www.assi.net">company's</a>home
page.
```

The sample regular expression is part of the substitute (s///) function. The regular expression's pattern is delimited by the exclamation point (!). Perl 5 uses the first character that follows the substitute character (s) or the pattern-match character (m) as the pattern delimiter. The pattern <NET>\s*(.*?)\s+(.*?)<ENDNET> contains six atoms. The six atoms work as follows:

<NET>	Matches the pattern <NET> (case-insensitive)
\s*	Matches the space character zero or more times.
(.*?)	Matches any characters that come after atom 2 and before atom 4
\s+	Matches the space character at least one time
(.*?)	Matches any characters that come after atom 4 and before atom 6
<ENDNET>	Matches the pattern <ENDNET> (case-insensitive)

An English interpretation of how the Perl interpreter reads these six atoms might look something like this: "First, find <Net>, in uppercase or lowercase (atom 1), followed by any number of optional space characters (atom 2). Then match and remember any characters (atom 3) up to the next one or more space characters (atom 4). Now match and remember any characters (atom 5) up to the characters <Endnet> (atom 6), in uppercase or lowercase."

The question meta-character (?) when it follows the asterisk (*) meta-character takes on an alternative meaning. The regular expression engine normally finds the longest possible string it can match, and then begins backtracking, trying to find the first valid pattern match (called a *greedy match*). Normally, the pattern (.*) would match the entire line. The question mark (?) meta-character changes the default action of the regular expression engine by making it match the first valid pattern. As the regular expression is processed, the question mark meta-character, when used with the asterisk (*) meta-character, stops the regular expression engine as soon as it finds a match.

Atoms 3 and 5 use the parentheses meta-characters to create a single atom from the multiple atoms ., *, and ?. The parentheses also have the effect of creating back reference variables, which are used in the replacement pattern of the substitution operation to create the HTML anchor and reference tags. In our example, there are two back reference variables, atoms 3 and 5, which are used later in the substitution pattern <a href="$1">$2</a>.

The substitute function replaces the search pattern with the replacement pattern. In this example, the replacement pattern uses a portion of the search pattern: the back reference variables, $1 and $2. The back reference variable $1 will equal a URL or e-mail address, and the back reference variable $2 will equal the text used as a link to the URL or e-mail address.

The entire pattern is modified by the pattern modifiers i and g that follow at the end of this substitution operation. The i pattern modifier tells the regular expression engine to ignore any character case in the pattern, which means atom 1 <NET> and atom 6 <ENDNET> will match any variation of uppercase and lowercase, such as `net` or `endNet`.

The g modifier tells the regular expression engine to match the pattern as many times as possible in the input string. This means that if there are multiple occurrences of the same pattern, the pattern will be matched for each occurrence in the input string. In our example, this means the substitution operation will match twice. The first pattern matches:

```
<NET> Eric.Herrmann@assi.net Eric Herrmann <ENDNET>
```

This creates two back reference variables: $1 equal to `Eric.Herrmann@assi.net` and $2 equal to `Eric Herrmann`. The resulting substitution string is:

```
<a href="Eric.Herrmann@assi.net"> Eric Herrmann </a>
```

Without the global pattern modifier g, the substitution operation would end with the first pattern match. The global pattern modifier tells the regular expression engine to repeat the pattern match again, beginning at the first character after the last pattern match. In our search string, the pattern now matches:

```
<NET> http://www.assi.net company's <endNet>
```

This creates the back reference variable $1 equal to `http://www.assi.net` and the back reference variable $2 equal to `company's`. The resulting substitution string is:

```
<a href="http://www.assi.net">company's</a>
```

What Next?

In this jump-start chapter, you learned the essentials of Perl 5's string functions and regular expressions. Perl 5 includes a host of functions, which make manipulating strings easier and faster than any other popular language. Regular expressions unleash the full power of Perl 5.

For all the details about the various string functions, read Chapter 15. That chapter provides many examples that demonstrate how each of the functions work. It also explains how to create custom sort subroutines, including sample subroutines that sort a hash by value and sort on multiple conditions.

Regular expressions are a rich feature of Perl 5. I encourage you to explore the details of regular expressions in Chapter 16. That chapter explains how to build regular expressions using meta-characters and pattern modifiers, as well as how to break down the individual parts of regular expressions so that you can understand precisely what they do. You'll also find some practical examples of programming with regular expressions.

CHAPTER
FIFTEEN

15

String Manipulation

- String manipulation functions

- Character functions

- String split and join functions

- Binary-encoded string conversion

- Custom sorting subroutines

Perl 5's soul is grounded in working with strings. Perl grew up manipulating strings, and its current popularity is still associated with strings.

In this chapter, you'll learn about Perl 5's string-manipulation features. The functions covered in this chapter allow you to work with multiple characters within a string, modify single characters within a string, separate and join strings, and translate character codes into other formats. The final section describes how to build custom sort routines for your programs.

Working with String Parts

Perl 5 has several useful functions for manipulating the contents of a string. When you are matching, changing, extracting, and just plain old manipulating a string, there are some standard tasks every programmer needs to do. These tasks include finding the position within a string of another string. A string within another string is called a *substring*. Once you've found the position of the substring, you may need to determine the length of the substring and then change its value. In Perl 5, the following functions perform these tasks:

- The index function returns the first position of a substring.

- The rindex function returns the last position of a substring.

- The length function returns the number of characters of a string.

- The substr function returns or modifies a substring.

- The s/// function substitutes one string for another string.

Getting the First and Last Position of a Substring

The index function returns the first position of a substring in a string. The syntax of the index function is:

```
lvalue = index (searchString,
                substring,
                beginningSearchPosition);
```

The search string and the substring may be a variable or a string literal.

The beginning search position is an optional offset position. If it is not supplied, the search begins from the first character position of the string. If you specify a beginning search position, the index function begins searching after the offset position, which means that the position returned by the index function may not be the first occurrence of the substring.

The value returned by the index function is actually the first occurrence of the substring after the offset position. If the substring is not found in the search string, the index function returns –1 (negative one), which can be used within a conditional expression.

NOTE   Using the **index** function for testing for the occurrence of a substring is not as general as a regular expression in determining the occurrence of a substring. However, it is usually faster than using a regular expression. Regular expressions are covered in Chapter 16.

You can use the beginning search position to search through an entire string, finding each occurrence of a substring, like this:

```
$offset = 0
while ( $offset>-1){
$offset = index($searchString,$substring,$offset);
    ...
}
```

This code will find each occurrence of the substring, saving its value into the $offset variable. When the search for $substring fails, $offset will be set to –1 and the loop will exit.

WARNING   The **index** function actually returns all values relative to the special first cell index variable ($[). The position returned by the **index** function is $[+ *position*. If the substring is not located, the return value is $[– 1. If you have modified the first cell index variable ($[), discussed in Chapter 6, the change affects the value returned by the **index** function.

When you need to search from the end of a string, use the rindex function. This function works in the same way as the index function, except that it begins searching from the end of the string or from an offset position from the end of the string. The syntax of the rindex function is:

```
lvalue = rindex(searchString, substring, offset)
```

The offset is optional, and if omitted, the search begins at the end of the search string. The offset is from the end of the search string.

Extracting Substrings

The `substr` function can be used to extract a substring or to modify a string. When used to extract a string portion, the `substr` function goes on the right side of the equal sign, like this:

```
lvalue = substr(expr, startingPosition, length);
```

The string being extracted from may be any valid expression. The `substr` function, beginning at the starting position and for as many characters as defined by the length parameter, copies that portion of the string into the lvalue. The length parameter is optional. If the length is not supplied, the substring is copied from the starting position to the end of the string.

You can specify a negative value for the length to indicate the number of characters to leave remaining at the end of the string, as shown here:

```
$string = "This_is_a short example";
$copyString = substr($string,10,-8);
```

In this example, the variable `$copyString` equals `short`.

You can also use a negative value for the starting position to count from the end of the string instead of the beginning. The starting position is included in the lvalue, but remember that the first position in the string is zero, not one. If you replace 10 with −10 in the previous example, the variable `$copyString` becomes `rt`.

The `substr` function can also be used to modify the contents of a string, which makes the expression of the `substr` function an lvalue. When the `substr` function is operating as an lvalue, the starting position defines where to begin inserting the new string. The `substr` function then inserts the expression on the right side into the position identified by the starting position and the length parameters.

The length parameter defines the number of characters to be replaced by the new string. If the length is zero, no character in the original expression will be replaced; the copied string will be inserted into the original string without modifying any characters in the original string. The original string will grow to accommodate the new string, as shown here:

```
$colors = "red, blue";
```

```
substr($colors,5,0) = " green,";
```

The resulting string, $colors, equals "red, green, blue".

When the length parameter is nonzero, the substr function deletes the number of characters identified by the length and inserts any new characters identified by the replacement string. Here is an example of using this format to delete characters:

```
$sentence = "The The was typed in error.";
substr($sentence,0,4) = "";
```

Here, the first four characters of $sentence are deleted.

If the length is negative, substr counts from the end of the string. All of the characters between the end character identified by length and the starting position will be replaced by the new string.

Getting the String's Length

As you've learned in the previous sections, when you work with strings, the length of a string or substring is usually important. You can use the length function to return the number of characters in a string. The syntax of the length function is:

```
lvalue = length(expression);
```

If the length function is used on a variable that has not been declared or defined, it returns zero.

The length function is frequently used for formatting data for output or verifying that something has been entered by the user. To verify user input, do this:

```
chomp $input;
if (length($input)){
   do something …
}
else {
  print "You must enter some data\n";
  exit;
}
```

The length function will return zero if the user entered no data. This will cause the if condition to fail and the else clause to tell the user what is wrong and exit.

Listing 15.1 illustrates the length function formatting the names in a text file to a fixed ten-character length each.

Listing 15.1: **Formatting Names**

```perl
1.  #!/usr/local/bin/perl
2.  use File::Copy;
3.  $filler = " ";
4.  $notOpened = 1;
5.  $index = 0;
6.  $infile = $ARGV[0];
7.  open(INFILE, "<$infile") || die "can't open file";
8.  copy ("$infile", "$infile.bak");
9.  while (<INFILE>){
10.     if ($notOpened){
11.         $notOpened = 0;
12.         open(OUTFILE, ">$infile") || die "can't open file";
13.     }
14.     ($first, $middle, $last) = split(/\W+/);
15.     $middleInitial = substr($middle, 0 , 1 );
16.     $middleInitial .= '.';
17.     $first .= $filler x (10 - length($first));
18.     $middleInitial .= $filler x (10 - length($middleInitial));
19.     $last .= $filler x (10 - length($last));
20.     print OUTFILE "$first$middleInitial$last\n";
21. }
22. close (INFILE);
23. close (OUTFILE);
```

Line 14 of Listing 15.1 splits the input line on any nonalphanumeric character into a first, middle, and last name:

```perl
($first, $middle, $last) = split(/\W+/);
```

Line 15 uses the substr function to remove just the first character of the middle name, and line 16 appends a period to the end of the middle initial:

```perl
$middleInitial = substr($middle, 0 , 1 );
$middleInitial .= '.';
```

Lines 17 through 19 use the length function to force each name to be at least ten characters long. The length function returns the number of characters in each line, which is then subtracted from 10. The filler character is then multiplied by this value and appended to the end of each name, which forces each name string to have at least ten characters:

```
$first .= $filler x (10 - length($first));
$middleInitial .= $filler x (10 - length($middleInitial));
$last .= $filler x (10 - length($last));
```

Line 20 prints the formatted name strings to the new output file:

```
print OUTFILE "$first$middleInitial$last\n";
```

TIP

When receiving data from an HTML form, each name/value pair will create an element in the input hash even if the value is empty. This means you can't test for the existence of one of the form inputs using the **defined** function. The element will be defined by the name of the name/value pair, but the value may be **null**. To solve this problem, I use the **length** function, which tells me if the value of the HTML element contains any data. That means instead of doing this:

```
if(defined ($form {'name'}
```

I do this:

```
if(length($form{'NAME'}))
```

The **defined** function will return true because the **NAME** is an entry in the **%form** hash, even when the value is empty. The **length** function will return zero unless some data was entered into the **NAME** file.

Replacing Strings

The s///, or substitute, function searches a string for a pattern and replaces that pattern with another pattern. Unlike the substr function, the substitute function searches a string for patterns, which may be regular expressions. Regular expressions are covered in detail in the next chapter; here, simple strings and scalar variables are used as examples. The substitute function searches either the default variable $_ or a bound string.

The bind operator (=~) is used to change the default action of the substitute function, the pattern-match operator, and other Perl utilities whose default action uses the $_ variable as an input parameter. The bind operator associates the operation on the right side of the operator with the expression on the left side of the operator. The expression can be a literal, a variable, or an operation that results in a value. The expression on the left of the operator, which is frequently a variable, is bound to the operation on the right of the operator. In the case of the substitute function, the expression must be an lvalue because the substitute function modifies the lvalue it searches.

NOTE   The equal sign in the bind operator can be replaced with the NOT operator (!). The expression on the left of the operator is still bound to the operation on the right of the operator, but the meaning of the operation is negated. When used with the pattern-match function, explained in the next section, the NOT bind operator (!~) forces the pattern-match operator to match anything not found in the bound string, like this: $name !~ m/COBOL/;

The syntax of binding a string to the substitute function is:

```
$searchString =~ s/oldPattern/newPattern/;
```

The variable $searchString, which may be any valid expression, is searched for the old pattern. The first occurrence of the old pattern is replaced with the new pattern. You can replace every occurrence of the old pattern with the new pattern by adding the global pattern modifier (g) to the end of the substitute function, like this:

```
$searchString =~ s/oldPattern/newPattern/g;
```

If a search string expression is omitted, the substitute function operates on the default special variable $_.

Table 15.1 lists the pattern modifiers that can be applied to the substitute function. You'll learn more about pattern modifiers in Chapter 16.

TABLE 15.1: Pattern Modifiers

Code	Description
g	Global—match all occurrences of the regular expression
i	Ignore case—match any case
m	Multiple lines—process the input as multiple lines
o	Only once—compile the regular expression the first time
s	Single line—ignore new lines
x	Extra spaces—allow comments and spaces in regular expression syntax

---

NOTE   The **s///** function works much like the pattern-match function **m//**, which is described in Chapter 16. The primary difference between these two functions is that the **s///** function modifies the bound string, searching for a pattern and replacing it with a new pattern, and the **m//** function simply searches for a pattern.

The substitute function and the functions described in the previous sections work with and modify multiple characters within a string. The next section explains how to modify single characters within a string.

Changing Characters

In any endeavor, the more you work with tools, the more you appreciate the right tool for the right job. Perl 5 certainly understands this philosophy and provides you with just the right character-translation tool when you need it.

Perl 5 offers the following functions for working with the ASCII character set:

- The chr and ord functions translate numbers to ASCII characters and ASCII characters to numbers, respectively.

- The lc, uc, lcfirst, and ucfirst functions change character case.

- The tr function performs single-character translations.

- The chop and chomp functions remove end-of-line characters.

These functions and their practical applications are described in the following sections.

Translating between Numbers and Characters

The chr and ord functions are specialized tools for translating between numbers and characters. This type of translation is helpful when working with the Perl interpreter, reading characters from a special terminal window, or building a specialized screen interface.

Converting Numbers to Characters

The chr function translates a number into a character. Programs that read the keyboard and work with video buffers use this function to send nonprintable characters to the screen. The syntax of the chr function is:

```
lvalue = chr(number);
```

The number may be any valid ASCII number. Octal and hex values are commonly used with the chr function because of their close relationship with the byte codes that define screen and control characters.

Listing 15.2, which comes with the standard Perl 5 distribution, demonstrates using the chr function to translate character code numbers into extended ASCII characters required for printing non-English characters. Figure 15.1 shows the output. The characters shown in Figure 15.1 are part of the ISO (International Organization for Standardization) Entity character codes.

Listing 15.2:   **Converting Non-English Characters**

```
1.  #!/local/bin/perl -w
2.
3.  open(E, "ISOlat1.sgml") || die;
4.
5.  while (<E>) {
6.      if (/^\s*<!ENTITY\s+
            (\w+)\s+CDATA\s+\"&\#(\d+);\"\s*-\s*(.*?)\s*->/) {
7.          print " $1\t=> '", chr($2), "',   # $3\n";
8.      } else {
9.   print STDERR $_;
10.     }
11. }
```

Lines 6 and 7 of Listing 15.2 work together, using regular expressions and the chr function to convert the results:

```
if (/^\s*<!ENTITY\s+(\w+)\s+CDATA\s+\"&\#(\d+);\"\s*-\s*(.*?)\s*->/) {
    print " $1\t=> '", chr($2), "',   # $3\n";
```

FIGURE 15.1:

Translating extended ASCII characters

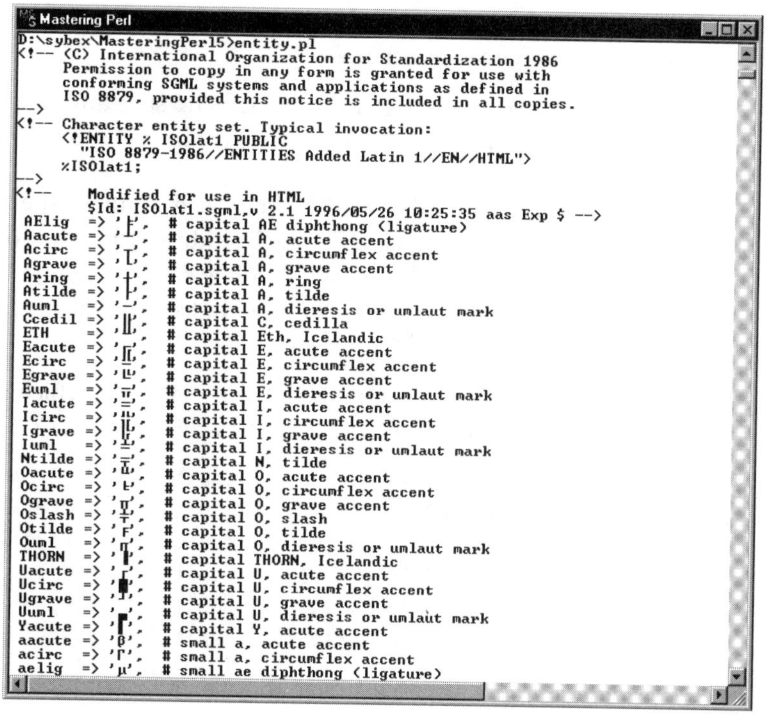

Line 6 uses regular expressions (which will be explained in more detail in Chapter 16), in the following steps:

1. The characters `^\s*<!ENTITY\s+` look for the characters `<!ENTITY` preceded at the start of a line by zero or more characters and followed by at least one space character.

2. The characters `(\w+)` match and save any single or multiple alphanumeric characters (*a–z*, *A–Z*, or 0–9).

3. The characters `\s+CDATA\s+` match one or more spaces, followed by CDATA, followed by one or more spaces.

4. The characters `\"&\#` match a quote character (`"`), followed by an ampersand (&), followed by a pound sign (#).

5. The characters `(\d+)` match and save one or more digits.

6. The characters `;\"\s*–\s*` match a dashed line preceded by a semicolon and a quote character. The dashed line may be preceded and followed by zero or more space characters.

7. The characters `(.*?)\s*–>/` match and save anything up until two dashes and a right arrow, which may be proceeded by zero or more spaces.

Steps 2, 5, and 7 save their matched characters into the special variables $1, $2, and $3, which are used on line 7. Line 7 produces each line you see in Figure 15.1 by printing the words matched in step 2, followed by a tab, and then converting the numbers matched in step 5 to their non-English equivalent characters, followed by the match found in step 7.

Several lines of input from the `ISOlatl.sgml` file, which is the ISO 1986 character entity set modified for use in HTML, opened on line 3, look like this:

```
<!ENTITY AElig  CDATA "&#198;" – capital AE diphthong (ligature) –>
<!ENTITY Aacute CDATA "&#193;" – capital A, acute accent –>
<!ENTITY Acirc  CDATA "&#194;" – capital A, circumflex accent –>
<!ENTITY Agrave CDATA "&#192;" – capital A, grave accent –>
<!ENTITY Aring  CDATA "&#197;" – capital A, ring –>
<!ENTITY Atilde CDATA "&#195;" – capital A, tilde –>
```

The number following the $# that you see in these lines is being translated by the chr function on line 7.

Converting Characters to Numbers

The ord function converts ASCII characters into their numeric value, which is the inverse of what the chr function does. The syntax of the ord function is:

```
lvalue = ord(expression);
```

The ord function converts only the first character of the expression. If the expression is omitted, the ord function will use the default special variable $_.

Listing 15.3, which is also delivered with the standard Perl 5 distribution, demonstrates the use of the ord function. This program converts octal values to their meta and control-code equivalents.

Listing 15.3:   Converting Octals to Control-Code and Meta Equivalents

```
1.  # assert.pl
2.  # tchrist@convex.com (Tom Christiansen)
3.  #
```

```
4.   # Usage:
5.   #
6.   #      &assert('@x > @y');
7.   #      &assert('$var > 10', $var, $othervar, @various_info);
8.   #
9.   # That is, if the first expression evals false, we blow up.  The
10.  # rest of the args, if any, are nice to know because they will
11.  # be printed out by &panic, which is just the stack-backtrace
12.  # routine shamelessly borrowed from the perl debugger.
13.
14.  sub assert {
15.      &panic("ASSERTION BOTCHED: $_[$[]",$@) unless eval $_[$[];
16.  }
17.
18.  sub panic {
19.      package DB;
20.      select(STDERR);
21.      print "\npanic: @_\n";
22.      exit 1 if $] <= 4.003;   # caller broken
23.      # stack traceback gratefully borrowed from perl debugger
24.      local $_;
25.      my $i;
26.      my ($p,$f,$l,$s,$h,$a,@a,@frames);
27.      for ($i = 0; ($p,$f,$l,$s,$h,$w) = caller($i); $i++) {
28.          @a = @args;
29.          for (@a) {
30.              if (/^StB\000/ && length($_) == length
                                              ($_main{'_main'})) {
31.                  $_ = sprintf("%s",$_);
32.              }
33.              else {
34.                  s/'/\\'/g;
35.                  s/([^\0]*)/'$1'/ unless /^-?[\d.]+$/;
36.                  s/([\200-\377])/sprintf("M-%c",ord($1)&0177)/eg;
37.                  s/([\0-\37\177])/sprintf("^%c",ord($1)^64)/eg;
38.              }
39.          }
40.          $w = $w ? '@ = ' : '$ = ';
41.          $a = $h ? '(' . join(', ', @a) . ')' : '';
42.          push(@frames, "$w&$s$a from file $f line $l\n");
43.      }
44.      for ($i=0; $i <= $#frames; $i++) {
45.          print $frames[$i];
```

```
46.    }
47.    exit 1;
48. }
49.
50. 1;
```

Line 35 of Listing 15.3 converts the octal values 200 through 377 to their meta equivalents:

```
s/([\200-\377])/sprintf("M-%c",ord($1)&0177)/eg;
```

Line 36 converts the octal values 0 through 37 and 177 to their control-code equivalents:

```
s/([\0-\37\177])/sprintf("^%c",ord($1)^64)/eg;
```

The AND operation (ord($1)&0177) at the end of line 36 is a binary AND, which sets the most significant bit of the result to zero. The ^64 on line 36 is an exclusive OR function (XOR), which toggles bit 7, making sure it is set to zero.

Changing Case

When you're writing something (including programs), case usually matters. Perl 5 has four functions for the character-case challenged: lc, lcfirst, uc, and ucfirst.

The syntax of the character-case functions is:

```
lvalue = characterCaseFunction(expression);
```

The expression is optional. If it is omitted, the default special variable $_ will be used as the expression.

The functions convert the entire expression or just the first character to its ASCII lowercase or uppercase equivalent, as follows:

- The lc function changes all the characters in the expression to lowercase.

- The lcfirst function changes only the first character of the expression to lowercase.

- The uc function changes all the characters in the expression to uppercase.

- The ucfirst function changes only the first character of the expression to uppercase.

If a character is not an ASCII character from *A* to *Z* or *a* to *z*, it will not be changed by the character-case function.

Listing 15.4 is a piece of code from a program distributed with the lib-www portion of Perl 5. Listing 15.4 is an example of formatting user input, which is a practical and reasonable use for the lc and uc functions.

Listing 15.4:   **Formatting User Input**

```perl
1.  #!/usr/local/bin/perl
2.
3.  $method = uc($opt_m) if defined $opt_m;
4.  $method = uc(lc($0) eq "lwp-request" ? "GET" : $0);
5.
6.  if ($c =~ /^ENTITY\s+(%\s*)?(\S+)\s+(.*)/is) {
7.      my($percent, $key, $val) = ($1, lc($2), $3);
8.      if ($percent) {
9.          $key = "%$key";
10.     }
11.     else {
12.         $key = "&$key";
13.         $val =~ s/CDATA\s+//;
14.     }
15.     $val =~ s/^"//s;
16.     $val =~ s/"$//s;
17.     $val =~ s/(%[\w\.\-]+);?/$entity{lc $1} || $1/eg;
18.
19.     $entity{$key} = $val;
20.     #print "E: $key => $val\n";
21. }
22. else {
23.     # Expand entities
24.     $c =~ s/(%[\w\.\-]+);?/$entity{lc $1} || $1/eg;
25.     #print "C: $c\n"
26.     if ($c =~ /^ELEMENT\s+\((([^\)]+))\)\s+([-O])\s+([-O])\s+(.*)/is)
    {
27.         my($elems, $start, $stop, $content) = (lc $1, $2, $3, lc $4);
28.         for ($elems, $content) {
29.             s/\s+//g;
30.         }
31.         $content =~ s/(\#pcdata)\b/\U$1/g;
32.         for $elem (split(/\|/, $elems)) {
```

```
33.              $element{$elem} = [$start, $stop, $content];
34.          }
35.      }
36.      elsif ($c =~ /^ELEMENT\s+(\S+)\s+([-O])\s+([-O])\s+(.*)/is) {
37.          my($elem, $start, $stop, $content) = (lc $1, $2, $3, lc $4);
38.          $content =~ s/\s+//g;
39.          $content =~ s/(\#pcdata)\b/\U$1/g;
40.          $element{$elem} =  [$start, $stop, $content];
41.      }
42.      elsif ($c =~ s/^ATTLIST\s+\(((([^\)]+)\)\)\s+//) {
43.          my $elems = lc $1;
44.          $elems =~ s/\s+//g;
45.          my $attrs = parse_attrs($c);
46.          for $elem (split(/\|/, $elems)) {
47.              $attr{$elem} = $attrs;
48.          }
49.      }
50.      elsif ($c =~ s/^ATTLIST\s+(\S+)\s+//) {
51.          $attr{lc $1} = parse_attrs($c);
52.      }
53.      else {
54.          print STDERR "?: $c\n";
55.      }
56. }
```

Lines 3 and 4 of Listing 15.4 are used to guarantee user input is in the correct format for later program use. Line 3 converts an optional flag to uppercase:

```
$method = uc($opt_m) if defined $opt_m;
```

Line 4 makes sure the HTTP method type is in uppercase:

```
$method = uc(lc($0) eq "lwp-request" ? "GET" : $0);
```

TIP Convert user input at the first reasonable point in your programs. This allows you to catch potential errors or special cases as early as possible and prevents a ripple effect throughout your code. This ripple effect occurs when your code repeatedly checks for exceptions and special cases. If you find your code is doing this, stop and look for a place earlier in your code where you can eliminate the special case, as done on lines 3 and 4 of Listing 15.4.

The lc function is used throughout the remainder of Listing 15.4 to convert the %entity hash keys to a consistent format. The %entity hash contains the HTML entity tags, which are accessed by a lowercase hash key. This is another excellent example of formatting varying data to a consistent format and thereby reducing overall code complexity.

Translating Single Characters

The tr, or translate, function is a general-purpose character-translation function. The translate function exchanges each occurrence of a character in the search string with its matching character in the replacement string. The syntax of the translate function is:

```
tr/searchString/replacementString/
```

The translate function modifies the string it is bound to via the bind (=~) or NOT bind (!~) operator. If the bound string is omitted, the translate function modifies the default special variable ($_).

Unlike most other Perl 5 functions, neither the search string nor the replacement string used with the translate function may be a variable. A translation table is built at compile time, which means both the search and replacement strings must be literal values.

The translation table built at compile time pairs each character in the search string with a character in the replacement string. If there are fewer characters in the replacement string than in the search string, the last character in the replacement string will be matched with the remaining characters in the search string. If the replacement string is omitted, the search string also becomes the replacement string.

The translate function provides a means to count the number of a specific set or type of characters in an input string. For example, if you want to count the number of vowels in an input string, use this code:

```
$numberOfVowels = ($inString =~ tr/aeiovy//);
```

If a character is replicated in the search string, only the first occurrence is used for translation, like this:

```
tr/01010/ABCDE/
```

This search string results in all 1 characters being translated to A characters and all 0 characters being translated to B characters.

The results of the translate function may be changed by the modifiers shown in Table 15.2.

TABLE 15.2: Translation (tr Function) Modifiers

Modifier	Description
c	Complement—match all characters that are not part of the search string
d	Delete—remove unpaired characters
s	Single—create only a single character from multiple translations of the same character

If your input accepts only alphabetical characters, you can translate all nonal-phabetical characters to a single value using both the c and s modifiers, like this:

```
$inputString =~ tr/a-z/*/cs;
```

The complement modifier (c) changes the translate function so that it matches all characters that are not part of the search string. The single modifier (s) changes the action of the translate function so that it generates only one replacement character when the same replacement character is generated more than once. The following are some examples of the translation and results using this input string:

```
$inputString = '844good38,*-input 721 data';
```

Translation	**Result**
`$inputString =~ tr/A-z/*/c;`	`***good****input***data`
`$inputString =~ tr/A-z/*/cs;`	`*good*input*data`
`$inputStirng =~ tr/A-z//cd;`	`goodinputdata`

Removing End-of-Line Characters

As you learned in Chapter 11, reading and writing to files are common program-ming tasks. Lines read from a file typically end in a newline character that is not part of the data and needs to be removed.

When I first started working with Perl, I used the chop function to get rid of the newline character at the end of lines. The chop function returns and removes the last character from a string. Because I have inadvertently mangled files using the chop function by removing valid characters when I only meant to remove trailing newline characters, I use the chomp function almost exclusively now. The chomp function removes only newlines, which is much safer than deleting any character that happens to be at the end.

The chop function has both a list and scalar context. In scalar context, chop function syntax is:

```
lvalue = chop($scalar);
```

The chop function removes the last character from the scalar variable, which may be a simple string literal. The lvalue is assigned the deleted character. The default special variable $_ will be modified if the scalar variable is omitted.

In list context, the syntax of the chop function is:

```
lvalue = chop(@array);
```

The chop function removes the last character of each element of the input list. The lvalue receives the last character deleted. Using this syntax, each element of the array will have its last character removed. You can strip all of the newline characters off of every line of an input file with this code:

```
open(INFILE, "input.txt");
@infile=<INFILE.;
close(INFILE);
chop(@infile);
```

This was the way I processed my files before I learned about the chomp function. The chop function indiscriminately removes the last character from a string. The chomp function removes only a newline character from the end of a string.

The chomp function also has both a scalar and list context. Its syntax is:

```
lvalue = chomp($scalar);
lvalue = chomp(@array);
```

The chomp function, unlike the chop function, returns the number of characters removed from either the list or scalar input variable. If you need to count the number of lines in a file, you could use the following code:

```
open(INFILE, "infile.txt");
@infile=<INFILE>;
```

```
close(INFILE)
$numberofLines = chomp(@infile);
print "This file has $numberofLines lines.\n";
```

The chomp function actually removes the value of the input record separator special variable $/, which defaults to the newline character. If you change the value of the input record separator variable, chomp will remove the new separator value from the end of your file-input lines.

As you've learned, the chop, chomp, and other functions that work on single characters can be very useful in your programs. The functions discussed in the next sections are also handy for many programming tasks that require separating strings into parts or putting strings together.

Separating and Joining Strings

The split function's versatility makes it one of my favorite functions. You've seen it in many of the examples presented in this and earlier chapters, and it was briefly discussed in Chapter 8. The opposite of splitting up strings with the split function is joining strings with the join function. These two functions are discussed in the following sections.

Splitting Strings

Delineating fields in a record, separating words, and determining directory locations are just a few of the tasks that the split function makes easy. The split function separates the expression into parts. The syntax of the split function is:

```
lvalue = split(/pattern/,expression, maxSplit);
```

If the lvalue is a scalar, a count of the delimited fields is returned. If the lvalue is an array or a list, each delimited field up to the maximum split value (the maximum number of times the expression may be separated) is saved into the array or list.

The pattern is interpreted as a regular expression and follows the same rules as the pattern-match function explained in the next chapter. The pattern may have pattern modifiers, which are the same as those in Table 15.1, and the pattern delimiters may be modified. If the pattern contains parentheses, the pattern matched will create an element of the list each time it is matched. If the pattern contains multiple parenthesis pairs, each pair will create an element in the return list. If a pair is matched, that value will be the element's value. If a pair is not matched, the element's value will be undef.

The expression will be interpreted as a string. The expression may be a scalar variable, string literal, or an expression that returns a string. If the expression is omitted, the default special variable $_ will be used.

The maximum split parameter defines the maximum number of times the expression may be separated. If this value is omitted, Perl 5 will separate the expression as many times as available for assignment plus one. If the assignment list is greater than or equal to the maximum split value, the remainder of the expression will be saved into the variable in the list.

NOTE   Without a maximum split value, Perl 5 stops working after it has separated the string the number of times the result will be used plus one for efficiency. Any further work would be a waste of processing time.

Listing 15.5 demonstrates using a list as the lvalue with the split function.

Listing 15.5:   Converting Time

```perl
1.  #!/usr/bin/perl
2.
3.  ($thisMonth, $thisYear, $thisDay) = split(/:/,`date +%m:%Y:%d`);
4.  ($thisMonth, $thisDay, $thisYear ) = MMDDYYYY();
5.
6.  sub MMDDYYYY(){
7.      my @timeList = localtime(time);
8.      my $MM = sprintf("%02d",$timeList[4]+1);
9.      my $YYYY = normalizeYear($timeList[5]);
10.     my $DD = sprintf("%02d",$timeList[3]);
11.     return ($MM,$DD,$YYYY);
12. }
13.
14. # Normalize years into 4-digit numbers corrected
15. # for any Y2K problems.
16. #
17. sub normalizeYear {
```

```
18.    local ($yearToNormalize) = @_;
19.    # Handle Y2K problem with a 1990 cutoff
20.    #
21.    if ($yearToNormalize < 90) {
22.        sprintf "20%.2d",$yearToNormalize;
23.    }
24.    elsif ($yearToNormalize < 100) {
25.        sprintf "19%.2d",$yearToNormalize;
26.    }
27.    else {
28.        sprintf "%.4d",$yearToNormalize;
29.    }
30. }
31. return 1;
```

This program in Listing 15.5 was first developed using the Unix **date** function as shown on line 3:

```
($thisMonth, $thisYear, $thisDay) = split(/:/,`date +%m:%Y:%d`);
```

The Unix **date** function allows you to define the output format. The expression date +%mi%Y:%d returns the current month, year, and day separated by colons. The **split** function separates these three fields using the colon delimiter and saves them into the list ($thisMonth, $this year, $thisDay). (Remember that surrounding the scalar variables with parentheses creates the list context.)

A combination of the maximum split value and the number of delimited fields in the expression defines the contents of the lvalue list, which may be an array. If the assignment list is greater than or equal to the maximum split value, the remainder of the expression will be saved into each variable in the list. Listing 15.6 demonstrates what happens when the list has more items than the maximum split value, and Figure 15.2 shows the output.

Listing 15.6:   **Splitting Local Time**

```
1.  #! /usr/local/bin/perl
2.  ($day, $month, $dayOfMonth, $rest) = split
                              (/\s+/,localtime(time),4);
3.  print "Day==>$day, Month==>$month, Day of Month==>$dayOfMonth,
        Remainder==>$rest\n";
4.  ($hour, $minute, $second, $rest) = split (/:/,$rest,4);
5.  print "Hour==>$hour, Minute==>$minute, Second==>$second,
```

```
                     Remainder==>$rest\n";
6.   ($second, $year) = split(/\s+/,$second);
7.   print "Second==>$second, Year==>$year\n";
8.   #A shorter solution
9.   ($day, $month, $dayOfMonth, $time) = split
                                    (/\s+/,localtime(time));
10.  ($hour, $minute, $second) = split (/:/,$time);
11.  print "Hour==>$hour, Minute==>$minute, Second==>$second\n";
```

FIGURE 15.2:

Splitting time

The output from localtime is separated into four fields. Each field is determined by splitting the result returned by localtime at each space character (one or more consecutive space characters, actually). Because there are more fields than available in the list on line 2 of Listing 15.6, the remainder of the expression is saved into the last variable in the list.

Line 4 then separates the time using the colon character as the field delimiter:

```
($hour, $minute, $second, $rest) = split (/:/,$rest,4);
```

In this case, there are more variables in the list than created by the split function, which is illustrated by the empty remainder in Figure 15.2. Because a colon does not separate the seconds and the year, they are again split using the space character as the delimiter.

Lines 9 and 10 illustrate a quicker means of separating out the hours, minutes, and seconds using the split function:

```
($day, $month, $dayOfMonth, $time) = split (/\s+/,localtime(time));
($hour, $minute, $second) = split (/:/,$time);
```

The delimiter used by the split function may be a regular expression. When the delimiter is a regular expression, if follows the same rules as the pattern-match function (summarized earlier in this chapter). Listing 15.7 demonstrates using the `split` function with a regular expression delimiter. The program in the listing is part of the standard Perl 5 distribution. This program changes the current directory and keeps the environment variable PWD the correct value.

NOTE   Listing 15.7 can be tested only on a Unix platform because the environment variable Env{'PWD'} is not available on a Windows computer.

Listing 15.7:   **The Unix chdir**

```
1.   sub main'chdir {
2.       local($newdir) = shift;
3.       $newdir =~ s|/{2,}|/|g;
4.       if (chdir $newdir) {
5.           if ($newdir =~ m#^/#) {
6.               $ENV{'PWD'} = $newdir;
7.           }
8.           else {
9.               local(@curdir) = split(m#/#,$ENV{'PWD'});
10.              @curdir = '' unless @curdir;
11.              foreach $component (split(m#/#, $newdir)) {
12.                  next if $component eq '.';
13.                  pop(@curdir),next if $component eq '..';
14.                  push(@curdir,$component);
15.              }
16.              $ENV{'PWD'} = join('/',@curdir) || '/';
17.          }
18.      }
19.      else {
20.          0;
21.      }
22. }
```

As shown on line 5 of Listing 15.7, the pattern delimiters (//) may be modified:

```
if ($newdir =~ m#^/#) {
```

If you add the character m to the beginning of a pattern match, the next character following the m will be used as your pattern delimiter. This allows the use of the forward slash in the pattern match without requiring the escape character.

Joining Strings Together

Anybody can take something apart; putting it back together is supposed to be the hard part. However, putting a list together to make a single delimited string is easy with Perl 5's join function. If you are building a simple database, sometimes all you need is a colon-delimited field, which can easily be accomplished like this:

```
$InventoryString = join(':', @inventory);
```

This simple line creates a single colon-delimited string of each element in the @inventory array.

The syntax of the join function is:

```
lvalue = join(delimiter, list);
```

The lvalue should be a scalar variable. The delimiter may be any expression. The delimiter will be used as a separator between each element of the list.

Listing 15.8 shows a practical example of using join to create a price list:

Listing 15.8:   **Building a Price List**

```
1. #!/usr/local/bin/perl
2.
3. %inventory = (car=>45_000.00,bike=>120.00,plane=>
                 450_000.00,lamp=>40.00);
4. open (INV, ">price.list");
5. foreach $item (sort keys %inventory){
6.    print INV join(":", ($item, $inventory{"$item"})), "\n";
7. }
8. close INV;
```

Listing 15.8 produces the following file:

```
bike:120
car:45000
lamp:40
plane:450000
```

Packing Characters

Probably one of the most commonly reused and least understood lines of code on the Internet is the URL-decoding routine that reads POST data. You may recall from Chapter 1 that CGI programs get their Internet input data in either GET or POST format. Listing 15.9 helps decipher that routine.

Listing 15.9:   **Reading HTML POST Input**

```
1.  sub readPostInput(){
2.     my (%searchField, $buffer, $pair, @pairs);
3.     if ($ENV{'REQUEST_METHOD'} eq 'POST'){
4.        # How many bytes are we supposed to receive?
5.        read(STDIN, $buffer, $ENV{'CONTENT_LENGTH'});
6.        # make a list of keyword/value pairs
7.        @pairs = split(/&/, $buffer);
8.        # cycle through each pair and decipher the values
9.        foreach $pair (@pairs){
10.          # get the name/value pair strings
11.          ($name, $value) = split(/=/, $pair);
12.          # translate "+" to a space
13.          $value =~ tr/+/ /;
14.          # decipher ASCI hexadecimal escaped characters, if any
15.          $value =~ s/%([a-fA-F0-9][a-fA-F0-9])/pack("C",
                                                    hex($1))/eg;
16.          $name =~ tr/+/ /;
17.          # decipher ASCI hexadecimal escaped characters, if any
18.          $name =~ s/%([a-fA-F0-9][a-fA-F0-9])/pack("C",
                                                   hex($1))/eg;
19.          $searchField{$name} = $value;
20.          #   print "val = $value name = $name <br>";
21.       }
22.    }
23.    return (%searchField);
24. }
25. return 1;
```

Listing 15.9 demonstrates many of the functions discussed so far in this chapter, including separating strings into parts using the split function, translating characters using the translate (`tr`) function, and converting one pattern to another using the substitute (`s///`) function. It also shows how to convert binary-encoded strings to characters using the `pack` function, which is the subject of this section.

Accomplishing these tasks in Perl 5 takes less than 15 lines of Perl 5 code (lines 7 through 18 of Listing 15.9). In another language, you might expect to use hundreds of lines of code to make the same character translations. These are the functions that make Perl 5 so popular on the Internet.

Lines 15 and 18 of Listing 15.9 use the `pack` function to translate hex character codes back to their ASCII values.

```
$value =~ s/%([a-fA-F0-9][a-fA-F0-9])/pack("C", hex($1))/eg;
$name =~ s/%([a-fA-F0-9][a-fA-F0-9])/pack("C", hex($1))/eg;
```

The `pack` function is designed to translate values, primarily for shipment across networks. Because you can never be sure what format the receiving platform will translate the data into, the data is packed into a known and consistent format.

The `pack` function takes a character code and translates a corresponding character to the format specified. The `pack` function is kind of like the translate (`tr`) function on steroids, because it can translate a lot more than just characters. Its syntax is:

```
pack TEMPLATE, inputList;
```

The character codes and their meanings are shown in Table 15.3.

TABLE 15.3: The pack Function Character Codes

Character Code	Meaning
a	Convert to its ASCII character value; pad empty characters with null
A	Convert to its ASCII character value; pad empty characters with spaces
b	Convert to a bit string from low to high order bit
B	Convert to a bit string from high to low order bit
c	Convert to a signed character
C	Convert to an unsigned character
d	Convert to a double-precision (floating-point number in the native platform format)

Continued on next page

TABLE 15.3 CONTINUED: The pack Function Character Codes

Character Code	Meaning
f	Convert to a single-precision (floating-point number in the native platform format)
h	Convert a hex string, putting the lower order nibble first
H	Convert a hex string to ASCII characters, putting the high order nibble first
I	Convert to signed integer format
I	Convert to unsigned integer format
l	Convert to signed long format
L	Convert to unsigned long format
n	Convert to short big endian order
N	Convert to long big endian order
p	Convert a pointer to string format
P	Convert a pointer to a fixed-length string
s	Convert to signed short format
S	Convert to unsigned short format
v	Convert to short little endian format
V	Convert to long little endian format
u	Convert to uu encoded format
x	Insert null byte
X	Back up one byte
@	Null fill to absolute position

The pack function formats data into a binary string, which is saved into a lvalue. That binary string may be interpreted into readable characters.

Listing 15.10 demonstrates the use of several of the character codes of the pack function, and Figure 15.3 shows its output. Each of the character codes in

Listing 15.10 has a number appended to it that replicates the code's actions. A code may also be repeated, like this:

```
pack "cccc" 101, 14, 105, 99;
```

Listing 15.10:   Pack Function Examples

```
1.  #!/usr/local/bin/perl
2.  $packed = pack "a10" , "Test";
3.  print "$packed Null Padded\n\n";
4.  $packed = pack "A10" , "Test";
5.  print "$packed Space Padded\n\n";
6.  $packed = pack "b32" , "01000101010100100100100101000011";
7.  print "$packed The right most bit is the most significant\n\n";
8.  $packed = pack "B32" , "01000101010100100100100101000011";
9.  print "$packed The left most bit is the most significant\n\n";
10. $packed = pack "c4", 0x45, 0x52, 0x49, 0x43;
11. print "$packed Numbers (hex) to ASCII, unsigned\n\n";
12. $packed = pack "C4", , 101, 114, 105, 99;
13. print "$packed Numbers (decimal) to ASCII, signed\n\n";
14. $packed = pack "h8", "54259434";
15. print "$packed Hex low Nibble first to  ASCII\n\n";
16. $packed = pack "H8", "45524943";
17. print "$packed Hex High Nibble first to ASCII\n\n";
18. $packed = pack "d", , 101.134;
19. print "$packed Double Precision native format packed for
            shipment\n\n";
20. $packed = pack "f", , 101.134;
21. print "$packed Single Precision native format packed for
            shipment\n\n";
22. $packed = pack "i5", , "97","98","99","100","101";
23. print "$packed Unsigned Packed Integers\n\n";
24. $packed = pack "I5", , "97","98","99","100","101";
```

After the packed data is received, it can be unpacked into the receiving platform's native format. The unpack function does the inverse of the pack function. The unpack function takes the packed binary string and creates a list from the input string. The list is determined by the unpack character codes, which are the same as the pack character codes. The syntax of the unpack function is:

```
lvalue = unpack code, string;
```

FIGURE 15.3:

Packing data

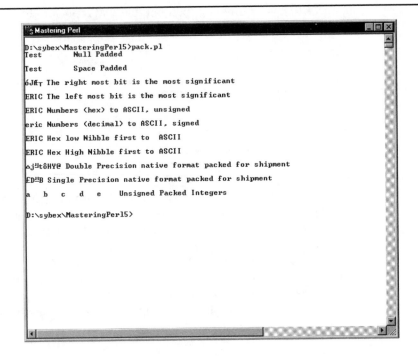

As you've seen in this section, Perl 5's character-translation features are well-suited for transferring data across the Internet and other networks. In the next section, you'll learn about another useful function for working with strings, the sort function, and how to build your own sort subroutines.

Creating Sorting Subroutines

The sort function was introduced in Chapter 6, in the discussion of built-in functions for working with arrays. Here, we'll focus on sort subroutines that extend the power of the sort function to infinity and beyond.

As you learned, the sort function uses the quick-sort algorithm, which is one of the fastest general-purpose sorting algorithms used in computer science.

However, this function only sorts strings in ascending order, and length is never part of the `sort` function's primary algorithm.

The syntax of the `sort` function without a special-purpose sort subroutine is:

```
lvalue = sort list
```

The lvalue must be an array or list. The list to be sorted may be an array, a list of scalars, or a list of strings. The list will be character sorted in ascending order. The length of each element in the string list is unimportant unless the strings are identical, up to the last character of the shorter string. In the case of identical strings, the shorter string will always be sorted before the longer string. As shown here, the comparison is always character by character with the short string winning any ties, like this:

add is sorted before addd

caa is sorted before caca

addd is sorted before caa

The sort routine can be controlled by the two variables, $a and $b, and the two operators, cmp and <=>. The sort routine's default action can be modified by building your own special-purpose sort subroutines. Here are a few examples:

- To sort in descending order:

  ```
  sortDescending(){$b cmp $a;}
  ```

- To sort numerically in ascending order:

  ```
  sortNumerically () {$a <=> $b;}
  ```

- To sort numerically in descending order:

  ```
  sortNumerically () {$b <=> $a;}
  ```

If you had any fears about creating your own sort routines, these examples should banish them. Now let's examine the details of creating sort subroutines.

Using Comparison Operators

The `sort` function's syntax for using user-created subroutines is:

```
lvalue = sort subroutineName list;
```

TIP The **sort** function also has a syntax that allows you to create the subroutine in place (an anonymous block): *lvalue* = sort *{statements} list*;. However, I don't recommend using this syntax because you'll end up recreating the same sort functions over and over again. Also, if you need to change your sort functions, you may have many copies of the same or similar code, which will not be updated properly. Instead, I recommend creating a sort **Utilitiy.pl** file that you can add to as needed and include in your code through the **require** or **use** statements.

Each subroutine you call for sorting is controlled by the cmp and <=> operators and the special variables $a and $b, which are references to the variables being sorted. The operators cmp and <=> are special trinary operators used for string or numeric comparison, respectively. Both of these operators return the following values:

- -1 if the left hand side is less than the right hand side
- 0 if the left hand side equals the right hand side
- 1 if the left hand side is greater than the right hand side

You must use the cmp or <=> operator for the final comparison in your special-purpose sort subroutine, or create your own comparison that returns -1 for less than, 0 for equality, and 1 for greater than. For example, to sort strings and ignore case, do this:

```
sub ignoreCase (){
    lc ($a) cmp lc($b);
}
```

To reverse the order of any sort, you only need to reverse the order of $a and $b. For example, to ignore case and sort in descending order, do this:

```
sub ignoreCaseDescending (){
    lc($b) cmp lc($a);
}
```

WARNING Never change the values of $a and $b.

Merging and sorting multiple arrays doesn't require any special-purpose code. Before the arrays are passed to the sort function, the Perl 5 interpreter merges them into a single array. To sort multiple arrays, do this:

```
lvalue = sort @array1, @array2, @arrayN;
```

Sorting a Hash by Value

Sorting a hash by value may seem a bit problematic at first, but Listing 15.11 shows how to solve this problem. Listing 15.11 produces the sorted list shown in Figure 15.4.

Listing 15.11:   **Hash Value Sorting**

```
1.  #!/usr/local/bin/perl
2.
3.  %Inventory = (car=>45_000.00,bike=>120.00,plane=>
                      450_000.00,lamp=>40.00);
4.  $sortHash = \%Inventory;
5.  @keyList = sort sortHashByValue keys %Inventory;
6.  foreach $key (@keyList){
7.     print "key==>$key, \tprice==>$Inventory{$key}\n";
8.  }
9.
10. sub sortHashByValue(){
11.    $$sortHash{"$a"} <=> $$sortHash{"$b"};
12. }
```

This sorted hash routine can be used by any function as long as the globally scoped reference $sortHash is created before the sort routine is called.

NOTE   The calling sequence used to invoke your special-purpose sort subroutine is outside the standard subroutine calling order, which you will learn about in Chapter 18. This unique calling order is efficient, but it also means that you cannot implement a recursive sort subroutine.

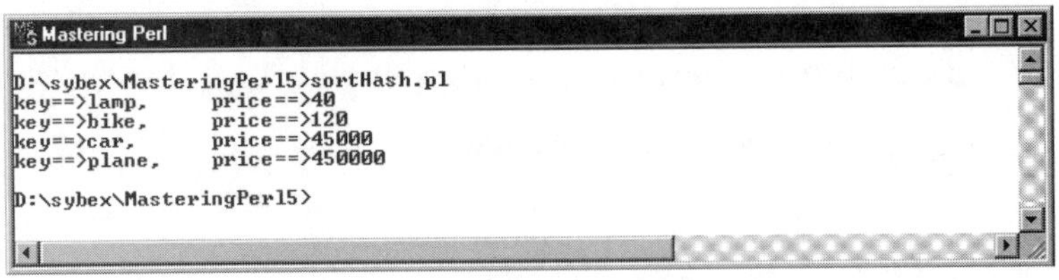

FIGURE 15.4:

Sorting a hash by value

```
D:\sybex\MasteringPerl5>sortHash.pl
key==>lamp,      price==>40
key==>bike,      price==>120
key==>car,       price==>45000
key==>plane,     price==>450000

D:\sybex\MasteringPerl5>
```

Sorting under Multiple Conditions

The final example in this chapter shows how to sort arrays and how to sort strings that require multiple conditions to determine the sort order. Listing 15.12 reads an employee database where every employee's last name is Smith. Some of these employees even have the same first name, but everyone has a different middle initial. This obviously is a contrived database, but sorting on fields that contain the same data, such as titles or salaries, is a common task. As you can see in the output shown in Figure 15.5, Listing 15.12 has a solution regardless of the sort field.

Listing 15.13:   Sorting on Multiple Conditions

```
1.  #!/usr/local/bin/perl
2.  open (DB, "<empDB.txt");
3.  @empDB = <DB>;
4.  close (DB);
5.  chomp @empDB;
6.  #file format ssn,name,salary,title
7.  my ($index) = 0;
8.  foreach $emp (@empDB){
9.     ($ssn,$name,$salary,$title) = split(/:/,$emp);
10.    $ssnList[$index] = $ssn;
11.    $nameList[$index] = $name;
12.    $salaryList[$index] = $salary;
13.    $titleList[$index] = $title;
14.    $index++;
15. }
16. @indexSSN = sort sortSSN 0..$#ssnList;
17. @indexName = sort sortName 0..$#nameList;
18. @indexSalary = sort sortSalary 0..$#salaryList;
19. @indexTitle = sort sortTitle 0..$#titleList;
20.
```

```perl
21. print "SORTED BY SSN\n";
22. foreach $item (@indexSSN){
23.     print "SSN:$ssnList[$item] \tName:$nameList[$item]
                                \tTitle:$titleList[$item]
                                \tSalary:$salaryList[$item]\n";
24. }
25.
26. print "SORTED BY Name\n";
27. foreach $item (@indexName){
28.     print "Name:$nameList[$item] \tSSN:$ssnList[$item]
                                \tTitle:$titleList[$item]
                                \tSalary:$salaryList[$item]\n";
29. }
30.
31. print "SORTED BY Title\n";
32. foreach $item (@indexTitle){
33.     print "Title:$titleList[$item] \tName:$nameList[$item]
                                \tSSN:$ssnList[$item]
                                \tSalary:$salaryList[$item]\n";
34. }
35.
36. print "SORTED BY Salary\n";
37. foreach $item (@indexSalary){
38.     print "Salary:$salaryList[$item] \tName:$nameList[$item]
                                \tTitle:$titleList[$item]
                                \tSSN:$ssnList[$item] \n";
39. }
40.
41. sub sortSSN(){
42.     $ssnList[$a] cmp $ssnList[$b]
43. }
44.
45. sub sortName(){
46.     ($fName1, $MI1, $lName1) = split(/\s+/,$nameList[$a]);
47.     ($fName2, $MI2, $lName2) = split(/\s+/,$nameList[$b]);
48.     ($lName1 cmp $lName2) or
49.     ($fName1 cmp $fName2) or
50.     ($MI1 cmp $MI2);
51. }
52.
53. sub sortTitle(){
54.     $titleList[$a] cmp $titleList[$b] or
55.     sortName();
```

```
56. }
57.
58. sub sortSalary(){
59.     $salaryList[$a] <=> $salaryList[$b] or
60.     sortName();
61. }
```

FIGURE 15.5:

Sorting out employees

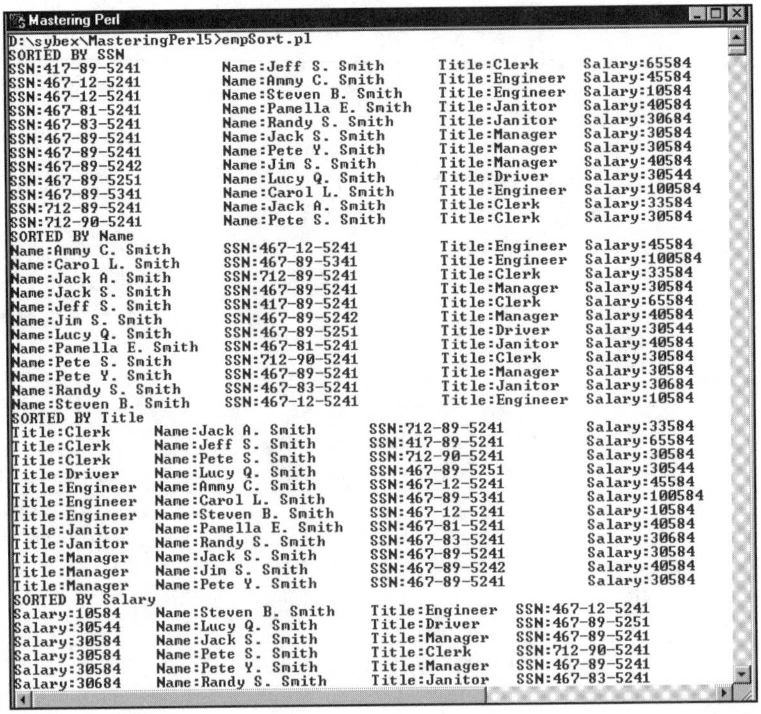

To accomplish these tasks, this code first reads the database and then separates it into multiple arrays based on the different fields of the database, which are social security number, employee name, title, and salary. Each array is built so that the same index number will access the same employee's information.

Next, the indexes are sorted based on the criteria defined in each sort subroutine. The sort subroutines are comparing the data in each array, but the value actually being saved is the array index. This allows you to use the list of sorted indexes across all four arrays to retrieve the sorted data associated with each employee.

The sortSSN subroutine on lines 41 through 43 is built with the knowledge that all social security numbers, which have the format *NNN-NN-NNN*, must be unique. Therefore, this special-purpose sort subroutine only needs to compare the two social security numbers:

```
sub sortSSN(){
   $ssnList[$a] cmp $ssnList[$b]
}
```

Note that this subroutine uses the string cmp operator, not the numeric <=> operator. The social security numbers include the dash character (-), which makes them strings instead of numbers.

The sortName subroutine on lines 45 through 51 is built to compare last names first, then first names, and finally middle initials when determining the sorting order of names that may be the same:

```
sub sortName(){
   ($fName1, $MI1, $lName1) = split(/\s+/,$nameList[$a]);
   ($fName2, $MI2, $lName2) = split(/\s+/,$nameList[$b]);
   ($lName1 cmp $lName2) or
   ($fName1 cmp $fName2) or
   ($MI1 cmp $MI2);
}
```

In order to make this comparison, the data must be separated first on lines 46 and 47 and then compared on lines 48 through 50. The or operator used on each of these lines is a short-circuit operator, as you learned in Chapter 4. As soon as the first nonzero result occurs, the or function stops further evaluation and returns its answer. In our example, it must always continue past the last name, and sometimes even the first name isn't sufficient, but the middle name always resolves the sorting conflicts. If there were a case where two names were completely identical, the name first read from the database would be printed first.

The sortByTitle subroutine is on lines 53 through 56:

```
sub sortTitle(){
   $titleList[$a] cmp $titleList[$b] or
   sortName();
}
```

First, the subroutine compares the titles. Whenever a title is not sufficient for a unique sort, the sortName subroutine is called. This is an excellent example of why named subroutines should be used whenever possible. Certainly, you could cut and paste the five lines of the sortByName subroutine into the sortTitle subroutine, but calling the existing subroutine takes less code. Also, if you need to change the sortName algorithm, you only have to change it in one place.

The sortSalary subroutine, on lines 58 through 61, uses the same logic as the sortTitle subroutine except for the comparison operator:

```
sub sortSalary(){
    $salaryList[$a] <=> $salaryList[$b] or
    sortName();
}
```

It is important to use a numeric comparison for numbers. A string comparison of salaries would sort the 100,584 salary before the 10,584 salary. In a string comparison, the characters 100 are determined to be less than 105 and the evaluation stops. This wasn't important in the social security number comparisons, because those numbers always have the same amount of digits.

Summary

In this chapter, you learned about some of Perl 5's most popular features. Perl 5's birth, growth, and popularity is centered on manipulating characters and strings. As you worked through this chapter, you learned about taking strings apart, putting them together, examining strings, and changing their contents.

You first learned how to determine the position in a string of another string. Perl 5 provides the index and rindex functions for this purpose. The index function finds the first occurrence of a string, starting from the front of a string. The rindex function finds the first occurrence of a string, starting from the end of a string. The substr function, explained next, operates something like the C/C++ strstr function, but of course, Perl always has a better solution. The substr function copies substrings from a string using offset and length parameters to determine the size of the copied substring. The substr function can also be used to modify a string, inserting the new string into the original string.

Using the substr function to modify strings is possible, but this task is more commonly accomplished using the substitute function (s///). The substitute function searches a string for a pattern and replaces that pattern with a second pattern. The substitute function modifies either the default special variable $_ or the string it is bound to by the bind operator (=~).

Next, you learned about Perl 5's functions for changing characters within a string. The lc function returns all lowercase characters, and the uc function returns all uppercase characters. You can change just the first character of a string's case using the lcfirst (lowercase) and ucfirst (uppercase) functions. One of Perl 5's most popular character-translation functions, the tr function, changes each occurrence of a search string to its corresponding replacement string. Though the tr function cannot be used with regular expressions or variables, you can modify the effect of the search and replacement strings using the translation modifiers c, d, and s. At the end of the character-translation section, you learned about the chop and chomp functions. Over the years, the chomp function has replaced the chop function as the tool to use for stripping off end-of-line characters.

The next topic in this chapter was Perl 5's split function. The split function uses a pattern, which may be a regular expression, to separate a string into a list. The expression is separated into substrings at each occurrence of the pattern. When the receiving lvalue is a scalar, the split function returns the count of the occurrences of a delimiter. The maximum split parameter controls the number of string extractions allowed by the split function. To complement the split function, Perl 5 has the join function, which creates delimited strings

If you're working in a networked environment, sending data across a socket, you need to know about the pack function. The pack function uses a character code to format data into a binary-encoded string.

This chapter closed with a discussion of sorting strings using the sort function. This section focused on the details of extending the sort function's string-oriented quick-sort algorithm. Using special-purpose subroutines, you can sort numbers, arrays, and even hash values. Sort subroutines must use either the string comparison operator cmp or the numeric comparison operator <=>. These trinary operators are unique and their return values of -1, 0, or 1 are required for the base sort routine to operate correctly.

This chapter described how to work with strings using standard string tools. In the next chapter, you'll learn how to manipulate strings using regular expressions.

CHAPTER

SIXTEEN

Regular Expressions

- ■ The pattern-match functions

- ■ Meta-characters and atoms

- ■ Pattern-match variables

- ■ Simple and complex regular expression examples

Regular expressions and pattern matching are fundamental to tapping into the power of Perl 5. Perl 5 is simply the best and easiest to use language for doing pattern matching and string manipulation. Perl 5 is such a popular Internet programming language because Internet programming is all about receiving ASCII strings, matching patterns, and manipulating regular expressions.

In this chapter, you'll learn the basic steps of building regular expressions. In the first part of this chapter, you'll learn the rules of building regular expressions. In the second part, you'll see those rules applied in a variety of examples.

An Introduction to Regular Expressions

A *regular expression* is a series of characters used to match a pattern that may be repeating. A *pattern* is a series of characters.

I used to hate regular expressions, but now that I understand them, I use them to solve many of my coding problems. What I disliked the most about them is that they can look like this:

```
$var =~ /([;<>\*\/'&\$!#\(\)\[\]\{\}:'"])/;
```

Now, some other programmer might say, "What's the problem? It's only a meta-character pattern match." To me, it just isn't clear until I take the time to study the pattern. In this chapter, you'll learn how to study the pattern so you can understand regular expressions. The first parts to understand are the pattern-matching functions and the meta-character pattern (which is what the example above is called).

The Functions for Matching Patterns

Perl 5 has three regular expression functions for matching patterns: substitution (s///), tokenizer (`split`), and pattern-match (m//). Each of these regular expression functions is used to solve a different type of coding problem.

You learned about the substitution and tokenizer functions in Chapter 15. The substitution function's syntax is:

```
s/patternToFind/replacementPattern/;
```

The substitution function tells Perl 5 to replace the pattern between the first pair of forward slashes with the pattern that is between the second and third forward slashes.

The tokenizer function's name is the `split` function. The `split` function's syntax is:

```
split (/pattern/,$variable, maxNumberOfTokens);
```

The parentheses are not required, but they are helpful reminders that you need to place a comma between each of the parameters passed to the function. The `split` function searches for the pattern in the variable. Every character preceding the pattern is returned in a scalar variable called a *token*. The pattern portion of the variable is discarded. This operation is repeated until all of the variable is processed or the maximum number of tokens is created. If the maximum number of tokens is reached before all of the variable is processed, everything in the variable following the next-to-last token is placed in the last token.

The pattern-match function is used with regular expressions to find patterns in a variable or string. The syntax of the pattern-match function is:

```
m/pattern/
```

The two forward slash characters delimit the pattern to be matched. The `m` is not required; you will frequently see the pattern-match function like this:

```
/pattern/
```

The `m` has one significant use, however. Perl 5 uses the first character following the `m` as the delimiter for the pattern. When you want to match strings that contain the forward slash, such as a directory separator, you can change the default delimiter (/) to another value, like this:

```
m!pattern!
```

NOTE   I use the term *function* to refer to the pattern-match (`m//`), substitute (`s///`), and tokenizer (`split`) functions. The pattern-match function can be used without the preceding `m`, like this `/pattern/`. In this form, it is commonly referred to as the pattern-match operator (`//`). I use the term *pattern-match function* to refer to both the operator and the function, which are actually the same thing.

The `m//`, `s///`, and `split` functions operate on the default input special variable (`$_`), which is the default storage variable for the last operation. If you don't want to match against the default input special variable, you need to use the binding operator (`=~`) with the variable you wish the regular expression to match against. The binding operator tells the function to match the variable on the left side of the expression instead of the default input special variable. You'll see examples of using the binding operator with regular expressions later in this chapter, in the "Regular Expressions Examples" section.

The pattern-match function is the most commonly used regular expression function. Therefore, the pattern-match function will be used throughout this chapter to explain the fundamentals of regular expressions. In the next section, you'll learn how to use the pattern-match function in a conditional expression.

Matches in Conditional Expressions

As you learned in Chapter 15, there are many ways to find patterns and pieces in strings. The pattern-match function is frequently used in conditional expressions to check for some character or characters in a string.

The example shown at the beginning of this chapter is frequently referred to as a *meta-character pattern*. You should always use that meta-character pattern when receiving input over the Internet. In fact, you should use it anywhere hackers could attack your program, which is everywhere unfortunately. The meta-character pattern checks for existences of particular characters that are considered dangerous because they can be used to start programs from the command-line interface. The semicolon, for example, can be used to end the current command and begin a completely new command.

The meta-character pattern is used here to illustrate the two most common means of using a conditional expression to check for patterns in a string.

```
if (/([;<>\*\/'&\$!#\(\)\[\]\{\}:'"])/;/) {
    invalidInput ($1);
}


if ($inputData =~/([;<>\*\/'&\$!#\(\)\[\]\{\}:'"])/;/){
    invalidInput ($1);
}
```

Both of these examples call the invalidInput subroutine shown in Listing 16.1, passing the subroutine the invalid data. The first example matches the meta-character pattern against the default variable $_. Both of these conditional expressions work because the pattern-match function (/ /) returns 1 when it finds a match for the pattern and 0 if no match is found. If the pattern is found, the conditional expression is true and the invalidInput subroutine in Listing 16.1 is called.

Listing 16.1:   Invalid Input

```
1.   sub invalidInput(){
```

```
2.      $invalidInput = shift;
3.      print<<"eof";
4.   Content-Type: text/html
5.
6.   </html>
7.   <body>
8.   The data you submitted is invalid. The following characters are
9.   <b> not <b> acceptable!
10.  <br>
11.  <center>
12.  <font size=+3>
13.  $invalidInput
14.  </font>
15.  </center>
16.  </body>
17.  </html>
```

TIP

You may find this example useful in your everyday programming. The `invalid-Input` subroutine in Listing 16.1 is suitable for use in your CGI programs. This subroutine returns a valid HTTP header and an HTML page to the calling web browser. The HTML page tells the user which input characters are unacceptable in their input.

Each of the examples that call the `invalidInput` subroutine passes the invalid input using the back reference variable $1. Back reference variables contain the characters that matched your regular expression, as explained in more detail later in this chapter.

To understand the details of regular expressions, it is important to understand the meta-characters used in the previous example. Meta-characters and other regular expression components are described in the next section.

Regular Expression Components

Patterns can be made up of simple characters or meta-characters that build a regular expression. Sometimes, all you need is a simple character-by-character match.

When you are searching for a word using your favorite text editor, you usually type in a simple word, like *hat*. The text editor's search function searches throughout the document looking for every occurrence of the word *hat*.

If you used the pattern-match function to search for *hat*, it might look something like this:

```
if (/hat/i){
    foundAmatch;
}
```

This tells Perl 5 to look for the characters *h*, *a*, and *t* in only that order. This pattern would match *HAT*, *hat*, and *that*. The pattern matches both uppercase and lowercase characters because the i included at the end of the pattern tells Perl 5 to ignore case when performing the match operation. The i and other pattern modifiers are explained later in this chapter.

With a text editor, you could avoid matches like *that* with *hat* by specifying that you want to find whole words only. There are many different ways to tell Perl 5 you only want to match *hat* and not *that*. The methods that tell Perl 5 to only match whole words or to match at the beginning or end of a string use regular expressions and meta-characters.

Meta-Characters

Meta-characters help you build regular expressions that match just the character you want without having to list all the characters you don't want, and vice versa. Table 16.1 lists each meta-character and its meaning. The use of these meta-characters is explained throughout this chapter.

TABLE 16.1: Meta-Characters

Character	Meaning
\	Escape, do not interpret the following meta-character
|	OR, match either of the alternatives
()	Create a single expression or atom
{}	Define the minimum and/or maximum repetitions of an atom
*	Match an atom zero or more times

Continued on next page

TABLE 16.1 CONTINUED: Meta-Characters

Character	Meaning
+	Match an atom one or more times
?	Match an atom zero or one times
^	Match an atom at the start of the string
$	Match an atom at the end of the string
[ ]	Match one of the enclosed atoms
.	Match any character
\A	Alternative to meta-character ^
\Z	Alternative to meta-character $

TIP

The meta-character pattern shown at the beginning of this chapter included the meta-characters of HTML and the command-line interface. The meta-characters of HTML and the meta-characters of Perl 5 regular expressions, which are covered in this chapter, are slightly different. In fact, you may find slight differences between the meta-characters of every language and every command-line interface (MS-DOS, Linux, HP-UX, Solaris, and so on). For more information about other meta-characters, refer to the documentation of that specific language or interface. For example, the HTTP and HTML specifications are available at www.w3.org.

Table 16.1 lists a lot of meta-characters that have to do with something called an *atom*. Regular expressions are made up of atoms, which are explained in the next section.

Atoms

Atoms are the fundamental building blocks of regular expressions. An atom is any single item in a pattern. A meta-character is not an atom; it must be paired with an atom to have meaning.

An atom can be any of the following:

- A single character or digit, A–Z, a–z, 0–9

- An escaped meta-character

- An escaped special-meaning character

- An octal code, a hexadecimal code, or a control code, such as \077, \xFF, or \cD

- A regular expression enclosed in parentheses

- A list of atoms enclosed in square brackets

- A back reference to a previous pattern match

Each of these types of atoms and its use in regular expressions is explained in the following sections.

Rules for Building Regular Expressions

You build regular expressions by combining atoms and meta-characters that specify the pattern that you want to match. Here, you'll learn the rules for putting together regular expressions, illustrated with some simple examples. Later in the chapter, you'll see some practical, more complex examples that use regular expressions.

Combining Atoms and Creating Back Reference Variables

Suppose that you are trying to find the name Steve in a phone book. You could create a pattern like /Steve/. If you were trying to match one or more instances of the pattern Steve, you might use the meta-character + , which matches an atom one or more times, in the pattern /Steve+/. This may seem correct, but a meta-character applies only to the preceding atom. The pattern /Steve+/ matches Steve, Stevee, and Steveee …, which is really the pattern Stev followed by one or more e characters. The meta-character + matches one or more characters of the preceding atom, and the preceding atom in this pattern is an e.

To match one or more of the pattern Steve, you must turn the pattern into an atom by enclosing it in parentheses, followed by the meta-character +, like this:

```
/(Steve)+/
```

This example will match one or more occurrences of Steve in a row. A regular expression or pattern surrounded by parentheses becomes an atom.

The parentheses around a regular expression also have another effect. The string matched by a regular expression in parentheses is saved in a back reference variable. A back reference variable is a variable created during a regular expression pattern match. The back reference variable contains the string matched by the pattern enclosed by the parentheses.

The back reference variable is always a variable of the name $1 to $n. (n is always equal to the number of the parentheses pairs used in the regular expression). The number of the parentheses pairs are determined by counting the pairs of parentheses in a regular expression, beginning from left to right and starting with the number 1. For example, if you had a regular expression that looked like this:

```
/(P1)(P2)(P3)ALPHA(p4)BETA(p5)/
```

The back reference variables would be $1, $2, $3, $4, and $5 and would contain the patterns matched by P1 through P5. There is always a one-to-one correspondence with the back reference variable name and the parentheses pair number. In the preceding pattern, the back reference variable named $1 contains the characters that matched pattern P1, the back reference variable named $2 contains the characters that matched pattern P2, and so on.

You can reference the back reference variable both inside and outside the regular expression. A back reference variable is created only when a pattern is matched. If you create a regular expression and the pattern does not match, then the back reference variable will be null. A back reference variable may contain zero characters if the pattern contains one of the quantity modifiers explained in the "Matching a Number of Times" section. Back reference variables are an important part of regular expressions, and you'll see examples of their use later in this chapter.

Using Escaped Characters

The escape character (\) is used to change the meaning of the character following it. When used in conjunction with other characters, the escape character allows you to match digits, words, and space characters.

NOTE As you learned in Chapter 12, the escape character is also used with the print function for sending printer control characters to a print device. For example, \n sends a newline command to the print device.

The escape character is always paired with another character in a regular expression. The paired character, which is the character following the escape character, takes an alternative regular expression meaning when preceded by the escape character.

When the escape character is paired with a meta-character, the pattern is designed to match the meta-character's ASCII value. For example, \+ in a regular expression matches the plus sign. Whenever you see the escape character in a regular expression and the next character is a meta-character, you know that the pattern is trying to match the meta-character itself.

When the escape character is paired with the ASCII characters shown in Table 16.2, the pattern matches the alternative regular expression meaning of the character.

TABLE 16.2: Meta-Character ASCII Values

Code	Meaning
\a	Alarm
\b	Word boundary
\B	Not word boundary
\d	Digit
\D	Not digit
\e	Escape
\f	Form feed
\n	Newline
\r	Carriage return
\s	Space character (space, \t, \n, \r, \f)
\S	Not space character
\t	Tab
\w	Word
\W	Not word
\oNN	Octal
\xNN	Hexadecimal
\cC	Control character

NOTE

The meta-characters listed in Table 16.2 are discussed later in the chapter. Many of these are convenience meta-characters that can be used instead of atom lists. Atom lists are also described later in this chapter.

For example, to match a telephone number, you need to match a pattern that is made up of parentheses, dashes, and digits. If you want to match all the phone numbers with the area code 800 in the phone book, your regular expression pattern might look like this:

```
\(800\) \d\d\d-\d\d\d\d
```

This pattern would match a number like (800) 374-0891. Escape characters are used to change the left and right parentheses meta-characters to their standard, uninteresting character format. The \d is an example of an alternative regular expression formed by pairing the escape character with the letter *d*. It matches a single digit.

In summary, the escape character has two main uses:

- It provides a means of matching meta-characters within a regular expression.

- It allows you to match a pattern of characters or numbers.

The next section, which covers matching an atom a specific number of times, shows another example of using the escape character in a regular expression.

Matching a Number of Times

All those \d codes in the pattern used to match 800 numbers (in the previous example) make my eyes cross. Another form for that pattern uses minimum and maximum values, like this:

```
\(800\) \d{3}-\d{4}
```

This pattern is easier to read than the one that includes a \d for each digit. The left and right parentheses meta-characters are escaped (\(and \)) as in the previous version, so the pattern must begin with (800) followed by a space character. The pattern must then be three digits (\d{3}), followed by a dash and then four digits (\d{4}). The new phone number pattern is controlled by the match quantifiers ({ }), which can take the forms shown in Table 16.3.

TABLE 16.3: Match Quantifiers

Quantifier	Meaning
{matchNumber}	The preceding atom must occur exactly *matchNumber* of times.
{minimum,}	The preceding atom must occur at least *minimum* number of times.
{minimum,maximum}	The preceding atom must occur at least *minimum* number of times, up to and including *maximum* number of times.

When you see the opening curly brace following an atom in a regular expression, you know the atom will be restricted in the number of times it may be repeated. That restriction is an exact match when the curly brace pair contains only a single number (as in the 800 number match pattern above). When the match quantifier contains a number followed by a comma, the match quantifier tells Perl 5 to match the previous atom by some range of numbers.

When a comma follows the first number, the number becomes a minimum match value. The maximum value is not required and defaults to infinity. For example, to match three or more digits, use this form:

    \d{3,}

If you want to match from one to five digits, use the minimum and maximum atom quantifiers, like this:

    \d{1,5}

This pattern says to match at least one digit but no more than five digits in a row.

The match quantifiers give you a way to match a pattern a specific number of times. In the next section, you'll learn about three meta-characters that provide a convenient way to achieve what can be done explicitly with the minimum and maximum quantifiers.

NOTE   Remember that meta-characters have no meaning by themselves. Meta-characters must be paired with the atom you are trying to match.

Matching Zero, One, or Infinity

There is an axiom in computer science: All rules should apply in zero, one, or infinity cases. The intent of this rule is to limit conditions that may occur eight, three, or some other less controllable number of times. Without this rule, your code becomes sprinkled with special conditional checks and your code becomes brittle—easy to break and hard to maintain.

Perl 5 provides three special meta-characters to deal with the match quantifiers of zero, one, or infinity, as listed in Table 16.4.

TABLE 16.4: Zero, One, or Infinity Match Quantifiers

Quantifier	Alternative	Meaning
*	{0,}	Match zero or more occurrences of the preceding atom.
?	{0,1}	Match zero or one occurrences of the preceding atom.
+	{1,}	Match one or more occurrences of the preceding atom.

If you use the zero-or-more quantifiers with the any character meta-character (.) at the beginning of a regular expression, your regular expression will match the entire line. The regular expression engine finds the longest possible string it can match, and then begins backtracking trying to find the first valid pattern match. This is called a *greedy match*. As the regular expression is processed, the zero-or-more quantifier tries to take as much of the pattern as possible. The zero-or-one quantifier (?) can be used to change this action by making the regular expression engine match the first valid pattern. As the regular expression is processed, the zero-or-one quantifier stops the regular expression engine as soon as it finds a match. This type of pattern match is called a short-circuit or *lazy match*.

Listing 16.2 demonstrates some of the effects of zero-or-more and zero-or-one quantifiers. Figure 16.1 shows its output.

Listing 16.2:   Greedy Matches

```
1.  $p="pattern";
2.  #A greedy match matches the entire pattern
3.  $p =~ /(.*)/;
```

```
4.   print "1==>$1<==\n";
5.   #This match allows zero "t"s to be matched. The first piece of
6.   #the regular expression matches the entire line
7.   $p =~ /.*(t*).*/;
8.   print "1==>$1<==\n";
9.   #This match makes the zero or more quantifier match the
10.  #smallest possible string, leaving two "t"s for the greedy match
11.  $p =~ /.*?(t+).*?/;
12.  print "1==>$1<==\n";
13.  #This match makes each quantifier match the smallest possible
14.  #string, which means only one "t" is required for a match
15.  $p =~ /.*?(t+?).*?/;
16.  print "1==>$1<==\n";
```

FIGURE 16.1:

Controlling greedy matches

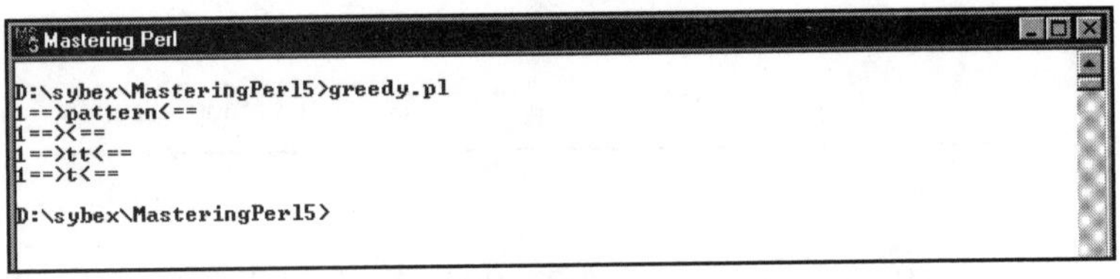

```
Mastering Perl

D:\sybex\MasteringPer15>greedy.pl
1==>pattern<==
1==>< ==
1==>tt<==
1==>t<==

D:\sybex\MasteringPer15>
```

Listing 16.3 demonstrates the use of some of the alternate meaning ASCII characters with the zero, one, or infinity quantifiers. Figure 16.2 shows its output.

Listing 16.3:   Zero, One, or Infinity Pattern Match

```
1.   $p = "This is a pattern test.";
2.   $spacer = "=" x 60;
3.   print "$spacer\n";
4.   #Match the first alphanumeric character
5.   if ($p =~ /(\w)/){ print "$1\n"; }
6.   #Match the one or more alphanumerics. This pattern and the next
7.   #pattern match the s because Perl tries to match the longest
8.   #pattern first and then backs up. The space character after
9.   #this ends the pattern (\w)* and (\w)+ pattern
10.  if ($p =~ /(\w)*/){ print "$1\n"; }
11.  if ($p =~ /(\w)+/){ print "$1\n"; }
12.  #Match zero or one characters
```

```
13. if ($p =~ /(\w)?/){ print "$1\n"; }
14. print "$spacer\n";
15. #Match an alphanumeric followed by a single space character
16. if ($p =~ /(\w\s)/){ print "$1\n"; }
17. #Match any number of alphanumerics followed
18. #by a single space character
19. if ($p =~ /(\w*\s)/){ print "$1\n"; }
20. #Match at least one alphanumeric followed
21. #by a single space character
22. if ($p =~ /(\w+\s)/){ print "$1\n"; }
23. #Match one or zero alphanumerics followed
24. #by a single space character
25. if ($p =~ /(\w?\s)/){ print "$1\n"; }
26. print "$spacer\n";
27. if ($p =~ /(\w\s)/){ print "$1\n"; }
28. #Match the pattern inside the parentheses any number of times
29. #Match any number of alphanumerics followed by a space character
30. #This pattern and the next pattern match the word pattern
31. #because Perl tries to match the longest pattern first and
32. #then backs up. Perl matches all the words followed by spaces
33. #and then returns the first solution it backs through
34. if ($p =~ /(\w*\s)*/){ print "$1\n"; }
35. if ($p =~ /(\w+\s)+/){ print "$1\n"; }
36. #Any empty line matches here
37. if ($p =~ /(\w?\s)?/){ print "$1\n"; }
38. print "$spacer\n";
```

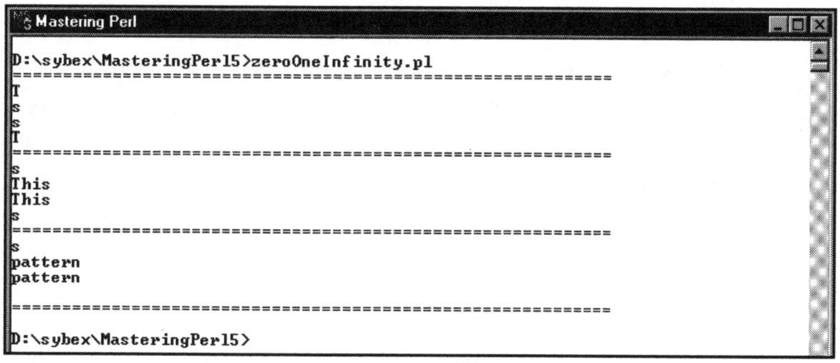

FIGURE 16.2:

Using the zero, one, or infinity match quantifiers

The \w meta-character pair matches any single alphanumeric character, which is any letter A through Z (lowercase or uppercase), any number 0 through 9, and the underscore. Line 5 of Listing 16.2 can be read as match the first alphanumeric character:

```
if ($p =~ /(\w)/){ print "$1\n"; }
```

The results shown in Figure 16.2 are what you would expect—line 5 matches the character T.

Line 10 indicates to match zero or more single alphanumeric characters:

```
if ($p =~ /(\w)*/){ print "$1\n"; }
```

The regular expression engine finds the longest possible match, which ends at the first space character. The engine then begins backtracking, finding the first valid match, which is the single character s. The zero-or-more quantifier (*) will always match the last valid pattern in the string.

Line 13 shows the effect of the zero-or-one quantifier (?) on the regular expression engine:

```
if ($p =~ /(\w)?/){ print "$1\n"; }
```

Instead of finding the longest possible match and then backtracking to find the first valid match, the regular expression engine searches from the front of the string for the first valid pattern.

Notice that the last line of Figure 16.2 is an empty string, which is produced by line 37 of Listing 16.3. The zero-or-more quantifier matches the longest possible string that will satisfy the regular expression. It searches the string finding all occurrences in a row of zero or more alphanumeric characters followed by a white space character. It then backtracks, returning the last valid pattern. The outer zero-or-one quantifier changes the search criteria, searching for the first occurrence of the atom, which is zero or one alphanumeric characters, followed by a white space character. Because it matches the first valid pattern, an empty string is a valid match. This is a case where the length of the back reference variable is actually zero. The pattern matches, but it contains no value.

Matching the Beginning and End of Lines

If you want to match a pattern at the beginning or end of a line, use the beginning-of-line meta-character (^) or the end-of-line meta-character ($).

The beginning-of-line marker should be placed in front of any atom you want to match at the start of a string. To match a pattern at the beginning of a line, use this syntax:

```
/^pattern/
```

For example, to match the word *This* at the beginning of the line in the string:

```
"This is the first this is this string of this"
```

use this pattern:

```
/^This/
```

The end-of-line marker should be placed at the end of any atom you want to match at the end of a string. To match a pattern at the end of a line, use this syntax:

```
/pattern$/
```

For example, to match the word *this* at the end of the line shown above, use this pattern:

```
/this$/
```

NOTE   The end-of-line marker can be confused with the scalar variable symbol ($). Scalar variables can be used in regular expressions, so the only time the end-of-line marker is valid as a meta-character in a regular expression is when it is physically the last thing in the regular expression or when it is followed immediately by a closing parenthesis or vertical bar.

Both of these meta-characters take on an alternative meaning based on context. When used inside the square brackets (the list meta-character) at the beginning of the list, the beginning-of-line marker negates the items in the list. For example, to match the first word in the same string used in the previous examples that was not *This*, use this pattern:

```
print "Does not contain THIS" if "This" =~ /[^this]/i;
```

You'll learn more about the list meta-character shortly.

Matching Any Character

Unlike the other meta-characters, the "any" meta-character (.) acts as an atom. The any meta-character matches every character except the newline character (\n), using this syntax:

```
/./
```

To match a single line of input excluding the newline character, use this pattern:

`/.*/`

You'll see some practical uses for the any meta-character later in this chapter, in the "Electronic Commerce Matches" section.

Matching One of Several Patterns

If you want to match any one of several possible alternatives, use the OR operator (|). The OR operator can be placed between two or more alternative patterns, directing the regular expression engine to match the first of the pattern alternatives it finds in the input search string. The pattern match begins from left to right. The first pattern to match ends the search. The syntax of the OR operator is:

`/pattern_1| pattern_2| pattern_3| pattern_n/`

WARNING   The OR operator should be used with discretion. The regular expression engine must search the entire input string for each pattern in the OR list until it finds a match. This can slow down your code if the input string is long, the OR pattern list is long, or the number of times the pattern is matched is frequent. If you can build a single pattern with meta-characters that includes the patterns of the OR list, your code will execute faster. For example, the pattern `/[abc]/` is faster than `/a|b|c/`.

Examples of using the OR meta-character are in the "Ignore Case Matches" and "A Whole Word Match" sections, later in this chapter.

Matching Lists

If you are trying to match the letters of the alphabet or several numbers or names, the list meta-character (`[]`) will solve your problems. Unlike parentheses, the list meta-character does not create atoms. The list meta-character creates a list of alternative atoms. Repeated atoms inside the list meta-character are ignored. The syntax of the list meta-character is:

`/[atomList]/`

The list meta-character will match the first atom of the atom list. For example, if you used this pattern:

`/[STEVE]/`

the match will include parts of SAM, VERONICA, STEVE, ETHEL, and TOM, because it is searching for one of the following: S, T, E, or V. The second E in the atom list STEVE is ignored because it repeats a previous atom. The atom list is processed one atom at a time. Each atom of the pattern is checked against the atom list. The first atom in the pattern to match one of the atoms in list stops at the S. If the patterns SAM, VERONICA, STEVE, ETHEL, and TOM were processed in order, the matched list would be SVSET.

You can think of the list meta-characters as acting like a continuous escape meta-character exclusively for the other meta-characters. Other meta-characters lose their special meaning inside the list meta-characters ([]). The exceptions to this rule are the beginning-of-line meta-character (^), the escape meta-character, and the range operator (-).

You can list a range of atoms inside the list meta-character without listing every atom in that range by using the range operator. To match a range of numbers, specify the minimum number, followed by the range operator, followed by the maximum number, like this:

```
/[minimum-maximum]/
```

For example, if you want to match the numbers 4, 5, 6, 7, and 8, you can use this pattern:

```
/[4-8]/
```

The range operator also works with characters. The smallest character is the uppercase *A*, and the largest character is the lower case *z*, using the ASCII character set values. To match any one of the letters of the alphabet, either uppercase or lowercase, use this pattern:

```
/[A-z]/
```

The beginning-of-line meta-character acts as a negation operator when used as the first character inside the list meta-character. When the beginning-of-line meta-character is the first character in the list, the list is negated. For example, to match everything except a lowercase letter, do this:

```
[^a-z]
```

The beginning-of-line meta-character loses any special meaning when it is used in a position other than the first position inside the list meta-character. This makes the list meta-character an excellent means of searching for meta-characters in an input string, as you learned earlier in this chapter. The following pattern matches the first meta-character in the input string:

```
/[{}()^.*+?]/
```

The escape character (\) maintains its meta-meaning inside the list meta-characters. To match the list meta-characters themselves, you must use the escape meta-character, like this:

```
[\[\]]
```

The escape character also works with the set of special-meaning characters, which are explained in the next section.

Using Special-Meaning Characters

Regular expressions are used to match all kinds of patterns, but the two most common patterns are digits and alphanumeric characters. Perl 5 provides several special characters that let you match a range of atoms:

- The \d meta-character, as you've seen in previous examples, matches any digit from zero to nine. Its equivalent is [0-9].

- The \D meta-character matches anything but from zero to nine. Its equivalent is [^0-9].

- The \s meta-character matches any white space character (tab, form feed, carriage return, space, and newline characters). Its equivalent is [\f\n\r\t].

- The \S meta-character matches any character but a white space character. Its equivalent is [^\f\n\r\t].

- The \w meta-character matches any alphanumeric character, including the underscore. Its equivalent is [a-zA-Z0-9_].

- The \W meta-character matches any character but an alphanumeric character, including the underscore. Its equivalent is [^a-zA-Z0-9_].

- The \b meta-character matches on the word boundary. A *word boundary* is defined as the position between two word characters (\w) that is not a word character (\W), which means that \b matches the position between the \w and \W in \w\W\w.

- The \B meta-character matches not on a word boundary.

- The \oNN meta-character matches octal numbers.

- The \xNN meta-character matches hexadecimal numbers.

- The \cC meta-character matches control characters.

Notice that each of the special characters is just a convenience code for ranges available in the list meta-characters. But convenience is a very nice thing. Also notice that each code has an opposite. The lowercase code is used to match a particular set of values. The uppercase code is used to find every character that is not in the list. For example, if you want to find a number, you use \d. If you want to find everything that isn't a number, use \D.

Pattern-Match Variables

Every regular expression includes three special variables that provide additional information about the results of your pattern match:

- The characters matched by your regular expression are in the special variable $&.

- The characters that preceded the characters matched by your regular expression are in the special variable $`.

- The characters that followed the characters matched by your regular expression are in the special variable $'.

The Perl interpreter assigns values to these variables only if you use them in your code. This means that the overhead associated with these variables exists only if you use them. Once you use any one of these pattern-match variables anywhere in your program, the Perl interpreter will continue to assign values to them, even if they are never used again. This means that once you have decided to use one of the pattern-match variables, you can use them throughout your code without paying any additional performance penalty.

Listing 16.4 uses the prematch ($`) and postmatch ($') variables to decode an input string. The decoding is positionally dependent on the results of the previous action. Each time a pattern is found, a new set of possibilities or states exists for the remaining portion of the input string. Data is extracted from the variable $limitedID during each pass through the while loop. The value of $limitedID is reset using the postmatch variable each time through the loop. The loop continues until all of $limitedID has been processed or there is an explicit exit by the last statement at the end of the loop. This program is part of a larger electronic commerce program that decodes formatted electronic commerce messages, which is discussed in more detail later in this chapter.

Listing 16.4:   **The Prematch and Postmatch Variables**

```perl
1.   #!/usr/local/bin/perl
2.   #
3.   foreach $limitedID (@limitedIDList){
4.       #This is an ordered search. The possibilities are:
5.       #(digit) : 0 or 1
6.       #* : 0 or 1
7.       #LIST of IDS : 0 or many - comma separated
8.       #{IDLIST} : 0 or 1
9.       #IDLIST : 0 or many IDS - comma separated
10.      while ($limitedID){
11.          #Look for text ordinal, save it and save remaining.
12.          #Possible matching input is (D), (D)*, (D)*{ID,
13.          #(D){ID, (D)ID{, (D)ID and some other permutations
14.          #Remaining could be *, *{}, *{ID, ID{, ID
15.          #STATE 1 LOOKING FOR TEXT ORDINAL
16.          if ($limitedID =~ /\((\d+)\)/){
17.              $limitedID = $';
18.              $textOrdinal = $1;
19.              next;
20.          }
21.          #Look for *
22.          #Possible matching input is *, *{, *{ID
23.          #Remaining could be {, {ID
24.          #STATE 2 LOOKING FOR ALL DED
25.          if ($limitedID =~ /(\*)/){
26.              $limitedID = $';
27.              $allDED = TRUE;
28.              next;
29.          }
30.          #Look for {,
31.          #Possible input is {ID, or {}
32.          #Remaining could be  }
33.          #STATE 3 LOOKING FOR {
34.          if ($limitedID =~ /[{]/){
35.              if ($`){
36.                  $IDString .= " $`";
37.              }
```

```
38.              $limitedID = $';
39.              $additionalIDs = TRUE;
40.              next;
41.          }
42.          #Look for ID,
43.          #Possible input is ID, ID{, or ID}, or ID{ID
44.          #Remaining could be { or } or {ID
45.          #STATE 4 LOOKING FOR ID
46.          if ($limitedID =~ /(\w+)/){
47.              $IDString .= " $1" ;
48.              $limitedID = $';
49.              next;
50.          }
51.          #Look for },
52.          #Possible input is  }
53.          #Remaining should be  empty
54.          if ($limitedID =~ /[}]/){
55.              last;
56.          }
57.          #CLEANUP - REMOVE TRASH SPACES
58.          $limitedID =~ s/\s+//g;
59.      }#end WHILE
60. #end foreach
```

Line 16 is looking for a numeric ID surrounded by parentheses. If the ID is found, the value is saved into $textOrdinal for later processing. The value of $limitedId is set to the remainder of the pattern, then the while loop is executed again using the next statement on line 19:

```
if ($limitedID =~ /\((\d+)\)/){
    $limitedID = $';
    $textOrdinal = $1;
    next;
}
```

This type of processing continues with each of the various states, extracting some information from the $limitedID. State 3 makes sure that data before the pattern match isn't lost. If any data is found in the prematch variable, it is saved into the $IDString.

```
if ($`){
    $IDString .= " $`";
}
```

It's relatively unusual to need either the prematch or postmatch variable in your code. However, as demonstrated in Listing 16.4, they can be useful for special purposes.

Pattern Modifiers

Regular expressions can be as complex or as simple as you choose to make them. In the previous section, you learned about several convenience codes that simplify regular expressions. Pattern modifiers can not only simplify your regular expression, but also make your regular expression more efficient and even return a list all of the occurrences of a pattern in the input string (this sounds a bit like an infomercial: "It slices, it dices, it even purees.")

The pattern modifiers are not really part of your regular expression. The pattern modifiers are appended to your regular expression, after the trailing delimiter. The pattern modifiers affect the entire regular expression. For example, you can change the regular expression so that it ignores case, matches across the entire input string instead of just the first occurrence, or compiles the regular expression so it is only evaluated the first time it is encountered.

There are six pattern modifiers: g (Global), i (Ignore case), m (Multiple lines), o (Only once), s (Single line), and x (eXtra spaces). Each of these is described in the following sections.

Global Matches

The global match modifier (g) modifies the number of times your regular expression is applied to the input string. A regular expression, by default, finds the longest single pattern match and stops. The global match modifier makes your regular expression match every occurrence of the pattern in the input string. Like many Perl 5 operators, the global match modifier operates differently based on context:

- The global match modifier in list context returns each occurrence of the pattern.

- The global match modifier in scalar context returns true for each occurrence of the pattern.

When the global match modifier is used in list context, your regular expression will return every occurrence of the pattern. The list context syntax of the global match modifier is:

```
@matchList = ($searchString =~/pattern/g);
```

Each occurrence of the pattern is saved into in its own cell in the array `@match-List`. Using this format, you can both capture each occurrence of the pattern and count the total number of occurrences of the pattern. The array `@matchList` contains each of the patterns. In scalar context, the array contains the number of occurrences of the pattern, like this:

```
$numberOfPatterns = @matchList;
```

You can also capture just a piece of the pattern matched by placing parentheses around the portion of the string you want to save. Each matched occurrence of the pattern within the parentheses will be returned. Everything outside the parentheses will be used as part of the regular expression, but only the pattern matched within the parentheses will be returned for you to save. (This mechanism uses the syntax you learned in the back reference variable section.)

When the global match modifier is used in scalar context, it traverses the input string one match at a time. Each match of the pattern returns true. The next time the pattern is matched against the input string, the global match modifier begins processing immediately after the position of the last match. If you only want to count the number of times a pattern is found, you can do this:

```
$count = 0
while ($searchString =~ /pattern/g) {
        $count ++;
}
```

The variable `$searchString` will be searched for the pattern from left to right. Each time the pattern is found, the value true is returned. If there are ten occurrences of the pattern in `$searchString`, your code will go through the `while` loop ten times.

Ignore Case Matches

The ignore case modifier (i) changes each alphabetical atom in the pattern so that it matches both uppercase and lowercase letters.

The ignore case modifier is great for text searches. For example, if you want to search for all occurrences of the word *this*, you could write:

```
/[Tt]his/
```

This pattern would find all occurrences of *this* that begin with an uppercase or lowercase *T*. On the other hand, you could use a pattern like this:

```
/This/i
```

Not only does this simplify your code, but this pattern also matches any case spelling of the word *this*, including typing errors like *tHis* or *THIS*.

The ignore case modifier also comes in handy when you're getting user input, especially from a question where you expect a yes or no response. For yes/no questions, use a pattern like this:

```
/(y(es)?|N(o)?)/i
```

With this pattern, your user can input a single Y or N in both uppercase and lower case. If your user wants to respond with a complete Yes or yes or YES, they also will be accepted by your pattern.

Multiple and Single Line Matches

When you're processing user input from the HTML text area tag, your data can come in a single line or in multiple lines. All of the data will be in one single variable associated with the text area tag. You could preprocess the user input looking for newline characters, or you could just tell your regular expression to ignore the newlines in `$searchString`. To ignore newline characters in a search string, do this:

```
/pattern/s
```

As you learned in the last chapter the substitute function uses the pattern operator. If your input has multiple lines and you want to convert that input to an HTML output with the same line format, do this:

```
$input =~ s/\n/<BR>/gs;
```

Each newline character will be converted to an HTML newline break command. If you want to treat the input string as a multiple-line string, do this:

```
/pattern/m
```

This helps when looking for the beginning and end of a line that may have embedded newline characters, as in this example:

```perl
$input = "This\nis\none\nscalar\n\object.\n That has multiple lines\n";
print "Matched object\n" if $input =~ m/^object/m;
print "Matched scalar\n" if $input =~ m/scalar$/m;
print "Matched scalar\n" if $input =~ m/^scalar/m;
```

In this example, the input text has embedded newline characters. Newline characters can be embedded into text when transferring text between e-mail programs and other nonstandard text readers. Each of the above lines matches because the input is treated as multiple lines. If you remove the m modifier from the pattern, the input does not match.

Only Once Please

Each time a regular expression is evaluated, Perl 5 takes some time to interpret the regular expression. If your pattern contains a variable and it is used inside a loop, Perl 5 must interpret that pattern each time through the loop. If the variable inside the pattern isn't changing each time through the loop, this is very inefficient. You can speed up your program by adding the interpret only once modifier (o) to your regular expression, like this:

```perl
/pattern/o
```

The only once pattern modifier compiles your regular expression the first time it is encountered by the Perl 5 interpreter.

WARNING   Having told you how to make your program more efficient, I now want to scream "Danger Will Robinson!" I'm afraid, however, that I would only be showing my age and not getting my point across. Be careful with this feature; you can end up creating a bug that is difficult to locate. When you use this modifier, be sure that the pattern will *never* change.

When I said Perl 5 will only interpret the regular expression once, I meant one time only for the entire program. If your regular expression is inside a subroutine, it will be interpreted the first time the subroutine is called and not again. Each subsequent time the subroutine is called, the value determined for the pattern the first time the subroutine was called will be used. This can be a useful feature, but be sure you know what you're doing.

Extra Spaces and Comments

The extra spaces and comments pattern modifier (x) has no effect on the pattern-matching capabilities of your regular expression. The extra spaces and comments modifier allows you to insert spaces and comments within your regular expression.

Regular expressions can be hard to read and understand. You can add comments to your regular expression with the extra spaces and comments modifier. You can add the comment character (#) to your regular expression using the same rules that apply to comments in your code. This means that everything after the comment character will be ignored.

For example, adding comments changes this regular expression:

```
if ($DED[$i] =~ /^$element\s+(\".*\")\s+(\w+)\s+(\d+)\s+(\d+)/){
```

to this more understandable regular expression:

```
if ($DED[$i] =~ /^$element\s+
(\".*\")\s+    #element description
(\w+)\s+       #element type
(\d+)\s+       #minimum value
(\d+)          #maximum value
/x){
```

If spacing is not important to your pattern and your pattern looks a bit cramped, the extra spaces and comments modifier allows you to separate your pattern atoms with spaces. All spaces are ignored in the regular expression pattern during the pattern-match operation. If your expression needs spaces, they can be added using the escape meta-character or by using the list meta-character, as illustrated here:

```
/T h i s [ ] i s [ ] i t/x
```

The spaces between the letters will be ignored. The spaces after each s are required and are included in the regular expression using the list meta-character.

Now you're finally finished with the components and rules for regular expressions and pattern modifiers. You need to know the rules, but if you don't feel comfortable with regular expressions, you probably won't use them. That would be a terrible shame. The rest of this chapter is devoted to practical examples of regular expressions and patterns.

Regular Expression Examples

You may have skipped over the first part of this chapter and began reading here. This is the good part, where you see the power of regular expressions in action. As you work through the examples, you will run across meta-characters, special meaning codes, and pattern modifiers, which were discussed earlier in the chapter. Even if you've read straight through to here, you should take the time to refer back to the early parts of this chapter so you can match the examples with the details of the rules.

The examples presented in the following sections teach you how to work with and interpret regular expressions. The first example is a simple pattern, which is expanded to a whole word search pattern in the next example. The other examples include code from an electronic commerce program and a global lazy match pattern.

A Simple Pattern

This section's example is just a series of alphabetical characters in a particular pattern. However, even a simple pattern like the following one has something to teach you.

```
/verse/
```

This pattern is made up of the five atoms: v, e, r, s, e. When this pattern is tested against an input search string, each atom is checked for its existence in the input string. As each atom is matched, the next atom is checked for its occurrence next to the previous atom. The input search string can be from one of two sources:

- The search string may be assigned using the binding operator (=~), like this:

```
$searchString = ~ /verse/
```

- If no search string is supplied, the default special variable $_ is tested for the pattern.

Perl 5 searches the search string from left to right trying to match the first atom in the pattern. When the first atom is matched, Perl 5 looks at the next atom in the pattern and then checks the search string. The search stops when the pattern is matched. In this example, the pattern matches any occurrence of the characters *v*, *e*, *r*, *s*, and *e* in a row. That means that this search string matches *conversely* as well as *verse* but does not match *Verse*.

In the next section, we'll take this basic pattern and build upon it to match just the word.

A Whole Word Match

A common task is to match a specific word inside a text document. To match just the word *verse*, you might consider surrounding the pattern with a check for white space characters, like this:

```
/\s+verse\s+/
```

The \s matches white space characters (tab, newline, form feed, and carriage return characters). The plus sign (+) tells the Perl 5 interpreter to match at least one of the previous atom, which is the white space character in this example. This pattern will match the word *verse* anywhere within a sentence, even at the end of a line, but it will not match at the end of a sentence like "It was a book of verse." This is because the period following *verse* is not a white space character. To match *verse* at the end of a sentence, you need to tell the Perl 5 interpreter to look for sentence ending punctuation marks: a period, a question mark, or an exclamation point.

The previous pattern also ignores sentence punctuation, such as the comma and semicolon. It would not match the word *verse* in a sentence like "You will write in verse, and only in verse, for this assignment."

A more complete pattern might look like this:

```
/(^|\s+)verse[\s,.!?;]/i
```

Somehow, the simple pattern /verse/ has begun to look like cryptography! Fear not, noble programmer, interpreting this regular expression is a snap!

The trick is to keep breaking down the regular expression until it's small enough to manage. This pattern breaks down into three manageable parts:

1. /i
2. [\s,!.?;]
3. (^|\s+)

First, the /i pattern modifier says ignore case. Any alphabetical characters in the pattern will match both uppercase and lowercase letters.

The second piece uses the list meta-character [], which creates a list of atom alternatives. Each item in the list is viewed by the interpreter as a candidate for a match. The list is particularly useful in this case because we want to match punctuation characters that normally double as meta-characters. Meta-characters lose the meta-meaning inside the list meta-character. However, the loss of meta-ness does not apply to the special-meaning characters like the white space character (\s). The special-meaning characters are preceded by the escape meta-character (\), which retains its meta-meaning inside the list meta-character. Inside the list meta-characters, we list all of the punctuation characters that might follow *verse*.

The third piece uses parentheses, which create a single atom made up of the pattern inside the parentheses. This means that the regular expression inside the parentheses is the first thing the interpreter must match. The beginning-of-line meta-character (^) means that anything following this meta-character must be the first item in the string. This takes care of the case, when *verse* is the first word of the sentence. The \s+ says to match at least one white space character. This handles the other cases when *verse* is a single word inside a sentence. Since both of these cases cannot be true at the same time, the OR meta-character (|) separates the two choices. This means that the regular expression will be matched when either case is true.

TIP

> Breaking a regular expression into each of its atoms and then solving the problem one atom at a time works for building regular expressions as well as decoding them. You shouldn't try to build the entire regular expression in one pass. Take each part of the input pattern and build an atom to match that part. As you work through each atom, combine them to create the final regular expression.

Now you may be wondering why I didn't use the list meta-characters for the third piece of the pattern, as I did for the second piece. The simple answer is it doesn't work! That is because the beginning-of-line meta-character (^) has a different meaning inside the list meta-characters. When the beginning-of-line meta-character is the first item inside the list meta-characters, it means match any atom except the atoms in this list. When the beginning-of-line meta-character is placed at any position other than the first position inside the list meta-characters, it loses its meta-ness and becomes a character atom. This means that if you are trying to match several alternatives and one of them is the beginning-of-string condition, you need to use the parentheses atom creator and the OR operator to create your own list of alternatives.

Electronic Commerce Patterns

This example presented in this section is a subroutine that is part of a larger electronic commerce program. Unlike the previous examples, the input to the regular expressions of Listing 16.5 is not a fixed word or sequence of letters. These regular expressions are matching patterns of characters and numbers. This subroutine, as part of a larger translation program, decodes formatted input strings. It illustrates the use of back reference variables and the binding operator, as well as using regular expressions to solve real-world problems.

Listing 16.5:   **The Decode Segment Subroutine**

```
1.   sub decodeSegment(){
2.      my ($sgmt, $sectionNumber) = @_;
3.      my $beginOfSegment = 1;
4.      #Is there something in the front of this segment?
5.      if ($sgmt =~ /(.+)\[/){
6.          decodeSegmentFront($1);
7.      }
8.      else {
9.          $beginOfLoop = 0;
10.     }
11.
12.     if ($sgmt =~ /\[(\w+)/){
13.         $sgmtName = $1;
14.     }
15.
16.     #if . then segment is not used
17.     if ($sgmt =~ /\[\./){
18.         $sgmtUsed = 0;
19.         if ($beginOfLoop){
20.             $loopUsed = 0;
21.             #Variable reset inside decodeSegmentFront because
22.             #loopCount frequently decremented/incremented together
23.             #loop that is not supposed to be used may be skipped
24.             $loopNotUsed = $loopCount;
25.         }
26.     }
27.     else {
28.         $sgmtUsed = 1;
29.     }
```

```
30.    ($sgmtNum, $rqrmt, $max) = split(/,/,$sgmt);
31.    if ($rqrmt){
32.        if ($rqrmt =~ /\]/){chop $rqrmt;}
33.        }
34.    else {$rqrmt = "0";}
35.    if ($max) {
36.        if ($max =~ /\]/){chop $max;}
37.        if ($max =~ />1/){$max = $MAX;}
38.    }
39.    else{$max = 1;}
40.    if ($loopMax =~ />1/){$loopMax = $MAX;}
41.
42.    #Get mask or new ordinal number
43.    if ($sgmt =~ /\[(\w+)([*@]\d+)/){
44.        $mask = $2;
45.        if ($mask =~ /(\@)(\d+)/) {
46.            $ordinal = $2;
47.            $ordinalSet = 1;
48.        }
49.    }
50.    else {
51.        undef $mask;
52.    }
53.    $level = $loopCount + $levelOffset;
54.    $ordinalOffset = ($sectionNumber +1) * 1000;
55.    $ordinal += $ordinalIncrement unless $ordinalSet;
56.    $ordinalSet = 0;
57.    $ordinalCount = $ordinal +$ordinalOffset;
58.
59.    if ($beginOfLoop && loopUsed){
60.        $positionID = $ordinalCount . "L";
61.        $savedMax = $max;
62.        $max = $loopMax;
63.        $fieldName = "SegmentLoopDescriptor";
64.        $class = "SegmentLoop";
65.        write;
66.    }
67.    if ($beginOfSegment && $loopUsed && $sgmtUsed){
68.        $positionID = $ordinalCount . "S";
69.        if ($beginOfLoop && loopUsed) {$max = $savedMax;}
70.        $fieldName = "SegmentDescriptor";
71.        $class = "Segment";
```

```
72.        write;
73.        decodeSegmentFields($sgmtName);
74.    }
75. }
76. format STDOUT_TOP =
77. Level Position ID Name   Min     Max   Class
                          Descriptor Class  Constraints
78. .
79. format STDOUT =
80. @>>>> @>>>>>>>>>   @>>> @>>> @>>>>>   @<<<<<<<< @
                       >>>>>>>>>>>>>>>>@>>,@>>>,@>>>>;
81. $level,$positionID,$sgmtName,$min,$max,$class, $fieldName
                       $rqrmt,$minLength, $maxLength
82. .
83.
```

Each input string in Listing 16.5 is made up of a list within the list meta-characters ([]). The data inside the list meta-characters must be processed individually. The data preceding the first list meta-characters contains information that affects the entire list.

Each of the regular expressions in Listing 16.5 is used within a conditional expression. The pattern-match function (//) returns a 1 if it finds a match for its regular expression or a 0 if no match is found. When the pattern is matched, the conditional expression passes. When the pattern is not matched, the conditional expression fails. As you can see in Listing 16.5, this feature is used to determine when to call subroutines, to set variable names, and to make other logic choices.

When the pattern is matched, the portion of the pattern that is surrounded by parentheses is captured in a back reference variable. As you learned earlier in the chapter, a back reference variable contains the characters of the input string that matched the corresponding portion of the regular expression surrounded by parentheses.

The patterns in Listing 16.5 also use the binding operator (=~) to have the pattern-match function match against something other than the default variable ($_). The binding operator binds the operator on the right side of the binding operator to the variable on the left side of the binding operator.

The following sections explain four of the regular expressions in Listing 16.5.

Matching Any Characters Followed by a Bracket

The first regular expression, beginning on line 5 of Listing 16.5, is checking for any information that might come before the first square bracket:

```
if ($sgmt =~ /(.+)\[/){
    decodeSegmentFront($1) ;
}
```

This regular expression has two main atoms: (.+) and \[.

Of the two atoms, I think the second one is the easiest to solve, so using the rule of solving the easiest problem first, let's get it out of the way. Because the square bracket ([) is a meta-character, you cannot include it in a pattern match without the escape character (\) in front of it. The escape character causes the first part of the list meta-character to lose its meta-ness. The regular expression's second atom, \[, is simply looking for a right square bracket ([).

The first atom is made up of the two atoms enclosed in the parentheses: the period (.) and the plus sign (+). The period is a meta-character that matches any character except the newline character. The + is the one or more quantifier, which must be paired with a previous character. It says there must be at least one but can be many more of the characters with which it is paired. Together, these two meta-characters can be read as "Match one or more of any character."

If you put the two main atoms together, they read "Match one or more of any characters followed by a square right bracket."

Because this example uses the binding operator, the pattern on line 5 of Listing 16.5 is matching against the variable $sgmt, which was passed to this subroutine on line 2.

Also in this example, one back reference variable, named $1, is created and then passed on line 6 to the subroutine decodeSegmentFront().

Matching Alphanumeric Characters Following a Bracket

The second regular expression begins on line 12 of Listing 16.5:

```
if ($sgmt =~ /\[(\w+)/){
    $sgmtName = $1;
}
```

In this example, we are looking for alphanumeric characters that follow the right square bracket ([). Our possible input strings are:

- Word and/or number, such as [MER], [P01], or [ST].

- Word and/or number, word and/or number, such as [MER,*2], [P01,0], or [ST,R].

- Word and/or number, word and/or number, number, such as [MER,*2,10], [P01,0,1], or [ST,R,5].

Because we are only interested in the first word and/or number, our regular expression needs to capture that information and can ignore the remaining information.

The pattern on line 12 breaks down into two atoms: \[and (\w+). The first atom is the same as the second atom in the pattern on line 5. It matches a right square bracket ([).

The second atom is made up of the two atoms enclosed in parentheses: \w and +. The \w atom matches any alphanumeric character and the underscore. The one-or-more modifier (+) works with the previous atom to match at least one alphanumeric character. The pattern (\w+) matches every alphanumeric character until it runs into a nonalphanumeric character, which is a comma or a left square bracket in this example.

The results of this match are saved in the back reference variable $1, which is saved for later use in the variable $sqmtName. The variable $sqmtName will end up containing patterns like MER, P01, CSH, and N1.

Matching Escaped Characters

The regular expression on line 17 of Listing 16.5 is another simple pattern match:

```
if ($sgmt =~ /\[\./){
```

Both of the meta-characters that make up the two atoms of this regular expression must be escaped so that the regular expression can match their ASCII character. In this example, the escape character (\) precedes the left bracket ([) and the period (.), so they lose their meta-meaning.

Matching Symbols and Digits

Our final example from Listing 16.5, on line 43, looks complex:

```
if ($sgmt =~ /\[(\w+)([*@]\d+)/){
```

Again, to see through the complexity, break the pattern down into its parts. This example contains the following three atoms:

```
\[
(\w+)
([*@]\d+)
```

You have already seen the first and second atoms in previous examples. The third atom is new.

The third atom is a single atom because it is surrounded by parentheses. It can be broken down into the following subparts:

```
[*@]
\d+
```

The list meta-character creates a list of alternatives. Only one of the values in the list of alternatives needs to match. The first atom matched ends the search of alternatives. In our example, the regular expression is searching either for an asterisk (*) or an at sign (@).

<table>
<tr><td>**NOTE**</td><td>Remember that the list meta-characters ([]) remove the meta-ness of most meta-characters. The exception is the negation meta-character (^) and the escape meta-character (\).</td></tr>
</table>

The second subpart of the third atom matches one or more digits. The \d meta-character matches any digit, and the one-or-more quantifier (+) tells Perl 5 to find one or more occurrences of the previous atom, which is a digit.

When you put the third atom together, it reads "Find either an asterisk or an at sign followed by one or more digits."

A Globally Lazy Match

Earlier in this chapter, you learned about greedy and lazy matches. The example in this section uses the lazy match quantifier, as well as the global pattern modifier. Listing 16.6 is part of the same larger program as Listing 16.5. The code shown here gets the data ready for Listing 16.5 to decode.

Listing 16.6:   A Lazy Match

```
1.  @tables = split(/\^/, $inputVector);
2.  #First index into tables is empty because string starts with a ^
```

```
3.   for ($tableIndex = 1 ; $tableIndex <= $#tables; $tableIndex++){
4.       $section = $tables[$tableIndex];
5.       my @allFields = ($section =~ /(.*?\])/g);
6.       $sgmtSection[$sectionIndex++] = \@allFields;
7.       }
8.
9.   foreach ($segmentIndex = 0 ; $segmentIndex <= $#sgmtSection;
                  $segmentIndex++){
10.      my $nextSegmentIndex = 0;
11.      #Reset ordinal for each segment
12.      $ordinal = 0;
13.      $loopCount = 0;
14.
15.      while ($sgmtSection[$segmentIndex]->[$nextSegmentIndex]){
16.          decodeSegment($sgmtSection[$segmentIndex]->
                           [$nextSegmentIndex++],
17.                            $segmentIndex);
18.      }
19. }
```

The data is first separated into several long strings on line 1 using the `split` function. Because the first cell of the `@tables` array is empty, Listing 16.6 uses a traditional `for` loop on line 3 instead of the more Perl-like `foreach` statement. This use of the `for` loop allows the program to skip the first cell of the `@tables` array, by starting the loop at an index of 1 instead of 0.

The regular expression on line 5 of Listing 16.6 is used to prepare the input string for Listing 16.5.

```
my @allFields = ($section =~ /(.*?\])/g);
```

The input into the regular expression on line 5 is a series of square brackets with coded information both outside and inside the square brackets. In addition to decoding each of the input square bracket pieces, the position of each square bracket pair in the string, relative to the other square brackets, is important. A typical line might look like this:

```
{:150+1[ARC,0,10][BMO,,6]+5[AP]}{[QX,M]…}
```

The special problem this regular expression must solve is separating the information by square brackets and yet keeping the data together for positional decoding.

This regular expression contains only one atom, (.*?\]), which is made up of four parts:

.

*

?

\]

The period (.) is a meta-character that matches any character except the newline character. The asterisk (*) says match zero-or-more of the preceding character. The question mark (?) normally says match zero or one, but it has a special meaning when used in this context. Here, the question mark changes the matching properties of the zero-or-many modifier.

The zero-or-many meta-character normally will match the longest string possible. If this expression looked like (.*\]), without the lazy match quantifier (?), it would match as many characters as possible before terminating on a left square bracket. Since the input string includes multiple left square brackets, it would match up to the last left square bracket (]) in the string. So, without the lazy match quantifier, the regular expression would match all the way up to the QX,M] position of the input string:

```
{:150+1[ARC,0,10][BMO,,6]+5[AP]}{[QX,M]…}
```

Our regular expression needs to match up to the first occurrence of a left square bracket, which is the effect of the lazy match quantifier on the regular expression. The question mark changes the pattern matching of the zero-or-many meta-character from match the longest to match the first case.

The regular expression (.*?\]) reads "Match any character until you find the first right square bracket." In the input string shown above, it matches:

```
{:150+1[ARC, 0, 10]
```

Our regular expression actually does more than this, because it includes the global match (g) pattern modifier: /(.*?\])/g. The global match pattern modifier does not change what the regular expression matches; it just affects the number of times it matches. An unmodifed regular expression matches once per input string. The global match pattern modifier makes the regular expression match all occurrences of the pattern in the input string. In addition, because the regular expression is enclosed in parentheses, each match creates a back reference variable.

The global match modifier and the back reference operator gobble up the entire string, creating one back reference variable for each occurrence of a right square bracket. The example saves each back reference variable as it is created by providing an assignment variable for the regular expression.

You can treat the regular expression as a single operation, much like a function call that returns some information. If you place parentheses around the entire regular expression operation, the regular expression operation is treated as a single expression, which gives you the ability to save the results of the single operation. To save the data returned by the regular expression, provide an assignment operator (=) and an assignment variable. The syntax for this operation is:

```
= (regularExpression);
```

The array @allFields is assigned each back reference variable as it is created.

Summary

With regular expressions in your programming tool belt, you can write some powerful code. I avoided regular expressions for many years because they just seemed too hard. My goal in this chapter was to demystify regular expressions so that you won't make the same mistake I did.

The first parts of this chapter introduced regular expressions and their components. You learned about the pattern-match function (/m/ or //), meta-characters, atoms, and the rules for creating regular expressions. With meta-characters, you can build regular expressions that match words, digits, word boundaries, and even special characters like tabs and newlines. Patterns are made up of individual atoms. You can combine atoms to make a new atom using parentheses. You can also use quantifier meta-characters to create regular expressions that match an atom an exact number of times or a combination of minimum and maximum number of times.

Back reference variables are created when any portion of the regular expression is surrounded by parentheses. The back reference variable contains the characters of the input string that matched the corresponding portion of the regular expression surrounded by parentheses. Back reference variables are numbered sequentially from 1 to n, where n is equal to the number of pairs of parentheses in the regular expression. Back reference variables are named in sequential order, corresponding with their regular expression parentheses pair. When counting parentheses pairs, begin with the number one and count from left to right.

You can use the list meta-character ([]) to create a list of alternative atoms. Most meta-characters lose their special meaning when used in a list.

Three special variables provide additional information about the results of your pattern match: $& contains the characters matched, the prematch variable ($`) contains the characters that preceded the characters matched, and the postmatch variable (`$) contains the characters that followed the characters matched. The Perl interpreter assigns values to these variables only if you use them in your code.

After the discussion of regular expression components, you learned about pattern modifiers. Pattern modifiers change the operation of the entire regular expression. For example, the global pattern modifier (g) repeats the match for the entire input string.

At the end of the chapter, you saw some more complex, real-world examples of programming with regular expressions. You learned that to decode a regular expression, you should break it into each of its atoms and then solve the problem one atom at a time. This mechanism also works for building regular expressions.

This chapter explained the details of regular expressions, but true understanding and ease of use comes only with regular use. You should start using regular expressions in your code whenever you get the chance. Remember to take one step at a time and do the easiest stuff first. Why the easy stuff first? Well, sometimes if you do the easy stuff first, there is nothing left when you are finished with the easy stuff. Also, it can't hurt to build up your confidence before you attack something you consider hard. The fun part is when something that looked hard turns out not to be such a big deal.

PART V

Advanced Perl Programming

CHAPTER

SEVENTEEN

Jump-Start on Advanced Programming Concepts

- Package scope

- Perl 5 data scope

- Subroutine calls and parameters

- Object-oriented programming

Packages, object-oriented features, and e-mail, all wrapped up in a tight little package—that's what you get in this chapter.

This chapter starts with an explanation of Perl 5 packages and their effect on data scope. You'll then learn about subroutine calls and parameter passing. Next, you'll get an overview of Perl 5's object-oriented features. At the end of this chapter, you'll be introduced to e-mail programming.

Jump-Start Definitions

Base class	An object class that has been added to the @ISA array (Perl 5's built-in array for providing inheritance). Also called a *superclass* or *ancestor class*.
Call-by-reference	A type of subroutine parameter passing, in which the parameter list refers to the actual variable in memory.
Call-by-value	A type of subroutine parameter passing, in which the value is copied into a subroutine variable. With this type of parameter passing, the actual value is not modified by the subroutine.
Class variable	An object variable that is global to the entire package and has persistence over the life of the program.
Class	The object-oriented term for the implementation of an object. Perl 5 uses a package to implement the class concept.
Constructor	An object class method (named new by convention in Perl 5) used for object initialization and to return an object reference.

Derived class	An object class that uses the methods of base classes as part of its implementation; also called a *subclass*.
Destructor	A subroutine (named DESTROY in Perl 5) that runs just before an object is freed or deleted from memory and allows the object to perform any cleanup required before it exits.
Dynamic binding	Calling a subroutine based on runtime conditions.
Dynamically scoped variable	A Perl 5 variable, defined using the keyword local, that is visible only to the enclosing block and any subroutines called within the enclosing block.
Fully qualified name	A name that begins with the type identifier, followed by the package name, followed by two colons (::) or a single quote ('), followed by the variable name. Package variables, subroutines, and file handles can be accessed using the fully qualified package naming scheme.
Function	A reusable block of code that returns a value. Because all Perl 5 subroutines return the value of the last expression evaluated, *function* and *subroutine* are synonyms.
Global variable	A variable that is visible to your entire program. Perl 5 variables are package global by default.
Handshake	A two-step communication. One side initiates a message, and the other side acknowledges the receipt of the message.

Inheritance	In object-oriented programming, the ability to use the methods and instance variables of ancestor classes. Perl 5 provides inheritance through the @ISA array.
Instance variable	An object variable that creates a unique identity for an object. Instance variables are created and associated with each new copy of an object.
Instantiate	To create an instance of a class or class object. Each time you instantiate a class object, you create a unique memory location for the object.
Lexical variable	A Perl 5 variable, defined using the keyword my, that is visible only within the enclosing scope. Lexical variables are not part of the package's symbol table.
Method	The object-oriented term for a subroutine associated with an object. The two types of object methods are class methods, which are frequently used as a interface programs between classes, and instance methods, which are used to access an object's instance variables.
Object reference variable	A variable that contains a reference to a package-scoped anonymous hash and that has been linked with the package through the bless function. An object reference variable is required to access the unique characteristics of an individual object.
Object-oriented programming	Designing a program around data structures. The combination of class, state, and methods (implemented in packages, instance variables, and subroutines) creates a Perl 5 object.

Overloaded variable	A variable that has the same name in multiple packages.
Overwritten variable	A variable whose definition has been replaced by another declaration or definition.
Package	A Perl 5 container for separating the namespace of functions and data. The variables and subroutines of one package are distinct from another package's variables and subroutines. Each package's variables and subroutines are usable by other packages, but they reside in their own unique namespace.
Polymorphism	The ability to use the same name for multiple subroutines. Perl 5 allows you to use the same subroutine name and gives you access to that subroutine through explicit subroutine calls or dynamic binding.
`sendmail`	A communication program that sends e-mail messages to one or more recipients, routing the messages over whatever networks are necessary.
SMTP (Simple Mail Transport Protocol)	The protocol used to transmit e-mail messages across the Internet.
SMTP server	An instance of a mail program that listens for incoming e-mail messages and routes them.
Socket	A file handle that is used to provide a network connection.
Subroutine	A reusable block of code that may be called for execution by other statements in a program.

Symbol table	A list of all of the symbols that can be addressed in a program. The symbol table includes subroutine names, file handles, formats, variables, and a mechanism to retrieve the symbols' values.
Typeglob	A Perl 5 data type that is used by the symbol table to represent the different types of symbols. The type indicator of a typeglob is an asterisk (*).
Unqualified variable name	A variable's name, without any preceding package identifiers. Throughout a package, a variable can be accessed by its unqualified name.

Jump-Start Program

Listing 17.1 illustrates many of the concepts discussed in this chapter. It demonstrates the scoping rules of packages, how symbols are accessed, and how to call an ancestor class in Perl 5. Figure 17.1 shows its output.

Listing 17.1: **Package Scope**

```perl
1.  #!/usr/local/bin/perl
2.  #By default everything not declared in a package
3.  #is part of package main.
4.  $globalMain = "Defined in default package main";
5.  $packageName = "Main ";
6.  sub validateNamedParams (\%\%){
7.      #Create two hash references to the formals and actual.
8.      my ($formalParams, $actualParams) = @_;
9.      #Now check each of the named actual parameter names.
10.     foreach $key (keys %$actualParams){
11.         #If the actual name is not part of the formal list,
12.         #then it must be a mistake.
13.         #Note that this does not force the actuals to have
14.         #all of the formals, it only looks for actuals that
```

```
15.        #are not part of the formals.
16.        if (!defined $$formalParams{$key}){
17.            #I want a comma space around my formal list.
18.            #The local will be reset, but since this routine dies,
19.            #it really doesn't matter.
20.            local $" = ', ';
21.            @formals = keys %$formalParams;
22.            print "$key is an invalid parameter name.\n";
23.            print "The valid parameter names are\n ";
24.            print "@formals\n";
25.            #For demonstration purposes, reset to die for installation.
26.            # die;
27.            warn ;
28.        }
29.    }
30. }
31.
32.
33. #Package main's scope ends here.
34. #To access anything of package Constants
35. #you must use a fully qualified name.
36. #
37. package Constants;
38. $lineSeparator = "=" x 60;
39. $packageName = "Constants ";
40.
41. #Package Globals contains the constants and
42. #subroutines that can be accessed by packages
43. #following globals.
44. package Globals;
45. $packageName = "Global ";
46. $global = "Defined in $packageName";
47. #You can see variables outside your package only if
48. #they are fully qualified.
49. #Variables that are part of your package do not need
50. #to be qualified.
51. print "In $packageName, $globalMain, $global\n";
52. print "In $packageName, $main::globalMain\n";
53. print "$Constants::lineSeparator\n";
54. #This subroutine can be used by other classes as their
55. #constructor.
56. sub new(){
```

```perl
57.     $packageName = shift;
58.     print "Building $packageName\n";
59.     $self = {};
60.     #The bless operation is generic, associating the
61.     #name passed in packageName with the instance hash.
62.     bless $self, $packageName;
63.     #Save the packageName; it is used in the mySymbols subroutine.
64.     $self->{name} = $packageName;
65.     return ($self);
66. }
67.
68. sub mySymbols(){
69.     #Get the packageName of this class.
70.     #The symbol table for the hash is named the same name
71.     #as the class.
72.     $hashName = "$self->{name}::";
73.     print "IN PACKAGE $self->{name}\n\n";
74.     #Print all the symbols of this class.
75.     while( ($name, *glob) = each %$hashName){
76.         if (defined ($glob)){
77.             print "Scalar $name, value $glob\n";
78.             print "$Constants::lineSeparator\n";
79.         }
80.         if (defined (@glob)){
81.             print "Array $name, value @glob\n";
82.             print "$Constants::lineSeparator\n";
83.         }
84.         if (defined (%glob)){
85.             print "Hash $name\n";
86.             if ($name !~ /main/i){
87.                 foreach $key (sort keys %glob){
88.                     print "NAME $key, VALUE \t$glob{$key}\n";
89.                 }
90.             print "$Constants::lineSeparator\n";
91.             }
92.         }
93.     }
94. }
95.
96. package Parameters;
97. @ISA = qw(Globals);
98. %tree = (mom => "Joan",
```

```
99.              dad => "Jim",
100.             GrandMa => "Mary",
101.             GrandPa => "Steven");
102. $packageName = "Parameters ";
103. $global = "Defined in $packageName";
104.
105. print "In $packageName, $globalMain, $global\n";
106. print "In $packageName, Globals name ==> $Globals::packageName\n";
107. print "$Constants::lineSeparator\n";
108.
109. #Use the inherited constructor.
110. sub new(){
111.    $class = shift;
112.    $class->SUPER::new();
113.    return ($self);
114. }
115.
116. sub mySymbols(){
117.    #Get my instance pointer.
118.    $self = shift;
119.    #Use the inherited mySymbols with this class's
120.    #instance pointer.
121.    $self->Globals::mySymbols();
122. }
123. #Call the family subroutine.
124. family(\%tree, "Keith", 25);
125.
126. #The age and religion parameters are optional.
127. sub family(\%$$;$$){
128.    my ($family, $name, $age, $sex, $religion) = @_;
129.    %familyHash = (Mom => 1, Dad => 1, GrandMa =>1, GrandPa => 1);
130.    main::validateNamedParams(%familyHash, %$family);
131. }
132. #Call the package Globals constructor.
133. $self = Globals->new();
134. #Print the Globals symbols.
135. $self ->mySymbols();
136. #Get the object reference to the Parameters package.
137. $self = Parameters->new();
138. #Print the Parameters symbols.
139. $self ->mySymbols();
```

FIGURE 17.1:

Demonstrating package scope

Packages

Packages are used for managing subroutine and variable visibility, which is another name for *scope*. All package variables and subroutines are global in scope by default, just like any other Perl 5 variable. All Perl 5 symbols are part of a package. If you don't declare a package, then the symbols are part of a package named main, which is the default package.

Package Namespaces

The Perl 5 package statement separates your program into unique namespaces. A namespace is the Perl 5 interpreter's mechanism for separating variables and subroutines from each other. The `package` statement declares the namespace, like this:

```
package packageName;
```

A Perl 5 package creates a lexical namespace. A *lexical* symbol is visible only within the block enclosing the symbol. Any statement outside the enclosing block, including subroutines that are called within the enclosing block, cannot access the lexical symbol.

The package namespace continues to the end of the enclosing block. A package namespace can be declared at any place in your program, including nesting a package within a package. A package that is within another package follows the same scoping rules as the package that contains it. The containing package cannot see into the enclosed package, and the enclosed package cannot see the variables and subroutines of the enclosing package.

A package's namespace is implemented as a hash variable. The hash variable is given the same name as the package. The name of the hash that contains the `main` package's symbols table is `%main::`. All program symbols are part of the default `main` package's namespace hash.

Qualified and Unqualified Names

A package variable always can be accessed using its fully qualified name. A package variable's fully qualified name begins with the type identifier, followed by the package name, followed by two colons (`::`) or a single quote (`'`), followed by the variable name. As demonstrated on lines 51 and 52 of Listing 17.1 (and shown in Figure 17.1), the global variable `$globalMain` is only visible to the other packages by using its fully qualified name, `$main::globalMain`, which includes the default package name `main`:

```
print "In $packageName, $globalMain, $global\n";
print "In $packageName, $main::globalMain\n";
```

Subroutines and file handles also may be accessed using the fully qualified package naming scheme, as you can see on line 137 of Listing 17.1, where the new subroutine of package `Parameters` is accessed using its fully qualified name:

```
$self = Parameters->new();
```

Throughout a package, a variable is visible by its unqualified name. The unqualified variable name is simply the variable's name, without any preceding identifiers. As you can see on line 124 of Listing 17.1, the `family` subroutine inside the package `Parameters` does not require a package qualifier:

```
family(\%tree, "Keith", 25);
```

Several examples of accessing symbols using unqualified and fully qualified variable names are shown in Table 17.1.

TABLE 17.1: Qualifying Package Variable Names

Type	Unqualified Name	Qualified Name
Scalar	$domain	$Cookie::domain
Array	@values	@Cookie::values
Hash	%expires	%Cookie::expires
Format	CUSTOMER	Cookie::CUSTOMER
File handle	DISK	Cookie::DISK
Subroutine	new()	Cookie::new()

Data Scope

Packages define the overall scope of your program, much like the walls of your home define the overall scope of your living space. Data scope defines the way you communicate within your program, much like the way doors, windows, and walls define the way you communicate within your home.

Perl 5 variables may be globally, lexically, or dynamically scoped. Globally scoped variables are like living in a glass house—everybody can see what is going on. Lexically scoped variables are like living in a bank vault—only those given the combination can get access. Dynamically scoped variables are a cross between the two. Dynamically scoped data are like having a speaker between the vault and the outside—you can control when you turn the speaker on, but you can't control who listens. When you call a subroutine, any code in the subroutine and any subroutine it calls has access to your dynamically scoped variables.

Global Scope

As explained earlier, all Perl 5 symbols are part of a package. That means that all Perl 5 symbols are limited to the lexical scope of their package, which seems to contradict the default global scope of a Perl 5 variable.

Perl 5 global variables are not truly global if you define *global* as one variable name having the same meaning throughout your program. Perl 5 global variables are global in that one fully qualified variable name has the same meaning throughout your code. In truth, global variables are actually package global variables. When a new package is declared, a separate symbol table for the new package is also declared, which you can see in the subroutine called mySymbols. This subroutine uses the package name to access the package's symbol table on lines 72 through 75 of Listing 17.1:

```
$hashName = "$self->{name}::";
print "IN PACKAGE $self->{name}\n\n";
#Print all the symbols of this class.
while( ($name, *glob) = each %$hashName){
```

Any global variables declared for the new package are also visible throughout the program. If the program changes package scope, the global variables are visible only through their fully qualified package names. To ensure you get the same global variable, you must use its fully qualified package name.

The package scope of Perl 5 symbols gives you the ability to overload and overwrite Perl 5 symbols. An *overloaded* symbol is a global symbol that has the same name in multiple packages. In Listing 17.1, the subroutines new() and mySymbols() and the variable $packageName are overloaded, because they are declared in multiple places but each declaration is within a new package scope.

An *overwritten* symbol is a symbol whose definition has been replaced by another declaration or definition, within the same scope. Lines 133 through 139 of Listing 17.1 demonstrate overwriting a variable, $self. The value of $self created on line 133 by the Globals->new() subroutine is overwritten by the return value from the Parameters->new() subroutine:

```
$self = Globals->new();
#Print the Globals symbols.
$self ->mySymbols();
#Get the object reference to the Parameters package.
$self = Parameters->new();
#Print the Parameters symbols.
$self ->mySymbols();
```

Dynamic Scope

A Perl 5 variable is dynamically scoped using the keyword local. A dynamically scoped variable temporarily overrides any global definition of the variable. Dynamically scoped variables are only visible to the enclosing block and to any subroutines called within the enclosing block. A dynamically scoped variable creates a copy of the previous value of a globally scoped variable. When the dynamically scoped variable goes out of scope, the previous value of the global variable is restored.

A common but potentially dangerous use for dynamically scoped variables is in subroutines that copy the input parameter list into local variables, like this:

```
local (variableList) = @_;
```

The implication, just by its name, local, is that dynamically scoped variables are local to the subroutine, which they are not. A local variable is visible to any subroutine called within its scope, which creates a temptation to use the dynamically scoped variable in the called subroutine. Using dynamically scoped variables in a called subroutine at best creates tightly coupled code and often creates spaghetti code that is hard to debug and modify. The better choice is to use the Perl 5 lexical declaration my, which is discussed in the next section.

Lexical Scope

A variable that is limited to the enclosing scope is called a lexical variable. Lexical variables, created using the keyword my, are not part of the package's symbol table. A lexical variable exists and is visible only within the enclosing scope. The subroutine family lexical variables created on line 128 of Listing 17.1 are visible only within the subroutine family and are automatically deleted when the subroutine goes out of scope:

```
my ($family, $name, $age, $sex, $religion) = @_;
```

A lexically scoped variable may remain in memory outside the execution of the enclosing block if its reference count remains greater than zero. Automatically deleting variables is called *garbage collection*. Perl 5 uses a simple reference count algorithm for garbage collection. When a variable can no longer be referenced by any statement, that memory location is freed for other uses.

A lexical variable is not part of a package's namespace and can be referred to only by the enclosing block. This structure creates a truly private variable that has visibility only within the block in which it is declared. This feature, along with the reference count garbage collection feature, gives Perl 5 a reentrant code capability. *Reentrant* code is code that can call itself safely, because each time it is called, it gets a new set of variables with which to work.

Subroutines

All Perl 5 subroutines return the value of the last expression evaluated, which means that in Perl 5, functions and subroutines are synonyms. A subroutine in Perl 5 is declared or defined using the keyword sub, which you can see throughout Listing 17.1, such as on line 127:

```
sub family(\%$$;$$){
```

Subroutines may be named or anonymous. Named subroutines are declared like this:

```
sub subName;
sub subName(parameterList);
```

Declaring a subroutine without defining it allows you to use the subroutine in a list. All Perl 5 subroutines are dynamically scoped and are accessible at compile time throughout your programs.

A subroutine is defined by adding the subroutine code block after the subroutine declaration, like this:

```
sub subName{code block}
sub subName(parameterList) {code block}
```

You can define an anonymous subroutine like this:

```
$subReference = sub {code block};
```

Subroutine Calls

The syntax used when calling a Perl 5 subroutine has a subtle impact on how the parameters are passed to the subroutine. The various ways to call a subroutine are summarized here.

This is a direct call that creates a local copy of the @_ array, set to the scalar values of the parameter list:

```
subName(paramList)
```

This is a direct call that creates a local copy of the @_ array, set to the scalar values of the parameter list (the subroutine must be predeclared):

```
subName paramList;
```

This is a direct call that passes the enclosing block's copy of the global @_array as the parameter list:

```
&subName;
```

This is an indirect call that uses a subroutine reference to call the subroutine:

```
&$subReference;
```

The ampersand is not optional in an indirect call. The global @_ array is passed as the parameter list. Prior to Perl 5, a subroutine call required an ampersand prefixing the subroutine name, as in &subName, but the ampersand has a specific effect on your code. A part of this effect is that users of your subroutine can force their own parameter lists on your subroutine by preceding the call to your subroutine with an ampersand, which overrides the declared parameter list, as explained in the next section.

This is an indirect call that creates a local copy of the @_ array equal to the scalar values of the parameter list:

```
&$subReference(paramList);
```

Subroutine Parameters

A subroutine defined with a parameter list must be called with exactly the parameters specified, or a compilation error occurs. Declared parameters are called *formal* parameters. The values and variables used when calling a subroutine are called the *actual* parameters. As you can see on line 130 of Listing 17.1, the parameters %familyHash and %$family are the actual parameters:

```
main::validateNamedParams(%familyHash, %$family);
```

Line 6 of Listing 17.1 declares the formal parameters of the validateNamed-Params subroutine:

```
sub validateNamedParams (\%\%){
```

Parameter lists define both the type and number of parameters your subroutine expects. A parameter list is defined by putting the type indicator of each parameter between parentheses when declaring or defining a subroutine. Each type indicator defines the parameter required for that position.

A semicolon inside the parameter list separates the mandatory parameters from the optional parameters. All parameters following the semicolon are optional. All parameters preceding the semicolon are required, as shown on line 127 of Listing 17.1:

```
sub family(\%$$;$$){
```

The parameters following the semicolon are part of the lexical variables read from the input array on line 128. The two optional scalar parameters represent the optional scalar variables $sex and $religion.

If the declared parameter is preceded by a backslash, the type of the input parameter must equal the type of the declared parameter, which you can also see on line 6 of Listing 17.1. A backslashed formal parameter forces a variable's reference to be passed. This allows you to define formal parameters of array and hash type and your actual parameters to be multiple arrays or hashes. A reference to the array or hash is passed in the parameter list instead of the array values, which also is demonstrated on line 130 of Listing 17.1.

Parameters that are not backslashed force the type indicator's context onto the actual parameter. If the formal parameter is a scalar type indicator and the actual parameter is an array, scalar context is applied to the actual parameter.

Like the reference parameters passed by backslashed formal parameters, the default input parameter list @_ is actually an array of references. Perl 5 does not copy each scalar variable to the subroutine, but instead passes a reference to the parameter in the default input array @_. If you modify the contents of the @_ array by directly referencing a cell in the array, such as $_[1], you are modifying the variable passed in the parameter list, not a copy of the variable.

There are two primary means of passing parameters: *call-by-reference* and *call-by-value*. A call-by-reference parameter has its actual value accessed and potentially modified by the called subroutine. A call-by-value parameter has its actual value copied into a subroutine variable; the actual value is never modified by the subroutine.

Call-by-reference is the Perl 5 default means of passing parameters because the default input array @_ contains references to the actual variables in the parameter list. You can also use the backslash character (\) to create a call-by-reference parameter.

To create a call-by-value parameter list, copy the default input array @_ into a list of subroutine lexical variables, like this:

```
sub programName (paramList){
```

```
    my (paramList) = @_;
    ...
}
```

Subroutine Return Values

All Perl 5 subroutines return the value of the last expression evaluated in the sub-routine. The context of the lvalue—list or scalar—in the calling statement deter-mines the context of the returning value.

Perl 5 has a `return` statement that explicitly states what values will be returned to the caller, as illustrated by line 65 of Listing 17.1:

```
return ($self);
```

The syntax of the `return` statement is:

```
return (list);
```

The `return` statement exits the subroutine and returns control to the calling statement. The contents of the list are the values returned. All arrays in the list will be expanded to their scalar values.

Object-Oriented Perl 5

All objects have two specific characteristics related to programming. First, you can do things to or with an object. Doing something with an object is called an *operation*, which is implemented in a subroutine. *Method* is the object-oriented term for a subroutine associated with an object.

The other characteristic of an object is its *state*. An object's state is implemented in *instance variables*. Instance variables capture the characteristics of an object that make each copy of the object unique. For example, line 64 of Listing 17.1 creates the instance variable name:

```
$self->{name} = $packageName;
```

Class is the object-oriented term for the implementation of an object. Perl 5 uses a package to implement the class concept. A class is the container that holds your Perl 5 object. A class is always a package, but a package is not always a class. A package becomes a class when it is used to create methods, variables, and modules that are associated with an object. A class becomes a module when the entire class, including all the methods and variables, are saved into one file, which has the same name as the class and has the extension .pm. In short, a module is no more than a file that has the same name as the class it contains with the filename extension .pm.

The combination of class, state, and methods—which are implemented in packages, instance variables, and subroutines—creates a Perl 5 object.

Object Methods

There are two types of methods in a Perl 5 object:

- The *class method* expects the package name as the first parameter of the parameter list.

- The *instance method* expects an object reference as the first parameter of the parameter list.

The calling syntax of object methods uses the right arrow notation. The right arrow notation invokes the class method and substitutes the parameter to the left of the arrow as the first parameter passed to the class method, which is demonstrated in the new methods on lines 56 and 57 and lines 110 and 111 of Listing 17.1:

```
56.  sub new(){
57.      $packageName = shift;
110. sub new(){
111.     $class = shift;
```

To call a class method, use this syntax:

```
className->methodName(paramList);
```

Perl 5 inserts the class name as the first parameter of the parameter list, which is illustrated on lines 133 and 137 of Listing 17.1:

```
133. $self = Globals->new();
137. $self = Parameters->new();
```

The first statements of a class method should always move the first parameter out of the parameter list into a lexical variable, like this:

```
my $class = shift;
```

A *constructor* is a class method used for object initialization and to return an object reference. By convention, a Perl 5 constructor is named new:

```
className->new();
```

TIP

Chapter 19 includes a brief listing (Listing 19.2) that you can use as a template for your constructors. That template performs the primary task of a constructor, creating and returning an object reference $self.

An object reference variable is required to access the unique characteristics of an individual object. An object reference variable is a variable that contains a reference to a package scoped anonymous hash and has been linked with the package through the bless function. The bless function takes two parameters: an object and a class name. If the class name is not supplied, the object is linked with the current package.

Here is the common usage of the bless function:

```
bless $referenceVariable, $className;
```

This usage implies that the bless function operates on a reference variable, but the function actually operates on the variable the reference variable points to. The bless function always returns a reference to the linked object. The complete syntax of the bless function is:

```
lvalue = bless object, className;
```

This syntax can replace the two-statement syntax:

```
my $self = {};
bless $self, $class;
```

with this single statement:

```
my $self = bless {}, $class;
```

The calling syntax of instance methods also uses the right arrow notation, but an instance method expects an object reference as its first parameter. This is shown on lines 135 and 139 of Listing 17.1, which each call their own instance of the instance method mySymbols():

```
135. $self ->mySymbols();
139. $self ->mySymbols();
```

An instance method is called like this:

```
$objectReference->methodName(parameterList);
```

Just as with the class method, the `object reference` is moved onto the parameter list and then shifted back off of the parameter list as the first statement of the instance method, like this:

```
my $self = shift;
```

The instance method then uses the lexical `$self` to access its instance variables. An instance method must always move its object reference into a lexical variable. The object reference gives the instance method access to the current state of the object.

A *destructor* is a subroutine that runs just before an object is freed or deleted from memory and allows the object to perform any cleanup required before it exits. In Perl 5, an object's destructor is identified by naming a subroutine DESTROY. The destructor is never explicitly called; instead, the destructor is executed by the Perl 5 interpreter just before the object is freed in memory.

Classes that want to use the methods of another module must use the `use` statement to include that module's exported methods and other symbols. The `use` statement includes the class name into the program's namespace by loading the file named `className.pm` from the disk. The `use` statement only looks for files with the filename extension `.pm`.

The syntax of the `use` statement is:

```
use className;
```

The `use` statement accepts only a class name as its single parameter, and that class name must reference a file of the same name with the `.pm` extension. Classes included using the `use` statement are compiled at the time they are loaded into the program. This is unlike the `require` statement, which compiles the loaded program during the execution of the overall program.

Object Variables

Class variables are global to the entire package and have persistence over the life of the program. (A variable is *persistent* as long as it remains in memory.) Class variables, such as the `$packageMain` variable, are used by the object methods to create state and identity across all the methods of a class.

Class variables can be created at any time in an object's existence, but they are most frequently created during construction or object compilation. Creating a class variable early in an object's existence helps guarantee that the class variable will be available whenever an object method is called. A class variable is global to the class and should always be available to all the methods of a class.

An *instance variable* creates a unique identity for an object. Instance variables are used to define both the state of an object and its uniqueness. Instance variables are created and associated with each new copy of an object. An instance variable is available only through a referenced variable that has been specially identified with a class, as demonstrated on lines 72 through 75 of Listing 17.1:

```
$hashName = "$self->{name}::";
print "IN PACKAGE $self->{name}\n\n";
#Print all the symbols of this class.
while( ($name, *glob) = each %$hashName){
```

These lines access the instance variable name on line 72, and then use that instance variable as a symbolic reference to the class's symbol table on line 75.

Inheritance

Inheritance is the ability to use the methods and instance variables of your ancestor classes. Perl 5 provides programming inheritance through a built-in array named @ISA.

A *base class*, also called a *superclass* or *ancestor class*, refers to a class that has been added to the @ISA array. A *derived class*, also called a *subclass*, is a class that uses the methods of ancestor classes as part of its implementation. The methods of a class added to the @ISA array are available to the derived class as if the derived class defined them.

Once a class is added to the @ISA array, that class's methods are treated as part of the derived class's methods. When a method that has not been defined in a derived class is called in that derived class, Perl 5 searches each class in the @ISA array for the method. Perl 5 uses a depth-first algorithm to find the missing method. The first method that matches the called method will be used.

To use another class's methods, the derived class includes its ancestor class name in the @ISA array, as demonstrated on line 97 of Listing 17.1:

```
@ISA = qw(Globals);
```

Explicit access to either class method is available using the double-colon notation, as on line 121:

```
$self->Globals::mySymbols();
```

The double-colon notation always calls the named class, overriding any dynamic binding in effect. This syntax explicitly invokes the method named by the class name to the left of the double colons.

When the keyword SUPER is used to invoke a method, Perl 5 begins looking in the @ISA array for a matching subroutine, as on line 112:

```
$class->SUPER::new();
```

The SUPER notation is a hybrid form of explicit access. The SUPER notation tells the Perl 5 interpreter to begin looking for the method in the @ISA hierarchy, overriding any method definition in the derived class. However, the SUPER notation does not define the specific ancestor class.

Polymorphism is the ability to use the same name for multiple subroutines, which is illustrated by the multiple new() subroutines in Listing 17.1. Perl 5 allows you to use the same subroutine name and gives you access to that subroutine through explicit subroutine calls or dynamic binding. *Dynamic binding* is the calling of a subroutine based on runtime conditions, which is illustrated on lines 135 and 139. The Perl interpreter cannot tell which mySymbols() method it is going to call until runtime, when it resolves the object reference variable $self:

```
135. $self ->mySymbols();
139. $self ->mySymbols();
```

E-Mail Transfer

SMTP, which stands for Simple Mail Transport Protocol, is the protocol used to transmit e-mail messages across the Internet. If you have an e-mail account, you use an SMTP server. The most popular SMTP server is sendmail, a Unix program.

An SMTP server is an instance of a mail program like sendmail that operates as a daemon listening for incoming e-mail messages on port 25. When a message is received, the SMTP server determines the correct routing for the e-mail message by examining the e-mail headers. Local e-mail messages are delivered to their mailboxes, and remote messages are forwarded to the next SMTP server along the route to the final destination.

The SMTP server requires that you communicate with it in a formatted manner. The SMTP server communicates in an asynchronous handshaking mode. Commands do not need to follow each other in a strict time frame. Commands can sometimes be minutes apart; however, the SMTP server will time out eventually. What is required is to follow a strict sequencing of commands. The sequence of commands requires that the receiver send and receive each command in the correct order.

> **NOTE** To receive the SMTP server response, read from the socket connection. The SMTP server should accept initial connections on port 25 and then return a unique socket for further communications.

Here are the steps involved in SMTP communications:

- Connect to the SMTP server on port 25. Read the response message, which should be a connection status of 220.

- Send `Helo yourIdentity`. Read the response message, which should be an OK status of 250.

- Send the From Header: `mail from: yourName@somewhere.com`. Read the response message, which should be an OK status of 250.

- Send the To Header: `rcpt to: recipientName@other.com`. Read the response message, which should be an OK status of 250.

- Tell the SMTP server you are ready to send the e-mail message by entering the `data` command. Read the response message, which should be a ready-to-receive-data status of 354.

- Send any additional To:, From:, Bcc:, Cc:, Reply-To:, Subject:, and other headers. When you're finished with the e-mail headers, enter a blank line. The SMTP server will not respond.

- Type in the body of the message. When you are finished entering the body of the message, type in a dot (`.`) in the left-hand column on a line by itself. Read the response message, which should be a 250 Requested mail action OK.

- Disconnect from the SMTP server by sending the `quit` command. Read the response message, which should be a 221 Goodbye.

The `Sender.pm` module creates an easy-to-use e-mail interface that implements all of the steps outlined above. The `Sender.pm` module runs on both Unix and Windows platforms.

TIP

Chapter 20 includes a very brief listing (Listing 20.5) that uses the `Sender.pm` module. The few lines of code in that listing show how easily you can send e-mail messages via your SMTP server.

What Next?

Like the other jump-start chapters, this chapter presents only an overview of the topics. For a complete understanding of packages, scope, object-oriented programming, and e-mail handling in Perl 5, read the next three chapters.

Chapter 18 is about functional programming—packages, data scope, subroutines, and functions. It includes examples that demonstrate how each type of Perl 5 data scope affects your programs. It also covers using subroutines and functions to perform repetitive tasks.

In Chapter 19, you learn the details of object-oriented programming, which is gaining popularity among modern programmers. The main example in that chapter is a program that provides a drag-and-drop interface for publishing interdepartmental information. Chapter 19 also explains how to use named parameters, which have several advantages over regular subroutine parameter lists.

Chapter 20 covers e-mail solutions. There you'll find details about SMTP servers and `sendmail`. It includes a separate set of solutions for Unix users, complete with examples of a registration application and a mailing list application. If you are working with a Windows system, you'll be interested in the coverage of Blat, a freeware Windows e-mail program. Both Windows and Unix users will want to get all the details about `Sender.pm`, a Perl module that provides a direct Perl interface to the SMTP server. You'll learn how easy it is to use `Sender.pm` and also examine the methods that perform the actual connections to the SMTP server. When you are finished with Chapter 20, you'll know how to extend `Sender.pm` or implement your own SMTP interface.

CHAPTER

EIGHTEEN

Functional Programming

- Packages and symbol tables

- Global data scope

- Dynamic data scope

- Lexical data scope

- Perl subroutines

Programming requires more than merely learning the syntax, rules, and capabilities of a language. Like building a house, programming is also about the design and structure of the program. A house is made up of different rooms, with each room designed for a particular function. A house builder considers the function of each room and how that function affects the other rooms in the house. A room for sleeping can also be used as a room for television viewing, but the two functions may conflict.

A program can be one communal space, where every task is done within the default `main` package. A program also can be broken into functional parts called subroutines, functions, packages, and modules, which are like the various rooms of a home.

This chapter is about designing a program's structure. In this chapter, you will learn about packages, subroutines, and the movement of data throughout a program. In the next chapter, you will learn about using objects and modules as alternatives to the program structures described in this chapter.

Perl 5 has three types of scope: lexical, dynamic, and global, which also will be explored in this chapter. *Scope,* as it is used in this chapter, defines how a symbol can be accessed within a program. A symbol's visibility and the ability to access a variable are programming synonyms.

Packages

When you build a one-room house, there isn't a lot of design involved. You need four walls, a roof, and probably some indoor plumbing. The same is true when you are building programs. Small programs don't need a lot of design. A small program might require some variables and a few subroutines, but mostly a small program just needs to work correctly.

As your construction project gets bigger, it takes a little more planning. If you're building a ten-story office building, you need a lot more coordination. For example, the plumbing between the bathrooms on each floor needs to be coordinated. Additionally, special rooms are required for plumbing and electrical facilities. Similarly, as a program gets bigger, it requires the same type of graduated additional planning, design, and coordination.

Packages are one of the coordination tools of Perl 5 programmers. A package is like a special room in your house or office building. More specifically, the variables and subroutines of one package are distinct from another package's variables and subroutines. This is like separating bathroom, living room, and bedroom functions and furniture. Each room has some similar functions, such as electrical switches and outlets, and some specialized items, such sinks, beds, and couches.

Packages define the "rooms" in your house. Each package's variables and functions are usable by other packages, but they reside in their own unique *namespace*. A namespace is the Perl 5 interpreter's mechanism for separating variables and subroutines from each other. You can think of a namespace as the physical room a variable or subroutine occupies. The package is the mechanism used for naming that room.

Package Definition

Packages allow you to give similar functions and variables the same name and still differentiate between them. As you will learn in the next chapter, most Perl 5 modules have an initialization routine called new. Perl programmers that use modules and packages expect to call the new function to initialize the package. This common interface is a great convenience for the programmer, but Perl 5 must distinguish between hundreds of functions with the same name, which is new in this case. Perl 5 uses the `package` statement and its unique namespace to distinguish between the new functions in modules such as `Mail::Sender` and `Mail::Internet`.

A package is a Perl 5 statement that declares all the symbols in the following lexical block to be grouped together. A *lexical* symbol is only visible within the block enclosing the symbol. Any statement outside the enclosing block, including subroutines that are called within the enclosing block, cannot access the lexical symbol.

The syntax of a package statement is:

```
package packageName;
```

The package name follows the same naming rules as a variable name (variable naming is explained in Chapter 5). The package name can be used to qualify the variables defined and declared in the package block. For example, the `Mail::Sender` module can name a variable `$connection` to refer to its connection to the SMTP server, and the `Mail::Internet` module can name a variable `$connection` to refer to its own connection. Outside the package, depending on data scope (scope is covered shortly), the two variables with the same name can be referred to uniquely by including their package name: $Mail::Sender::connection or $Mail::Internet::connection.

Packages are a programmer's tool for controlling complexity, but many programs don't require a package declaration. Packages that never use a package statement are part of the default package named main.

The package namespace is the Perl 5 interpreter's way of controlling and organizing a program's symbols. If you don't declare a package namespace, the interpreter defaults all symbols to the default package namespace, which is main.

The Lexical Scope of Packages

Because a package declaration is a lexical statement, its scope is limited to the enclosing block. The enclosing block begins with the package statement and continues until either the next package statement or the end of the block containing the package statement. Listing 18.1 demonstrates accessing package variables within variable lexical blocks. Figure 18.1 shows the results of running this program.

Listing 18.1:   **Package Scope**

```
1.  #!/usr/local/bin/perl
2.  $a = "MAIN";
3.  $b = "MAIN";
4.  $c = "MAIN";
5.  print "Package main $main::a, $main::b, $main::c\n";
6.  print "Package main $a, $b, $c\n\n";
7.  print "Begin package one scope.\n";
8.  package one;
9.  $a = 1;
10. {
11.    $b = 1;
12. }
13. {
14.    $c = 1;
15. }
16. #package one block ends
17. print "Package one variables $a, $b, $c\n";
18. print "End package one scope\nBegin package two scope\n\n";
19. package two;
```

```
20.  $a = 2;
21.  $b = 2;
22.  {
23.     $c=2;
24.  }
25.
26.  print "Package one $one::a, $one::b, $one::c\n";
27.  print "Package two $two::a, $two::b, $two::c\n";
28.  print "Package two $a, $b, $c\n\n";
29.
30.  #a new block scope begins
31.  print "Begin new enclosing block scope\n";
32.  {
33.     print "Begin package three scope\n";
34.     #package three scope begins
35.     package three;
36.     $a = 3;
37.     {
38.        $b = 3;
39.     }
40.     {
41.        $c = 3;
42.     }
43.     print "Package one $one::a, $one::b, $one::c\n";
44.     print "Package two $two::a, $two::b, $two::c\n";
45.     print "Package three $three::a, $three::b, $three::c\n";
46.     print "Package three $a, $b, $c\n";
47.     print "End enclosing block scope and package three scope\n\n";
48.  #this ends package three's scope
49.  }
50.
51.  #package two's scope continues
52.  print "Continue package two scope scope\n";
53.  print "Package two $a, $b, $c\n";
```

In Listing 18.1, the lexical scope of package one begins on line 8 and continues until line 19, where the lexical scope of package two begins. This illustrates the first means of terminating a package's scope. A package's scope ends with the declaration of a new package within the same enclosing block. Line 32 begins a new block scope, which illustrates the other way to end package scope.

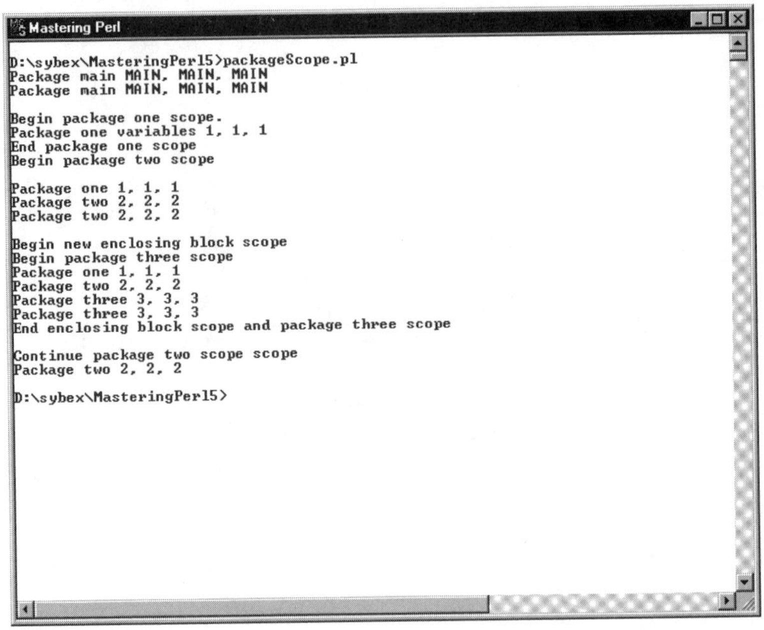

FIGURE 18.1:

Accessing package variables within lexical blocks

```
D:\sybex\MasteringPerl5>packageScope.pl
Package main MAIN, MAIN, MAIN
Package main MAIN, MAIN, MAIN

Begin package one scope.
Package one variables 1, 1, 1
End package one scope
Begin package two scope

Package one 1, 1, 1
Package two 2, 2, 2
Package two 2, 2, 2

Begin new enclosing block scope
Begin package three scope
Package one 1, 1, 1
Package two 2, 2, 2
Package three 3, 3, 3
Package three 3, 3, 3
End enclosing block scope and package three scope

Continue package two scope scope
Package two 2, 2, 2

D:\sybex\MasteringPerl5>
```

Package three's scope begins with the `package` statement on line 35. Package three's scope ends when the block enclosing the `package` statement ends on line 49. The end of package three's scope and the continuation of package two's scope is illustrated by the `print` statement on line 53:

```
print "Package two $a, $b, $c\n";
```

This shows that the global variables $a, $b, and $c are actually only global to the enclosing packages.

Unqualified and Fully Qualified Package Variable Names

Listing 18.1 also illustrates that package variables can be accessed using their package-qualified name or their unqualified name. Within the scope of a package, a package variable can be accessed using the unqualified variable name. The unqualified variable name is simply the variable's name, without any preceding identifiers.

A package variable always can be accessed using its fully qualified name. A package variable's fully qualified name begins with the type identifier, followed by the package name, followed by two colons (::) or a single quote ('), followed by the variable name. Subroutines and file handles also may be accessed using the fully qualified package naming scheme, as shown in Listing 18.2.

Listing 18.2:   **Package Subroutines**

```
1.  #!/usr/local/bin/perl
2.  #
3.  package one;
4.  sub common{
5.      print "package one\n";
6.  }
7.  package two;
8.  sub common{
9.      print "package two\n";
10. }
11. package three;
12. sub common{
13.     print "package three\n";
14. }
15. common();
16. one'common();
17. two'common();
18. three'common();
```

The subroutine call on line 15 of Listing 18.2 is within the lexical scope of package three, which means common() prints "package three." Lines 16 through 18 each call the subroutine common() using the fully qualified subroutine name, which allows Perl 5 to determine the correct namespace from which to retrieve the subroutine definition. This is like turning on the light switch in your house by telling someone else to turn on the bathroom light. They know which light to turn on because you fully qualified the "light" function.

Lines 16 through 18 of Listing 18.2 use the single quote to delimit the package name from the subroutine name to demonstrate this alternative delimiter. However, in practice, the double colon is the most common delimiter used between the package name and the package variable, subroutine, or file handle.

Table 18.1 shows examples of unqualified and fully qualified naming conventions for each of the unique namespaces created by a package declaration.

TABLE 18.1: Unqualified and Fully Qualified Package Variable Names

Type	Unqualified Name	Qualified Name
Scalar	`$cup`	`$kitchen::cup`
Array	`@forks`	`@kitchen::forks`
Hash	`%flatware`	`%kitchen::flatware`
Format	`SPICES`	`kitchen::SPICES`
File handle	`CABINET`	`kitchen::CABINET`
Subroutine	`diner()`	`kitchen::diner()`

Symbol Tables

Each package declaration is assigned its own symbol table. A *symbol table* is a list of all of the symbols that can be addressed in a program. The symbol table includes subroutine names, file handles, formats, variables, and a mechanism to retrieve the symbols' values.

A package's namespace, or symbol table, is implemented as a hash variable. The hash variable is given the same name as the package. The name of the hash that contains the `main` package's symbol table is `%main::`. All program symbols are part of the default `main` package's namespace hash.

The `main` hash can be used to access all of the symbols of a program. Global variables that are declared outside a specific package scope are implicitly part of the `main` package namespace. When you declare a new package namespace, the new package's namespace hash becomes a symbol in the `main` package's namespace hash.

NOTE   A global symbol is visible to any statement in your program. Perl 5 variables are global by default. Every Perl 5 global variable may be accessed by any Perl 5 statement using the global variable's fully qualified name.

If a package contains another package, the contained package's symbol table is named in the containing package's symbol table. The best way to clarify how a

package symbol table contains another package's symbol table is through an
example, which is the purpose of Listing 18.3.

Listing 18.3:   **Package Symbol Tables**

```
1.   #!/usr/local/bin/perl
2.   $a = "MAIN";
3.   $b = "MAIN";
4.   $c = "MAIN";
5.   package one;
6.   $a = 1;
7.   {$b = 1;}
8.   {$c = 1;}
9.   #package one block ends
10.  package two;
11.  $a = 2;
12.  $b = 2;
13.  {$c=2;}
14.  #a new block scope begins
15.  {
16.      #package three scope begins
17.      package three;
18.      $a = 3;
19.      {$b = 3;}
20.      {$c = 3;}
21.  #this ends package three's scope
22.  }
23.  $lineSeparator = "=" x 60;
24.  open (OUT, ">pkgAll.txt");
25.  select (OUT);
26.  while ( ($name, *glob) =  each %main::){
27.      if (defined ($glob)){
28.          print "Scalar $name, value $glob\n";
29.      }
30.      if (defined (@glob)){
31.          print "Array $name, value @glob\n";
32.      }
33.      if (defined (%glob)){
34.          print "Hash $name\n";
35.          if ($name !~ /main/i){
36.              foreach $key (sort keys %glob){
37.                  print "NAME $key, VALUE \t$glob{$key}\n";
```

```
38.              }
39.          }
40.      }
41.      if (!(defined($glob) || defined (@glob) || defined (%glob))){
42.          print "FILE HANDLE $name\n"
43.      }
44.      print "$lineSeparator\n";
45. }
46. close (OUT);
```

Listing 18.3 repeats the structure of Listing 18.1 up to line 22. Line 26 of Listing 18.3 begins retrieving the symbols of package main. The symbol tables of all packages of a program are accessible through the main package's symbol table. Line 26 iterates through the main package hash, retrieving each symbol's name (without the type indicator) and typeglob.

A *typeglob* is a Perl 5 data type that is used by the symbol table to represent the different types of symbols. The type indicator of a typeglob is an asterisk (*).

When searching through the symbol table, you can replace the typeglob indicator with a scalar, array, or hash indicator to determine if the symbol's type exists. Lines 27, 30, and 33 of Listing 18.3 perform these replacements:

```
if (defined ($glob)){
if (defined (@glob)){
if (defined (%glob)){
```

TIP   Before the Perl 5 reference variable existed, typeglobs were used as a pseudo reference type for passing arrays and hash to subroutines. Typeglobs are still useful for saving references to file handles, like this: $filehandle=*STDOUT;.

The output from Listing 18.3 is shown in Listing 18.4. This listing is the main package's symbol table.

Listing 18.4:   **The main Package Symbol Table**

```
1.   Scalar _<pkgAll.pl, value pkgAll.pl
2.   ================================================================
3.   Scalar @, value
4.   ================================================================
5.   FILE HANDLE stdin
```

```
6.    ================================================================
7.    Hash Win32::
8.    NAME DomainName, VALUE          *Win32::DomainName
9.    NAME FormatMessage, VALUE       *Win32::FormatMessage
10.   NAME FsType, VALUE              *Win32::FsType
11.   NAME GetCwd, VALUE              *Win32::GetCwd
12.   NAME GetLastError, VALUE        *Win32::GetLastError
13.   NAME GetNextAvailDrive, VALUE *Win32::GetNextAvailDrive
14.   NAME GetOSVersion, VALUE        *Win32::GetOSVersion
15.   NAME GetShortPathName, VALUE    *Win32::GetShortPathName
16.   NAME GetTickCount, VALUE        *Win32::GetTickCount
17.   NAME IsWin95, VALUE             *Win32::IsWin95
18.   NAME IsWinNT, VALUE             *Win32::IsWinNT
19.   NAME LoginName, VALUE           *Win32::LoginName
20.   NAME NodeName, VALUE            *Win32::NodeName
21.   NAME SetCwd, VALUE              *Win32::SetCwd
22.   NAME Sleep, VALUE               *Win32::Sleep
23.   NAME Spawn, VALUE               *Win32::Spawn
24.   ================================================================
25.   Scalar , value 256
26.   ================================================================
27.   Hash UNIVERSAL::
28.   NAME VERSION, VALUE             *UNIVERSAL::VERSION
29.   NAME can, VALUE                 *UNIVERSAL::can
30.   NAME isa, VALUE                 *UNIVERSAL::isa
31.   ================================================================
32.   FILE HANDLE
33.   ================================================================
34.   Hash DynaLoader::
35.   NAME boot_DynaLoader, VALUE    *DynaLoader::boot_DynaLoader
36.   ================================================================
37.   Scalar , value D:\ACTIVE~1\5~1.005\BIN\MSWIN3~1\PERL.EXE
38.   ================================================================
39.   Hash main::
40.   ================================================================
41.   Array INC, value D:\ACTIVESTATE\5.00502\lib/MSWin32-x86-object
      D:\ACTIVESTATE\5.00502\lib
      D:\ACTIVESTATE\site\5.00502\lib/MSWin32-x86-object
      D:\ACTIVESTATE\site\5.00502\lib D:\ACTIVESTATE\site\lib .
42.   ================================================================
43.   FILE HANDLE _
44.   ================================================================
```

```
45.   Scalar a, value MAIN
46.   ================================================================
47.   Scalar ", value
48.   ================================================================
49.   FILE HANDLE STDIN
50.   ================================================================
51.   Scalar b, value MAIN
52.   ================================================================
53.   FILE HANDLE STDOUT
54.   ================================================================
55.   FILE HANDLE stdout
56.   ================================================================
57.   Scalar c, value MAIN
58.   ================================================================
59.   Scalar _<perlmain.c, value perlmain.c
60.   ================================================================
61.   Scalar $, value -208533
62.   ================================================================
63.   Scalar _<.\win32.c, value .\win32.c
64.   ================================================================
65.   Hash ENV
66.   NAME BLASTER, VALUE    A220 I5 D1
67.   NAME CMDLINE, VALUE    perl pkgAll.pl
68.   NAME COMSPEC, VALUE    C:\WINDOWS\COMMAND.COM
69.   NAME PATH, VALUE       D:\ACTIVESTATE\5.00502\BIN
      \MSWIN32-X86-OBJECT;D:\ACTIVESTATE\5.00502\BIN;
      C:\PERL5\5.00471\BIN\MSWIN32-X86;C:\PERL5\5.00471\BIN;
      C:\WINDOWS;C:\WINDOWS\COMMAND;C:\PERL5\BIN;
70.   NAME PERL5DB, VALUE    BEGIN{require 'd:\ActiveState\PerlDB.pl'}
71.   NAME PROMPT, VALUE     $p$g
72.   NAME TEMP, VALUE       C:\WINDOWS\TEMP
73.   NAME TMP, VALUE        C:\WINDOWS\TEMP
74.   NAME WINBOOTDIR, VALUE C:\WINDOWS
75.   NAME WINDIR, VALUE     C:\WINDOWS
76.   ================================================================
77.   Hash three::
78.   NAME a, VALUE    *three::a
79.   NAME b, VALUE    *three::b
80.   NAME c, VALUE    *three::c
81.   ================================================================
82.   Hash IO::
83.   NAME Handle::, VALUE  *IO::Handle::
```

```
84.  ============================================================
85.  Hash two::
86.  NAME OUT, VALUE                    *two::OUT
87.  NAME a, VALUE                      *two::a
88.  NAME b, VALUE                      *two::b
89.  NAME c, VALUE                      *two::c
90.  NAME glob, VALUE                   *main::two::
91.  NAME key, VALUE                    *two::key
92.  NAME lineSeparator, VALUE          *two::lineSeparator
93.  NAME name, VALUE                   *two::name
94.  ============================================================
95.  Scalar /, value
96.
97.  ============================================================
98.  Scalar 0, value pkgAll.pl
99.  ============================================================
100. FILE HANDLE ARGV
101. ============================================================
102. FILE HANDLE STDERR
103. ============================================================
104. FILE HANDLE stderr
105. ============================================================
106. Hash one::
107. NAME a, VALUE     *one::a
108. NAME b, VALUE     *one::b
109. NAME c, VALUE     *one::c
110. ============================================================
111. FILE HANDLE DB::
112. ============================================================
113. Scalar _<..\universal.c, value ..\universal.c
114. ============================================================
115. Hash CORE::
116. NAME GLOBAL::, VALUE    *CORE::GLOBAL::
117. ============================================================
```

Listing 18.4 illustrates how the typeglob is a placeholder for the various Perl 5 symbol types. Each of the type tests on lines 27, 30, and 33 of Listing 18.3 check for the existence of a particular variable type. Lines 1, 3, 5, and 7 of Listing 18.4 display the types of the built-in variables $_, @, and stdin and the Win32 hash:

```
Scalar _<pkgAll.pl, value pkgAll.pl
```

```
Scalar @, value
FILE HANDLE stdin
Hash Win32::
```

These results show that symbols do have specific types.

Listing 18.4 also points out the many built-in symbols of Perl 5. Several hash variables and special variables exist within the main package's symbol table on all Perl 5 programs run on a Windows computer. For example, you can see STDOUT on line 53, the process ID variable ($$) on line 61, and ARGV on line 100.

NOTE   Listing 18.4 shows each variable name without its type indicator, which might be a little confusing. For example, the built-in scalar variables such as $ and $$ show up without their preceding type indicator ($). The process ID variable on line 61 appears as $.

Finally, Listing 18.4 illustrates that each package contains the hash table of each package it contains. Lines 85 through 93 are the variables defined in package two of Listing 18.3. The symbol table printed between lines 85 and 93 is accessed from within the symbol table of another package. This access to another package's symbols becomes important when you try to understand the scoping details of the keywords my and local, which are covered next.

Data Scope

If packages define the rooms in your house, then data scope defines the way you communicate between rooms. Data scope gives you choices about how much privacy you want between rooms. Perl 5 variables may be globally, lexically, or dynamically scoped.

Globally scoped data has no privacy at all. Anyone can see what's going on in your room anytime they want to. Perl 5 variables are global by default.

Having lexically scoped data is like having a solid door with a lock on it between rooms. You can't get behind that door without some help. Perl 5 packages are always lexically scoped.

Dynamically scoped data is a little less secure. Having dynamically scoped data is like having an extension on your phone. Only those people who use the extension can listen in on your conversations, but you can't control who can listen and when they can listen. Perl 5 subroutines and formats are always dynamically scoped.

Global Scope

A global variable can be declared at any place in your code and will be visible from that point to your entire program. Perl 5 global variables are not truly global if you define *global* as one variable name having the same meaning throughout your program. As you learned in the earlier discussion of packages, each package variable is unique to that package. The variable `$connection` from the `Mail::Sender` package does not have the same meaning or value as the variable `$connection` from the `Mail::Internet` package. Perl 5 global variables are global in that one fully qualified variable name has the same meaning throughout your code, which means that `$Mail::Sender::connection` has the same meaning and value throughout your program.

In truth, global variables are actually package global variables. When a new package is declared, a separate symbol table for the new package is also declared. Any global variables declared for the new package are also visible throughout the program. If the program changes package scope, the global variables are visible only through their fully qualified package names. To ensure you get the same global variable, you must use its fully qualified package name.

An *overloaded* variable is a global variable that has the same name in multiple packages. An *overwritten* variable is a global variable whose global definition has been replaced by another declaration or definition.

As shown in Listing 18.3, the global variables of one package may be overloaded by the global variables of another package, but they are not actually overwritten. Each package global variable is actually a different variable, even when it has the same, overloaded, name as a variable in another package. Just as you know that David Smith and David Jones are two different people, Perl 5 knows that `$main::scalar` and `$math::scalar` are two separate variables, even though their unqualified package global name, `$scalar`, is the same.

In the most trivial and common case, you overwrite a variable each time it is assigned a new value. You can overwrite a variable by declaring it more than once in the same scope, however. A variable that is declared as `my $editor = "doug";` and then later in the same scope is declared as `my $editor = "Marilyn Smith";` has been overwritten. Even in the case where the declaration does not include the assigning of a value, such as my `$editor;`, the previous values have been overwritten by the most recent declaration.

WARNING   Overwriting a variable by declaring it a second time can create confusing code. By using the same variable name to mean two different things in the same scope, you create a potential bug. You may forget which meaning of the variable you currently intend, and it is likely another programmer will miss the second declaration and not know what you expect the overwritten and twice-declared variable to mean. You should always use unique variable names throughout your code. When you need a new variable, declare a new variable with a different name. A variable name requires very little computer memory—only a byte or a word in most cases.

Dynamic Scope

A Perl 5 variable may also be dynamically scoped using the keyword `local`. A dynamically scoped variable temporarily overrides any global definition of the variable. Dynamically scoped variables are only visible to the enclosing block and any subroutines called within the enclosing block. A dynamically scoped variable creates a copy of the previous value of a globally scoped variable. When the dynamically scoped variable goes out of scope, the previous value of the global variable is restored.

This feature has some practical use when used with built-in global variables such as ARGV, $_, @INC, and $". When modifying any global variable for an enclosing scope, you should always make allowances for returning the global variable to its previous value. Since dynamically scoped variables save and restore the previous copy of a variable, you can use this feature to automatically save and restore modified copies of global variables. Listing 18.5 demonstrates how to use dynamically scoped variables to restore global variables to their previous values.

Listing 18.5:   **Dynamically Scoped Variables**

```
1.  #!/usr/local/bin/perl
2.  require common.pl ;
3.  while (<>){
4.     ($name, $title) = split(/:/);
5.     @departments = common();
```

```
6.      print "Now searching @departments\n";
7.      #Create a new enclosing block scope
8.      {
9.          #Create dynamically scoped copies of the special variables
10.         local ($_, @ARGV, @INC, $name, $title);
11.         @INC =("c:\testing\private","c:\testing\private\testData");
12.         @ARGV = ("c:\testing\private\testData\$department[0]",
13.                  "c:\testing\private\testData\$department[1]");
14.         require common.pl;
15.         while(<>){
16.             ($name, $title) = split(/:/);
17.             @employee = common($name);
18.             ($name, $title, $salary) = split(/:/,@employee);
19.         }
20.         #All dynamic variables restored to their previous values
21.     }
22.     if (/ENGINEERING/){
23.         $salary += ($salary * .20);
24.     }
25. }
```

The local variables are created on line 10 of Listing 18.5:

```
local ($_, @ARGV, @INC, $name, $title);
```

The require statements on lines 2 and 14, although identical in syntax, load two different files. Line 2 of Listing 18.5 searches the default @INC array directories for common.pl. Line 14 also loads common.pl based on the @INC array. However, in this case, it is searching a local copy of the @INC array, which includes only the two private directories loaded on line 11:

```
@INC =("c:\testing\private","c:\testing\private\testData");
```

Lines 12 and 13 load a local copy of the @ARGV array:

```
@ARGV = ("c:\testing\private\testData\$department[0]",
         "c:\testing\private\testData\$department[1]");
```

The local copy of @ARGV is used on line 15:

```
while(<>){
```

The file-input operator (<>) uses the @ARGV array for file-input arguments. By default, the @ARGV array is loaded with command-line arguments, but in this case, the @ARGV array is loaded with new information on line 13.

The split function on line 16 also operates on a local copy of the default-input variable $_. The utility of all of the local copies of these special variables comes into play on line 19, which ends the enclosing block for the local variables created on line 10.

The values of each of the global variables are restored by line 22. Line 21 is operating on the value loaded into the default special variable ($_) on line 3, not the value of $_ loaded on line 15. When this code continues execution on line 3, the while loop's input operators will be reading from an unmodified global @ARGV array.

In practice, the use of local variables, except in special cases where the dynamic scoping is the purpose, should be replaced with lexical my variables. Because local variables can be seen and modified by any subroutine called within the enclosing block, they are not truly limited in scope. This can lead to unexpected side effects when one of your subroutines modifies a local variable. The local variable may go out of scope or be used for another purpose elsewhere in the code. This problem becomes more acute as your program grows, and it becomes more difficult to keep track of each variable's use and definition throughout the code. In practice, when you want to create a variable that is truly local to the enclosing scope, use the keyword my, which is discussed next.

Lexical Scope

A variable that is limited to the enclosing scope is called a lexical variable. Lexical variables, created using the keyword my, are not part of the package's symbol table. A lexical variable exists and is visible only within the enclosing scope, with the following exception.

Perl 5 uses a reference count to determine how long a variable should remain in existence, which means a lexical variable does not go out of existence just because the enclosing scope ends. Every variable has an associated reference count. When a variable is defined or declared, its reference count is set to one. If a lexically scoped variable's enclosing block ends, the variable's reference count is decremented by one. If a variable's reference count is zero, Perl 5 automatically frees the space allocated for the variable in memory. Freed memory may be used for other memory tasks as needed.

A lexically scoped variable may remain in memory outside the execution of the enclosing block if its reference count remains greater than zero. Each Perl 5 reference to a variable increments the variable's reference counter. The reference counter is decremented when the variable counting the reference is deleted.

This means of automatically deleting variables is called *garbage collection*. Languages such as C++, Perl, and Java have built-in algorithms for determining when a variable is no longer needed in a program. When a variable can no longer be referenced by any statement, that memory location should be freed for other uses.

As stated earlier, a lexical variable is not part of a package's namespace and can only be referred to by the enclosing block. This structure creates a truly private variable that has visibility only within the block in which it is declared. This feature, along with the reference count garbage-collection feature, gives Perl 5 a reentrant code capability. *Reentrant* code is code that can call itself safely, because each time it is called, it gets a new set of variables with which to work. The most classic example of reentrant code is the calculation of the Fibonacci number, as shown in Listing 18.6.

Listing 18.6:   **A Reentrant Program to Calculate the Fibonacci Number**

```perl
1.  #!/usr/local/bin/perl
2.  foreach $value (0 .. $ARGV[0]){
3.      $fib = fibonacci($value);
4.      print "fibonacci of $value is $fib\n";
5.  }
6.
7.  sub fibonacci ($){
8.      local ($fib) = @_;
9.      return ERROR if $fib < 0;
10.     return 0 if $fib == 0;
11.     return 1 if $fib == 1;
12.     return (fibonacci($fib-1) + fibonacci($fib-2));
13. }
```

The Fibonacci algorithm is often used to calculate just how quickly two opposite-sex rabbits can produce a whole lot of new rabbits. The definition of a Fibonacci function is:

- The result equals the result of adding $n - 1$ and $n - 2$.

- The result is 1 if n equals 1.

- The result is 0 if n equals 0.

Lines 7 through 13 of Listing 18.6 are a recursive implementation of the Fibonacci function. According to this function, it takes just 25 generations to produce 75,025 rabbits, if only one female rabbit lives to maturity during each generation and if rabbits live forever. These results are shown in Figure 18.2.

FIGURE 18.2:

Eternal rabbits

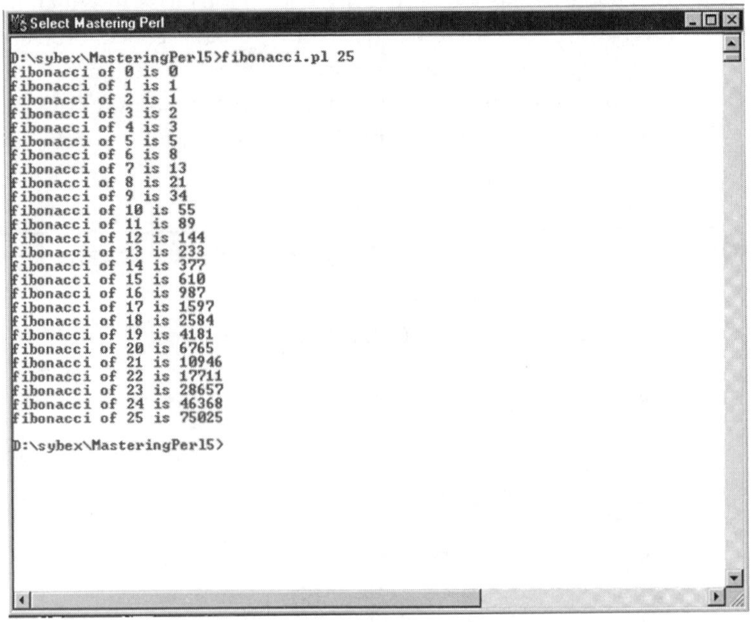

```
D:\sybex\MasteringPerl5>fibonacci.pl 25
Fibonacci of 0 is 0
Fibonacci of 1 is 1
Fibonacci of 2 is 1
Fibonacci of 3 is 2
Fibonacci of 4 is 3
Fibonacci of 5 is 5
Fibonacci of 6 is 8
Fibonacci of 7 is 13
Fibonacci of 8 is 21
Fibonacci of 9 is 34
Fibonacci of 10 is 55
Fibonacci of 11 is 89
Fibonacci of 12 is 144
Fibonacci of 13 is 233
Fibonacci of 14 is 377
Fibonacci of 15 is 610
Fibonacci of 16 is 987
Fibonacci of 17 is 1597
Fibonacci of 18 is 2584
Fibonacci of 19 is 4181
Fibonacci of 20 is 6765
Fibonacci of 21 is 10946
Fibonacci of 22 is 17711
Fibonacci of 23 is 28657
Fibonacci of 24 is 46368
Fibonacci of 25 is 75025

D:\sybex\MasteringPerl5>
```

Lexically scoped my variables are the only truly private variables in Perl 5. All other variables are part of a package namespace. Whenever possible and practical, you should use the keyword my to create local variables instead of the keyword `local`.

Caution: A Potential Memory Leak

When a program fails to delete memory references, it makes the computer prone to a computer bug called a *memory leak*. Memory leaks can cause a computer to crash because the computer runs out of memory resources. Perl 5's garbage-collection algorithm has a potential memory leak.

Lexically scoped variables that contain a reference to themselves or are part of a circular reference will never be deleted. For example, suppose that the variable my $name refers to itself, like this:

```
$name=\$name;
```

The reference count for this variable will equal 2 (one for the variable itself, plus one for the reference to the variable). When the enclosing block goes out of scope, the reference count is decremented by one, leaving a positive reference count. Even though the lexically scoped variable $name cannot be accessed by any other Perl 5 statement, its memory location will never be freed, because the variable has a positive reference count. This also can occur if a variable is part of a circular reference, like this:

```
my $hisName, $herName;

$hisName = \$herName;

$herName = $hisName;
```

Each of these lexically scoped variables has a reference count of 2 and will never be deallocated from memory.

On the other hand, this example does allow for memory deallocation:

```
my($hisName, $herName, $their Name);

$hisName = \$herName;

$theirName = \$hisName;
```

Both $hisName and $herName have a reference count of 2, and $theirName has a reference count of 1. When the enclosing block ends, each variable's reference count will be decremented by one, leaving $theirName at a reference count equal to zero and $hisName and $herName at a reference count equal to one. Because the $theirName reference count is zero, its memory location is marked as free. All variables referred to by a freed variable have their reference count decremented by one. This sets $hisName's reference count to zero, decrementing the reference count of all the variables it referenced, which frees the last lexically scoped variable, $herName, from memory.

Subroutines and Functions

If packages define the rooms in your house and data scope defines the way you communicate between rooms, then subroutines define the way you do things in each room. Subroutines perform repeatable operations, similar to turning on a light, vacuuming the floor, or washing the dishes in a room.

A *subroutine* is a reusable block of code. A *function* is a reusable block of code that returns a value. All Perl 5 subroutines return the value of the last expression evaluated, which means that in Perl 5, functions and subroutines are synonyms.

My first programming boss had a rule about creating subroutines. Her subroutine rule was that if you repeat it three times or more, then it should be a subroutine. Subroutines can be one line long or hundreds of lines long, but they are usually short sections of code that perform a distinct operation.

Subroutine Definition

A subroutine in Perl 5 is declared or defined using the keyword `sub`. Subroutines may be named or anonymous and are declared like this:

```
sub subName;
sub subName(parameterList);
```

Declaring a subroutine without defining it allows you to use the subroutine in a list. All Perl 5 subroutines are dynamically scoped and are accessible at compile time throughout your programs.

A subroutine is defined by adding the subroutine code block after the subroutine declaration, like this:

```
sub subName{code block}
sub subName(parameterList) {code block}
```

You also can define an anonymous subroutine, like this:

```
$subReference = sub {code block};
```

The lvalue, `$subReference`, is not required. However, if it is omitted, there is no way to call the anonymous subroutine. Because the anonymous subroutine is created as part of an assignment statement, a semicolon is required after the closing curly brace (`}`). The semicolon completes the assignment statement operation.

Subroutine Calling Syntax

The syntax used when calling a Perl 5 subroutine has a subtle impact on how the parameters are passed to the subroutine. The @_ array is the only mechanism for receiving the parameter list. The details of parameter passing are discussed in the next section. The various ways to call a subroutine are listed in Table 18.2.

TABLE 18.2: Subroutine Calling Syntax

Call	Type	Action
subName(*paramList*)	Direct	Creates a local copy of the @_ array set to the scalar values of the parameter list.
subName *paramList*;	Direct	Creates a local copy of the @_ array set to the scalar values of the parameter list. Must be a predeclared subroutine.
&subName;	Direct	Passes the enclosing block's copy of the global @_ array as the parameter list.
&$subReference;	Indirect	Uses a subroutine reference to call the subroutine. The ampersand is not optional in an indirect call. The global @_ array is passed as the parameter list.
&$subReference(*paramList*);	Indirect	Creates a local copy of the @_ array equal to the scalar values of the parameter list.

Prior to Perl 5, a subroutine call required an ampersand prefixing the subroutine name, as in &subName. This syntax is still acceptable in Perl 5 but *Practically Perfect Perl 5 Programmers Practice Ampersand Prefix Abstinence*. Not only will some of the upper-crusty Perl programmers frown on your use of the ampersand, but the ampersand has a specific effect on your code. A part of this effect is that users of your subroutine can force their own parameter lists on your subroutine by preceding the call to your subroutine with an ampersand. The ampersand is used for an indirect call—as a reference to a subroutine. The ampersand tells the Perl 5 interpreter to look in its list of subroutines for the reference address.

Here is a summary of how subroutine calls work:

- If the parameter list is absent and the ampersand is used as part of the calling sequence, the global copy of @_ array is passed to the subroutine.

- If a parameter list is used in the subroutine call, the @_ array becomes a local copy of the parameter list.

- If the ampersand is used along with a parameter list, and the parameter list is surrounded by parentheses, the parameter list is passed to the called subroutine.

- If the parameter list is not surrounded by parentheses, the global copy of the @_ array is passed to the called subroutine.

Listing 18.6 demonstrates the different types of subroutine calls, and Figure 18.3 shows its output.

Listing 18.6:   **Subroutine Calls**

```
1.  #!/usr/local/bin/perl
2.  sub printParams($$$){
3.     my @paramList = @_;
4.     $paramCount = @_;
5.     print " $paramCount Parameters passed which are @paramList\n";
6.  }
7.  @_ = (5,6,7,8,9,10);
8.  #creates a local copy of @_ for printParams
9.  printParams (1,2,3);
10. #passes the global copy of @_ to printParams
11. &printParams;
12. #creates a local copy of @_ for printParams
13. #overrides the prototype definition, passing one fewer
14. #than the required parameters
15. &printParams (-4, -3);
16. #passes the global copy of @_ to printParams
17. &printParams -4, -3;
18. #creates a local copy of @_ for printParams
19. #overrides the prototype definition, passing more than
20. #the allowed parameters
21. &printParams(-13,-14,-15,-16,-17);
```

Lines 11 and 17 of Listing 18.6 use global copies of the @_ array as parameter lists:

```
&printParams;
&printParams -4, -3;
```

FIGURE 18.3:

Calling subroutines

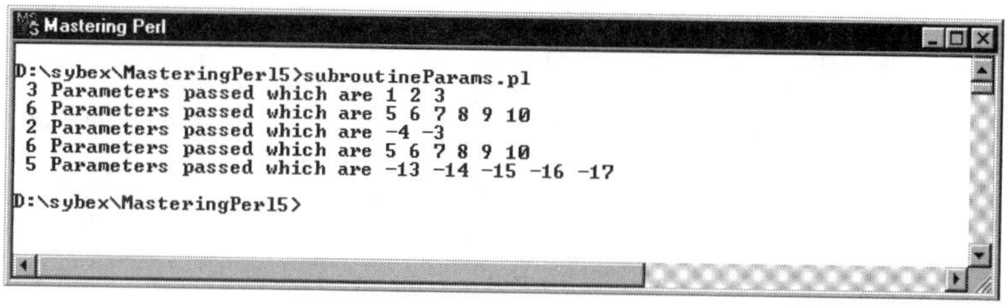

```
 Mastering Perl                                                    _ □ X

D:\sybex\MasteringPerl5>subroutineParams.pl
 3 Parameters passed which are 1 2 3
 6 Parameters passed which are 5 6 7 8 9 10
 2 Parameters passed which are -4 -3
 6 Parameters passed which are 5 6 7 8 9 10
 5 Parameters passed which are -13 -14 -15 -16 -17

D:\sybex\MasteringPerl5>
```

You can see the result of using global @_ array copies versus local copies in Figure 18.3.

Subroutine Parameter Lists

A subroutine defined or declared without a parameter list can be called without any restrictions on the number or type of parameters passed to the subroutine. A subroutine defined with a parameter list must be called with exactly the parameters specified, or a compilation error occurs. Declared parameters are called *formal* parameters. The values and variables used when calling a subroutine are called the *actual* parameters.

Parameter lists define both the type and number of parameters your subroutine expects. A parameter list is defined by putting the type indicator of each parameter between parentheses when declaring or defining a parameter. Each type indicator defines the parameter required for that position. Several sample parameter lists are shown in Table 18.3.

T A B L E 18.3: Sample Parameter Lists

Parameter List	Meaning
()	Zero parameters required or accepted.
($)	One parameter required.
($;\@)	One parameter required. The second parameter is optional but must be an array. A reference to the array, not the array elements, will be copied into @_.
($$$@)	The first three parameters are scalar; the remaining actual parameters will be gobbled up by the ending array.

Continued on next page

TABLE 18.3 CONTINUED: Sample Parameter Lists

Parameter List	Meaning
(\@\%$;$$)	The first parameter must be an array; a reference to the array will be passed to the subroutine. The second parameter must be a hash; a reference to the hash will be passed to the subroutine. The third parameter must be scalar in context. The fourth and fifth scalar parameters are optional.

A semicolon inside the parameter list separates the mandatory parameters from the optional parameters. All parameters following the semicolon are optional. All parameters preceding the semicolon are required.

If the declared parameter is preceded by a backslash, the type of the input parameter must equal the type of the declared parameter. A backslashed formal parameter forces a variable's reference to be passed. This allows you to define formal parameters of array and hash type and your actual parameters to be multiple arrays or hashes. A reference to the array or hash is passed in the parameter list instead of the array values.

Parameters that are not backslashed force the type indicator's context onto the actual parameter. If the formal parameter is a scalar type indicator and the actual parameter is an array, scalar context is applied to the actual parameter. This means that the size of the array, not the array values, will be passed to the subroutine.

Arrays and Hashes as Parameters

Unless you have placed a backslash before an array or hash formal parameter type, it makes little sense to define an array or hash as the input parameter type except in the last parameter position. Any array or hash variable passed as a parameter will be copied into its list of scalar variables, creating an undetermined number of parameters. In practice, scalar variables and backslashed hash and array variables are the most commonly used formal parameters because the hash and array type indicators effectively gobble up all remaining parameters.

Listing 18.7 illustrates passing scalar variables and array and hash references to a subroutine.

Listing 18.7:   Parameter Lists for Subroutines

```
 1.  #!/usr/local/bin/perl
 2.  sub parameterList (\@$\@\%$){
 3.      my ($array1Ref, $size, $ array2Ref, $hashRef, $scalar) = @_;
 4.      foreach $item (@$array1Ref){print "$item " ;}
 5.      foreach $item (@$array2Ref) {print "$item " ;}
 6.      print "$size, $scalar\n";
 7.      while (($key, $value) = each %$ hashRef)
                 {print "$key, $value ";}
 8.  }
 9.  @actualParam1 = (a, b, c, d, e);
10.  $param1Size = @actualParam1;
11.  @digits = (1 .. 10);
12.  $digitsSize = @p2;
13.  %hash = (z => 11, q => -1, t =>12);
14.
15.  parameterList (@actualParam1,$param1Size,@digits, %hash,
                 $digitsSize);
```

On line 2 of Listing 18.7, the subroutine `parameterList` declares five formal parameters.

```
sub parameterList (\@$\@\%$){
```

The first and third formal parameters declare that the actual first and third parameters must be arrays. The second and fifth formal parameters declare that the context of the actual second and fifth parameters will be scalar. The fourth formal parameter declares that the actual fourth parameter must be a hash. If the actual calling parameters did not meet these criteria, the program creates a compile-time error.

Line 15 calls the subroutine with the correct number and type of actual parameters:

```
parameterList (@actualParam1,$param1Size,@digits, %hash,
                 $digitsSize);
```

These actual parameters are copied into a dynamically scoped @_ array, which is copied into the lexically scoped variables of the subroutine on line 3:

```
my ($array1Ref, $size, $ array2Ref, $hashRef, $scalar) = @_;
```

Copying the @_ array into lexically scoped variables is the preferred means for accessing the @_ array because it prevents accidental modification of the actual parameters.

Like the reference parameters passed by backslashed formal parameters, the default input parameters list @_ is actually an array of references. Perl 5 does not copy each scalar variable to the subroutine, but instead passes a reference to the parameter in the default input array @_. If you modify the contents of the @_ array by directly referencing a cell in the array, such as $_[1], you are modifying the variable passed in the parameter list, not a copy of the variable.

Suppose that you tried to modify the input array and the passed parameter was a constant, like this:

```
subName ($VAR, 1,2,)1
sub SubName
    $_[1]=5;
```

Your program would generate a runtime error and stop executing, which is called crashing. Your program crashes because you cannot modify a literal—the number 1 in this example.

Call by Reference versus Call by Value

Another type of parameter passing, which is demonstrated in Listing 18.7, is called *call-by-reference* because your parameter list refers to the actual variable in memory. An alternative to call-by-reference is *call-by-value*, which can be simulated in Perl 5 by copying your actual parameters into a lexical list of variables, like this:

```
sub employee ($$$){
    my ($size, $Name, $salary)=@_;
```

This employee subroutine requires three input parameters, which are immediately copied into lexical variables. The lexical variables may then be manipulated without fear of actually modifying the actual variables passed into the subroutine.

Although it may seem like a good idea to modify the input parameters directly, this is usually bad programming practice because it creates a tight link between the calling code and the subroutine. Modifying the input parameters directly by modifying the @_ array cells requires your subroutine to be aware of what is expected to happen to the input parameters, because it will be modifying their contents. Modifying the input parameters also means the calling code must use variables that your subroutine can modify. The calling program can never use a literal as an actual parameter, because the subroutine is modifying the input parameters, and modifying a literal will create a runtime error (your program will crash). If your subroutine does modify the input parameters, then the calling code must be aware of this practice so it will never use a literal as an input parameter.

Creating tight couplings like this between your code makes your code harder to modify. If your subroutine changes how it uses its parameters, every place that subroutine is called must be examined for the effect of the change.

WARNING   Tightly coupled code is called brittle code because it is rigid and inflexible. You should avoid modifying the input array @_, which then directly returns the results of the subroutine in the actual parameters, if at all possible. Instead, you can take advantage of Perl 5's `return` statement, which makes it easy for you to return any type of data to the calling code.

Creating subroutines that use lexical variables as copies of the input array @_ creates loosely coupled code. Modifications to the lexical variables do not affect the calling code. Loosely coupled code is easier to modify, which is why call-by-value is preferred over call-by-reference.

Returning Data

All Perl 5 subroutines return the value of the last expression evaluated in the subroutine. The context of the lvalue—list or scalar—in the calling statement determines the context of the returning value.

For example, if the returned value of the subroutine is a list, such as (a, b, c, d), and the lvalue receiving the return value is a scalar, like this:

```
$scalarContext = subName();
```

the lvalue will receive the last element of the list. If the lvalue is an array, like this:

```
@arrayContext=subName();
```

the lvalue will be set to the contents of the list (a, b, c, d).

If the last expression of the subroutine is an array and the lvalue is a scalar, the value received is the size of the array. In fact, any number of return values are possible, but it is not possible to declare what you will return.

Perl 5 has a `return` statement that I prefer to use to exit my subroutines, because it explicitly states what values the code is expected to return to the caller and where the subroutine is expected to end. When I need to return to the code to modify or debug it, I know exactly where the final statement in the subroutine is located.

The syntax of the `return` statement is:

```
return (list);
```

The `return` statement exits the subroutine and returns control to the calling statement. The contents of the list are the values returned. All arrays in the list will be expanded to their scalar values.

If you want to return arrays or hashes, I recommend returning a reference to the array or hash. Returning a reference to an array or hash has a two-fold effect:

- Because Perl is not required to make a copy of the data, it is faster to return a reference to an array or hash.

- It is safer to return a reference to a hash.

A hash is made up of key/value pairs. If the returned hash contains a key with no value, then when the hash is expanded to a list, the key/value pairs will become unordered.

For example, if the returned hash was a name/value pair from an HTML form, all of the form's names will be defined as keys into the hash, but some of the values may be undefined. If the hash defined a person's address, the name/value pair for street might be defined, but the name/value pair for apartment might have only the apartment as the hash key, with no value. When the hash is expanded in the `return` list, you will end up with a list that contains an unbalanced hash array, such as this:

```
(Name, Beatrice, Street, "1304 Kinsington", Apartment, City, Alwurst,
State, Calif, Zip, 45875)
```

If the calling code tries to create a hash from the expanded values, everything after the hash key `Apartment` will be incorrect.

The `return` statement is not required to exit a subroutine. As stated previously, the value of the last statement executed in the subroutine will be the value returned to the calling code. If an assignment statement is the last statement executed, the value of the assignment statement will be returned to the calling code.

Summary

This chapter explained how to use tools that let you organize your programs. The tools Perl 5 provides are packages, subroutines, and lexical variables.

The chapter first described how packages are used to organize the overall structure of your program. A package definition declares a new lexical namespace. A package's namespace, which is called a symbol table, is implemented as a hash. The namespace continues in scope until the next package statement or the enclosing block ends. All of the symbols of a package are accessible through the package's symbol table.

You learned that even if you never declare a package, your program is still part of a package. Perl 5 defaults all programs to the package main. All the symbols of a program are accessible through the main package's symbol table.

Next, the chapter explained how you can control the communication between packages using Perl 5's data scope rules. Perl 5's variables are globally scoped by default, but that global visibility is controlled by the variable's package. When a variable is accessed using its unqualified name, the variable is global to its package. A global variable can be accessed across packages by any statement in your program if the variable is accessed by its fully qualified package name. Dynamic variables are created using the keyword local. Dynamic variables are accessible only to statements and subroutines called within the enclosing block. Lexical variables are Perl 5's truly private variables. A lexical variable is visible and exists only within the enclosing block in which it was defined or declared. A lexical variable is created using the keyword my.

The final tool covered in this chapter was the subroutine. A subroutine is a reusable block of code that may be called for execution by other statements in your program. Whenever you find yourself repeating the same code three or more times, you should create a subroutine. A subroutine is executed by using the subroutine's name in a statement. If the subroutine name is preceded by an ampersand (&), the subroutine receives a copy of the default array @_ from the enclosing scope of the calling statement. If the subroutine name is followed by a parameter list enclosed by parentheses, the parameter list will be copied into a dynamically scoped @_ array, which is accessible in the subroutine's scope.

Perl 5 subroutines may define the number and type of parameters that should be used when calling the subroutine. If the parameter type is preceded by a backslash in the formal declaration, the actual parameter must be of that type. A reference to the actual parameter is passed in the @_ array for all formal parameters preceded by a backslash. Formal parameters that are not preceded by a backslash force their type context—scalar or array—onto the actual parameters.

All subroutines in Perl 5 are also functions because all Perl 5 subroutines return the value of the last expression executed in the subroutine. The Perl 5 `return` statement can be used to explicitly exit a subroutine, which returns execution control to the calling statement. Any values in the `return` statement are returned to the lvalue of the calling statement.

Packages, data scope, and subroutines are a Perl 5 programmer's tools for creating functionally built programs. Functional programs segment the namespace and operations of the program into logically related parts. In the next chapter, you will learn about the Perl 5 features that allow you to design your programs around data structures. This type of programming is called *object-oriented design*.

Object-Oriented Programming

- ■ Object classes

- ■ Object methods

- ■ Object variables

- ■ Named parameters

- ■ Programming inheritance

In this chapter, you'll learn the programming techniques required for creating Perl 5 objects. This chapter doesn't teach the philosophy of object-oriented design, but it does explain how to implement objects in Perl 5. You'll learn about the major parts of an object and how to implement them.

Object-oriented programming techniques include creating constructors, destructors, class methods, and instance variables. All of these techniques are explained in this chapter. You'll also learn how to pass named parameters. The final section of this chapter describes how Perl 5 implements multiple inheritance and the syntax for calling base methods explicitly.

TIP   Object-oriented programming is a broad and worthwhile subject. I will admit that I was skeptical of this discipline at first, but now I am a fully converted to the object-oriented paradigm. I believe object-oriented–designed programs are easier to maintain and build. I highly recommend you take some time to study and practice this discipline. There are many books available on this topic. One that I recommend is *Design Patterns*, by Erich Gemma, et al. (Addison-Wesley, 1994).

An Introduction to Objects and Classes

An object can be a car, a house, or your computer's monitor. Objects are easy to visualize. For many programmers, being able to visualize the solution you are building makes the programming task easier.

Object Characteristics

All objects have two specific characteristics related to programming. First, you can do things to or with an object, such as turning on or off the computer monitor or driving the car down the road. Doing something with an object is called an *operation*, which is implemented in a subroutine. *Method* is the object-oriented term for a subroutine associated with an object.

The other characteristic of an object is its *state*. A computer monitor's state might be on or off. Your car has many states—it might be in first gear, the radio may be on or off, and so on. An object's state is implemented in *instance variables*.

Instance variables capture the characteristics of an object that make each copy of the object unique. *Instance variable* is the object-oriented term for a variable associated with an object.

Object Classes

A *class* is the container that holds your Perl 5 object. A class is always a package, but a package is not always a class.

As you learned in the previous chapter, a package can be used to create functional designs and functional libraries. A package becomes a class when it is used to create methods, variables, and modules that are associated with an object. A class becomes a module when the entire class, all the methods, and all of the variables are saved into one file, which has the same name as the class and has the extension `.pm`.

The module `Win32` is a module because its package name is `Win32` and it is saved into a file called `Win32.pm`. In short, a module is no more than a file that has the same name as the class it contains, with the filename extension `.pm`. To create a class, you declare a package and then create class variables and methods and instance variables and methods that are part of the class.

NOTE   The term *class* will be used throughout this chapter as a synonym for package. When the syntax of functions and statements, such as **bless** and **use**, is explained, you can always substitute the keyword **package** for the keyword **class**.

Class is the object-oriented term for the implementation of an object. Perl 5 uses a package to implement the class concept. The combination of class, state, and methods—which are implemented in packages, instance variables, and subroutines—creates a Perl 5 object.

Object Methods

There are two types of methods in a Perl 5 object: class methods and instance methods. The class method expects the package name as the first parameter of the parameter list. The instance method expects an object reference as the first parameter of the parameter list.

The calling syntax of object methods uses the right arrow notation. The right arrow notation invokes the class method and substitutes the parameter to the left of the arrow as the first parameter passed to the class method.

The following sections describe class methods, constructors, object references, instance methods, and instance variables.

Class Methods

Class methods are called with the class name as the first parameter of the parameter list. Class methods are frequently used as interface programs between classes.

To call a class method, use this syntax:

```
className->methodName(parameterList);
```

Perl 5 adds the class name as the first parameter of the parameter list. The first statements of a class method should always move the first parameter out of the parameter list into a lexical variable, like this:

```
my $class = shift;
```

The class method can then use the lexical $class variable as a means of defining which package the class method is associated with.

With Perl 5, the most frequently used class method is the constructor, which is described next.

Constructors

A *constructor* is a class method used for object initialization and to return an object reference. By convention, a Perl 5 constructor is named new:

```
className->new();
```

The object reference is used by other classes to access instance methods and by the instance methods to access the class instance variables. Since constructors end up creating the object references that are later used by instance methods, the constructor is always a class method. Any program that includes the class name can use class methods.

Listing 19.1 calls the constructor of a larger program, called NewsUpdate, used by companies (such as the Knight Ridder Charlotte Observer at www.ThatsRacing.com) to display news articles for various departments within the company. The program provides a drag-and-drop interface for publishing interdepartmental information. Pieces of this program will be used throughout this chapter to explain various object-oriented concepts and implementations in Perl 5.

Listing 19.1:   The Department Page Call

```
1.  #!/usr/local/bin/perl
2.  use DepartmentPage;
3.  require "readPostInput.cgi";
4.  #The department's name is passed via a server-side Include
5.  #exec format, which makes the argument list available in ARGV
6.  #just as if it came from the command line.
7.  my ($trash, $departmentName)= split(/=/,$ARGV[0]);
8.  my $department =
            DepartmentPage->new(departmentName=>$departmentName);
```

Listing 19.1 includes the class name `DepartmentPage` through the `use` statement on line 2. The `use` statement includes the class `DepartmentPage` in the program's namespace by loading the file named `DepartmentPage.pm` from the disk. Here are the rules for the `use` statement:

- The syntax of the use statement is:

   ```
   use className;
   ```

- The `use` statement only looks for files with the filename extension `.pm`.

- The `use` statement accepts only a class name as its single parameter, and that class name must reference a file of the same name with the `.pm` extension.

- Classes included using the `use` statement are compiled at the time they are loaded into the program. (The `require` statement compiles the loaded program during the execution of the overall program.)

Listing 19.1 invokes the `DepartmentPage` constructor on line 8, which contains the new method, using the special syntax for calling class methods:

```
my $department =
```

```
DepartmentPage->new(departmentName=>$departmentName);
```

The new method receives the class name as its first parameter. It then shifts the first parameter into the lexical variable $class. The variable $class is then used to bless a reference to an anonymous hash, linking the instance variable $self to the class named in $class. This is what is done in the department page constructor (Listing 19.3). But before we get to that example, let's simplify and consolidate our example with the standardized code in Listing 19.2.

Listing 19.2:   **A Constructor Template**

```
1.  sub new{
2.      my $class = shift;
3.      my (%params) = @_;
4.      my $self = {};
5.      bless $self, $class;
        ...
N-1     return $self;
N   }
```

Listing 19.2 is a simplified and standardized constructor that you can use as a template for your constructors. This template performs the primary task of a constructor, creating and returning an object reference $self. Line 2 of Listing 19.2 shifts the class name out of the input array @_.

The class name is then shifted into the $class variable. Line 4 creates a reference to an anonymous hash, which will be used to access the class's instance variables. This anonymous hash will remain in existence as long as there is at least one reference to it. Line 5 creates a·link between the anonymous hash and the class name passed in the $class lexical variable. The $class variable is used in the bless function on line 5 to create a link between the anonymous hash and the class name.

Once the association is created between the anonymous hash and the class, the object reference variable is returned to the calling program. The variable $self, which contains the object reference, can then be used by the calling program to refer to the class's instance variables.

Object Reference Variables

An object reference variable is required to access the unique characteristics of an individual object. An object reference variable is a variable that contains a reference to a package-scoped anonymous hash and that has been linked with the package through the bless function.

The object reference variable is created by the bless function, which makes a link between an object and a class name. In this example, the bless function modifies the hash reference variable by creating a link between the anonymous hash and the class name. The bless function takes two parameters: an object and a class name. If the class name is not supplied, the object is linked with the current package.

The constructor template (Listing 19.2) shows the common usage of the bless function:

```
bless $referenceVariable, $className;
```

However, this syntax actually hides some of the details of the bless function. This usage implies that the bless function operates on a reference variable, but the function actually operates on the variable the reference variable points to. This means that changes to the reference variable do not modify the link between the object and the class. If you created a new reference to the object, you would not need to bless it (the reference or the object) into the class a second time, because the object retains its link to the class.

Also, although an lvalue isn't normally supplied in the commonly used bless format, the bless function always returns a reference to the linked object. The complete syntax of the bless function is:

```
lvalue = bless object, className;
```

This syntax can replace the two-statement syntax:

```
my $self = {};
bless $self, $class;
```

with this single statement:

```
my $self = bless {}, $class;
```

The two-statement syntax of the bless function is used throughout this book because it is the form you will see most often in Perl 5 programs.

Listing 19.3 shows the constructor of the departmentPage class, which was called in Listing 19.1. Although this listing contains 64 lines (including a generous number of comment lines), it follows the same structure of the constructor template shown in Listing 19.2.

Listing 19.3:   **The Department Page Constructor**

```
1.  #!/usr/local/bin/perl
2.  #The extension of the file is not included in the use statement.
3.  use Constants;
4.  use Relationship;
5.  use Article;
6.
7.  #This package defines the class for the department's main page.
8.  #Class and package are synonyms.
9.  package DepartmentPage;
10.
11. open(DEPARTMENTS,"departments.txt") || die $!;
12. @departments = <DEPARTMENTS>;
13. close (DEPARTMENTS);
14.
15. sub new {
16.    #I know who I am and it is passed in the first parameter.
17.    my $class = shift;
18.    #PARAMETER LIST
19.    #departmentName Scalar string
20.    #Copy the remaining param list into the params hash.
21.    #Using a hash, the param list does not need to be ordered.
22.    #The param list may even be incomplete.
23.    #If there is no data for the parameter,
24.    #the instance variable will be created as null OR
25.    #you can create defaults for your instance variable.
26.    my (%params) = @_;
27.
28.    #Create the object that will contain all of the instance
29.    #variables. Notice that the hash is a package global variable.
30.    my $self = {};
31.
32.    #Create the link between the package and the object.
33.    #Remember even though you are blessing the reference to the
34.    #object, the bless is actually done on the object.
35.    bless $self, $class;
36.
37.    #By naming the hash cell, it is created. Determine if
38.    #the named parameter was passed to the constructor. Use
39.    #defaults if the initialization parameter is not available.
```

```
40.
41.    #INITIALIZE MY INSTANCE VARIABLES
42.    $self->{name} = (defined $params{departmentName}) ?
                         $params{departmentName} : "Main";
43.    my $department;
44.    #The @departments array is a class variable, visible to all
45.    #methods and NOT accessed using the $self instance variable.
46.    foreach $department (@departments){
47.       chomp $department;
48.       #Find the department that matches the departmentName used
49.       #to instantiate this object.
50.       if ($department =~ /^$self->{name}/){
51.       #When the correct department is found, initialize my
52.       #instance variables, creating my unique instance identity.
53.          ($fileName, $self->{linkLimit}, $self->{template},
             $self->{imageSource},$self->{imageAltText}) =
54.             split(/:\^/,$department);
55.          last;
56.       }
57.    }
58.    #Create the relationship object, which has the info about
59.    #the relationships between department page and news stories
60.    $self->{relationship} = Relationship->new
                         (department=>$self->{name});
61.    #Build my department's Main HTML news page.
62.    $self->buildDeptPage();
63.    return ($self);
64.    }
```

The constructor begins on line 15 and continues to line 64. The class itself is declared on line 9:

```
package DepartmentPage;
```

Lines 17, 26, 30, 35, and 63 are almost a direct copy of Listing 19.2. Notice the two-statement syntax of the bless function on lines 30 and 35:

```
17.    my $class = shift;
26.    my (%params) = @_;
30.    my $self = {};
35.    bless $self, $class;
```

Lines 42 through 62 perform the initialization processing, which is the other main task of a constructor. Lines 62 and 63 are used to call an instance method of the NewsUpdate program and return the object reference:

```
$self->buildDeptPage();
return ($self);
```

Instance methods are discussed in the next section.

Instance Methods

The calling syntax of instance methods also uses the right arrow notation, but an instance method expects an object reference as its first parameter. An instance method is called like this:

```
$objectReference->methodName(parameterList);
```

Just as with the class method, the object reference is moved onto the parameter list and then shifted back off the parameter list as the first statement of the instance method, like this:

```
my $self = shift;
```

The instance method then uses the lexical $self to access its instance variables. Listing 19.4 is an instance method from the NewsUpdate program introduced in Listing 19.1 and called on line 62 of Listing 19.3.

Listing 19.4:   **Building the Department Page**

```
1.   sub buildDeptPage(){
2.       #Return HTML for this department's Main Page
3.       #Get this department's story list
4.       #Read template
5.       #Look for a line with :^\w+^:
6.       #Determine substitution type
7.       #Make substitution
8.       #
9.       #Substitution Types:
10.      #MainStoryLink
11.      #MainStoryHeadLine
12.      #DepartmentImageSource
13.      #DepartmentImageAlternativeText
14.      #MainStoryFirstParagraph
```

```perl
15.     #DepartmentStoryLinks
16.     my $self = shift;
17.     my $storyListRef = $self->{relationship}->
                                    getDepartmentStories();
18.     my @unorderedStoryList = @$storyListRef;
19.     #This returns the indexes in sorted order
20.     @storyListIndexes = sort uidSort 0.. $#unorderedStoryList;
21.     sub uidSort(){
22.         $unorderedStoryList[$b]->{uid} <=>
                                    $unorderedStoryList[$a]->{uid} ;
23.     }
24.     my ($storyIndex, @storyList) ;
25.     #Take list of indexes and move unordered list to ordered list
26.     for ($storyIndex = 0; $storyIndex <= $#storyListIndexes;
                                    $storyIndex++){
27.         $storyList[$storyIndex] =
28.             $unorderedStoryList[$storyListIndexes[$storyIndex]];
29.     }
30.
31.     my $mainStory;
32.     foreach $story (@storyList){
33.         if ($story->{mainStory} =~ /y(es)?/i){
34.             $mainStory = $story;
35.             last;
36.         }
37.     }
38.     $mainStory->{firstParagraph} = $self->getFirstParagraph
                                    ($mainStory->{uid});
39.
40.     open(TEMPLATE,"$self->{template}");
41.     #List context is required?
42.     my (@template) = <TEMPLATE>;
43.     close(TEMPLATE);
44.     my $line;
45.     for ($i=0; $i <= $#template; $i++){
46.         #Does this line contain the magic characters?
47.         if ($template[$i] =~ /:\^\w+:\^/){
48.             #This copies only the pattern string to @allmatches
49.             my @allMatches = ($template[$i] =~ /:\^(\w+):\^/g);
50.             my $match;
51.             foreach $match (@allMatches){
52.                 SWITCH:
```

```
53.              {
54.                  if ($match =~ /mainStoryLink/){
55.                      my $subString = q|"http://www.assi.net/
                                cgi-bin/viewNews.cgi?article=|;
56.                      $subString .= qq|$mainStory->{uid}"| ;
57.                      $template[$i] =~ s/:\^mainStoryLink:
                                \^/$subString/;
58.                      last SWITCH;
59.                  }
60.                  if ($match =~ /mainStoryHeadline/){
61.                      #Insert main story headline
62.                      $template[$i] =~ s/:\^mainStoryHeadline:
                                \^/$mainStory->{headline}/;
63.                      last SWITCH;
64.                  }
65.                  if ($match =~ /mainStoryFirstParagraph/){
66.                      #Insert main story first paragraph
67.                      #$template[$i] =~ s/:
                                \^mainStoryFirstParagraph:
                                \^/This is a test/;
68.                      $template[$i] =~ s/:
                                \^mainStoryFirstParagraph:
                                \^/$mainStory->{firstParagraph}/;
69.                      last SWITCH;
70.                  }
71.                  if ($match =~ /DepartmentImageSource/){
72.                      $template[$i] =~ s/:
                                \^DepartmentImageSource:
                                \^/\"$self->{imageSource}\"/;
73.                      last SWITCH;
74.                  }
75.                  if ($match =~ /DepartmentImageAlternateText/){
76.                      $template[$i] =~ s/:
                                \^DepartmentImageAlternateText:
                                \^/\"$self->{imageAltText}\"/;
77.                      last SWITCH;
78.                  }
79.                  if ($match =~ /DepartmentStoryLinks/){
80.                      #Delete this line from the template
81.                      #Insert the story links into the template
82.                      $template[$i] = "";
83.                      my $subString = "http://www.assi.net/
                                cgi-bin/viewNews.cgi?article=";
```

```
 84.                     for ($storyIndex = 0;
 85.                         $storyIndex <= $self->{linkLimit};
 86.                         $storyIndex++){
 87.                       $story = $storyList[$storyIndex];
 88.                       my $printSubString = $subString .
                                                   $story->{uid};
 89.                       $template[$i] .= qq|
 90. <LI>
 91. <FONT SIZE=-1>
 92. <A HREF="$printSubString">
 93. $story->{headline}
 94. </FONT>
 95. </LI>
 96. |;
 97.                     }
 98.                   last SWITCH;
 99.                 }
100.                 DEFAULT:{
101.                     print<<"eof";
102. INVALID MATCH IN BUILDING DEPARTMENT PAGE
103.                 $match
104. is an invalid template identifier
105. eof
106.                 }
107.               }#END OF SWITCH BLOCK
108.             }#end of foreach allMatches
109.         }#end we have found a template identifier
110.     }#end looping through template
111. print "@template\n";
112. }#end buildDeptPage subroutine
```

This instance method moves its object reference out of the parameter list on line 16. An instance method must always move its object reference into a lexical variable. The object reference gives the instance method access to the current state of the object. For the buildDeptPage method, this means it has access to a relationship object that is already intialized with the correct department name. The buildDeptPage method can get its department's stories without special logic to determine which department it belongs to, as shown on line 17 of Listing 19.4:

```
my $storyListRef = $self->{relationship}->getDepartmentStories();
```

The capturing of an object's state and identity in instance variables allows each method to concentrate on its particular task, without requiring special logic or additional variables to determine its unique identity. Listing 19.4 outputs the department page shown in Figure 19.1 without any special logic to determine which department it belongs to. Instance variables, which are discussed in the next section, can help you create more reusable methods by decreasing the amount of logic required to determine a method's identity.

FIGURE 19.1:

A departmental news page

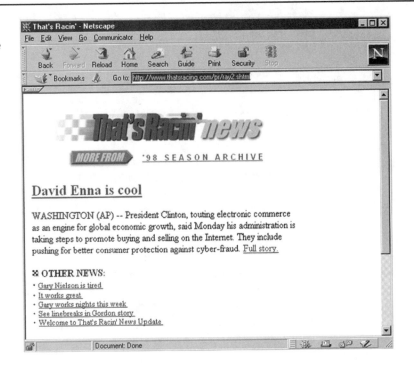

Object Variables

There are two types of variables in a Perl 5 object: class variables and instance variables. Class variables are global to the entire package and have persistence over the life of the program. (A variable is *persistent* as long as it remains in memory.) Both class methods and instance methods use class variables as a means of modifying the object's overall state. Class variables are used by the object methods to create state and identity across all the methods of a class.

An instance variable creates a unique identity for an object. Instance variables are used both to define the state of an object and its uniqueness. Instance variables are created and associated with each new copy of an object. Some instance variables have persistence throughout the life of the object, but an instance variable is available only through a referenced variable that has been specially identified with a class.

Instance Variables

When General Motors puts out one more car, that car has the same basic parts as the last one, but each car has different options. These options include color, radio, engine type, air conditioning, and many, many more choices. Each of these options creates a car with identifiable properties, which distinguish it from another car. These options that make a particular car different from another car are like instance variables in object-oriented programming.

Each time you invoke an object, you get the same basic object and a reference variable to that object. The class methods and class variables are the common part of the object. The instance variables and instance methods that are accessed using the reference variable are the unique characteristics of the object you created.

Instance Variables of the DepartmentPage Object

Lines 41 through 60 of Listing 19.3 create the instance variables of the Department-Page object. The instance variables give each department's page its own identity.

```
41.    #INITIALIZE MY INSTANCE VARIABLES
42.    $self->{name} = (defined $params{departmentName}) ?
                         $params{departmentName} : "Main";
43.    my $department;
44.    #The @departments array is a class variable, visible to all
45.    #methods and NOT accessed using the $self instance variable.
46.    foreach $department (@departments){
47.       chomp $department;
48.       #Find the department that matches the departmentName used
49.       #to instantiate this object.
50.       if ($department =~ /^$self->{name}/){
```

```
51.        #When the correct department is found, initialize my
52.        #instance variables, creating my unique instance identity.
53.           ($fileName, $self->{linkLimit}, $self->{template},
                 $self->{imageSource},$self->{imageAltText}) =
54.              split(/:\^/,$department);
55.           last;
56.        }
57.     }
58.     #Create the relationship object, which has the info about
59.     #the relationships between department page and news stories
60.     $self->{relationship} = Relationship->new
                                      (department=>$self->{name});
```

The first instance variable is created on line 42:

```
$self->{name} = (defined $params{departmentName}) ?
                    $params{departmentName} : "Main";
```

The anonymous hash is referenced using the reference object, and assigned a value using the hash key name. Remember that a hash cell comes into existence when a key is assigned a value. In this case, the input array %params is checked to see if departmentName was defined. If the test returns true, then the parameter is used as this department's name; otherwise, the name is set to "Main".

Next, the constructor searches the class variable @departments for the department's initialization information. The @departments array, which is read from a file on the hard disk, is shown in Listing 19.5.

Listing 19.5:   The Departments Initialization Data

```
1. Medical :^5 :^templates/medical.template :^/images/news_image.gif
            :^Medical Center News
2. Main :^5 :^templates/Main.template :^/images/Main_image.gif
            :^Main Center News
3. Education :^5 :^templates/Education.template
            :^/images/Education_image.gif :^Education Center News
4. Business :^5 :^templates/Business.template
            :^/imagesBusiness_image.gif
            :^Business Center News
5. Sports & Fitness :^5 :^templates/Sports.template
            :^/images/Sports_image.gif :^Sports & Fitness Center News
6. Classifieds :^5 :^templates/Classifieds.template
            :^/images/Classifieds_image.gif :^Classifieds Center News
```

The foreach loop searches through the @departments array, looking for a line that begins with this objects' name. The test for the object's name on line 50 of Listing 19.3 uses the object reference variable $self to access the anonymous hash that contains the instance data:

```
if ($department =~ /^$self->{name}/){
```

Once the correct department data is identified, line 53 of Listing 19.3 saves the data into the hash cells linkLimit, template, imageSource, and imageText. Each of the hash keys becomes an instance variable creating a department ID entity for this object. Line 60 of Listing 19.3 creates a Relationship object, which we'll use to study how instance variables can make programming much simpler:

```
$self->{relationship} = Relationship->new(department=>$self->{name});
```

Instance Variables of the Relationship Object

Listing 19.6 is part of the Relationship object of the NewsUpdate program. The Relationship object keeps track of the stories and which department pages they are part of.

Listing 19.6:   **Story Relationships**

```
1.  #!/usr/local/bin/perl
2.  package Relationship;
3.
4.  #This object must read and write to the disk - keeping a copy of
5.  #itself after each run.
6.  #
7.  #Package globals should not be modified outside this package
8.  $storyIndex = 0;
9.  #RELATIONSHIP = DEPARTMENT:^UID:^HEADLINE:^MAINSTORY
10. open(RELATIONSHIP,"relationship.txt") || die $!;
11. @relationship = <RELATIONSHIP>;
12. close (RELATIONSHIP);
13. foreach $relation (@relationship){
14.     my ($department,$uid,$headline,$mainStory) =
                                split(/:\^/,$relation);
15.     my %relationshipHash = (department=>$department,
16.                             uid=>$uid,
17.                             headline=>$headline,
18.                             mainStory=>$mainStory);
19.     push @storyList, \%relationshipHash;
```

```
20. }
21.
22. sub new {
23.     my $class = shift;
24.     my (%params) = @_;
25.     $self = {};
26.     bless $self, $class;
27.     $self->{departmentName} = $params{department};
28.     return $self;
29. }
30.
31. sub getDepartmentStories {
32.     my $self = shift;
33.     #Search the story list and return a list of all of the
34.     #stories that have this department's name.
35.     my (@departmentStories, $i);
36.
37.     #Story list is an array that points to a hash of story data.
38.     foreach $story (@storyList){
39.         if ($$story{department} eq $self->{departmentName}){
40.             #Save the hash reference into department story list.
41.             $departmentStories[$i++] = $story;
42.         }
43.     }
44.     return (\@departmentStories);
45. }
```

Like the DepartmentPage object, the Relationship object reads from the hard disk some initial data about itself. Unlike the DepartmentPage object, the Relationship object is also responsible for saving any modifications to itself. You'll learn how this is done in the section on destructors, a bit later in this chapter.

Lines 22 through 29 of Listing 19.6 contain the Relationship constructor. The constructor initializes one instance variable on line 27 and then returns its reference object:

```
$self->{departmentName} = $params{department};
return $self;
```

Lines 31 through 45 demonstrate how to use an instance variable and provide some insight into how instance variables can simplify programming interfaces. The instance method getDepartmentStories can be called by another class, such as `DepartmentPage`, with a reference object that points to one instance of the object, like this:

```
my $storyListRef = $self->{relationship}->getDepartmentStories();
```

Creating the `Relationship` object, which was done on line 60 of Listing 19.3, saves it into the instance variable `relationship`, an object reference to the `Relationship` object. When the `getDepartmentStories` instance method of the `Relationship` object is invoked, the first parameter it receives is the reference object variable.

The parameter is shifted into a lexical variable `$self`, which can then be used to access the `Relationship` object's instance variables. Recall that the `Relationship` object's instance variable was set to the `departmentName` on line 27 of Listing 19.6.

Even though neither the calling code nor the receiving method explicitly received any identification about which department stories to get, the instance method has all the information it needs. The instance method retrieves the department name from the instance variables and then searches the class variable `@storyList` array for every occurrence of a story associated with this department on line 39 of Listing 19.6:

```
if ($$story{department} eq $self->{departmentName}){
```

Each story that is identified with the department is added to the lexical array `@departmentStories` on line 41:

```
$departmentStories[$i++] = $story;
```

which is returned to the calling method on line 44:

```
return (\@departmentStories);
```

Object-oriented programming allows each object to keep the information relevant to the object with the object. In this example, the object information was the department name. The methods of the object can then operate with the instance data, returning object information with very little coupling between the calling and receiving object. This decoupling of data and methods creates an environment where modification of one object's methods has little or no impact on another object. These decoupled objects are more flexible because they can accept modification with fewer concerns about the effect throughout the larger program.

The instance method examples discussed in this section use both class variables and instance variables. Class variables create a coupling between the methods of an object and should be used with care. Class variables are explained in the next section.

Class Variables

When Ford builds its millionth Taurus, it uses a common set of materials and templates. The common features of a car that identify a particular car model are called class variables in object-oriented programming.

Class variables can be created at any time in an object's existence, but they are most frequently created during construction or object compilation. Creating a class variable early in an object's existence helps guarantee that the class variable will be available whenever an object method is called. A class variable is global to the class and should always be available to all the methods of a class. A class variable is persistent throughout the object's life. Both the DepartmentPage and Relationship objects of the NewsUpdate program use class variables to facilitate object persistence and initialize the object's state.

The DepartmentPage object reads from disk into the @departments array each department's unique information. The class variable @departments is a means of creating class identity in a dynamic environment. Each time the DepartmentPage class is instantiated, it reads a set of initialization data from a file on the hard disk. A class is *instantiated* when its constructor is called, creating a new instance of the class. Later, as different instances of the class are created, each instance will use the data read from the hard disk to create part of its unique identity.

This mechanism of initialization keeps the maximum amount of unique information separate from your object code and provides a means of externally configuring an object, which helps create more general code. General, or generic, code is often more readily modifiable and reusable, which are attributes that help reduce both the cost of code maintenance and the cost of creating new code.

The Relationship object also uses the hard disk as an initialization medium, but with a different overall goal. The Relationship object creates a class array @storyList, which contains a hash of individual story information. The @storyList array contains the Relationship object's current state. Reading and writing an object's state to disk creates object persistence between object invocations and across different processes. This is a means of creating object persistence in a dynamic environment, such as CGI programming, which is, in fact, the NewsUpdate environment.

A snapshot of the `Relationship` data and the object itself is shown in Listing 19.7.

Listing 19.7:   The Relationship Data

```
1.  Sports:^912480848:^Gary Nielson is tired:^No
2.  Front_Page:^912480848:^Gary Nielson is tired:^No
3.  PR:^912480848:^Gary Nielson is tired:^No
4.  PR:^912480756:^David Enna is cool:^Yes
5.  Front_Page:^912480062:^It works great:^Yes
6.  PR:^912480062:^It works great:^Yes
7.  PR:^912478162:^Gary works nights this week:^No
8.  Sports:^912478162:^Gary works nights this week:^No
9.  PR:^912204099:^Welcome to That's Racin' News Update:^No
10. Sports:^912204099:^Welcome to That's Racin' News Update:^No
11. Sports:^912204683:^See linebreaks in Gordon story:^No
12. PR:^912204683:^See linebreaks in Gordon story:^No
13. Front_Page:^912205983:^No HTML required! :^No
14. Sports:^912205983:^No HTML required! :^No
15. PR:^912205983:^No HTML required! :^No
```

The `Relationship` data shown in Listing 19.7 captures one unique instance of a `Relationship` object. Each time the object is instantiated, it reads a copy of its current state into memory, using the hard disk as a persistent data store. When the `Relationship` object is modified, it writes a new copy of itself to disk. The mechanism used for writing a copy of itself to disk is described in the next section.

Destructors

The standard way to create a Perl 5 object is through the new subroutine, which takes the place of a constructor. A good object-oriented language also has a means to automatically call a subroutine when the object ceases to exist. A *destructor* is a subroutine that runs just before an object is freed or deleted from memory and allows the object to perform any cleanup required before it exits. In Perl 5, an object's destructor is identified by naming a subroutine DESTROY.

The destructor is never explicitly called; instead, the destructor is executed by the Perl 5 interpreter just before the object is freed in memory. The first question asked by most programmers is, "Why would you want to execute just before the object is being removed from memory?" And the most frequent answer is, "To close sockets or file handles." As you learned in Chapter 11, explicitly closing open file handles guarantees any buffered data is flushed from the buffer.

TIP   I recommend taking the time to create the DESTROY subroutine and making sure that all open file handles are closed before the object is freed from memory.

A destructor can do more than close sockets and file handles, however. Listing 19.8 illustrates a quite reasonable and rather clean example of why destructors are so handy.

Listing 19.8:   The DESTROY Subroutine

```
1.  #The DESTROY subroutine runs just before the object is removed
2.  #from memory. I don't have to call this routine; it will be
3.  #called automatically for me. This means that I don't
4.  #have to think about when to write out the Relationship
5.  #object. It will be written once each time the Relationship
6.  #object is created and destroyed.
7.  sub DESTROY {
8.    my $self = shift;
9.    #I have a complete and up-to-date copy of the Relationship
10.   #object in memory, so destroy the old copy and dump out the
11.   #latest copy.
12.   open(RELATIONSHIP,">relationship.txt") || die $!;
13.   foreach $story (@storyList){
14.     my $outString;
15.     $outString .= $story->{department} . ':^';
16.     $outString .= $story->{uid} . ':^';
17.     $outString .= $story->{headline} . ':^';
18.     $outString .= $story->{mainStory};
19.     chomp $outString;
20.     print RELATIONSHIP "$outString\n";
21.   }
22.
23.   close (RELATIONSHIP);
24. }
```

Listing 19.8 is the destructor for the Relationship object in the NewsUpdate program. The Relationship object is responsible for keeping track of which stories belong with which department page. Stories can be added, deleted, and modified from each department page, and each modification to the story list must be recorded. The story list modifications are kept in memory and then written to disk. The Relationship object reads this information from the disk when it is created but must decide when is the best time to write the modified information to the disk.

The program could write to the disk each time the data is modified. However, writing to the disk is a slow process. The destructor is the perfect solution to this problem. Each modification to the story list is maintained in memory, then just before the Relationship object is removed from memory, the DESTROY subroutine is executed. This is an efficient and timely solution because the destructor writes a fresh copy of the Relationship object to memory once, and only once, and it always has the latest modification in it. As an added bonus, no special logic is required to determine when to save the data to disk—it happens automatically just because the subroutine is named DESTROY.

Named Parameters

In Chapter 18, you learned about passing parameters to subroutines. That chapter explained how to pass parameters in an array to a list of lexical variables. In the examples in this chapter, you may have noticed that after the object reference or class name is shifted out of the @_ array, the parameter list is copied into a lexical hash, like this:

```
my (%params)= @_;
```

Using a hash as the receiving variable for the parameter list means you can declare a parameter list, as in functional programming, but you can use a named parameter list. A named parameter list has the calling program pass the parameters to the subroutine just as if it were initializing a hash variable with a name/value pair. Listing 19.1 (line 8) used this syntax to call the department-Page constructor:

```
my $department = DepartmentPage->new(departmentName=>$departmentName);
```

The departmentPage is the parameter name, and the value is $departmentName.

Named parameters allow you to call a subroutine with parameters out of order and with parameters missing. The receiving routine expects the parameters as a hash, which doesn't have a specific order. It also allows the receiving subroutine to set defaults if the calling subroutine doesn't define an expected parameter, which is exactly what line 42 of Listing 19.3 does:

```
$self->{name} = (defined $params{departmentName}) ?
$params{departmentName} : "Main";
```

If the named parameter departmentName is defined, that value is used; otherwise, the default value of "Main" will be used as the department page name.

Some programmers (myself included) prefer the additional features of a named parameter list, which are enumerated here:

- You can explicitly associate a value with each parameter. This feature makes your code easier to understand, because each parameter passed is identified with its destination name.

- Because named parameter lists are position independent, you can insert your parameters in whatever order is convenient for the calling code. This feature allows the receiving subroutine the luxury of changing the order of the parameters at any time.

- Your parameter lists can be of varying length. In a defined parameter list, optional parameters can occur only at the end of the parameter list. In a named parameter list, optional parameters are position independent.

- Named parameter lists can be validated. This feature provides a means of verifying the input parameters.

When I first discovered named parameters, I was concerned about passing invalid parameter names. I could call a subroutine with a named parameter that would never be used because I mistyped the parameter name. For example, what if I typed in:

```
depatmentName=>$departmentName
```

instead of:

```
departmentName=>$departmentName
```

The default value would always be used because the named parameter departmentName would not be defined—just because I left out that *r*.

My partner, Tim Coats, came up with a slick solution for validating input parameter names, which is shown in Listing 19.9.

Listing 19.9:   Named Parameter Validation

```
1.   sub validateNamedParams (\%\%){
2.       #Create two hash references to the formals and actual
3.       my ($formalParams, $actualParams) = @_;
4.       #Now check each of the named actual parameter names
5.       foreach $key (keys %$actualParams){
6.           #If the actual name is not part of the formal list,
7.           #then it must be a mistake.
8.           #Note that this does not force the actuals to have
9.           #all of the formals, it only looks for actuals that
10.          #are not part of the formals.
11.          if (!defined $$formalParams{$key}){
12.              #I want a comma space around my formal list.
13.              #The local will be reset, but since this routine dies,
14.              #it really doesn't matter.
15.              local $" = ', ';
16.              @formals = keys %$formalParams;
17.              print "$key is an invalid parameter name.\n";
18.              print "The valid parameter names are\n ";
19.              print "@formals\n";
20.              die;
21.          }
22.      }
23. }
```

The validateNamedParams subroutine in Listing 19.9 takes two parameters: a hash with the expected named parameters (called formal parameters) and a hash with the actual parameters. It then loops through the actual parameters, on line 5, checking to see if each key in the actual parameter list is a key in the formal parameter list. If the actual parameter does not exist in the formal parameter list, it must be an error.

The calling code can send fewer named parameters, which allows the calling routine to use whatever predefined defaults exist in the called routine. However, the calling code cannot send additional named parameters that haven't been defined by the called routine. This prevents a potentially silent but deadly bug, where the caller is sending data but the subroutine is quietly ignoring the data and neither the caller nor the called code gives or gets any indication that there is a potential problem. Thus, if an input parameter name is not part of the defined list of expected parameters, an input error has occurred. When this happens, the list of valid parameters is printed out and the program dies. Missing parameters do not create an error because the program only checks for existence of the actual parameter names.

Named parameter validation is a great tool to use when you are developing your code. You can call the validateNamedParams program using the if $DEBUG syntax, like this:

```
validateNamedParams (\%formalParams,%\actualParams) if $DEBUG;
```

Using this syntax, you validate the parameter list only when you are testing or debugging. If your program changes, you can set the debug switch on to verify that all your parameters are being named correctly. Listing 19.10 demonstrates how to use the validateNamedParams subroutine (the named parameters UID and headLine have capitalization errors), and the resulting output is shown in Figure 19.2.

Listing 19.10:   **Input Parameter Checking**

```
 1. #!/usr/local/bin/perl
 2. $self->addStory(departmentName => "Medical",
 3.                 UID => $UID,
 4.                 headLine => $headline,
 5.                 mainStory => $mainStory);
 6.
 7. sub addStory {
 8.     #PARAMETER LIST
 9.     #departmentName Scalar string
10.     #uid Scalar Unique story ID
11.     #mainStory Scalar string Y/N
12.     #headline Scalar string The stories headline
13.     %formalParams = (departmentName => 1,
14.                      uid           => 1,
15.                      headline      => 1,
16.                      mainStory     => 1);
17.     my $self = shift;
18.     my (%params) = @_;
19.     validateNamedParams (\%formalParams, \%params) if $DEBUG;
```

```
20.     my %story;
21.     $story{department} = $params{departmentName};
22.     $story{uid} = $params{uid};
23.     $story{mainStory} = $params{mainStory};
24.     $story{headline} = $params{headline};
25.     unshift @storyList, \%story;
26.     return 1;
27. }
```

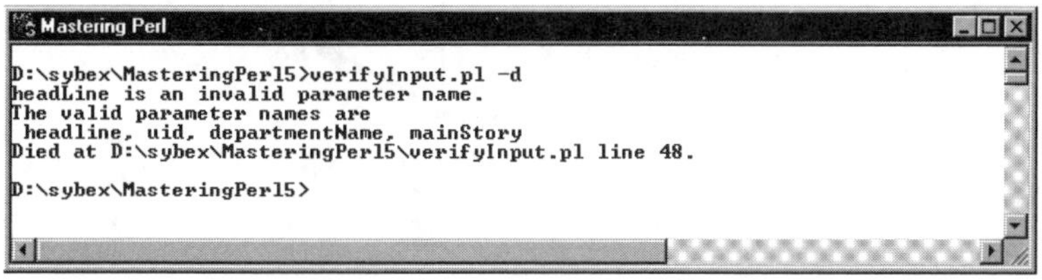

FIGURE 19.2:

Checking for invalid named parameters

```
Mastering Perl                                                      _ □ ×

D:\sybex\MasteringPerl5>verifyInput.pl -d
headLine is an invalid parameter name.
The valid parameter names are
  headline, uid, departmentName, mainStory
Died at D:\sybex\MasteringPerl5\verifyInput.pl line 48.

D:\sybex\MasteringPerl5>
```

Inheritance

Inheritance is the ability to use the methods and instance variables of your ancestor classes. Perl 5 provides programming inheritance through a built-in array named @ISA.

Several terms are associated with inheritance. The terms *base class*, *superclass*, and *ancestor class* are synonyms. Each term refers to a class that has been added to the @ISA array. The terms *derived class* and *subclass* also are synonyms. These terms define classes that use the methods of ancestor classes as part of their implementation. The methods of a class added to the @ISA array are available to the derived class as if the derived class defined them.

There are two types of inheritance: single and multiple. Multiple inheritance is similar to the type of inheritance you get through your genes. You can inherit something from each of your ancestors and each of their ancestors, although in Perl 5, each derived class can have as many direct ancestors as desired. Single inheritance allows for only one ancestor per derived class. Figure 19.3 shows the two types of programming inheritance in a family tree format.

FIGURE 19.3:

Multiple and single
inheritance trees

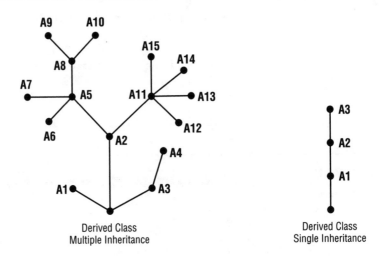

Derived Class
Multiple Inheritance

Derived Class
Single Inheritance

To use another class's methods, the derived class includes its ancestor class name in the @ISA array, like this:

```
@ISA=qq(Ancestor);
```

This method of adding classes to the @ISA array is becoming a standard, but you may use any method you prefer to add classes to the @ISA array, such as:

```
push @ISA, "Ancestor";
```

Once a class is added to the @ISA array, that class's methods are treated as part of the derived classes methods. When a method is called in the derived class that has not been defined in the derived class, Perl 5 searches each class in the @ISA array for the method. Perl 5 uses a depth-first algorithm to find the missing method. The first method that matches the called method will be used.

To build the multiple inheritance tree shown in Figure 19.3, the derived class would add its three ancestors to the @ISA array like this:

```
@ISA=qq(Ancestor1, Ancestor2, Ancestor3);
```

Each Ancestor class then adds to the @ISA array. Using the elements shown in Figure 19.3, the additions would look like this:

Ancestor1	No changes
Ancestor2	@ISA=qq(Ancestor5,Ancestor11);
Ancestor3	@ISA=qq(Ancestor4);

Ancestor5	@ISA=qq(Ancestor6, Ancestor7, Ancestor8);
Ancestor8	@ISA=qq(Ancestor9, Ancestor10);
Ancestor11	@ISA=qq(Ancestor15, Ancestor14, Ancestor13, Ancestor12);
Ancestors 6, 7, 9, 10, 15, 14, 13, 12, 4	No changes

The depth-first algorithm searches each @ISA class for the inherited method. If Ancestor4 contained the inherited method, Perl 5 would first look through every other class in the inheritance before finding the inherited method in Ancestor4. If both Ancestor9 and Ancestor15 defined a method with the same name, the inheritance tree would find the method in Ancestor9 first, searching like this: Ancestor1, Ancestor2, Ancestor5, Ancestor6, Ancestor7, Ancestor8, Ancestor9.

The first inherited method is returned and placed in the Perl 5 inheritance cache. The inheritance cache keeps track of all methods that have been retrieved from the @ISA array. This increases program efficiency because Perl 5 only searches the @ISA inheritance tree when an inherited method is requested the first time. Subsequent requests for inherited methods are drawn directly from cache. Any modifications to the @ISA array reset the inheritance cache.

It is possible to explicitly call an Ancestor class method by using the class name in the method call, like this:

```
$self->Ancestor4::test();
```

This syntax explicitly invokes the method named by the class name to the left of the double colons. The object reference is still passed as the first parameter of the parameter list. Listing 19.11 shows inheritance from the derived class of the test subroutine.

Listing 19.11:   Method Inheritance

```
1.  #!/usr/local/bin/perl
2.  package base;
3.
4.  sub new{
5.      my $class = shift;
6.      my $self = {};
7.      #By using the shifted $class variable the object reference to
8.      #the hash can be blessed into a derived class.
```

```
9.    bless $self, $class;
10.   $self->{name} = "base";
11.   return $self;
12.
13. }
14.
15. sub test (){
16.    my $self = shift;
17.    print "I am in the base class\n";
18.    print "My name is $self->{name}\n";
19. }
20.
21. package derived;
22. @ISA = qw (base);
23. sub new{
24.    my $class = shift;
25.    #Call my base class without explicity naming which base class
26.    #has the new method.
27.    my $self = $class->SUPER::new();
28.    #This overwrites the base class's instance variable.
29.    $self->{name} = "derived";
30.    return $self;
31. }
32.
33. my $self = derived->new();
34.
35. $self->test();
```

When Listing 19.11 is run, the `test` subroutine in the base class runs, but the instance variable name has been changed to the value `"derived"`, as shown in Figure 19.4. As long as you use the hash mechanism of creating instance variables, the derived class has access to the base class instance variables.

FIGURE 19.4:

Inheriting a method

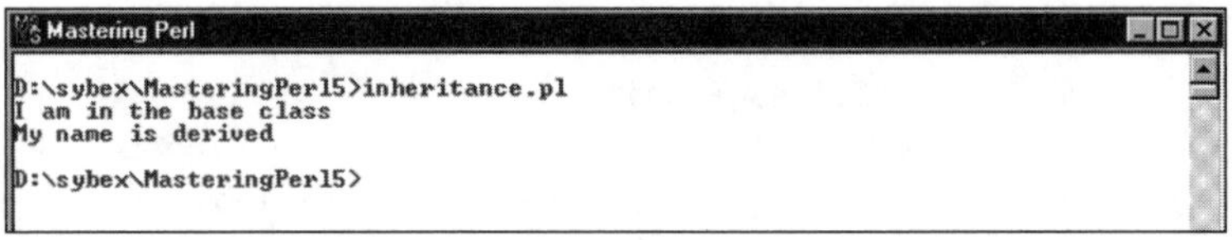

If you add a test method to the derived class, the subroutine overrides the base class method, as shown in Listing 19.12. The same method call, $self->test();, now calls the derived class method, which is shown in Figure 19.5.

Listing 19.12:   The Base Class Method Call

```
1.  #!/usr/local/bin/perl
2.  package base;
3.
4.  sub new{
5.      my $class = shift;
6.      my $self = {};
7.      #By using the shifted $class variable the object reference to
8.      #the hash can be blessed into a derived class.
9.      bless $self, $class;
10.     $self->{name} = "base";
11.     return $self;
12.
13. }
14.
15. sub test (){
16.     my $self = shift;
17.     print "I am in the base class\n";
18.     print "My name is $self->{name}\n";
19. }
20.
21. package derived;
22. @ISA = qw (base);
23. sub new{
24.     my $class = shift;
25.     #Call my base class without explicity naming which base class
26.     #has the new method.
27.     my $self = $class->SUPER::new();
28.     #This overwrites the base class's instance variable.
29.     $self->{name} = "derived";
30.     return $self;
31. }
32.
33. sub test (){
34.     my $self = shift;
35.     print "I am in the derived class\n";
```

```
36.    print "My name is $self->{name}\n";
37. }
38.
39. my $self = derived->new();
40.
41. #Call the derived class test method.
42. $self->test();
43. #Call the base class test method.
44. $self->SUPER::test();
```

FIGURE 19.5:

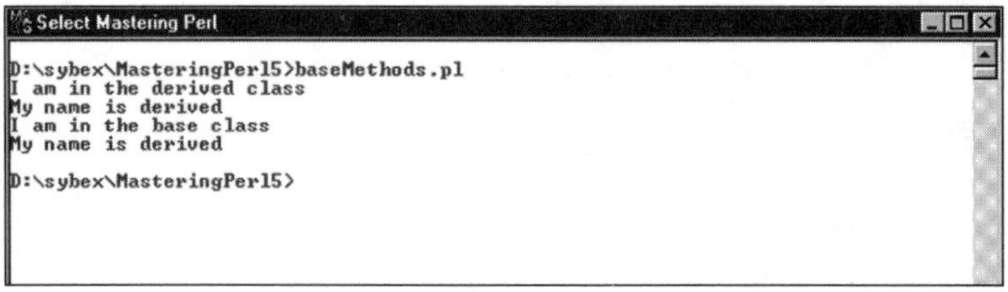

Calling the base
class method

```
Select Mastering Perl                                    _□×
D:\sybex\MasteringPerl5>baseMethods.pl
I am in the derived class
My name is derived
I am in the base class
My name is derived

D:\sybex\MasteringPerl5>
```

Listing 19.12 shows the base class **test** method being overridden by the derived class **test** method. The call on line 42 calls the derived class **test** method. The call on line 44 explicitly calls the next class in the inheritance hierarchy that has a **test** method.

When the keyword SUPER is used to invoke a method, Perl 5 begins looking in the @ISA array for a matching subroutine. Lines 42 and 44 are examples of polymorphism and dynamic binding. *Polymorphism* is the ability to use the same name for multiple subroutines. Perl 5 allows you to use the same subroutine name and gives you access to that subroutine through explicit subroutine calls or dynamic binding. *Dynamic binding* is the calling of a subroutine based on runtime conditions. The **test** subroutine is both polymorphic and dynamic. The **test** subroutine is defined in two different classes, making it polymorphic. Each method can be accessed explicitly or dynamically.

Explicit access to either class method is available using the double-colon notation, like this:

```
$self->derived::test();
$self->base::test();
```

The double-colon notation always calls the named class, overriding any dynamic binding in effect. The SUPER notation is a hybrid form of explicit access. The SUPER notation tells the Perl 5 interpreter to begin looking for the method in the @ISA hierarchy, overriding any method definition in the derived class. However, the SUPER notation does not define the specific ancestor class. This decouples the derived class from the ancestor class and hierarchy, allowing the ancestor classes to evolve without affecting the derived classes. An evolving ancestor hierarchy means the ancestor classes can change over time without requiring changes in the derived class.

Dynamic binding is in effect when there are multiple subroutines with the same name in the hierarchy tree. Perl 5 executes the method that the reference object is blessed into, or begins searching up the hierarchy tree from that point.

Summary

Object-oriented design is as much a philosophy as it is a programming discipline. In this chapter, you learned about Perl 5 object-oriented programming techniques—the philosophy has been left for another book.

In Perl 5, you use the `package` statement to declare your class. Throughout the chapter, the keyword `package` and the keyword `class` are interchangeable. A *class* is a container for related object methods and variables. *Method* is the object-oriented programming term for subroutine. Object-oriented methods come in two forms: class methods and instance methods. In this chapter, you learned how to call class methods with the class name as the first parameter of the parameter list. You also learned about the Perl 5 constructor, which is the most frequently used class method (named `new`). The constructor is primarily responsible for returning an object reference and initializing object variables.

Next, the chapter covered instance methods. These methods expect an object reference as their first parameter. An object reference is created using the `bless` function. The `bless` function links an object with the named class. If a class name is not supplied to the `bless` function, the current class is linked with the blessed object. An instance method operates primarily on instance variables, which define the state and identity of an individual object. Instance variables and class variables are the two types of object variables implemented in Perl 5. Instance variables use a blessed anonymous hash to create a unique reference to object data. An instance variable is added, modified, and deleted through a lexical reference to the object's anonymous hash. Class variables, on the other hand, are global to the entire class. Class variables are used to communicate a common identity and state to the Perl 5 object.

Then the chapter discussed destructors. Perl 5 will free your object in memory when the last reference to the object is deleted. You cannot control when your object will be freed in memory, but you can guarantee that you will get a final opportunity to perform your own object cleanup. If you name a subroutine DESTROY, Perl 5 will call the subroutine just before the object is freed in memory. The DESTROY method is called a destructor in object-oriented program terminology. A destructor is primarily used for closing sockets and file handles, but it can have many useful functions. For example, in this chapter, you saw how a destructor could be used to save data to disk automatically.

One of the features of object-oriented programming is the ability to use methods from other class as if they were part of your object. This feature is called *inheritance*, which was discussed in the final section of this chapter. Perl 5 implements inheritance through the global @ISA array. To add an ancestor class to a derived class hierarchy tree, the derived class adds the ancestor class name to the @ISA array. Perl 5 uses a depth-first search mechanism to find inherited methods.

CHAPTER

TWENTY

E-Mail Solutions

- The sendmail program and SMTP servers

- Unix e-mail programming

- Windows e-mail programming

- The Sender.pm module

Despite the popularity of the World Wide Web, e-mail is still the most commonly used application on the Internet. The SMTP protocol and the Unix `send-mail` program are well-established tools for transferring e-mail messages. The Windows mail interface has been problematic over the years, but there are now several options that you can use.

In this chapter, you will learn how to apply some e-mail solutions for both Unix and Windows computers. The first two examples you'll work through require you to have a connection to a Unix `sendmail` process. I connected to my local ISP via a telnet connection to build these examples. In the second part of this chapter, you'll learn about two Windows e-mail solutions: the Blat program and the `Sender.pm` module. The Blat application is a Windows-only solution. The `Sender.pm` module runs on any system with a connection to an SMTP server, which you have if you can receive e-mail on your computer.

An Introduction to E-Mail Programs and Protocols

SMTP (Simple Mail Transport Protocol) is the protocol used to transmit e-mail messages across the Internet. The most popular implementation of SMTP is the `sendmail` program. The `sendmail` program is the e-mail backbone of the Internet. SMTP and `sendmail` have been around since the 1980s. If you have an e-mail account, you use an SMTP server.

TIP　　　The full definition of the SMTP protocol can be found in RFC821. RFC stands for Request For Comments. RFCs are used as a means to document new and emerging Internet protocols. You can learn more about RFCs at http://www.faqs. org/rfcs/. RFC821 is also available from this book's companion page at the Sybex web site.

To communicate with an SMTP server, you must follow an exacting protocol. Doesn't that sound ominous—an exacting protocol? In practice, it is not difficult to make SMTP connections. The SMTP server will reject your e-mail request if you don't talk to it correctly, but if you know the secret handshake, you can talk to any SMTP server.

The following sections provide an overview of the `sendmail` program and SMTP servers. You'll learn how to use these in Unix and Windows programs later in the chapter.

The sendmail Program

The `sendmail` program sends messages to one or more recipients, routing the messages over whatever networks are necessary. If `sendmail` is invoked without a switch, it can be used to send mail from a file. In this mode, `sendmail` reads to the end-of-file marker or a single line that contains the period character (`.`) in the leftmost column.

The following are the most common switches used with `sendmail`:

- With the `-bd` switch (`sendmail -bd`), the `sendmail` program is started as a daemon; this is usually done by the system administrator. (A *daemon* is a process that runs in the background, performing its task without human intervention.) The `sendmail` daemon listens on port 25 for incoming SMTP connections, routing messages appropriately.

- With the `-t` switch, `sendmail` scans the message for recipient addresses. Each line that contains a To:, Cc:, or Bcc: will be searched for e-mail addresses. The Bcc: line, which is used as a recipient address, is deleted before the message is actually sent.

- With the `-bv` switch, `sendmail` will verify e-mail names but not try to collect or deliver a message. This is a convenient tool for managers of mailing lists.

- With the `-f` switch and the correct privileges, you can use `sendmail` to set the From: line in an e-mail header. You need normal privileges to set the From: value the same as your user name or superuser, or root privileges to set the From: value to an address that is different from the user name.

The `sendmail` program returns a status code when it exits. The status codes are shown in Table 20.1.

TABLE 20.1: The sendmail Program Status Codes

Status Code	Meaning
EX_OK	Successful completion on all addresses
EX_NOUSER	User name not recognized

Continued on next page

TABLE 20.1 CONTINUED: The sendmail Program Status Codes

Status Code	Meaning
EX_UNAVAILABLE	Necessary resources were not available
EX_SYNTAX	Syntax error in address
EX_SOFTWARE	Internal software error, including bad arguments
EX_OSERR	Temporary operating system error, such as "cannot fork"
EX_NOHOST	Host name not recognized
EX_TEMPFAIL	Message could not be sent immediately but was queued

SMTP Servers

An SMTP server is an instance of a mail program like sendmail that operates as a daemon listening for incoming e-mail on port 25. When operating as an SMTP server, sendmail (or any other SMTP server program) listens for incoming e-mail messages. When a message is received, the SMTP server determines the correct routing for the e-mail message by examining the e-mail headers. Local e-mail messages are delivered to their mailboxes, and remote messages are forwarded to the next SMTP server along the route to the final destination.

The SMTP server only requires that you communicate with it in a formatted manner. You don't need a special e-mail tool to talk to your SMTP server. You can use telnet to connect to your SMTP server and send an e-mail message directly from the command line. However, using telnet to send an e-mail message does present one minor problem. This problem is apparent in Figures 20.1 and 20.2.

Figure 20.1 is the telnet session I used to produce the e-mail message shown in Figure 20.2. Unfortunately, one of the things you may notice in Figure 20.1 is that only the response from the SMTP server is visible. The input to the SMTP server during the telnet session is not echoed to the terminal. This means that you cannot see what you are typing, opening the door for typos and other errors. Sending an e-mail message via telnet is a little impractical, but you might want to use this method in an emergency.

FIGURE 20.1:

A telnet session to produce
an e-mail message

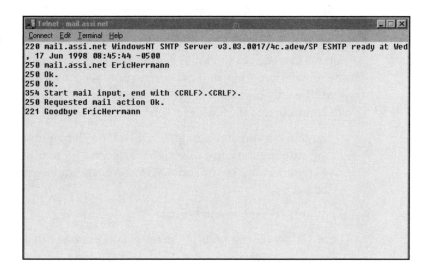

FIGURE 20.2:

A telnet e-mail message

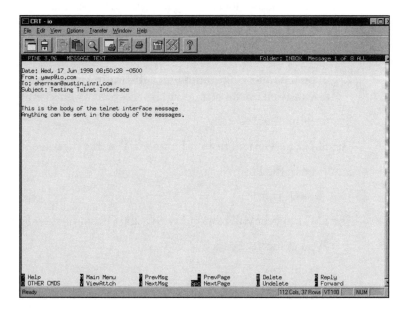

The following steps show the procedure for using a telnet session to send an e-mail message. The messages and their sequence are the same, whether you are connected to port 25 via telnet or through a programmatic socket interface. After you issue each SMTP command, the SMTP server will respond with the appropriate status message, as shown in Figure 20.1. By following the steps outlined below in your program, you can successfully send e-mail messages from anywhere. The only difference is that in your program, you replace step 1 with a valid connection to the SMTP server.

1. From the command prompt (DOS or Unix), enter the following command substituting the name of your SMTP server for mail.somewhere.com (press Enter after each command; SMTP commands are terminated with a newline character).

    ```
    telnet mail.somewhere.com 25
    ```

The SMTP server responds to the telnet connection with a 220 status message.

NOTE   Not all SMTP servers are named `mail`. You must know the name of the SMTP server to which you wish to connect. The SMTP server is the same name your e-mail client uses for receiving and sending e-mail. Look in the definition of the outgoing and incoming e-mail server in your favorite e-mail program. You can use that name as your SMTP server name.

---

2. Type the following command, substituting a computer name or something else (any character string will be accepted as an identity) for *YourIdentity*.

    ```
    Helo YourIdentity
    ```

The SMTP server will respond with a 250 status message.

3. Type in the From: header:

    ```
    mail from:
    ```

The SMTP server will respond with a 250 Ok status message.

4. Type in the To: header.

    ```
    rcpt to:
    ```

The SMTP server will respond with a 250 Ok status message.

5. Tell the SMTP server you are ready to send the e-mail message by entering the following command:

    ```
    data
    ```

The SMTP server will respond with a 354 status message.

6. Type in additional To:, From:, Bcc:, Cc:, Reply-To:, Subject:, and other headers you want to send. When you're finished with the e-mail headers, enter a blank line. The SMTP server will not respond.

7. Type in the body of the message. When you are finished entering the body of the message, type in a dot (.) in the left-hand column on a line by itself, then press Enter. The SMTP server responds with a 250 Requested mail action Ok message.

8. Disconnect from the SMTP server by typing:

   ```
   quit
   ```

The SMTP server responds with a 221 Goodbye message.

Later in the chapter, you'll learn how to configure a Windows program, Blat, which uses the steps you just used to communicate with the sendmail SMTP server to send e-mail messages. The next section shows how to use the sendmail program from a Unix machine.

Unix E-Mail Solutions

From a Unix platform, you can use the sendmail program directly, without going through an e-mail client program such as Netscape mail or Eudora. The examples presented here include two common e-mail applications: one for sending and responding to an HTML registration form and one for sending personalized e-mail messages to a list of contact names.

A Registration Application

Let's begin with one of the more common uses for e-mail—transferring registration forms. This type of application includes a little HTML and CGI programming. Using an e-mail message is one of the easiest ways to process HTML form data and to notify yourself or your users of the new information.

The HTML E-Mail Form

Figure 20.3 shows an example of a registration form made up of text boxes, a pull-down menu, a text area box, and Register and Reset buttons. The form is generated by the HTML shown in Listing 20.1.

Listing 20.1: **An HTML E-Mail Form**

```
1.   <HTML>
2.     <HEAD>
3.       <TITLE>Email Registration Form</TITLE>
4.     </HEAD>
5.     <BODY>
6.         <H1>Registration Form</H1>
7.       <form method=post action=http://www.practical-inet.com/
                              cgi-bin/perlBook/registerEmail.cgi>
8.       <TABLE>
9.         <TR>
10.          <TH width=10% Align=left>Name</TH>
11.          <TD colspan=5><INPUT ALIGN=Left NAME="Name" SIZE=60
                    TYPE=Text></TD>
12.        </TR>
13.        <TR>
14.          <TH width=10% Align=left>Company</TH>
15.          <TD colspan=5><INPUT ALIGN=Left NAME="Company" SIZE=60
                    TYPE=Text></TD>
16.        </TR>
17.        <TR>
18.          <TH width=10% Align=left>Title</TH>
19.          <TD colspan=5><INPUT ALIGN=Left NAME="Title" SIZE=60
                    TYPE=Text></TD>
20.        </TR>
21.        <TR>
22.          <TH width=10% Align=left>Address</TH>
23.          <TD colspan=5><INPUT ALIGN=Left NAME="Address" SIZE=60
                    TYPE=Text></TD>
24.        </TR>
25.        <TR>
26.          <TH width=10% Align=left>City</TH>
27.          <TD width=20%><INPUT ALIGN=Left SIZE=20
                    TYPE=Text Name=City></TD>
28.          <TH width=10% Align=left>State</TH>
29.          <TD width=20%><INPUT ALIGN=Left SIZE=10
                    TYPE=Text Name=State></TD>
30.          <TH width=10% Align=left>Zip</TH>
31.          <TD width=20%><INPUT ALIGN=Left SIZE=15
                    TYPE=Text Name=Zip></TD>
```

```
32.        </TR>
33.        <TR>
34.          <TH width=10% Align=left>Phone</TH>
35.          <TD width=20% ><INPUT ALIGN=Left SIZE=20
                              TYPE=Text Name=Phone></TD>
36.          <TH width=10% Align=left>Email</TH>
37.          <TD width=20% colspan=3><INPUT ALIGN=Left SIZE=20
                              TYPE=Text Name=Email></TD>
38.        </TR>
39.        <TR>
40.          <TH colspan=2 align=left>How did you learn about
                              us?</TH>
41.          <TD>
42.            <select name="Learn">
43.              <option value="radio">Radio</option>
44.              <option value="Television">Television</option>
45.              <option value="Lycos">Lycos </option>
46.              <option value="Yahoo">Yahoo </option>
47.              <option value="InfoSeek">Infoseek</option>
48.              <option value="other">Other</option>
49.            </select>
50.          </TD>
51.        </TR>
52.        <TR>
53.        <TH colspan=6>Comments</TH>
54.        </TR>
55.      </TABLE>
56.      <center>
57.        <TextArea rows=5 cols=60 name="Comments" ></textarea>
58.        </center>
59.        <TABLE>
60.          <TR>
61.            <TD><INPUT NAME="EmailRegister"
                    TYPE=Submit VALUE="Register"></TD>
62.            <TD><INPUT TYPE=Reset></TD>
63.          </TR>
64.        </TABLE>
65.      </form>
66.    </BODY>
67. </HTML>
```

FIGURE 20.3:

An e-mail registration form

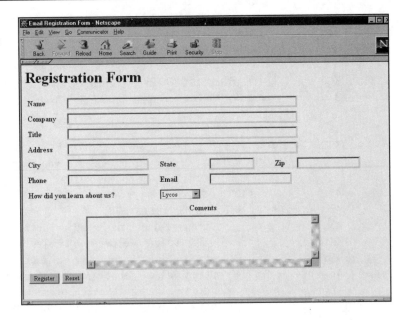

Your CGI program doesn't care how the data is entered on your HTML form. All data generated from your HTML form and sent via the HTTP POST method header is translated the same way. Each HTML input tag, text area, text box, radio button, or option list is converted into URL-encoded name/value pairs, which your CGI program must decode. The address of the CGI program to receive and decode the data is on line 7 of Listing 20.1:

```
<form method=post action=http://www.practical-inet.com/
                    cgi-bin/perlBook/registerEmail.cgi>
```

TIP   I prefer to use an absolute URL in the `action` field when identifying the program the form should send the data to. That way, regardless of how the server is configured, I'm sure the server has the correct address for calling my CGI program.

When your web client selects the Register button (created on line 61 of Listing 20.1), the browser generates the correct HTTP request headers, URL-encodes the data, and ships it to the web server identified in the `action` field of the HTML `form` tag.

One other thing to notice about Listing 20.1 is the handling of the HTML table formats and text areas. On line 55, the first table with all the input fields is terminated with the closing </TABLE> tag. On line 59, a new table begins just for the Register and Reset buttons. I created two tables because the extra TextArea tag doesn't work well inside a table format. The TextArea tag spans multiple columns and rows, and that conflicts with the table row tag <TR> and the column tags <TD> and <TH>. It's possible to make the TextArea tag work with the table tags by setting the table rows and colspan fields precisely; however, it's easier to work with the TextArea tag outside the HTML table format.

The CGI Program to Respond to the HTML Form

Listing 20.2 processes the input received from the HTML registration form in Listing 20.1 and returns the page shown in Figure 20.4. The returning of a "Thank You" page is more than just a courtesy to your web client—your CGI program must respond to every HTTP request with a valid HTTP response. The simplest HTTP response is another HTML web page.

Listing 20.2:   An E-Mail HTTP Response

```
1.  #!/usr/bin/perl
2.  require "readPostInput.cgi";
3.
4.  %postInputs = readPostInput();
5.  $dateCommand = "date";
6.  $time = `$dateCommand`;
7.  open (MAIL, "|/usr/sbin/sendmail -t") || return 0;
8.
9.  select (MAIL);
10. print<<"EOF";
11. To: Eric.Herrmann\@assi.net
12. From: $postInputs{'email'}
13. Subject: Email Registration Received
14.
15. $time
16. Email Registration
17. Name: $postInputs{'Name'}
18. Email: $postInputs{'Email'}
19. Company Name: $postInputs{'Company'}
```

```
20. Street Address: $postInputs{'Address'}
20. City: $postInputs{'City'}
22. State : $postInputs{'State'}
23. Zip: $postInputs{'Zip'}
24. Phone: $postInputs{'Phone'}
25. Learn: $postInputs{'Learn'}
26. Comments: $postInputs{'Comments'}
27.
28. EOF
29.    close(MAIL);
30.    select (STDOUT);
31.    printThankYou();
32.
33. sub printThankYou(){
34. print<<"EOF";
35. Content-Type: text/html
36.
37. <HEAD>
38. <TITLE>THANK YOU FOR REGISTERING!</TITLE>
39. <META HTTP-EQUIV="Content-Type" CONTENT="document">
40. </HEAD>
41. <BODY>
42. <TABLE CELLSPACING=2 CELLPADDING=2 border=0 width=600>
43. <TR>
44. <BR>
45. <CENTER>
46. <FONT SIZE=+3><B>Thank You</b></font></center><BR><BR>
47. <CENTER><B><FONT SIZE=+1>
48. <P>Thank you $postInputs{'Name'} for registering <BR>
49. </FONT></B><CENTER>
50. </TD>
51. </TR>
52. </TABLE>
53.
54. </BODY>
55. </HTML>
56.
57. EOF
58. }
```

FIGURE 20.4:

E-mail Thank You web page

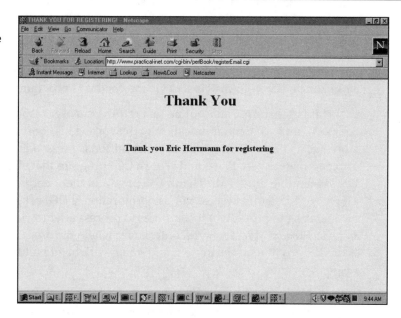

Listing 20.2 communicates with the Unix `sendmail` program, which you learned about at the beginning of this chapter. Line 4 of Listing 20.2 reads the HTML POST input into the hash `%postInputs`:

```
%postInputs = readPostInput();
```

NOTE   The `readPostInputs` subroutine was first introduced in Chapter 1 and revisited in Chapter 15. This subroutine uses a standard algorithm for decoding the URL-encoded data. You should include this standard algorithm in your CGI programs, via one of the standard CGI modules or libraries, such as `CGI.pm` or `cgi-lib.pl`.

The interface with the `sendmail` program begins on line 7:

```
open (MAIL, "|/usr/sbin/sendmail -t") || return 0;
```

Line 7 links the file handle with the `sendmail` program. As you learned in Chapter 12, if you want to communicate with a program, open a pipe to it using the open function with the pipe symbol (|) instead of the file-input operator (<>). Line 9 selects the MAIL file handle as the default output device:

```
select (MAIL);
```

The sendmail program requires the standard format, or e-mail headers, you see at the top of most e-mail messages. This format require the To: and From: lines; the Subject: line is optional. The e-mail headers end with a blank line, which is then followed with the optional body of the e-mail message. You can send any information you want inside the body of the e-mail message. When the file handle MAIL is closed on line 29, your mail is sent via the sendmail program.

The printThankYou subroutine that returns the user response in Figure 20.4 isn't sent until your communication with sendmail is completed. This can create a time delay between when the Register button is pressed and the HTML Thank You page is received. You could write a CGI program that eliminates this delay by first sending the HTML Thank You page and then sending the e-mail message. However, based on a web server's configuration, a CGI program is considered to be operating improperly if it continues to process after responding to the HTML request. Since you rarely have control over where the final CGI program will be hosted, I recommend finishing your e-mail work before returning the HTTP response headers.

Listing 20.2 generates the e-mail message shown in Figure 20.5. As you can see, no special formatting or processing of the HTML form hash %postInputs is required to interface with the sendmail program.

FIGURE 20.5:

The e-mail message received

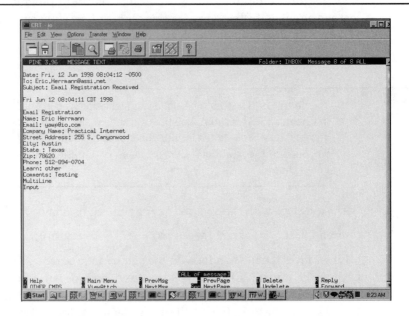

A Mailing List Application

Many text editors, such as Microsoft Word, offer a mail merge feature that allows you to generate multiple personalized letters using a single letter template. You can write one form letter and send it to different people, with each person's name used in strategic places in your letter.

These days, many of us prefer to communicate via e-mail. Rather than producing multiple personalized letters, you can send e-mail to a lot of friends, relatives, or business clients by using the program in Listing 20.3.

Listing 20.3:   **Personalized E-Mail to a Contact List**

```perl
1.  #!/usr/bin/perl
2.  if ($#ARGV < 1){
3.      print "contact file first letter file 2nd\n";
4.      exit 1;
5.      }
6.  $contactFile = $ARGV[0];
7.  $letterFile = $ARGV[1];
8.
9.  open (CONTACTLIST, "<$contactFile") || die "Can't open
                                    $contactFile\n";
10. open (LETTER, "<$letterFile") || die "Can't open $letterFile\n";
11. @contactList = <CONTACTLIST>;
12. @letter = <LETTER>;
13. close (CONTACTLIST);
14. close (LETTER);
15. $count = 0;
16. for $line (@contactList){
17.
18.     if ($line =~ /@/){
19.         $count++;
20.         open (MAIL, "|/usr/sbin/sendmail -t") || die "Can't open
                                        pipe to sendmail \n";
21.         ($companyName, $emailAddress, $FLName) = split(/,/,$line);
22.         $emailAddress =~ s/\t//g;
23.         $FLName =~ /\s*(\w+)\s*(\w+)/;
24.         $firstName= $1;   $lastName = $2;
25.         chomp $lastName;
26.         select (MAIL);
27.         $subjectLine = $letter[0];
```

```
28.        chop $subjectLine ;
29.        $subjectLine = "$companyName";
30.        $returnAddress = "Eric.Herrmann\@assi.net";
31.        print<<"EOF";
32. To: $emailAddress
33. From: $returnAddress
34. Subject: $subjectLine
35.
36. EOF
37.        for $index (0 .. $#letter){
38.            $letterLine = $letter[$index];
39.            chop $letterLine;
40.            if ($letterLine =~ /companyName/) {
41.                $letterLine =~ s/companyName/$companyName/g;
42.            }
43.            if ($letterLine =~ /firstName/) {
44.                $letterLine =~ s/firstName/$firstName/g;
45.            }
46.            if ($letterLine =~ /lastName/) {
47.                $letterLine =~ s/lastName/$lastName/g;
48.            }
49.            print "$letterLine\n";
50.        }#end for loop
51.    close (MAIL);
52.        }#end if
53. }
54.
55. print STDOUT "\nYou sent $count emails\n";
```

Listing 20.3 uses a contact list and a form letter to send personalized e-mail messages to a list of e-mail address and names. The program gets both file-names—for the contact list and the form letter files—from the command line. This is a Unix interface, but later in this chapter you'll learn how to use the Sender.pm module, which allows you to create a Perl e-mail interface on both a Unix and Windows computer.

The contact list read in on line 9 of Listing 20.3 is formatted so that each line is made up of an e-mail address and the recipient's name separated by a space. The contact list is read into an array and then processed one line at a time. Because the file can include blank lines and comment lines, line 18 specifies that only lines that have the e-mail at sign (@) in them are processed:

```
if ($line =~ /@/){
```

A pipe to the `sendmail` program is opened on line 20, then the e-mail address and contact name are extracted on line 21:

```
open (MAIL, "|/usr/sbin/sendmail -t") || die "Can't open pipe to
                                              sendmail \n";
($companyName, $emailAddress, $FLName) = split(/,/,$line);
```

Each time a new e-mail message is sent, a new connection is made to the `sendmail` program. Making a connection to a program always requires some extra processing time. Usually, it is faster to open a connection and keep it open as long as you are communicating with the other program. In the case of Listing 20.3, opening and closing a pipe to `sendmail` is slower than opening a connection and sending multiple e-mail messages through that one connection. If it is slow and I know it is slow, why do I do it this way? I open and close a pipe to `sendmail` for two important reasons:

- You can start the program in Listing 20.3 and leave it running. You don't need to be concerned whether it takes ten minutes or ten hours to run. It's not slowing your machine or your work. The time involved in running the program revolves around making a single connection to `sendmail` to send a single letter.

- Each mailing is an individual e-mail delivery, which keeps the e-mail message as personal as possible, considering it is a form letter. The letter may read like a form letter (depending on the author's writing skill), but it will look like an individual e-mail message because it is sent individually.

One alternative to this method of sending e-mail involves opening a connection to `sendmail` and sending a blast of e-mail messages with a lot of CC: or BCC: lines. But how personal would the e-mail message seem when its recipients see a lengthy CC: list?

The message is personalized on lines 29 through 34 of Listing 20.3:

```
        $subjectLine = "$companyName";
        $returnAddress = "Eric.Herrmann\@assi.net";
        print<<"EOF";
To: $emailAddress
From: $returnAddress
Subject: $subjectLine
```

The subject line of each e-mail includes the recipient's name. (If your recipients are like me, they will probably toss any e-mail that looks like a spam that has nothing to do with them.)

Lines 37 through 50 process each line of the letter, looking for the unique characters, companyName, firstName, and lastName. Each time one of these character strings is matched, all occurrences of those characters are replaced with the actual company name, first name, or last name, which was retrieved from the contact list:

```
for $index (0 .. $#letter){
    $letterLine = $letter[$index];
    chop $letterLine;
    if ($letterLine =~ /companyName/) {
$letterLine =~ s/companyName/$companyName/g;
    }
    if ($letterLine =~ /firstName/) {
$letterLine =~ s/firstName/$firstName/g;
    }
    if ($letterLine =~ /lastName/) {
$letterLine =~ s/lastName/$lastName/g;
    }
    print "$letterLine\n";
}#end for loop
```

TIP   If you're going to send form letters, take the time to personalize them. Your recipients will appreciate the extra time, and they are more likely to read the letter.

Windows E-Mail Solutions

Sending e-mail from a Perl program running on a Windows computer can be a pain in the neck if you don't have some type of interface to an SMTP server. As explained earlier in this chapter, opening up a telnet session on port 25 to your Internet service provider's SMTP server is possible but not very practical. Here, you'll learn about two interfaces to SMTP servers. One is a freeware program, and the other is a module that provides a direct Perl–to–e-mail interface.

Blat: A Windows E-Mail Program

Originally intended as only a command-line interface, Blat became popular as a programming interface because it is the cheapest game in town. Blat is freeware. The authors of Blat are Mark Neal (mjn@aber.ac.uk) and Pedro Mendes (prm@aber.ac.uk).

Blat is available in the public domain for you to use and/or modify. As is the case with all types of public domain programs, many people have helped to make Blat a useful and easy-to-install SMTP interface. The following sections explain how to install and use Blat.

Blat Installation

To install Blat on your Windows computer, you need to copy two DLLs (dynamic link libraries) to your WinNT/System32 directory and tell Blat how to communicate with your SMTP server. The two DLLs are gqinsock.dll and cw3215.dll. You can get these files from http://gepasi.dbs.aber.ac.uk/softw/blat.html or from this book's companion pages on the Sybex web site.

Next, run the Blat installation program, which takes two parameters: your SMTP server name and your e-mail address. Enter the following command:

```
blat -install
```

If you don't know your SMTP server's name, look in your existing mail program's configuration setup. For example, my Internet service provider's SMTP server is located at mail.io.com.

After you install Blat this way, when you send mail from the command line using Blat, it will try to connect to an SMTP server at *mail.yourDomain.com* and will identify all e-mail messages as from *yourName@yourDomain.com*.

Blat in Action

Blat is designed as a command-line program for sending the contents of a file as the body of an e-mail message. You can also use Blat from within Perl programs.

To send a file as an e-mail message, use this syntax:

```
blat filename.txt -t yourName@yourDomain.com
```

This sends the contents of the specified filename to the specified e-mail address.

Blat version 1.7 (the current release at the time of this writing) has several command-line options that allow you to send binary files, send the same message multiple times, and read input from STDIN. These options are listed in Table 20.2.

TABLE 20.2: Blat Options

Option	Parameter	Description
-	None	For console input, end input with Ctrl+Z
-attach	*<file>*	Attach a binary file to the message (may be repeated)
-c	*<recipient>*	Carbon-copy recipient list (comma-separated)
-b	*<recipient>*	Blind carbon-copy recipient list (comma-separated)
-base64	None	MIME Base64 content transfer encoding
-f	*<sender>*	Override the default sender address (the new address must be known to server)
-h	None	Display help
-i	*<address>*	A From: address, not necessarily known to the SMTP server (<sender> is included in the message header's Reply-to: and Sender: fields)
-mime	None	MIME quoted printable content transfer encoding
-o	*<organization>*	Set Organization: to appear in the header fields
-p	*<profile>*	Use stored profile for server, sender, try, and port
-port	None	Override the default port on the server
-q	None	Suppress all output
-s	*<subject>*	Subject line (if you do not include a subject line, the subject "contents of console input" will be sent)
-server	*<address>*	Override the default SMTP server to be used
-t	*<recipient>*	Recipient list (comma-separated)
-try	None	Set how many times Blat should try to send a message

The -q (suppress all output) and the - (console input) options are important from a programmer's viewpoint. The -q option means your program doesn't have to worry about output from Blat interrupting your web server or any other program. The - option means your program can send data directly to the Blat program.

The programmer's interface to Blat can be downright finicky. Blat works flawlessly from the command line, but a misplaced switch or quote character stops the program without any helpful error messages. If you use Blat in your code, I suggest using one of the two subroutines in Listing 20.4.

Listing 20.4:   The Blat Interface

```
1.   $msg = "Testing the Blat Interface\n";
2.   blatSTDIN("Eric.Herrmann\@assi.net", "dummy\@noWhere.com",
                 "test blat", $msg);
3.   sub blatSTDIN ($$$$){
4.      my ($toName, $fromName, $subject, $message) = @_;
5.      $blat = "c:\\Winnt\\system32\\blat.exe - -t $toName  -s
                 \"$subject\" -q";
6.      open (MAIL, "| $blat -f \"$fromName\" ") || die $!;
7.      print MAIL $msg;
8.      print MAIL "TESTING BLAT STDIN\n";
9.      close MAIL;
10.     }
11.
12.  blatFILE("Eric.Herrmann\@assi.net", "dummy\@noWhere.com",
                 "test blat", $msg);
13.  sub blatFILE ($$$$){
14.     my ($toName, $fromName, $subject, $message) = @_;
15.     open (OUTFILE, ">$$");
16.     print OUTFILE $msg;
17.     print OUTFILE "Testing FILE interface\n";
18.     close (OUTFILE);
19.     `c:\\Winnt\\system32\\blat.exe $$ -t $toName  -s
                \"$subject\" -q`;
20.     unlink ($$);
21.     }
```

On line 5, the subroutine blatSTDIN uses the − (console input) option to force Blat to get its input from STDIN, or in this case, from the open MAIL file handle. It also uses the -q (suppress all output) option:

```
$blat = "c:\\Winnt\\system32\\blat.exe - -t $toName  -s \"$subject\" -q";
```

The blatSTDIN subroutine produces the mail message shown in Figure 20.6.

FIGURE 20.6:

Sending a Blat mail message from the open file handle

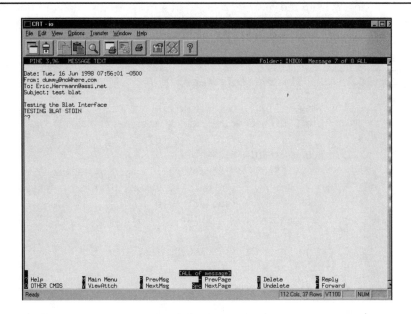

You might notice that Figure 20.6 uses a spoofed e-mail address (hiding the original address). Obviously, dummy@noWhere.com did not send this message. Blat allows you to change the From: e-mail address, but it always includes the registered e-mail address of the login process executing the Blat program in the Reply-to: headers.

When you test Blat on your computer, expand the headers to show the entire path. You'll see name of the SMTP server that Blat connects to, the name of the computer that connected to the SMTP server, and the e-mail address of the person logged in to the computer that executed the Blat program. Blat is not a good tool if you are trying to hide the original sender's address.

Blat uses an SMTP feature called server relay. This feature is often used to spoof e-mail addresses, hiding the original sender of the e-mail. My primary Internet service provider does not allow this type of e-mail routing. It compares the address of the original message with the address of the sender. If the address did not originate on my Internet service provider's domain, it does not relay the message. However, most SMTP servers allow this type of relay traffic.

The ^? characters that you see at the bottom of the e-mail message in Figure 20.6 are the result of a bug in release 1.7 of Blat. The ^? characters are always sent when a message uses the - option. The subroutine `blatFILE`, on lines 13 through 21 of Listing 20.4, solve this problem by writing the message to a temporary file.

Line 15 creates an output file handle to a file named as the current process ID of the script:

```
open (OUTFILE, ">$$");
```

The process ID is guaranteed to be unique among all the processes currently executing, thereby creating a unique temporary filename.

Lines 16 and 17 write your message to the file:

```
print OUTFILE $msg;
print OUTFILE "Testing FILE interface\n";
```

Before you send your message, you must close your temporary file. This makes sure the output buffers are flushed and any system file locks are released.

Line 19 uses the command-line interface of Blat to send the temporary file as an e-mail message:

```
`c:\\Winnt\\system32\\blat.exe $$ -t $toName  -s \"$subject\" -q`;
```

As shown in Figure 20.7, those pesky extra ^? characters are no longer included in the e-mail message.

Line 20 cleans up the temporary file, deleting it from your computer.

```
unlink ($$);
```

The two subroutines of Listing 20.4 make Blat a useful e-mail tool for Windows programmers.

Sending a Blat mail message from a file

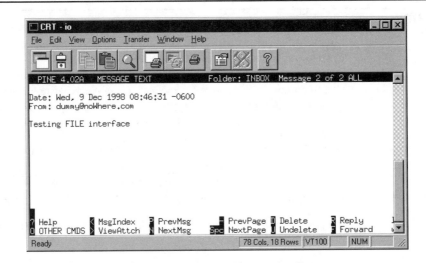

Sender.pm: A Perl E-Mail Interface

In this section, you'll learn about Sender.pm, a Perl module that provides a direct Perl interface to the SMTP server. The Sender.pm module can be used on any platform that has a connection to an SMTP server. If you can send and receive e-mail, you probably can use Sender.pm. The CPAN site includes an older module called Net::SMTP, which can also be used as a programmer's e-mail interface. However, I think Sender.pm is easier to use. To send an e-mail, you only need to create a Sender object and call the MailMsg method. That's it!

In this section, you'll learn how easy it is to use Sender.pm and then you will progressively step into the methods that perform the actual connections to the SMTP server. This way, when you are finished with this chapter, you'll know how to use Sender.pm and why and how Sender.pm works. If you should decide to extend Sender.pm or implement your own SMTP interface, you'll know how to proceed.

TIP	The `Sender.pm` module was written by Jan Krynicky (Jenda@Krynicky.cz). She says that this is her first module, and she has only been writing Perl code for 1.5 years. Congratulations are certainly in order. Her code makes the interface to an SMTP server easier to understand. `Sender.pm` and other modules by Jan are available from http://Jenda.Krynicky.cz. Jan tells me she lives in the Czech Republic, which is East of Germany, South of Poland, and North of Austria. As far as I am concerned, Jan is at the end of the next e-mail message, only a click away. Country boundaries just don't matter any more!

Why do I like the `Sender.pm` module so much? Listing 20.5 shows the reason.

Listing 20.5:   The Sender.pm Module

```
1.  use Mail::Sender;
2.  $sender = new Mail::Sender({from => 'yawp@io.com',
3.                              smtp => 'mail.assi.net'});
4.
5.  if (!(ref $sender) =~ /Sender/i){
6.    die $Mail::Sender::Error;
7.  }
8.
9.  $sender->MailMsg({to =>'Eric.Herrmann@assi.net',
10.                  subject => 'Testing Sender',
11.                  msg => "An easy email interface?"});
12.
13. if ( ($sender->{'error'}) < 0) {
14.     print "ERROR: $Mail::Sender::Error\n";
15. }
16. else {
17.     print "Msg Sent Ok\n";
18. }
```

What could be easier than that? There are only two real lines of functional code in Listing 20.5. The rest of it is error-checking code. All that is required to send a mail message using `Sender.pm` is initializing the `$sender` object with a From: address and a valid SMTP server to connect to. This is done on lines 2 and 3, which actually contain just one Perl statement:

```
$sender = new Mail::Sender({from => 'yawp@io.com',
                            smtp => 'mail.assi.net'});
```

Then all you need to do is call `MailMsg` method with your instance of a **Sender** object providing the recipient address, subject line, and a message. This is done on lines 9 through 11, which again contain only a single Perl statement:

```
$sender->MailMsg({to =>'Eric.Herrmann@assi.net',
                  subject => 'Testing Sender',
                  msg => "An easy email interface?"});
```

If you want to send a longer message, create a variable—either a scalar or an array of strings—and send the variable in the message field. If you want to send a file or several files, just use the `MailFile` syntax, as explained in the section about Sender methods, coming up soon.

Listing 20.5 uses several groups of **Sender** methods that work together to send an e-mail message. You'll learn more about using the **Sender** methods shortly. First, you'll see how to use the lower-level and more direct methods of this module, which better illustrate the steps involved in communicating with the SMTP server.

Sender.pm Communication with an SMTP Server

Rather than the code in Listing 20.5, you can use the more direct methods shown in Listing 20.6 to send an e-mail message. This example, which sends a binary file as an e-mail attachment, illustrates each of the steps you learned in the section on using an SMTP server through a telnet connection. Listing 20.5 is more practical for every day use, but it doesn't demonstrate the SMTP interface through `Sender.pm` as well as Listing 20.6.

Listing 20.6: **Sender.pm Module Lower-Level Methods**

```
1.   use Mail::Sender;
2.   $sender = new Mail::Sender({from => 'yawp@io.com',
3.                               smtp => 'mail.assi.net'});
4.
5.   if (!(ref $sender) =~ /Sender/i){
6.     die $Mail::Sender::Error;
7.   }
8.
9.   $sender->OpenMultipart({to =>'eherrmann@austin.inri.com',
10.                 subject => 'Testing Sender Direct I/F'});
11.  $sender->Body;
12.  $sender->SendLine("Attached is a our new Logo jpg file\n");
13.  $sender->SendFile({description => 'Chapter 6 image 2',
```

```
14.                       ctype => 'Image Tif type',
15.                       encoding => 'Base64',
16.                       disposition => 'attachment;
                          filename="f0602.tif";
                          type="tiff image"',
17.                       file => 'f0602.tif'});
18. $sender->Close;
19.
20. if ( ($sender->{'error'}) < 0) {
21.    print "ERROR: $Mail::Sender::Error\n";
22. }
23. else {
24.    print "Msg Sent Ok\n";
25. }
```

Listing 20.6 shows the steps required when communicating with the SMTP server. The SMTP communication works in the following order:

1. Connect

2. Say hello

3. Tell the server who is sending the e-mail

4. Tell the server whom you are sending e-mail to

.5. Tell the SMTP server you are sending it data

6. Send the mail headers

7. Complete the OpenMultipart message headers line on line 11 by sending the body.

The remaining lines separate the message from the file attachment and then disconnect from the SMTP server.

The following section describes the syntax and use of the various methods. After you learn the complete syntax of the main methods of Sender.pm, you'll step through the lower-level code that makes the actual connection to the SMTP server.

Sender.pm Method Syntax

The Sender.pm module uses the object-oriented syntax explained in Chapter 19. The new method of Sender.pm initializes the Sender object so that the Sender methods listed in Table 20.3 can use the default values. Table 20.4 lists the default Sender method parameters. Each of the default parameters may be overridden by explicitly passing the value in the appropriate method.

TABLE 20.3: Sender.pm Methods

Method	Description
Body	Send the head of the multipart message body. You can specify the character set and the encoding. The default is "US- ASCII","7BIT".
Cancel	Cancel an opened message.
Close	Close and send the mail.
MailMsg(msg)	Send a message.
MailFile(msg, file)	Send one or more files by mail.
New	Prepare a Sender.
Open	Open a new message.
OpenMultipart	Open a multipart message.
Part	Print a part header for the multipart message. The **undef** or empty variables are ignored.
Send(@strings)	Print the strings to the socket. Doesn't add any end-of-line characters. Use \r\n as the end-of-line characters.
SendEnc(@strings)	Print the strings to the socket. Doesn't add any end-of-line characters. Use \r\n as the end-of-line characters. Encodes the text using the selected encoding (Base64/Quoted-printable).
SendEx(@strings)	Print the strings to the socket. Doesn't add any end-of-line characters, but changes all end-of-line characters to \r\n.
SendLine(@strings)	Print the strings to the socket. Adds the end-of-line character at the end.
SendLineEnc(@strings)	Print the strings to the socket. Adds the end-of-line character at the end. Encodes the text using the selected encoding (Base64/Quoted-printable).
SendLineEx(@strings)	Print the strings to the socket. Doesn't add any end-of-line characters, but changes all end-of-line characters to \r\n.
SendFile(file)	In multipart mode, send a file as a separate part of the mail message.

WARNING	Do not mix up **SendEx** and **SendEnc** or **SendLineEx** and **SendLineEnc**! **SendEnc** and **SendLIneEnc** do some buffering necessary for correct Base64 encoding, and the **Send** method, which does the actual sending of the message, is not aware of that. Usage of **SendLine** and **SendLineEx** in non–7-bit parts is not recommended. In particular, if you use **SendLine** or **SendLineEx** to send several lines, eventually creating a single message, the data is likely to become corrupted.

TABLE 20.4: Default Sender Method Parameters

Parameter	Description
From	The address of the sender of the e-mail message
Replyto	The address the e-mail message should be replied to
To	The recipient's e-mail address
Smtp	The IP or domain address of the SMTP being connected to
Subject	The subject line of the e-mail message
Headers	Any additional headers sent before the body of the message
Boundary	The message boundary

The Sender.pm methods return detailed failure information as shown in Table 20.5. The method Mail::Sender::Error contains a textual description of last error.

TABLE 20.5: Sender.pm Method Failure Codes

Code	Meaning
-1	SMTP host unknown
-2	Socket failed
-3	Connect failed
-4	Service not available

Continued on next page

TABLE 20.5 CONTINUED: Sender.pm Method Failure Codes

Code	Meaning
-5	Unspecified communication error
-6	Local user `$to` unknown on host `$smtp`
-7	Transmission of message failed
-8	Argument `$to` empty
-9	No message specified in call to `MailMsg` or `MailFile`
-10	No filename specified in call to `SendFile` or `MailFile`
-11	File not found
-12	Not available in single-part mode

Most of the methods of `Sender.pm` are straightforward and don't require a special explanation. The following are some of the more important methods or those that do not follow the default syntax.

new

This method is used to initialize a `Sender` object and must be called before any other `Sender` method. It initializes the default parameters listed in Table 20.4. You can set `smtp`, `from`, and other parameters here and then use the information in all messages.

The `new` method does not open a connection to the SMTP server. You must use `$Sender->Open` or `$Sender->OpenMultipart` to start talking to the server. The parameters passed to the new method are used in subsequent calls to `$Sender->Open` and `$Sender->OpenMultipart`. Each call to a method with new default parameters, such as the `to` or `from` address, changes the variables initialized by the new method. If the `new` method is successful, it returns a reference variable to a `Mail::Sender` object. If a mail message in `$sender` is opened, it is closed and a new mail message is created and sent. `$sender` is then closed. The file parameter may be a filename, a list of filenames (separated by commas), or a reference to a list of filenames.

Close

Although this method does not require any parameters, it is important to note that the mail message being sent to the server is not processed until the Sender object is closed. The Close method should be called automatically when destroying the object, but you should call it yourself just to be sure—and you should do it as soon as possible to close the connection and free the socket.

Part

This method prints a part header for the multipart message. It accepts the following special parameters:

- ctype defines the content type (MIME type) of this part. This parameter defaults to "application/octet-stream".

- encoding defines the encoding used for this part of message. This parameter defaults to "7BIT".

- disposition defines the type of e-mail as a message or an attachment. This parameter defaults to "attachment".

SendFile

This method sends a file as a separate part of the mail message and operates only in multipart mode. SendFile accepts the same parameters as the part method and, in addition, accepts the file parameter. The file parameter identifies the name of the file to send, a list of filenames, or a reference to a list of filenames. Each file will be sent as a separate part.

MailFile

This method lets you send a file or several files. For example, using the MailFile method, you can replace lines 9 through 18 of Listing 20.6 with this one simple call:

```
MailFile ({msg=> "msg",
          file => 'f06022.tif'});
```

MailMsg

This method sends the message. If a mail message in $sender is already open, it is closed, which sends the message, and a new mail message is then created and sent. `$sender` is then closed. The `MailMsg` method shows the exact sequence and syntax necessary for your program to communicate with the SMTP server. If you want to build your own interface to the SMTP server, you should study this method. You'll do that in the next section.

SMTP Server Communication Revisited

The SMTP server communicates in an asynchronous handshaking mode. Commands do not need to follow each other in a strict time frame. Commands can sometimes be minuted apart; however, the SMTP server will timeout eventually. What is required is to follow a strict sequencing of commands. Therefore, as you examine Listing 20.7, take note of the communication sequence over the socket connection. The socket connection is the connection to the SMTP server. If you decide to further investigate `Sender.pm`, you will see the same sequence of communication regardless of the type of e-mail message being sent.

Listing 20.7:   **The SMTP Server Connection**

```
1.   sub MailMsg {
2.     my $self = shift;
3.     my $msg;
4.     if (ref $_[0] eq 'HASH') {
5.         my $hash=$_[0];
6.         $msg=$hash->{msg};
7.         delete $hash->{msg}
8.     } else {
9.         $msg = pop;
10.    }
11.    return $self->{'error'}=NOMSG unless $msg;
12.
13.    $self->Open(@_);
14.    $self->SendEx($msg);
15.    $self->Close;
16.    return $self;
17. }
```

Listing 20.7 does not include the constructor or initialization routines of `Sender.pm`. The constructor saves the SMTP information, but the communication to the SMTP server isn't started until one of the `Open` methods is called.

The `MailMsg` subroutine, which begins on line 1 of Listing 20.7, establishes the sequence of events for communication with an SMTP server. Lines 13 through 16 open communications with the SMTP server (this involves some initial handshaking and header transfer), send the body of the message, and then close communication:

```
$self->Open(@_);
$self->SendEx($msg);
$self->Close;
return $self;
```

Let's examine the steps involved. Knowing how they work will help you to understand how to design and build your own module.

As implemented in the `Sender.pm` module, the `Open` method is where all the action occurs. With this design, the `Open` method connects to the SMTP server and then tells the SMTP server whom the message is coming from, where it is going, and that the data is about to be sent. From that point, the SMTP server will accept almost any data you send it. Listing 20.8 steps through the initial communication sequence with the SMTP server.

Listing 20.8:   SMTP Connection Initialization

```
1.   sub Open {
2.     my $self = shift;
3.     if ($self->{'socket'}) {
4.       if ($self->{'error'}) {
5.         $self->Cancel;
6.       } else {
7.         $self->Close;
8.       }
9.     }
10.    delete $self->{'error'};
11.    my %changed;
12.    $self->{multipart}=0;
13.
14.    if (ref $_[0] eq 'HASH') {
15.      my $key;
16.      my $hash=$_[0];
17.      foreach $key (keys %$hash) {
18.        $self->{lc $key}=$hash->{$key};
19.        $changed{$key}=1;
```

```
20.    }
21.    } else {
22.      my ($from, $reply, $to, $smtp, $subject, $headers ) = @_;
23.
24.      if ($from) {$self->{'from'}=$from;$changed{'from'}=1;}
25.      if ($reply) {$self->{'reply'}=$reply;$changed{'reply'}=1;}
26.      if ($to) {$self->{'to'}=$to;$changed{'to'}=1;}
27.      if ($smtp) {$self->{'smtp'}=$smtp;$changed{'smtp'}=1;}
28.      if ($subject) {$self->{'subject'}=$subject;$changed
                                          {'subject'}=1;}
29.      if ($headers) {$self->{'headers'}=$headers;$changed
                                          {'headers'}=1;}
30.    }
31.
32.    $self->{'to'} =~ s/[ \t]+/, /g if ($changed{to});
33.    $self->{'to'} =~ s/,,/,/g if ($changed{to});
34.    $self->{'boundary'} =~ tr/=/-/ if $changed{boundary};
35.
36.    if ($changed{from}) {
37.      $self->{'fromaddr'} = $self->{'from'};
38.      $self->{'fromaddr'} =~ s/.*<([^\s]*?)>/$1/; #get from address
39.    }
40.
41.    if ($changed{reply}) {
42.      $self->{'replyaddr'} = $self->{'reply'};
43.      $self->{'replyaddr'} =~ s/.*<([^\s]*?)>/$1/; #get reply address
44.      $self->{'replyaddr'} =~ s/^([^\s]+).*/$1/; #use first address
45.    }
46.
47.    if ($changed{smtp}) {
48.      $self->{'smtp'} =~ s/^\s+//g; #remove spaces around $smtp
49.      $self->{'smtp'} =~ s/\s+$//g;
50.      $self->{'smtpaddr'} = ($self->{'smtp'} =~
51.      /^(\d{1,3})\.(\d{1,3})\.(\d{1,3})\.(\d{1,3})$/)
52.      ? pack('C4',$1,$2,$3,$4)
53.      : (gethostbyname($self->{'smtp'}))[4];
54.    }
55.
56.    if (!$self->{'to'}) { return $self->{'error'}=TOEMPTY; }
57.
58.    if (!defined($self->{'smtpaddr'})) { return
            $self->{'error'}=HOSTNOTFOUND($self->{smtp}); }
```

```
59.
60.   my $s = &FileHandle::new(FileHandle);
61.   $self->{'socket'} = $s;
62.
63.   if (!socket($s, AF_INET, SOCK_STREAM, $self->{'proto'})) {
64.     return $self->{'error'}=SOCKFAILED; }
65.
66.   if (!connect($s, pack('Sna4x8', AF_INET, $self->{'port'},
          $self->{'smtpaddr'}))) {
67.     return $self->{'error'}=CONNFAILED; }
68.
69.   my($oldfh) = select($s); $| = 1; select($oldfh);
70.
71.   $_ = <$s>; if (/^[45]/) { close $s; return
          $self->{'error'}=SERVNOTAVAIL; }
72.
73.   print $s "helo localhost\r\n";
74.   $_ = <$s>; if (/^[45]/) { close $s; return
          $self->{'error'}=COMMERROR; }
75.
76.   print $s "mail from: <$self->{'fromaddr'}>\r\n";
77.   $_ = <$s>; if (/^[45]/) { close $s; return
          $self->{'error'}=COMMERROR; }
78.
79.   foreach (split(/, /, $self->{'to'})) {
80.     print $s "rcpt to: <$_>\r\n";
81.     $_ = <$s>; if (/^[45]/) { close $s; return
            $self->{'error'}=USERUNKNOWN($self->{to}, $self->{smtp}); }
82.   }
83.
84.   print $s "data\r\n";
85.   $_ = <$s>; if (/^[45]/) { close $s; return
          $self->{'error'}=COMMERROR; }
86.
87.   print $s "To: $self->{'to'}\r\n";
88.   print $s "From: $self->{'from'}\r\n";
89.   print $s "Reply-to: $self->{'replyaddr'}\r\n"
              if $self->{'replyaddr'};
90.   print $s "X-Mailer: Perl Mail::Sender Version
              $Mail::Sender::ver Jan Krynicky  <Jan\@chipnet.cz>
              Czech Republic\r\n";
91.   if ($self->{'headers'}) {print $s $self->{'headers'},"\r\n"};
```

```
92.  print $s "Subject: $self->{'subject'}\r\n\r\n";
93.
94.  return $self;
95. }
```

Lines 3 through 9 of Listing 20.8 clean up after any previous communication:

```
if ($self->{'socket'}) {
    if ($self->{'error'}) {
        $self->Cancel;
    } else {
        $self->Close;
    }
}
```

Each call to the Open method closes any previously opened sockets, completing any communication currently in progress.

Lines 14 through 30 are involved in reading the incoming parameter list and determining if any of the initialized parameters have changed. Lines 32 through 54 make sure e-mail and SMTP addresses are in the correct format. The network communication begins on line 60. The protocol used in establishing the initial socket on line 63 is a standard Internet socket protocol.

The actual communication with the SMTP server begins on line 66, which establishes the initial connection with the SMTP server on the public port 25:

```
if (!connect($s, pack('Sna4x8', AF_INET, $self->{'port'},
    $self->{'smtpaddr'}))) {
```

After the initial connection on line 66, the server responds on the socket with a 220 status message, briefly describing itself. If the response status code is a 400 or 500 series message, the message sequence has failed in some manner and communication must be reestablished. The server response is read off the socket on line 71, followed by the if check to verify a valid status response code:

```
$_ = <$s>; if (/^[45]/) { close $s; return $self->{'error'}=
    SERVNOTAVAIL; }
```

This is part of the handshaking process. You must use the correct sequence of commands to the SMTP server, but you must also read, and thereby clear, each response communication from the SMTP server.

Reading the response from the SMTP server is critical, and it is called completing the handshake. A *handshake* is a two-step communication. One side initiates a message, and the other side acknowledges the receipt of the message. If the receipt of the message is not acknowledged, then the message sender never knows if the message is received. By reading the SMTP server's response message, you are actually removing the message from the connection, called a *socket*. By removing the message, you have acknowledged the message, which completes the handshake.

After successfully connecting to the SMTP server, it's polite to say hello and identify yourself. In fact, it's required to say helo and identify yourself, which is done on line 73:

```
print $s "helo localhost\r\n";
```

The identity value can be any value. The Sender.pm module uses a hard-coded localhost value. It would be more polite to get your actual local host name and send that value. The SMTP server's response to the helo message is a 250 status message, echoing back the SMTP server name and your identity.

Next, on line 76, you must tell the SMTP server who the mail is from:

```
print $s "mail from: <$self->{'fromaddr'}>\r\n";
```

The response should be a 250 Ok status message. Then on line 80, each recipient's name is sent to the SMTP server:

```
print $s "rcpt to: <$_>\r\n";
```

The server responds with a 250 Ok status message for each recipient.

At this point, you've completed the initial communication exchange. Your next step, on line 84, is to tell the SMTP server that you're going to send it some real data:

```
print $s "data\r\n";
```

The SMTP server responds with a 354 status message telling you it is ready to receive mail input.

Now you're ready to send the actual e-mail headers. In this implementation, the To:, From:, Reply-to:, X-mailer:, Subject:, and any other e-mail headers are sent to the SMTP server in the Open method. From this point forward, the SMTP server will not respond with a new status message until you have completed sending the e-mail message. The headers are sent between lines 87 through 92:

```
print $s "To: $self->{'to'}\r\n";
print $s "From: $self->{'from'}\r\n";
print $s "Reply-to: $self->{'replyaddr'}\r\n" if $self->{'replyaddr'};
print $s "X-Mailer: Perl Mail::Sender Version $Mail::Sender::ver Jan
         Krynicky <Jan\@chipnet.cz> Czech Republic\r\n";
if ($self->{'headers'}) {print $s $self->{'headers'},"\r\n"};
print $s "Subject: $self->{'subject'}\r\n\r\n";
```

You can put any value in the X-mailer: header. This header is essentially used as a comment line to let the programmer identify the tool used to send the e-mail message. Also, you can change the From: address, but this will not hide the actual Sender. The protocol requires the SMTP server to identify the originating computer, the hops made through the SMTP chain, and the original login user name. When you send the message, these additional headers show up when your e-mail receiver clicks on the option to show all headers. Finally, notice that all communication with the SMTP server ends with \r\n. You must send a carriage return character (\r) in addition to the newline character (\n) to the SMTP server.

NOTE   I'm not sure I agree that the headers sent from lines 87 through 92 of Listing 20.8 should be in an **Open** method. The e-mail headers are part of the e-mail message and are not required as part of the initial communication sequence.

The rest of the SMTP communication is anticlimactic. Listing 20.9 shows how the body of the message is sent to the SMTP server using the SendEx method.

Listing 20.9:   **The E-Mail Body**

```
1.  sub SendEx {
2.  my $self = shift;
3.  my $s;
4.  $s = $self->{'socket'};
5.  my $str;
6.  foreach $str (@_) {
7.    $str =~ s/\n/\r\n/;
8.  }
9.  print $s @_;
10. return 1;
11. }
```

As you can see from Listing 20.9, sending the body of the message only involves writing to the SMTP socket after the standard newline character (\n) has been replaced with the carriage return/linefeed character (\r\n).

The SMTP server has nothing to say until you complete the e-mail message, which is done in Listing 20.10.

Listing 20.10:   E-Mail Message Completion

```
1.  sub Close {
2.    my $self = shift;
3.    my $s;#=new FileHandle;
4.    $s = $self->{'socket'};
5.    if ($self->{buffer}) {
6.      my $code = $self->{code};
7.      print $s (&$code($self->{buffer}));
8.      delete $self->{buffer};
9.    }
10.   if ($self->{'multipart'}) {print $s "\r\n-",$self->{'boundary'},
                                  "-\r\n";}
11.   print $s "\r\n.\r\n";
12.
13.   $_ = <$s>; if (/^[45]/) {close $s; return $self->{'error'}=
                                TRANSFAILED;}
14.
15.   print $s "quit\r\n";
16.   $_ = <$s>;
17.
18.   close $s;
19.   delete $self->{'socket'};
20.   return 1;
21. }
```

Line 11 of Listing 20.10 actually completes the sending of one e-mail message. The SMTP server responds on line 13 with a 250 requested mail action Ok message. At this point, if you wanted to send multiple e-mail messages, you could begin the data sequence again.

Sender.pm chooses to only send one e-mail per SMTP connection. Line 15 of Listing 20.10 closes the connection to the SMTP server with a quit command. The SMTP server responds with a polite "Goodbye" response. Your communication with the SMTP server is now complete.

This communication process is basically the same, regardless of the type of e-mail being sent. A multipart e-mail message with a file attachment only requires a boundary header separating the different parts of the e-mail message. The file itself should be binary encoded using a protocol like Base 64. This process is fully covered in the `Sender.pm` module's `MailFile` method. If you examine that method, you'll see that you can easily use `MailFile` to send any type of attachment, or you can build your own method or module.

TIP   The functions for binary encoding a file are available in the `Mime::Base64` and the **MIME** modules. These modules are freely available from the CPAN web site, www.perl.com/CPAN.

Summary

What happens when you learn how to program in Perl 5? You get to use and write some really cool applications. In this chapter, you learned about coding Perl applications that use one of the earliest and most widely used tools of the Internet—e-mail. You can use the examples presented in this chapter as a starting point for your own HTML and e-mail programs.

Most e-mail programs on the Internet communicate through the `sendmail` daemon. The `sendmail` program, when run as a daemon, is frequently referred to as your SMTP server. The STMP server is responsible for routing e-mail messages from domain to domain, across the network.

Although it's more convenient to use an interface program to talk with your SMTP server, in this chapter, you also learned the commands necessary to communicate with an SMTP server using a telnet session.

After you learned about the `sendmail` program and SMTP servers, you saw an example of one of the more common CGI applications—reading an HTML registration form and sending an e-mail response. Then you learned more about the `sendmail` program through a Perl 5 interface program that sends form letters to a mailing list.

There is a growing demand for e-mail applications that run on a Windows computer. In this chapter, you learned about a Windows freeware program called

Blat. Blat is an interface program to your SMTP server. To avoid problems with the Blat interface, you can use the two subroutines that were included in this section. The blatSTDIN subroutine sends e-mail messages directly through your program. The blatFILE subroutine uses a file interface to send e-mail messages.

Finally, you learned about the Sender.pm module. Perl 5 comes delivered with an SMTP interface module called Net::SMTP, but I think Sender.pm is easier to use. The module Sender.pm is an e-mail interface built by a Perl 5 user. With fewer than 20 lines of code and this module, you can send e-mail messages and attached files.

PART VI

Windows Only

Jump-Start on Windows Solutions

- ■ Win32 extensions to Perl 5

- ■ A menu-driven interface to Windows utilities

- ■ Registry and event log information

- ■ Perl 5 database applications

The number of Perl 5 modules available to handle Windows tasks has grown dramatically over the past few years. There are more than 30 special-purpose Win32 modules that can be added to your Perl 5 Windows installation.

In this chapter, you'll get an overview of the use of the Win32 modules. The jump-start program for this chapter is a menu-driven interface to a set of utilities for your Window's computer. It gives you access to information about your computer, network, Registry, and event log. This chapter also outlines how to connect to and use Windows databases.

Jump-Start Definitions

Access control list (ACL)	A basic part of the Windows NT security model. The ACL defines who has access to your files. Each ACL is specific for an individual user, global group, or local group that is granted or denied permission to access your files.
Database engine	The application, such as Microsoft Access or Oracle, that manipulates the data in your database. The database engine is the heart of your database management system.
Database management system	A set of tools for managing data in a particular format.
DSN (Data Source Name)	A common set of information that all databases must supply. A DSN defines the location of the database, the type of database, and the user name and password of a database. You must create the DSN on your computer before you can connect your program to your database. A *User DSN* is accessible by only the account that created it. A *System DSN* is accessible by any account.

Dynamic-link library (DLL)	A compiled module of functions and data, which is linked with your code at runtime. Windows uses DLLs to load in functions and data as your program needs them.
Event log	A Windows log maintained by the Registry that contains information about system and application events. Windows NT systems have three types of event logs: Application, Security, and System.
ODBC (Open Database Connectivity)	A commonly agreed upon standard for connecting to the major database engines of the world.
Registry	A central database where Windows keeps all of its information about the software and hardware on your computer. The Registry is separated into branches of related information called *keys* and *subkeys*.
Relational database	A database made up of tables, each containing related information. A row in a table is made up of columns of information that describe an individual object. Each column defines an individual feature of the object, such as a car's color, make, or model.
SQL (Structured Query Language)	A programming language designed specifically for database operations. SQL is a common language among many database engines.

Jump-Start Program

Listing 21.1 is part of a nearly thousand-line program I wrote for this book. The program provides easy access to Windows utilities. The portion of the program in Listing 21.1 shows an overview of how the entire program works (you can download the entire program from this book's companion web site at www.sybex.com or www.MasteringPerl5.com).

Listing 21.1:   Windows Utility Programs

```
1.  use Cwd;
2.  use Win32;
3.  use Win32::FileSecurity;
4.  use Win32::AdminMisc;
5.  use Win32::Console;
6.  use Win32::Registry;
7.  use Win32::EventLog;
8.
9.  #Define global constants
10. @months = (Jan, Feb, March, April, May, June,
11.                 July, Aug, Sep, Oct, Nov, Dec);
12. @days = (Sun, Mon, Tue, Wed, Thur, Fri, Sat);
13. $SEC = 0; $MIN = 1; $HOUR = 2; $DAYOFMONTH = 3;
14. $MONTH = 4; $YEAR = 5; $WEEKDAY=6;
15. $separator = ("=" x 60) . "\n";
16.
17. #Print the initial screen
18. printMainMenu();
19.
20. while ($input = <STDIN>){
21.    #Get rid of the newline
22.    chomp $input;
23.    #Exit if just hit enter
24.    exit if length ($input) == 0;
25.    #Decode the input from the main menu
26.    #This returns a symbolic reference to the
27.    #correct submenu to execute
28.    $menuName = decodeMainMenu($input);
29.    #Using a symbolic reference, call the menu requested
30.    &$menuName();
31.    #Get the input from the submenu
```

```
32.     $input = <STDIN>;
33.     #All the implementation routines are named the
34.     #same as the print menu. This means we remove
35.     #print from the symbolic reference and we now
36.     #have a symbolic reference to the utility routine
37.     #
38.     $menuName =~ s/print//;
39.     $utilityName = $menuName;
40.     #Call the utility routine that handles the menu input
41.     &$utilityName($input);
42.     #Pause after the results are printed
43.     print "\n\n<ENTER> to continue";
44.     $trash = <STDIN>;
45.     #Print the Diagnostic Utility screen again
46.     printMainMenu();
47. }
48.
49. sub decodeMainMenu($){
50.     my ($menuRequest) = @_;
51.     print "\n";
52.     SWITCH:{
53.         if ($menuRequest =~ /^0|Drive/i){
54.             $menuName = "printDriveMenu";
55.             last SWITCH;
56.         }
57.         if ($menuRequest =~ /^1|File/i){
58.             $menuName = "printFileMenu";
59.             last SWITCH;
60.         }
61.         if ($menuRequest =~ /^2|User/i){
62.             $menuName = "printUserMenu";
63.             last SWITCH;
64.         }
65.         if ($menuRequest =~ /^3|Net/i){
66.             $menuName = "printDiagUtils";
67.             last SWITCH;
68.         }
69.         if ($menuRequest =~ /^4|Registry/i){
70.             $menuName = "printRegistryMenu";
71.             last SWITCH;
72.         }
73.         if ($menuRequest =~ /^5|Event/i){
```

```
74.             $menuName = "printEventMenu";
75.          last SWITCH;
76.       }
77.       if ($menuRequest =~ /^q|^e/i){
78.          exit;
79.       }
80.    DEFAULT:{
81.       print "INVALID COMMAND $menuRequest\n";
82.       }
83.    }#END SWITCH
84.    return ($menuName);
85. }
86.
87. sub printMainMenu(){
88.    print<<"eof";
89.
90.
91. Windows UTILITIES
92.
93.           Display Drive Utilities Menu
94. Enter [0] or Drive
95.
96.           Display File System Utilities Menu
97. Enter [1] or File
98.
99.           Display User Information Menu
100. Enter [2] or User
101.
102.           Display Network Utilities Menu
103. Enter [3] or Net
104.
105.           Display The Registry Utilities Menu
106. Enter [4] or Registry
107.
108.           Display The Event Log Utilities Menu
109. Enter [5] or Event
110.
111. (Blank line to exit)
112. eof
113. print "ENTER COMMAND: ";
114. }
115.
```

```perl
116. sub DriveMenu($){
117.     my ($menuRequest) = @_;
118.     my ($utilityName);
119.     print "\n";
120.     SWITCH:{
121.         if ($menuRequest =~ /^0|Drives/i){
122.             $utilityName = "justDrives";
123.             last SWITCH;
124.         }
125.         if ($menuRequest =~ /^1|Disk/i){
126.             $utilityName = "diskConfiguration";
127.             last SWITCH;
128.         }
129.         if ($menuRequest =~ /^2|Space/i){
130.             $utilityName = "diskSpace";
131.             last SWITCH;
132.         }
133.         DEFAULT:{
134.             print "INVALID COMMAND $menuRequest\n";
135.             return;
136.         }
137.     }#END SWITCH
138.     &$utilityName();
139. }
140.
141. sub diskSpace(){
142.     foreach $drive (@allDrives){
143.         #Get the Drive Type
144.         $driveType = Win32::AdminMisc::GetDriveType($drive);
145.         if ($driveTypes{$driveType} =~ /REMOTE|FIXED/){
146.             ($driveSize, $freeSpace) =
                        Win32::AdminMisc::GetDriveSpace($drive);
147.             $drive =~ s/\\//;
148.             print "Drive $drive\n";
149.             print "Free Space: $freeSpace\nTotal Size:
                    $driveSize\n\n";
150.         }
151.     }
152. }
153.
154. sub diskConfiguration(){
155.     foreach $drive (@allDrives){
```

```
156.      #Get the Drive Type
157.      $driveType = Win32::AdminMisc::GetDriveType($drive);
158.      if ($driveTypes{$driveType} =~ /REMOTE|FIXED/){
159.         print "$drive is a $driveTypes{$driveType}\n";
160.         #Only get geometry on disks I can guarantee have
161.         #something to read in them.
162.         @driveDetails =  Win32::AdminMisc::
                                    GetDriveGeometry($drive);
163.         $size = $driveDetails [$GEOSECTORS] *
164.                   $driveDetails [$GEOBYTES] *
165.                   $driveDetails [$GEOTOTALCLUSTORS];
166.         $freeSpace = $driveDetails [$GEOSECTORS] *
167.                       $driveDetails [$GEOBYTES] *
168.                       $driveDetails [$GEOFREECLUSTERS];
169.         print<<"eof";
170. With the following Drive Details:
171.    Sectors per cluster:      $driveDetails[$GEOSECTORS]
172.    Bytes per sector:         $driveDetails[$GEOBYTES]
173.    Free clusters:            $driveDetails[$GEOFREECLUSTERS]
174.    Total clusters:           $driveDetails[$GEOTOTALCLUSTORS]
175.    Free Space Available:     $freeSpace
176.    Total Space Available:    $size
177. eof
178.         }
179.      }
180. }
181.
182. sub justDrives(){
183.
184.    #Get all the drives on my computer
185.    @allDrives = Win32::AdminMisc::GetDrives();
186.    #List the drives and types
187.    foreach $drive (@allDrives){
188.       $driveType = Win32::AdminMisc::GetDriveType($drive);
189.       print "\t$drive is a $driveTypes{$driveType}\n";
190.    }
191. }
```

Line 18 of Listing 21.1 prints the main menu, as shown in Figure 21.1, and then the program goes into an infinite loop waiting for user input on line 20:

```
while ($input = <STDIN>){
```

FIGURE 21.1:

The main menu for the
Windows Utilities program

This loop exits if the user enters a blank line or the keyword `quit` or `exit`:

```
exit if length ($input) == 0;
if ($menuRequest =~ /^q*|^e/i){
```

The user input is passed to an input handler subroutine (`decodeMainMenu`) that decides which submenu should be displayed to the user:

```
$menuName = decodeMainMenu($input);
```

The `decodeMainMenu()` subroutine loads a scalar variable with the name of the correct submenu, such as the submenu named on line 54:

```
$menuName = "printDriveMenu";
```

This submenu name is then used as a symbolic reference to call the correct print menu subroutine on line 30:

```
&$menuName();
```

If you enter 0 from the main menu, the program calls the `printDriveMenu()` subroutine, which prints the menu shown in Figure 21.2.

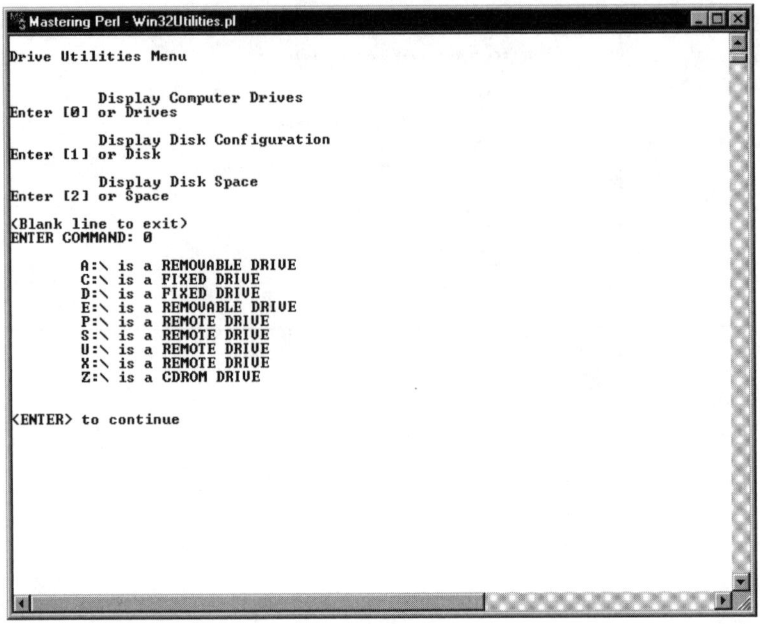
Mastering Perl - Win32Utilities.pl
Drive Utilities Menu
Display Computer Drives
Enter [0] or Drives
Display Disk Configuration
Enter [1] or Disk
Display Disk Space
Enter [2] or Space
<Blank line to exit>
ENTER COMMAND: 0
A:\ is a REMOVABLE DRIVE
C:\ is a FIXED DRIVE
D:\ is a FIXED DRIVE
E:\ is a REMOVABLE DRIVE
P:\ is a REMOTE DRIVE
S:\ is a REMOTE DRIVE
U:\ is a REMOTE DRIVE
X:\ is a REMOTE DRIVE
Z:\ is a CDROM DRIVE
<ENTER> to continue

FIGURE 21.2:

The Drive Utilities menu

The subroutine printDriveMenu() uses the same logic as the printMainMenu() subroutine (on lines 87 through 114). Each print*Utility*Menu() subroutine is accompanied by a companion *Utility*Menu() subroutine, which decodes the user input for that submenu. The symbolic reference that calls the printDriveMenu() subroutine is modified on line 38 to call the companion *Utility*Menu() subroutine:

```
$menuName =~ s/print//;
```

For example, the DriveMenu() subroutine is called using the symbolic reference on line 41:

```
&$utilityName($input);
```

Each companion subroutine creates a symbolic reference to the correct implementation subroutine, such as the justDrives() subroutine symbolic reference created on line 122:

```
$utilityName = "justDrives";
```

The subroutine is actually called on line 138:

```
&$utilityName();
```

The Windows Utilities program shown in Listing 21.1 is designed so that you can expand and modify the utility routines. You can download the entire program and add your own utility programs to each of the `printUtilityMenu()` subroutines and their companion `UtilityMenu()` subroutines. All you need to do is add your own utility routines to the `SWITCH` logic of the `UtilityMenu` routines, inserting the name of your subroutine. You'll learn about some expansion possibilities in Chapter 22.

Windows System Information

There are numerous Win32 extensions to Perl 5 that you can use to get information about your computer and your network. The following sections describe how to use Win32 modules to obtain information about your computer's drives, file system, users, Registry, and event log.

Drive Information

In Listing 21.1, the Drive Utilities menu calls the three subroutines `just-Drives()`, `diskConfiguration()`, and `diskSpace()`. These subroutines use the `Win32::AdminMisc` module created by Dave Roth. The `justDrives()` subroutine calls the `GetDrives()` AdminMisc subroutine, which returns all the drives on your computer:

```
@allDrives = Win32::AdminMisc::GetDrives();
```

The `GetDriveType` AdminMisc subroutine is then used to decode each drive type, on line 188:

```
$driveType = Win32::AdminMisc::GetDriveType($drive);
```

The second option on the Drives Utilities menu gets detailed information about a disk drive's sectors, bytes, and clusters using the `GetDriveGeometry()` subroutine, on line 162:

```
@driveDetails = Win32::AdminMisc::GetDriveGeometry($drive);
```

The drive details are reported to the user on lines 169 through 177:

```
        print<<"eof";
With the following Drive Details:
        Sectors per cluster:        $driveDetails[$GEOSECTORS]
```

```
         Bytes per sector:          $driveDetails[$GEOBYTES]
         Free clusters:             $driveDetails[$GEOFREECLUSTERS]
         Total clusters:            $driveDetails[$GEOTOTALCLUSTORS]
         Free Space Available:      $freeSpace
         Total Space Available:     $size
    eof
```

You can determine just the total disk size and space available using the third menu option, Display Disk Space. This option calls the AdminMisc subroutine GetDriveSpace(), on line 146:

```
    ($driveSize, $freeSpace) = Win32::AdminMisc::GetDriveSpace($drive);
```

File System Information

The File System Utilities menu produced by Listing 21.1 displays the authorized users for the current directory and the permissions associated with the files of the directory. Figure 21.3 shows an example of this menu.

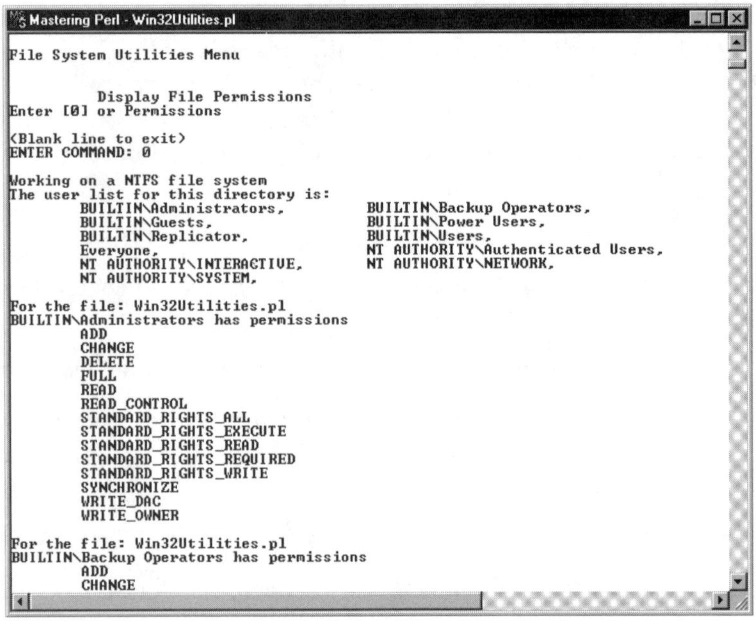

FIGURE 21.3:

The File System Utilities menu

The subroutine that prints this menu and the implementation routines that return the file system information are part of the larger program, which is available on the book's web site. The subroutine that prints the menu and the subroutine that calls the correct subroutine for responding to the user's input are in the same format as described previously, as are all the other menu and implementation programs.

The File System Utilities menu has one option, which uses the `FileSecurity` module to get the discretionary access control list (ACL) for the files in the current directory, on line 391 of the complete program:

```
Win32::FileSecurity::Get($fileName, \%DACL);
```

The %DACL hash contains a list of users who have access to the directory, which is retrieved by getting the keys to the %DACL hash on line 392:

```
@userList = sort keys %DACL;
```

After displaying the user list, the program uses the %DACL keys to retrieve the permission values for each user using the `EnumerateRights` subroutine, on lines 407 through 414:

```
foreach $name (@userList){
Win32::FileSecurity::EnumerateRights($DACL{$name}, \@values);
    $prevSeparator = $";
    $" = "\n\t";
    @values = sort (@values);
    print "\nFor the file: $fileName\n";
    print "$name has permissions\n\t@values\n";
}
```

User Information

The User Utilities menu generated by Listing 21.1 has two options: one displays login information about the current user of your computer and the other shows more detailed user information. Figure 21.4 shows the detailed user information display.

The User Utilities menu calls two subroutines, `loginInformation()` and `userInformation()`, to get details about the current computer user. The `login-Information()` subroutine uses the Win32 module subroutines `LoginName()`,

`DomainName()`, `NodeName()`, and `GetOSVersion()` to get information about this user session, on lines 459 through 479 of the complete program:

```
$loginName  = Win32::LoginName();
$domainName = Win32::DomainName();
$nodeName   = Win32::NodeName();
@windowsInfo = Win32::GetOSVersion();
```

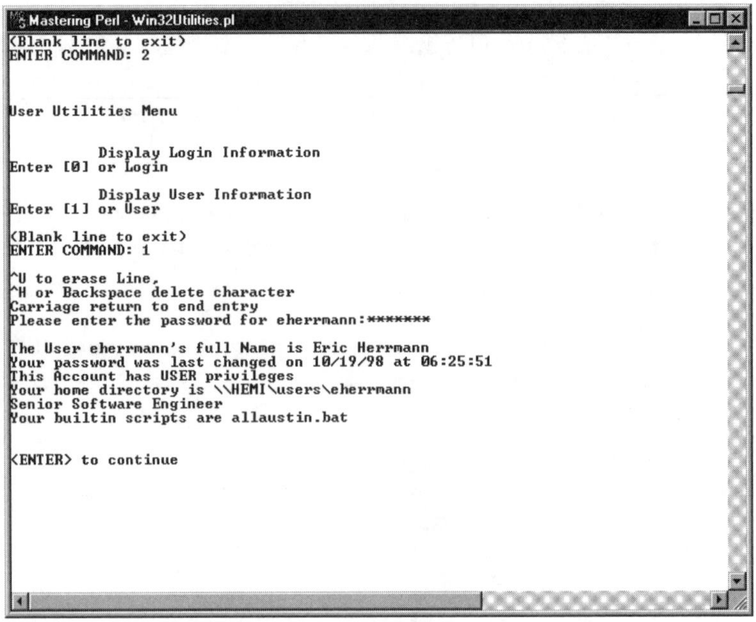

FIGURE 21.4:

The User Utilities menu

The `userInformation()` subroutine, whose results are displayed in Figure 21.4, gets the user's password using the `Console` module. The password is saved and the typed in characters are covered with an asterisk on lines 535 through 542 of the complete program:

```
#Almost anything but control characters
#and the space character are valid
if ( $char >= 0x21 && $char <= 0x7E){
     #Convert the number to an ASCII character
      $password .= chr $char;
      print "*";
```

```
        last SWITCH;
    }
```

The password is used as input to the `AdminMisc::UserGetAttributes` subroutine on lines 548 through 555:

```
#Supply login Name and Password
#Leave Server Name blank
#Returns Full Name, Password Age, User Privilege Mask
#Home Directory, comments, flags and scripts
#
Win32::AdminMisc::UserGetAttributes("", "$loginName",
        $fullName,      $password, $passwordAge, $privileges,
        $homeDirectory, $comment,  $flags,        $scripts);
```

Network Information

The Network Diagnostic Utilities menu displayed by Listing 21.1 provides access to the built-in network diagnostic utilities loaded with the Windows NT installation, as shown in Figure 21.5. If your Windows 95/98 computer is part of a network, these utilities may be available to you.

FIGURE 21.5:

The Network Diagnostic Utilities menu

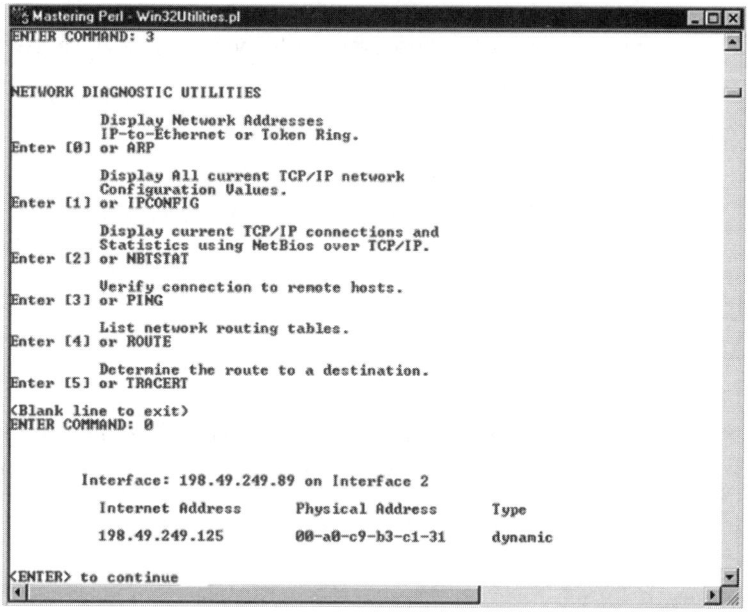

The Network Diagnostic Utilities menu calls one of six built-in programs. The program uses the back quote operator to access each utility. Line 147 of the entire program calls the Address Resolution Protocol (ARP):

```
@arp = `arp -a`;
```

ARP displays and modifies physical addresses related to your network IP-to-Ethernet or Token Ring address.

Line 152 of the entire program calls the IPCONFIG program:

```
@ipconfig = `ipconfig/all `;
```

The IPCONFIG program displays all of the TCP/IP (Transport Control Protocol/Internet Protocol) configuration values, configured by the DHCP (Dynamic Host Configuration Protocol) process. You can use the IPCONFIG program to display a subset of the TCP/IP configuration values, update the configuration data, and disable TCP/IP on DHCP clients.

After doing some data validation and formatting, line 172 of the entire program calls the NBTSTAT program:

```
@nbtstat = `nbtstat $getNames`;
```

The NBSTAT program displays a list of a remote connection's TCP/IP statistics using the NetBIOS protocol.

Line 188 of the entire program calls the PING program (which also requires data validation and formatting):

```
@ping = `ping -n 5 $destination`;
```

The PING program sends an echo packet to the remote computer's network connection. The PING program keeps statistics on the length of time it takes each echo packet to be returned.

Line 193 of the entire program calls the ROUTE program to print the active routes from the computer's routing table:

```
@route = `route print`;
```

The ROUTE network utility program can be used to modify, delete, add, and change the network routing tables of local and remote computers.

Line 207 of the entire program calls the TRACERT program (which again requires some data validation and formatting):

```
@tracert = `tracert $destination`;
```

The TRACERT program collects data on each of the intermediate connections, called *hops*, along the route. Detailed information about the route taken to a destination and the length of time used by each hop along the route is returned.

The Network Diagnostic Utilities program is discussed in much more detail in Chapter 22.

Registry Information

The Windows Registry keeps track of the hardware in your computer and every piece of software. The Registry Utilities menu produced by Listing 21.1 gives you a user interface to list your Registry's hardware keys, to create and delete Registry keys, and to view the values associated with Registry keys. This menu is shown in Figure 21.6.

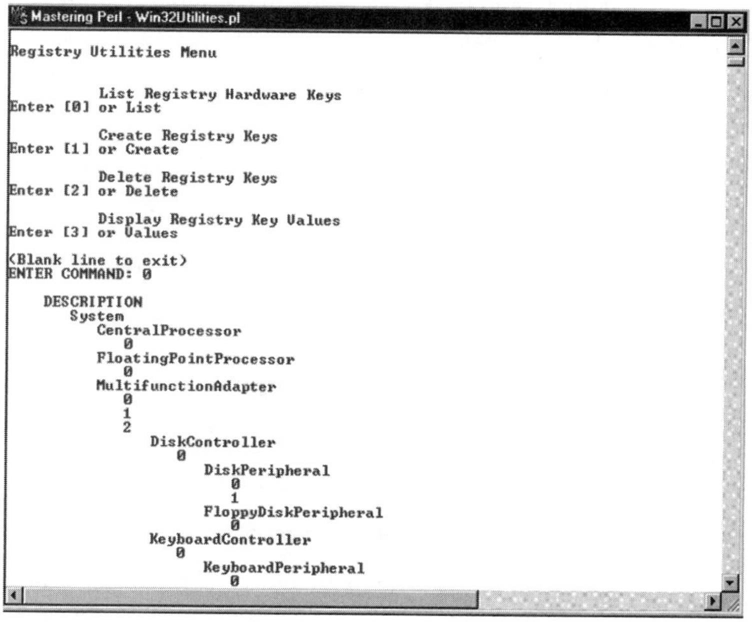

FIGURE 21.6:

The Registry Utilities menu

WARNING   A corrupted Registry can prevent your computer from running. Before you run any program that modifies the contents of your Registry, you need to export a copy of your entire Registry (see Chapter 23 for instructions). Make sure that you put the exported copy of your Registry some place other than the computer on which you are working.

The List Registry Hardware Keys menu option calls the `listRegistryKeys()` subroutine of the complete program, which uses three `Win32::Registry` methods: `Open`, `GetKeys`, and `Close`.

A Registry key, such as `$HKEY_LOCAL_MACHINE`, is used like an object reference with the `Win32::Registry` module, on line 711 of the complete program:

```
$HKEY_LOCAL_MACHINE->Open($key, $nextKeyList);
```

This creates a connection to your computer's Registry. The `Registry::Open` method uses the key variable as a pointer to an internal object root. This object root defines the beginning location for all searches through the Registry. The `GetKeys` method uses an open Registry key (the object reference returned by the `Open` method) and returns an array of the subkeys under the open Registry key, which happens on line 718:

```
$keyList->GetKeys(\@subKeys);
```

You should always remember to close an open Registry key. The `Close` method is called on line 726, using the open `$keyList` as the object reference variable:

```
$keyList->Close();
```

The Registry Utilities menu also allows you to create Registry keys. This version adds a key to the ActiveWare key list for demonstration purposes. The key is created on line 696 of the complete program:

```
$keyList->Create("Perl6",$newKeyList);
```

The `Create` method requires an open key before it can be called. Its syntax is:

```
$keyList->Create($newSubKey, $subKeyList);
```

If `$newSubKey` already exists, it will not be created.

The Registry Utilities menu includes an option for deleting a Registry key. On line 647, the program deletes the key added by the Create Registry Keys menu option, using the Registry method `DeleteKey`:

```
$keyList->DeleteKey("Perl6");
```

The DeleteKey method requires an open key that points to a folder that contains the key to be deleted. Its syntax is:

```
$keyList->DeleteKey($subKey);
```

The DeleteKey method returns true if it was successful.

Finally, the Registry Utilities menu provides an interface to display the values that each Registry key contains. The values of a Registry key are retrieved using the Registry method GetValues, on line 671 of the complete program:

```
$keyList->GetValues(\%keyValues);
```

The GetValues method creates a hash of the values of an open key. The hash contains three keys: Name (the name of the value), Type (the data type of the value), and Value (the data of the key value). The keys of the returned hash point to an array that contains the value's name, its data type, and its value. The hash %keyValues is processed from lines 672 through 685:

```
foreach $valueIndex (keys %keyValues){
    print "\nThe index is the same as the name: $valueIndex\n";
    print "$separator\n";
      #The name of the value being retrieved is in the first cell
      #of the array reference
    print "\tName     => $keyValues{$valueIndex}->[0]\n";
      #The data type of the value is in the second cell (cell 1)
      #but the data type is only a number. So that number is
      #used as an index in the data type names array created
      #at the beginning of this program.
    print "\tData Type => $registryDataTypes[
                        $keyValues{$valueIndex}->[1]]\n";
      #The actual value of the key is in cell 2
    print "\tValue     => $keyValues{$valueIndex}->[2]\n";
}
```

Event Log Information

Windows event logs contain information about each login event, the location of device driver message files, and application error messages. All security, system, and application programs are supposed to log significant events into the event log.

The Event Log Utilities menu displayed by Listing 21.1, shown in Figure 21.7, provides a user interface to list the event log entries, create a new entry, and create a backup copy of the event log. The program uses `Win32::EventLog` methods for these tasks.

The Event Log Utilities menu lists the events of your System log. Line 779 of the complete program creates an object reference to the event log:

```
$eventLog = Win32::EventLog->new('System') || die $!;
```

The object reference, `$eventLog`, is then used on lines 786 through 788 to read a system event:

```
$eventLog->Read((EVENTLOG_SEEK_READ | EVENTLOG_BACKWARDS_READ),
                 $eventIndex,\%eventLogData);
```

FIGURE 21.7:

The Event Log Utilities menu

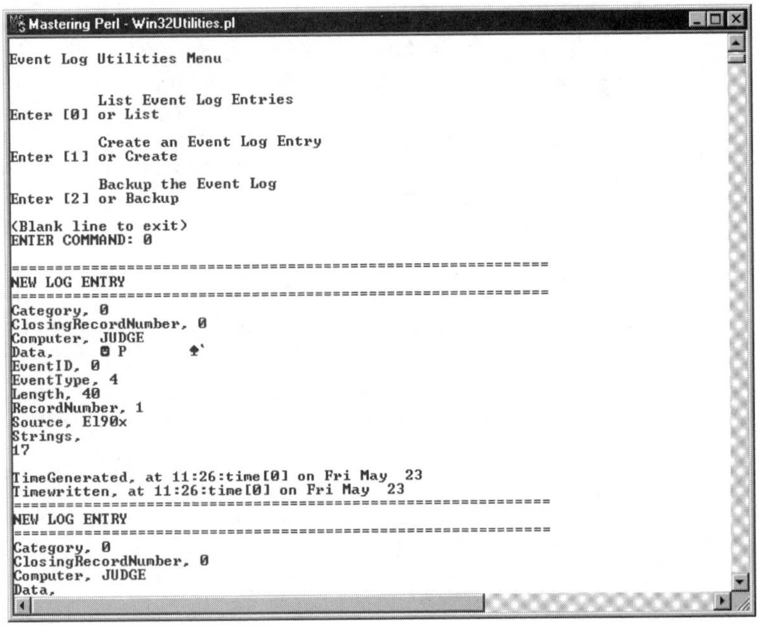

The Read method requires an object reference and takes three parameters:

```
$classRef->Read(READ_MASK, $RecordIndex,$hashReference);
```

The `$RecordIndex` defines the record number to read. The contents of the hash pointed to by the `$hashReference` will be overwritten by the Read method.

Therefore, the hash reference should refer to a lexical hash. The *READ_MASK* defines how to read the event log file.

Creating an event log record is accomplished through the `writeEvent()` subroutine, on lines 827 through 845. This subroutine calls the `Report` method, [passing it a event record hash], as shown here:

```
sub writeEvent(){
    $eventLog = Win32::EventLog->new('System') || die $!;
    %eventRecord = (
    'Source'        => 0,
    'Computer'      => 0,
    'Length'        => 0,
    'RecordNumber'  => 0,
    'TimeGenerated' => 0,
    'TimeWritten'   => 0,
    'ClosingRecordNumber' => 0,
    'Category'      => 2,
    'EventID'       => 4242,
    'EventType'     => EVENTLOG_INFORMATION_TYPE,
    'Strings'       => "Used to identify the data",
    'Data'          => "Informational data about the message",
    );

    $eventLog->Report(\%eventRecord);
}
```

The final option on the Event Log Utilities menu creates a backup copy of your System log file, using the `EventLog::Backup` method, on line 870 of the complete program:

```
$eventLog->Backup($fileName);
```

Perl and Your Windows Database

A *database management system* is a set of tools for managing data. A *database engine* is the application, such as Microsoft Access or Oracle, that manipulates the data in your database. Microsoft Access is an example of a relational database management system. A relational database is made up of tables. Each table contains rows of information about each object stored in the table. A row is made up of columns of information that describe an individual object.

ODBC (Open Database Connectivity) provides the connections for your database. SQL (Structured Query Language) is the common language that all major databases understand.

The Database Interface

The `Win32::ODBC` module has become a standard for connecting Win32 applications to various database programs. `Win32::ODBC`, written by Dave Roth, is an extension module to Win32 Perl. Using `Win32::ODBC` methods, you can connect to your database, create tables, insert data, and retrieve data.

The module and other ODBC applications connect to your Microsoft Access database through a Data Source Name (DSN). The DSN contains a common set of information that all databases must supply. You must create the DSN on your computer before you can begin connecting your program to your database.

When configuring the DSN driver, you must use the exact format of the driver definition. The `Win32::ODBC::ConfigDSN()` method uses the common ODBC API (Application Program Interface) ODBC_ADD_DSN. The parameters, driver type, and DSN definition are common across ODBC modules. The parameters define the DSN name, description, the location of the database file, the default directory, and the user name and password assigned to the DSN. The database file must be created through Access before a connection to the file can be made. Here is an example of code to configure a DSN:

```
$DSN = "DSN Name";
Win32::ODBC::ConfigDSN(ODBC_ADD_DSN,
        "Microsoft Access Driver (*.mdb)".
        ("DSN=$DSN",
         "Description=Description of database",
         "DBQ=c:\\\\dataBaseDirectory\\MyDatabase.mdb",
         "DEFAULTDIR=c:\\\\dataBaseDirectory",
         "UID=",
         "PWD="));
```

Table 21.1 lists some of the methods in the `Win32::ODBC` module.

TABLE 21.1: Win32::ODBC Module Methods

Method	Description
close	Disconnects your program from the database engine. The `close` method requires an object reference as its first and only parameter: `$myDb->close();`.
ConfigDSN	Configures a DSN. The parameters define the DSN name, description, the location of the database file, the default directory, and the user name and password assigned to the DSN.
Data	Retrieves the columns from the current row. You can retrieve all the columns of a row in unspecified order, like this: `lvalue = $myDb->Data();`. You can retrieve an ordered list of the columns in a row by specifying which columns you wish to retrieve: `lvalue = $myDb->Data(columnNameA, columnNameE, column-NameC);`. The column names can be in any order and can a subset of the entire column list.
DataHash	Returns a hash containing the column name and column values of the current row. You can retrieve specific columns by providing the column names, like this: `%columnData = $myDb->DataHash(ColumnA, ColumnE, ColumnC);`. The `DataHash` method is usually used to retrieve an entire row of data, like this: `%columnData = $myDb->DataHash();`.
DumpError	Prints a formatted output, showing which database connection produced the error, the error number, and the text of the error message, returned by the database engine. The `DumpError` method prints error information about the last error condition. You can use the `DumpError` method with an object reference or class notation, like this: `$myDb->DumpError();`.
FetchRow	Retrieves the next row of data from the latest SQL query of your database. The `FetchRow` method must be used with an object reference, which points to a valid ODBC connection, like this: `$myDb->FetchRow();`.
new	Acts as the `Win32::ODBC` class constructor. The `new` method takes one parameter, a valid DSN, and returns an ODBC object reference: `my $myDb = Win32::ODBC ->new("Valid DSN Name");`.
Sql	Takes a SQL statement as an input parameter, like this: `$SQL = "Select FirstName, LastName, Age, Occupation From Employees ";` `$myDb->Sql($SQL);` The `Sql` method makes a call to `ODBCExecute`, which passes the SQL statement to the database.

SQL Statements

SQL is a programming language designed specifically for database operations, and it is a common language among many database engines. The common form of SQL is called ANSI-SQL. Table 21.2 shows the ANSI-SQL data types that are compatible with the Microsoft Access database engine. The data types are used to define the columns of data that make up a table.

TABLE 21.2: ANSI-SQL and Access-Compatible Data Types

ANSI-SQL	Access SQL Equivalent	Description
BIT, BIT VARYING	BINARY	A Boolean data type (True/False)
DATE, TIME, TIMESTAMP	DATETIME	A data type for date-specific operations
REAL	SINGLE	A single-precision real number
DOUBLE PRECISION, FLOAT DOUBLE	FLOAT, FLOAT8	A double-precision real number
SMALLINT	SHORT	A small integer, usually two bytes
INTEGER	LONG	A long integer, usually two words
CHARACTER, CHARACTER VARYING	TEXT	Character strings

Each of the SQL statements listed in Table 21.3 can be loaded into a scalar variable and then passed to your database engine as described for the `Win32::ODBC::Sql` method.

TABLE 21.3: SQL Statements for Manipulating Tables

Statement	Syntax	Description
Alter Table	Alter Table *tableName modify-Type columnDefinition*	Modifies or deletes a column definition. Only one column definition may be changed per **Alter Table** statement. The table name must already exist in the database.

Continued on next page

TABLE 21.3 CONTINUED: SQL Statements for Manipulating Tables

Statement	Syntax	Description
Create Table	Create Table *tableName* (*column-NameList*)	Creates a new table. The table name should be a single string of alphanumeric characters. The column name list is a comma-separated list that defines the column names, their data types, and constraints on the column.
Delete From	Delete From *tableName* Where *selectionCriteriaList*	Deletes rows from a database. The selection criteria list is a list of column names and relational operators that define the matching criteria used to select a row for deletion.
Insert Into	Insert Into tableName (*column-NameList*) Values (*valueList*)	Adds data to a table. The column name list is an optional parameter that allows you to insert the values in a row in any order. The values in the value list will be inserted into the table in a one-to-one correspondence with the column order defined in the column name list.
Select	Select (*columnList*) From (*tableList*) *selectionCriteria*	Retrieves data from a table. You can use functions, selection criteria, and predicates in the column list. The table list may be one or more tables or views. The selection criteria are used to determine which rows of the table the **Select** statement will return.
Update	Update *tableName* Set *column-NameValueList* Where *selection-Criteria*	Updates a column in a table. The column-name value list is a comma-separated list of column names and the new value. You may also define selection criteria to select a particular column for updating.

What Next?

When I wrote the chapters in this part of the book, I was forced to choose the best features among many great modules. This chapter provided a brief introduction to some of the Win32 modules that you can use to get information about your Windows system and to connect to ODBC databases.

Chapter 22 provides a list with descriptions of the Windows modules available for download with the ActivePerl build. In that chapter, you'll explore the Windows methods that report information on your hard drive, the file system, and your computer's network. At the end of the chapter, you'll learn how to connect your Perl 5 program to any DLL on your computer.

In Chapter 23, you'll learn the details of how your computer uses the Registry and how to write code to modify keys in your Registry. Chapter 23 also provides details about event log methods. The in-depth discussion of the event log module `EventLog.pm` module gives you the information you need to extend that module or to create your own modules.

Chapter 24 covers connecting to ODBC databases through the `Win32::ODBC` module. In Chapter 24, you'll get step-by-step instructions for setting up a Microsoft Access database and then for connecting it to the Internet.

CHAPTER

TWENTY-TWO

Win32 System Administration

- Disk drive information

- File system information

- User information

- A network utilities interface

- DLL functions

This chapter is about Win32 modules, your computer, and your network. The Active State build for Perl now includes the GS port of Perl for Windows, which was the other major Win32 port of Perl 5. The Active State build is, for all practical purposes, the Perl 5 build for Windows. In the first section in this chapter, you'll learn the correct directories for installing Perl modules. Then you'll step through a manual installation of a Win32 extension.

There are numerous Win32 extensions to Perl 5, and many of them are listed in this chapter. The examples focus on managing your computer hardware and its network. With an understanding of the modules explained in this chapter, you will be able to work with your disk drive, manipulate file permissions, manage your network, and connect to any Win32 DLL (dynamic-link library).

Win32 Extensions

One of the most marvelous things about Perl is that everybody contributes to it. Perl 5 is a great language in its own right, but the extensions added to it greatly increase your power as a programmer. Table 22.1 lists Active State Win32 modules.

TABLE 22.1: Win32 Modules

Name	Author	Zip Name	Purpose
Win32-API	Aldo Calpini	win32-api.zip	Implement Win32 APIs and load DLLs
Win32-AdminMisc	Dave Roth	win32-adminmisc.zip	Manage network groups and users
Win32-Asp	Matt Sergeant	win32-asp.zip	Provide PerlScript Programming interface
Win32-ChangeNotify	Christopher J. Madsen	win32-changenotify.zip	Monitor events related to files and directories.
Win32-Clipboard	Aldo Calpini	win32-clipboard.zip	Provide Windows Clipboard interaction
Win32-Console	Aldo Calpini	win32-console.zip	Create a low-level MS-DOS window interface

Continued on next page

TABLE 22.1 CONTINUED: Win32 Modules

Name	Author	Zip Name	Purpose
`Win32-DDE`	Doug Wegscheid	`win32-dde.zip`	Provide Dynamic Data Exchange interface
`Win32-DomainAdmin`	ellis@kkc.com	`win32-domainadmin.zip`	Add access to the few LAN Manager functions in `Win32::NetAdmin` or `Win32::AdminMisc`
`Win32-Event`	Christopher J. Madsen	`win32-event.zip`	Use Win32 event objects
`Win32-EventLog`	Jesse Dougherty	`win32-eventlog.zip`	Provide Event Log interface
`Win32-File`	Douglas Lankshear	`win32-file.zip`	Manage file attributes
`Win32-FileSecurity`	Monte Mitzelfelt	`win32-filesecurity.zip`	Manage FileSecurity discretionary access control lists (DACLs)
`Win32-IPC`	Christopher J. Madsen	`win32-ipc.zip`	Provide base class for Win32 synchronization objects
`Win32-Internet`	Aldo Calpini	`win32-internet.zip`	Provide class object for reading, creating, manipulating, and writing messages with RFC 822 compliant headers
`Win32-Message`	Dave Roth	`win32-message.zip`	Provide `HTTP::Message` object that contains home headers and a content, or body (the class is abstract—only used as a base class for `HTTP::Request` and `HTTP::Response`—and should never be instantiated as itself)
`Win32-Mutex`	Christopher J. Madsen	`win32-mutex.zip`	Creates access to Win32 mutex objects (`Wait` and `WaitForMultipleObjects` calls are inherited from the `Win32::IPCmodule`)

Continued on next page

TABLE 22.1 CONTINUED: Win32 Modules

Name	Author	Zip Name	Purpose
Win32-NetAdmin	Douglas Lankshear	win32-netadmin.zip	Provide control over the administration of network groups and users
Win32-NetResource	Jesse Dougherty	win32-netresource.zip	Provide control over Win32 network resources (disks, printers, etc.)
Win32-ODBC	Dave Roth	win32-odbc.zip	Provide an ODBC Perl interface (see Chapter 24)
Win32-OLE	Jan Dubois	win32-ole.zip	Provide OLE Automation
Win32-PerfLib	Jutta M. Klebe	win32-perflib.zip	Access the Windows NT Performance Counter
Win32-Pipe	Dave Roth	win32-pipe.zip	Provide an interface to creating pipes between processes
Win32-Process	Unknown	win32-process.zip	Provide process control
Win32-RasAdmin	Dave Roth	win32-rasadmin.zip	Provide RAS administration
Win32-Registry	Unknown	win32-registry.zip	Provide Registry interfaces (see Chapter 25)
Win32-Semaphore	Christopher J. Madsen	win32-semaphore.zip	Use Win32 semaphore objects
Win32-Service	Douglas Lankshear	win32-service.zip	Manage system services
Win32-Shortcut	Aldo Calpini	win32-shortcut.zip	Create an object-oriented interface to the Win32 Shell Links (IShellLink interface)
Win32-Sound	Aldo Calpini	win32-sound.zip	Play WAV files and system sound files
Win32-TieRegistry	Tye McQueen	win32-tieregistry.zip	Manipulate the Registry
Win32-WinError	Unknown	win32-winerror.zip	Load Win32 error messages

Unfortunately, until recently, installing those new modules under Windows could be troublesome. With the new Active State 500 series builds, the automatic Perl module installer program, named **ppm**, is supposed to solve all your problems. The **ppm** module installer is supposed to go get the module and install it for you in one step. In my case, I continued to have problems because my computer sits behind a corporate firewall. If **ppm** doesn't work for you, you can use the manual method described here.

First go to the Active State module distribution center at:

```
http://www.ActiveState.com/packages/default.prk?list=1
```

This site lists all the modules that Active State supplies.

Choose the module you wish to install and download the Active State distributions by appending `.zip` to the end of the package name:

```
http://www.ActiveState.com/packages/zips/<packageName>.zip
```

Download this file to a temporary directory. For example, if you are installing the `Win32::API` module, type:

```
http://www.ActiveState.com/packages/zips/win32-api.zip
```

The double colons in the module class name are replaced with a dash, and all the characters are lowercase.

Once you have saved the zipped file onto your disk, open the archive and extract the .ppd file and the .gz file. Place the .ppd file in your Perl 5 `bin` directory and the .gz file in a directory called `x86` under the `bin` directory. If the `x86` directory does not exist, create the subdirectory under the `Perl5\bin` directory, which looks like this on my computer: `C:\Perl5\bin\x86`.

The **ppm** program is located in the `Perl5\bin` directory. Open an MS-DOS window and change directories to your Perl installation `bin` directory. On my computer, I type `cd \Perl5\bin` at the C: prompt. From the `bin` directory, type:

```
perl ppm.pl install  package-name.ppd
```

For example, if you are installing the `Win32::API` module, type:

```
perl ppm.pl install win32-api.ppd
```

Many of the modules listed in Table 22.1 require DLLs that must be compiled to match the particular Perl 5 build you installed. It's a good idea to get these builds from the Active State site when you can. These libraries are dynamically loaded, creating a runtime link with your built-in Windows function by the dynaloader and autoloader modules. If you don't use the ppm module, you should place the module file, such as API.pm, in the Win32 library directory, like this:

```
C:\Perl5\site\lib\Win32
```

The .dll, .exp, .lib, and .bs file should go into the autoload directory, like this:

```
C:\Perl5\site\lib-auto\Win32-className
```

If you are loading the Win32::API module, the class name is API.

The Disk Drive

You already know how to read files and directories, but those tasks are common across all platforms. Here, we are concerned with only your Windows computer. We'll start at the lowest level, your hard drive, and work up to your file system.

TIP   Many of the listings in this section and others use the Win32::AdminMisc module created by Dave Roth. You can get further documentation on this module and other modules written by Dave Roth at www.roth.net.

Getting the Drives

To automatically decode information about your file system, you need to be able to move around the various drives connected to your computer. Listing 22.1 returns all the drives connected for your computer and prints them, as shown in Figure 22.1.

Listing 22.1:   **Just the Drive**

```
1.   use Win32::AdminMisc;
2.   %driveTypes = (1 => "RAMDISK DRIVE ",
3.                  2 => "REMOVABLE DRIVE ",
4.                  3 => "FIXED DRIVE ",
5.                  4 => "REMOTE DRIVE ",
6.                  5 => "CDROM DRIVE "
7.                  );
```

```
8.  #Get all the drives on my computer
9.  @allDrives = Win32::AdminMisc::GetDrives();
10.
11. #In scalar context, this gives me the size of the array
12. $numberOfDrives = @allDrives;
13.
14. $computerName = Win32::AdminMisc::GetComputerName();
15.
16. print "\nThere are $numberOfDrives drives on $computerName\n";
17. #List the drives and types
18. foreach $drive (@allDrives){
19.    $driveType = Win32::AdminMisc::GetDriveType($drive);
20.    print "\t$drive is a $driveTypes{$driveType}\n";
21. }
```

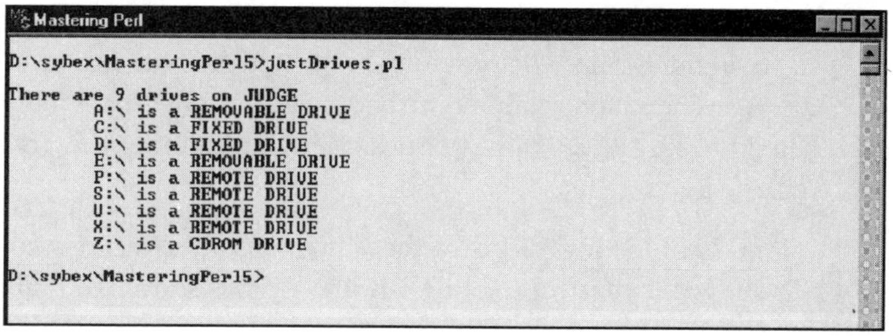

FIGURE 22.1:

Getting the drives
connected to the computer

The Win32::AdminMisc method GetDrives, which returns a list of all of the drives connected to the computer, does most of the work. It is used on line 9 of Listing 22.1:

```
@allDrives = Win32::AdminMisc::GetDrives();
```

The syntax of the GetDrives method is:

```
@driveList = GetDrives($driveType);
```

The $driveType parameter to the GetDrives method is optional. If it is not included, GetDrives returns all the drives on your computer. My copy of Admin-Misc did not export the drive type constant, so I created the hash you see on lines 2 through 7 to provide an English-like response from the GetDriveType method call on line 19:

```
$driveType = Win32::AdminMisc::GetDriveType($drive);
```

Table 22.2 lists the drive types and the integer values that the `GetDriveType` method equates to each drive type.

TABLE 22.2: Drive Types for the GetDriveType Method

Drive Type	AdminMisc Constant	Integer Value
CD-ROM	DRIVE_CDROM	5
Fixed	DRIVE_FIXED	3
RAM disk	DRIVE_RAMDISK	1
Remote	DRIVE_REMOTE	4
Removable (floppy, zip, etc.)	DRIVE_REMOVABLE	2

The `GetDriveType` method requires an input drive letter followed by a back-slash, in the format `'DriveLetter:\'`, which is the format returned by `Get-Drives`. The integer value returned by `GetDriveType` equates to the drive type listed in Table 22.2. If an error occurs in determining the drive type, zero is returned.

Line 20 of Listing 22.1 uses these integer values as an index into the hash `%driveTypes` to print the English-drive types shown in Figure 22.1:

```
print "\t$drive is a $driveTypes{$driveType}\n";
```

Getting the Disk Configuration

Now let's take a closer look at the details of your computer's drive using the `AdminMisc` method `GetDriveGeometry`. Listing 22.2 gets the drives on your computer (as in Listing 22.1) and then goes down to the sector level to get the actual disk configuration.

Listing 22.2:   **Drive Details**

```
1.  use Win32::AdminMisc;
2.  #Define constants for ease of use
3.  %driveTypes = (1 => "RAMDISK DRIVE ",
4.              2 => "REMOVABLE DRIVE ",
```

```
5.                    3 => "FIXED DRIVE ",
6.                    4 => "REMOTE DRIVE ",
7.                    5 => "CDROM DRIVE "
8.                  );
9.  $GEOSECTORS = 0;
10. $GEOBYTES = 1;
11. $GEOFREECLUSTERS = 2;
12. $GEOTOTALCLUSTORS = 3;
13. #Get all the drives on my computer
14. @allDrives = Win32::AdminMisc::GetDrives();
15. #In scalar context, I get the size of the array
16. $numberOfDrives = @allDrives;
17. #Get the Name of my computer
18. $computerName = Win32::AdminMisc::GetComputerName();
19. print "There are $numberOfDrives drives on $computerName\n";
20.
21. foreach $drive (@allDrives){
22.    #Get the Drive Type
23.    $driveType = Win32::AdminMisc::GetDriveType($drive);
24.    if ($driveTypes{$driveType} =~ /REMOTE|FIXED/){
25.       print "$drive is a $driveTypes{$driveType}\n";
26.       #Only get geometry on disks I can guarantee have
27.       #something to read in them.
28.       @driveDetails = Win32::AdminMisc::GetDriveGeometry($drive);
29.       $size = $driveDetails [$GEOSECTORS] *
30.               $driveDetails [$GEOBYTES] *
31.               $driveDetails [$GEOTOTALCLUSTORS];
32.       $freeSpace = $driveDetails [$GEOSECTORS] *
33.                    $driveDetails [$GEOBYTES] *
34.                    $driveDetails [$GEOFREECLUSTERS];
35.       print<<"eof";
36. With the following Drive Details:
37.    Sectors per cluster:      $driveDetails[$GEOSECTORS]
38.    Bytes per sector:         $driveDetails[$GEOBYTES]
39.    Free clusters:            $driveDetails[$GEOFREECLUSTERS]
40.    Total clusters:           $driveDetails[$GEOTOTALCLUSTORS]
41.    Free Space Available:     $freeSpace
42.    Total Space Available:    $size
43. eof
44.    }
45. }
```

Line 24 checks each of the drive types returned by GetDriveType, looking for remote or fixed drives:

```
if ($driveTypes{$driveType} =~ /REMOTE|FIXED/){
```

Each of these drives is then interrogated for its low-level formatting information, which is printed in Figure 22.2.

Listing 22.2 depends on the GetDriveGeometry of line 28 to get the drive's details:

```
@driveDetails = Win32::AdminMisc::GetDriveGeometry($drive);
```

The GetDriveGeometry method takes one parameter, the mounted drive, to be interrogated. The drive parameter must end in a backslash. The syntax of the GetDriveGeometry method is:

```
@driveDetails = GetDriveGeometry($DRIVE);
```

The array returned by GetDriveGeometry lists the drive details shown in Table 22.3, which also shows the array index for each array item.

TABLE 22.3: Drive Details Array Indexes and Values

Array Index	Drive Information
0	Sectors per cluster
1	Bytes per sector
2	Total disk clusters
3	Total free disk clusters

To calculate the total available bytes on a disk, use this formula:

TotalBytes = BytesPerSector * SectorsPerCluster * NumberOfClusters

To calculate the free space on your disks, use this formula:

FreeSpace = BytesPerSector * SectorsPerCluster * NumberOfFreeClusters

If you just want to get the total size and amount of free space on your hard disk, you can use Listing 22.3, which produces Figure 22.3.

Listing 22.3:   Total Size and Space

```
1.  use Win32::AdminMisc;
2.  %driveTypes = (1 => "RAMDISK DRIVE ",
3.                 2 => "REMOVABLE DRIVE ",
4.                 3 => "FIXED DRIVE ",
5.                 4 => "REMOTE DRIVE ",
6.                 5 => "CDROM DRIVE "
7.                 );
8.  #Get all the drives on my computer
9.  @allDrives = Win32::AdminMisc::GetDrives();
10. foreach $drive (@allDrives){
11.     #Get the Drive Type
12.     $driveType = Win32::AdminMisc::GetDriveType($drive);
13.     if ($driveTypes{$driveType} =~ /REMOTE|FIXED/){
14.         ($driveSize, $freeSpace) =
                    Win32::AdminMisc::GetDriveSpace($drive);
```

```
15.        $drive =~ s/\\//;
16.        print "Drive $drive\n";
17.        print "Free Space: $freeSpace\nTotal Size:
                    $driveSize\n\n";
18.    }
19. }
```

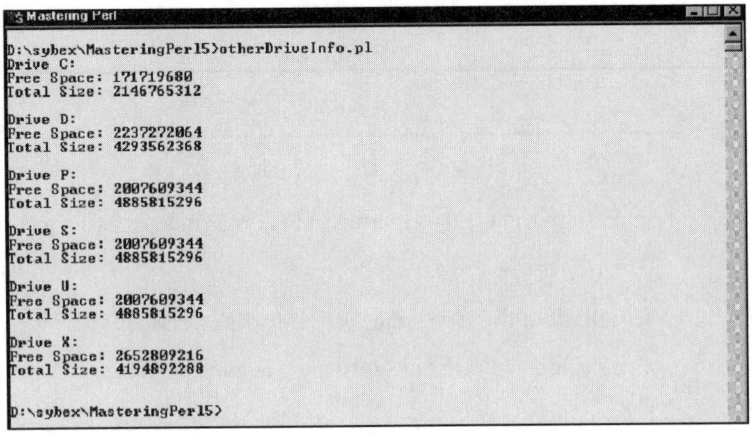

FIGURE 22.3:

Getting the drive's size and space

Line 14 of Listing 22.3 uses the AdminMisc method GetDriveSpace, whose syntax is:

```
(@TotalSpaceAvailable, $FreeSpace) = GetDriveSpace($Drive);
```

GetDriveSpace requires a $DRIVE input parameter and returns the drive size and free space in bytes.

The File System

Now let's look at your Windows NT file system security and something called access control lists, or ACLs for short. ACLs are a basic part of your Windows NT security model. Every file on your computer has its own security attribute, which defines the owner of the file and the file's ACL. Each ACL is specific for an individual user, global group, or local group that is granted or denied permission to access your files.

NOTE

System security is one of the best features of Windows NT. Unfortunately, this type of file security is not part of the Windows 95/98 operating system. The programs in this section were only tested on a Windows NT computer.

The ACL defines who has access to your files. Each user is then given specific permission to modify the file. Each file has a set of specific rights, which apply to an individual user, and a set of standard rights, which apply to the generic user called *everyone*. Table 22.4 lists the rights of a file object.

TABLE 22.4: File Access Rights

Name	Type	Description
`ReadData`	Specific	Read data privileges granted to this user
`WriteData`	Specific	Write data privileges granted to this user
`AppendData`	Specific	Append data privileges granted to this user
`ReadEA` (extended attribute)	Specific	Read extended attribute privileges granted to this user
`WriteEA` (extended attribute)	Specific	Write extended attribute privileges granted to this user
`Execute`	Specific	Execute privileges granted to this user
`ReadAttributes`	Specific	Read attribute privileges granted to this user
`WriteAttributes`	Specific	Write attribute privileges granted to this user
`SYNCHRONIZE`	Specific	Synchronize file access
`WRITE_OWNER`	Specific	Assign the write owner
`WRITE_DAC`	Specific	Write access to the DACL
`READ_CONTROL`	Specific	Read access to the security descriptor
`DELETE`	Specific	Delete privileges granted to this user
`STANDARD_RIGHTS_ALL`	Generic	All rights extended to the generic user (everyone)
`STANDARD_RIGHTS_EXECUTE`	Generic	Execute rights extended to the generic user (everyone)

Continued on next page

TABLE 22.4 CONTINUED: File Access Rights

Name	Type	Description
STANDARD_RIGHTS_READ	Generic	Read rights extended to the generic user (everyone)
STANDARD_RIGHTS_REQUIRED	Generic	Required rights for the generic user (everyone)
STANDARD_RIGHTS_WRITE	Generic	Write rights extended to the generic user (everyone)

Listing 22.4 reads all the files in a directory and returns the ACL object for itself, as you can see in Figure 22.4.

Listing 22.4:   File Permissions

```perl
1.  use Win32;
2.  use Win32::FileSecurity;
3.  use Cwd;
4.  my $dir = cwd();
5.  #Get the file system we are working with
6.  $fileSystem = Win32::FsType();
7.  print "Working on a $fileSystem file system\n";
8.  #open and read the current directory
9.  opendir(THISDIR, $dir);
10. @dirList = readdir (THISDIR);
11. close (THISDIR);
12. #Delete the directories . and ..
13. splice @dirList, 0, 2;
14. foreach $fileName (@dirList){
15.    #For space purposes only, report on this file
16.    if ( $0 =~ /$fileName/){
17.       Win32::FileSecurity::Get($fileName, \%DACL);
18.       @userList = sort keys %DACL;
19.       if (!defined $firstPass){
20.          $firstPass = 1;
21.          print "The user list for this directory is:\n";
22.          foreach $user (@userList){
23.             $count++;
24.             print "\t$user,";
25.             print "\t" unless length ($user) > 22;
26.             print "\t" if length ($user) < 15;
```

```
27.              if ($count%2 == 0){
28.                  print "\n";
29.                  }
30.              }
31.          }
32.      print "\n";
33.      foreach $name (@userList){
34.          Win32::FileSecurity::EnumerateRights($DACL{$name},
                                                  \@values);
35.          $prevSeparator = $";
36.          $" = "\n\t";
37.          @values = sort (@values);
38.          print "\nFor the file: $fileName\n";
39.          print "$name has permissions\n\t@values\n";
40.          }
41.      }
42. }
```

FIGURE 22.4:

Getting drive details

Line 17 of Listing 22.4 gets the file's DACL using the `Win32::FileSecurity` method `Get`:

```
Win32::FileSecurity::Get($fileName, \%DACL);
```

The `Get` method requires the name of an NT object, which may be a file, directory handle, socket, filename, or any other NT object, and returns a hash. The hash is a security object, which contains the rights of each user, global group, and local group, to the NT object. You can see all of the users who have access to a particular object by retrieving all the keys of the hash, as on line 18:

```
@userList = sort keys %DACL;
```

Each user's permissions mask is passed to the `Win32::FilesSecurity` method `EnumeratedRights`. The `EnumeratedRights` method takes a permissions mask and returns an array that describes each value in the mask in an English format.

Line 39 prints the returned permissions mask you see in Figure 22.4:

```
print "$name has permissions\n\t@values\n";
```

User Information

The built-in Win32 module contains several functions for getting information about the current user, which we will explore in this section.

Getting Login Information

Listing 22.5 retrieves information about the computer and the user who is currently logged in.

Listing 22.5:   Login Data

```
1.  use Win32;
2.  %windowsName = (0=> "Generic " Win32,
3.                  1=> "Windows 95",
4.                  2=> "Windows NT");
5.  $WIN_IDENTIFIER = 0;
6.  $WIN_VERSION = 1;
7.  $WIN_SUBVERSION = 2;
```

```
8.  $WIN_BUILD = 3;
9.  $WIN_NAME = 4;
10.
11. $loginName  = Win32::LoginName();
12. $domainName = Win32::DomainName();
13. $nodeName   = Win32::NodeName();
14. @windowsInfo = Win32::GetOSVersion();
15. print<<"eof";
16. User: $loginName
17. Is logged into the Domain $domainName on Node $nodeName
18. Running $windowsName{$windowsInfo[$WIN_NAME]}
        $windowsInfo[$WIN_VERSION].$windowsInfo[$WIN_SUBVERSION]
19. With $windowsInfo[$WIN_IDENTIFIER] Build $windowsInfo[$WIN_BUILD]
20. eof
```

As you can see in Figure 22.5, the Win32 methods on lines 11 through 13 retrieve current information about the logged-in user. The syntax of each method requires only a scalar lvalue to store the returned information, like this:

```
$name = Win32::LoginName( );
$domain = Win32::DomainName( );
$node = Win32::NodeName( );
```

FIGURE 22.5:

Getting current user information

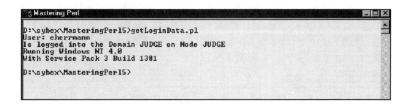

The Win32 method `GetOSVersion` must be called in array context, like this:

```
@windowsInfo = Win32GetOSVersion( );
```

The `GetOSVersion` method returns an array that contains information about your Windows operating system and the current upgrades loaded, as shown in Table 22.5.

TABLE 22.5: GetOSVersion Return Values

Name	Index	Meaning
Service Pack	0	Windows NT Service Pack
Version	1	Major version number
Subversion	2	Minor version number
Build	3	Compiled build number
Windows Type	4	An integer value that equates to the operator system 0=Generic Win32, 1=Windows 95/98, 2=Windows NT

Getting User Details

Now let's take some of the information from Listing 22.5 and get some more details about an individual user. Some platforms require password information to get details about a user. However, it's not a good idea to have users type their passwords onto the screen and have it remain visible.

Perl handles user I/O easily, but low-level control of the keyboard is a little more difficult. This next listing uses the `Win32::Console` module to retrieve a user's password. The `Console` module gives you character-by-character control of input from the keyboard. Listing 22.6 gets the current user and then requests the user's password.

Listing 22.6: **Passwords and Attributes**

```
1.  use Win32;
2.  use Win32::Console;
3.  use Win32::AdminMisc;
4.  $CARRIAGE_RETURN = 13;
5.  $SEC        = 0; $MIN    = 1; $HOUR = 2;
6.  $DAYOFMONTH = 3; $MONTH  = 4; $YEAR = 5;
7.  $WEEKDAY    = 6; $DAYOFYEAR = 7;
8.  $STANDARDTIME = 8;
9.  @privileges = (GUEST, USER, ADMINISTRATOR);
10. #Create a console object connect to STDIN
11. $console = Win32::Console->new(STD_INPUT_HANDLE);
```

```
12.
13. #Get the username
14. $loginName  = Win32::LoginName();
15. #Get the password
16. print<<"eof";
17. ^U to erase Line,
18. ^H or Backspace delete character
19. Carriage return to end entry
20. eof
21. print "Please enter the password for $loginName:";
22.
23. #Keep getting characters until we get a carriage return
24. #The label GETPASSWORD is used to exit
25. #both the interior SWITCH block
26. #and the data entry while loop
27. GETPASSWORD:
28. while (($char = ($console->Input())[5]) != $CARRIAGE_RETURN ){
29.    #Set up a switch block for future additions to input control
30.    SWITCH:{
31.        #^H or backspace
32.        if ($char == 8){
33.           #backup up one character
34.           # print a blank
35.           # back up one character
36.           print "\b \b";
37.           chop $password;
38.           last SWITCH;
39.        }
40.        #^U
41.        if ($char == 21){
42.           #Erase all input
43.           $currentInputSize = length($password);
44.           print "\b \b" x $currentInputSize;
45.           last SWITCH;
46.        }
47.        #Carriage return
48.        if ($char == 13){
49.           #EXIT if no password entered
50.           if (length ($password) == 0){
51.              print "PASSWORD REQUIRED\n";
52.              exit;
53.           }
```

```
54.              #Stop data entry, exit the while loop
55.              last GETPASSWORD;
56.         }
57.         #Almost anything but control characters
58.         #and the space character are valid
59.         if ( $char >= 0x21 && $char <= 0x7E){
60.             #Convert the number to an ASCII character
61.             $password .= chr $char;
62.             print "*";
63.             last SWITCH;
64.         }
65.     }#end SWITCH
66.     #must call Console::Input twice
67.     $char = ($console->Input())[5]
68. }#end get password
69. #
70. #Supply login name and password
71. #Leave server name blank
72. #Return full name, password age, user privilege mask,
73. #home directory, comments, flags and scripts
74. #
75. Win32::AdminMisc::UserGetAttributes("", "$loginName",
76.         $fullName,       $password, $passwordAge, $privileges,
77.         $homeDirectory, $comment,  $flags,        $scripts);
78.
79. #To get the
80. @changedDate = localtime(time - $passwordAge);
81. #Month dates begin at zero
82. $dateString = $changedDate[$MONTH] + 1;
83. $dateString .= '/' . $changedDate[$DAYOFMONTH];
84. $dateString .= '/' . $changedDate[$YEAR];
85. foreach $timeValue ($changedDate[$HOUR],
86.                     $changedDate[$MIN],
87.                     $changedDate[$SEC]){
88.     $twoChars = sprintf ("%02d", $timeValue);
89.     $timeString .=  $twoChars . ':';
90. }
91. chop $timeString;
92. print<<"eof";
93.
94.
95. The User ${loginName}'s full Name is $fullName
```

```
96.  Your password was last changed on $dateString at $timeString
97.  This Account has $privileges[$privileges] privileges
98.  Your home directory is $homeDirectory
99.  $comment
100. Your built-in scripts are $scripts
101. eof
```

Listing 22.6 uses the $loginName retrieved on line 14 to get a password for a specific user. This limits the control the user has to experiment with different username and password combinations. This program only works with the logged-in user and that user's password. Lines 23 through 68 get the user's password one character at a time using the while loop on line 27 to get individual characters:

```
while (($char = ($console->Input())[5]) != $CARRIAGE_RETURN ){
```

Each character is checked within the SWITCH block for validity and character control. Because this listing uses a SWITCH block for input control, you can expand the code for your own needs. All keyboard characters excluding control codes and space characters are accepted as password characters on line 59:

```
if ( $char >= 0x21 && $char <= 0x7E){
```

Because line 59 accepts only valid input characters, all invalid characters are quietly ignored. The keyboard may send an initial Ctrl or Shift character, which is ignored because it will be used in combination with another character on the next keystroke. The Ctrl or Shift character, which is ignored when received as a single key, is required to deal with the combination keyboard characters, such as Ctrl+U and Ctrl+H, which are received as a single key code.

TIP
The Console module, which is responsible for getting characters one keystroke at a time, is built for low-level control of an MS-DOS window. Use the Win32::Console module to manually control the cursor, text size, color, and other MS-DOS window attributes.

Once the password is entered, lines 75 through 77 call the Win32::AdminMisc method UserGetAttributes. This method's input and output parameters are listed in Table 22.6.

TABLE 22.6: UserGetAttributes Parameters

Name	Type	Description
SERVER	Input	The server name, which should be preceded by two backslashes
USERNAME	Input	The logged-on username
USERFULLNAME	Output	The full name of the logged-on user
PASSWORD	Input	Ignored
PASSWORDAGE	Output	The number of seconds from the date when the password was changed
PRIVILEGE	Output	An integer representing the user account privilege: 0=guest, 1=user, 2=administrator
HOMEDIRECTORY	Output	The default directory for user files
COMMENT	Output	Any value
FLAGS	Output	Account flags
SCRIPTPATH	Output	The user's login script and path

NOTE   A server name of * means a server can respond. Null server names send the request to the domain controller.

The input parameter password is included for backward compatibility with older LAN Manager software. The server name is not included, so this program will get its information from my local domain controller. The output parameter $passwordAge contains the number of seconds since you last changed your password. This time it is converted as the date and time of the last password change on line 80:

```
@changedDate = localtime(time - $passwordAge);
```

The $passwordAge is subtracted from the current time and then converted to local time. The localtime array is then converted into *MM/DD/YY* and *HH:MM:SS* format on lines 81 through 91. The listing produces the output shown in Figure 22.6.

Getting user details

Now it's time to turn from your individual computer to your network. The next section discusses network administration tools.

Network Administration

In this section, you will explore six Windows NT built-in network diagnostic tools and their Perl interface program. The interface program presented here provides basic use of the utilities. You can extend the program to suit your own needs, as described in the discussions of the individual utilities.

Building a Network Diagnostic Utilities Interface

When I went looking for Perl 5 networking diagnostic modules, I came up short-handed. After exploring the networking tools built into Windows NT, I decided to create the network diagnostic utilities interface program, shown in Figure 22.7.

Each of the utilities shown in Figure 22.7 is part of your Windows NT installation. Listing 22.7 is a prototype of a simple user interface to each of these utilities. This interface is fully functional, but you may wish to extend it for your own purposes.

> **NOTE**   Network administration is primarily a Windows NT task. These functions are not automatically loaded onto a Windows 95/98 system. The program in Listing 22.7 will run on your computer if you have loaded onto your computer the Windows networking programs that the program uses.

FIGURE 22.7:

Network diagnostic utilities

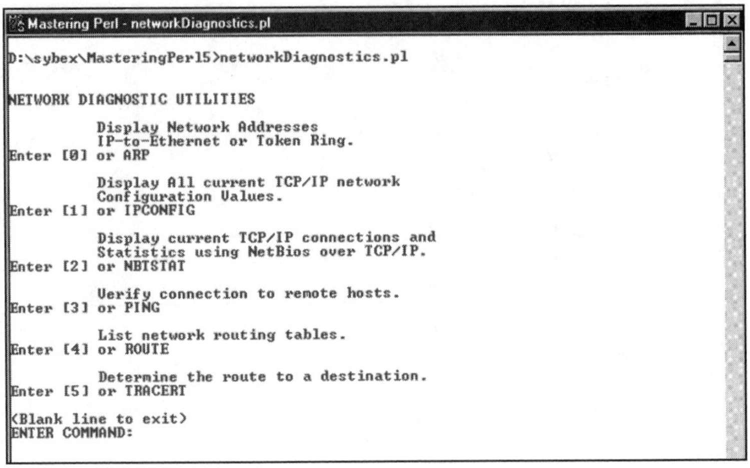

Listing 22.7:   Network Diagnostics

```
1.   #Print the initial screen
2.   printDiagUtils();
3.
4.   while ($input = <STDIN>){
5.       #Get rid of the newline
6.       chomp $input;
7.       #Exit if just hit enter
8.       exit if length ($input) == 0;
9.       #Go execute the command
10.      runDiagnostic($input);
11.      #Pause after the results are printed
12.      print "\n\n<ENTER> to continue";
13.      $trash = <STDIN>;
14.      #Print the Diagnostic Utility Screen again
15.      printDiagUtils();
16.  }
17.
18.  sub runDiagnostic($){
19.      my ($diagnostic) = @_;
20.      print "\n";
21.      SWITCH:{
22.          if ($diagnostic =~ /^0|arp/i){
23.              @arp = `arp -a`;
```

```
24.            print "@arp";
25.            last SWITCH;
26.        }
27.        if ($diagnostic =~ /^1|ipconfig/i){
28.            @ipconfig = `ipconfig/all `;
29.            print "@ipconfig";
30.            last SWITCH;
31.        }
32.        if ($diagnostic =~ /^2|nbtstat/i){
33.            ($cmd, $computerName) = split(/\s/,$diagnostic);
34.            if (length ($computerName) == 0){
35.                print<<"eof";
36. NBTSTAT displays statistics on current connections
37. To get a list of available connects enter -r
38. Enter a connection after the command [2|NBSTAT]\n
39. eof
40.                $diagnostic = getNewCommand();
41.                redo SWITCH;
42.            }
43.            else {
44.                if ($computerName!~ /-/){
45.                    $ computerName = '-a ' . $ computerName;
46.                }
47.            }
48.            @nbtstat = `nbtstat $ computerName `;
49.            print "@nbtstat";
50.            last SWITCH;
51.        }
52.        if ($diagnostic =~ /^3|ping/i){
53.            ($cmd, $destination) = split(/\s/,$diagnostic);
54.            if (length ($destination) == 0){
55.                print<<"eof";
56. PING verifies connections and prints statistics
57. to a remote host.
58. Enter a remote host name after the command [3|PING]\n
59. eof
60.                $diagnostic = getNewCommand();
61.                redo SWITCH;
62.            }
63.            print "This command may takes several seconds.\n";
64.            @ping = `ping -n 5 $destination`;
65.            print "@ping";
66.            last SWITCH;
```

```
67.        }
68.        if ($diagnostic =~ /^4|route/i){
69.            @route = `route print`;
70.            print "@route";
71.            last SWITCH;
72.        }
73.        if ($diagnostic =~ /^5|tracert/i){
74.            ($command, $destination) = split (/\s/,$diagnostic);
75.            if (length ($destination) == 0){
76.                print "TRACERT traces domain routes\n";
77.                print "Enter a domain name after the command
                         [5|TRACERT]\n";
78.                $diagnostic = getNewCommand();
79.                redo SWITCH;
80.            }
81.            print "This command may take several minutes.\n";
82.            print "TRACING $destination ... ";
83.            @tracert = `tracert $destination`;
84.            print "@tracert";
85.            last SWITCH;
86.        }
87.        if ($diagnostic =~ /^q(uit)*|^e(xit)/i){
88.            exit;
89.        }
90.        DEFAULT:{
91.            print "INVALID COMMAND $diagnostic\n";
92.        }
93.    }#END SWITCH
94. }
95.
96. sub getNewCommand(){
97.    print "ENTER COMMAND: ";
98.    my $newInput = <STDIN>;
99.    chomp $newInput;
100.    return $newInput;
101. }
102.
103.
104. sub printDiagUtils(){
105.    print<<"eof";
106.
107.
108. NETWORK DIAGNOSTIC UTILITIES
109.
```

```
110.            Display Network Addresses
111.            IP-to-Ethernet or Token Ring.
112. Enter [0] or ARP
113.
114.            Display All current TCP/IP network
115.            Configuration Values.
116. Enter [1] or IPCONFIG
117.
118.            Display current TCP/IP connections and
119.            Statistics using NetBios over TCP/IP.
120. Enter [2] or NBTSTAT
121.
122.            Verify connection to remote hosts.
123. Enter [3] or PING
124.
125.            List network routing tables.
126. Enter [4] or ROUTE
127.
128.            Determine the route to a destination.
129. Enter [5] or TRACERT
130.
131. (Blank line to exit)
132. eof
133. print "ENTER COMMAND: ";
134. }
```

Listing 22.7 begins printing the menu you see in Figure 22.7 by calling the `printDiagUtils` subroutine on line 2. The `printDiagUtils` subroutine is nothing more than a couple of `print` statements. This code prints a user interface screen (the menu shown in Figure 22.7), reads the user's response, responds to the user input, and then starts over. That bit of logic is only 12 lines of 134 lines of code. It is important, however, to remove the 30 lines of code required to print the menu from the main program. It would be easy to lose track of the simplicity of lines 4 through 16 in the overall program if the code that prints the menu and responds to the user input were included in the main program. As the program is written, it's easy to see the overall flow of logic in the 12 lines of code that make up the heart of this program:

```
while ($input = <STDIN>){
    #Get rid of the newline
    chomp $input;
    #Exit if just hit enter
```

```
        exit if length ($input) == 0;
        #Go execute the command
        runDiagnostic($input);
        #Pause after the results are printed
        print "\n\n<ENTER> to continue";
        $trash = <STDIN>;
        #print the Diagnostic Utility Screen again
        printDiagUtils();
    }
```

TIP
　　　　Take the opportunity to separate major blocks of code from the primary logic when such opportunities present themselves. Especially when handling user I/O, you should look for large chunks of code that can be separated into input and output subroutines. Moving logical blocks of code to subroutines allows you to stay focused on the primary task in the main part of your program.

Listing 22.7 loops infinitely, getting user input as long as the user enters new requests. The data is stored into the $input variable on line 4, and the trailing newline character is removed on line 6:

```
while ($input = <STDIN>){
    #Get rid of the newline
    chomp $input;
```

User input from the command line almost always includes a newline character. Because the chomp function removes only trailing newline characters, you can safely remove the newline character without needing to first confirm that the newline is part of the user input.

Line 8 is the first opportunity to exit the program. If the user enters a blank line, the program exits:

```
    exit if length ($input) == 0;
```

Otherwise, the diagnostic utilities subroutine runDiagnostics is called on line 10. The diagnostic utilities respond to the user's request and then pause, giving the user an opportunity to see the results. The pause, which is implemented by waiting for user input, is created on lines 11 through 13:

```
    #Pause after the results are printed
    print "\n\n<ENTER> to continue";
    $trash = <STDIN>;
```

Once the user presses Enter, the program continues by calling `printDiagUtils`, which prints the Network Diagnostic Utilities menu again.

Now let's take a look at each of the network diagnostic utilities and their interface programs. The following sections explain the individual utilities and provide information that you can use to add further functionality to Listing 22.7.

Managing Physical Addresses

The ARP (Address Resolution Protocol) program in Listing 22.7 displays the physical addresses related to your network IP-to-Ethernet or Token Ring address. You can use the ARP program available to you on your computer to modify these physical addresses. Lines 22 through 26 of Listing 22.7 display only the IP-to-Ethernet physical address, as shown in Figure 22.8:

```
if ($diagnostic =~ /^0|arp/i){
    @arp = `arp -a`;
    print "@arp";
    last SWITCH;
}
```

FIGURE 22.8:

Displaying IP-to-Ethernet address tables

```
Mastering Perl - networkDiagnostics.pl                          _ □ ×

D:\sybex\MasteringPerl5>networkDiagnostics.pl

NETWORK DIAGNOSTIC UTILITIES

            Display Network Addresses
            IP-to-Ethernet or Token Ring.
Enter [0] or ARP

            Display All current TCP/IP network
            Configuration Values.
Enter [1] or IPCONFIG

            Display current TCP/IP connections and
            Statistics using NetBios over TCP/IP.
Enter [2] or NBTSTAT

            Verify connection to remote hosts.
Enter [3] or PING

            List network routing tables.
Enter [4] or ROUTE

            Determine the route to a destination.
Enter [5] or TRACERT

<Blank line to exit>
ENTER COMMAND: 0


 Interface: 198.49.249.89 on Interface 2
   Internet Address      Physical Address      Type
   198.49.249.125        00-a0-c9-b3-c1-31     dynamic

<ENTER> to continue
```

You can modify Listing 22.7 so that the ARP interface takes additional parameters. Table 22.7 lists the parameters of the ARP program.

TABLE 22.7: ARP Parameters

Parameter	Description
-a [*inet_addr*]	Display the current ARP TCP/IP entries. If an optional Internet address (*inet_addr*) is specified, only that address's data will be displayed.
-d *inet_addr*	Delete the specified Internet address.
-s *inet_addr ether_addr*	Add an entry into the ARP cache, associating the Internet address (*inet_addr*) with the physical Ethernet address (*ether_addr*).

Configuring TCP/IP

From lines 27 through 31, the IPCONFIG program in Listing 22.7 displays all of the TCP/IP (Transport Control Protocol/Internet Protocol) configuration values, configured by the DHCP (Dynamic Host Configuration Protocol) process:

```
if ($diagnostic =~ /^1|ipconfig/i){
    @ipconfig = `ipconfig/all `;
    print "@ipconfig";
    last SWITCH;
}
```

These values include the IP address, the subnet mask, the WINS (Windows Internet Naming Service) configuration, and the DNS (Domain Name Server) configuration. These are shown in Figure 22.9. The Ethernet adapter name in Figure 22.9 (E190x1) is displayed by the `ipconfig/all` command.

FIGURE 22.9:

Displaying TCP/IP network configuration values

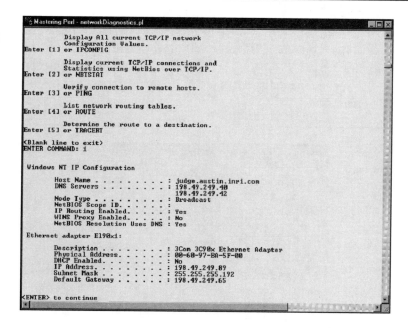

You can also use the IPCONFIG program available to your on your computer to display a subset of the data in Figure 22.9, update the configuration data, and disable TCP/IP on DHCP clients. Table 22.8 lists the parameters of the IPCONFIG program.

TABLE 22.8: IPCONFIG Parameters

Parameter	Description
None	Display the IP address, subnet mask, and default gateway values.
all	Display the IP address, subnet mask, default gateway values, WINS configuration, and DNS configuration.
renew [*adapter*]	Renew the DHCP configuration parameters or the optional Ethernet adapter.
release [*adapter*]	Disable the TCP/IP running on the local DHCP client.

Getting NetBIOS Statistics

The NBTSTAT program in Listing 22.7, between lines 32 through 51, lists a remote connection's TCP/IP statistics using the NetBIOS protocol, as shown in Figure 22.10. The NBTSTAT program in Listing 22.7 shows the remote computer's name table, but you can modify it to handle additional parameters. Table 22.9 lists the NBSTAT parameters.

FIGURE 22.10:

Diplaying NetBIOS statistics

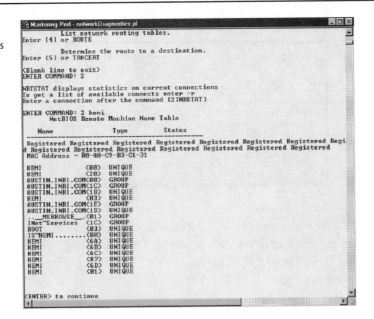

TABLE 22.9: NBTSTAT Parameters

Parameter	Description
-a *computer name*	List the remote computer's name using the computer name.
-A *IP address*	List the remote computer's name using the IP address.
-c	List the NetBIOS name cache and IP addresses.
-n	List the NetBIOS local name table.
-r	List the number of names resolved and registered, for WINS-configured computers.

Continued on next page

TABLE 22.9 CONTINUED: NBTSTAT Parameters

Parameter	Description
-R	Reload the LMHOSTS file.
-s	Display the NetBIOS connection table, displaying both the IP addresses and server names if possible.
-S	Display the NetBIOS connection table, displaying only the IP addresses.

WARNING   Be careful using the −R parameter to reload the LMHOSTS file. This command purges all names from the NetBIOS name cache.

Even the limited interface to NBTSTAT in Listing 22.7 requires additional parameters, however. Line 33 separates the user input into the command and the computer name:

```
($cmd, $computerName) = split(/\s/,$diagnostic);
```

If the computer name is not supplied, lines 34 through 39 present a help message to the user, explaining the type of format required:

```
if (length ($computerName) == 0){
print<<"eof";

NBTSTAT displays statistics on current connections
To get a list of available connects enter -r
Enter a connection after the command [2|NBSTAT]\n
eof
```

Requesting new input from the user takes the program out of its normal input cycle, which means it must call a new input handler on line 40:

```
$diagnostic = getNewCommand();
```

The getNewCommand subroutine between lines 96 and 101 requests, receives, and formats the new input data, returning properly formatted user input for further processing:

```
sub getNewCommand(){
    print "ENTER COMMAND: ";
    my $newInput = <STDIN>;
```

```
    chomp $newInput;
    return $newInput;
}
```

The redo command on line 41 short-circuits the flow of execution, sending control to the first statement in the SWITCH block:

```
redo SWITCH;
```

If the user has entered the data in the correct format, the remote computer's table data is retrieved on line 48 and displayed on line 49:

```
@nbtstat = `nbtstat $ computerName `;
print "@nbtstat";
```

Using PING

PING is a program Unix users have been using for decades. When you are having problems connecting to a remote computer, you "ping" it. Much like a sonar system sending out one ping to identify another ship, PING sends out an echo packet checking the remote computer's network connection. The PING program in Listing 22.7 tests a remote computer's network connection by sending it five echo packets of data. PING keeps statistics on the length of time it takes each echo packet to be returned, as you can see in Figure 22.11.

Much like the NBTSTAT program of the previous section, the PING program interface between lines 52 through 67 of Listing 22.7 requires an additional parameter. If the name of the remote computer is not supplied, a help message is printed and new user input is requested:

```
if ($diagnostic =~ /^3|ping/i){
   ($cmd, $destination) = split(/\s/,$diagnostic);
   if (length ($destination) == 0){
      print<<"eof";

PING verifies connections and prints statistics
to a remote host.
Enter a remote host name after the command [3|PING]\n
eof
      $diagnostic = getNewCommand();
      redo SWITCH;
   }
   print "This command may takes several seconds.\n";
```

```
@ping = `ping -n 5 $destination`;
print "@ping";
last SWITCH;
}
```

FIGURE 22.11:

Getting PING timing statistics

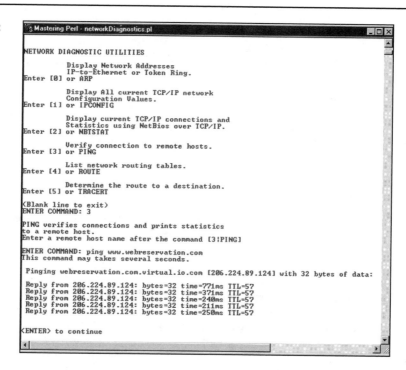

Like the other network administration commands, the PING program can take other parameters than those used in the interface program (Listing 22.7). Those additional parameters are listed in Table 22.10.

TABLE 22.10: PING Parameters

Parameter	Description
-a	Convert IP addresses to host names.
-f	Send a flag that tells all gateways along the route to not fragment the data packet.
-i *time*	Set the Time to Live field of the data packet to time.

Continued on next page

TABLE 22.10 CONTINUED: PING Parameters

Parameter	Description
-j *route-list*	The packet must follow the route identified in the route list to the destination. Consecutive hosts can be separated by intermediate gateways.
-k *route-list*	The packet must follow the route identified in the route list to the destination. Consecutive hosts are not allowed.
-l *bytes*	Send echo packets containing the amount of data specified in bytes. The minimum packet size is 64 bytes. The maximum packet size is 8192 bytes.
-n *count*	Send only the number of echo packets specified by count.
-r *count*	Record the outgoing and return routes of the data packet. Count identifies the maximum number of routing hosts to be recorded. The maximum value for count is 9.
-s *count*	Specify a timestamp and limit the number of hops along the route to count.
-t	Send echo packets to the destination until interrupted.
-v *service*	Set the Type of Service field of the data packet to the specified service.

Getting Network Routing Tables

The network utility ROUTE program in Listing 22.7 prints the active routes from the computer's routing table, as you can see in Figure 22.12.

Lines 68 through 72 do not accept any parameters and print only the existing routes:

```
if ($diagnostic =~ /^4|route/i){
    @route = `route print`;
    print "@route";
    last SWITCH;
}
```

ROUTE is an extremely powerful network utility. It not only can list the active routes, but also can modify, delete, add, and change the network routing tables of local and remote computers. The syntax of the route command is like this:

```
route [-f] [command[destination][MASK netmask][gateway]]
```

FIGURE 22.12:

Displaying active network routes

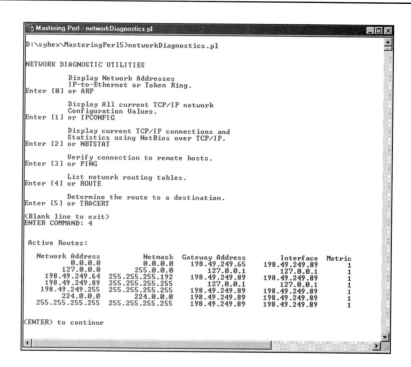

The parameters to the route command are listed in Table 22.11. If a destination is not provided with a change, add, delete, or print command, the command defaults to the local routing table.

TABLE 22.11: ROUTE Parameters

Parameter	Description
-f	Clear the routing tables of all gateway entries. If this parameter is used along with a command, the routing tables will be cleared before the command is executed.
add	Add the specified route to the routing table of the computer listed in destination.
add -p	Add the specified route to the routing table of the computer listed in destination and make the new route persistent across system reboots.
change	Modify the specified route in the routing table of the computer listed in destination.
delete	Delete the specified route to the routing table of the computer listed in destination.

Continued on next page

TABLE 22.11 CONTINUED: ROUTE Parameters

Parameter	Description
print	Print the contents of the routing table.
print -p	Print only the persistent routes in the routing table.
MASK *netmask*	Add the netmask as subnet mask value to the route entry.
gateway	Specify the gateway used.

Tracing Internet Routes

The TRACERT program uses much of the same logic of the PING program, but focuses on each of the intermediate connections, called *hops*, along the route. Detailed information about the route taken to a destination and the length of time used by each hop along the route is returned, as shown in Figure 22.13.

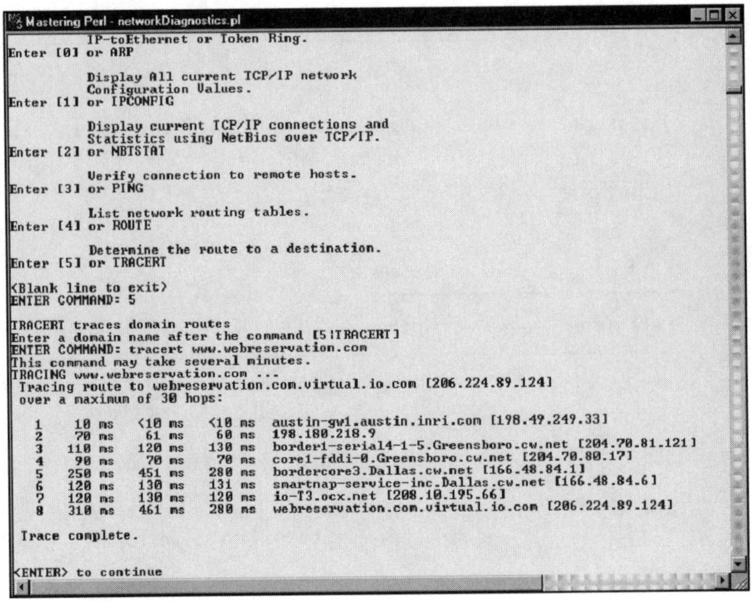

FIGURE 22.13:

Tracing Internet routes from here to there

The interface program between lines 73 and 86 of Listing 22.7 requires a destination input parameter, so a simple help message is required, along with the additional command-entry logic:

```
if ($diagnostic =~ /^5|tracert/i){
    ($command, $destination) = split (/\s/,$diagnostic);
    if (length ($destination) == 0){
        print "TRACERT traces domain routes\n";
        print "Enter a domain name after the command [5|TRACERT]\n";
        $diagnostic = getNewCommand();
        redo SWITCH;
    }
    print "This command may take several minutes.\n";
    print "TRACING $destination ... ";
    @tracert = `tracert $destination`;
    print ."@tracert";
    last SWITCH;
}
```

TIP

The TRACERT program can take a significant amount of time to execute. Whenever the user executes a program that is going to take more than three seconds, you should give the user feedback that something is happening. A simple message that tells the user that the TRACERT program can take several minutes to run is usually sufficient, and your users will appreciate it.

As with the other network utility programs, the TRACERT program takes additional parameters that you may wish to add to Listing 22.7. These parameters are listed in Table 22.12.

TABLE 22.12: TRACERT Parameters

Parameter	Description
-d	Do not convert IP addresses to host names.
-j *route-list*	Follow the route identified in the route list.
-h *count*	Limit the number of hops to count.
-w *time*	Wait the amount of milliseconds specified in time for each reply.

DLL Functions

Your Windows installation comes with hundreds of libraries that Perl 5 can use if it can just create an interface to these libraries. There are more than 1400 DLL (dynamic-link library) files on my C disk alone. Windows uses DLLs to load in functions and data as your program needs them. DLLs are compiled modules of functions and data, which are linked with your code at runtime.

The Win32 API functions are part of a DLL called Kernel32.dll, which is in my C:\WINNT\System32 directory. You can see each of the functions exported by a DLL using the Quick View application. Figure 22.14 shows just a few of the Win32 APIs that are part of the Kernel32.dll file on my computer. (To learn more about an individual function, you can refer to a Win32 programming book or look on the Microsoft web site.)

FIGURE 22.14:

Export API functions from Kernel32.dll

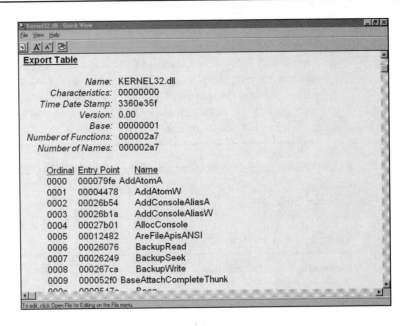

Once you have determined which library and function you wish to use, you can dynamically load and call that function through the Win32::API module, which was written by Aldo Calpini. The Win32::API module allows you to load any DLL on your computer. This wonderful module extends the power of Perl to an endless set of prebuilt libraries. For example, you can use the `Win32::API` module to create an interface to the native Win32 API `GetFullPathName`, which is part of the Kernel32.dll library.

The link to the DLL is created through the `Win32::API` constructor. The constructor, `new`, requires the following information:

- The name of the library (DLL) that will be loaded
- The name of the function that will be exported from that library
- A reference to a list that contains the type of input parameters to the function
- The type of data that will be returned by the function

This information is used to create a calling interface to the library function.

Each of the parameters passed to the `Win32::API` new method must be in the proper case, because the DLL links are case-sensitive. The syntax of calling the `Win32::API` new method is:

```
$handleName = Win32::API->new(libraryName,
                              functionName,
                              referenceToListOfInputParameterTypes,
                              returnParameterType);
```

The input parameter types must be passed as a list reference using the parameter types listed in Table 22.13.

T A B L E 2 2 . 1 3 : Function Parameter Types

Type Symbol	Meaning
I	Integer
N	Double word (long number)
P	Pointer (reference)

Many functions in the Win32 API library have both an ASCII and Unicode method. The ASCII methods end in an *A*; the Unicode methods end in a *W*. The syntax of the `GetFullPathName` ASCII method is:

```
N GetFullPathNameA (P fileName,
                    N bytesInPathBuffer,
```

```
                    P pathBuffer,
                    P fileNameReferencePointer);
```

To load this function using the `Win32::API` module, do this:

```
@parameterList = (P, N, P, P);
$getFullPath = Win32::API->new("Kernel32",
                               "GetFullPathNameA",
                               \@parameterList, N);
```

The `Win32::API` module will load the Kernel32.dll and return an object reference linked to the API function named in the new method.

It is not necessary to name the path to the DLL when loading the library. Perl will search the Windows PATH environment variable, looking through the directory listings for the library. If you have problems loading the DLL, try explicitly defining the library path, like this:

```
$DLL = "c:\\WINNT\\system32\\Kernel32";
```

Do not add the .dll extension to the library names—the `Win32::API` `new` method assumes a .dll file extension.

Once you have created an object reference to the Win32 function, you call the function, as shown in Listing 22.8.

Listing 22.8:   **DLL Function Loading**

```
1.  use Win32::API;
2.  $functionName = "GetFullPathName";
3.  $BUFFER_SIZE = 256;
4.  $pathBuffer = '\0' x $BUFFER_SIZE;
5.  @parameterList = (P, N, P, P);
6.  $fileName = "getFullPath.pl\0";
7.
8.  #Load the Win32 DLL Kernel32
9.  $getFullPath = Win32::API->new("c:\\WINNT\\system32\\Kernel32",
10.                                "GetFullPathNameA",
11.                                \@parameterList, N);
12. #Call the Win 32 API
13. $returnSize = $getFullPath->Call($fileName,
14.                                  $BUFFER_SIZE,
15.                                  $pathBuffer,
16.                                  $filenameRef);
```

```
17. #Separate the null terminated string into Perl format
18. ($filePath, $trash) = split (/\0/,$pathBuffer,2);
19. print "$filePath\n";
```

Line 4 of Listing 22.8 forces Perl 5 to allocate memory for the $pathBuffer variable. Because a linked library will be writing into the memory location, you must allocate all memory before calling any interface functions. Also, as you can see on line 6, Perl strings need to be null-terminated, like this:

```
$fileName = "getFullPath.pl\0";
```

Summary

This chapter began with a look at the Win32 modules that you can install onto your Windows computer. The Active State 500 series builds include an installation module called ppm, which simplifies module installation. If your computer resides behind a firewall, which inhibits the ppm module installer, you can manually retrieve and install Win32 modules.

Next, you learned about the Win32 methods that allow you to access your hard disk and get access to discretionary access control lists (DACLs). The AdminMisc method GetDrives returns a list of all of the drives connected to your computer. The AdminMisc method GetDriveType returns an integer that defines the drive type. You can get exact sector and byte information on your hard disk using the AdminMisc method GetDriveGeometry, or just collect the amount of space available and total disk size using the AdminMisc method GetDriveSpace. Once you completed your investigation of the AdminMisc drive interface methods, you learned about the FileSecurity DACL interface program. Using the FileSecurity method Get, you can read each of the access control permissions associated with a Windows NT object.

Then you learned how to use the built-in methods that collect information about the current user. The Win32 methods `LoginName`, `DomainName`, `NodeName`, and `GetOSVersion` supply the user's login name, the domain and node the user is running on, and the type of operating system, including the build number being used. This section included a module that gives you direct control of the console, creating a hidden password interface. Using the `AdminMisc` method `UserGetAttributes`, you can collect information about the user's full name, the home directory, and the type of script run at login.

Most system administrators in today's world must deal with both individual computers and networks. In the section on network administration, you learned about a program that provides a user interface to a set of Windows NT network diagnostic utilities. The diagnostic utilities discussed here included ARP, IPCON-FIG, NBTSTAT, ROUTE, PING, and TRACERT. The individual discussions of these utilities included details on how to extend the prototype interface program.

Your computer comes with hundreds DLL files. All you need to do is link your Perl program with a DLL, and you can use all of the exported DLL functions. In the last section in this chapter, you learned how to use the `Win32::API` module to connect your Perl program with the DLLs on your computer. With this additional feature in your Perl programming toolkit, you can add the power of hundreds (or thousands) of existing functions to any Win32 program.

CHAPTER

TWENTY-THREE

The Registry and Event Log

- An overview of the Registry

- Registry key access and manipulation

- Registry data retrieval and modification

- Event log access and manipulation

In this chapter, you will explore the mysteries of the Windows Registry. First, you will learn about the internals of your Registry. You will learn how to read and create Registry keys, as well as how to add and delete data from within a Registry key. Once you have learned how to manipulate your Registry, you will learn about one of the hidden but major Registry functions—the event log.

The event log can track every step you make through your computer. Through the event log, which is part of your Registry, all software programs, including Windows, have a means of recording significant events in a central location and consistent format. In the section on the event log, you will learn how to add your own events, save copies of event logs, read event logs, and process the contents of an event log record. At the end of this chapter, you will learn how to add new functionality to a Win32 module.

An Introduction to the Registry

The Registry is the Windows operating system keeper of all knowledge. When Windows needs to know how to start a program, find a file, or determine just who is using this computer, it looks in the Windows Registry.

The Registry is created during the Windows installation and updated throughout the life of your computer. The Registry keeps track of the hardware in your computer and every piece of software also. When you double-click on a file, Windows goes to the Registry and asks it what program to run based on its type (which is usually determined by its three-letter extension). The Registry is stored in simple text files, but you can't edit the Registry with a simple text editor. The user interface to the Registry is through a program called REGEDIT (Registry Editor).

Running the Registry Editor

To run REGEDIT, select Start➤Run, type **regedit** in the Run box, and select OK. The Registry Editor will start with a top-level view of your Registry, which will look something like Figure 23.1.

Your Registry contains six major groupings of information, which you can see in Figure 23.1. You can think of each of these groupings as knowledge databases.

Each knowledge database contains domain-specific information about your computer. These knowledge domains, which are called Registry *keys,* hold the following information:

HKEY_CLASSES_ROOT   Your file associations and other software settings that tell Windows how and when to start up certain programs.

HKEY_CURRENT_USER   Information about the current user of your computer.

HKEY_LOCAL_MACHINE   The hardware and software settings of your computer.

HKEY_USERS   Each user's settings, including the default user.

HKEY_CURRENT_CONFIG   The current settings of both the hardware and software configuration.

HKEY_DYN_DATA   The hardware settings used during bootup and information about your Plug-and-Play settings (these settings change dynamically).

FIGURE 23.1:

Running the Registry Editor

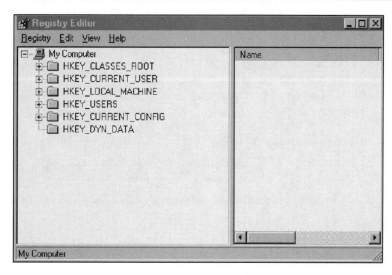

Because the Registry is the source of all knowledge for your computer, it is of great interest to programmers. The Registry is usually part of installing your program or creating a user license, which makes it important for most software developers.

Needless to say, if your Registry is broken, so is your computer. Heed all the warnings you've read in other documents and the ones you'll see in this chapter! Additionally, back up your Registry before running any of the programs in this chapter. Instructions for backing up your Registry follow.

WARNING   Back up your Registry! DO IT NOW! If you don't know how, see the "Backing Up Your Registry" section below.

Backing Up Your Registry

To create a backup file for your Registry, run REGEDIT as described in the previous section. From the Registry Editor, select Registry>Export Registry. This will bring up the Export Registry File dialog box, shown in Figure 23.2.

FIGURE 23.2:

Exporting the Registry

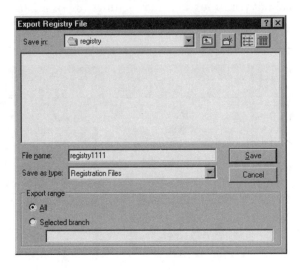

To save all of your Registry to a file, select the All radio button in the Export Range portion of the dialog box. This created a 4MB file on my computer. I used WinZip to compress the Registry file and put a copy of my Registry on floppy disk for safekeeping. You, too, should store your exported Registry file somewhere other than on the computer on which you are working.

Registry Manipulation

The following sections describe how to read and modify the keys and values in your Registry. Before you begin modifying your Registry, make sure that you have a backup of your Registry (see the preceding section for instructions).

Reading the Registry

In this section, you will learn how to read the keys in your Registry, using three Win32::Registry methods: Open, GetKeys, and Close. The Registry module provides an easy-to-use, object-oriented interface to your computer's Registry. Using the Registry module, you can retrieve all keys of any branch in your Registry in fewer than 20 lines of code. Listing 23.1, which produces Figure 23.3, follows the HARDWARE subkey of the HKEY_LOCAL_MACHINE branch on your local Windows computer.

Listing 23.1:   **A Registry Branch**

```
1.  use Win32::Registry;
2.  $| = 1;
3.  $key = "HARDWARE";
4.  $HKEY_LOCAL_MACHINE->Open($key, $nextKeyList);
5.  listKeys($nextKeyList);
6.  sub listKeys(){
7.      $count++;
8.      my ($keyList) = @_;
9.      my ($nextObj, @subKeys, $subKey);
10.     $keyList->GetKeys(\@subKeys);
11.     foreach $subKey (@subKeys){
12.         $tabString = "    " x $count;
13.         print "$tabString $subKey\n";
14.         $keyList->Open($subKey, $nextKeyList);
15.         listKeys($nextKeyList);
16.         $count-;
17.     }
18.     $keyList->Close();
19. }
```

FIGURE 23.3:

Following the HARDWARE key branch

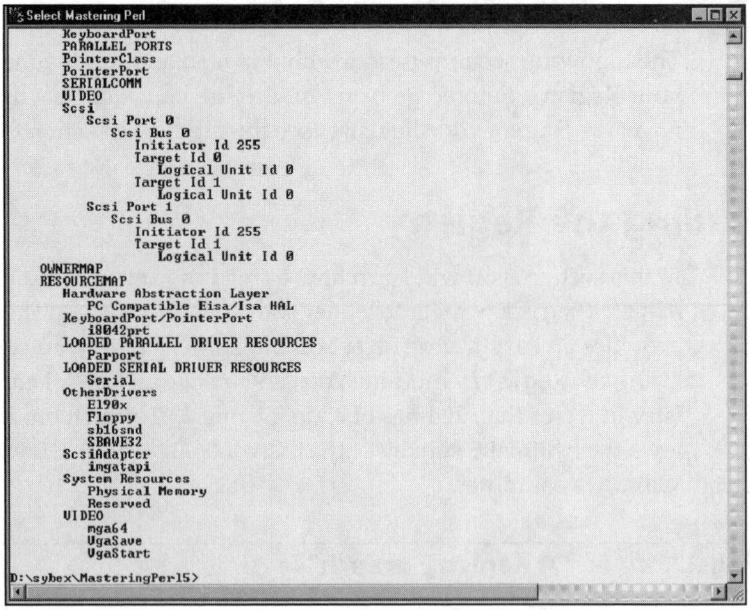

The Registry module uses a different method from most other Perl modules for creating an object reference. On line 3 of Listing 23.1, the variable $HKEY_LOCAL_MACHINE is used like an object reference. Most Perl 5 modules have a constructor, called new, that returns an object reference. The Registry module exports the variables shown in Table 23.1. The variables listed in Table 23.1 can be used to open the major branches of your Registry.

TABLE 23.1: Exported Registry Keys

Key	Contents	Version
$HKEY_LOCAL_MACHINE ($HKLM)	Hardware and software settings	95/98/NT
$HKEY_CLASSES_ROOT ($HKCR)	File associations and OLE information	95/98/NT
$HKEY_USERS ($HKU)	All user profiles	95/98/NT
$HKEY_CURRENT_USER ($HKCU)	The logged-in user	95/98/NT
$HKEY_CURRENT_CONFIG	Current hardware and software configuration	95/98/NT
$HKEY_DYN_DATA	Current devices loaded and status	95/98

Continued on next page

TABLE 23.1 CONTINUED: Exported Registry Keys

Key	Contents	Version
$HKEY_PERFORMANCE_DATA	Performance values	NT
$HKEY_PERFORMANCE_NLSTEXT	Performance text	NT
$HKEY_PERFORMANCE_TEXT	Performance text	NT

Opening the Registry

The `Registry::Open` method uses the key variable as a pointer to an internal object root. This object root defines the beginning location for all searches through the Registry. The `Open` method creates a connection to the Registry and returns an object reference to the subkey passed in the `Open` method call. The syntax of calling the `Open` method is:

```
RegistryKey->Open(RegistrySubKey, $subKeyReference);
```

The *RegistryKey* must be a valid Registry key. The *RegistrySubKey* must be a Registry key that is part of the *RegistryKey* branch. The `Open` method returns an object reference to the subkey, which can then be used to traverse the opened Registry branch. Listing 23.1 shows how to traverse a branch of the Registry using the `Open` method and the `GetKeys` method (discussed next).

Getting Registry Keys

The `GetKeys` method uses an open Registry key (the object reference returned by the `Open` method) and returns an array of the subkeys under the open Registry key. The `GetKeys` method can be used in array context, like this:

```
@subKeys = $openKey->GetKeys();
```

It can also be used in scalar context (as in Listing 23.1), like this:

```
$openKey->GetKeys(\@subKeys);
```

In either context, `GetKeys` returns in the array `@subKeys` an array of Registry keys under the `$openKey`, which may contain more Registry subkeys.

Listing 23.1 uses recursion to traverse an entire branch of a Registry key:

```
6.  sub listKeys(){
7.      $count++;
```

```
8.     my ($keyList) = @_;
9.     my ($nextObj, @subKeys, $subKey);
10.    $keyList->GetKeys(\@subKeys);
11.    foreach $subKey (@subKeys){
12.        $tabString = "    " x $count;
13.        print "$tabString $subKey\n";
14.        $keyList->Open($subKey, $nextKeyList);
15.        listKeys($nextKeyList);
16.        $count--;
17.    }
```

Recursion occurs when a program calls itself. Recursion stops when the program can no longer follow the particular branch or inquiry that caused it to begin calling itself. Listing 23.1 is a rather nice example of a depth-first search of the Registry using recursion. In the listKeys subroutine, a Registry key branch is opened each time through the foreach loop that processes the @subkeys array. The branch is opened on line 14, just before the subroutine calls itself on line 15:

```
$keyList->Open($subKey, $nextKeyList);
listKeys($nextKeyList);
```

The new branch of subkeys is referenced by the lexical variable $nextKeyList, which is copied by that listKeys subroutine, into the lexical $keyList. Each branch of subkeys continues to open the next level of the branch until there are no further levels to traverse. At that point, the lexical array @subkeys contains no elements and the foreach loop has nothing further to process. The current instance of listKeys will exit, and the foreach loop of the previous @subkey array will continue processing until it reaches the end of a branch. Recursion always sounds like circular logic, which it is, so if you find yourself scratching your head right now, you can simulate the recursion of Listing 23.1 through REGEDIT.

To simulate this program's recursion, open REGEDIT and begin opening the HKEY_LOCAL_MACHINE key's subfolders. Always open the next folder that has a subfolder. When a folder has no more subfolders, back up the folder list until you can find a folder with subfolders and repeat the process. Figure 23.4 shows all of the folders (that are visible on the screen) underneath the HARDWARE subkey, which is a subfolder under my HKEY_LOCAL_MACHINE Registry branch.

FIGURE 23.4:

Viewing the HARDWARE
branch in the Registry
Editor

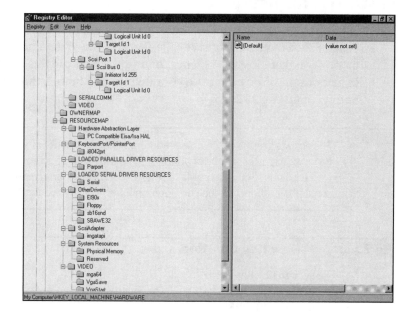

You can compare this graphical representation of the Registry to the one generated by Listing 23.1, shown in Figure 23.3, and see that they show the same information.

Closing the Registry

The Close method closes the Registry connection for the open key. This method must be called with an open key as the object reference:

```
$keyReference->Close();
```

The last line of Listing 23.1 closes the open Registry key:

```
$keyList->Close();
```

The Registry reference returned by the Open method is a connection to your computer's Registry, which is a system resource. Make sure you release this system resource by closing the Registry keys you are no longer using.

Creating a Registry Key

Listing 23.2 creates a new Registry key under an old branch of my HKEY_LOCAL_
MACHINE\SOFTWARE key ActiveWare. This was the old name for the Win32 Perl
distribution that I installed on my computer. I now use this Registry branch for
Registry testing. You can create your own testing branch through REGEDIT or by
modifying Listing 23.2.

WARNING   The listings presented in this section modify the contents of your Registry. If you
have not exported a copy of your entire Registry, please do so before running any
of the listings shown here. Make sure you put the exported copy of your Registry
some place other than the computer on which you are working.

Listing 23.2:   New Key Creation

```
1.   use Win32::Registry ;
2.   #Define the key that will be opened
3.   $key = "SOFTWARE\\ActiveWare";
4.
5.   #Open the subkey under the root directory
6.   $HKEY_LOCAL_MACHINE->Open($key, $keyList);
7.
8.   #Print the keys under ActiveWare before
9.   #we add the new key. ActiveWare is the
10.  #old name for the new ActivePerl
11.  print "Under HKEY_LOCAL_MACHINE\n\tActiveWare\n";
12.  $keyList->GetKeys(\@subKeys);
13.  $numberOfSubKeys = @subKeys;
14.  print "\tThere is $numberOfSubKeys key\n";
15.     foreach $subKey (@subKeys){
16.         print "\t\t$subKey\n";
17.     }
18.
19.  #Create a new key under the
20.  #opened key referenced by keyList
21.  print "\nCreating the Perl6 Key\n";
22.  $keyList->Create("Perl6",$newKeyList);
23.
```

```
24. #Print the key list now that we have added
25. #a new key
26. print "Under HKEY_LOCAL_MACHINE\n\tActiveWare\n";
27. $keyList->GetKeys(\@newSubKeys);
28. $numberOfSubKeys = @newSubKeys;
29. print "\tThere are now $numberOfSubKeys keys\n";
30.    foreach $subKey (@newSubKeys){
31.       print "\t\t$subKey\n";
32.    }
33. #Close both opened keys
34. $keyList->Close();
35. $newKeyList->Close();
```

If you don't have an ActiveWare branch under your HKEY_LOCAL_MACHINE\ SOFTWARE, you must modify line 3 of Listing 23.2 to point to an existing branch of your Registry:

```
$key = "SOFTWARE\\ActiveWare";
```

Notice that line 3 uses a double backslash to list the subfolder under the SOFT-WARE branch of the Registry. The Registry subfolders are treated just like directories and files in your Perl programs. Each subfolder is considered a new directory under the previous folder. Follow the same rules for Registry subfolders as you learned for creating directory names. Running Listing 23.2 on my computer produces Figure 23.5.

FIGURE 23.5:

Creating a Registry key

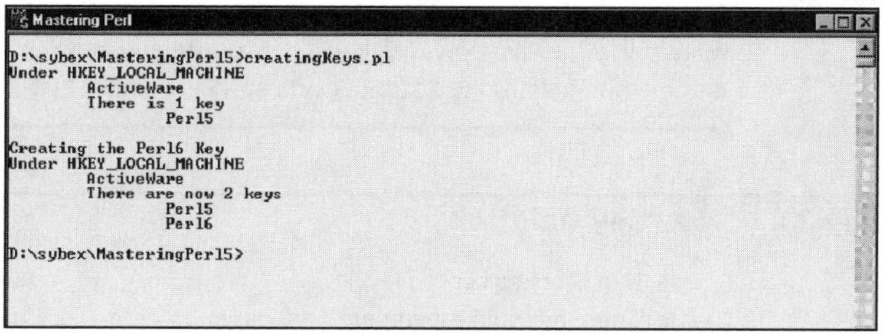

The Create method requires an open key before it can be called. Its syntax is:

```
$keyList->Create($newSubKey, $subKeyList);
```

where:

- $newSubKey is the new key to create under the $keyList key.

- $subkeyList is the pointer to the newly created key.

- $keyList is a previously opened key.

If $newSubKey already exists, it will not be created. Instead, the Create method acts like the Open method and returns an opened key reference. If you run Listing 23.2 twice, you will see that the Perl 6 key is created only once.

Deleting Registry Keys

Any self-respecting program offers an uninstall capability, which should include cleaning up the Registry. If you modify the Registry with your program, the Win32::Registry module makes it easy for you to remove any Registry entries if your program is uninstalled.

Removing Registry keys is demonstrated in Listing 23.3, which produces the result shown in Figure 23.6. If you remove the code used for creating Figure 23.6, Listing 23.3 collapses down to calling the three methods: Open, DeleteKey, and Close.

WARNING   The DeleteKey method works differently on Windows 95/98 than it does on Windows NT. In Windows NT, it will only delete an empty key. In Windows 95/98, this method deletes the $subkey and every key under that $subkey branch.

Listing 23.3:   **Key Deletion**

```
1.  use Win32::Registry;
2.  #Define the subkey under the main branch
3.  $key = "SOFTWARE\\ActiveWare";
4.  #Using the Main branch open the sub branch
5.  $HKEY_LOCAL_MACHINE->Open($key, $keyList);
6.  print "Under HKEY_LOCAL_MACHINE\n\tActiveWare\n";
7.  $keyList->GetKeys(\@subKeys);
8.  $numberOfSubKeys = @subKeys;
```

```
9.  print "\tThere are $numberOfSubKeys keys\n";
10.    foreach $subKey (@subKeys){
11.        print "\t\t$subKey\n";
12.    }
13.
14. $key = "Perl6";
15. print "\nDeleting the $key Key\n";
16. #Delete the key we added
17. if (!$keyList->DeleteKey($key)){
18.    print "Failed to delete $key\n";
19. }
20.
21. #Display that the key was deleted
22. #for confirmation purposes
23. print "Under HKEY_LOCAL_MACHINE\n\tActiveWare\n";
24. $keyList->GetKeys(\@newSubKeys);
25. $numberOfSubKeys = @newSubKeys;
26. print "\tThere are now $numberOfSubKeys key\n";
27.    foreach $subKey (@newSubKeys){
28.        print "\t\t$subKey\n";
29.    }
30. $keyList->Close();
```

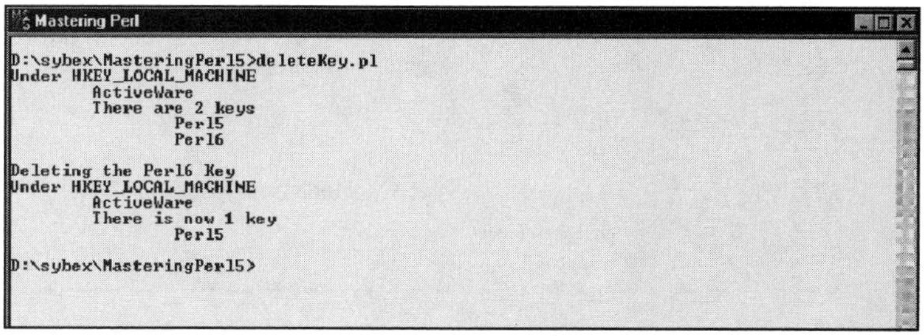

FIGURE 23.6:

Deleting a Registry key

```
Mastering Perl                                                      _ □ ×
D:\sybex\MasteringPerl5>deleteKey.pl
Under HKEY_LOCAL_MACHINE
        ActiveWare
        There are 2 keys
                Perl5
                Perl6

Deleting the Perl6 Key
Under HKEY_LOCAL_MACHINE
        ActiveWare
        There is now 1 key
                Perl5

D:\sybex\MasteringPerl5>
```

The DeleteKey method requires an opened key that points to a folder that contains the key to be deleted before it is called. Its syntax is:

```
$keyList->DeleteKey($subKey);
```

where:

- $subkey is the Registry subkey (and its subfolders in Windows 95/98) to be deleted.

- $keyList is a previously opened key that points to the folder that contains $subkey.

The DeleteKey method returns true if it was successful.

Getting Registry Data

As explained earlier, Registry keys normally contain data that is used to manage your computer's hardware and software. Most of your hardware component information will be in binary format. You can retrieve this data and view it in hexadecimal format. Table 23.2 lists the different types of data in the Registry.

TABLE 23.2: Registry Data Types

Type	Meaning
REG_BINARY	Binary data
REG_DWORD	A 32-bit integer
REG_DWORD_LITTLE_ENDIAN	A 32-bit integer in little-endian format (the default)
REG_DWORD_BIG_ENDIAN	A 32-bit integer in big-endian format
REG_EXPAND_SZ	A text string that contains references to environment variables (the string will expand to the size of the environment variable when it is dereferenced)
REG_LINK	A symbolic link to another Registry key
REG_MULTI_SZ	A list of text strings
REG_NONE	An undefined data type
REG_SZ	A text string

The GetValues method creates a hash of the values of an open key. The hash contains three keys:

Name   The name of the value

Type   The data type of the value

Value   The data of the key value

The keys of the returned hash point to an array that contains the value's name, its data type, and its value. Listing 23.4 retrieves the values under the License subkey for my Perl 5 debugger. Each value is displayed in Figure 23.7. (The last value in Figure 23.7 must be how they determine if you should have a license, because my copy is licensed and not expired.)

Listing 23.4:   **Registry Key Values**

```
1.   use Win32::Registry ;
2.      $separator = "="x65;
3.      #Set the registry data types up for display
4.      @registryDataTypes = (
5.          "REG_NONE",
6.          "REG_SZ",
7.          "REG_EXPAND_SZ",
8.          "REG_BINARY",
9.          "REG_DWORD",
10.          "REG_DWORD_BIG_ENDIAN",
11.          "REG_LINK",
12.          "REG_MULTI_SZ");
13.
14. $key = "SOFTWARE\\ActiveState\\License\\PLDB10";
15. $HKEY_LOCAL_MACHINE->Open($key, $keyList) ;
16. $keyList->GetValues(\%keyValues);
17.      foreach $valueIndex (keys %keyValues){
18.          print "\nThe index is the same as the name: $valueIndex\n";
19.          print "$separator\n";
20.          #The name of the value being retrieved is in the first
21.          #cell of the array reference
22.          print "\tName      => $keyValues{$valueIndex}->[0]\n";
23.          #The data type of the value is in the second cell (cell 1)
24.          #but the data type is only a number. So that number is
25.          #used as an index in the data type names array created
26.          #at the beginning of this program.
27.          print "\tData Type => $registryDataTypes
                                 [$keyValues{$valueIndex}->[1]]\n";
28.          #The actual value of the key is in cell 2
29.          print "\tValue     => $keyValues{$valueIndex}->[2]\n";
30.      }
31. $keyList->Close();
```

FIGURE 23.7:

Getting key values

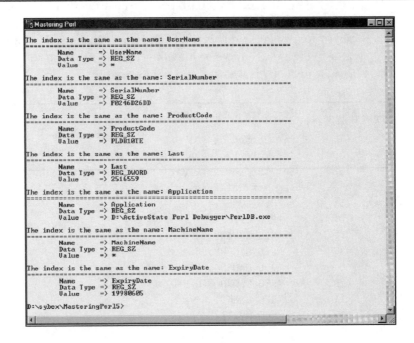

The syntax of the GetValues method is:

```
$keyList->GetValues(\%keyValues);
```

The hash passed to the GetValues method must be a hash reference and, as with all the other Registry methods, the $keyList used to call the GetValues method must be an open key.

The data type returned by the GetValues method is actually an integer, which isn't very informative, unless you know what each integer means. Table 23.3 lists the data types and their integer values.

TABLE 23.3: Getting Key Values

Type	Integer Returned by GetValues
REG_BINARY	3
REG_DWORD	4
REG_DWORD_LITTLE_ENDIAN	4

Continued on next page

TABLE 23.3 CONTINUED: Getting Key Values

Type	Integer Returned by GetValues
REG_DWORD_BIG_ENDIAN	5
REG_EXPAND_SZ	2
REG_LINK	6
REG_MULTI_SZ	7
REG_NONE	0
REG_SZ	1

This information is used between lines 4 and 13 of Listing 23.4 to create an array of the names of the Registry data types that has a one-to-one correspondence with their integer values. Line 27 uses this array and the integer data type returned by GetValues to display the data type in a more understandable format than some number between 0 and 7:

```
$registryDataTypes[$keyValues{$valueIndex}->[1]]\n";
```

The data type is first retrieved from the %keyValues hash. Remember that the %keyValues hash points to an array of name, data type, and value. Since the first array cell contains the data type and the data type is an integer, that integer can be used as an index into the array @registryDataTypes. As long as the @registryDataTypes array elements are in the correct order, you get the nice English-like names shown in Figure 23.7.

Modifying Registry Data

Now that you can see the data in your Registry keys, it's time to assign the values you want in those keys. You can change any value in your Registry using the SetValueEx method. Its syntax is:

```
$keyList->SetValueEx($valueName, 0, $dataType, $value);
```

$valueName is the name of the value to be modified. This value is reserved for future use. The number zero represents an undefined or reserved variable.

$dataType is the type of data to be added. It must match the data added in the $value parameter. The valid data types are shown in Table 23.2. Take note that you use the names in Table 23.2, not the indexes in Table 23.3. $value is the data to be added to the $valueName.

Listing 23.5 illustrates how to use SetValueEx. Figure 23.8 shows the results.

Listing 23.5:   Registry Key Values

```
1.   use Win32::Registry ;
2.   $separator = "="x65;
3.   #Set the registry data types up for display
4.   @registryDataTypes = (
5.         "REG_NONE",
6.         "REG_SZ",
7.         "REG_EXPAND_SZ",
8.         "REG_BINARY",
9.         "REG_DWORD",
10.        "REG_DWORD_BIG_ENDIAN",
11.        "REG_LINK",
12.        "REG_MULTI_SZ");
13.
14.  #Define the key that will be opened
15.  $key = "SOFTWARE\\ActiveWare";
16.
17.  #Open the subkey under the root directory
18.  $HKEY_LOCAL_MACHINE->Open($key, $keyList);
19.
20.  $HKEY_LOCAL_MACHINE->Open($key, $keyList);
21.  #Create a new key under the
22.  #opened key referenced by keyList
23.  $keyList->Create("Perl6",$newKeyList);
24.
25.  $keyList->SetValueEx("FutureBin",0,REG_SZ,"d:\\Perl6\\Bin");
26.  $keyList->GetValues(\%keyValues);
27.     foreach $valueIndex (keys %keyValues){
28.        print "\nThe index is the same as the name:
                    $valueIndex\n";
29.        print "$separator\n";
30.        #The name of the value being retrieved is in the first
31.        #cell of the array reference
32.        print "\tName      => $keyValues{$valueIndex}->[0]\n";
33.        #The data type of the value is in the second cell (cell 1)
```

```
34.          #but the data type is only a number. So that number is
35.          #used as an index in the data type names array
36.          #created at the beginning of this program.
37.          print "\tData Type => $registryDataTypes
                                  [$keyValues{$valueIndex}->[1]]\n";
38.          #The actual value of the key is in cell 2
39.          print "\tValue       => $keyValues{$valueIndex}->[2]\n";
40.      }
41. $keyList->Close();
```

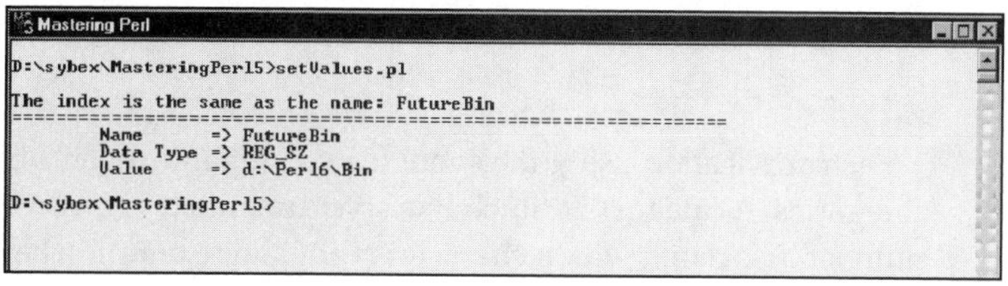

FIGURE 23.8:

Adding values to your keys

> **TIP**
>
> The `Win32::Registry` module has other methods that you might find useful.
> These are documented at http://Jenda.Krynicky.cz. This site is maintained by Jan
> Krynick, who has done some wonderful Perl and Win32 work.

An Introduction to the Event Log

Windows provides a central messaging system for all programs to record their status. All security, system, and application programs are supposed to log significant events into the event log. After reading the first half of this chapter, you should expect that job to fall to the Registry, which it does. Your Registry contains keys for each of the log files on your computer.

Event logging begins when you turn on your computer. The default log files on an NT computer are Application, System, and Security. (A Windows 95/98 computer contains only an Application key under the event log Registry entry.) Within these log files is information about each login event, the location of device driver message files, and application error messages. A log file is actually a subkey in your Registry with the values shown in Table 23.4.

TABLE 23.4: Log File Subkey Values

Name	Type	Description
CategoryCount	REG_DWORD	The number of categories supported
CategoryMessageFile	REG_EXPAND_SZ	The path to the category message file
EventMessageFile	REG_EXPAND_SZ	The path to the event identifier message file
ParameterMessageFile	REG_EXPAND_SZ	The path to the event source's message file
TypesSupported	REG_DWORD	The types supported in bit mask format

Each application using the event log can separate events based on user-defined categories. A category is much like an enumerated value, which is a consecutive number associated with a character string. For example, the security log files contain the categories Logon/Logoff, File System Access, Privileged Actions, and Change in Security Policy.

Event message files contain events. Like the categories type, each event identifier should be associated with a character string, which can be understood by the user. Identifying a number with a character string uses the same type of processing you saw in Listing 23.5, where the Registry data types and a number were associated with a character string through an array:

```
@registryDataTypes = ("REG_NONE", "REG_SZ", "REG_EXPAND_SZ",
                      "REG_BINARY","REG_DWORD", "REG_DWORD_BIG_ENDIAN",
                      "REG_LINK", "REG_MULTI_SZ");
```

You can register your program's log file by using the `RegisterEventSource` method. If your program has a key in the Registry, a reference to your event log file will be returned. If your program is not part of the Registry, the default event log application is returned. Using the methods identified in the Registry section, you can add your program to the application keys under the Event log. The correct Registry branch for application programs is:

```
HKEY_LOCAL_MACHINE
    System
        CurrentControlSet
```

```
Services
    EventLog
        Applications
```

In the next section, you will learn about the Perl methods available for accessing your event log. If you are using a Windows NT computer, you can view your event log using the Event Viewer. The Event Viewer is a GUI to the event log. To bring up the Event Viewer, choose Start➤Program Files➤Administrative Tools (Common)➤Event Viewer.

Event Log Manipulation

Included with the latest ActiveState build is a module called `EventLog.pm`. The module provides a Perl 5 object-oriented interface to your computer's built-in event log functions.

Like many of the Windows modules, `EventLog.pm` is a Perl 5 interface to existing native functions. The `EventLog` methods and their corresponding native methods are listed in Table 23.5. Sometimes, that interface requires significant operations inside the `EventLog` module. Other times, the `EventLog` method is a *pass-through* method, which just calls a native method, passing the input and output parameters between the calling program and the native method. Later in the chapter, you'll learn how to add an interface for calling native methods.

TABLE 23.5: EventLog Cross Reference to Native Functions

EventLog Method	Native Method	Description
Backup	BackupEventLog	Pass-through method
Clear	ClearEventLog	Pass-through method
GetOldest	GetOldestEventLogRecord	Pass-through method
GetNumber	GetNumberOfEventLogRecords	Pass-through method
new	OpenEventLog	Keeps the log handle as an instance variable
Open	None	Deprecated; now calls the **new** method

Continued on next page

TABLE 23.5 CONTINUED: EventLog Cross Reference to Native Functions

EventLog Method	Native Method	Description
Read	ReadEventLog	Creates a hash from the returned log values
Report	WriteEventLog	Converts the input hash data into the correct format for writing to the log file

Reading the Event Log

As you have learned, there are three main log files on your Windows NT computer: Application, Security, and System. Your process must have administrator access privileges to view the Security and System log files. The Application log file is used as the default if your input file is not matched.

Reading the System Log

Listing 23.6 connects to the System log file and reads the records. Figure 23.9 shows its output.

Listing 23.6: **The System Log**

```
1.  use Win32::EventLog;
2.  #Define Global Constants
3.  @months = (Jan, Feb, March, April, May, June,
4.             July, Aug, Sep, Oct, Nov, Dec);
5.  @days = (Sun, Mon, Tue, Wed, Thur, Fri, Sat);
6.  $SEC = 0; $MIN = 1; $HOUR = 2; $DAYOFMONTH= 3;
7.  $MONTH = 4; $YEAR = 5; $WEEKDAY=6;
8.  $separator = ("=" x 60) . "\n";
9.
10. #The new method takes 2 parameters:
11. #the event log to access and the computer name
12. #If the computer name is blank, it uses the local computer
13. $eventLog = Win32::EventLog->new('System') || die $!;
14.
15. for $eventIndex (1..10){
16.     my %eventLogData;
```

```
17.    #The SEEK and FORWARDS read flags are required.
18.    #They create a bit mask which tells the native function
19.    #$eventIndex is the location to read forward from
20.    $eventLog->Read((EVENTLOG_SEEK_READ |
                       EVENTLOG_BACKWARDS_READ),
                       $eventIndex,\%eventLogData);
21.
22.    print "${separator}NEW LOG ENTRY\n$separator";
23.    foreach $logEntry (sort keys %eventLogData){
24.       switch:{
25.          #If the entry is time-oriented, then put it into a
26.          #standard human-usable format
27.          if ($logEntry =~ /Time/){
28.             @time = localtime($eventLogData{$logEntry});
29.             for ($timeIndex = 0; $timeIndex < $YEAR;
                    $timeIndex++){
30.                $time[$timeIndex] = sprintf("%02d",
                                       $time[$timeIndex]);
31.                $month = $months[$time[$MONTH]] ;
32.                $day = $days[$time[$WEEKDAY]];
33.             }
34.             print "$logEntry, at $time[$HOUR]:
                                   $time[$MIN]:
                                   $time[$SEC]
                                   on $day $month
                                   $time[$DAYOFMONTH]\n";
35.             last switch;
36.          }
37.          #Event ID is double word format. The higher order
38.          #bits must be cleared or a negative number is assumed
39.          if ($logEntry eq EventID){
40.             $eventLogData{$logEntry} = $eventLogData{$logEntry}
                                       & 0xFFFF;
41.          }
42.          #Strings are C/C++ null terminated
43.          #Perl wants a newline character
44.          if ($logEntry eq Strings){
45.             #Convert null terminated strings to newline
46.             $eventLogData{$logEntry} =~ tr/\0/\n/;
47.          }
48.          #Now that the data is formatted, print it out
49.          DEFAULT:{
```

```
50.                  print qq|$logEntry, $eventLogData{$logEntry}\n|;
51.              }
52.          }#switch
53.      }
54. }
```

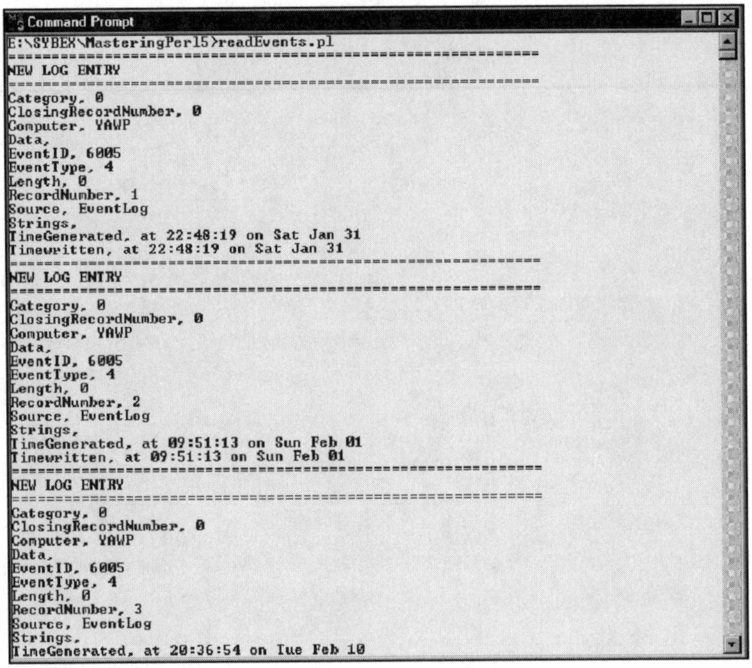

FIGURE 23.9:

Reading the oldest log
events

The first few lines of Listing 23.6 initialize indexes and arrays, which are used
for formatting the data returned from the event log. Line 13 makes the connection
to the event log:

```
$eventLog = Win32::EventLog->new('System') || die $!;
```

The new method calls the built-in function OpenEventLog. The native function
OpenEventLog takes a log filename and a computer name as input parameters
and returns a reference to the log file. The new method creates an anonymous
hash that contains a reference to the log file, the log filename, and the computer
name. These instance variables are blessed into the EventLog class, and a reference to the blessed object is returned. The syntax of the new method is:

```
$eventLog = Win32::EventLog->new(logFileName, computerName);
```

where:

- The object reference will be saved into $eventLog.

- The log filename is required and must reference a valid log file.

- The computer name is optional. If it is missing, this parameter defaults to the local computer.

Without a valid log file reference, all of the other EventLog functions will fail. Hence, on line 13 of Listing 23.6, if the new function fails, the program dies and prints the system error message ($!).

Line 20 begins reading the System log file at record number one, which is the oldest record in the System log file:

```
$eventLog->Read((EVENTLOG_SEEK_READ | EVENTLOG_BACKWARDS_READ),
                               $eventIndex,
                               \%eventLogData);
```

The System log file record numbers are sequential in order. The oldest record has the smallest number, and the newest record has the largest value. The record numbers are set by the native function and cannot be modified.

The Read method requires an object reference and takes three parameters:

```
$classRef->Read(READ_MASK, $RecordIndex,$hashReference);
```

The $RecordIndex defines the record number to read. The contents of the hash pointed to by the $hashReference will be overwritten by the Read method. Therefore, the hash reference should refer to a lexical hash.

The READ_MASK defines how to read the event log file. The READ_MASK of Listing 23.6 tells the Read method to begin reading at the record index, and record processing will continue backwards from that point. The READ_MASK is a bit string with each bit identifying an individual action for the Read method. To create a bit string with more than one option turned on, you OR (|) the options together, as shown on line 20 of Listing 23.6. Table 23.6 shows each of the values of the READ_MASKS and their corresponding bit values.

TABLE 23.6: Read Masks

Mask Name	Integer Value	Bit Value	Description
EVENTLOG_BACKWARDS_READ	8	1000	Read from this position backward in reverse chronological order.

Continued on next page

TABLE 23.6 CONTINUED: Read Masks

Mask Name	Integer Value	Bit Value	Description
EVENTLOG_FORWARDS_READ	4	0100	Read from this position forward in chronological order.
EVENTLOG_SEQUENTIAL_READ	1	0001	Read forward from the last **Read-EventLog** call position.
EVENTLOG_SEEK_READ	2	0010	Read from the position specified in the record index. EVENTLOG_FORWARDS_READ or EVENTLOG_BACKWARDS_READ must be used with this flag.

Reading the Most Recent Entries First

The Read method uses the record index to identify which record should be read next. Because the record numbers begin with one and are sequentially incremented as each new record is added, it's fairly easy to read from the end of the log file. Reading backwards feels awkward to me, so I created Listing 23.7, which reads the most recent entries in the log file first. The result of running Listing 23.7 is shown in Figure 23.10.

Listing 23.7: **Recent Events First**

```
1.   use Win32::EventLog;
2.   @months = (Jan, Feb, March, April, May, June,
3.            July, Aug, Sep, Oct, Nov, Dec);
4.   @days = (Sun, Mon, Tue, Wed, Thur, Fri, Sat);
5.   $SEC = 0; $MIN = 1; $HOUR = 2; $DAYOFMONTH= 3;
6.   $MONTH = 4; $YEAR = 5; $WEEKDAY=6;
7.   $separator = ("=" x 60) . "\n";
8.
9.   #Open the System log file
10.  $eventLog = Win32::EventLog->new('System') || die $!;
11.  #Get the current number of events in the event log
12.  $eventLog->GetNumber($totalEvents);
13.  #Assign number of records to input or all the records available
14.  $numberToRead = ($ARGV[0] > 0 && $ARGV[0] < $totalEvents) ?
                     $ARGV[0] : $totalEvents;
15.  #Turn on bits 1 and 3
```

```
16. $readFlag = EVENTLOG_SEEK_READ | EVENTLOG_FORWARDS_READ;
17. #set the Read index to the latest event
18. for ($eventIndex = $totalEvents;
19.      $eventIndex > $totalEvents - $numberToRead;
20.      $eventIndex-){
21.    my %eventLogData;
22.    #The SEEK and FORWARDS read flags are required.
23.    $eventLog->Read($readFlag, $eventIndex, \%eventLogData);
24.    print "${separator}NEW LOG ENTRY\n$separator";
25.    foreach $logEntry (sort keys %eventLogData){
26.       switch:{
27.          #Format time to human-usable format
28.          if ($logEntry =~ /Time/){
29.             @time = localtime($eventLogData{$logEntry});
30.             for ($timeIndex = 0; $timeIndex < $YEAR;
                       $timeIndex++){
31.                $time[$timeIndex] = sprintf("%02d",
                                       $time[$timeIndex]);
32.                $month = $months[$time[$MONTH]];
33.                $day = $days[$time[$WEEKDAY]];
34.             }
35.             print "$logEntry, at $time[$HOUR]:
                                   $time[$MIN]:
                                   $time[$SEC]
                                   on $day $month
                                   $time[$DAYOFMONTH]\n";
36.             last switch;
37.          }
38.          #The Event ID is a double word format
39.          #The higher order bits must be cleared
40.          if ($logEntry eq EventID){
41.             $eventLogData{$logEntry} =
                    $eventLogData{$logEntry} & 0xFFFF;
42.          }
43.          #Now that the data is formatted, print it out
44.          DEFAULT:{
45.             print qq|$logEntry, $eventLogData{$logEntry}\n|;
46.          }
47.       }#switch
48.    }
49. }
```

FIGURE 23.10:

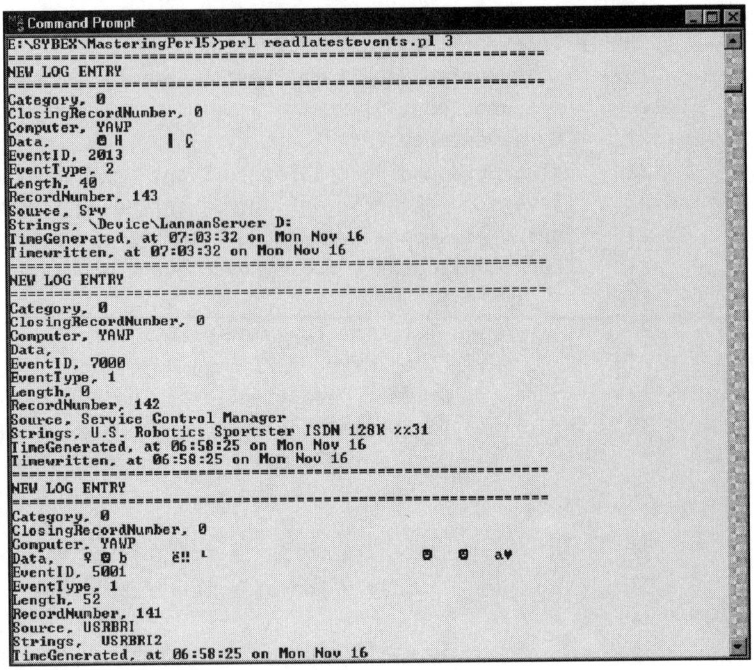

Reading the most recent log events

Listing 23.7, on line 12, uses the GetNumber method to determine the first index into the log file:

```
$eventLog->GetNumber($totalEvents);
```

The GetNumber method sets the parameter $totalEvents to the number of records in the log file, which is the same value as the record number of the most recently added event. Line 14 gives you the option to limit the number of events displayed by Listing 23.7:

```
$numberToRead = ($ARGV[0] > 0 && $ARGV[0] < $totalEvents) ? $ARGV[0] :
$totalEvents;
```

You can limit the number of returned events to any value greater than zero up to the total number of events. The for loop on lines 18 through 20 controls the next event read from the log file:

```
for ($eventIndex = $totalEvents;
     $eventIndex > $totalEvents - $numberToRead;
     $eventIndex-){
```

The event index is initialized to the total number of events in the log file, which is also the most recent event in the log file. The conditional expression on line 19, which controls the for loop, checks to see if the event index has been decremented by the limit on the number of times to read. Because we are reading from the most recently entered record back to the first record entered, the loop-increment expression on line 20, which would usually increment the for loop index, decrements the loop index. Line 22, using the bit mask set back on line 16, reads the next requested record from the log file:

```
$eventLog->Read($readFlag, $eventIndex, \%eventLogData);
```

Writing to the Event Log

Your programs will probably spend more time adding events to the event log than reading them. One of the hardest tasks every programmer faces is responding to bug reports on delivered programs. (Of course, all of the easy-to-fix bugs were squashed before you released your program for general use.) If you take the time to save significant information about your program's state when an error occurs, you will have the data necessary to solve customer bug reports. Listing 23.8 demonstates how to record an event into an open log file.

Listing 23.8:   **An Event Report**

```
1.   use Win32::EventLog;
2.   $eventLog = Win32::EventLog->new('System') || die $!;
3.   %eventRecord = (
4.        'Source'        => 0,
5.        'Computer'      => 0,
6.        'Length'        => 0,
7.        'RecordNumber'  => 0,
8.        'TimeGenerated'=> 0,
9.        'Timewritten'   => 0,
10.       'ClosingRecordNumber' => 0,
11.       'Category'      => 2,
12.       'EventID'       => 4242,
13.       'EventType'     => EVENTLOG_INFORMATION_TYPE,
14.       'Strings'       => "Used to identify the data",
15.       'Data'          => "Informational data about the message",
16.       );
17.
18. $eventLog->Report(\%eventRecord);
```

The hash %eventRecord lists each of the items stored into a log event record. The first seven items in %eventRecord are initialized to zero and later set by the native method WriteEventLog. Table 23.7 lists each item in the event log and who has the eventual control over its value. Any data written to a record item that is controlled by the native method WriteEventLog will be overwritten by WriteEventLog before it is stored into the event record.

TABLE 23.7: Event Log Record Items

Item Name	Controlling Method	Description
Category	Perl method	A user-defined integer
Computer	WriteEventLog	The value assigned when the log file was opened
Data	Perl method	Any character string
EventID	Perl method	A user-defined integer
EventType	Perl method	A predefined integer value (see Table 23.8)
Length	WriteEventLog	The number of characters stored into the data key
RecordNumber	WriteEventLog	The next sequential record number
TimeGenerated	WriteEventLog	The time WriteEventLog was called
TimeWritten	WriteEventLog	The time WriteEventLog wrote the record to the event log
Source	WriteEventLog	The log file opened by the **new** method
Strings	Perl method	Any character string

Much of the data recorded into the event log is designed for a C/C++ interface. If you expect to read the events through the Windows Event Viewer, then you should conform to the C/C++ interface format. If you plan on using a Perl 5 program, such as Listing 23.7, to read the log events, then you can record simple text strings into both the Strings and Data hash keys. Your program controls which event type is stored into the event log record, but the event type should be limited to the four values shown in Table 23.8. The event type is stored as a bit value much like the *READ_MASK* bit mask. However, unlike the *READ_MASK*, the event type can be only one value at a time.

TABLE 23.8: Event Types

Log Type	Value	Description
EVENTLOG_ERROR_TYPE	1	Use to indicate failures in programs or devices
EVENTLOG_WARNING_TYPE	2	Use to identify potential problem areas, such as low memory, too many processes, and other areas that your computer can temporarily work around
EVENTLOG_INFORMATION_TYPE	4	Use to record programming events
EVENTLOG_AUDIT_SUCCESS	8	Use to record a successful auditable security event, such as logging onto your computer account
EVENTLOG_AUDIT_FAILURE	16	Use to record a failed auditable security event, such as logging onto your computer account

TIP   If you are developing a new application, you can use the **EVENTLOG_ INFORMATION_TYPE** to record the application's progress. When you deliver applications, be sure to limit your logged events.

Both the Read and Report methods modify the interface data between the Perl methods and the native functions. This is one of the primary purposes of any of the Perl 5 wrapper methods. Your code is shielded from the internal data structures of the native methods. Listing 23.8 calls the EventLog method Report on line 18:

```
$eventLog->Report(\%eventRecord);
```

The Report method requires a reference to a hash initialized with the data you want stored into your log file. Converting the data to the native method format is accomplished in the Report method.

Using Other EventLog Methods

Each of the EventLog methods described in the following sections assists in providing a consistent object-oriented interface to the event log. Each method calls a native event log function, passing to the native method the open log file refer-ence, also called a *handle*. The native method performs all additional operations.

Backing Up the Event Log

The Backup method creates a copy of the open event log in the filename passed in the input parameter $fileName. Use the Backup method as shown here:

```
use Win32::EventLog;
$eventLog = Win32::EventLog->new('System') || die $!;
$fileName = 'e:\sybex\MasteringPerl5\SystemLogFile.evt';
$eventLog->Backup($fileName);
```

The backup log file is in log file format and cannot be read with a text editor. Later in this chapter, you will write an extension to the EventLog.pm class so you can read the backup file.

Clearing the Event Log

The Clear method erases the open event log. Use this method only if you want to destroy the contents of your event log.

The Clear method takes an optional $fileName parameter. If a filename is pro-vided to the Clear method, the log file will be copied to the filename. If the file-name refers to a file that already exists, the Clear method will fail. If a filename is not provided, the log file will be erased and a backup copy will not be created. When the log file is cleared, the record number index is reset to one. Use the Clear method as shown here:

```
use Win32::EventLog;
$eventLog = Win32::EventLog->new('Application') || die $!;
$fileName = 'e:\sybex\MasteringPerl5\OldSystemLogFile.evt';
$eventLog->Clear($fileName);
```

Getting the Oldest Record

The GetOldest method returns the record number of the first record in the open event log, which is also the oldest record. This record number is initialized to one. Use the GetOldest method as shown here:

```
use Win32::EventLog;
$eventLog = Win32::EventLog->new('System') || die $!;
$eventLog->GetOldest($totalEvents);
```

Extending the EventLog Class

The EventLog class is missing interfaces to several native methods that you might find useful, three of which are listed in Table 23.9. To create an interface to these native methods, add a call to the native method inside the EventLog class.

TABLE 23.9: Native Event Log Functions

Function	Parameters	Description
OpenBackupEventLog	*LogFileHandle*, *LogFileName*, *ComputerName*	Opens a reference to a backup log file
CloseEventLog	*LogFileHandle*	Closes an open log file handle
RegisterEventSource	*LogFileHandle*, *LogFileName*, *ComputerName*	Opens a reference to the named log file (which must be a valid subkey of a log file entry in the event log Registry keys)

The EventLog class has established the structure of calling the native methods through the AutoLoad method. You can use that structure to add additional native method calls. Listing 23.9 adds two new methods to the EventLog class: Close and OpenBackupFile.

Listing 23.9:   EventLog Class Extension

```
1.   sub Close {
2.      my $self = shift;
3.      my $result = CloseEventLog($self->{'handle'});
4.      $! = Win32::GetLastError() unless ($result);
5.      return $result;
6.   }
7.
8.   sub OpenBackupFile
9.   {
10.      #Get the class name we were instantiated under
11.      my $class = shift;
12.      die "usage: PACKAGE->OpenBackupFile(Backup File Name[,
                 SERVERNAME])\n" unless @_;
```

```
13.    my $source = shift;
14.    my $server = shift;
15.    my $handle;
16.
17.    #Create new handle
18.    OpenBackupEventLog($handle, $server, $source);
19.    my $self = {'handle' => $handle,
20.               'Source' => $source,
21.               'Computer' => $server };
22.    bless $self, $class;
23.    return $self
24. }
```

Both of the methods of Listing 23.9 are simple pass-through functions. The Close method calls the native method CloseEventLog, and the OpenBackupFile method calls the native method OpenBackupEventLog.

Listing 23.10 uses the new methods added in Listing 23.9 to create a backup log file and then read the file. As Listing 23.10 illustrates, the same methods used to read and write to the System file also can be used on the backup log file.

Listing 23.10:   A Backup Log File

```
1.  use Win32::EventLog;
2.  #Define global constants
3.  @months = (Jan, Feb, March, April, May, June,
4.             July, Aug, Sep, Oct, Nov, Dec);
5.  @days = (Sun, Mon, Tue, Wed, Thur, Fri, Sat);
6.  $SEC = 0; $MIN = 1; $HOUR = 2; $DAYOFMONTH= 3;
7.  $MONTH = 4; $YEAR = 5; $WEEKDAY=6;
8.  $separator = ("=" x 60) . "\n";
9.  #Open the System log file
10. $eventLog = Win32::EventLog->new('System') || die $!;
11. %eventRecord = (
12.          'Source'       => 0,
13.          'Computer'     => 0,
14.          'Length'       => 0,
15.          'Category'     => 2, #Warning
16.          'RecordNumber' => 0,
17.          'TimeGenerated'=> 0,
```

```
18.              'Timewritten'  => 0,
19.              'EventID'       => 1442,
20.              'EventType'     => EVENTLOG_INFORMATION_TYPE,
21.              'ClosingRecordNumber' => 0,
22.              'Strings'       => "Last record before copying file",
23.              'Data'          => "This record will be the first record
                                     of the backup file",
24.          );
25. $eventLog->Report(\%eventRecord);
26.
27. $fileName = 'e:\sybex\MasteringPerl5\SystemLogFile.evt';
28. #Create a backup copy of the log file
29. #If this filename exists, the backup method will fail
30. $eventLog->Backup($fileName);
31.
32. %eventRecord = (
33.              'Source'        => 0,
34.              'Computer'      => 0,
35.              'Length'        => 0,
36.              'Category'      => 2, #Warning
37.              'RecordNumber'  => 0,
38.              'TimeGenerated' => 0,
39.              'Timewritten'   => 0,
40.              'EventID'       => 1442,
41.              'EventType'     => EVENTLOG_INFORMATION_TYPE,
42.              'ClosingRecordNumber' => 0,
43.              'Strings'       => "First record after the backup file
                                     created",
44.              'Data'          => "Danger-This Record is Not part of
                                     the backup file",
45.          );
46. $eventLog->Report(\%eventRecord);
47. #Close the System file
48. $eventLog->Close();
49.
50. #Open the backup log file
51. #The methods used on the system file now work on the backup file
52. $eventLog = Win32::EventLog->OpenBackupFile
             ('e:\Sybex\MasteringPerl5\SystemLogFile.evt') || die $!;
53.
54. #Get the current number of events in the event log
```

```
55. $eventLog->GetNumber($totalEvents);
56. #Assign number of records to input or all the records available
57. $numberToRead = ($ARGV[0] > 0 && $ARGV[0] <  $totalEvents) ?
                        $ARGV[0] : $totalEvents;
58. #Turn on bits 1 and 2
59. $readFlag = EVENTLOG_SEEK_READ | EVENTLOG_FORWARDS_READ;
60. #Set the Read index to the latest event
61. for ($eventIndex = $totalEvents;
62.     $eventIndex > $totalEvents - $numberToRead;
63.     $eventIndex-){
64.   my %eventLogData;
65.   #The SEEK and FORWARDS read flags are required.
66.   $eventLog->Read($readFlag, $eventIndex, \%eventLogData);
67.   print "${separator}NEW LOG ENTRY\n$separator";
68.   foreach $logEntry (sort keys %eventLogData){
69.     switch:{
70.       #Format time to human-usable format
71.       if ($logEntry =~ /Time/){
72.         @time = localtime($eventLogData{$logEntry});
73.         for ($timeIndex = 0; $timeIndex < $YEAR;
                  $timeIndex++){
74.           $time[$timeIndex] = sprintf("%02d",
                  $time[$timeIndex]);
75.           $month = $months[$time[$MONTH]];
76.           $day = $days[$time[$WEEKDAY]];
77.         }
78.         print "$logEntry, at $time[$HOUR]:
                                $time[$MIN]:
                                $time[$SEC]
                                on $day $month
                                $time[$DAYOFMONTH]\n";
79.         last switch;
80.       }
81.       #Event ID is double word format. The higher-order
82.       #bits must be cleared or a negative number is assumed
83.       if ($logEntry eq EventID){
84.         $eventLogData{$logEntry} = $eventLogData{$logEntry}
                                                & 0xFFFF;
85.       }
86.       #Now that the data is formatted, print it out
87.       DEFAULT:{
```

```
88.                print qq|$logEntry, $eventLogData{$logEntry}\n|;
89.           }
90.       }#switch
91.    }
92. }
93. $eventLog->Close();
```

Listing 23.10 opens the System log file and writes a new record on line 25:

```
$eventLog->Report(\%eventRecord);
```

Lines 27 through 30 create the backup log file:

```
$fileName = 'e:\sybex\MasteringPerl5\SystemLogFile.evt';
#Create a backup copy of the log file
#If this filename exists, the backup method will fail
$eventLog->Backup($fileName);
```

A second record is then written to the System log file to differentiate the System log file from its earlier copy. Line 48 closes the System log file so the method created in Listing 23.9 can open a handle to the backup log file (multiple references to different log files are permissible):

```
$eventLog->Close();
```

Line 52 opens the backup log file, and the remaining code uses the same interface to the backup log file as created and used for the System log file:

```
$eventLog = Win32::EventLog->OpenBackupFile
            ('e:\Sybex\MasteringPerl5\SystemLogFile.evt') || die $!;
```

Figure 23.11 shows the first two records of the backup log file and the first record of the System log file. Because the System log file was created after the backup log file, the first record of the System log file is not part of the backup log file. The System log file is shown in Figure 23.12. However, the second record of the System log file is equal to the first record of the backup log file, as it should be.

Listing 23.10 is a brief example of modifying a Win32 class, which you can see is within the capabilities of most programmers. Using this example of modifying a Win32 class, you can learn to extend other Win32 classes to suit your particular programming needs.

TIP

You can refer to Win32 documentation for more information about Win32 classes and how to modify them. One of my favorite locations for retrieving Win32 documentation is at http://www.inforoute.cgs.fr/leberrel/perldoc.html.

FIGURE 23.11:

The backup log file

```
Command Prompt

E:\SYBEX\MasteringPerl5>readBackupFile.pl 2
===========================================================
NEW LOG ENTRY
===========================================================
Category, 2
ClosingRecordNumber, 0
Computer, YAWP
Data, This Record will be the First Record of the backup file
EventID, 1442
EventType, 4
Length, 55
RecordNumber, 170
Source, System
Strings, Last record before copying file
TimeGenerated, at 16:28:59 on Mon Nov 16
Timewritten, at 16:28:59 on Mon Nov 16
===========================================================
NEW LOG ENTRY
===========================================================
Category, 0
ClosingRecordNumber, 0
Computer, YAWP
Data,
EventID, 10
EventType, 4
Length, 0
RecordNumber, 169
Source, Print
Strings, 12 Collage Complete Administrator HP DeskJet 560C LPT1: 1440398 1
TimeGenerated, at 16:27:40 on Mon Nov 16
Timewritten, at 16:27:40 on Mon Nov 16
```

FIGURE 23.12:

The System log file

```
Command Prompt

E:\SYBEX\MasteringPerl5>perl readlatestevents.pl 2
===========================================================
NEW LOG ENTRY
===========================================================
Category, 2
ClosingRecordNumber, 0
Computer, YAWP
Data, Danger This Record is Not part of the backup file
EventID, 1442
EventType, 4
Length, 49
RecordNumber, 171
Source, System
Strings, First Record after the Backup File Created
TimeGenerated, at 16:28:59 on Mon Nov 16
Timewritten, at 16:28:59 on Mon Nov 16
===========================================================
NEW LOG ENTRY
===========================================================
Category, 2
ClosingRecordNumber, 0
Computer, YAWP
Data, This Record will be the First Record of the backup file
EventID, 1442
EventType, 4
Length, 55
RecordNumber, 170
Source, System
Strings, Last record before copying file
TimeGenerated, at 16:28:59 on Mon Nov 16
Timewritten, at 16:28:59 on Mon Nov 16
```

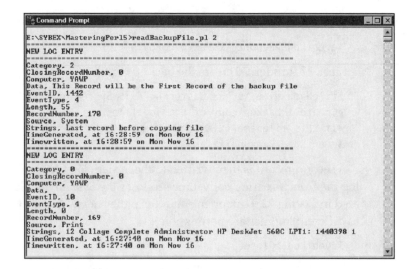

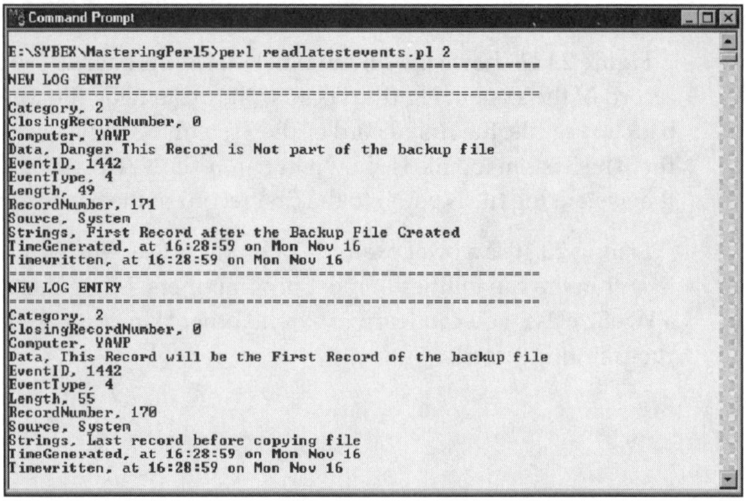

Summary

The Registry is a central database where Windows keeps all of its information about the software and hardware on your computer. The Registry is separated into branches of related information called keys and subkeys. In this chapter, you learned how to read, write, and modify the Registry's keys and values.

You learned that you can use the Win32::Registry module's Open method to create a connection to a Registry key. Once a Registry key is opened, you can use the GetKeys method to read all of the subkeys beneath the opened key. The Close method is used to break the connection with the Registry key. To add keys to the Registry, you use the Create method. To delete a key, use the DeleteKey method.

A Registry key is like a directory on your computer; it doesn't have much use unless it contains information inside the key. This chapter described how to add data to your Registry key with the SetValueEx method and to retrieve that data with the GetValues method.

One of the branches under the HKEY_LOCAL_MACHINE key in your Registry is the EventLog key. The event log acts as a central messaging center for tracking software events. The event log uses the structure of the Registry as a common location for storing information about Application, Security, and System events. Also like the Registry, the event log interface is through a Win32 class, which is called EventLog.

In this chapter, you learned how the EventLog methods allow you to read an event log report, which always contains when the event occurred, the source of the event, and the computer name on which the event occurred. EventLog records must be read through a special interface. The EventLog method Read is used to retrieve records from the event log. Reading from the event log is controlled by a record number and a read mask. Writing to the event log is accomplished through the Report method.

New events are always added in sequential order to a previously opened event log file. The process writing to the event log controls which file the data is recorded into, the event type and category, and additional recorded data, but the time of the event and the event number are controlled by built-in native methods.

The EventLog class, like many of the Win32 classes, is a work in progress. At the end of this chapter, you learned how to extend the EventLog class by adding a Close method and an OpenBackupFile method. These new methods were then used to retrieve information from a backup log file.

# CHAPTER TWENTY-FOUR

Databases and the Web

■ An introduction to database management systems

■ ODBC connections

■ Data importing techniques

■ An introduction to SQL

■ Databases and the Internet

Business applications all seem to have one thing in common: a lot of data. Whether your program deals with sales figures, inventory, employee salary, or any other common business information, the data is made up of rows and columns of names and numbers that need to be sorted, extracted, entered, updated, and manipulated. Once a program collects information, people want to see that data in a variety of forms.

Quite often, you may be tempted to write all the code yourself to sort, track, and store your program's information. You usually end up wishing you had an easy way to meet the growing demands for reports, sorts, and more. The solution is to transfer most of the data manipulation to a database. In this chapter, you will step through the process of importing a growing list of data into a new database.

Ultimately, the Internet is extending into all forms of programming and business applications, and database programming is no exception. Once you have learned how to build and manipulate your database, you'll learn how to export it to the web.

An Introduction to Databases

The data you collect (about your business, your family, your hobbies, and so on) and the medium used to store and organize that data is called a *database*. That means the shoe box of receipts you pull out for the auditor is a database. As your business grows, you may decide you need something more than a shoe box—perhaps a ledger. Later, you may decide to copy the data into a file on your computer. Each of the previous storage mediums represents a database. The problem with those types of databases is that they don't provide any built-in means of automatically sorting, printing, or managing the data. You need a database management system to do these things.

A database management system is a set of tools for managing data in a particular format. You could create your own tool set, or you could buy an existing one. One thing all database management systems include is a database engine. A *database engine* is the application, such as Microsoft Access or Oracle, that manipulates the data in your database. The database engine is the heart of your database management system, and it will usually be either an object-oriented or relational database engine. The object-oriented system, which is gaining in popularity, is still not available on the average desktop PC.

NOTE   The examples in this chapter use Microsoft Access, one of the more popular database engines, but the process applies to all the major database programs available today.

If you have a copy of Microsoft Access on your desktop PC, you have a copy of an inexpensive relational database management system. A relational database is made up of *tables*. Each table contains rows of information about each object stored in the table. A *row* contains data about one object of information, such as an e-mail contact. A row is made up of columns of information that describe an individual object. In an e-mail table, an e-mail contact object would include columns about the e-mail address, the name of the e-mail contact, and other information. In a database table for car data, the car object row would include columns about the make and model of the car, specific options, and other information. Each database file may contain multiple tables, and each table may contain multiple columns.

A single table or multiple tables may also be accessed via a *view*. A view is a logical subset of a table or a combination of tables. The view defines a different way to access, or see, the table's data, but it does not contain data itself. The view allows you to create further logical relationships between tables without creating a second copy of the data. You might create a single view from the relationships between several different contact tables, such as an e-mail contact table, a business contact table, and a party guest contact table.

The ODBC Connection

Are you familiar with Esperanto? Well neither am I, and that's probably because it didn't have the support of every major government in the world. Esperanto was supposed to be the common language of our globe. Are you familiar with ODBC and SQL? If you are a database programmer, the answer is almost certainly yes. That's because ODBC and SQL have the support of every major software company in the world, including Microsoft, Sun, and IBM.

ODBC stands for Open DataBase Connectivity. You can think of it as a universal connector. In this section, you'll learn how to connect your program to your database. SQL (pronounced "sequel"), which stands for Structured Query Language, is the common language that all major databases understand. It will be explained after you are connected to your database.

We'll be using two applications to accomplish this first step: Microsoft Access and `Win32::ODBC`. The module `Win32::ODBC` has become a standard for connecting Win32 applications to various database programs. Its interface to your database engine will be a common thread throughout this chapter.

Creating a DSN

The `Win32::ODBC` module and other ODBC applications connect to your Access database through a Data Source Name (DSN). For ODBC to work across many different database engines, it requires a standard way to communicate with all databases. The DSN contains a common set of information that all databases must supply. You must create the DSN on your computer before you can begin connecting your program to your database.

The DSN supplies the following information:

- The locations of the database
- The type of database driver (Microsoft Access in our example)
- User name and password information

There are two primary types of DSNs:

- A User DSN is accessible by only the account that created it. If you are creating a DSN for your own use, you should create a User DSN.
- A System DSN is accessible by any account. If you are creating a DSN that will be used by multiple users, you should create a System DSN.

The DSN created for this example will eventually be accessed through a web server, so it should be a System DSN.

You can create a DSN through the Windows Control Panel or by using the `Win32::ODBC` module. As a programmer, I prefer the `Win32::ODBC` programmatic method to the GUI interface of the Control Panel, because I can handle the whole process easily through my code. However, I think understanding both the GUI and programmatic interface to a DSN gives you a better concept of the entire process and the links involved. The following sections describe both methods.

Using the Control Panel

To create a DSN for your Access database, open your Control Panel and click on the ODBC icon. In Figure 24.1, the ODBC icon is in the middle of the first line of icons.

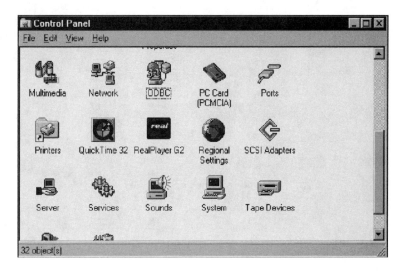

Clicking on the ODBC icon brings up the ODBC Data Source Administrator, which is used to define and configure DSN entries. Select the System DSN tab and then click on the Add button to bring up the Create New Data Source dialog box. In this dialog box, select the specific driver used for your database engine. I have selected the Microsoft Access Driver, as shown in Figure 24.2.

Selecting the Access driver brings up the ODBC Microsoft Access 97 Setup dialog box. Here, you enter the name of your DSN, which is the same name you will use in your program to reference the DSN. You also can enter a brief description of the DSN. Then select the Database radio button in the System Database portion of the dialog box (for a System DSN) and click on the System Database button. The Select System Database dialog box appears, as shown in Figure 24.3. Navigate to the directory that contains your database and select it.

FIGURE 24.2:

Selecting a data source
driver

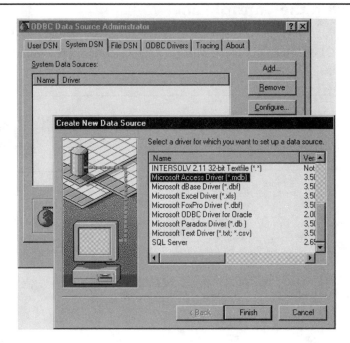

Using the Win32::ODBC Module

To create a DSN via a program, you first need to know what drivers are on your
computer. Listing 24.1 uses the Win32::ODBC module to collect a list of all the
ODBC drivers on your computer and print them to your computer monitor. Figure 24.4 shows the list for my computer.

Listing 24.1:   Getting the ODBC Drivers

```
1.  use Win32::ODBC;
2.  #Get the available drivers
3.  %drivers = Win32::ODBC::Drivers();
4.  #I want to print the driver attributes comma separated
5.  #Load the dynamic copy of array separator with a new separator
6.  local $" = ", ";
7.  foreach $driver (sort keys %drivers){
8.      @attributes = split (/;/,$drivers{$driver});
9.      print "Driver = $driver\n";
10.     print "@attributes\n\n";
11. }
```

FIGURE 24.3:

Selecting the database

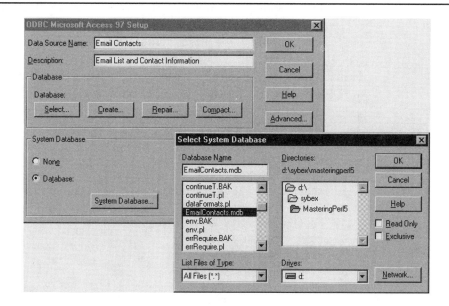

FIGURE 24.4:

Listing the ODBC drivers

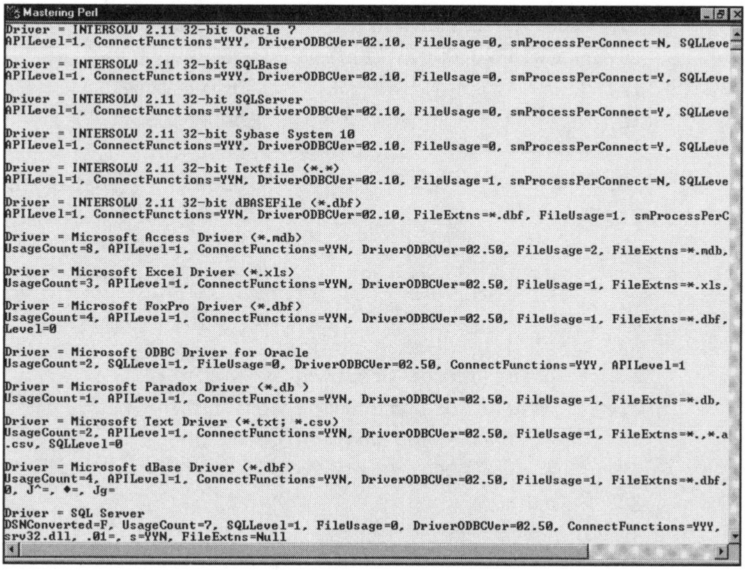

Although Listing 24.1 prints the driver types to screen, I recommend sending the output to file for later reference. When configuring the DSN driver, you must use the exact format of the driver definition. If you created a file of your driver types from Listing 24.1, use the same format captured in the file. I used the driver format returned by Listing 24.1 in the program shown in Listing 24.2 to configure the DSN driver type. Listing 24.2 creates and configures the DSN.

Listing 24.2:   Creating a Data Source Name (DSN)

```
1.  use Cwd;
2.  use Win32::ODBC;
3.  #Define the driver type for this database
4.  $DriverType = "Microsoft Access Driver (*.mdb)";
5.  #Define the Data Source Name
6.  $DSN = "Email Contacts";
7.  #Describe the Data Source Name
8.  #The format is required
9.  $Description = "Description=Email List and Contact Information";
10. #The filename of the database.
11. #This must be created before you can connect to the DSN
12. $DataBase = "EmailContacts.mdb";
13. #Set the directory to current directory
14. $dir = cwd();
15. #Configure the DSN
16. if (Win32::ODBC::ConfigDSN(ODBC_ADD_DSN,
17.                            $DriverType,
18.                            ("DSN=$DSN",
19.                            $Description,
20.                            "DBQ=$dir\\$DataBase",
21.                            "DEFAULTDIR=$dir",
22.                            "UID=", "PWD="))){
23.     print "Successful configuration of $DSN!\n";
24. }
25. else{
26.     print "Error Creating $DSN\n";
27.     #Always use the DumpError routine.
28.     #It tells you what is going on
29.     Win32::ODBC::DumpError();
30.     die;
31. }
32.
33. #Create a Win32::ODBC object
```

```
34. #Lots of Perl programmers use this notation:
35. #$myDBConnection = new Win32::ODBC($DSN);
36. #But I prefer this syntax
37. my $myDb = Win32::ODBC->new($DSN);
38. #Create a lexical that will be accessible outside the else block
39. my $connection;
40. #Verify the connection is valid
41. if (! $myDb){
42.     print "Failed to Connect $DSN\n";
43.     Win32::ODBC::DumpError();
44.     #You can't do anything without a connection so die here
45.     die;
46. }
47. else {
48.     $connection = $myDb->Connection();
49.     print "Successful Connection $connection, $DSN\n";
50. }
51. #Always close the database connection
52. $myDb->Close();
```

Line 4 of Listing 24.2 assigns the driver type, which was retrieved by Listing 24.1, for connecting to the Access database.

```
$DriverType = "Microsoft Access Driver (*.mdb)";
```

The DSN is created on lines 16 through 22:

```
if (Win32::ODBC::ConfigDSN(ODBC_ADD_DSN,
                           $DriverType,
                           ("DSN=$DSN",
                           $Description,
                           "DBQ=$dir\\$DataBase",
                           "DEFAULTDIR=$dir",
                           "UID=", "PWD="))){
```

This uses the common ODBC API (Application Program Interface), ODBC_ADD_
DSN. The parameters, driver type, and DSN definition are common across ODBC
modules. The parameters define the DSN name, description, the location of the
database file, the default directory, and the user name and password assigned to
the DSN. The default directory will be used as a location for writing temporary
working files by Access. Access must have privileges to write into the default
directory.

The database file (emailContacts.mdb in this example) must be created through Access before a connection to the file can be made. The only way I know to do this is by creating a blank database in Access and then saving it to a file. The name of the file is the database parameter to the Win32::ODBC ConfigDSN method, as you can see on lines 12 and 20:

```
$DataBase = "EmailContacts.mdb";
"DBQ=$dir\\$DataBase",
```

Lines 26 through 30 perform error processing for an invalid DSN configuration:

```
print "Error Creating $DSN\n";
#Always use the DumpError routine.
#It tells you what is going on
Win32::ODBC::DumpError();
die;
```

It's relatively easy to corrupt a database. Error processing, which is sometimes overlooked in other applications, should never be ignored. The DumpError routine prints to the selected file handle the error number, text of the error message, and current connection information. I like to include one additional line, such as line 26, which prints a message that tells me what the code was doing when the error occurred.

Once you have created the DSN, you can connect to your new database. Connecting to the database is accomplished on line 37:

```
my $myDb = Win32::ODBC->new($DSN);
```

This line calls the class constructor, which initializes the connection to the Access database.

The last thing this program does is close the connection to the database. This is extremely important with all database applications. An open database is likely to become corrupted. The Win32::ODBC class contains a destructor that disconnects from the database and clears the class's error codes.

The Win32::ODBC module will be used throughout this chapter to connect and manipulate a database. The primary functions of the Win32::ODBC module are explained in the next section. After that, you will learn how to create rows and columns in a database and then insert new data into that database.

The Win32::ODBC Module

Win32::ODBC, written by Dave Roth, is a module extension to Win32 Perl. Dave Roth has created a wonderful set of methods that make connecting to your Win32 database a portable and simple task. Using Win32::ODBC methods, you can connect to your database, create tables, insert data, and retrieve data. Here, you will learn about the more frequently used methods of Win32::ODBC. There are many more methods in the Win32::ODBC class, and I recommend that you read the online documentation.

> **TIP**
>
> You can download the Win32::ODBC module and find further documentation at www.roth.net. Installing the module on your computer is a relatively easy process. Win32::ODBC expects two files to be in the Win32 and odbc subdirectories. Beneath your Perl 5 installation, you have a lib directory. Copy ODBC.pm to C:\Perl5\lib\Win32 and copy ODBC.pll to C:\Per5\lib\auto\Win32\odbc. If the Win32 and auto\Win32\odbc subdirectories do not exist below the lib directory, create them. Both of these files and detailed installation instructions are available at ftp://ftp.roth.net/pub/ntperl and http://www.perl.com/CPAN/ authors/ Dave_Roth.

The close Method

The close method disconnects your program from the database engine. You should always close your database connection. Do not depend on Perl 5 to close the open file handle. Your database engine is likely to have opened working files, which may not be properly closed when your program exits.

The close method requires an object reference as its first and only parameter.

```
$myDb->close();
```

The Data Method

The Data method accesses a data structure internal to the Win32::ODBC module to retrieve the column values of an individual row. The Data method has meaning only after your program has retrieved data from your database through a SQL statement. The Data method retrieves the columns from the current row; use the FetchRow method to get the next row of data.

You can retrieve all the columns of a row in unspecified order like this:

```
lvalue = $myDb->Data();
```

You can retrieve an ordered list of the columns in a row by specifying which columns you wish to retrieve, as in this example:

```
lvalue = $myDb->Data(lastName, firstName, emailAddress);
```

The data will be returned in the same order as requested. If the lvalue is a scalar, the Data method returns the column values in one concatenated string. If the lvalue is a list, the data is returned in list context, where each item in the list is a column value.

```
while ($myDb->FetchRow()){
    ($lastName, $firstName, $emailAddress =
$myDb->Data(lastName, firstName, emailAddress);
    sendLetter($emailAddress, $lastName, $firstName);
}
```

The DataHash Method

The DataHash method accesses an internal data structure to retrieve the column values of an individual row. The DataHash method only has meaning after your program has retrieved data from your database through a SQL statement. The DataHash method retrieves the columns from the current row; use the FetchRow method to get the next row of data.

The DataHash method returns a hash containing the column name and column values of the current row. You can retrieve specific columns by providing the column names, like this:

```
%columnData = $myDb->DataHash(Model, Year, Price);
```

The DataHash method is usually used to retrieve an entire row of data, like this:

```
%columnData = $myDb->DataHash();
```

There is usually very little time and space penalty for retrieving the entire contents of a row using the DataHash method. Because the DataHash method retrieves both the column name and the column value, you can get the entire contents of a row and still access only the columns you need. Later, if you need to change your program to access more or fewer values from the column, you will have the data available without needing to modify your program:

```
while ($myDb->FetchRow()){
    %model = $myDb->DataHash();
    print<<"EOF";
    <tr>
```

```
        <td Align=left>$model{model}
        <td Align=left>$model{year}
        <td Align=left>$model{price}
        <td Align=left width=70%>$model{comments}
    </tr>
EOF
}
```

The DumpError Method

Though you don't really want to see the response from the DumpError method (because it means your program has a bug), it should be liberally sprinkled throughout your code. Use the DumpError method to verify the successful completion of every call to your database engine.

The DumpError method prints a formatted output, showing which database connection produced the error, the error number, and the text of the error message, returned by the database engine. The DumpError method prints error information about the last error condition, which may not be instance-specific. The DumpError method prints only the last error message. Usually, that message is related to the last error your object created. If the error your object created did not cause a new error message, the message printed will be the last error message created, even though it may not be relevant to the error your object created. You can use the DumpError method with an object reference or class notation, like this:

```
#class notation calling syntax
Win32::ODBC::DumpError();

#object reference calling syntax
$myDb->DumpError();
```

The DumpError method tells you information about the type of error but it doesn't tell you where the error occurred in your program. Listing 24.3 illustrates a method of calling the DumpError method that tracks when your program was running and what your code was doing at the time the error occurred. Listing 24.4 shows the output when an error occurred from running Listing 24.3.

Listing 24.3:   **Calling DumpError**

```
1.   #Log the errors to file for later review
2.   #The filename will be unique because the Process ID is
3.   #appended using the special variable $$
```

```
4.   open (ERRORFILE, ">errorList$$.txt") || die ;
5.   (@times) = localtime(time);
6.   #Date the file
7.   $time = $times[2] . ':' . $times[1] . ':' . $times[0];
8.   select ERRORFILE;
9.   print  "$time\n";
10.
11.  $SQLStatment = qq|Create Table $make (ad_ID char(20) NOT NULL,
12.                                         model char(20) NOT NULL,
13.                                         year Integer,
14.                                         price Integer,
15.                                         phone char(10),
16.                                         comments char(80))|;
17.  if ($myDb->Sql($SQLStatment)){
18.     print  "error creating table $make\n";
19.     $myDb->DumpError();
20.  }
```

Listing 24.4:   **Output from Calling DumpError**

```
15:52:15
error creating table Buick

----- Error Report: -----
Errors for "16" on connection 1:
Connection Number: 1
Error number: -1303
Error message: "[Microsoft][ODBC Microsoft Access 97 Driver] Table
'Buick' already exists."
--------------------
```

The FetchRow Method

The FetchRow method retrieves the next row of data from the latest SQL query of your database. The FetchRow method must be used with an object reference, which points to a valid ODBC connection:

```
my $myDb = Win32::ODBC->new($DSN);
$myDb->FetchRow();
```

The FetchRow method populates an internal data structure. After calling the FetchRow method, you must call either the Data or DataHash method to retrieve the column values of a row. The FetchRow method returns undef if there is an error or no more data to retrieve, which makes it suitable for use in a while loop, like this:

```
while ($myDb->FetchRow()){
    %model = $myDb->DataHash();
```

The new Method

The new method is the Win32::ODBC class constructor. The new method takes one parameter, a valid DSN, and returns an ODBC object reference:

```
my $myDb = Win32::ODBC->new("Auto Ads");
```

The ODBC object reference is then used to communicate further ODBC commands to the connected database

If the new method fails, it returns undef. Always check the result returned by the new method. If an invalid result is returned, your best solution is to print or log the error message and exit your program:

```
my $myDb = Win32::ODBC->new($DSN);
#Verify the connection is valid
if (! $myDb){
    print "Failed to Connect $DSN\n";
    Win32::ODBC::DumpError();
    #You can't do anything without a connection so die here
    die;
}
else {
    print "Connected to $DSN\n";
}
```

The RowCount Method

Sometimes, you just want to count the number of rows in a table. The quickest method to accomplish this task is the RowCount method. The RowCount method returns the number of rows that were traversed by the last SQL command:

```
$myDb->Sql($SQL)
$numberOfRows = $myDb->RowCount();
```

NOTE   The **RowCount** method is an ODBC extension and may not work for all database engines.

The Sql Method

The Sql method is the real workhorse of the **Win32::ODBC** class, but it really isn't an ODBC command. The Sql method makes a call to **ODBCExecute**, which passes the SQL statement to the database:

```
$SQL = "Select model, year, price, comments From $cars{Make} ";
if ($myDb->Sql($SQL)){
        $prevFH = select(ERRORFILE);
        print "Error selecting car make.\n";
        Win32::ODBC::DumpError();
        select ($prevFH);
    }
```

The Sql method returns **undef** on success. This means your error-checking syntax is reversed. Instead of checking for a positive response to indicate success, you check for a positive response to indicate failure. In the example above, the error-handling code will be called when anything other than **undef** is returned by the Sql method.

Existing Data

I can type, but it is an error-prone operation that takes way too much time. If you already have your database information in some type of electronic media, manually entering it into a database table should be one of your last options. With Perl 5, **Win32::ODBC**, and a little SQL, you can import your data into a new database in a matter of moments.

Creating a Database Table

A database makes it easy to keep track of all sorts of information. For example, I used to keep my e-mail contact list in Netscape Messenger. My data in Netscape Messenger was simple—just an e-mail address and a name for each contact.

However, once I had a database, I decided to put my list there and track several additional items.

Listing 24.5 creates an e-mail contact table in the emailContact.mdb Access database.

Listing 24.5:   Creating a Database Table

```
1.  use Win32::ODBC;
2.
3.  #Define the Data Source Name
4.  $DSN = "Email Contacts";
5.
6.  #Create a Win32::ODBC object
7.  #Lots of Perl programmers use this notation:
8.  #$myDBConnection = new Win32::ODBC($DSN);
9.  #But I prefer this syntax
10. my $myDb = Win32::ODBC->new($DSN);
11. #Verify the connection is valid
12. if (! $myDb){
13.    print "Failed to Connect $DSN\n";
14.    Win32::ODBC::DumpError();
15.    #You can't do anything without a connection so die here
16.    die;
17. }
18.
19. #Create the table rows and columns
20. #This statement should be run only once during initialization
21. $SQLStatment = qq|Create Table emailContacts
                                (address char(40) NOT NULL,
22.                              lastName char(20),
23.                              firstName char(10),
24.                              MI char (2))|;
25.
26. if ($myDb->Sql($SQLStatment)){
27.    print "Error creating the initial Table\n";
28.    Win32::ODBC->DumpError();
29. }
30.
31. #Always close the database connection
32. $myDb->Close();
```

Lines 21 through 24 illustrate how to create a SQL statement for the Win32::ODBC Sql method:

```
$SQLStatment = qq|Create Table emailContacts(address char(40) NOT NULL,
                                             lastName char(20),
                                             firstName char(10),
                                             MI char (2))|;
```

I prefer to use the quote operators, which allow me the freedom to define the SQL statement on several lines. (The SQL Create command and other SQL commands will be explained in the next section.)

Importing Text Data

Listing 24.6 imports a text file into the table created in Listing 24.5. You'll learn how to add columns to database tables later, so it doesn't matter if this table doesn't have all the items you might want in a normal contact list.

Listing 24.6:   **Importing Text Data**

```
1.  use Win32::ODBC;
2.  if ($#ARGV < 0){
3.     die "You must enter the contact list file name as the first
           argument";
4.  }
5.  #Define the Data Source Name
6.  $DSN = "Email Contacts";
7.
8.  #Create a Win32::ODBC object
9.  #Lots of Perl programmers use this notation:
10. #$myDBConnection = new Win32::ODBC($DSN);
11. #But I prefer this syntax
12. my $myDb = Win32::ODBC->new($DSN);
13. #Verify the connection is valid
14. if (! $myDb){
15.    print "Failed to Connect $DSN\n";
16.    Win32::ODBC::DumpError();
17.    #You can't do anything without a connection so die here
18.    die;
19. }
20.
21. #Read the contact data in and add it to the new table
```

```
22. open (CONTACTS, "<$ARGV[0]") ||
            die "Invalid file name specified: $ARGV[0]";
23. @contacts = <CONTACTS>;
24. close (CONTACTS);
25. #Log the errors to file for later review
26. #The filename will be unique because the process ID is
27. #appended using the special variable $$
28. open (ERRORFILE, ">errorList$$.txt") || die;
29. (@times) = localtime(time);
30. #Date the file
31. $time = $times[2] . ':' . $times[1] . ':' . $times[0];
32. print ERRORFILE "$time\n";
33.
34. #Read each line of the contact list and add it to the database
35. foreach $contact (@contacts){
36.    ($firstName, $MI, $lastName, $emailAddress) =
            split(/:/,$contact);
37.    chomp $emailAddress;
38.    #Insert the contact list into the emailContacts table
39.    $SQL = qq|Insert Into emailContacts ( address,
40.                                    firstName,  MI, lastName)
41.                      Values ('$emailAddress',
42.                              '$firstName',
43.                              '$MI',
44.                              '$lastName')|;
45.    if ($myDb->Sql($SQL)){
46.       #Force the output from DumpError into the error file
47.       $prevFH = select(ERRORFILE);
48.       print "Error Creating emailContacts\n";
49.       Win32::ODBC::DumpError();
50.       select ($prevFH);
51.    }
52. }
53.
54. close (ERRORFILE);
55.
56. #Always close the database connection
57. $myDb->Close();
```

Line 22 of Listing 24.6 reads from the command line the name of the file that contains the e-mail contact information:

```
open (CONTACTS, "<$ARGV[0]") ||  die "Invalid file name specified:
$ARGV[0]";
```

Because you may be importing a large amount of data, this program creates a file for collecting errors. The file is initialized with a time stamp on line 32, so you can distinguish between import runs. The time stamp uses the `localtime` function (on line 29). This function returns an array of information based on the current time, which is returned by the `time` function:

```
(@times) = localtime(time);
```

The array that is returned by the `localtime` function is time formatted in the order shown here:

- The seconds from 0 to 60

- The minutes from 0 to 60

- The hour of the day from 1 to 12

- The day of the month from 1 to 31

- The month of the year from 0 to 11

- The year in four-digit format

- The day of the week from 0 to 6

- The day of the year from 1 to 365

- Whether or not it is daylight saving time (1 indicates true)

This time is formatted into an hours, minutes, seconds format on line 31:

```
$time = $times[2] . ':' . $times[1] . ':' . $times[0];
```

Each error file is also given a unique name by appending the special variable `$$`, which contains the process ID, to the filename (on line 28):

```
open (ERRORFILE, ">errorList$$.txt") || die;
```

This program then connects to the DSN and begins adding data to the e-mail contacts database on lines 39 through 45:

```
$SQL = qq|Insert Into emailContacts (address,
                                    firstName,  MI, lastName)
                    Values ('$emailAddress',
                               '$firstName',
```

```
                                    '$MI',
                                    '$lastName')|;
         if ($myDb->Sql($SQL)){
```

Lines 39 through 44 take the data retrieved from the contact list file and create a SQL statement from the data. You may notice that the column names listed first are not in the same order as they are stored in the database. If you list the names of the columns first in a SQL Insert statement, the values will be inserted into the table in the correct order. Running Listing 24.6 imports from a file into the emailContacts table, as shown in Figure 24.5.

FIGURE 24.5:

Imported Microsoft Access data

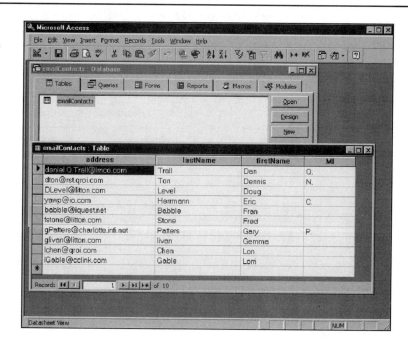

SQL is a large part of interacting with any database. The next section provides an introduction to SQL.

SQL—The Database Language

SQL is a programming language designed specifically for database operations, and it is a common language among many database engines.

You can do almost any database task with SQL, but sometimes it can be a little cumbersome. To make SQL easier to use, most database engines extend SQL. These SQL extensions create unique dialects of SQL that are no longer portable between the various database engines. The ability to use the same queries between different database engines is the entire purpose of SQL, so I urge you to avoid SQL extensions whenever possible.

The common form of SQL is called ANSI-SQL. Like every other programming language, SQL has data types, keywords, and operators. Table 24.1 shows the subset of the ANSI-SQL data types that are compatible with the Microsoft Access database engine. The data types are used to define the columns of data that make up a table.

TABLE 24.1: ANSI-SQL and Access Compatible Data Types

ANSI SQL	Access SQL Equivalent	Description
BIT, BIT VARYING	BINARY	A Boolean data type (True/False)
DATE, TIME, TIMESTAMP	DATETIME	A data type for date-specific operations
REAL	SINGLE	A single-precision real number
DOUBLE PRECISION, FLOAT DOUBLE	FLOAT, FLOAT8	A double-precision real number
SMALLINT	SHORT	A small integer, usually two bytes
INTEGER	LONG	A long integer, usually two words
CHARACTER, CHARACTER VARYING	TEXT	Character strings

The following sections provide a brief overview of using SQL to create tables and to manipulate tables and the data that they contain.

The file that contains the 1993 definition of ANSI-SQL is more than 3000 lines long, without comments. Here, you will spend only a few pages learning about the most common SQL commands. If you want to learn more about SQL, I recommend three resources: the Internet, your local bookstore, and the help function of Microsoft Access or the database engine of your choice.

Creating a Table

You create a table using the `Create Table` SQL statement. The syntax of the `Create Table` statement is:

```
Create Table tableName (columnNameList)
```

The table name should be a single string of alphanumeric characters. The column name list is a comma-separated list that defines the column names, their data types, and constraints on the column. Column names may include spaces; if the name has spaces, surround it with single quotes. The valid constraints on a column are listed in Table 24.2.

TABLE 24.2: Column Constraints

Constraint	Description	Example
Check	Before the column's data is added, it is validated. If the data does not pass validation, it is not added to the row.	`Price Integer Check (Price > 1000)`
Default	When a new object is added to the table, any columns that are not filled in will be assigned their default value.	`Salary Real Default = 28000.42`
Foreign Key	Declares this column as a foreign key. A foreign key creates a relationship between two or more tables.	`ad_id char (20) Foreign Key References UsedCars`
NOT NULL	Generates an error if the column data is not assigned a value. (NULL is also a constraint, but it is the default for all columns.)	`Year Integer Not Null`
Primary Key	Declares this column as the table's primary key. A primary key must be a unique value	`emailAddress char (60) Primary Key`
Unique	Prevents the same column in two rows from containing the same value.	`nickName char(20) Unique`

As an example, Listing 24.7 creates a set of tables for the headings in the transportation section of a newspaper's classified ads. When I ran this program against my local newspaper online classified section, it produced the tables shown in Figure 24.6.

Listing 24.7: **Creating Transportation Tables**

```perl
1.  use Win32::ODBC;
2.
3.  #Define the Data Source Name
4.  $DSN = "Auto Ads";
5.
6.  #Create a Win32::ODBC object
7.  #Lots of Perl programmers use this notation:
8.  #$myDBConnection = new Win32::ODBC($DSN);
9.  #But I prefer this syntax
10. my $myDb = Win32::ODBC->new($DSN);
11.
12. #Verify the connection is valid
13. if (! $myDb){
14.    print "Failed to Connect $DSN\n";
15.    Win32::ODBC::DumpError();
16.    #You can't do anything without a connection so die here
17.    die;
18. }
19. else {
20.    print "Connected to $DSN\n";
21. }
22.
23. #Read the classified section
24. open (ADS, "<$ARGV[0]") || die "Invalid file as first param
                                  $ARGV[0], $!";
25. @ads = <ADS>;
26. close ADS;
27.
28. #Log the errors to file for later review
29. #The filename will be unique because the process ID is
30. #appended using the special variable $$
31. open (ERRORFILE, ">errorList$$.txt") || die;
32. (@times) = localtime(time);
33. #Date the file
```

```
34. $time = $times[2] . ':' . $times[1] . ':' . $times[0];
35. print ERRORFILE "$time\n";
36. select ERRORFILE;
37. for ($i=0; $i<=$#ads; $i++){
38.     #Match the transportation line
39.     #Classified file has unique header before each car info line
40.     if ($ads[$i] =~ /^\d+\s+-\s+(.*)<\/a>/){
41.         $make = $1;
42.         #Remove commas and spaces
43.         $make =~ s/[,\s]//g;
44.         #Create the table rows and columns
45.         #This statement should be run only once during initialization
46.         #If the table already exists, it's okay
47.         #Creating the table will fail but processing can continue
48.         $SQLStatment = qq|Create Table $make
                                        (ad_ID char(20) NOT NULL,
49.                                      model char(20) NOT NULL,
50.                                      year Integer,
51.                                      price Integer,
52.                                      phone char(10),
53.                                      comments char(80))|;
54.     if ($myDb->Sql($SQLStatment)){
55.         print ERRORFILE "error creating table $make\n";
56.         $myDb->DumpError();
57.     }
58.     }
59. }
60. close ERRORFILE;
61. $myDb->Close();
```

Lines 48 through 53 create the tables shown in Figure 24.6:

```
$SQLStatment = qq|Create Table $make (ad_ID char(20) NOT NULL,
                                      model char(20) NOT NULL,
                                      year Integer,
                                      price Integer,
                                      phone char(10),
                                      comments char(80))|;
```

Each table will contain information about a specific transportation heading.

Modifying a Table

Once you create a table, its column definitions can be modified, deleted, and added to with the `Alter Table` statement. Only one column definition may be changed per `Alter Table` statement. The syntax of the `Alter Table` statement is:

```
Alter Table tableName modifyType columnDefinition
```

FIGURE 24.6:

Transportation tables

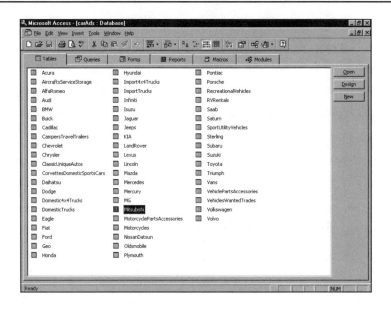

The table name must already exist in the database. The modify type can be one of three values shown in Table 24.3. The column definition follows the same rules as defined in the previous section.

TABLE 24.3: Alter Table Modify Types

Type	Description	Example
Add	Adds a new column to the table	`Alter Table emailContacts Add ('Last Contact' Date)`
Drop	Deletes a column from an existing table	`Alter Table emailContacts Drop (MI)`
Modify	Modifies the column definition	`Alter Table emailContacts Modify (emailAddress char (80))`

The following code adds the last contact date to the emailContacts database:

```
$SQLStatment = qq|Alter Table emailContacts
                    Add (lastContact Date Default = LastUpdated)|;
if ($myDb->Sql($SQLStatment)){
   print ERRORFILE "error adding Column lastContact\n";
   $myDb->DumpError();
}
```

NOTE   The `LastUpdated` function used in the `Default` statement may not be available in all database engines.

Inserting Data into a Table

A database, no matter how well defined, is useless without data. To add data to your database table, use the `Insert Into` statement. This statement has the following syntax:

```
Insert Into tableName (columnNameList) Values (valueList)
```

The column name list is an optional parameter that allows you to insert the values in a row in any order. The column name list is an unordered list of the names of the columns in the named table. The values in the value list will be inserted into the table in a one-to-one correspondence with the column order defined in the column name list. The column name list does not need to name all of the columns in a table; any missing column names will be filled in with their default values.

For example, suppose that you created a table with First, Middle, and Last Name columns (in that order), but you have data on only the first and last names. You could use the `Insert Into` statement to add the data like this:

```
$SQL = qq|Insert Into emailContacts (Last, First)
            Values ('$lastName', '$firstName')|;
```

The single quotes are required in the value list when using the `Insert Into` statement with `Win32::ODBC` and Microsoft Access. Single quotes are only used on text column data, however.

Deleting Data from a Table

Most databases will grow to unmanageable sizes if they don't receive regular maintenance. To delete rows from a database, use the `Delete From` statement. Its syntax is:

```
Delete From tableName Where selectionCriteriaList
```

The selection criteria list is a list of column names and relational operators that define the matching criteria used to select a row for deletion. The selection criteria may be several expressions connected by the logical operators. Table 24.4 lists the relational and logical operators.

TABLE 24.4: Relational and Logical Operators

Operator	Meaning
=	Equality
>	Greater than
<	Less than
>=	Greater than or equal to
<=	Less than or equal to
!=	Not equal
And	Logical AND
Not	Logical NOT
Or	Logical OR

As an example, Listing 24.8 deletes all of the rows in the tables of the Auto Ads DSN whose date is 10 days old or older or whose sold column is True.

Listing 24.8:   Deleting the Sold and the Old

```
1.  use Win32::ODBC;
2.  open (OUTFILE, ">searchCars.htm");
3.  select (OUTFILE);
4.  #Define the Data Source Name
```

```
5.   $DSN = "Auto Ads";
6.
7.   #Create a Win32::ODBC object
8.   my $myDb = Win32::ODBC->new($DSN);
9.
10.  #Verify the connection is valid
11.  if (! $myDb){
12.      print "Failed to Connect $DSN\n";
13.      Win32::ODBC::DumpError();
14.      #You can't do anything without a connection so die here
15.      die;
16.  }
17.  @makes = $myDb->TableList;
18.  (@times) = localtime(time);
19.  #Date is stored in the tables as a day of year and year
20.  $oldDay = $times[7] - 10;
21.  $year = $times[5];
22.  #If we are in a new year, back up to the previous year
23.  if ($oldDay < 1){
24.      $oldDay += 365;
25.      $year-;
26.  }
27.  foreach $make (@makes){
28.      $SQL = qq|Delete From $make Where (
29.                              (Day <= $oldDay AND Year = $year)
30.                              OR Sold = True)|;
31.      if ($myDb->Sql($SQL)){
32.         print "Error deleting from $make, $oldDay, $year\n";
33.         $myDb->DumpError();
34.      }
35.  }
36.  $myDb->Close();
```

Lines 28 through 30 of Listing 24.8 delete the items:

```
$SQL = qq|Delete From $make Where (
                        (Day <= $oldDay AND Year = $year)
                        OR Sold = True)|;
```

Note that comparisons are made to the columns Day and Year, which are integer in format. If you are comparing character data, be sure to place single quotes around the actual data values.

Updating Data in a Table

To update a column in a table, you use the `Update` statement. The `Update` statement requires that you define which column you are going to modify and the new value to place in the column. You may also define selection criteria to select a particular column for updating. If you do not define selection criteria, all the columns in the table will be updated. The syntax of the `Update` statement is:

```
Update tableName Set columnNameValueList Where selectionCriteria
```

The column-name value list is a comma-separated list of column names and the new value. A single column-name value pair looks like this:

```
columnName=value
```

For example, suppose that you just sent an e-mail message to all of the recipients on your contact list and you want to update the last contact date. You could use this program fragment, which updates all of the rows in the emailContacts table to the current year and current day of the year:

```
(@times) = localtime(time);
#Date is stored in the tables as a day of year and year
$day = $times[7] ;
$year = $times[5];
$SQL = qq|Update emailContacts Set Day = $day, Year = $year|;
```

Selecting Data from a Table

Now that you've created your table and filled it with useful data, you need some way to retrieve all that information. The SQL statement for retrieving data is the `Select` statement. The basic syntax of the `Select` statement is:

```
Select (columnList) From (tableList) selectionCriteria
```

You can use functions, selection criteria, predicates, and more in the column list. The table list may be one or more tables or views. The selection criteria are used to determine which rows of the table the `Select` statement will return. The selection criteria may be a combination of one or more of the criteria clauses listed in Table 24.5.

TABLE 24.5: Selection Criteria Clauses

Keyword	Syntax	Description
Group By	Group By *columns*	Combines rows with the same values in the **Group By** *columns* into a single row.
Having	Having *conditionalExpression*	Used with the **Group By** criteria, returns only the records that meet the **Having** conditional expression.
Like	Like *partialString*%	Used in the **Where** clause as a wildcard to select all strings that match the partial string value. You may use multiple percent signs and multiple partial strings to create a pattern.
Order By	Order By *columnName* ASC|DESC	Returns the selected data in ascending or descending order, ordered by the data in the named column. The default is ascending.
Where	Where *conditionalExpression*	Returns the data that meets the criteria in the conditional expression.

For example, to select all the models in a table ordered by model, year, and price, you would use the following Select statement:

```
$SQL = qq| Select model, year, price, comments From $cars{Make}
                    Order By Model, Year, Make|;
```

NOTE   There are many variations on the basic Select statement. For more information on this and other SQL statements, you can refer to the resources mentioned earlier—the Internet, a book devoted to SQL, or the help function for your database engine.

Your Database and the Internet

In this section, you will create an Internet connection to the transportation database created in Listing 24.7. You will step through each phase of this project, importing the data, querying for data from the web, and displaying the data on the Internet. The database is a live connection to a Microsoft Access database engine through the Internet Information Server (IIS) 3.0.

This application uses the standard ODBC APIs and ANSI-SQL. Because we use these standards, changing to another database engine such as FoxPro or a low-cost Unix solution like MiniSQL will require only a few changes in the program. Your computer requires a little setup to deal with the idiosyncrasies of the Microsoft Access database, so you will begin by taking care of that setup.

Setting Up for Access and the Web

If you plan on displaying or updating your data through Microsoft's IIS, make sure you give it read and write access to the directories and subdirectories where your database is located. The Microsoft Access database engine needs to write working files out to your disk when you access and update your database. Access must have the privileges necessary to create and delete these temporary files. When your program is accessed from the web, Access will be running under the privileges of your web server, which will be named something like IUSR_MAIN. You must explicitly add read and write access through the Properties window for the Web Server User.

NOTE   This code was tested with the Microsoft IIS server, which runs on Windows NT.

To explicitly set the permissions for a directory, first select the directory in Windows Explorer, then select the Properties option from the File menu, as shown in Figure 24.7.

From the Properties dialog box, select the Security tab and click on the Permissions button. This brings up the Directory Permissions dialog box. Check the Replace Permissions on Subdirectories and Replace Permission on Existing Files checkboxes at the top of the dialog box, as shown in Figure 24.8. Then click on the Add button at the bottom of the dialog box to display the Add Users and Groups dialog box, as shown in Figure 24.9.

Search through the list until you find your web server. You may need to change the List Names From selection (use the drop-down list box). You also may need to click on the Show Users button in the middle of the window. Give the web server (named something like IUSR_MAIN) full control over the directory in which your database file is located. Because you are giving open access to this directory, I recommend separating this directory from your regular directory tree.

FIGURE 24.7:

Selecting directory
properties

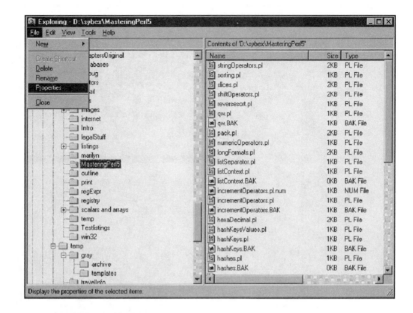

FIGURE 24.8:

Setting directory
permissions

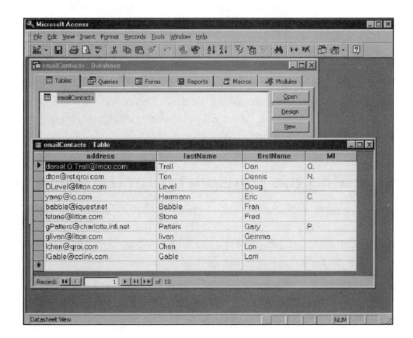

FIGURE 24.9:

Adding users

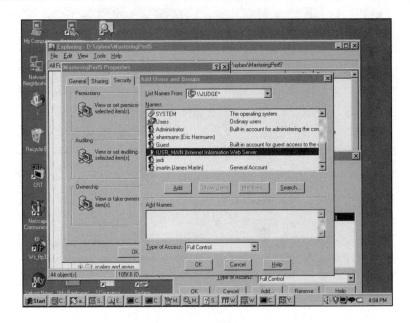

Once you click on OK from the Add Users and Groups dialog box, you should select OK and continue to answer Yes at each of the several confirmation dialog boxes.

In the following examples, Access is executed through a web server. Access writes temporary working files and then later deletes them from the directory where your database file is located. This means the web server must have full control of the directory (and subdirectories) that contains your Access database files, which you have just set up.

Initializing the Transportation Database

The first step after design is creating the DSN and the tables that will be populated with your database's data. For this example, I accessed the classified section of my local online newspaper and downloaded a transportation list. I used this list as an input to Listing 24.9.

Listing 24.9 creates the DSN and adds a new table for each transportation entry in the input file. If the DSN or a table exists, Access returns an error, but processing on other tables continues.

Listing 24.9:   **Initializing the Transportation Database**

```
1.  use Cwd;
2.  use Win32::ODBC;
3.  #Define the driver type for this database
4.  $DriverType = "Microsoft Access Driver (*.mdb)";
5.  #Define the Data Source Name
6.  $DSN = "Auto Ads";
7.  #Describe the Data Source Name
8.  #The format is required
9.  $Description = "Description=Transportation Classifieds";
10. #The filename of the database.
11. #This must be created before you can connect to the DSN
12. $DataBase = "carAds.mdb";
13. #Set the directory to current directory
14. $dir = cwd();
15. #Configure the DSN
16. if (Win32::ODBC::ConfigDSN(ODBC_ADD_DSN,
17.                           $DriverType,
18.                           ("DSN=$DSN",
19.                           $Description,
20.                           "DBQ=$dir\\$DataBase",
21.                           "DEFAULTDIR=$dir",
22.                           "UID=", "PWD="))){
23.    print "Successful configuration of $DSN!\n";
24. }
25. else{
26.    print "Error Creating $DSN\n";
27.    #Always use the DumpError routine.
28.    #It tells you what is going on
29.    Win32::ODBC::DumpError();
30.    die;
31. }
32.
33. #Create a Win32::ODBC object
34. my $myDb = Win32::ODBC->new($DSN);
35. #Verify the connection is valid
36. if (! $myDb){
37.    print "Failed to Connect $DSN\n";
38.    Win32::ODBC::DumpError();
39.    #You can't do anything without a connection so die here
```

```perl
40.    die;
41. }
42. else {
43.    #I like giving myself confirmation that things are going well
44.    print "Connected to $DSN\n";
45. }
46.
47. #Read the classified section
48. open (ADS, "<$ARGV[0]") || die "Invalid file as first param
                                    $ARGV[0], $!";
49. @ads = <ADS>;
50. close ADS;
51.
52. #Log the errors to file for later review
53. #The filename will be unique because the process ID is
54. #appended using the special variable $$
55. open (ERRORFILE, ">errorList$$.txt") || die ;
56. (@times) = localtime(time);
57. #Date the file
58. $time = $times[2] . ':' . $times[1] . ':' . $times[0];
59. print ERRORFILE "$time\n";
60. select ERRORFILE;
61.
62. for ($i=0; $i<=$#ads; $i++){
63.    #Match the transportation line
64.    #Classified file has unique header before each car info line
65.    if ($ads[$i] =~ /^\d+\s+-\s+(.*)<\/a>/){
66.       my $make = $1;
67.       #Remove commas and spaces
68.       $make =~ s/[,\s]//g;
69.       #Create the table rows and columns
70.       #This statement should be run only once during initialization
71.       #if the table already exists, it's okay
72.       #Creating the table will fail but processing can continue
73.       $SQLStatment = qq|Create Table make
                                    (ad_ID char(20) NOT NULL,
74.                                 model char(20) NOT NULL,
75.                                 year Integer,
76.                                 price Integer,
77.                                 phone char(10),
78.                                 comments char(80))|;
79.       if ($myDb->Sql($SQLStatment)){
```

```
80.                print ERRORFILE "error creating table $make\n";
81.                $myDb->DumpError();
82.        }
83.     }
84. }
85. close ERRORFILE;
86. $myDb->Close();
```

This program expects to be run in the same directory as the Access database and will fail if this is not true. The directory is explicitly set using the cwd() method of the Cwd class on line 14:

```
$dir = cwd();
```

The DSN is created beginning on lines 16 through 22:

```
if (Win32::ODBC::ConfigDSN(ODBC_ADD_DSN,
                           $DriverType,
                           ("DSN=$DSN",
                           $Description,
                           "DBQ=$dir\\$DataBase",
                           "DEFAULTDIR=$dir",
                           "UID=", "PWD="))){
```

Once the DSN is created, the transportation list is read into memory on lines 48 and 49:

```
open (ADS, "<$ARGV[0]") || die "Invalid file as first param
                          $ARGV[0], $!";
@ads = <ADS>;
close ADS;
```

Each transportation table is created between lines 63 through 78. The transportation file has a unique header format that looks like this:

```
1930 - Aircrafts, Service, Storage</a>
```

which is matched by the regular expression on line 65:

```
if ($ads[$i] =~ /^\d+\s+-\s+(.*)<\/a>/){
```

The type of transportation item is saved in a back reference variable, which is stored into a lexical variable on line 66:

```
my $make = $1;
```

A database table name in Access should not contain spaces or commas, so these offending characters are removed on line 68:

```
$make =~ s/[,\s]//g;
```

Once the data is formatted correctly, the SQL statement to create each new table is generated on lines 73 through 78:

```
$SQLStatment = qq|Create Table $make (ad_ID char(20) NOT NULL,
    model char(20) NOT NULL, year Integer, price Integer,
    phone char(10), comments char(80))|;
```

Line 79 executes the SQL statement through the `Win32::ODBC Sql` method:

```
if ($myDb->Sql($SQLStatment)){
```

If an error occurs, it is logged but processing continues:

```
    print ERRORFILE "error creating table $make\n";
    $myDb->DumpError();
}
```

Now that the tables have been created for our transportation database, we need to import the data into each transportation table, which is accomplished in the next section.

Importing Data into the Transportation Database

You will populate the database tables with today's classified ads. To load the tables, I downloaded the transportation listings and then ran the files through Listing 24.10, which uses the `Insert Into` SQL statement to load each transportation table with data. When I ran Listing 24.10 on the Mitsubishi classified listings, it produced the table shown in Figure 24.10.

Listing 24.10:   Importing the Transportation Data

```
1.  use Win32::ODBC;
2.  #Define the Data Source Name
3.  $DSN = "Auto Ads";
4.  #Create a Win32::ODBC object
5.  my $myDb = Win32::ODBC->new($DSN);
6.  #Verify the connection is valid
7.  if (! $myDb){
8.     print "Failed to Connect $DSN\n";
```

```
9.    Win32::ODBC::DumpError();
10.   #You can't do anything without a connection so die here
11.   die;
12. }
13.
14. #Read the classified section
15. open (ADS, "<$ARGV[0]") || die "Invalid file as first param
                                    $ARGV[0], $!";
16. @ads = <ADS>;
17. close ADS;
18.
19. #Log the errors to file for later review
20. #The filename will be unique because the process ID is
21. #appended using the special variable $$
22. open (ERRORFILE, ">errorList$$.txt") || die;
23. (@times) = localtime(time);
24. #Date the file
25. $time = $times[2] . ':' . $times[1] . ':' . $times[0];
26. print ERRORFILE "$time\n";
27.
28. for ($i=0; $i<=$#ads; $i++){
29.     #Match the transportation line
30.     #Classified file has unique header before each car info line
31.     if ($ads[$i] =~ /TRANSPORTATION\s+-\s+(\w+)H/){
32.         my $make = $1;
33.         #Get the next line that has the car data
34.         my $carLine = $ads[++$i];
35.         #This regular expression pulls the relevant info from an ad
36.         #All the ads list the year model price and phone number
37.         #If an ad doesn't have this info, it will be ignored
38.         ($year,$model,$comments1, $price, $comments2, $phone) =
39.         ($carLine =~ /.*?(\d+)\s*(\w+)\s*(.*)\$(\d+,?\d*)\s*(.*)
                          (\d{3}-\d{4})/);
40.         #This creates a 2030 bug but we'll live with it
41.         if (length ($year) <= 2){
42.           if ($year > 30){
43.               $year = "19" . $year;
44.           }
45.           else{
46.               $year = "20" . $year;
47.           }
48.         }
```

```
49.          #The price has to match a comma that occurs sometimes
50.          #so remove it to keep all the prices in the same format
51.          $price =~ s/,//;
52.          #Create a unique table ID
53.          $ad_ID = $i . "_" . time;
54.          #Put all the extra stuff into one scalar
55.          $comments = $comments1 . $comments2;
56.      #Insert the car data into the model table
57.      $SQL = qq|Insert Into $make (ad_ID, model, year,
58.                                   phone, comments, price)
59.               Values ('$ad_ID', '$model', '$year',
60.                          '$phone','$comments', '$price')|;
61.      if ($myDb->Sql($SQL)){
62.          $prevFH = select(ERRORFILE);
63.          print "Error Creating $make\n";
64.          Win32::ODBC::DumpError();
65.          select ($prevFH);
66.      }
67.   }
68. }
69.
70. close ERRORFILE;
71.
72. #Always close the database connection
73. $myDb->Close();
```

Lines 28 through 55 prepare the input data for the SQL statement that begins on line 57. Each classified entry is actually made up of two lines in the transportation file. Each line of the ad's file must be processed, looking for a line that identifies itself as a classified information. A typical classified ad looks like this:

```
<!-H#TRANSPORTATION - MitsubishiH#->
 '91 3000 GTSL; gold ext.; charcoal int. Lthr. 70K miles. AT; fully
loaded. 1 owner. Exc. cond. Must sell; $10,500. Marble Falls area.
915-388-4064. <HR>
```

FIGURE 24.10

The Mitsubishi table

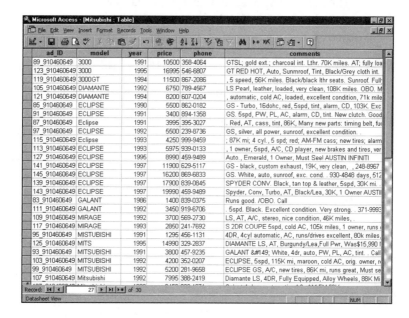

These two lines of data must be processed together. The first line, which is identified by line 31 of Listing 24.10, always occurs before the actual classified data, so this line is used to mark the beginning of a new ad:

```
if ($ads[$i] =~ /TRANSPORTATION\s+-\s+(\w+)H/){
```

If this line is not found, the `for` loop increments the index variable and we continue processing with the next line. If this line is found, we save the next line into the lexical `$carLine` at the same time the index to the next line of data is incremented. This is one way to process two lines at a time, where the first line is used to identify that the next line has significance to the program:

```
my $carLine = $ads[++$i];
```

Now that we have identified a line for importing into the database, a decision must be made on the minimum set of required data. The regular expression on lines 38 and 39 requires that a classified ad contain the year, model, price, and phone number. If this data is not included in the ad, the regular expression will fail and the data will not be added to the database:

```
($year, $model, $comments1, $price, $comments2, $phone) =
($carLine =~ /.*?(\d+)\s*(\w+)\s*(.*)\$(\d+,?\d*)\s*(.*)
         (\d{3}-\d{4})/);
```

The regular expression, which looks rather daunting, is really quite straightforward when you break it into pieces, as you learned in Chapter 16. Here is a breakdown of this regular expression:

`.*?(\d+)`	The year is preceded by an arbitrary amount of data until the first digit is located. Then all consecutive digits are saved into the first back reference variable.
`\s*(\w+)`	The next part of the regular expression matches the first word to follow the model year; the model may be preceded by zero or more space characters.
`\s*(.*)`	After the model name, everything goes into a comments variable until we find a price.
`\$(\d+,?\d*)`	The price is always preceded by a dollar sign and then a series of digits that are saved into the fourth back reference variable. Some prices contain commas, and some don't, so the price regular expression looks for a series of digits followed by zero or one commas, which is followed by zero or more digits.
`\s*(.*)`	After the price is another set of freeform characters that are followed by a phone number.
`(\d{3}-\d{4})`	The phone number must be three digits followed by a dash followed by four digits, which means we will match only local phone numbers.

Each regular expression that is surrounded by parentheses is saved into a back reference variable and, in this example, into the lvalue list on the left of the assignment operator.

NOTE   The details of regular expressions were covered in detail in Chapter 16, but that was a long time ago. If you've forgotten or tried to ignore regular expressions, I encourage you to investigate their usefulness further.

Lines 40 through 55 make sure the data is all in the same format. Each piece of data will eventually be queried, and invalid comparisons will occur if prices include commas or two-digit years versus four-digit years are included in the data. As a database programmer, it is your responsibility to make sure the data is properly formatted before it is inserted into the database.

The creation of the SQL statement used to make the actual insertion of the data begins on line 57:

```
$SQL = qq|Insert Into $make (ad_ID, model, year,
                        phone, comments, price)
```

```
Values ('$ad_ID', '$model', '$year',
        '$phone','$comments', '$price')|;
```

This SQL statement uses the column list and values format to insert data into each transportation table. You should use this format whenever possible, because it allows you to modify the column order and add new columns within your database without changing your import code. Each of the values in the value list is surrounded by single quotes, a requirement of the Access database engine.

Searching for Cars on the Web

Now that you've got something to display on the web, you need to create a means for people to query your classified ads database. I don't think the average user wants to enter SQL queries, so it's up to you to make the query request intuitive to the user. A reasonable goal is to come up with something simple that will satisfy 80 percent of most users' queries. An example of this type of search page is shown in Figure 24.11, which is generated by Listing 24.11.

Listing 24.11:   **Searching for Transportation**

```
1.  use Win32::ODBC;
2.  #Define the Data Source Name
3.  $DSN = "Auto Ads";
4.
5.  #Create a Win32::ODBC object
6.  #Lots of Perl programmers use this notation:
7.  #$myDBConnection = new Win32::ODBC($DSN);
8.  #But I prefer this syntax
9.  my $myDb = Win32::ODBC->new($DSN);
10.
11. #Verify the connection is valid
12. if (! $myDb){
13.    print "Failed to Connect $DSN\n";
14.    Win32::ODBC::DumpError();
15.    #You can't do anything without a connection so die here
16.    die;
17. }
18. @makes = $myDb->TableList;
19. #Remember whenever you return an HTML page
20. #from a CGI program you must include a valid HTTP header
21. #followed by at least one blank line
```

```
22. print<<"EOF";
23. Content-Type: text/html
24.
25. <html>
26. <body>
27. <form method=POST action="cgi-bin/classifiedCarSearch.cgi">
28. <center>
29. <h1>Search Our Transportation<br>
30. Classified ADS</h1>
31. <table>
32.    <tr>
33.       <th width=20%>Select a Make </th>
34.       <th Align=Left> Order By: </th>
35.    </tr>
36.    <tr>
37.       <td><select name="Make">
38. EOF
39. #This foreach loop creates option list values that
40. #are part of the previous select HTML statement
41. #The value is returned as a part of the CGI data
42. #The $make outside the Option tag is what the user sees.
43. #The newline is for convenience if debugging is required
44. foreach $make (@makes){
45.    print  qq|<Option value="$make"> $make\n|;
46. }
47. #After the option list is created we just need to
48. #list the order that they want to see their cars
49. print<<"EOF";
50.            </select>
51.       </td>
52.       <td witdh=80%>
53.          <table>
54.             <tr>
55.                <td><input type=checkbox name="Price"> Price </td>
56.                <td><input type=checkbox name="Model"> Model </td>
57.                <td><input type=checkbox name="Year"> Year </td>
58.             </tr>
59.          </table>
60.       </td>
61.    </tr>
62. </table>
63. <input type=submit Value="Get Search Results">
```

```
64. <input type=reset>
65. </form>
66. </center>
67. </body>
68. </html>
69. EOF
```

FIGURE 24.11:

Searching online

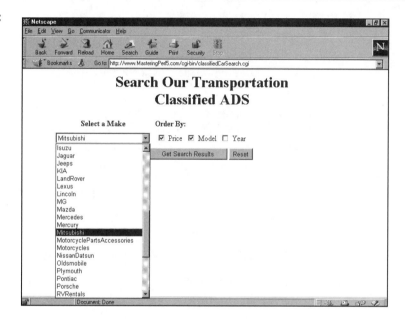

When the CGI program in Listing 24.11 is called, it makes a connection to the database, as you have seen in almost all of the examples in this chapter. In fact, the initial CGI program is no different from any other database program. Line 18 uses the Win32::ODBC method TableList to get all of the tables of the transportation database:

```
@makes = $myDb->TableList;
```

Lines 22 through 24 fulfill the basic requirement of a CGI program, which is returning a valid HTTP header followed by a blank line. (The blank line signifies the end of the HTTP headers.) You can have as many HTTP headers as needed, but a blank line must follow the last HTTP header:

```
print<<"EOF";
Content-Type: text/html

<html>
<body>
```

The selection list shown in Figure 24.11 is created by the `foreach` loop on lines 44 through 46, which processes the table list created on line 18. Each table is presented to the user as part of the option list:

```
foreach $make (@makes){
    print  qq|<Option value="$make"> $make\n|;
}
```

The checkboxes that print (lines 55 through 58) have a unique characteristic that you will see in the `classifiedCarSearch.cgi` program in the next section. The `classifiedCarSearch.cgi` program is called when the user selects the Get Search Results button, which is created on line 63:

```
<input type=submit Value="Get Search Results">
```

The submit button knows which program to call based on the action field in the HTML form tag printed on line 27:

```
<form method=POST action="cgi-bin/classifiedCarSearch.cgi">
```

In the next section, you'll complete your online database project by returning the request made in Figure 24.11.

Displaying the Online Search Results

The CGI program in Listing 24.11 calls the CGI program in Listing 24.12, which reads the transportation database and generates the HTML page shown in Figure 24.12.

Listing 24.12:   **Classified Ads Online**

```
1.  use Win32::ODBC;
2.  require "readPostInput.cgi";
3.  %cars = readPostInput();
4.  #Define the Data Source Name
5.  $DSN = "Auto Ads";
```

```
6.   #Create a Win32::ODBC object
7.   my $myDb = Win32::ODBC->new($DSN);
8.   #Verify the connection is valid
9.   if (! $myDb){
10.     print "Failed to Connect $DSN\n";
11.     Win32::ODBC::DumpError();
12.     #You can't do anything without a connection so die here
13.     die;
14. }
15. #Using the data read by readPostInput in the cars hash,
16. #create the SQL statement
17. $SQL = "Select model, year, price, comments From $cars{Make}";
18. #Checkboxes are only returned if they are checked. We can
19. #use this to our advantage to determine if the user wants
20. #an ordered search result
21. if ((defined ($cars{Model} || defined ($cars{Year})
        || defined $cars{Price}))){
22.     $SQL .= " Order By ";
23.     my $count = 0;
24.     #At least one type of ordered search was requested.
25.     #The foreach processes only those list items that are defined
26.     foreach $order (  $cars{Model}, $cars{Year}, $cars{Price}){
27.        #Each time through the loop at the order request to
28.        #the SQL statement
29.        $orderList .= " $order,;
30.        #If count is greater than zero we know we have an
31.        #ordered search
32.        $count++;
33.     }
34.     if ($count){
35.        #Get rid of the trailing comma
36.        chop $orderList;
37.        $SQL .= $orderList ;
38.     }
39. }
40.
41. if ($myDb->Sql($SQL)){
42.     print "Error getting Make info for $car{Make}\n";
43.     $myDb->DumpError();
44. }
45.
46. print<<"EOF";
```

```
47. Content-Type: text/html
48.
49.
50. <html>
51. <title> $cars{Make} Classifieds </title>
52. <body>
53. <center>
54. <h1> You Searched for $cars{Make} </h1>
55. EOF
56. #If there is any data in orderlist then tell the user the
57. #type of order requested
58. if ($orderList){
59.    @orderRequested = split(/,/,$orderList);
60.    #Save the list separator's previous value
61.    $prevSeparator = $";
62.    #This will print out , AND between each element of the array
63.    local $" = ", AND";
64.    print "<h2> Ordered by  @orderRequested </h2>\n";
65.    #Return the list separator to its previous value
66.    $" = $prevSeparator;
67. }
68.
69. #The cell padding puts some space around the data in the table cell
70. #The 70% width forces the last cell to take up most of the screen
71. print<<"EOF";
72. <table border=1 cellpadding=5>
73.    <tr>
74.       <th Align=left>Model
75.       <th Align=left>Year
76.       <th Align=left>Price
77.       <th Align=left width=70%>Additional Information
78.    </tr>
79. EOF
80. while ($myDb->FetchRow()){
81.    %model = $myDb->DataHash;
82. print<<"EOF";
83.    <tr>
84.       <td Align=left>$model{model}
85.       <td Align=left>$model{year}
86.       <td Align=left>$model{price}
87.       <td Align=left width=70%>$model{comments}
88.    </tr>
```

```
89. EOF
90. }
91.
92. print<<"EOF";
93. </table>
94. </center>
95. </body>
96. </html>
97. EOF
```

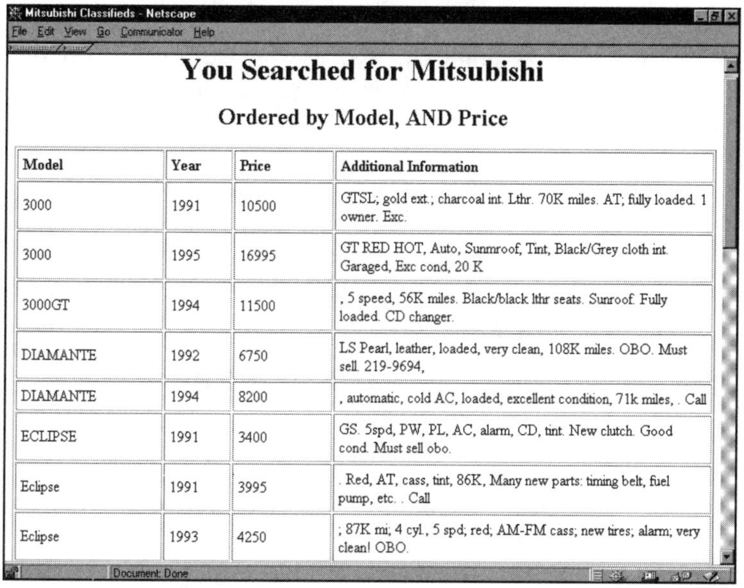

FIGURE 24.12:

Displaying classified ads online

FIGURE 24.12:

Displaying classified ads online

Listing 24.12 reads the data sent to it via the POST method into the %cars hash on line 3:

```
%cars = readPostInput();
```

The %cars hash contains each of the name/value pairs of the input items generated from the HTML form in Listing 24.11. The first thing this program uses from the %cars hash is the name of the table it will be querying. The data is available via the hash key Make ($car{Make}), which was created in the option list generated in Listing 24.11. This name/value pair is retrieved on line 17, which initializes the SQL query statement:

```
$SQL = "Select model, year, price, comments From $cars{Make}";
```

At this point, the program must check the input values from the Order By checkboxes to determine if the SQL query statement is complete.

Unlike other HTML form input tags, the checkbox name/value pair is sent only when the checkbox is selected. Line 21 determines if any name/value pairs from the Order By checkboxes were selected:

```
if ((defined ($cars{Model} || defined ($cars{Year}) ||
    defined $cars{Price}))){
```

If at least one of the checkboxes was selected, the SQL query will use the Order By constraint clause. The Order By portion of the SQL query is added on line 22:

```
$SQL .= " Order By ";
```

Lines 26 through 33 check to see which checkboxes were actually selected. The foreach loop contains a list of each of the checkboxes, one list item for each checkbox name. The foreach loop processes only defined elements of a list, however, so the $order variable will be set only to checkbox values that were selected. As the loop is processed, the $orderList is built, one checkbox item at a time:

```
foreach $order ($cars{Model}, $cars{Year}, $cars{Price}){
    #Each time through the loop at the order request to
    #rhe SQL statement
    $orderList .= " $order,";
    #If count is greater than zero we know we have an
    #ordered search.
    $count++;
}
```

Once the $orderList is complete, a trailing comma must be removed, which is accomplished by the chop function on line 36:

```
chop $orderList;
```

The $orderList variable is appended to the formatted $SQL variable on line 37, and the actual SQL query is made on line 41:

```
$SQL .= $orderList;
if ($myDb->Sql($SQL)){
```

If the user made a request for an ordered search, the type of request is echoed back to the user on lines 58 through 67:

```
if ($orderList){
    @orderRequested = split(/,/,$orderList);
    #Save the list separator's previous value
    $prevSeparator = $";
    #This will print out , AND between each element of the array
    local $" = ", AND";
    print "<h2> Ordered by  @orderRequested </h2>\n";
    #Return the list separator to its previous value
    $" = $prevSeparator;
}
```

Line 63 takes advantage of the list separator variable to produce the formatted output: `Ordered By Model, AND Price` (shown in Figure 24.12).

Each row returned by the SQL query is displayed in HTML format in the `while` loop from lines 80 through 90. The row of the query result is fetched on line 80 and then the data is retrieved through the `Win32::ODBC` method `DataHash`:

```
while ($myDb->FetchRow()){
    %model = $myDb->DataHash;
```

This creates the hash data used to display each row of the table data between lines 84 and 87:

```
print<<"EOF";
    <tr>
        <td Align=left>$model{model}
        <td Align=left>$model{year}
        <td Align=left>$model{price}
        <td Align=left width=70%>$model{comments}
    </tr>
EOF
```

As with most programming projects, producing the final result is a matter of taking one step at a time and then stringing those steps together until the project is completed. Here, you stepped through each of the processes required to create an online database. You can now apply this simple solution to your more complex problems.

Summary

In this chapter, you first learned about the requirements for database applications. ODBC is a commonly agreed upon standard for connecting to the major database engines of the world. To connect to a database, you must create a Data Source Name (DSN), which defines the location of the database, the type of database, and the user name and password of a database.

You can create a Microsoft Access Database DSN through the Windows interface or via the `Win32::ODBC` method `ConfigDSN`. The `Win32::ODBC` class contains a set of methods (written by Dave Roth) that provides an ODBC interface to your `Win32::ODBC` compliant database engines.

Next, the chapter covered `Win32::ODBC` and SQL statements. The `Win32::ODBC` methods allow you to create a DSN and connect and close your database. They also include several debugging routines to help you interpret the errors returned from your database engine. SQL is used after you connect to your database to manipulate tables and the data tables contain.

Using the `Win32::ODBC` APIs, you can send SQL statements to your database and retrieve the results:

- To create tables, use the `Create Table` statement.
- To modify the columns defined in the table, use the `Alter Table` statement.
- To add data to a table, use the `Insert Into` command.
- To delete from a table, use the `Delete From` statement.
- To modify data in a table, use the `Update` statement.
- To retrieve data from a table, use the SQL `Select` statement.

At the end of this chapter, you stepped through the complete process of creating an online database. First, you set permissions on your directories so the web server and Microsoft Access would have the correct privileges to read and write from your database directory. Then you created a new DSN and more than 50 tables in a transportation database. Once the database was defined, you imported data into the database through a Perl 5 program. With your database populated, you then built a CGI program to query your transportation database. The last step was displaying the results of an online query in HTML format to the user.

Index

Note to the Reader: Throughout this index **boldfaced** page numbers indicate primary discussions of a topic. *Italicized* page numbers indicate illustrations.

(

R

X

Y

Z

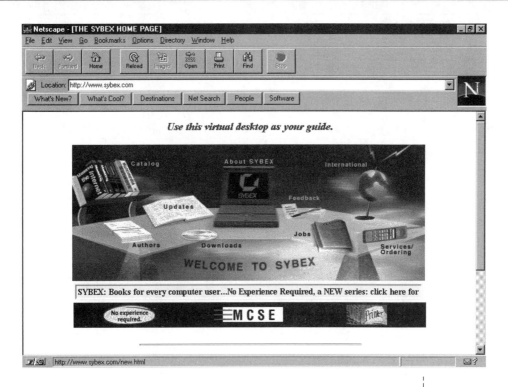

Variable	English Name	Description
$@	$EVAL_ERROR	The Perl syntax error message from the last eval() command
$$	$PROCESS_ID	The process number of the Perl running this script
$<	$REAL_USER_ID	The real uid of this process
$>	$EFFECTIVE_USER_ID	The effective uid of this process
$(	$REAL_GROUP_ID	The real gid of this process
$)	$EFFECTIVE_GROUP_ID	The effective gid of this process
$0	$PROGRAM_NAME	The name of the file (without the filename extension) used to invoke the executing program
$[		The index of the first element in an array and of the first character in a substring
$]	$PERL_VERSION	The version and patch level of the Perl interpreter
$^D	$DEBUGGING	The current value of the debugging flags
$^F	$SYSTEM_FD_MAX	The maximum system file descriptor
$^H		The current set of syntax checks enabled by use strict and other pragmas
$^I	$INPLACE_EDIT	The current value of the in-place edit extension
$^M		An emergency pool of allocated memory, used after an out-of-memory condition for printing error messages
$^O	$OSNAME	The name of the operating system under which this copy of Perl was built, as determined during the configuration process
$^P	$PERLDB	The internal variable for debugging support